D0903258

Donated by
*Friends of Muskoka Lakes
Library*

Books of Merit

BATTLE LINES

BATTLE

EYEWITNESS
ACCOUNTS FROM
CANADA'S
MILITARY HISTORY

LINES

J. L. GRANATSTEIN
NORMAN HILLMER

Thomas Allen Publishers
Toronto

National Library of Canada Cataloguing in Publication

Battle lines : eyewitness accounts from Canada's military history / J. L. Granatstein & Norman Hillmer, eds.

Includes index.

ISBN 0-88762-156-2 (bound)

I. Canada—History, Military.   I. Granatstein, J.L., 1939–   II. Hillmer, Norman, 1942–

FC226.B377 2004   355'.00971   C2004-902545-7

Editor: Jim Gifford
Jacket and text design: Gordon Robertson
Jacket image: Archives of Ontario/c22-0-0-10-37

Page 467 constitutes a continuation of this copyright page.

Published by Thomas Allen Publishers,
a division of Thomas Allen & Son Limited,
145 Front Street East, Suite 209,
Toronto, Ontario M5A 1E3 Canada
www.thomas-allen.com

  **Canada Council
for the Arts**

The publisher gratefully acknowledges the support of the Ontario Arts Council for its publishing program.

We acknowledge the support of the Canada Council for the Arts, which last year invested $21.7 million in writing and publishing throughout Canada.

We acknowledge the Government of Ontario through the Ontario Media Development Corporation's Ontario Book Initiative.

We acknowledge the financial support of the Government of Canada through the Book Publishing Industry Development Program (BPIDP) for our publishing activities.

08 07 06 05 04   1 2 3 4 5

Printed and bound in Canada

For Tess Johnson, Michael Hillmer,
and Melinda Hillmer

CONTENTS

Introduction   1

Wolfe Takes Quebec, 1759   13
ANONYMOUS

The Battle on the Plains of Abraham   19
CAPTAIN JOHN KNOX

The Assault on Detroit, 1763   24
MAJOR DUNCAN

The Americans Fail to Take Quebec, 1775–76   27
SIR GUY CARLETON

The Indian Way of War   28
THOMAS ANBUREY

Fighting with Brock   30
W.H. MERRITT

Honour and Glory   34
ANNE PREVOST

Corporal Chrétien Fights Off the Invaders, May 1813   36
CAPTAIN JACQUES VIGER

The Difficult British–Indian Alliance, 1813   38
    LIEUTENANT-COLONEL MATTHEW ELLIOTT

An Officer's Wife on a Campaign in Upper Canada, 1814   41
    ANONYMOUS

Seizing the *Caroline*, 1837   46
    ANDREW DREW

The Battle of the Windmill, 1838   50
    LIEUTENANT ANDREW AGNEW

Fighting the Fenians at Ridgeway, 1866   52
    CAPTAIN W.D. OTTER

They Could Teach a Lesson to Many:
   French Canadians in the Militia, 1871   54
    COLONEL P. ROBERTSON-ROSS

Aboriginal Boatmen on the Nile, 1884   55
    COLONEL SIR WILLIAM BUTLER

The Midland Battalion Moves to Battle, 1885   58
    WALTER F. STEWART

The Trek Around Lake Superior, 1885   65
    LIEUTENANT-COLONEL GEORGE T. DENISON

Letters Home from Battleford, 1885   68
    HARRY BROCK

Fighting the Cree at Frenchman's Butte, 1885   71
    CAPTAIN WILLIAM PARKER

A Gentleman Cadet at the Royal Military College, 1898   74
    F.H. MAYNARD

Going to War in South Africa, 1899–1900   79
    TOM WALLACE

Plenty of Fighting to Suit Everybody:
   The RCR at Paardeberg   83
    DOUGLAS MCPHERSON

A Journalist Reports on Paardeberg, February 1900   84
STANLEY M. BROWN

We Have to Do or Die:
    A Strathcona in South Africa, April 1900   89
    J.C. WALKER

The Volunteers Melt Away, 1900   89
C.F. HAMILTON

Cavalry in South Africa   90
CHARLES AND BERT ROOKE

In the Militia, 1912–14   96
ARTHUR TURNER

HMCS *Rainbow* Forces the *Komagata Maru*
    out of Vancouver Harbour, July 1914   98
    REAR ADMIRAL WALTER HOSE

The Outbreak of War, 1914   103
ALBERT HERBERT JOHN ANDREWS

Gathering at Valcartier   104
LIEUTENANT ALEXANDER THOMAS THOMSON

From Valcartier to Salisbury Plains   110
PRIVATE WILLIAM PEDEN

Winter Training on the Prairies, 1915   113
ROBERT G. COMBE

Trench Life, March 1915   114
PRIVATE WILLIAM PEDEN

War in the Air, April 1915   118
ANONYMOUS

The Canadian Battle of Ypres   119
ALBERT EDWARD ROSCOE

In Flanders Fields   121
MAJOR JOHN MCRAE

An Acadian Reports from Overseas, 1915   122
    PRIVATE ATHANASE POIRIER

What an Officer Needs in the Trenches, 1915   125
    LIEUTENANT ALEXANDER THOMAS THOMSON

Training Woes in Calgary, December 1915   127
    PRIVATE S.E. ADAM

I Was Frightened: Dealing with Fear in the Trenches   128
    LIEUTENANT JAMES THORPE

We All Shook As Though We Had the Ague:
   A Bomber at the Front, March 1916   130
    ERNEST M. TAYLOR

Trench Life, April 1916   132
    ARCHER TOOLE

Sea Sick, May 1916   133
    PRIVATE MICHAEL DUGGAN

Flying with the No. 7 Squadron, Royal Flying Corps,
   in France, May 1916   135
    LIEUTENANT E.J. WATKINS

Explaining War to the Home Folk, 1916: I   136
    ARCHIE MACKINNON

Explaining War to the Home Folk, 1916: II   137
    HAROLD W. MCGILL

The Newfoundland Regiment Is Wiped Out
   at Beaumont Hamel, July 1, 1916   138
    CAPTAIN GEORGE HICKS

He Probably Won't Try to Lead Us Again:
   The RFC Stages a Bombing Raid, July 1916   140
    SECOND LIEUTENANT JOHN B. BROPHY

Explaining War to the Home Folk, 1916: III   143
    HART LEECH

Shooting Down a Zeppelin over London, October 1916   144
SECOND LIEUTENANT W.J. TEMPEST

An Amputee Breaks the News, 1917   146
JAMES HEPBURN

The Terrible Poignancy of War, 1917   147
ARCHIBALD MACKINNON

The Guns of Vimy   149
THOMAS EARL WALKER

The Best Show I Have Been In   151
HAROLD W. MCGILL

Narrow Escapes at Vimy   152
MAJOR PERCY MENZIES

A "Reprisal" Bombing Raid on Freiburg, Germany,
April 1917   154
SUB-LIEUTENANT WALTER P. FLETT

Learning to Fly, May 1917   156
CHARLES HENDERSHOT

The Call of Duty, 1917   157
PRIVATE THOMAS P. HARRIS

The Hell of Passchendaele I:
I Shivered Alongside Stephens, October 1917   160
PRIVATE JOHN P. SUDBURY

The Hell of Passchendaele II: October 1917   163
ARTHUR TURNER

The Hell of Passchendaele III: A Next-of-Kin Letter   172
LIEUTENANT ARTHUR G. STARKINGS

The Hell of Passchendaele IV:
The Hardest Tour I Have Ever Made   172
KEITH MACGOWAN

A Stout Effort in the Air, 1917   179
WILBERT C. GILROY

Until You Hear from Me Again   181
JOHN ALLEN HUNTER/CHAPLAIN J.S. DARCEY

A Hot Fight, November 1917   182
LIEUTENANT ANDREW WILSON

General Currie on Conscription, November 1917   184
LIEUTENANT-GENERAL SIR ARTHUR CURRIE

Not a Window Anywhere:
    The Halifax Explosion, December 1917   185
LAMBERT GRIFFITH

It Was the End of the World: Halifax Destroyed,
    December 1917   187
FRED LONGLAND

A Nursing Sister Near the Front, May 1918   191
NURSING SISTER KATHERINE MACDONALD

Cracking the Hindenburg Line, August 1918   192
IVAN CLARK MAHARG

Oh, For Three Months' Leave . . .   198
LIEUTENANT LEWIS HONEY

My First Aerial Scrap, September 1918   199
WARREN HENDERSHOT

Following Fritz, October 1918   201
JOHN MENZIES

At 11 a.m. It Went Quiet   205
CLARENCE ELDER

The Last .303 Cartridge I Will Ever Fire   209
JOHN GAITZ

Veterans and the Political Mood in Winnipeg, 1919   210
OFFICER COMMANDING, MILITARY DISTRICT NO. 10

Bush Pilots in Uniform, 1925   211
    T.F. COOPER

Strike Duty, Sydney, Nova Scotia, 1925   212
    LIEUTENANT-GENERAL GUY SIMONDS

The Chief of Staff Resigns, 1927   214
    CHARLES VINING

Militarism in the Nation's Schools, 1927   217
    AGNES MACPHAIL, MP

The American Enemy, 1927   223
    COLONEL J. SUTHERLAND BROWN

The Navy Deals with Revolution in Latin America, 1932   225
    REAR-ADMIRAL FRANK HOUGHTON

The Non-Permanent Active Militia in
    the Great Depression   229
    MAJOR J. MURRAY SAVAGE

Cadet Life at the Royal Military College in the 1930s   231
    BRIGADIER-GENERAL ROBERT BENNETT

We Owed It to Our Country, 1936, 1938   236
    W.L. MACKENZIE KING

The Army Goes to War, 1939   239
    MAJOR E.G. WEEKS

Creating the 1st Canadian Division, 1939   242
    LIEUTENANT-GENERAL GUY SIMONDS

General McNaughton Talks to the Prime Minister, 1939   245
    W.L. MACKENZIE KING

A Small Boat Captain at Dunkirk, May 1940   247
    REAR ADMIRAL R.W. TIMBRELL

The Canadians Go to France—After Dunkirk, 1940   250
    MAJOR-GENERAL HARRY FOSTER

Prejudice Against Aboriginals in the Navy   252
MAX BASQUE

A Nursing Sister in Britain, February 1941   252
NURSING SISTER ELAINE WRIGHT

Training Seamen, 1941   256
LIEUTENANT WILLIAM H. PUGSLEY

HMCS *Chambly* Boards a U-Boat, September 1941   259
LIEUTENANT E.T. SIMMONS

The Hong Kong Disaster, 1941   262
BRIGADIER JOHN H. PRICE

"Studied Brutality" in Hong Kong, 1942–43   265
GEORGE S. MACDONELL

Requests for Special Privileges "Simply Not Done"   268
LIEUTENANT-GENERAL MAURICE POPE

Recruiting CWACs   269
CATHRYNE BLACKLEY ARMSTRONG

Monty on Canada's Senior Officers, 1942   271
FIELD MARSHAL MONTGOMERY OF ALAMEIN

Striking Against Germany, 1942   273
DENNIS JOHN QUINLAN

From Alberta to Camp Borden, 1942   274
KEN HUTCHINSON

A Padre on the Tragedy of Dieppe, August 1942   278
MAJOR THE REVEREND MIKE DALTON

The Calgarys at Dieppe, 1942   280
GRANT ODUM PHILLIP

I Am a Prisoner, August 1942   281
LIEUTENANT H.W. HOCKIN

The Men Belittled Us at Every Turn, 1942   282
NEVA BAYLISS

A Jolly Good Chance: Trying to Escape,
    Hong Kong, 1942   283
SERGEANT JOHN PAYNE

The Sinking of the SS *Caribou*, October 1942   284
ALEX BATEMAN

This Can't Last Forever:
    A Dieppe POW at Christmas, 1942   286
PRIVATE JACK GRISS

A Day on a Bomber Squadron and a Last Letter   287
FLIGHT LIEUTENANT F. LAWRENCE PARKER

The Three Rivers Regiment Lands in Sicily, July 1943   294
JACK WALLACE

Doubts About General McNaughton's Abilities, 1943   295
VINCENT MASSEY

Ike on McNaughton, Canada, and the Empire, 1943   296
CAPTAIN HARRY BUTCHER

The Fears of German POWs, Sicily, July 1943   298
MAJOR ROY DURNFORD

Characteristics of Canadian Soldiers, Sicily, 1943   299
MAJOR A.T. SESIA

There Is Great Hope That He Is Alive:
    Caring for Those at Home, 1943   301
VARIOUS

Washing Out of Pilot Training, 1943   305
JAMES KESHEN

Tank Training in England, 1943   306
BRIGADIER-GENERAL CHRISTOPHER DE L. KIRBY

The Strains of High Command, 1943   307
LIEUTENANT-GENERAL GUY SIMONDS

As Tough a Go as Anything We've Encountered:
    Italy, December 1943   311
CAPTAIN HARRY JOLLEY

There Are No Trenches: At Ortona, December 1943   312
GREGORY CLARK

Dining with Colonel Zabotin in Halifax   315
LEO HAMSON

The Problem of Home Defence Conscripts, 1943   321
LIEUTENANT-GENERAL MAURICE A. POPE

Service in Italy Behind the Front, 1943   323
JACK AINSWORTH

Politics and Food in the Navy, February 1944   325
FRASER MCKEE

Young Officers Emerge in Battle, 1944   326
MAJOR-GENERAL CHRIS VOKES

The Rise of the Militia Officer, 1944   327
BRIGADIER WILLIAM MURPHY

The Generals Ready for D-Day, 1944   328
LIEUTENANT-COLONEL G.S. CURRIE

The Opening of the Hitler Line Battle, Italy, May 1944   330
BRIGADIER WILLIAM MURPHY

We Are Going In Tomorrow Morning, D-Day, 1944   331
SERGEANT EDWARD WORDEN

Beach Head Taken:
    A Journalist Lands in Normandy, June 6, 1944   332
ROSS MUNRO

We French Canadians Are in No Way Subordinate, 1944   335
MAJOR T.L. BULLOCK

So Long Without Eat & Sleep:
   In the Normandy Beachhead   338
   TROOPER KEN HUTCHINSON

I Saw French Women Throwing Roses:
   Liberation, June 1944   339
   MATTHEW HALTON

Night Flying Training in Wales, July 1944   342
   PILOT OFFICER WILLIAM WATSON

Write Often and Send Grub   344
   JACQUES GOUIN

The Normandy Diary of Gunner Brady   346
   GUNNER JAMES P. BRADY

Falaise Is at Last Ours:
   The Closing of the Gap, August 1944   350
   FREDERICK GRIFFIN

A Nursing Sister on German POWs and
   Canadian Slackers, September 1944   354
   NURSING SISTER JEAN M. ELLIS

Outarmoured and Outgunned by the German Panthers:
   Tanks in Italy, 1944   356
   BRIGADIER WILLIAM MURPHY

The Loyal Edmonton Regiment at the Gothic Line,
   September 1944   358
   BILL BOSS

Letters from the Mud, November–December 1944   360
   LIEUTENANT J.E. BOULET

What the Hell Is the Matter with Everything?:
   Manpower Bungles, November 1944   361
   FLIGHT LIEUTENANT ALEX GRAHAM

A First Christmas in Stalag Luft III, 1944   362
   IAN H. FOWLER

The Luftwaffe's Last Throw, New Year's Day, 1945   363
SERGEANT W.L. LARGE

Battle Fatigue, February 1945   364
BURTON FITCH

A Passover Seder at Cleve, Germany, March 1945   366
CHAPLAIN SAM CASS

Free at Last: An RCAF POW Writes Home, April 1945   367
WARRANT OFFICER DON SCOWEN

V-E Day in Germany, May 1945   368
GUNNER JAMES P. BRADY

V-E Day in London, May 1945   369
EDNA WILSON

The End of the War in London and Toronto   371
CAPTAIN PAT BATES AND PEGGY BATES

Occupying Germany, May–June 1945   374
STANLEY WINFIELD

I Have Just Seen Belsen, June 1945   379
SQUADRON LEADER TED APLIN

A Soldier's Suicide   383
CAPTAIN KEN CALDER

The Difficult Re-adjustment to Peace   384
RODOLPHE CORMIER

Our Grandchildren Will Ask Us Who Liberated Us   385
EDITOR, *Our Free Holland*

A Commander for Korea, August 1950   388
MAJOR-GENERAL JOHN M. ROCKINGHAM

The Chinese Intervene in Korea, December 1950   390
MAJOR RODERIC BRIAN MEREDITH

Hands Off Korea:
    Captain Pope and the Trotskyist Blonde, April 1951   394
    HARRY POPE

With the Guns in Korea, 1951   396
    LIEUTENANT DON DALKE

Crossing the Imjin River, 1951   398
    MAJOR-GENERAL JOHN M. ROCKINGHAM

There Sure Isn't Much News:
    Private Roy Dooley Writes Home from Korea, 1951   400
    PRIVATE ROY DOOLEY

Problems in the NATO Brigade, 1953   401
    LIONEL SHAPIRO

What Problems in the NATO Brigade?   406
    COLONEL CHARLES P. STACEY

Keeping the Peace in Suez, UNEF, 1959   408
    CAPTAIN G.R. TOMALIN

Governor General Vanier on His Beloved Vandoos   409
    MAJOR-GENERAL GEORGES P. VANIER

The World's Most Provincial Animal:
    Canadian Peacekeepers Abroad, 1962   410
    ANONYMOUS

Getting Out of Egypt Ahead of the Six Day War,
    May 1967   412
    FLIGHT LIEUTENANT MICHAEL BELCHER

Keeping Peace in a Troubled Cyprus, 1975   415
    ROBERT BURNS

At War in the Gulf, January 1991   419
    LIEUTENANT (N) RICHARD GIMBLETT

The Canadian Airborne Regiment in Somalia, 1993   422
    ROBERT PROUSE

The Killing of Shidane Arone, Somalia, 1993   429
COURT MARTIAL TESTIMONY

Squaring Off with Serbian Forces in Croatia, 1993   435
SERGEANT PAUL GÉLINAS

Medical Risks in Croatia, 1994   439
DR. ERIC SMITH

Dealing with Serbs and Croats, 1994   442
ANONYMOUS

The Nightmare of Rwanda—and After   442
ANONYMOUS

Serving in Kosovo, 1999   447
CAPTAIN PAUL DE GRANDPRÉ

Making a Difference in Kosovo   451
LIEUTENANT ELEANOR TAYLOR

Stopping Smugglers in the Straits of Hormuz, 2002   453
ANONYMOUS

Fighting in Afghanistan, 2002   457
STEPHEN J. THORNE

Operating in Kabul, December 2003   462
MAJOR KEITH CAMERON

Source Acknowledgments   467

Index   479

INTRODUCTION

War made Canada. The struggles between France and England set the future of what was New France and what soon would become British North America. The Revolutionary War and the War of 1812 determined that Canada would not be part of the United States, and the crushing of the Riel rebellions confirmed that Canada would be a settler nation from sea to sea. The South African War demonstrated the force of British imperialism, enough to send Canadian troops to a territory thousands of miles away to wage a strenuous three-year campaign. The two world wars, vast in scope and cost, advanced Canadian independence and ensured Canadian democracy. Dozens of peace operations under the auspices of the United Nations, the North Atlantic Treaty Organization (NATO), and other international organizations, and alliance warfare in Korea, the Persian Gulf, Kosovo, and Afghanistan, proved Canadians' modern commitment to collective security in defence of significant interests and values. Through conflict, the country was formed in attitude and institution.

At first, the wars were here, on our soil, in our homes. The settler in Montmorency in 1759, the Loyalist farmer on the Niagara Frontier in 1812, the townspeople at Ridgway in 1866, and the Métis families near Batoche in 1885 all faced up to the depredations of an invading army. The men in the household had to decide if they would join the militia and resist the enemy, or if they would hide in the woods. The women and children struggled to hold the family's possessions and property together while the men were away and, frequently, while battles were fought to a bloody conclusion in their fields and farmhouses.

It was different in 1899, 1914, and 1939. Canadians went abroad to fight for Empire and Country in wars that did not directly threaten their territory, at least at the outset. They enlisted for emotional reasons, because of ties to Britain and Europe, or because of a desire for adventure, to flee obligations to their families and creditors, or because social pressures forced them to do so. During the First and Second World Wars, they believed, or came to believe, that the enemy threatened the way they lived and the causes for which they lived. They might have much martial ardour, but were almost certain to possess little military training. They learned in action. Those wars were fought elsewhere—in the kopjes of the Transvaal, in Flanders fields, or on the North Atlantic, in the air over Europe, or on Italian or French and Dutch territory. The immediate impact of war fell on others, but many of the casualties were Canada's.

No one knows how many soldiers and civilians died or were wounded in the Seven Years War or the War of 1812 or the 1885 Northwest Rebellion. For the modern wars, there are calculations of military casualties for South Africa, 244 dead and 252 wounded; for the Great War, 59,769 dead, 172,950 wounded, and 2,084 prisoners of war (POWs); for the Second World War, 42,042 dead, 54,414 wounded, and 8,995 POWs; and for Korea, 320 dead, 1,152 wounded, and 30 POWs. There have been dozens of fatalities in United Nations and other operations, and soldiers have died recently in Afghanistan. Canadians have paid their full price to keep the world they live in.

In the wars of the twentieth century, Canadians served abroad for years. The men of the First Canadian Division went overseas in December 1939 and some did not return home, if they returned at all, until late 1945 or 1946. They changed overseas, and so too did their wives change, their children grow, and their futures alter. Consider Bruce Matthews, a well-off Toronto militia artilleryman, who went overseas with that First Division as a junior officer. He brought his wife to Britain soon after and sent her home, pregnant with twins, when France fell in the early summer of 1940. He would not see her again for five years, and when his children greeted him, by now a much-decorated major-general, they asked, "Mommy, who is that man?" That painful question captures so much: the dislocation of war, the separation of families, and the ruin of individuals' hopes and plans. The Matthews family survived and prospered. Yet many relationships could not stand the strain of prolonged absence. Soldiers returned home to be told that their wives or fiancées had made "other" arrangements. They had to make the best of it. But some could not cope. Captain Ken Calder's family fell apart, and he took his life in despair.

The political and social costs of conflict cannot be calculated precisely, but the hothouse atmosphere of the century's great wars had huge implications for Canada and Canadians. Religious and ethnic groups suffered persecution because they were branded as uncooperative, or as "enemy aliens." The battlefront's constant and ever-growing need for reinforcements led to huge pressures for conscription in the two world wars, and this exacerbated the historic racial and regional tensions between Canadians. Those who would not fight overseas during the Second World War were called "zombies," conjuring up half-dead creatures from the horror movies of the time. Leaders had to struggle to find ways to meet the military's needs without ripping apart the country that their soldiers were fighting to protect. Prime Minister Sir Robert Borden largely failed the national unity test in 1917–18; Liberal leader William Lyon Mackenzie King largely succeeded between 1939 and 1945.

At the same time, war led directly to the imposition of Prohibition, the first income tax, and the adoption of women's suffrage during the Great War, and to serious steps towards a Canadian social security system in the Second World War. Great international conflicts moved tens of thousands of women to work in war factories, and vastly accelerated the flow of people from rural to urban areas. War brought prosperity by increasing wages and offering almost all the overtime work anyone could want, but rationing and shortages frequently meant there was little to spend money on, other than exorbitantly priced liquor or automobile tires sold by blackmarketeers. War's dislocation meant that children, growing up with their fathers overseas and their mothers on a munitions factory production line, found themselves on their own. Delinquency was the result, critics insisted.

Canadians overseas had their own very real concerns, not least their fear of death or disability, but they too were interested in home, in loved ones, in life and conditions in the country they were defending. What is striking is that over almost two and a half centuries the human preoccupations during war remain so constant: love and loss, fear and idealism, work, money, and security. Canada's military men and women wrote to tell their family and friends that they had survived, that they were well, that the thoughts of home and country were very much in their minds, in battle or out. Those who remained in Canada were just as eager for news from abroad or at sea. Often, too often, the news was terrible: the impersonality of a letter from Ottawa with a terse report of a young person dead or wounded or missing in action was a cold demonstration that bureaucratic norms had to be served, even in the midst of the most awful of tragedies.

Military history has the reputation of being too bloody and too male, too full of tales of derring-do and heroic slaughter. For us, and for our colleagues who are reinterpreting the national military experience for a new century of Canadians, it is a rich mosaic of the social, the intellectual, the psychological, the political, strategic, and economic, the home front and the battle front, the led and the leaders. Military history is more than the history of combat. War cannot be understood unless it is understood broadly.

This book concentrates on the battle lines, the personal accounts of military life in Canada and Canadians at war, ranging from the Seven Years War and the fall of New France to service in Afghanistan with NATO's International Security Assistance Force in 2003–04. Inevitably, and deliberately, the emphasis is on first-hand documents written when the moment described is new and fresh. We sought the liveliest and best-written material that could be found. The ideal was a perceptive letter written immediately after a great event, but we discovered that this is rare. Soldiers are tired and psychologically battered after a battle. They have duties to perform, from burying their dead comrades to ensuring that they have supplies of food and ammunition for the next action. They might snatch a moment to write a line to their family, but most often that task is met after they come out of the line. "Didn't know one could go so long without eat & sleep," wrote Trooper Ken Hutchison to his family from Normandy on June 14, 1944, eight days after D-Day.

Sometimes, the poignancy of a moment is caught precisely. "The chances of a 'sub[altern]' getting back alive are about nix," Lieutenant Hart Leech scribbled to his mother just before he went into action on the Somme. "If I do get back, why you can give me the horse laugh. If not this'll let you know that I kicked out with my boots on." Leech's letter reached his family in September 1916, after he was killed in battle. Sometimes, though, the poignancy is retrospective. Thinking back on his Second World War many years after, the Acadian Rodolphe Cormier could think of nothing ennobling about the experience. Entering the army at eighteen and serving in it until he was 23, he could not leave the war behind. It robbed him of his youth and his peace of mind. He became an alcoholic, simply trying to forget. We might wish that all the pieces carried that wrenching wallop, driving home the sadness and madness of war, but who could bear to read such a book?

We do not present front-line reports exclusively or only battle accounts. The military canvas includes the boredom of soldiers, sailors, and airmen in the "hurry up and wait" wartime system of the armed forces; the tedious memoranda with numbered paragraphs and the mindless bureaucracy; the propaganda aimed to cow the enemy and bolster the morale of soldiers and citizens; the stultification of peacetime service, when planning for war is of little interest to anyone except the professionals; and, always, the close, frequently disagreeable encounters with civilians and politicians.

Memoirs, personal papers, and the odd reflection by generals and ministers help fill out the picture. Sailor Walter Hose's tale of the HMCS *Rainbow* as it prevented a boatload of desperate Indians from entering Canada in the summer of 1914 is a reminder that the military serves at the behest of government. Colonel Buster Brown's preparations for war with the United States demonstrates that American aggression in North America was feared in certain quarters as late as the 1920s.

Canadians have almost always been uninterested in their soldiers in peacetime. While we have material from generals and admirals and from privates and airmen and airwomen, readers ought not to be surprised if there is little on the periods when Canada had no armed forces that could train well or fight. This was certainly the case for most of the years before and after the Great War. During the years between the two world wars, the battle lines became commentaries on the weaknesses of the militia, the stories of cadets at the Royal Military College, or accounts of bush flying in the 1920s by Canadian air force crews.

For the period before 1914, we print accounts by those who were at Quebec with Wolfe, those who fought in the War of 1812 and the South African War, and those who participated in the skirmishes and rebellions of the nineteenth century. The report by Captain W.D. Otter that his Toronto militia regiment fled in "a regular panic" from the Fenians at Ridgeway in 1866 portrays the perils of sending untrained troops into battle, a lesson Canadians proved slow to learn. The bulk of the volume is taken from the First and Second World Wars, amounting to almost two-thirds of the total. This is natural enough, because close to one in ten of the nation's population served in the armed forces during those monumental struggles. We also include a substantial array of narratives by those Canadians who served in the Korean War and in the peacekeeping, nation-building, and peace-enforcing roles that Canada has taken up in the last fifty years.

Most of our documents were written by soldiers and by men. There are reasons for this. Canada has been a land power throughout its history. We sent soldiers to fight against Riel's uprisings and we sent soldiers to South Africa. In the Great War, all but 30,000 or so of the more than 600,000 serving Canadians were in the army. Even in the Second World War, when Canada had a large air force, with 250,000 men and women, and a navy of 100,000 men and women, the army still accounted for almost three quarters of those 1.1 million who put on a uniform.

Women did not play a direct military role until the Northwest Rebellion and the South African War, when a few nurses accompanied the troops. In the 1914–18 war, nurses numbered in the low thousands, and in the Second World War there were 50,000 women in the CWACs, Wrens, and WDs, as the women's services in the army, navy, and air force were popularly known, in addition to thousands of Nursing Sisters. After 1945, women continued to serve and today number up to one quarter of Canada's small regular force and perhaps a higher percentage in Canada's even smaller reserves. In this collection, there are letters, memoirs, and accounts by women, but we have not sought to impose a false balance where none existed.

Not everyone who served in 1759 or 1914 or 1950 was literate. Tens of thousands were not, most especially in the country's early history. There are no letters here from those who could not read or write. Not all soldiers or sailors had someone to whom they wanted to or could write. Some simply found letter-making or keeping a journal foreign to the way they thought; for others, what they saw and experienced was too searing to relive in description. For much of the world wars, in fact, soldiers were ordered not to keep diaries for fear they might fall into enemy hands. Happily for us, some disobeyed their orders. If some of the letters we publish are graceless or lacking proper punctuation or spelling, we offer no apologies. We have corrected just enough to ensure that the meaning is clear. Nor have we wanted to clutter up the text with all manner of editorial devices. Introductions are provided where they seemed helpful for context or understanding; explanations are added in the texts themselves only when they are absolutely necessary.

The question of preservation is crucial. Private Jones may have written brilliantly perceptive letters from Batoche back to his parents in Halifax, but unless they were passed on from father to son to grandson and great-granddaughter or, even better, donated to a museum or an archives, they most likely are now irretrievably lost. Much of Canada's history has regrettably ended up in rubbish heaps across the land. We have had to work with what was left.

Fortunately, there are huge archival collections and more and more online depositories that make military letters available to everyone at their computer. The best electronic military collection is the extraordinarily useful Canadian Letters and Images Project maintained (and continuously expanded) by Professor Stephen Davies at Malaspina College in Nanaimo, B.C. (www.mala.bc.ca/history/images). This is a national treasure that deserves Canadians' support. The Directorate of History and Heritage at National Defence Headquarters in Ottawa also maintains a web site (www.forces.gc.ca/hr/dhh/engraph/home_.asp) on which some hundreds of historical reports and many books are available, many including first-person accounts. The Canadian War

Museum recently acquired the rich Second World War clipping files of the *Hamilton Spectator* and put them on-line (www.warmuseum.ca) with a fine search engine. The reportage of Canadian war correspondents is now readily available. There are dozens of other web sites that collect and preserve our past.

We are historians, and historians are apt to think chronologically. The documents that make up this book are almost all organized by date primarily because events follow one upon the other and are usually best comprehended that way. When a letter from a sailor on a corvette precedes three 1944 letters from infantry soldiers in Italy and France, and a Lancaster bomber pilot's diary entry follows those, an important fact is conveyed. With their straitened armed forces today, most Canadians might not realize that we once had a huge navy, army, and air force, all operating at the same time in far-flung parts of the globe. A chronological approach also mixes together the banal and the life-altering moments. When the soldiers of No. 1 Platoon of A Company of the Umpty-umph Battalion of the 142nd Division were fighting for their lives at Passchendaele, Ortona, Kapyong, or in the Medak Pocket, a recruit in training was griping about the food he was being fed at Camp Ennui. Military service is always unfair, with some exposed to repeated risks and some safe as church mice. A chronological organization, in our view, sharply exposes the dichotomy.

An editorial comment from a 1946 Dutch weekly newspaper that bade goodbye to the Canadian soldiers is one of the very few pieces in this book that is not a first-person account. Yet in its frank gratitude— "We have coals for our stoves and food for our children. That was your work"—it offers the best of reasons to explain why Canadians fought and died.

Many, many friends and colleagues have helped with this book. Jack Saywell went to the York University Archives on our behalf. Laurel Halliday did superb research in the voluminous and excellent material in the Museum of the Regiments and the Glenbow Museum and Archives in Calgary. Patricia Grimshaw energetically dug into the Canadian War Museum's growing manuscript archives. Stephen Davies of the Canadian Letters and Images Project was enormously cooperative, as was Mac Johnston of *Legion* magazine. Ryan Shackleton pored through pre-Confederation sources at the National Archives.

John G. Armstrong, Michael Bliss, Major Michael Boire, Kenneth J. Calder, Robert L. Calder, Major Doug Delaney, Paul Dickson, Richard Gimblett, Leo Hamson, Stephen Hoogenraad, Jeff Keshen, Philippe Lagassé, Hector Mackenzie, Tony Michel, Hilary Neary, Peter Neary, Richard Newport, Jeff Noakes, Roger Sarty, and Marie-Eve Vaillancourt graciously provided us with excellent material they uncovered in the course of their own research, or had in their possession as family treasures. Serge Bernier, Isabel Campbell, Steve Harris, and Michael Whitby assisted mightily at the Directorate of History and Heritage at National Defence Headquarters, as did Serge Durflinger, Dean Oliver, and Roger Sarty at the Canadian War Museum. Karen Baldree-O'Neill, Steven Beattie, Trista Grant, and Eliza Marciniak were expert letter-decipherers and proofreaders. Susan B. Whitney carefully reviewed the final manuscript. Gillian Watts prepared the index. Our literary agent, Linda McKnight, again worked her magic. Patrick Crean was the model of benevolent publishing, and managing editor Jim Gifford's involvement in the book was extraordinary. We are grateful to them all for their generosity.

Battle Lines is not the history of Canada. It is, however, a substantial and sometimes neglected part of the national story written in the words of those who made and continue to make it. The tale is not consistently inspiring, populated by pride, ambition, avarice, and cowardice as it sometimes is. Yet there are many great and stirring moments here, moments of great heroism, courage, and fortitude that are the underpinnings of our heritage. Canada's history was made by ordinary men and women performing extraordinary deeds in the most difficult of times, and we can all draw strength for the future from those who prepared the way for us.

J.L. Granatstein
Norman Hillmer
Toronto and Ottawa,
24 May 2004

BATTLE LINES

Wolfe Takes Quebec, 1759

ANONYMOUS

July 4th, A flag of truce was sent by the general to the town, to acquaint the governor of our design of attacking it on the part of his Britannick majesty; and also to inform him, that he was order'd by his master to carry on the war in this country with the utmost lenity; that he expects the troops under his command will follow his example, and that the inhuman practice of scalping, either by Indians or others, may be put a stop to, as he shall answer the consequence of its being severely revenged: at the same time we set at liberty twenty-five women, that were taken by us in the river. Monsieur Le Marquis de Vandreuil, who commands in the town, return'd a very polite answer, and desir'd the admiral might be acquainted, that as two gentlemen had been taken off the isle Condre by his people, belonging to Admiral Durell, the greatest care should be taken of them, and that as soon as he thought proper to remove our fleet and army he would return them: they made no scruple of informing our officer, that they were well acquainted with our force, and were surprised we should attempt the conquest of this country with such a handful of men. . . .

July 10th, Our bombs threw several shells into the French camp near Beauport, which they return'd with shot from their batteries, that is large boats with a gun each, of 12 to 24 pounders, of these they have about twenty, in different parts of the river, who keep so close under

their own breast, that we can get no opportunity of cutting them off.—
In the evening the Captain dropt as close in shore as the depth of the
water would allow, and fir'd several broad-sides at their camp, which
they were oblig'd to move a little farther back; but as they are entrenched close to their breast-works on the bank, cannot drive them
from thence. At night the enemy, having got a mortar down to their
camp, threw several shells very near the Captain and the Bombs, upon
which they weigh'd and drop'd out of their reach. . . .

July 31. In the morning two armed transports got under way, and at
high-water ran ashore, close to the enemies batteries, a little above the
falls of Montmorency, and began a very smart fire upon them, which
they returned. At seven the troops from Point Levi and Orleans embarked in the boats, and at eight rendezvoused in two lines between
the island and the north shore. The grenadiers, in the first line, supported by 200 Royal Americans, and Amhersts, and the Highlanders in
the second line, at the same time the Centurion dropt as near as possible to their batteries, and kept a continual fire upon them, which they
returned upon the boats with eight pieces of cannon and two mortars;
which, notwithstanding our being within point-blank shot for several
hours, suffered very little. The enemy's troops in the mean time filled
their breast-works and trenches, and behind them paraded with an
army greatly superior to ours in number. Notwithstanding this, their
batteries, the height of the bank, steep and difficult of access, and many
other disadvantages, the greatest spirit and chearfulness was discern-
able through our whole army, and all waited with the utmost impa-
tience for the moment of attack. General Wolf row'd at the head of us,
and gave his orders with great calmness, and so did the rest of our general officers. Admiral Saunders was greatly exposed, and the fleet had
like to have lost in him a gallant commander, a shell falling so near his
boat as to damage some of the oars and half fill her with water; at noon
the first line of boats was ordered in a-breast of the batteries, but some
of the boats grounding upon a bank some distance from the shore,
were ordered off again; General Townsend, with all the troops from
Montmorency, except the light infantry, were in readiness at the same
time to march a-cross the strand and passing between the falls and
river to join us at our landing. Colonel How, with the light infantry,

were at the same time to make a faint of passing Montmorency river, some distance above the falls, to divert the attention of the enemy. At four the first line of boats was landed, and the grenadiers, without waiting for form, or orders, rushed on with the greatest impetuosity for the bank, where they received from the enemy such an incessant fire of musquetry, as must be far easier to conceive than to describe; but firm to their purpose, and nothing daunted, true Englishmen, they endeavoured to surmount all difficulties, and attempted to gain the steep bank; and would, in all probability have fallen a sacrifice to their bravery, if a violent and sudden squall of wind and rain had not put a stop to the enemy's fire, and at the same time made it impossible for those brave fellows to proceed further, occasioned by the excessive slipperiness of the ground. During this time General Townsend with his brigade passed below the falls, and advanced to join us, but the General finding the difficulty of the attempt, and unwilling to sacrifice such brave fellows with so little probability of success, ordered the retreat to be beat, and fortunately for us, the lower part of the strand was out of musquet shot. After getting the wounded into the boats, General Wolf, with the remainder of the grenadiers and highlanders, joined General Townsend, and marched in good order along the strand towards the falls, and embarked Amherst's in the boats, saluted all the time by the infernal clamours of the Indians, and the Vive le Roy of the French; though the Poltroons, who were twice our numbers, dared not come down to us, though often invited by the hats waved at them from our general officers and troops: at five we took the people out of our armed transports and set fire to them; the enemy kept a continual fire from their batteries on our troops as they marched along the strand, but providentially did little execution; our grenadiers had possession of one of their small batteries, but in the confusion forgot to spike up the guns; the evening was employed in transporting the troops to their respective posts. Our loss this day was sixty killed, and between 3 and 400 wounded, all which we got off in the boats, except a Captain of the Royal Americans, who we hear is prisoner among the French, but mortally wounded; the Indians, according to their barbarous custom, stripped and scalped the dead, and with difficulty this officer escaped, being rescued by some French officers. What loss the

French have sustained we can only guess at, but suppose it to be considerable, as a continual fire was kept from our train at Montmorency, and from the Centurion and two armed ships: our whole body of troops at this attack did not amount to 5000, while the enemy acknowledge theirs to be 16000; but the advantage of the ground, not their number, fought against us; and it is the general opinion, that half our troops in their situation would have been a sufficient match for their whole number. . . .

August 15th, Six marines were surpriz'd and carried off from our camp at St. Anthony's. General Murray sent out parties from thence to destroy all the houses in that district; parties were detach'd likewise from our camps at Montmorency and Point Orleans, to destroy all the buildings (churches excepted) and their corn: one of these detachments from Montmorency fell in with a party of Canadians, headed by a priest, twenty of which they took prisoners, and killed several. In return for many acts of cruelty, the priest and the rest of the prisoners were put to death, and scalp'd by our rangers. . . .

September 12th, At nine in the evening 1600 of the troops were embark'd in the boats, commanded by General Monckton, who was to make the first landing at midnight: the boats rendezvous'd in a line a-breast of Admiral Holmes, who lay about five leagues above Quebec.

13th, At one in the morning the boats that had the troops in were order'd to row down the river (it being then ebb-tide) in the same order as the troops were to land, *viz.* the light infantry first, then Bragg's, Anstruther's, Kennedy's, Lascelle's, and a detachment of Frazier's; at two the frigates and transports, with the rest of the troops follow'd them. In rowing down the boats were discover'd by the enemy, but they expecting some boats down with provisions, under cover of the night, let us pass without examination. At Four we landed the troops about two miles from Quebec, with small loss, none but the enemy's centinels being there.

An attack is resolv'd on, and, let it be remember'd, for the honour of England, that though the enterprize is hazardous, exceeding doubtful, and attended with the utmost danger in every shape, not the least dejection or sign of fear appears among the troops: on the contrary, an uncommon eagerness in them to attack the foe is plain in every countenance: they are impatient to be lead on, and the General officers but with great difficulty can restrain their impetuosity; it should seem as if their courage rose in proportion to the labours they have to surmount; or perhaps they are fir'd with the resolution of revenging their companions who fell ill in the late attack, and are determin'd to punish the infamous and inhuman practice of scalping, if the place should fall into our hands, which however, seems greatly doubtful: it will in all probability be owing to the resolution the men have taken, of not being made prisoners, deter'd from falling into the enemy's hands, from the infernal practice above-mention'd being so often exercis'd upon those who are unhappy enough to fall into their hands.

From this disposition of the men, and the conduct and prudence of a very good set of officers, great things may be expected, especially from the Gentleman who commands in chief, who, in his military capacity, is perhaps equalled by few, and exceeded by none; and when riper years have matured a sound judgment, the great talents he possesses in the art of war will shew themselves to advantage; yet, if I can read right, though no man doubts his courage, he is not sanguine in his expections of reducing the place, and can depend on nothing but surprise, some bold and unexpected stroke, or as the French call it, *coup de main*; for this no troops in Europe are so fit as ours for resolution, and a contempt of death are characteristic of an English soldier.

How many lives must be lost of the few troops we have before we can hope to succeed; had General Amherst been able to have joined us, something might have been done: as it is, he comes too late, for either the place will be taken, or we must return to England before he arrives: in the latter case he must fail as well as we, and owing to the same cause, want of numbers.

Could the junction have taken place, we might bid defiance to united strength, of French, Indians, and Canadians.

There can be but little hopes of taking the place by assault, for though the Men of war might be of infinite service in silencing the batteries of the Lower Town, yet the greatest, and indeed an almost insurmountable difficulty would yet remain; for the few passages that lead from the Upper to the lower town are strongly intrenched, and our ships can by no means reach the upper batteries.

The country is extremely strong, and the enemy have added much to its natural strength; and have now, for the defence of the river, floating batteries and boats, which in a great measure frustrate our designs: several parties of Indians are likewise troublesome to us, by hovering round our advanced posts, and we have hitherto found it impossible to elude their vigilance.

Every thing is in motion, and a few hours will probably determine the fate of Canada.

If the General should attempt to ascend the rock, it is a work of much labour and difficulty, if at all practicable; and should our troops perform this difficult undertaking, I shall for the future think little of Hanibal's leading an army over the Alps; the rock is almost steep, and the summit seems to me inaccessible to an army; this at least appears to be the Opinion of the French, who place no centinel there, and seem perfectly secure that it will never be attempted.—All difficulties have been surmounted, and such a blow struck as will amaze posterity: our brave General lead on the troops to the hills above-mentioned, and was the first man that began to clime it; the men followed their leader with the utmost alacrity, and at length ascended the summit: as soon as they were formed the enemy advanced, and sent a party to the bottom of the hill to cut off our retreat, but they were themselves cut off by the troops that remained below. Those above being attacked by the enemy, had reserved their fire till the French advanced within forty yards of them, then made a general discharge, which threw the enemy into confusion; our people improved the advantage, and with their bayonets pushed them over the river St. Charles, and into the town: this success was dearly purchased by the loss of our brave General, who was wounded in the beginning of the action, and died soon after, but not before he had the satisfaction of being told the day was ours. I die contented then the hero cry'd, my life was due to my country, happy if I have been the means of adding conquest and glory to it: he died with calmness, and closed a well-spent life by an action which throws a lustre upon the arms of Britain; like the old Theban, he died and conquered: the affliction of the army best speaks his merit; he was the sincere friend, the gentleman, and the soldier: at a time of life when many have but the command of a company, he had raised himself by his merit almost to the top of his profession: it is to be hoped his grateful country will decree those honours to his breathless corps, as living he would undoubtedly have received.

The enemy, after their first repulse, made a stand at some distance, but were soon broke by the bravery of our troops, and ran into the town for shelter in the greatest confusion imaginable; there was dreadful slaughter on their side: the conflict was short but bloody, upwards of 600 of our men being wounded, though not above 40 killed outright: the disparity in the number of killed and wounded was, no doubt, owing to the enemy's firing at too great a distance, for their balls were almost spent before they reached our men; several of our people having received contusions on parts where the blow must have been mortal, had they reserved their fire a little longer: thus ended the thirteenth day of September, a day which will reflect honour on the British arms for ever.

The Battle on the Plains of Abraham

CAPTAIN JOHN KNOX

Sept. 11, 1759. Great preparations are making throughout the fleet and army to surprise the enemy, and compel them to decide the fate of Quebec by a battle. All the long-boats below the town are to be filled with seamen, marines, and such detachments as can be spared from Points Levi and Orleans, in order to make a feint off Beauport and the Point de Lest, and endeavor to engross the attention of the Sieur de Montcalm, while the army are to force a descent on this side of the town. The officer of our regiment who commanded the escort yesterday on the reconnoitring party, being asked in the general's hearing, after the health of one of the gentlemen who was reported to be ill, replied "he was in a very low indifferent state," which the other lamented, saying, "He has but a puny, delicate constitution." This struck his Excellency, it being his own case, who interrupted, "Don't tell me of constitution: that officer has good spirits, and good spirits will carry a man through everything."

September 12. A soldier of the Royal Americans deserted this day from the south shore, and one came over to us from the enemy, who informed the General "that he belonged to a detachment composed of two officers and fifty men who had been sent across the river to take a prisoner; that the French generals suspect we are going higher up to lay waste the country and destroy such ships and craft as they have got above; and that Monsieur Montcalm will not be prevailed on to quit his situation, insisting that the flower of our army are still below the town; that the reduction of Niagara has caused great discontent in the French army, that the wretched Canadians are much dissatisfied, and that Monsieur de Levis is certainly marched, with a detachment of the army, to Montreal, in order to re-enforce Mr. Bourlemacque and stop General Amherst's progress." This fellow added "that, if we were fairly landed on the north side of the river, an incredible number of the French regulars would actually desert to us." . . .

Sept. 13, 1759. Before daybreak this morning we made a descent upon the north shore, about half a quarter of a mile to the eastward of Sillery; and the light troops were fortunately by the rapidity of the current carried lower down between us and Cape Diamond. We had in this debarkation thirty flat-bottomed boats, containing about sixteen hundred men. This was a great surprise on the enemy, who from the natural strength of the place did not suspect, and consequently were not prepared against so bold an attempt. The chain of sentries which they had posted along the summit of the heights galled us a little, and picked off several men and some officers before our light infantry got up to dislodge them. This grand enterprise was conducted and executed with great good order and discretion. As fast as we landed, the boats put off for re-enforcements, and the troops formed with much regularity. The General, with Brigadiers Monckton and Murray, was ashore with the first division. We lost no time here, but clambered up one of the steepest precipices that can be conceived, being almost a perpendicular, and of an incredible height. As soon as we gained the summit, all was quiet, and not a shot was heard, owing to the excellent conduct of the light infantry under Colonel Howe. It was by this time clear daylight. Here we formed again, the river and the south country in our rear, our right extending to the town, our left to Sillery, and halted a few minutes. The general then detached the light troops to our left to rout the enemy from their battery, and to disable their guns, except they could be rendered serviceable to the party who were to remain there; and this service was soon performed. We then faced to the right, and marched toward the town by files till we came to the Plains of Abraham, an even piece of ground which Mr. Wolfe had made choice of, while we stood forming upon the hill. Weather showery. About six o'clock the enemy first made their appearance upon the heights between us and the town, whereupon we halted and wheeled to the right, thereby forming the line of battle. The first disposition then was "grenadiers of Louisburg on the right, forty-seventh regiment on the left, twenty-eighth on the right, forty-seventh regiment on the left, twenty-eighth on the right, and the forty-third on the left." Part of the light infantry took post in the houses at Sillery, and the remainder occupied a chain of houses which were opportunely situated for that purpose and covered our left flank, inclining toward our rear. The general then advanced some platoons from the grenadiers and twenty-eighth regiment below the height on our right, to annoy the enemy, and prevent their getting round the declivity between us and the main river, which they had attempted. By this time the fifteenth and thirty-fifth regiments joined us, who formed a second line, and were soon after followed by the forty-eighth and fifty-eighth, two battalions of the sixtieth and seventy-eighth regiments (Highlanders), by which a new disposition was made of the whole, namely: "first line, thirty-fifth to the right, in a circular form on the slope of the hill; fifty-eighth, left; grenadiers, right; seventy-eighth, left; twenty-eighth, right; forty-seventh, left; forty-third, in the centre." General Wolfe, Brigadiers Monckton and Murray, to our front line; and the second was composed of the fifteenth and two battalions of the sixtieth regiment under Brigadier Townshend, with a reserve of the forty-eighth regiment, under Colonel Burton, drawn up in four grand divisions with large intervals. The enemy had now likewise formed the line of battle, and got some cannon to play on us, with round and canister shot; but what galled us most was a body of Indians and other marksmen they had concealed in the corn opposite to the front of our right wing, and a coppice that stood opposite to our centre inclining toward our left. But the Colonel Hale, by Brigadier Monckton's orders, advanced some platoons alternately from the forty-seventh regiment, which after a few rounds obliged these sculkers to retire. We were now ordered to lie down, and remained some time in this position. About eight o'clock we had two pieces of short brass six-pounders playing on the enemy, which threw them into some confusion, and obliged them to alter their disposition; and Montcalm formed them into three large columns. About nine the two armies moved a little nearer each other. The light cavalry made a faint attempt upon our parties at the battery of Sillery, but were soon beat off; and Monsieur de Bougainville, with his troops from Cape Rouge, came down to attack the flank of our second line, hoping to penetrate there. But, by a masterly disposition of Brigadier Townshend, they were forced to desist; and the third battalion of Royal Americans was then detached to the first ground we had formed on after we gained the heights, to preserve the communication with the beach and our boats. About ten o'clock the enemy began to advance briskly in three columns, with loud shouts and recovered arms, two of them inclining to the left of our army, and the third toward our right, firing obliquely at the two extremities of our line, from the distance of one hundred and thirty, until they came within forty yards, which our troops withstood with the greatest intrepidity and firmness, still reserving their fire and paying the strictest obedience to their officers. This uncommon steadiness, together with the havoc which the grape-shot from our field-pieces made among them, threw them into some disorder, and was most critically maintained by a well-timed, regular, and heavy discharge of our small arms, such as they could no longer oppose. Hereupon they gave way, and fled with precipitation, so that by the time the cloud of smoke was vanished our men were again loaded, and, profiting by the advantage we had over them, pursued them almost to the gates of the town and the bridge over the little river, redoubling our fire with great eagerness, making many officers and men prisoners. The weather cleared up, with a comfortably warm sunshine. The Highlanders chased them vigorously toward Charles River, and the fifty-eighth to the suburb close to John's gate, until they were checked by the cannon from the two hulks. At the same time a gun which the town had brought to bear

upon us with grape-shot galled the progress of the regiments to the
right, who were likewise pursuing with equal ardor, while Colonel
Hunt Walsh, by a very judicious movement, wheeled the battalions of
Bragg and Kennedy to the left, and flanked the coppice where a body
of the enemy made a stand as if willing to renew the action; but a few
platoons from these corps completed our victory. Then it was that
Brigadier Townshend came up, called off the pursuers, ordered the
whole line to dress and recover their former ground. Our joy at this
success is inexpressibly damped by the loss we sustained of one of the
greatest heroes which this or any other age can boast of,—General
James Wolfe,—who received his mortal wound as he was exerting
himself at the head of the grenadiers of Louisburg; and Brigadier
Monckton was unfortunately wounded upon the left of the forty-third
and right of the forty-seventh regiment at much the same time,
whereby the command devolved on Brigadier Townshend, who, with
Brigadier Murray, went to the head of every regiment and returned
thanks for their extraordinary good behavior, congratulating the officers on our success. There is one incident very remarkable,—that the
enemy were extremely apprehensive of being rigorously treated; for,
conscious of their inhuman behavior to our troops upon a former occasion, the officers who fell into our hands most piteously (with hats
off) sued for quarter, repeatedly declaring they were not at Fort
William Henry (called by them Fort George) in the year 1757. A soldier of the Royal Americans who deserted from us this campaign, and
fought against us to-day, was found wounded on the field of battle.
He was immediately tried by a general court-martial, and was shot
to death pursuant to his sentence. While the two armies were engaged
this morning, there was an incessant firing between the town and our
south batteries. By the time that our troops had taken a little refresh-
ment, a quantity of intrenching tools were brought ashore, and the regiments were employed in redoubting our ground and landing some
cannon and ammunition. The officers who were prisoners say that
Quebec will surrender in a few days. Some deserters who came out to
us in the evening agree in that opinion, and inform us that the Sieur
de Montcalm is dying, in great agony, of a wound he received to-day
in their retreat. Thus has our late renowned commander by his superior

eminence in the art of war, and a most judicious *coup d'état*, made a conquest of this fertile, healthy, and hitherto formidable country, with a handful of troops only, in spite of the political schemes and most vigorous efforts of the famous Montcalm, and many other officers of rank and experience at the head of an army considerably more numerous.

The Assault on Detroit, 1763

MAJOR DUNCAN

The British war against the French transformed into a war against France's Indian allies, notably the tribes led by Pontiac. Fighting them was no easy task, as suggested by this account of the attack on the fort at Detroit on July 30, 1763.

On the Evening of the 30th July Capt. Dalyell being fully persuaded that *Pondiack* the Indian Chief, with his Tribes, would soon abandon his Designs, and retire, insisted with the Commandant, Major Gladwin (contrary to his Opinion, and that of two French Gentlemen, who well knew the Disposition of the Enemy as also the Intelligence they had received from the disaffected French) that they might be surprized in their Camp, totally Routed, and drove out of the Settlement: after many arguments for, and against the Interprize, Capt. Dalyell at last said that Major Gladwin might do as he pleased, but, that, really he saw no Difficulty in the Execution, and in giving them an Irrecoverable Blow, or Words to that Purpose; on which, it was soon determined that Captain Dalyell was to march out with 240 of the best troops. Thereupon we marched half after two in the Morning, two deep along the great Road, by the River side, two Boats up the River along shore, with a Paterrara in each, with Orders to keep up with the Line of March, cover our Retreat, and take off our dead, and wounded, Lieut. Bean with the Queen's Independants being ordered on a Rear Guard to cover the dead and wounded to the Boats. About a mile and half from the Fort, we had Orders to form into Platoons, and if attacked in the Front, to fire by Street Firings; We then advanced, and in about half a Mile further *our Advanced Guard commanded by Lieutenant Brown* of the 55th. had been fired upon just close to the Enemy's Breast Works, and Cover, so close that the Fire being very heavy, not only killed, and wounded the most of his Party, but communicated to the main Body, killed, and wounded several, which being unexpected staggered, and put the whole in some Confusion; but soon Recovered their order, and gave the Enemy, or rather their Works a Discharge, or two from the Front, commanded by Capt. Gray, at the same time, the Rear commanded by Capt. Grant, was fired upon from a House and some Fences, about 20 Yards on his left, on which, he ordered his own and Capt. Hopkin's Company to face to the left, and give a full Fire that way. The Enemy then (it appeared) giving way every where Capt. Dalyell sent Orders to Capt. Grant to take Possession of the above said House, and Fences, which he immediately did, and entered; he found in the House two men, who told him the Enemy had been there long, and well apprized of our Design. Captain Grant then asked them the number, they answered 300, and that they intended as soon as they attacked us in the Front to get in our Rear and between us, and the Fort. Capt. Dalyell soon after Firing ceased, came where Capt. Grant was, who told him what the Frenchmen had said, on which he went to the House, and spoke to the Frenchmen, then went towards the Front, and soon Returned again, telling Capt. Grant that he was wounded, and that one of our Pateraras was broke, and that he had ordered the Boat back to the Fort with some dead, and wounded. Capt. Grant some time before hearing the Enemy Whooping on our Flank, went, and asked the Frenchman what it was, who answered that they (the Indians) were endeavoring to get in our Rear, and (as far as he understood it) that we were, or would be lost. Dalyell returned again with Major Rogers, who hearing the Enemy Whooping, as before, and being told again what the Frenchman said, Capt. Grant tooke liberty to say we should not give the Enemy time to recollect, and recover themselves, that if he intended to go on, we should push them, and if to retire, we should do it before they got in our Rear: to which Capt. Dalyell, made no Reply, and went with Major Rogers to the main Body again. Captain Grant then begged of Lieut. McDugal, who acted as Adjutant to the Detachment to go up to Capt. Gray to the Front, and tell him what he said to Capt. Dalyell, and to know if he approved of the same, and if he did, to tell him it. Lieutenant McDougal being gone, Capt. Grant told Capt. Dalyell, who came in ab^t an hour after (with Mr. Babby, and Mr. St. Martin two French Gentlemen who had gone with him as Volunteers, and Guides) & said that he intended to Retire, and ordered Capt. Grant to march in the Front conducted by Mr. Babby and post himself in an Orchard and house which would be shown him by him.—he then marched, and in about half a Mile further had some shots fired on his Flank at a distance, but got Possession of an Orchard wall fence, and just as he got there, heared a warm firing in the Rear, having at the same time a Firing on his own Post from the Fences & Cornfields behind it. Lieut. McDougal then came up to him, and told him that Capt. Dalyell was killed, and Capt. Gray very much wounded, in making a rush on the Enemy, and Driving them out of a Breast Work of Cord Wood, & an Intrenchment they had made, and that the Command then divolved upon him Capt. Grant; Lieutenant Bean *Immediately came up, and told him*, that Captain Rogers had desired him to tell him, that he had taken Possession of a House with the Rear of the troops that Capt. Grant had better retire with what numbers he had, as Major Rogers could not get off without the Boats to cover him, he being hard pushed by the Enemy from the Enclosures behind him, some of which scoured the Road, thro' which he must retire. Capt. Grant had by this time de-tached all the men he could get, and took Possession of all the Enclo-sures, Barns, Fences &c. from his own Post to the Fort, in which Posts he put Lieut. Cuyler, Lieut. Bean, and Ensign Fisher, as soon as they came up with sufficient men to prevent the further Advance of the Enemy, he also sent Ensign Pawly with 20 men back, to attack a party of the Enemy, which not only annoyed his own Post a little, but galled those who were joining him from the attack where Capt. Dalyell was killed, and Capt. Gray, and Lieut. Luke & Lieut. Brown wounded, which Ensign Pawly did, and killed some of the Enemy in their flight.—he then sent back to Capt. Rogers to tell him what he had done, and desired that he would come off, that the Retreat was quite secured, and the different Parties ordered to cover one another suc-cessively until the whole had joined—but Capt. Rogers not finding it safe, chose to wait for the armed Boats, one of which appear'd imme-

diately with Lieut. Bremm, whom Capt. Grant had directed to go &
cover Capt. Roger's Retreat, who was in the next house about 80 yards
distance. Lieut. Bremm accordingly went & firing a few shots, Lieut.
Abbot with the other Boat sent down with Capt. Gray, Lieut. Brown,
and some wounded men returned, which I suppose the Enemy seeing,
did not wait her arrival, but retired on Lieut. Bremm's firing, and gave
Capt. Rogers an Opportunity to come off; so that the whole from different Posts joined without any confusion, and marched into the Fort
in good order about eight o' the clock covered by the Armed Boats
on the Water Side, and by our own Parties on the Countryside in
View of the Enemy all joined, and much stronger than at the Beginning of the Affair, as was afterwards told by some Prisoners who made
their escape many [having] joined them from the other side of the
River, and other Places.

The Americans Fail to Take Quebec, 1775–76

SIR GUY CARLETON

> *Even before their Declaration of Independence, the American
> colonies sent an army to "liberate" Quebec from the British. But the
> attack, led by General Benedict Arnold, failed in the dead of winter,
> and by May 1776, the Americans were forced to withdraw when a
> British fleet arrived.*

[They had] marched out of the [gates] of St Louis and St Johns [*sic*] to
see what those mighty Boasters were about. They were found very
busy in their preparations for a retreat, a few shot being exchanged,
the line marched forward and the plains were soon cleared of those
plunderers, all their artillery, military stores, scaling ladders, petards,
etc. were abandoned . . . Thus ended our siege and blockade during
which the mixed garrison of soldiers, sailors, British and Canadian
militia with [help] from Halifax and Newfoundland showed great zeal
and patience under very severe duty and uncommon vigilance, indis-
pensable in a place liable to be stormed, besides great labor necessary
to render such attempts less practical.

The Indian Way of War

THOMAS ANBUREY

The War of Independence pitted the British against the revolutionary Americans, both sides having Aboriginal allies. This account illustrates the fascination inspired by the First Peoples.

Camp at Button-Mole Bay
upon Lake Champlain
June 24, 1777

After the meeting of the Indians at River Bouquet, the General ordered them some liquor, and they had a war-dance, in which they throw themselves in various postures, every now and then making most hideous yells; as to their appearance, nothing more horrid can you paint to your imagination, being dressed in such an *outré* manner, some with the skins of bulls with the horns upon their heads, others with a great quantity of feathers, and many in a state of total nudity: there was one among them at whose modesty I could not help smiling, and who, rather than be divested of any covering, had tied a blackbird before him. Joined to these strange dresses, and added to the grotesque appearance, they paint their faces of various colours, with a view to inspire an additional horror. It is almost incredible to think what a prodigious degree of conceit and foppery reigns amongst the savages in decorating their persons, perhaps not inferior to that by which alone some of our pretty fellows of the present age so conspicuously distinguish themselves. The following striking instance of it several other officers, as well as myself, were eye-witnesses to, and it afforded us no small entertainment.

In our way to their encampment, we observed a young Indian who was preparing for the war-dance, seated under a wigwam, with a small looking-glass placed before him, and surrounded with several papers, filled with different paints. At our stopping to observe him, he was at first a little disconcerted, and appeared displeased, but soon after proceeded to adorn himself. He first smeared his face with a little bear's grease, then rubbed in some vermilion, then a little black, blue, and green paints, and having viewed himself for some time in the glass, in a rage he wiped it all off, and began again, but with no better success, still appearing dissatisfied. We went on to the council, which lasted near two hours, and on our return found the Indian in the same position, and at the same employment, having nearly consumed all his stock of colours! What a pity it is the ladies in England, adepts in this art, have not such a variety of tints to exercise their genius with!—in my mind, if they must paint, the more ridiculous they appear, the better.

Bear's grease, indeed, would not be a very delicate perfume, but no matter—if nature must be patched up, it little signifies with what!— I could laugh at the streaks on an Indian, but am struck with contempt at the airs put on by your flirts, from a pennyworth of carmine, and touched with pity when sixty would assume the glow of fifteen, through a false shame or a childish want of admiration!

An Indian's idea of war consists in never fighting in an open field but upon some very extraordinary occasion, for they consider this method as unworthy an able warrior, and as an affair in which fortune governs, more than prudence or courage.

They are of essential service in either defending or invading a country, being extremely skilful in the art of surprising, and watching the motions of an enemy.

On a secret expedition they light no fire to warm themselves, nor prepare their victuals, but subsist merely on the miserable pittance of some of their meal mixed with water; they lie close to the ground all day, and only march in the night; while halting to rest and refresh themselves, scouts are sent out on every side to reconnoitre the country, and beat up every place where they suspect an enemy can lie concealed. Two of the principal things that enable them to find out their enemies, is the smoke of their fires, which they smell at a vast distance, and their tracks, in the discovery and distinguishing of which they are possessed of a sagacity equally astonishing, for they will discern by the footsteps, that to us would appear extremely confused, nearly the number of men, and the length of time since they passed; this latter circumstance was confirmed to me by an officer who has the superintending of their tribes. Being out upon a scout with them, they discerned some footsteps, when the Indians told him that seven or eight people had passed that way, and that only two or three days since: they had not gone far before they came to a plantation with a house upon it, and as is the custom with the Indians, ran up to it, and surprised a scouting party of the Americans, consisting of seven, who had come there overnight.

In travelling through the woods, they carefully observe the trees, especially the tall pines, which are for the most part void of foliage, on the branches that are exposed to the north wind, the trunk on that side having the bark extremely rugged, by which they ascertain the direction to be taken; and for the more easy discovery of their way back again, their tomahawks are continually blazing the trees, which is cutting off a small piece of the bark, and as they march along they break down the underwood.

Every Indian is a hunter, and their manner of making war is of the same nature, only changing the object, by skulking, surprising, and killing those of their own species, instead of the brute creation.

There is an indisputable necessity of having Indians, where Indians are employed against you, unless we had men enough of our own trained up in that sort of military exercise, as our European discipline is of little avail in the woods against savages.

The reason of my dwelling so much on the subject of Indians is because I am sensible how repugnant it is to the feelings of an Englishman to employ them, and how much their cruelty and barbarity has been exaggerated.

They fight as those opposed against them fight; we must use the same means as our enemies, to be but on an equal footing with them.

Fighting with Brock

W. H. MERRITT

On the 27th June, 1812, a man arrived at Thos. Clark's, Esqr., with the news of war being proclaimed by the Pres[iden]t of [the] U[nited] S[tates]. The news flew like lightning over the country. The flank companies and other volunteer corps were immediately ordered out. We had one Regt. of regulars the 41st, in the Upper Province, that is, above Kingston, say, York, Ft. George, Queenston, Chippawa, Fort Erie, Amherstburg, Sandwich and St. Joseph. The country was well aware of the strength and population of the U.S. and turned out with a desire and determination of doing their duty. At the same time they were acting under the impression of being eventually conquered. I heard [at] 12 o'clock P.M. on the night of the 27th of the declaration of war, by Mr. Culp. . . .

Capt. G. Hamilton, Askin, Rolph, &c., were volunteers with M[ajor] Chambers. On the 9th August the gallant and celebrated Brock arrived with the flank companies of the York Militia, and Capt. Hatt's f[lank] c[ompany] from the Niag[ara] Dist[rict]. He addressed all the militia present [and] told them of his determination of proceeding immediately to Amherstburg and driving the enemy out of the country, requesting all willing to defend their country at the risque of their lives to volunteer their services, which they all did to a man. He selected 350 of the best men [and] sent the rest home, as the boats would hold no more. I was sent by land to Del[aware] Town to prevent any party penetrating by that direction. [I] went by way of Port Talbot [and] was placed under Col. Talbot's com[man]d. After remaining three days there [I] sent an express to C[olonel] Tal[bot], requesting permission to proceed on as far as practicable towards Sandwich. Accordingly, on the 15th inst., I received a discretional order to act as I thought proper, and moved on. Most unfortunately, the day before I reached Sandwich Detroit was captured. I could hardly have met with a more serious disappointment; being the first that was sent on the expedition and having more fatigue and trouble than any other corps, and being deprived of the glory in sharing in the capture was truly annoying to both the men and myself.

Gen. Brock arrived at Amherstburg on Friday, the 14th Aug. Again addressed the men. [On the] 15th [he] moved up to Sandwich. The enemy retired on his approach. [He] erected a couple of batteries opposite Detroit fort and town, summoned Hull to surrender, which he refused, opened the batteries in the afternoon. [They] had little or no effect. On the 16th, Sunday, with that promptness so very conspicuous in his character, [he] crossed the river with about 700 Indians under the celebrated *Tecumthe*, 350 regulars and about 430 militia. [His] whole force [was] 1480. [The] Indians were sent in[to] the wood. [The] reg[ulars] and militia marched up the plain, or rather road, till within

300 yards of the fort where they filed off to the left in a deep ravine. At the same time our batteries were playing away from the opposite shore with effect. The exterminating General, thinking warm work was about commencing, thought proper to surrender with 2500 men, &c., &c. . . .

On 7th September left [Sandwich] for Fort George, where we arrived on the 15th. We were in momentary expectation of an attack from Gen. Rennselaer, who had collected a large force opposite Queenston and Ft. Erie.

Our duty at this time was very severe. [We were] up all night and slept in the day. Cornet Pell Major was stationed with a party at Ft. Erie. On the *9th October* the enemy succeeded in cutting out two schooners near Ft. Erie, the *Caledonia* and *Detroit*. Cornet Major volunteered to bring off the latter with a few men from under the enemy's shore, [but] was mortally wounded and several of his men slightly, some severely. [He] was taken down to Chippawa. I went to see him on the 12th but a few minutes before I arrived he made his exit. I returned to make arrangements for his interment on the following day. Early in the morning Capt. H[amilton] and myself, who slept in the same room, were alarmed by a gun. We had just slipped on our jackets and swords when they were repeated, and a sad scene ensued. Women and children [were] running in all directions and soldiers [were] repairing to their posts. We ran to our barracks and with much difficulty and danger succeeded in getting out our horses, as the stables were in range of the American guns which were leveled at the court house. We received orders to repair to Queenston as soon as possible, as the enemy had landed. We galloped up as far as Durham's where we met our troops that had been driven from the field and the wounded coming out. Gen. Brock, we heard, was killed a few moments before. In short, for young soldiers we had the most dismal prospects before us that possibly can be conceived. The enemy was magnified to 5000 men and continually crossing without our being able to annoy them. Our few but gallant fellows that had been beaten back and dispersed over the field were now collecting. The wounded [were] meeting us from the field. Col. McDonald, Prov[incial] A. D. C. to the Gen[eral] was brought three miles by two soldiers, mortally wounded. A circumstance that damped our minds most was the loss of our gallant and much lamented Brock. In him we lost a host. All ranks and descriptions of people placed such implicit reliance on his skill, bravery, and good judgment, that led by him they were confident of success. To revenge his death they were determined to make an effort. (The 49th Regt. had arrived while we were at Detroit.) Gen. Sheif arriving from Ft. George at this moment took the command, collected the flank companies of militia, a few of the 41st and the remainder of the 49th companies who had been engaged in the morning. I was sent on the right to prevent their coming down the mountain undiscovered. Capt. Norton with 70 Indians was before me. He crossed the fields, gained the mountain, drove in their flanking parties and attacked their main body. [He] was repulsed with some loss, as he had so few men. G[eneral] Sheif made an oblique movement to the right, gained the mountain and advanced to Phelp's fields. We remained here an hour [waiting] for a detachment of the 41st from Chippawa. Col. Clark arriving with his men the attack was made. I was previously sent to hurry on Capt. Bullock. They came on *double-quick*, gained the field about five minutes after the action commenced [and] pushed on. The enemy fled in a few minutes in the greatest disorder. We made 900 and odd prisoners. Capt. Holcroft behaved with the greatest coolness [and] kept his 6 pounder exposed to [the] fire of the enemy's long guns during the action. Mr. McKenney's conduct was conspicuous for bravery during the day. It would be impossible to describe the feelings of our young soldiers at this moment, having entered the action with the idea, if successful, of two-thirds being killed or wounded, in 10 minutes to have all the enemy in our possession with a loss of not more than 12 or 13 on our side. It was a most fortunate circumstance for us [and] gave new life to everything. Only the loss of our brave general. On the night before Maj. Merritt and a number of officers were with him. He expected an attack, was round himself giving orders for a strict lookout, was very anxious for it to take place, as he had great confidence in his new raised men. At 4 A.M. a dragoon arrived with the intelligence of an attack having been made at Queenston. He mounted and rode up without an attendant. The morning was breaking as he arrived. Perceiving our shells [were] not reaching the enemy's batteries he rode up [and] ordered more powder. The mortar threw one or two with great effect. At that moment 500 of the enemy appeared within

20 yards of the battery on the mountain in his rear. He ordered the few artillerymen with him to retreat and ran down the mountain exposed to a very heavy fire. Capt. Dennis, 49th, com[manding] the post with 2 flank companies 49th and part of 4 comp[anie]s militia, expecting an attack gave orders for the guard to fire on the first boat that was launched. About ½ after 3 the enemy launched a boat, the guard fired, the men repaired to their posts and drove them back with immense slaughter [and] took 150 prisoners. About 500 had succeeded in landing above under cover of the darkness and bank and gained the brow of the mountain. The guard at that place had left it and joined their comrades under the hill. They were not perceived till they were in the rear of Gen. Brock's battery. He rallied about 30 of the grenadiers [and] was preparing to charge the 500 when he received a random shot through the left breast. He fell in the act of cheering his men. His last words were, *Push on, my brave fellows.* Col. McDonald, who was near them, called on the men about him to revenge his death, which they were well disposed to do. He succeeded with about 75 militia and regulars in gaining the mountain on their left, exposed to a cross fire all the time. They formed and advanced, drove the enemy to the summit of the hill, when Capt. Williams, 49th, was badly wounded in the head, C[olonel] McD[onald] had his horse shot and received a mortal wound through his body. The loss of the two com[manding] officers threw the men in[to] disorder. The enemy took courage [and] advanced. Our men made a precipitate retreat down the mountain and retired to Durham's, where we met them.

Honour and Glory

ANNE PREVOST

Anne Prevost, the daughter of the Governor General of British North America, kept a diary through the War of 1812. These entries are from the opening months of the war.

June 25th: I was summoned in the midst of my French lesson to hear some news that had arrived. It was indeed an important piece of intelligence:—"America has declared War against England." The news had arrived by an Express to some of the Quebec merchants. . . .

On this day I saw nothing before me but my Father's honour and glory. Although I knew how small a force we had to defend the Canadas, such was my confidence in his talents and fortune, that I did not feel the slightest apprehension of any reverse. I thought those abominable Yankees deserved a good drubbing for having dared to think of going to War with England, and surely there was no harm in rejoicing that the War had happened during my Father's Administration, because I thought he was the person best calculated to inflict on the Yankees the punishment they deserved. Stars and Ribbons glittered in perspective. Yet I must do myself the justice to say it was *pure fame* I longed my Father to win—I thought of *fame* more than of its accompaniments. . . .

July 27th: We had an account of General Brock's victory—the particulars of the capture of Detroit arrived on Saturday 29th. Several houses were illuminated in the evening, and on Monday the whole town was lighted up.

August 12th: The American prisoners arrived: the Officers were placed on parole in some of the adjacent villages. It was said they boasted General Dearborn would soon release them as he was going to overrun Canada with an army of a hundred thousand men. . . .

October 22nd: An Express brought the news of the Battle of Queenston, and the death of our noble defender, General Brock. Had he lived how different every thing might have turned out. His energy and talents were invaluable to my Father, for it was impossible for one individual to watch over both Upper and Lower Canada in the way that was necessary for their complete defence. This excellent Officer was only "too prodigal of life,"—he fell while leading on the Grenadiers of the 49th Regiment: his own favourite corps. If he had but reserved his personal exertions till the reinforcements came up—which ultimately drove back the invaders—his Country might have had him still. A General ought to sometimes recollect how valuable his life is to his army.

Corporal Chrétien Fights Off
the Invaders, May 1813

CAPTAIN JACQUES VIGER

"Corporal or Lance Sergeant Chrétien."—Cananocoui as before stated is 18 miles lower down than Kingston; we have there a redoubt. The garrison consists of local militia and a detachment from this post. Nine Voltigeurs under the order of Corporal Chrétien were on duty there on the 14th of May, when Lieutenant Marjoribanks, R.N., in command of a gun vessel cruising among the islands, arrived and landed 30 militiamen. He had discovered one of the enemy's gun boats on the river. He proposed to his men to attack this boat, but these good people thought otherwise; they were not yet I presume tired of life; they offered many objections to the lieutenants hostile and bloodthirsty intentions. The poltroon has powers of eloquence quite equal to those of the brave man; these philosopher soldiers used their rhetoric to such good purpose that the Lieutenant saw the futility of risking the attack with such a crew, and decided to land them at Cananocoui. From what precedes you may perhaps conclude that under the weighty arguments of these braves this bloodthirsty officer had yielded and had come to more humane and rational sentiments. Alas, no! you are wrong. They are case-hardened villains, these English tars; they live for knocks and thumps; they know positively nothing of our college logic, or, if they speak of it it is merely to ridicule and despise it; they affect to believe that there is more argument and sound sense in a grape shot than in the best argument. Strange people, do you say? Well, they are. Anyway, after landing his thirty rhetoricians (an epithet which our friend the officer emphatically qualified, it is said, with heavy words) he invited volunteers to accompany him on his venture, for he was still bent on the same sanguinary designs; one subaltern and 10 men of the 104th Regiment, Corporal Chrétien and the nine voltigeurs volunteered to form part of the expedition and were permitted to do so by Colonel Stone of the militia, who was commandant. These, with the boat's crew of six men, gave chase to the enemy's vessel, but failed to overtake her.

Feeling very sore and disappointed at the failure of this second attempt to close with the enemy, Marjoribanks had made up his mind not to return empty handed; he therefore decided to make a descent at the nearest American port, which was Gravelly Point. His pilot had told him that the Yankee boats repaired to the Cape every night. He conceived the evil pleasure of cutting them out by way of surprise, and his wicked followers accepted the idea with the greatest enthusiasm.

About one o'clock on the morning of the 25th of May, two countrymen were taken prisoners off the shore, and forced to guide the marauders to the village, still a good distance off. Gravelly Point was at last reached at two o'clock. Alas! the enemy's boats were not there. A landing, however, was effected, a few soldiers of the 104th left to keep guard over the boat, and the troops, headed by Chrétien, advanced noiselessly, following each other in Indian file; they reached the barracks, which stood at about 20 acres from the village, smashing in the windows and doors with their axes, they found them quite deserted. They then advanced towards the commandant's quarters without meeting the slightest resistance. A sentry was found on duty; he was told to keep quiet or have his brains battered. He managed to break away, however, taking his unbattered brains away with him. A light was burning in the officers' apartments. Chrétien took but an instant to knock in the door; he was met by the officer (a major) who attempted to discharge his pistol at him (it was loaded with 20 slugs); it missed fire, however. Chrétien was more fortunate; he let him have his musket charge in the stomach, laying him dead. Three other loaded pistols were found on a table, 20 cartridges loaded with slugs; there were also 2 sabres. These were the only articles the men were permitted to take away. The retreat was now ordered. When they had pushed away a good distance the Yankees, (who had run away from their barracks in a most disgraceful way even before our people had landed), now reappeared on the shore, and, for the purpose, we presume, of frightening the fishes, kept up for quite a while a desultory musketry fire. It was "mustard *after dinner*." The two countrymen who had been seized and forced to serve as guides were then put ashore and the expedition returned to Cananocoui.

The naval lieutenant in his official report to Commodore Yeo, gave a detailed statement of Chrétien's coolness and courage, together with the peril he had exposed himself to during this brush with the enemy. He further charged him to convey the despatch to Kingston.

Sir George Prevost sent for him, and, besides promoting him to the rank of sergeant, presented him with the sabre and pistols looted at Gravelly Point.

The Difficult British–Indian Alliance, 1813

LIEUTENANT-COLONEL MATTHEW ELLIOTT

Britain's Aboriginal allies risked their all by fighting against the invading Americans. Frequently, they objected to tactics and strategy; occasionally, they were left in the lurch, as this letter by Lieutenant-Colonel Matthew Elliott to Colonel William Claus illustrates.

Dundas, 24th Oct., 1813.

Dear Sir,—I have to inform you of the arrival of myself and about 2,000 Indians, (men, women and children,) at this place from the Western District. The causes that led to this event will be best explained by a simple narrative of facts that have occurred since the loss of our fleet on the 10th September.

A few days after that event Major-General Procter gave orders to remove the stores and dismantle the fort preparative to the retreat of the troops. This being done without the Indians being consulted caused a very great jealousy, from the supposition that their father was about to desert them. This was heightened by the uncertainty they labored under with respect to the fate of the fleet. To obtain an explanation Tecumtha and the other chiefs requested General Procter and myself to meet them in council, which took place on the 17th September, when Tecumtha, in the name of the whole, delivered a speech, the purport of which was to call on the General for information of his intentions, and to urge his making a stand with the Indians and the physical force of the country at Amherstburg before he retreated, stating that until we were beaten it would be impolitic to give ground. On the 19th the General returned his answer, in which he stated it was not his intention to leave the District but only to fall back to the river Thames at Chatham where he would be out of reach of their shipping. He was determined to make a stand. To this place he invited them to accompany him. Agreeable to the arrangements which took place at the Council the Shawanese, Hurons and other Indians crossed and proceeded to Sandwich. On the 23rd the enemy landed at Amherstburg, and the same day the troops retreated to Levalle's. The Indian goods which had come up I met at Sandwich and sent them back as far as Mrs. McIntosh's, where the next day I distributed part of them to the Indians, with whom I remained, and kept two days march in rear of our troops. On our arrival at the river Thames I had the number of the Indians taken, when it appeared that the Pottewatomies, Miamies, Ottawas, (a part of them,) and Chippewas had remained behind and it was supposed had crossed the river Detroit. This desertion reduced our number to 1000, (the number we should have had, had the stand been made at Amherstburg was 3000.) This number was again lessened on the 2d of October by the desertion of the Hurons and a few of the Shawanese, who, finding from our movements that we did not intend to make a stand at Chatham, as had been agreed at the Council, embraced an opportunity afforded them by a flag borne by the Indians of Sandusky to take the Americans by the hand. The enemy's ships were at this time off the mouth off the River Thames. The inhabitants, who were the bearers of the flag, told the Hurons that General Harrison would, on the 3d at 12 o'clock, make his headquarters at Colonel McKee's farm. This information I communicated to General Procter on the morning of the 3d, shortly after which he proceeded towards the Moravian Town, 28 miles distant, and about an hour after he set off our scouts brought word that the enemy had crossed the forks and were rapidly advancing up the river. An express was immediately sent to apprise the General, (the express overtook him at Shaw's,) and Colonel Warburton made arrangements to meet them at or near McCrae's. A party of Indians attacked and compelled their advance guard to retire. The Indians, in consequence of the General's absence, drew off across the forks at that time and sent word to Colonel Warburton that they were determined not to fight as the General had deceived them by leaving them. I was enabled to change their minds and they agreed to wait and meet the enemy at Chatham. The troops fell back opposite this place on the morning of the 4th October. The enemy advanced up to Chatham, where a partial skirmish took place between the advance guards. At about 11 o'clock A.M. General Procter arrived and found fault with Colonel Warburton for leaving Dolson's. Yet he very soon after ordered the troops to retreat to Moravian Town. From the manner in which this was conducted the greater part of the provisions and stores fell into the enemy's hands. The Indians kept up a fire across the fork for some time after the troops moved off and then followed, after burning a house in which was a quantity of arms and stores. We halted this evening at Sherman's, five miles from the Moravian Town. The women and most of the baggage had been sent forward a few days previous. Early on the morning of the 5th our scouts brought word that the enemy was advancing on both sides of the river rapidly and in force. The General determined to halt and wait for their arrival, for which purpose the troops were halted about two miles from Jackman's. The troops were posted in two lines on the left, so as to have their flank, covered by the river, supported by a six-pounder which was posted in the road, the Indians in one line on the right. In this position we waited about two hours, when the enemy commenced the attack. Our six-pounder was carried by a few American horse without its being once discharged. The conduct of the troops was shameful in the highest degree; a great part of them never fired one round until they retreated. This threw the Indians in the centre into confusion and they broke. On the right they remained firing and compelled the enemy's left wing to retreat about a mile and a half. I have as yet been unable to ascertain the enemy's loss but judge it must have been considerable. The Indians on their return from the pursuit were much surprised to find that we had not been equally successful on the left, and the unexpectedness threw them into confusion and a retreat ensued, which put the whole of our baggage, both public and private, into the hands of the enemy. At daylight next morning I overtook General Procter at Delaware, and, making every arrangement in my power for the accommodation of the Indians, I proceeded to Burford, from whence Captain Wm. Elliott was by me sent back to Delaware to meet the Indians and to purchase provisions for them on the route. He joined me at Burford on the 22d with the last of the Indians, about 700 in number, when I proceeded with them to this place. Should there be any more coming in I have made such arrangements as will insure them provisions on the road.

I am, dear Sir, your obedient, humble servant,

M. Elliott.

An Officer's Wife on a Campaign in Upper Canada, 1814

ANONYMOUS

> *This account by an officer's wife begins in Kingston in June 1814. Soon after, with her baby, she managed to accompany the troops, despite the disapprobation of officers and other men.*

The evening was just leaving us when our little party marched into Kingston. An officer of the quarter master general's department met us a few miles from the town and returned with us. He said that the tents belonging to our flank companies that had been embarked for the frontier that day had been left standing with all their camp furniture in expectation of being of service and offered to escort us to the spot. Charles asked me whether I would prefer taking my chance for a night and a day in a tent or remaining in the waggon until he could dispose of the men and return to find a lodging for us. I was quite charmed with the alternative and declared for the tent.

. . . and so we took possession of our tent by the light of a brilliant moon—can you imagine anything more delightful or novel than there being at the end of a long day's journey in a very crowded waggon. I could not tear myself away from the door of my tent for hours. The encampment was on a quiet declivity sheltered from the winds by a green hill covered by a magnificent forest and before was the calm expanse of water in the Harbour, reflecting in the moonbeams, and all around us the snow white canvas tents with the bustling soldiers assembling their campfires for cooking their suppers, or resting on the grass, or posting sentinels. It was a beautiful scene and I enjoyed it thoroughly, fortunately without any presentiment of the change which was approaching.

We opened our provision basket, our kettle was boiled and our camp table spread and never did two lighter or happier hearts join in thanksgiving for the blessings of good shelter and rest. We were soon sound asleep, Tilly as usual in her little crib which we always carried with us.

Toward morning we were awakened by the sound of a deluge of rain which pounded steadily for several hours without penetrating our canvas roof but at length began to descend in a sort of mist and made everything we had found so comfortable the night before damp and wretched.

Charles left us as soon as the day dawned to ascertain if there was any chance to secure Tilly and myself better quarters in town. The rain continued in torrents and my possessions were well soaked through altho' I managed to have another spare tent brought and spread over ours by some of the men and then almost suffocated Tilly and me by a large fire of coals which succeeded in drying our cloathes and the walls of the tent so that by the time Charles returned we were rather warm and in no danger of suffering from exposure.

"We are not to travel today" was the first announcement I heard on the return of my Husband. I did not express any disappointment nor ask any questions but knew that he had something more to say and waited for information until he would be pleased to communicate it. He made some very flattering remarks on my arrangements and expressed a great deal of appreciation of all I had done and a great deal of confidence in what I could do but still for some time said nothing of what was uppermost in his mind and I began to feel a little angry and at last said, "If you have any reason to keep up my spirits, I would ask no questions but do not look so excessively important without letting me know that there is some reason for it. I am resigned to anything."

My Husband laughed and said that he had gone to the General in the morning to report himself and receive his orders, that it was so arranged that we should embark for the Frontier in our Gunboats that were to make a coasting voyage along the shore but that in the course of his interview with the General something had occurred which altered this arrangement. It appeared that there was a small schooner to be sent off in the Evening on an expedition the object of which was of very great importance to the garrison. If the expedition was successful it would return to Kingston but if it failed it would go on to Niagara if circumstances would admit. An old officer belonging to the Commissariat had been in recent conversation on this subject (the object of the expedition being concerned with his Department) with the General when Charles was admitted, he expressed a wish that he might be furnished with a party of twenty reliable followers and he would go with them himself and stake his life and reputation on success. Charles had at once volunteered himself and his party and his wishes had been accepted.

"I knew you would not blame me, dear Heart," said he, "and yet I felt I acted cruelly in undertaking to leave you and Tilly friendless and alone as you will be in this strange Land." My heart beat quickly for a few moments but I managed to reply that he had done exactly what was incumbent upon him under the circumstances and that we must do our best.

After a little consultation it seemed there was a possibility that the schooner might go on to Niagara and he would be on board with his whole party. He consented to my coming if I could smuggle Tilly and myself on board and take my chances with him. Our being there, as we thought, could do no injury to the public service and the risque and discomfort would be all our own and balanced against reputation and the various expenses in securing us a lodging, if he could get them, the alternative of going or staying was not long in being decided in my mind. . . . If I succeeded in getting aboard no one could interfere with Mr. Maund and that the General had expressed great approbation of his conduct and had thanked him repeatedly and the old Commissariat officer had been very warm in his expressions on the subject. He felt satisfied that he had done his duty as a soldier though as a Husband and a Father he had his doubts whether he had any business to incur any risque that was not strictly in the "way of business."

The rain ceased in the middle of the day and the sun looked out from the black clouds as Charles marched his little detachment to the place of embarkation. Our travelling bags were already on board and with Tilly in my arms I followed at a short distance, not wishing to make myself conspicuous as I would have been had I kept with the party. This, thought I, is one of the consequences for which I thought myself quite prepared. The moment was approaching when I must either be separated from my Husband or take my chances with him on an actual perilous mission. It is exactly what I expected and wished and I tried to think it very exhilarating and kept up my spirits and my courage by talking to Tilly and telling her as we walked what a Hero and Heroine she had for a Papa and Mama and what a fearless girl she ought to be with such an example of valour.

I was obliged to recall all my resolutions never to let an expression of alarm or discontent pass my lips under any possible extremity when I saw the little sloop in which I was to embark not only my own life and fortune but all heads that I could boast in the world. It was extremely small, there was no cabin but a sort of dark round tunnel under which a dozen inadvertently sized persons might creep for shelter in stiff weather. It had an old and crazy look and the single mast was swaying and creaking in the wind although it was not yet violent, the sun too had disappeared and the clouds were ominous of tempest. The evening was fast approaching. The craft seemed already crowded with soldiers and their arms, no prospect of quarter deck privileges for any of the party.

In spite of this discouraging appearance I was resolved not to flinch from my determination never if I could help it to be separated from my Husband. Indeed there seemed no easy tempting alternative for . . . I did not know a single human being in the garrison, we were so suddenly leaving. I depended upon my own courage and [illegible words] with sufficient conviction never to feel ashamed that Charles would find his wife a troublesome appendage and it was an object with me to habituate him to my being with him without allowing him to feel my presence a burdensome impossibility.

Influenced by these notions which every woman can or ought to feel, I suppressed the momentary conviction to "turn the white feather" and putting my plaid mantle closely round little Tilly I quickly stept on board without raising any objections from any one so that the first glance of my Husband looking for us found me seated very comfortably in a corner of the deck upon a pile of greatcoats which I had arranged for my own accommodation. From seeing there was an expression of dismay on his countenance which he endeavoured to turn off with a laugh to which I responded rather in the same part. No one spoke to us but I heard in reply to a question the words, "Sure, it is our Captain's lady, God help him" in a tone of commiseration.

My worst fear for myself was unfortunately realized for just as I was trying to persuade myself that no one would interfere with us, the old commissary came on board accompanied by a young naval officer who it appeared was to command the sloop and the expedition. Mr. T___, the commissary, was a very old gentleman whose views had been heard long before that it was necessary to get out of the Harbour before it was dark. His glance fell upon us as I sat crouching on the pile of greatcoats and making myself as small as I could in the hope of escaping observation.

"Hallo, what the devil have we here?" was his first exclamation. "Maund, sergeants, corporals, yay, hello! here is a woman on board . . . walk off Madam, if you please, who in the name of wonder brought you here or gave you leave to come."

"I am here with my Husband," was my reply.

"Your Husband! My goodness are you a mad woman to talk of Husbands and think of following them in an affair as this. Walk off, Madam, go on home and thank your stars that I found you before it was too late."

Charles, who had just come on board, having gone on shore for biscuits for his men, came to my rescue and very ceremoniously presented "Mrs. Maund, my wife" to Mr. T___ and said that we really had no choice but to bring me as we had not a single friend in the country and had been encamped for four and twenty hours of torrential rain in Kingston and I was accustomed of late to fatigue and exposure in my life and he would trust us to meet them without complaining.

"It might be all very true," Mr. T___ said, "but at present there is but one course to pursue, she must go on shore without a moment's delay and there is no time to argue about it." The service on which they were going was not likely to be very Lady like and I was stark mad and so was my Husband fit for Bedlam for thinking of such a thing.

I now thought to try the aspect of my pretty face which I have sometimes found a very powerful ally when all other means failed so I thereon gave the old gentleman the full benefit of my most insinuating smile while I pleaded for permission to stay where I was. I gained however only a small measure of success, he offered me his arm very decidedly and cleared off to place a hand on the other side and seeing that there was no alternative, I gave up the point with as good a grace as I could and requested him to have my travelling bag put on shore as well as I myself. Charles was more distressed than I was but I assured him that situated in point of comfort and security on shore was perhaps better and that he need not fear my taking good care both of myself and Tilly. We had small time to sentimentalize over this our first separation for in a very few minutes the sloop had glided from the wharf and I saw a look of agony from my Husband which made my heart feel for him much more than for myself.

Even as the *Woodpecker* was fairly under weigh I began to resort to a habit which I have tried to acquire of looking my fate full in the face with a view to seeing the worst and making the best of it, though my cheerfulness . . . had hitherto been exerted without the supporting calm of my Husband. . . . We were separated for the first time. I would not let myself possibly think how long it would be before we were to meet again but I did not and would not despair. . . . My innocent child still sleeping quietly in my arms, so far from adding weight to my anxieties seemed only a pledge that her Mother would not be disconsolate . . .

Standing under the growing clouds of a stormy evening on a wharf crowded with soldiers and Sailors with baggage and myself the only female in sight and my poor child sleeping in my arms and the only human being upon whom I had depended now flying from us toward the wild Lakes in a vessel which seemed clearly incapable of weathering the coming tempest, I stood still for a moment watching the receding sail of the *Woodpecker*, trying to collect my thoughts and decide what next was to be done.

Seizing the Caroline, 1837

ANDREW DREW

After the failed 1837 rebellion in Upper Canada, there was a series of "alarums and excursions" along the border, with American supporters of William Lyon Mackenzie's rebels preparing attacks and

opponents sometimes striking first. This 1863 account is of the
seizure and sinking of a "rebel" vessel on the night of December 29,
1837.

I directed the boats to move their oars as gently as possible, just enough
to stem the current, and not to talk, or even whisper. Being able to
expend half an hour here unseen was a great event for us, to allow it to
become darker, as everything depended upon our being able to reach
the vessel unseen. At last I judged it dark enough, and we dropped
silently down upon our prey literally without moving an oar until we
were close alongside of her. These were anxious moments for me,
knowing how hazardous it is to climb a vessel's side and make good a
footing upon the deck without being knocked on the head; however,
in this, as in everything else, fortune favoured us. When within a
boat's length of the vessel, one of the watch (who had apparently just
awoke out of a sleep) cried out, "Boat, ahoy! boat, ahoy!"

"Give us the countersign," I answered, in a low tone of voice.
"Silence, silence! Don't make a noise, and I'll give you the countersign
when we get on board." I then mounted the vessel's side, which I had
some difficulty in doing for want of a ladder, and when fairly on deck
I drew my sword, and found three men lounging over the starboard
gangway unarmed, and quite unconcerned. I said to them, "Now I
want this vessel, and you had better go ashore at once." She was laying
alongside a wharf, to which she was secured. I waved my sword over
their heads to make them go, and I do not think that until this moment
they fairly understood their position. Then they moved leisurely over
to the port-side, I thinking they were going on shore; but as they saw
none of my party on the deck but myself they took up their fire-arms,
which it appeared had been left on that side the deck, and the foremost
man fired his loaded musket at me. Not more than a yard from him,
how the ball missed me I do not know; but he was too close to take aim,
and it passed me. I thought this an act of treachery, and that I need
show him no mercy, so with the full swing of my arm I gave him a cut
with my sword over the left temple, and he dropped at my feet. In
another second one of the other men put a pistol close to my face and
pulled the trigger; fortunately it flashed in the pan, or I should not
have been here to have told the tale. Why I was so lenient with this

man I do not know, for he deserved death at my hands as much as the other; but I merely gave him a sabre-cut on the inside of the right arm, which made him drop his pistol, and he was unarmed. The other man I disarmed, and drove them both over the side; but as they did not seem to move as fast as I thought they ought, I gave them about an inch or two of the point of my sword, which quickened their pace wonderfully.

All this did not appear to have taken up more than a minute of time, and we were in complete possession of the after-part of the vessel. Three of the boats boarded forward, where there was a good deal of firing going on, and, as the quarter-deck was clear, I mounted the idle-box and gave orders for the firing to cease immediately, fearing from the darkness of the night we might take friends for foes; and Lieutenant MacCormick had already received a desperate wound.

The vessel was now entirely in our possession, and, to guard against an attack from the shore, I directed Lieutenant Elmsley to head a small party as an advanced guard, to warn us should an attack be meditated. We then roused everybody out of their beds and sent them on shore, a considerable number of persons having been sleeping on board. After this the vessel was set on fire in four different places, and soon began to burn. The next thing was to cast her off from the jetty, which at one time I feared we should have had great difficulty in doing, as she was made fast with chains under water, or rather under ice for this was the middle of a Canadian winter, where water freezes to the thickness of a foot in a short time; but a young gentleman of the name of Sullivan, understanding the difficulty, seized hold of an axe, jumped down upon the ice, and in a short time cleared the chain and set the vessel adrift.

This done, and the vessel in flames fore and aft, I ordered everyone to the boats, which became the more necessary as the enemy had opened a fire of musketry from the shore, and some shot came disagreeably near to me standing on the paddle-box. The order was soon obeyed, for it was also getting too hot to stand upon the deck. I did not give any particular orders to the officer of my own boat; but I intended to be the last person out of the vessel, and naturally thought they would wait for me, and, when just ready to embark, I saw a man coming up the fore hatchway. I went forward to ascertain whether it was likely anyone else was down below; but the man said it was not possible, for it was so hot he could not have lived there another minute. I then went to get into my boat, when to my horror I found that every boat had left the vessel. I cannot describe my feelings at that moment, nor shall I ever forget the sensation that came over me: the vessel in flames and fast drifting down the stream. I looked around, and could just see one boat in the distance; another minute would have been fatal to me. I hailed her to come back, calling out as loud as I could that they had left me behind; fortunately, they heard me, and returned and took me and the man on board.

Having now accomplished our object, we had only to find our way safely back; and when we rounded the point of the island before named we saw a tremendous blazing fire on the Canadian shore, not only enough to guide us, but almost to light us on our way back. It was most welcome, for by this time it had become quite dark. Not caring about discovery now, and as little for shot from Navy Island, we kept much closer to it, and felt safe in so doing. We landed between two and three o'clock in the morning at the spot from whence we started, and found hosts of people to receive us with good hearty British cheers. Sir Allan Macnab was most particularly cordial in his welcome, and candidly acknowledged he never expected to see me again, but that our success had far exceeded his most sanguine expectations.

By this time the burning vessel was fast approaching the Canadian shore, and not far distant. Of all the marvels attending this novel expedition, the course which the steamer took of her own accord was the most wonderful. When free from the wharf at Fort Schlosser, her natural course would have been to follow the stream, which would have taken her along the American shore and over the American Falls; but she acted as if she was aware she had changed owners, and navigated herself right across the river, clearing the Rapids above Goat Island, and went as fairly over the centre of the British Falls of Niagara as if she had been placed there on purpose.

There were hundreds of people on the banks of the river to witness the splendid sight, for it was perfectly beautiful, and the descent took place within a quarter of an hour after our landing; and no human ingenuity could have accomplished what the vessel had so easily done for herself.

The Battle of the Windmill, 1838

LIEUTENANT ANDREW AGNEW

The skirmishes along the border culminated in a large party of rebels and American sympathizers trying to seize Fort Wellington, Upper Canada, to cut communications between Upper and Lower Canada. The effort failed, the invaders ultimately being trapped in a windmill and destroyed by British regulars and Canadian militia. This account is by an officer of the 93rd Highland Regiment of Foot.

The rebels . . . had taken possession of a windmill and six adjacent stone houses. They completely commanded the road and part of the river. The mill was almost impregnable being round and solid masonry many feet thick. Two gun boats and small field pieces making no impression upon it. The numbers of these villains decreased as we came nearer and we actually ascertained that their number was rather under 300 and three field pieces. Round all the houses they had built up the lower windows and got from one to the other by ladders to the other windows which they pulled up after them. They made light breast works of stone and mounted their field pieces at the doors.

Since the action on Tuesday the militia had come in great numbers and surrounded the mill on three sides with guard houses at intervals beyond musket shot and keeping a regular cordon prevented any possibility of escape by land, wilst several government gun and steamboats on the river prevented their sneaking off by water. Here these "Sympathizers" remained till Friday afternoon when we came up and Colonel Dundas of the 83rd landing with 4 companies of his corps and two 18 pounders under Major Macbean. We immediately took up position in front of the mill turning off the high road at long shot from them. We crossed the fields and the 93rd Grenadiers took their place on the Prescott side but almost fronting the mill. The 18 pounders passed us and were placed on our left at 400 yards distance. The 83rd forming in line to their left and an immense force of militia from the right and left of the regulars extending to the river. An armistice of a few hours was granted in the morning for the purpose of burying the dead as the Prescott people of course were anxious to have the bodies of their friends, the field of battle being too near the mill for them to attempt to approach it; the greatest indignation prevailed owing to the body of [Lieutenant William] Johnstone of the 83rd having been found stuffed and badly mutilated, the 83rd vowed vengeance and the militia swore to a man they would give no quarter. We began the attack at 3 o'clock by firing on one of the 6 stone houses and the first shot (fired by major Macbean) Struck the wall and made a considerable breach in the building, the artillery practice was beautiful, immense charing at every shot which almost invariably told the rascals finding this past a joke, showed a flag of truce from two of the houses, but having tried this trick before and fired upon the officers who came to parley no notice of it was taken, after about ¾ of an hour firing the 83rd advanced in extended order, the militia remaining as an outer circle and we advanced to about 100 yards of the chief cluster of houses on the right. Advancing field by field, the rebels now began a short flanking fire, and one of the 83rd being immediately killed and another wounded. Col. Dundas, who was determined to lose as few men as possible sounded the bugle to lie down and the artillery fired on over the heads of the soldiers. Evening was now fast closing in and as the incessant and very random fire of the militia was very nearly as dangerous as the rebels in the dark, a howitzer was brought up and fired at the outermost (on the left hand side) house till set on fire it was immediately stormed and carried by the 83rd who did their work most gallantly, brands were instantly taken and the next house lighted and thus they carried them one after the other and driving the rebels like rats from one to the other at the point of the bayonet and as their wounded of course perished in the flames, their courage began to fail, and coming out in a body begged to surrender, the troops immediately commenced to bayonet when Colonel D. anxious to close the affair offered them if every man came out unarmed and made an unconditional surrender, they should have *present* personal security, this they did and the colonel, riding in front with great difficulty kept back the troops and placing a guard round them, considered them prisoners. He has been much blamed for this, as it is impossible to hang wholesale so large a body and great dissatisfaction is naturally felt in the country that such ruthless [?] should in any measure escape, but having been on the spot and heard his own arguments I think he acted with discretion when it is considered that it was night, that the tired troops must have remained otherwise in the field all night and had great loss storming so strong a natural position against desperate and well armed men next day. I think he saved much trouble by taking prisoners. We fortunately lost not a man though as we closed up on the right bullets whistled pretty sharply among our bonnets.

Fighting the Fenians at Ridgeway, 1866

CAPTAIN W.D. OTTER

> *The adjutant of the Queen's Own Rifles, Captain Otter wrote this frank report after the difficult action at Ridgeway against the Fenians, Irish-Americans who hoped to advance the cause of Ireland's independence by attacking British colonies in North America.*

Second June, 1866 (Saturday), paraded at Port Colborne at 12:30 A.M. and marched to a train, on which was the 13th Battalion of Hamilton and the York and Caledonia Rifle Companies, who had arrived the night before. At 4 A.M. a detachment of 125 officers and men of our own corps arrived from Toronto.

It was intended that the force should leave at 2 A.M., but further orders detained us til 5 A.M. These orders were from Colonel Peacock, H. M. 16th Foot, who was to be in command, and was brought by Capt. Akers, R. E.

At 5 A.M., in obedience to Colonel Peacock's orders, the force left Port Colborne, the strength being, Queen's Own 480, 13th Battalion, York and Caledonia Companies about 400, in all say 880, under the command of Colonel Booker, 13th Battalion. Moved to Ridgeway station on the B & L. H. Railway, where we left the train and marched toward Stevensville, for the purpose of forming a junction with Colonel Peacock's column.

No. 5 Company, Q.O.R. (armed with Spencer repeating rifles), formed the advance guard, followed by the remaining companies of the battalion, the 13th Battalion and York Company, the Caledonia

Company finding the rear guard. In this order the column moved about two miles, when at 7 A.M. the Fenians were discovered to our front. The advance guard was immediately extended from its centre, Nos. 1 and 2 on its left and right. No. 3 centre supports, No. 4 left, No. 7 as a flanking party to the left, supported by No. 8, and No. 6 flanking to the right, No. 9 and 10 in reserve. After an advance of say half a mile, No. 6 was sent as a support to No. 2 on the right, immediately the Fenians, who were extended behind the fences, their main body being well posted in a wood, opened fire, which was immediately returned by our men, who continued steadily advancing. The firing became general, being heaviest on our centre and right. At almost the first fire Ensign McEachren was hit in the stomach, and being taken to the rear, died in twenty minutes.

We continued driving them for about an hour, when our skirmishers being reported out of ammunition, Nos. 9 and 10 companies were sent to the right, and the 13th Battalion order to relieve us, which they did by sending out three companies to skirmish, and who had not being engaged fifteen minutes, when the cry of "Cavalry" was raised at seeing two or three Fenian horsemen advancing towards us. Colonel Booker ordered the reserve (Queen's Own) to "Prepare for Cavalry" and the companies forming it, *viz.*: Nos. 1, 2, 3, 5, and 8, formed square. The mistake was immediately seen, the order given to "Re-form Column" and two leading companies (Nos. 1 and 2) to "extend." On re-forming, the reserve being too close to the skirmish line, was ordered to retire, the left-wing of the 13th who were in our rear, seeing our men retire and thinking we were retreating, broke and retired in a panic, on seeing which our men also broke and ran. Just previous to this the retire was sounded to Nos. 1 and 2 of the Queen's Own, who not seeing the necessity of the order, disobeyed, until it was again sounded, when they reluctantly moved to the rear, the remainder of the skirmish line doing the same, though not understanding the reason of their recall, but on seeing the reserve in disorder, they too became demoralized and fled. The fire of the now pursuing Fenians became hotter than ever, and the volunteers being crowded up in a narrow road, presented a fine market to their rifles, causing our poor fellows to fall on all sides.

It was in vain the officers endeavored to rally the men, several times squads, and even a company were collected, but never in sufficient force to check the pursuit, though a constant fire was kept up until the Fenians ceased following. For the first two or three hundred yards it was a regular panic, but after that the men fell into a walk, retiring in a very orderly manner, but completely crestfallen.

The enemy followed to Ridgeway Station and there gave up the pursuit, moving onto Fort Erie. We've returned to Port Colborne, arriving at about 1 P.M. very tired and hungry, not having had any sleep the previous night nor any food that day.

Had the "retire" not been sounded we should have beaten them in 10 minutes more, for part of their force was actually retreating before we commenced to retire.

General O'Neill in command of the Fenians, and other officers of their force, owned to some of our wounded whom they captured (owing to our not having ambulances or vehicles of any description) that we "behaved splendidly and were mistaken by them for regulars, owing to our steadiness, and that had we fought five minutes longer they must have succumbed, as their men were fast becoming demoralized."

They Could Teach a Lesson to Many:
French Canadians in the Militia, 1871

COLONEL P. ROBERTSON-ROSS

> *The adjutant-general of militia, Robertson-Ross, reported on the summer camp held at Laprairie, Quebec, in 1871.*

On mustering the force, I found nearly the whole of the 3rd Brigade to be composed of French speaking Canadians, and in the two other brigades, although the great majority of the men were English speaking, being struck with the number of French Canadian names while calling the rolls of the different companies, I obtained an accurate return of the number of French speaking Canadians in the camp, and they exceeded 2000 in number. The appearance and condition of the

majority of the infantry corps in this camp, in respect to drill, condition of arms, accoutrements, and soldierlike bearing, was inferior on
the whole to the majority of the infantry corps assembled in the
Province of Ontario, although there were exceptions; but the men,
although generally speaking not so tall, looked at least as hardy and
robust, indeed some of the rural companies, of both French and
British descent, looked fit to undergo great hardship, and the adapt-
ability of all to camp life was most striking; indeed in this very important part of military instruction, not only have both French and English
speaking Canadians little to learn from any army, but they could teach
a lesson to many.

Lieutenant-colonel Osborne Smith reports that the general conduct of the troops was excellent, that he believes "so large a number
of men was never assembled for the time with such an entire absence
of crime, and so little irregularity."

Aboriginal Boatmen on the Nile, 1884

COLONEL SIR WILLIAM BUTLER

*In 1884, General Garnet Wolseley requested the services of Cana-
dian Aboriginals and voyageurs to help the Khartoum Relief Expedition ascend the Nile. Some 400 Canadian boatmen guided the
British army through a series of treacherous cataracts into the Sudan.
Colonel W.F. Butler's account recalls the Red River Expedition of
1870, where he and Wolseley served with several of the Canadian
"Nile voyageurs."*

One day, the 4th of November [1884], I was engaged in the daily work
of the dockyard, when across the river a strange object caught my
sight—strange only in this Nile land, for in other lands it had been a
well-known friend, but one now so far off in memory, and so distant
in the scenes of river and shore which were connected with it, that it
might well have seemed a shadow called up from the past—a mirage
of pine-cliff and canoe, destined to vanish again into the dead world
from which it had arisen.

There, hugging the black eddy of the muddy Nile, a small American birch-bark canoe, driven by those quick down-strokes that seem to be the birthright of the Indian voyageur alone, was moving up the further shore. When this strange craft had got well abreast of our dockyard, it steered across the swift river and was soon underneath my tent. Out of the canoe, with all the slow gravity of his race, stepped a well-remembered figure—William Prince, Chief of Swampy Indians, from Lake Winnipeg in North America. After him came seven other Indian and half-breed voyageurs, all from the same distant land—they were the pioneers of the 400 Canadian voyageurs whose services we have already seen secured in the preceding August; but personally to me there was something more in this visit of these Indians than the advent of the pioneers from the North-West who were to aid the Expedition in its fight with the rocks and rapids of the Nile.

Fourteen years earlier this same William Prince had been the best Indian in my canoe when we forced our way up the rapids of the Winnipeg to meet the advance of the Red River Expedition through the wilderness of the North-West. And here to-day, on the Nile above the Second Cataract, stood William Prince, now chief of his tribe, grown more massive of frame and less agile of gait, but still keen of eye and steady of hand as when I last saw him standing bow-man in a bark canoe. among the whirling waters whose echoes were lost in the endless pine-woods of the Great Lone Land.

Seated in my tent in old Indian fashion, cross-legged on the ground, Prince and his companions soon found themselves at home in this strange land, for dry and arid as these deserts were, there were drops of whisky and plugs of tobacco to be found in them, and these are keys to unlock the tongue of a Redman just as potent in the sands of Nubia as in the pine-islands or prairies of the North.

"How many Indians had come from Winnipeg?" "About a dozen; but had longer time and fuller notice been given, fifty or even a hundred would have come."

"Were the voyageurs taking them all together up to the old North-West mark?" "No; but there were a good proportion among them able boatmen. The Iroquois and French Canadians were nearly all first-class men; there were also several excellent boatmen from the Ottawa, but there were some 'dead-beats' who knew nothing of the work."

Then it was their turn to ask questions.

"How long would it take to reach Khartoum?" "From two to three months."

"Were there many rapids?" "Yes; but no rapid longer or more difficult than this Second Cataract they had just passed."

"Well, if that was the case and they were to start at once they could get there by Christmas."

Then we talked about old times and friends. Their world had changed, they said, towns had grown up along the silent river-shores, farms and fences covered the far-stretching prairies, the buffalo were all gone, the lonely lakes had steamboats on them. People said the new times were better, but for themselves they liked the old days, the old days of the log-house along the river, the wilderness lying out to the west with its free life, its herds and hunts, its trading and its trapping.

"People were friendly towards each other then," was their final summing up of the case of old versus new.

They went back in the evening to the foot of the Second Cataract, and on the following day Prince and a Cree half-breed, named Cochrane, again appeared with a batch of voyageurs who were to act as guides and pilots to the 38th or Stafford Regiment, which was about to embark for the ascent of the river. Our fleet lying ready for service at the foot of the steep clay-bank at Gemai was daily growing in number. On the morning of November 1st, five boats carrying a pioneer party of Engineers started for Dongola, and a few days later the embarkation of the first infantry battalion began. It did not take long to accomplish; thirty-two boats carried the half-battalion which was the first to start. The embarkation commenced at 7:30 A.M. and at 8, the last boat was under weigh. It was a very simple business: the men were marched down to the shore, told off in tens, put into the boats; arms and packs were soon stored, and then in succession from the front, or upstream side, the fleet moved off. A light breeze blew from the north; the lug-sails were loosened, and with oars pulled in many fashions, the white flotilla moved up the broad river, and was soon out of sight. It was the 5th of November; just thirty years had passed since this same battalion of the 38th Regiment was engaged in stemming the strong tide of the Russian hosts up the slopes of Inkermann. It was a soldiers' fight then, and in the coming months it was to be a soldiers' fight too.

The Midland Battalion Moves to Battle, 1885

WALTER F. STEWART

> *Staff Sergeant Stewart's diary details his enlistment, rapid promotion, and move to the Northwest as Canada scrambled to field an army to fight Louis Riel, the Métis, and the Indians.*

March 29, 1885—In Toronto staying with Nellie and Artie. Going back to the North West on Tuesday via the States. Trouble commenced with Riel. A rebellion breaking out throughout the North West. Queen's Own and Grenadiers ordered out. Drove to Armories with Artie in his dog cart to witness the preparations. Wished myself going with them. Home again at 6. The soldiers will start west tomorrow.

March 30—Drove to city in the morning. Called for Bill Heath who goes back to the west with me tomorrow. We went to Artie's office and saw the Queen's Own and Grenadiers pass to the train for the west to the scene of the troubles. Afternoon, on taking up a paper I read the account of Col. Williams, about to get up a battalion to go to the North West. At once telegraphed to him to take me. Got answer late at night to report myself at Port Hope at once. Too late to go tonight. Will leave in the morning. Delighted at the prospect of being able to take part in defending our country. Archie wishing to go with me.

March 31—Off by 7:30 A.M. train for Port Hope and reached there on time. Proceeded to drill shed where I found Col. Williams, Uncle Harry and others I knew, also those of the company I was to be attached to, then at drill. Got on my uniform, certainly not the very best, and took my place in the ranks. Orders were to move east to Kingston tomorrow morning. Spent my spare time at Grandmother's and visiting old friends, but most of the time learning my drill.

April 1—General muster at drill shed at 8 A.M., preparing to depart. Marched up Main and John Streets, to Grand Trunk Station, the whole town turning out to see us off. Were joined at station by Millbrook and Bowmanville, also Lindsay and Peterboro Companies. Off on train at 9 A.M., the 46th Band playing "Auld Lang Syne." Two more companies came on at Belleville. Arrived at Kingston at 3 P.M. and went into barrack. Col. Williams sent for me in evening and appointed me a staff sergeant. Took my place in sergeants' mess.

April 2—All busy serving and receiving outfits of clothing, etc., all day. Expect to start for North West on Saturday.

April 3—Still busy serving out goods and getting them to readiness for starting. Cannot now get away till Monday. All anxious to get away.

April 4—On getting up found about two feet of snow on the ground and still snowing. Heard later in the day that trains were blocked and some of the telegraph lines down. A poor lookout for starting.

April 5—Had church parade in the morning in barrack yard standing in slush. Snow going fast. Self went for walk in the evening. Orders to leave for west in morning.

April 6—Whole battalion named now "Midland Battalion," left the barracks and moved into the train at 10:15 A.M. About 450 strong. Left at 10:30 A.M. on Kingston and Pembroke Railway. Reached the CPR at dark and commenced our western course by Lake Superior and north shores. Three gaps of unfinished line to cross over; we will be a long time getting even to Winnipeg.

April 7—Had very little sleep during the night. Car too crowded. Making good time, going sometimes at the rate of 40 miles an hour. A private named Keller from Bowmanville, being drunk ever since he started from home, got the D.T.s, suddenly jumped through the car window carrying away glass and all. Backed up train but could only find his tracks in snow leading to heavy bush land. Reached Biscotasing about 6 P.M. Tea, bread and chunks of beef served us at railway camp for our supper. An awful scramble is getting to the tables only seating 40 at a time. Trains moved off at 8.

April 8—Had a better night's sleep so felt better. Making good time on the road. Reached Gap No. 1 at 10 A.M. and took to sleighs. Found the roads very bad; for a few miles; deep snow, but got better as we went. Some places snow three feet deep, other places quite bare. All day. Reached railway contractor's log camp where they had tea prepared for us. All very hungry, having had no dinner. After tea changed horses and drove on. Reached end of the first gap, 45 miles, at 2:30 in the morning. All glad to get over so quickly, but so cold. Made the best of it around the fires that had been lighted for us by railway men, and in the open bush.

April 9—Did not feel quite myself, having had no sleep, but after a breakfast of hardtack and tea felt all right. A train of flat cars boarded up at the sides backed in for us. Then all aboard, and we were off on a cold ride westward to next gap, 85 miles distant. All in good spirits though it was so cold. The excitement of being jolted and jerked about over the rough road kept up some circulation. Had hardtack and cheese and tea (made from hot tap on the engine). Reached Gap No. 2 just at dark; had a mile to march to get to our quarters for the night: "Hell-Fire-Bay" it was named, on the north shore of Lake Superior, consisted of some large tents for sleeping quarters for some; others in the hold of a schooner. All had tea at about midnight, only about 50 being able to get to the tables at a time. Lou Macdougald and I could only find sleeping space in the blacksmith shop, slept with our heads against the anvil for pillow.

April 10—Up early to find it snowing and blowing like fury, but in spite of it all, will march over the gap, not having more than enough teams to take our baggage. All had to march. At 8 A.M. we struck westward over the ice of a large bay of Lake Superior. Very soon every man was wet to the knees, with snow and water under the snow, for 22 miles. Guide took us the wrong way, making our march three miles longer. We men just wanted to lynch him. Reached end of Gap No. 2 at 3 P.M., had dinner and took to flat cars again. Another cold ride for 43 miles. Arrived at big camp at Jack Fish Bay, beginning of Gap No. 3, a very comfortable camp.

April 11—Had a good night's sleep, all of us. Had my blanket stolen so had to make the best of my overcoat. We here lose a day. Teams not returned from taking the 65th French Battalion across Jack Fish Bay. Weather very stormy, snowing and blowing all day. Col. George T. Denison's Cavalry Corps arrived in camp towards evening. All day had a deal of waiting and scrambling over getting meals, the cooks at each meal being able to seat only about 60 at the tables at a time. I slept in a big store shed that night. Smells and smells. Got word that teams had just got back, 9 P.M., ready to take us on in the morning.

April 12—All off over the gap, about 120 teams conveying us over the 20 miles. Nothing important during the trip, only our driver proved ugly and we had to threaten him with throwing him out and taking possession of the team. Arrived at end of gap and all on a train of flat cars by 5 P.M. Traveled by flats 33 miles, then at 10 o'clock that night marched 12 miles and got on board a train of emigrant sleeping cars to once more have a good rest right through to Winnipeg. A good day's work. Driving 20 miles, on flat cars over a rough and dangerous track for 33 miles, then a midnight march of 12 miles.

April 13—Self slept in baggage car, did not get much sleep; the baggage guards kept on talking all night. Passed Port Arthur during night. On the train all day flying along towards Winnipeg. Stopped at Rat Portage late in the evening 10 minutes. All the town turned out to see us passing through. Gave us mighty cheers as we were leaving.

April 14—All hands up early and found ourselves in Winnipeg. Had breakfast at the CPR restaurant, then fell into ranks to march up Main Street to camp and await orders. Self detailed to help in moving the baggage. Battalion only marched to end of Main Street when Col. Williams got a telegram to proceed direct to the front. All right about-turned and marched back to station. I was rather disappointed at not being able to go home to see them all, but glad to get into action. Had tobacco served out to us at the station, one pound each. Lieut. Wal. Smart, who does not smoke, gave me his. Father, Mother, Frances, Fred and Grace appeared in time to see me off. And later Lou came in his uniform, just had joined Col. Scott's regiment (91st). Off by train for Qu'Appelle at 1:30 P.M. Arrived at Brandon at 6, where the ladies kindly served us tea, ham sandwiches and cakes. Here Col. W. got telegram to proceed to Swift Current. On the train all night.

April 15—Got a good night's sleep in emigrant sleepers. Arrived at Swift Current at 2 P.M. It was raining hard. Pitched camp beside the York Rangers, who had got there before us. Received us with cheers. We had a splendid camp ground on the level prairie.

April 16 and 17—Drilled on the camp grounds both days all day. We go north from here 300 miles to Batoche, our main objective. Louis Riel is waiting there for us.

April 18—Two of our companies, "E" and "F," left early this morning for Saskatchewan Ferry, 33 miles north, on the march, to load supplies on the "Northcote." York Rangers took train back to Qu'Appelle.

April 19, 20, 21—Our remaining six companies at drill and target practice. The mounted Intelligence Scouts arrived and camped near us; a fine body of men, 50 in all, commanded by Capt. Dennis. All impatient to get away north.

April 22—Got orders to move north (hurry, hurry) to go on boat up the South Saskatchewan to join General Middleton and escort the transport. Made an early start with remainder of battalion. We marched all day, arrived by dark. A good march of 33 miles. All pretty tired. Went on boat and threw ourselves anywhere for a sleep. We didn't want to eat, just sleep.

April 23—The "Northcote" started with us all on board, four companies and officers. A barge on one side of the boat, a large scow on the other, all heavily loaded with provisions and ammunition for Middleton's forces, also a Gatling gun. Got stuck on a sand bar before we got five miles, but with heaving and twisting about got clear. Went through similar operations a dozen times during the day. Anchored for the night only 15 miles from where we started. Made a bunk for myself, with three others, in hold of barge. Had fairly comfortable quarters. Fortified ourselves with bags of oats and bales of hay in case of attack from Indians on shore.

April 24—Wooded up early and started off, but still did not go far before the old "Northcote" found another sand bar to run into. Had heavy rain storm lasting about three hours, during which time we ran on to another sand bar; got off only to get high and dry on another. Only made about eight miles today. Boys all in good spirits, as usual, singing and joking all day long, but feeling sorry for the old boat.

April 25—A fine bright warm day. The same story continued, running on sand bars about every half hour, and only getting off by all hands going ashore and pulling on a long rope, or shifting about from boat to scow or from scow to boat. About twenty times a day the cry was by the officer of the day, "All hands on the flats." Then getting off and on the way again, we would hear the sounding pilot taking soundings with a 12-foot pole, call: "4 ft. scant, 4½ ft., 5 ft., 6 ft., no bottom. No bottom!" Then it would be "6 ft., 5 ft., 4½ ft., 4 ft. scant, 3 ft., 3 ft. small, 2½ ft.," and chuck up on a sand bar to rest for an hour. About noon ran on a sand bar. Worked all the rest of day with the spars and windlasses, one of which got broken towards evening so have to suspend operations until tomorrow. All went to bed feeling more or less out of sorts.

April 26—Sunday was no day-of-rest for us. We spent the day, all hands working hard unloading scows and boat, taking everything ashore. The only way of releasing the old tub. The worst stick-stack-stow we have had yet, deep in mud. We got steaming away again, but only ran a mile, when we got stuck fast again. All hands went ashore with a long rope and after a great deal of long and strong pulling got her off, but it was nearly dark and had to anchor for the night.

April 28, 29, 30—Had the same kind of routine day after day: running for about half an hour and then running on a sand bar and sticking fast for two solid hours at the least. We are all getting sick of it. Wishing some of the rebels would show themselves to vary the monotony. Got news through a rider on horse, that General Middleton had had a fight with the rebels, but no particulars.

May 1, 2—The same story continued of running on sand bars and all hands pulling her off. Very slow work. Amused myself sketching during the monotonous run.

May 3—Had church parade in the morning on the port side scow, Col. Williams reading the service. The boat took a notion and ran all this time without getting stuck, but would not let us have dinner though. The damd [*sic*] old tub ran hard aground just as the bugle sounded. All pulling on the rope again and after an hour's hard work we got her going once more. Towards evening about a dozen teams came and met us from Middleton's camp; wanting oats and hay. Told us that all were anxious about us, thinking we had fallen into enemy hands. Ran boat ashore and tied up for the night. Teams loaded up and went back to camp. Pete Robertson of Port Hope came aboard with Col. Williams and stayed all night. He is farming here near Saskatoon; he looked like a tramp.

May 4—Made an early start and reached Saskatoon about 8 A.M. In small village, a big barn had been made over into a hospital for wounded. Amongst them I met Sangford and Thompson, each wounded in the left arm, and Herb Perrin had his arm shot off. Told me Capt. Gardner was badly wounded and now in the hospital, and that Ted had been appointed Captain in his place. Left Saskatoon at 9 A.M., after wooding up. Had good running all day, the best we had since starting, the river being narrower and deeper. More houses to be seen along the banks, looking more like civilization. We have to keep a sharp lookout for the enemy the rest of the way; expect to come in contact with it at any time. Reached Clarke's Crossing at 2 P.M., and Col. Williams had orders from the General to make all possible haste; thought it advisable to leave off two companies here. Left off "B" & "D" companies with 10 days' provisions and ammunition. Got within about 10 miles of Middleton's camp and anchorage for the night, placing a double picquet on shore. All's well! at midnight.

May 5—Nothing unusual happened during the night. The boat steamed off at 5 A.M. Reached Middleton's camp at 9 A.M. after 12 days and nights on the boat. Saw some of the Shell River boys as soon as we landed. Self took the cash box, etc., and made my way to Major Boulton's camp, where I saw Ted and all the boys just going out on parade. Stayed at their camp until own tents were put up. Our boys marched past headed by the 90th Band at 9:30 A.M., and they looked fine. General Middleton very much provoked at our coming in with only two companies, 86 men instead of 428; not according to his orders. Not our fault; done by some officious brat back east. Ted spent most of the afternoon with me; weather quite cold. This is the Fish Creek battle ground.

May 6—Spent a good deal of the morning with Ted in Major Boulton's tent. Going to start tomorrow on our march to storm Batoche, where the enemy is strongly entrenched and commanded by Louis Riel. All anxious to be on the march. Visited the Fish Creek battle field with the rest of the staff sergeants, Sgt. Major Sproule, Lou McDougall and Hooper. Expected to go with Ted and Sandy Stewart but they did not want to go with me. Picked up a few relics and were shown the field by Sgt. Hughes of the 90th. Saw dead horses, broken wagons and dead Indians, and graves being dug. The smells were none too good. Got separated from the rest of my companions in the woods covering rough ground. Wandered back to camp alone to view the scenery. Well, it was nice to be alone once more with my thoughts and situation. Saw neat log houses and farms, belonging to the rebels, some in ruins. Land very rich. Had Will Shepherd of Winnipeg and some of the Shell River boys, Ted among them, spending the evening with us. In brigade orders, "The whole brigade will move on Batoche tomorrow, in full marching order. The Regulars, 60 men, to go up-river on the steamer 'Northcote.'" An alarm was sounded at midnight but turned out to be a hoax.

The Trek Around Lake Superior, 1885

LIEUTENANT-COLONEL GEORGE T. DENISON

The Canadian Pacific Railway was not yet complete in 1885, and troops moving west had to traverse some very rough country in the dead of winter. Colonel Denison's graphic account remains the best description.

We moved off then on what was the hardest experience on the campaign. We had thirty-five miles to go on the ice across a great inlet of Lake Superior, along the front of which, some ten or fifteen miles out, were one or two islands, which held the ice together and made a firm stretch of ice over which we had to march. After we had gone some twelve or fifteen miles we came to a point where the sleighs with our baggage stores and dismounted men left us, and turning to the right went up an inlet for some miles, to a place called McKellar's Bay, from which a short piece of track had been finished to Jackfish Bay. Here we halted for our mid-day meal. The horses were drawn up in a line facing the south, as there was a strong north wind. The horses were fed from their nose-bags, and the officers and men stood in the shelter of the horses, and with a chunk of corned beef in one hand and a chunk of bread in the other we made our dinners. A hole was cut in the ice and our horses watered from it, and we drank from the same source of supply.

When leaving Toronto the supplies were short, or the officers in charge thought anything would do for the cavalry, for we were issued blankets that had been condemned, in most of which there were holes more or less. I insisted on an extra supply and obtained three for each man, and, as the holes were not all opposite one another, they were of some use. We were issued water bottles just as we were leaving, and when we got to Biscotasing I arranged to have tea made to fill them all. They were all filled, but would not remain in that condition, as they all leaked, and in a few minutes the men had got rid of their so-called water bottles. These also were condemned water bottles, but unfortunately we could not, by any means, turn them to any use whatever. As soon as we got a chance the men got soda water bottles, and made out to get along with them.

From Port Monroe to the point at which the sleighs left us to go to McKellar's Bay, the track along the ice was packed and clearly marked by the sleighs, which for some days had been plying between these points; but when we left the track to go some twenty miles across a vast prairie or desert of ice, with snow in drifts everywhere, there was no track and we had to pick our way. In the early spring there had been rain and thaw, and all over the solid ice there had accumulated some few inches of water. This had frozen to a depth of about two or three inches, and on this crust-ice several snowfalls had been deposited. The snow, as usually happens, had been blown by the wind, so that in places there would be smooth glare ice, and in others snow, from a quarter of an inch to perhaps a foot or even more in depth. The glare ice was, of course, strong and solid, but where the snow was deep it had protected the ice under it, so that it did not become nearly so strong. As we marched on the glare ice the horses without their hind shoes slipped about and travelled with difficulty. When the snow was deep, and the deeper it was, the more certain the result, the horses' hoofs would go through the snow to the crust-ice, and through it down two or three inches to the solid ice below that.

Where the snow was deep the horses were almost mired, so to speak, their hoofs catching and tripping them in the crust-ice. We pushed on as fast as we could, trying all the while to pick our way, avoiding as much as possible the glare ice, or the deep snow. This made the distance longer, and the wind from the north kept constantly getting colder and stronger. A man on horseback had been provided as a guide to go with us. He was afraid a blizzard was coming up and got considerably alarmed, for we were miles from shore, and along the whole stretch and on the islands it was an absolute wilderness. He kept urging us on, and we kept moving as fast as possible. About four or five o'clock we came to where the snow on the ice seemed to have gathered much more extensively, and we could hardly move, the horses going through the crust-ice every step. I halted the column, and sent several men out like a fan to see if a place could be found where the snow was not so deep. William Hamilton Merritt, my adjutant, was one, and when he had got about a quarter of a mile off he signalled us to follow him, and we struggled through the deep snow and found a clearer stretch.

He and I rode on ahead after that, to pick the way. I think the spot where I halted was by some current of the wind much more covered with snow than other parts, for after that it was not nearly so difficult to find a way through the drifts. The wind, however, was very high, the temperature, as we found out afterwards, about zero, and some flakes of snow began to fall. I was very uneasy lest a real blizzard should come on, which would leave us without food all night on the ice. Many lives would have been lost. Fortunately it was only a slight flurry of snow, which soon blew over, enabling us to see our way.

By six o'clock the exertions we had gone through made me at any rate, very hungry, and then I thought of my piece of bread I had picked up in the morning at Port Monroe. It was rather cruel of me, but I was determined to teach a lesson. I took it out of my holster, picked the mud off it carefully and commenced eating it. As I was doing it I dropped back and let the column pass me as I rode, slowly eating my supper. Every man in the command saw me eating it and they had all seen me save it. I did not have to complain of wastefulness after that.

We kept on marching and pushing on as fast as we could, but did not reach Jackfish Bay, then a small contractors' camp of tents and a few buildings, until about 8 P.M., just at dusk. Our men who had gone by McKellar's Bay had arrived many hours before us, and we found there the Midland Battalion, who were under the command of my old friend and schoolmate, Lieut.-Colonel Arthur Williams, M.P. They all came down to the shore to meet us and received us with loud cheers, for they had been very anxious on account of our delay, and the threatened blizzard. Colonel Williams came up and shook hands with me and said: "Supper is just ready and my men want your men to come and eat it, and they will wait till another meal is cooked." We were much pleased at this evidence of kindly feeling, but I told him to let his men have their meal at once, as we would have to look after our horses before we had supper.

Letters Home from Battleford, 1885

HARRY BROCK

May 18, 1885

My dear Mother,

Since my last the Indians have grown demonstrative and captured a provision train about 10 miles from here, killing one of the Escort and wounding another, but saddest of all this news will prevent Hume Blake and his train of luxuries from advancing till they get a proper escort from Swift Current. In the meantime we will have to stick to Pork and hardtack and from what Col. Otter says we have not too much left of that. Poundmaker had better beware for if the Q.O.R. get really hungry nothing can or will stop them in pursuit of it. A strange instance happened the other day. Captain Hughes and a small party were out scouting through the bushes about two miles out. They espied a pig about one hundred yards in front and with a strange infatuation the pig committed suicide by running up against five of the men with fixed swords. Nothing could stop the poor beast on its wild career and the men sorrowfully carried the remains into camp. At least Captain Hughes says so and we all believe him. The other night the Sentry on an outpost saw something advancing on the lines and called out, "Halt, who goes there?" No answer. He repeated the question three times and still no answer. He then fired and called the attention of the officer of the picket to the circumstances in the morning. They went forward and found a cow dead but how the bullet cut the cow's throat still remains a mystery. Until this is solved the officer does not feel called upon to report the matter at headquarters. Seriously, we are being gouged in the matter of prices of provisions by the storekeepers here. Milk is 20¢ a qt, sugar 40¢ a pound, oatmeal 35¢ a lb, butter 60¢, coal oil $5.00 a gal, bread 50¢ a large loaf, jam $1.50 a pot, etc. etc. So you can see where most of the money will go. The Colonel has wisely issued an order to go into force tomorrow forbidding the men to pay more than 10¢ a qt for milk. If they do they get two hours at pack drill for each qt they buy. Washing is $1.20 a doz. Since the attack on the provision train the Brigadier has ordered all the force to stay inside the lines as he does not wish the Indians to get any pot shots. This put a stop to our fishing and shooting and the ducks and plover are in abundance all around us. We have two services in camp, one with us (the main body) and one in South Battleford with the outpost, both Church of England. All Protestants are forced to go and the Presbyterian Minister here is raising Cain. He wants to hold a service for his flock but the Colonel would not allow it and on his giving the Colonel a piece of his mind the Colonel seized his church and we use it now as a mess room and kitchen. They have a good service at South Battleford in Government House. Cassels plays the melodeon very well and he has trained a choir. It consists of himself, organist, (Presbyterian), Captain Hughes, 2nd tenor, (R.C.), three Episcopalians, two Methodists and a "tough" who does not know what church he belongs to but has a splendid voice. You may imagine how well they do when they yesterday sang Jackson's Te Deum without a single mistake, complete in all the parts. We heard of Riel's defeat and capture but my satisfaction was lessened very much at the news of Lieut. Fitch's death. When I consider—now that I can look back on it with deliberation—my own chances on May 2nd I feel very thankful at my escape and wonder I was not even hit. However, on an expedition of this sort we have all to take our chances. I expect to hear from Wem next mail, that is if it arrives safely. Lil's letters set me up for a week. I have not written to Father, knowing that it's all the same when I write to you and if he happens to be away from town you would be kept waiting for the news. All here are doing well and in spite of hard fare still growing fat.

June 2, 1885

After being practically locked up for two weeks without any news your letters were most welcome, but I'm afraid in my last I was rather premature in expecting to go home soon, Big Bear having changed his mind and resolved not to surrender. Our Regiment and, in fact, the whole Brigade feel very keenly the insult cast on us by General Middleton in leaving us here and taking the other brigade to the front. It was done to spite Col. Otter who was put over the head of the General's nominee, General Laurie, for this position. Col. Otter, being

simply a Militia man, was rising too fast and the General being a regular, is determined to give him no more chances to distinguish himself,
although he proved by his coolness and valour at "Cut Knife" that he
is thoroughly worthy of the highest command that can be given him. I
know, however, that the people in Toronto will see that it was no fault
of ours that we did not get a better chance to show what we are good
for. Only 50 of us got any chance at "Cut Knife" and I know the rest of
the Regiment could be depended on for any service. I only hope the
General gets no more fighting and that Big Bear will surrender to
General Strange. The only consolation we have is that General Middleton is thoroughly hated by his own Brigade. What on earth do the
Toronto papers mean by publishing letters against Col. Otter about
his being a martinet etc., etc. In every body of men there are always
some grumblers and fellows only too glad to get an opportunity to
malign any one over their heads. There are always the people to strike
a man behind his back especially when he has no chance to defend
himself. All stories adverse to Col. Otter in regard to his harsh treatment of the men under his command are utterly false and without
foundations. On the contrary, he has been most kind and considerate
and his conduct in these matters is a complete contrast to General
Middleton's treatment of his men and especially General Middleton's
treatment of his officers. Hume Blake has arrived but came on two
days in advance of his convoy of goodies. They will arrive tomorrow
and will be quite acceptable, to say the least of it. The Grenadiers
heard when they were at Prince Albert that the goodies had been taken
by Poundmaker and were greatly nettled over it. After they were all in
their tents after dark they would go on this way:

    Solo Q. Who lost their Jam?
        A. The Queen's Own.
    Solo Q. Who got the Queen's Own Jam?
        A. Poundmaker.

One man would yell out the question and the whole camp would yell
out together the answer. The effect must have been very comical. The
90th are splendid fellows, nearly 100 of them old Queen's Own men.
We fraternized immediately on our meeting. They are over one whole

Company short since they left Winnipeg, killed and wounded. That is one company out of six, they having lost over 50 men. Our wounded will all get well although two of them will never quite get over the effects of the bullets. The wounded of the other corps here will all not be so lucky. Two B Battery may have to have their arms amputated and one who is shot in the abdomen twice and they have not got out either bullet yet.

Fighting the Cree at Frenchman's Butte, 1885

CAPTAIN WILLIAM PARKER

On the following morning the 28th, of May, 1885, with Steele's Scouts in advance, the Column marched forward, here and there we found camping places, and an amount of discarded loot, so we knew the Indians and their prisoners were quite close. About 10 A.M. we arrived at a valley running across our front, with a bad muskeg between us and the opposite bank, the banks on each side being quite steep, thirty or forty feet above the muskeg. We were at the west side, which was covered with brush, interspersed with trees, the east bank opposite was clear of brush but fringed all along the top with heavy poplar trees, the writer was one of the advance Scouts, and we had just started to ride down the slope, when our Interpreter and guide, Alec Rowland said he was sure the Indians were on the opposite side, so the Column was halted, when a horse neighed from the opposite side, the Interpreter then said, "The Indians are there sure." General Strange said, "We will find out," and ordered the nine-pounder gun up and to fire a shell across. It was no sooner fired than the engagement was on, the Indians poured a heavy fire into us, the 65th. Battalion with the Kildonan Red Coats, and one troop of Steele's Scouts were fighting down the bank in the heavy brush, the nine-pounder firing over their heads shelling the Indian position, Steele's Scouts were on the left flank, the Alberta Rifles on the right flank. On the first shell bursting in the heavy fringe of woods in the Indian position, several shrieks and screams were heard, evidently from the prisoners, so the General ordered the gun not to be fired again in that particular spot.

After about two hours of steady fighting by both sides, Steele's Scouts were ordered to go further to the left flank to try and find a crossing over the muskeg. We proceeded there, and the writer was detailed to take two men and find a crossing; leaving one man to hold the horses under cover, the two of us started on foot, and when about half way over fired at an Indian pony standing at the edge of the muskeg on the opposite side, there was no return fire, so we went to the other side and found a fairly good crossing, this was reported to Major Steele who sent a message to General Strange. While waiting, I asked permission of Major Steele to climb a very tall pine tree, that would overlook the Indian position, he consented, and on going up about sixty feet a clear view over the position was obtained, and as I suspected, the Indians, in twos and threes, were getting out and treking in a northerly direction. A message having arrived from the General, the writer was called down, and was informed by Major Steele that the General had decided to retire two or three miles back from the position to more open ground, and to bivouac for the night, that the Alberta Rifles had reported the Indians were getting around the right flank, Steele's Scouts covered the retirement which was carried out without further fighting.

All ranks behaved splendidly. The 65th. Montreal boys were very keen to make use of their bayonets, and clamored more than once to be led across the muskeg, in a bayonet charge against the Indians.

At day-light the next morning the Column moved forward again, Steele's Scouts in advance, and on arriving at the Indian position found it unoccupied. It was observed they had excellent rifle pits all along the top of the bank just inside the fringe of trees, and had dug a large cellar with logs over the top, in which they kept the prisoners, evidently the place where the screams had come from. The camp ground in the rear of the position was a wonderful sight, being covered with bales of prime furs, roughly valued at between forty and fifty thousand dollars, also an enormous quantity of house-hold furniture, etc. etc. ornaments, silver-ware, cook stoves, bedding, etc.

In the fight we had only three casualties, two Privates of the 65th. Battalion, one shot through the chest, the other through the shoulder, the third, Constable McCrae of the Mounted Police and also of Steele's Scouts, was very badly wounded in the leg; this man refused to be brought out by the Stretcher Bearers until he had fired away all his ammunition. As he was liable to bleed to death, it was reported to General Strange, who said, "I guess I will have to go myself," which he did, and brought the man out from the front firing line.

After leaving the Indian position the Column went on a few miles and camped. The General received a despatch that General Middleton had just arrived at Fort Pitt with three hundred Mounted Men, so an Escort of one Lieutenant, one Sergeant and twelve men was ordered to escort General Middleton from Fort Pitt to our camp, the writer was the Sergeant. As we left late in the evening for Fort Pitt, it soon got dark, and in riding through some woods we heard shouting from quite a long way off, we shouted in return, and kept it up until we heard them say, "We are escaped prisoners," we told them we were Soldiers, there were four of them who came staggering up to us. Two of them I knew personally, the Rev'd Quinney of the Church of England and W. B. Cameron; a very affecting scene took place, the four of them crying with joy. The Rev'd Quinney on recognizing me, placed his head on my stirrup and wept like a child. They were weak and very hungry, stating they had escaped from the Indians during the fighting, and had been wandering through the woods since then, that all the other prisoners were well. We sent them to report themselves to General Strange. The next morning we escorted Gen'l Middleton up to General Strange's camp at Frenchman's Butte. The writer was present when the two Generals met. General Strange told General Middleton what he had done, stating he had sent Major Steele and his Scouts after the Indians, to hold them in check and at that very time was probably in action with them, and requested General Middleton to send his three hundred Mounted men on to help Steele. Well does the writer remember the answer. "Not a man! not a man!, who is this Major Steele, it should not have been done." They then went into the tent and nothing further was heard. It appears just after we had left on Escort Duty, Steele's Scouts left to follow the Indians. On my return I begged the Brigadier to allow me to follow after them, but he refused and said that General Strange wanted me to look after the few Scouts left behind.

The next morning, May the 30th. The Alberta Column (minus Steele's Scouts) pulled out for Cold Lake, as Big Bear and his Indians were supposed to be heading in that direction. We arrived there the second day and found no signs of the Indians having been there. On the second night about mid-night, some firing was heard at one of our out-posts, and I was immediately called to go and investigate. I took Alec Rowland, the Guide, with me, and found Lieut. Starnes of the 65th. Battalion in charge of the outpost, he said they had a sentry watching a small path coming out of the woods. That when he arrived on the scene the sentry reported, an Indian on his pony had come out of the woods, dismounted, knelt down, and fired at him, and the Indian rode into the woods and disappeared. This was the third or fourth time that I had been called out in the night under similar circumstances, and decided to put a stop to it if possible. Rowland was sent to examine the small pathway, and reported that although the ground was wet and soft, there were no signs of a horse having been there, that there were numerous boot marks in the grass at the edge of the wood. To my enquiry Mr. Starnes stated he had doubled his men up there to look for the Indian. The sentry was placed under arrest, and pleaded guilty to the offense of perpetrating a false alarm, he was given three weeks imprisonment, and this put a stop to further incidents of this kind.

A Gentleman Cadet at the Royal Military College, 1898

F.H. MAYNARD

When I was a boy most of us attended the ordinary day schools in the city. In those days there were a few boarding schools run on the lines of British Public Schools, but they were few and far between. Education at the Day Schools was quite good. The pupils were drawn from every walk of life, and if you thought yourself socially superior to some, you were quickly cured of your snobbery. You learnt to call everyone by their Christian names, and this continued in after life when perhaps a former class-mate delivered milk at your door, or served you in a shop, when you would shake hands across the counter and say: "Hello, Bill, how are you, haven't seen you for a long time." In those days there were no "A," "O" Level exams nor did one acquire a school leaving certificate. For this reason my father, quite rightly, decided that I might achieve some recognized standard of education, which would be of use when job hunting after leaving school. I suggested going up for the entrance exam for the R.M.C. He agreed and I put in my application. In due course the exam took place. It lasted 4 days. On the second day we were given a document for our parents to sign—that in the event of passing the exam we would go to the R.M.C. My father signed the paper cheerfully.

After the exam I went on a camping expedition down the Ottawa. Mixed camps were a feature of life in those days, when boys and girls shared the same camping site. We spent the time boating, bathing, and fishing, and went on excursions in the neighbourhood. A steam boat used to leave Ottawa daily and sail to Grenville and back. On the way it called near our camp site. My brother was on board, and he announced the news that I had passed into the R.M.C. I received warm congratulations from my campmates. The news opened a new vista to me, quite an unknown one, because few of us knew anything about the R.M.C. We used to see the odd cadet walking about, looking very smart and soldierly, but what we had heard about life there was anything but pleasant. The press had made the most of the "Plummer row" in which a recruit called Plummer, having become alarmed at what he was to expect at the initiation, armed himself with a revolver and threatened to shoot anyone who touched him. He then ran across to Kingston, and told the tale to the press, who took all they could out of it.

Shortly after returning home from camping I received a document regarding a medical exam, to be signed by one's own doctor. This document intrigued me because, beside having a list of diseases that would preclude your entry into the R.M.C., there was a curious note about the limbs being of equal length. I worried about this note and set about measuring my limbs. Every time I did so I got a different result, and came to the conclusion that one leg was shorter than the other, and one arm longer than the other. As for the list of diseases, I decided that I suffered from at least half of them, if not all. However, I took the paper to my doctor, and he made a thorough examination. He said I was perfectly fit except for being slightly short-sighted in my left eye, but he decided not to mention this because one shot with the right eye. Much relieved, I posted the document to the R.M.C. Nothing further happened until early in September I received orders to report to the Adjutant of the R.M.C. on a certain date in September.

I travelled by boat to Kingston via the Rideau Canal. One other Ottawa boy accompanied me. On arrival at Kingston we booked in at the British American Hotel, and spent the night there with about 10 others. We had a cheerful evening. The next morning we got into cabs and drove across the bridge to the R.M.C. which in those days consisted of 3 buildings; the Main Building containing the Commandant's office, class rooms and dining room; the Stone Frigate containing dormitories; and a small building on the edge of the parade ground fitted up as a gymnasium. Later on we were to become closely acquainted with this building and its contents.

We reported to the Adjutant, Major McGill, who directed us to report to Cadet Sgt. Poole in the Stone Frigate. We were kindly received by Poole and shown where to sleep, eat, etc. Nothing further happened that day, but the next day we started to learn drill under Poole's direction. In the afternoon we were free and explored the grounds, walked over to Kingston and explored the town. In the evenings Poole used to give us talks on what was expected of us. After a few days of this the senior cadets arrived. We helped them hump their kit to their rooms, answered the call "Recruit!" and watched the college come to life. On the call of "Recruit!" one moved with all speed because the last arrival got the job. This practice made for speed of movement.

The most distasteful job recruits had to do was that of Bath Orderly. Fortunately the job didn't come round very often. It involved drawing the seniors' baths in the morning, which meant getting up earlier than usual. Some seniors wanted a cold bath, some a hot one, and some only tepid. Although times were laid down for each bath, more often than not the senior, after being roused, would fall asleep again and by the time he was roused the next one on the list would arrive. This led to double recrimination and abuse of the Bath Orderly.

The hazing of recruits was at times severe. The worst practice was when we were roused in the middle of the night, ordered to put our equipment on over our naked bodies and then run the gauntlet, the seniors being armed with stick canes or anything handy. After this experience we returned to bed somewhat sore in places.

Looking back one wonders why boys between 16 and 20 were sub-jected to treatment that may have been suitable for little boys at a Prep School but quite unsuitable for older boys. At the time I suppose we thought this was the R.M.C. that our predecessors had suffered in the same way, and that if we couldn't stick it out we were no good.

A week or so later came the initiation. This was a noisy business. The recruits were herded into the Bridging pit and blindfolded. Then giant fire crackers were exploded. After this each recruit was taken charge of by a senior and led away. If he resisted he was beaten over the head with a sock filled with sand. The seniors used to make blood-curdling noises to frighten the recruit and they were required to run, walk and jump imaginary ditches. Being blindfolded they could not see. Some were marched into the Lake until the water was up to their nostrils, after which they were ordered to about turn and returned to the bank. Another practice was to tell the recruit he was to be branded with a hot iron. As he was blindfolded he didn't realize the branding was done with a piece of ice.

I remember that when I was a senior we carried out the initiation in somewhat the fashion as described above, but, by chance, we had cho-sen one of those glorious evenings which occur in Canada, at the Fall of the year, when the air is still with a slight hint of frost—a night when sound seems to travel for miles. In no other country have I experienced such a night, which seems peculiar to Canada. On this night we made the usual hullabaloo of sounds which, unfortunately, travelled across the water to Kingston. The girl friends of the recruits, hearing the awful row and having heard tales of the way recruits were treated, thought something terrible was happening to their boy friends. So they started calling the Commandant on the telephone saying they were sure the recruits were being murdered by those brutal seniors. He hadn't heard the noise as he was indoors, but he went outside and was convinced something was amiss. So he proceeded to the parade ground and yelled for the BSM. When the BSM arrived he asked him, "What the hell is that bloody row? I have been pestered by telephone calls from Kingston about it and a lot of young ladies are alarmed." The BSM explained that the initiation was being carried out, but that it was more noise than hurt. The Commandant said, "Carry on, but no more noise or you will find yourselves on the mat in the morning." He returned to his house and we carried on, but the spirit had gone out of the affair and soon we all went to bed, the recruits enormously relieved.

After the initiation, two more events remained in the recruit's life, one the obstacle race, and two, the St. Patrick's Day Cake Walk. The obstacle race was of the usual kind surmounting walls, ditches, wire entanglement, barrels, etc. The Cake Walk was a traditional entertainment put on by the recruits who appeared in fancy dress, and put on a number of turns. No one quite knows the origin of the Cake Walk but it was good fun for all. After St. Patrick's Day things eased off a bit as everyone was thinking of the end of term exams, and of going home in June when the recruit year ended.

The life of a recruit was spartan in that one had no heat in the bedrooms and nothing but cold baths. The cold bath in those days was supposed to cure all ills. It had been extolled by Charles Kingsley, the novelist, and there was much about its benefit in the Boy's Own Paper, a periodical of that time. Anyway, what with cold baths, daily drill and daily P.T. we were all gloriously fit and, in spite of the odd incident we objected to, we were happy, and when we departed for home leave felt considerable pride in what we had survived and experienced in our first year.

The general routine was six hours study, one hour P.T., and one hour drill daily, but recruits had to put in an extra hour between 9 and 10 P.M. in the gym doing whatever we fancied.

We had made many friends amongst the people of Kingston who went out of their way to entertain us and, above all, to give us a good meal whenever we went to their homes. The food at the College was plain and good, but monotonous. Each day of the week had its menu which never varied throughout the three years I was there, so any change provided by the kind hearts of our Kingston friends was most welcome. Sometimes after a visit we would be given a cake to take back with us. It was difficult to carry a cake inside a tight tunic, but we were an ingenious lot of boys.

So far I haven't touched on the subject of recreation. As the College was situated on the shores of Lake Ontario it was natural that canoeing, sailing small boats, and swimming should be the principal recreations. We soon became experts in the handling of these small craft. In addition to these activities there was rugby football for the few, and also ice hockey. There was also a cricket team, for the few, a couple of tennis courts, and ice boating during the short season between the freezing over of the Lake and the advent of snow. It was an exhilarating sport as one travelled at great speed.

After the term exams we all went home. The year at Kingston had left its mark on me. Instead of the rather weedy boy who left home in September the previous year, I was so changed physically and mentally that few people recognized me. I was indeed a good advertisement for the mysterious College.

Going to War In South Africa, 1899–1900

TOM WALLACE

> *Canada sent volunteers to fight against the Boers in 1899, and among the soldiers in the Royal Canadian Regiment was Tom Wallace, the son of a Conservative MP. Three of his letters home convey much about Canadian attitudes at the time.*

Quebec
Oct. 29th

My Dear Papa

I received your letters and papers all right and you don't know how glad I was to hear from you all. It has been raining here all day. We just been issued with our kit which includes two pairs of heavy boots, 1 pair leggings, 1 pr. trousers, 1 serge, 1 good big overcoat and cape, two flannel shirts, two undershirts, 2 pr. drawers, 1 heavy sweater, the new Oliver equipment that is brown leather belts and a valise on our back, a rifle and a bayonet, a knife, spoon, fork, 3 brushes. We have to get the rest of the kit in the morning. Mr. Brown of the Mail and Empire is doing all he can for us. I know Hamilton the Correspondent of the Globe also. We are getting along all right. A great many of the Toronto co'y were transferred to another co'y but I am going to stay with "C" Company all right. We had a fine church parade here to-day to Holy Trinity Church. Hendrie and McGee and I sleep next to each other. Lord Minto and Sen. Hutton were at church. The minister preached a grand sermon and a great many of the Contingent took the Sacrement. I enclose you a form of the service. Alf. Sherritt the amateur champion bicycle rider of Canada is with us too. There are no accounts that I left unpaid. The Armory in Bolton is all paid up. We have a fine Co'y. Young Rorke is a nice chap. H.V. Rorke of Customs Ottawa is down here to-day. A great many of the boys are Orangemen. We get all the papers sent to us. World, Globe, Mail and Montreal Star. We go on board the boat to-morrow. With love to all. I am

Your loving son

Tom

It is 9:30 P.M. and Col. Sergt. is calling the role so I must stop.

S.S. Sardinian
Sunday, Nov. 26th, 1899

My Dear Mamma and
all the rest.

I have written two letters home since I have been on the ship and I suppose you will receive them all right. This is our fourth Sunday on board and we are beginning to feel as if we would like to get on land again. We expect to arrive in Cape Town on Wednesday, Nov. 29th. We have had a very good trip so far and I thought I would write to-day because I may not have a chance to write a very long one from Cape Town. We can't tell anything about the War yet. We have two newspaper reporters on board, Mr. Brown of Mail and Empire and Mr. Hamilton of Globe. I know them both. So you will be able to get all the news from the papers after we arrive in Cape Town. We have all our outfit now and we are ready to march as soon as we land. Sam Hughes is on board but he does not belong to this contingent. I think that he is going to be attached to the Dublin Fusiliers. Of course, we have not much room to drill on board but we are kept busy doing something all the time. We can't complain very much about the *"grub"* but it might be better. We are all pretty good tailors by this time because we are kept busy sewing on buttons and cutting our clothes to fit us. We have an English Church preacher, a priest, a presbyterian minister and a Y.M.C.A. representative on board. There are also four nurses on board. I am in with a fine lot of boys. We have two suits of uniform. One is dark green and the other is the "karkee." When we are in marching order we carry 61 lbs. on our back. It was very warm for a while but it is getting cool again. We drew our first pay on Thursday last $15.35. I am a full private in the front rank of No. 3 Section "C" Company. We had target practice on board with the Morris tube and I happened to make enough to be classed as a 1st class marksmen. I have been acting as Colonel Otter's Orderly (not the one who shines his boots) this last few days and it is a pretty good job. I am not sure but I may be able to keep it when we get on land. I hope I can because there will be a good chance on a job like this. We were all at Church this morning and we had communion Service also. While I am the Colonel's Orderly I am down in the Officer's quarters in the Orderly Room and I carry messages from the Colonel to the different officers. I got good many letters from Woodbridge before I left Quebec and I will try to get time to answer them. I got letters from Leader and Recorder and Weston Times asking me to write to them once in a while and I will try to do so. Tell Ed Brown I will write from Cape Town if I have time. When I am the Colonel's I get out of all parades and don't have sentry duty to do and get out of a lot of dirty work. There is not very much news on board it is the same thing day after day.

　　With love to all
　　I am your loving Son

　　Tom

Bloemfontein
late Capital Orange Free State
S. Africa
Saturday, March 16th, 1900

My Dear Mother

After four weeks of marching, fighting and hardships we have at last arrived in Bloemfontein the capital of Orange Free State. We are camped about ½ mile outside of the town on a nice plain. It is a fine country around here, the farther we go the country gets better. We took part in Lord Robert's general advance on Bloemfontein. When we started from Graspaan Feb. 12th it was the intention to march to Kimberley but as we advanced the Boers evacuated Magersfontein and all around Kimberley and retreated towards here. We followed them and overtook Cronje at Paardeberg Drift and you would see a full account in the papers about what we did to Mr. Cronje. And we were under fire for four days and one night. (I have just come back from the spring where I was getting water for tea. I had to carry two pots of water about 1¼ miles. I am orderly to-day)—We marched from Grasspan and Bloemfontein a distance the way we came of 176 miles. We had to carry our overcoats (part of the time) and our accoutrements and rifles all the way. We marched side by side with the Gordon Highlanders Highland Brigade Guards, Brigade Cornwalls and Shropshires and we can hold our own as far as marching goes. I wasn't sick one day on the whole march. Sometimes we marched all night and other times all day in the heat of the day. We were on half rations all the way here and everbody says it is remarkable how we kept up the way we did. We marched a good many more than 176 miles but that was marching on outpost and back again. We slept out in the open rain or shine and we were very often lying on the wet ground all night. Of course I haven't time to write account of march and experiences to-day as the mail closes in five minutes. We are staying here for a few days now and I will [?] a full account. Don't publish this letter I am going to write to Ed Brown a pretty full account of our trip if I get a chance soon. We are all in fine shape now we are getting fed up. Our fellows didn't grumble at all but just took things as they came. I think the Boers will soon be finished now as soon as they feel another good trimming.

Hoping you are all well.

Love to all

I am

Your loving Son

Tom

Plenty of Fighting to Suit Everybody:
The RCR at Paardeberg

DOUGLAS MCPHERSON

The Dutton Advance, *a small-town Ontario newspaper, regularly published letters written home by men from the area. This letter, from a member of the Canadian contingent in South Africa, gives a view of the Paardeberg battle.*

Paardeberg Drift, March 3, 1900.

Dear Mamie,—You have heard all about our wanderings long before this no doubt. We have had plenty of fighting to suit everybody, and we all hope it requires no more. We have also found out that campaigning is no fun but hard work and very bad for one's health without the hard fighting we have had.

We started from Belmont on Sunday night, and while we were marching to the train not a sound was made, for we all felt that we were going to a dangerous part of the country. We bivouacked at Gras Pan that night and at three A.M. we started our march along with three other regiments which formed our brigade (the nineteenth). We had to carry two days' rations, emergency rations, overcoats and ammunition and when the heat of the day came we felt like dropping, and before we reached Ram's Dam about 80 had fallen out overdone with thirst. Here we got some very dirty water to drink, and some weak coffee with biscuits for supper.

Again at five we were off for the Riet River 14 miles away and it became terribly hot about 9:30. Still we plugged along, until about one o'clock, when we were halted and our company and D Company were sent about two miles away to reconnoitre a kopje where we remained until the rear guard of the column had passed. The sun was terrible, not a cloud, not a speck of shade and among burning stones with no water. But even that ended and we stumbled, almost fainting, up to the banks of the river, where we stayed, eating nothing until after six o'clock at night except our hard tack biscuits. During the afternoon we dragged the naval guns across the river and at night we had soup. Next morning we had only nine miles to go, so we did that by 8:30 but had to furnish outposts on arriving, so we had no rest that night, and next morning we pressed on to Jacobsdal, where we had a good feed of meat and hoped for rest but had to go on twelve miles that night to the Modder River, all the time hoping to come up with Cronje and the Boers, but he was a veritable Will'o the Wisp to us. The next night we went twenty three miles to this place, arriving at 6 A.M. After a hasty drink of coffee and some rum to revive us we forded the Modder River and advanced on the enemy's position. At eight we were firing at the place where we saw smoke, for no Boers were visible, although only 500 yards from their trenches. Here we lay all day with the bullets whistling and cracking all around us and no cover except the ant hills which were far too scarce. Well, at about 5:30 P.M. we got the order to fix bayonets which was received with satisfaction, for we were being cut up very badly and were unable to move from our scanty cover all day. Well, we charged but we lay down where we were and when darkness came retired, but all night we were bringing in wounded. Next day, when the Boers left the position I went all through their trenches and the place seemed to me to be impregnable to anything but artillery, and my only wonder was that more of us were not killed.

A Journalist Reports on Paardeberg, February 1900

STANLEY M. BROWN

Two journalists accompanied the Royal Canadian Regiment to South Africa. Stanley Brown was the first to get his reportage into book form.

Officers commanding companies were told precisely what the plan for the night attack was.

Shortly, it was this: Six companies, "C," "E," "D," "F," "G" and "H," were to start at two o'clock in the morning (February 27th), from the advanced trench, 550 yards from the Boers' nearest shelters, and proceeding in the dark were to get as near the enemy as possible covering a front of about 240 yards from left to right. The front rank men were to push on with bayonets fixed and magazines charged; fifteen paces behind them the rear rank were to proceed, with rifles slung and carrying spades and picks. In case the front rank were not seriously opposed, they were to enter the Boer trenches; if they were opposed they were to lie down and return the fire, covering the rear rank who were to at once open a trench for the firing line to fall back on, a dozen yards behind. Thirty engineers were also to help with the trench digging on our right. "B" Company, on account of losses and previous hard work, was in reserve, with "A" Company in their old place in the trench across the river. The Gordons (two companies only) were to man the left of the advanced trench with fixed bayonets and orders not to fire for fear of hitting our men ahead. They were to be a sort of moral support behind the stealthy advancers. To the left, 800 yards from the river and almost facing it, the Shropshires were to be stationed with orders to open a heavy fire when they saw that our men were engaged, in order to divert the Boers' attention and make the danger lighter for the Royal Canadians. These plans were all well carried out, except that the Boers decided to open fire instead of allowing our men to walk into their trenches at will.

Between the time of issuing these orders and the beginning of the move the men rested, ate a little, and many had a much needed sleep in the trenches.

"How do you feel?" asked one of the two city regiment chums of the other, as they waked up from a short chilly sleep.

"All right," replied the other, "though I could do with half a tin of 'bully beef' to give me ballast. I'm a little light in the middle."

"Well, you can run all the faster," continued the first one, "but I mean how do you feel about this attack?"

"I don't fancy this night work," was the answer, "and look what Gen. Wauchope's men got at Magersfontein in the dark! I like the daylight for my business. I'd almost carry a lantern if I had one, but that's what brought grief to the Highland Brigade. I guess we had better travel incog.," and the two peered out into the black night above the trenches.

"No sounds towards the laager," one went on. "I guess they've all—"

"Ready, men!" whispered the Sergeant, "now look sharp! Steady getting out of the trench! Ease off—no more than an arm's length. Quiet. Not a sound!"

The whole line was up on the veldt in a long row of black shadows, "C" and "E" companies with Major Buchan on the left in order, then came in succession to the right "D," "F," "G," and "H" companies in charge of Major Pelletier.

Col. Otter and his Adjutant, Lieut. Ogilvy, remained in the advanced trench.

It was twenty minutes past two in the morning.

The soldiers walking cautiously like blind men went carefully forward, keeping in touch with one another by the clasp of hands or the feel of the next man's tunic. There was no sound, and the anxious waiters in the trenches behind felt that each minute prolonged itself into an hour.

Trees here and there on the open were the cause of breaking touch between "G" and "F" companies, and two hundred yards from the starting point the men halted till the whole line in blackest darkness was put in order again. They were then but two hundred and fifty yards from the enemy, and to halt there on the open and perfect their further arrangements, was a feat in itself. It proved what discipline and courage was in the ranks of the Royal Canadian Regiment.

Then the advance continued, and stealing on like velvet-footed burglars, they slowly put more yards of gained ground behind them.

Every foot was a wonderful advance, and a yard then was as good as twenty any other time.

Could the Boers *see* them? No. Could they *hear* them coming? No one could say. Did they *know* they were coming? That was hard to tell.

What thoughts crammed the men's heads! What strange and uncanny feelings they had! What horrible recollections of other night attacks, disastrous beatings many times during the campaign!

Still, without a waver, they forged on, waiting for a dashing bayonet charge or—anything to relieve their minds in those restless moments.

Slow steps and cat-like movements brought them practically face to face with their enemy, for, on the right "G" and "H" companies were within thirty yards of the Boer trenches, and on the left "C" and "E" companies were but eighty yards from the Dutchmen, when— Bang! came from hundreds of rifles in the Boer trenches. The enemy's hiding-place was alive with the incessant click of triggers, and the air was full of bullets from the muzzles of rifles, practically staring in the faces of the Canadians. From right to left Cronje's men swept the advancing line, no longer advancing, but lying prostrate on the sand.

Before the Canadians had a chance to fire, men dropped dead in the ranks. Then did the rear rank ply their picks and spades, and dig with a well-nigh insane frenzy. Hotter came the continual fire, and quieter lay the first line, with their trembling bodies stretched on the open veldt, till they began to use their rifles in return.

At once it was found a mistake to keep shooting, since it only drew more aimed shots around them—then they stopped.

Still the burghers blazed away, and in the first ten minutes of their fiendish fusilade twelve of our regiment lay dead—one in "C" Company, three in "D," one in "E," three in "F," and four in "G,"—and in the course of the fierce fight thirty more lay wounded. Some person near the centre of the line shouted "Retire!"—no person ever knew who was the instigator of the order—and from centre to left the word soon ran along the line, and the men started back in groups as best they could, halting at times on the way to seek shelter from the pouring lead, scooping up little piles of sand with which to protect their heads, and then dashing back farther, when the Boers' fire quieted the least.

They did not scamper back in a confused mob; they retreated in a common-sense way. In the dark some got too far from the river and dropped into the trench where the Gordons' bayonets gave them a piercing reception, others edged too much to the right, but luckily for them they were able to retire in more safety through the bushes on the river bank.

When the rifles had rattled ceaselessly for fifteen minutes, the Shropshires on the left opened a heavy fire on the Boer trenches.

Meanwhile the order to retire had never reached "G" and "H" companies, who held on bravely, looking down the barrels of the Boer rifles but thirty yards away. "H" Company, under Capt. Stairs, had the position at the river bank, and "G" Company, with Lieut. Macdonnell in command, were next to the left. The former company of eastern Canadian soldiers escaped without a casualty, but the latter company in a few moments suffered one corporal and three privates killed and ten men wounded. Lieut. Kaye of "G" Company had heard the order to retire and took back with him part of the half company.

While the galling fire kept up, the men of these companies in the rear rank dug away at the trenches, knowing it was a matter of life and death, and the sappers who were with them worked with lightning speed. Amid a steady fire part of "G" Company were able to crawl back to the dongas in the river's high banks and kept up a continuous fire to cover the trench-diggers.

As soon as he could Lieut. Macdonnell drew back to the newly-made trench, and Lieut. Jones of the same company soon followed this example, with his men. Shortly, "H" Company's soldiers swooped into the trench, and while they kept sending their volleys of lead into the Boers' trenches, the men of "G" Company took up the shovels and made the shelter more secure.

It was a brief fight, but a long half hour of deadly combat. Ten minutes of triple hell and twenty minutes of an ordinary inferno.

The Canadians still hanging on in the firing-line sniped away till dawn came, and then, with the faint light at five o'clock they kept it up for nearly another hour, searching out the Boer rifle pits strung along the river.

An old burgher jumped from the Boer trenches and waved his hands. The Canadians ceased firing and hollered for him to "come on in"; his heart failed him and he jumped into his burrow again, and the Canadians once more showered their bullets in.

Another appearance of the elderly Boer was a signal for the Canadians to cease firing, another disappearance of the Dutchman and another splash of lead followed him.

"Come in and surrender!" cried the Canadians, but the enemy paid no attention till the aged fighter had made two more sudden appearances from out his cover, and two as quick leaps back to his stinking rifle pit.

By six o'clock the Boer leader had rigged a dirty pillow-cover to the cleaning-rod of a rifle, and with no mistake in his slouchy movements, he slunk to the Canadian lines, and the eastern Canadians received the surrender. The hard-fighting Gen. Cronje, with his 4,200 men, gave himself up unconditionally to Lord Roberts, and the Canadians, with their trenches built exactly 63 yards from the enemy's lines, had, by their gallant work, been "the last straw to break the camel's back." They had forced home the last thrust which he was not able to parry, and which brought him to the ground a beaten man.

The Royal Canadian Regiment had been the fighting germ in the heart of the British army that had wiped out at last the sorrowful remembrance of Majuba Day.

We Have to Do or Die:
A Strathcona in South Africa, April 1900

J.C. WALKER

> *The Lord Strathcona's Horse, a mounted regiment raised by Canada's High Commissioner in Britain, Lord Strathcona, arrived in South Africa in April 1900. Trooper Walker's jingoism and prejudices reflect those of his time.*

We arrived here a week ago and went into camp the next day. We had a pleasant voyage, but lost 160 head of horses. We were to have gone to Kimberley this week and help to relieve Mafeking, and thence on to Pretoria, but unfortunately glanders has broken out among our horses and unless we can get new mounts we may be here six weeks. I think Strathcona's influence will get us to the front in time, for it is an understood thing we have to do or die. We can do both, if necessary. You need not expect many letters from me as we are very busy from 5 A.M. until dark, and besides I have to go on sentry two nights a week. This is a beautiful place but strongly pro-Boer, as there are so many Dutch and Jews here. Our boys are getting into scraps with them. Our favorite amusement is to get around them, make them take off their hats and sing "God Save the Queen," give them a good kick and let them go.

The Volunteers Melt Away, 1900

C.F. HAMILTON

> *The Toronto Globe war correspondent in South Africa kept up a confidential correspondence with his editor, J.S. Willison. Some hard truths that did not make it into the newspaper were spoken here.*

The battalion is thinning down dreadfully. With the draft, Canada must have sent out from 1250 to 1300 men in the Royal Canadian

Regt. Today I doubt if it could place more than 450 rifles in the firing line. Death & wounds, about 150; sickness of one sort & another (including a peculiar disease known locally as Mauseritus, possessing many & diverse symptoms & one cause) perhaps 650. That's war. Our regiment has shot its bolt. That's volunteers—good as the best for 6 months—after that, not so good. The men are fervently homesick. When a fight occurs, none the less, they go ahead in a way which arouses the praise of Imperial officers. It is a very lucky regiment & at Yster there was a bally run, which Otter & Ogilvy (the adjutant) stopped. Otter was shot rallying the men. But the right was by itself, got steadied, & went ahead & did its job & got mentioned by general Hamilton as doing particularly well. There's luck, if you like. Otter has taken command again—time, too, for Buchan is a coward and Pelletier, while brave enough & a particularly fine fellow, loses his head & has no judgement. I have every hope that the war will end soon—it can't end too soon for me, altho' I have got to like campaigning, as I do it now, very much. I can make myself comfortable now with anyone.

Cavalry in South Africa

CHARLES AND BERT ROOKE

> *Charlie and Bert Rooke enlisted in Lord Strathcona's Horse in early 1900 and returned home after service in South Africa. Then they both re-enlisted in the Canadian Mounted Rifles in 1901 along with their brother George, and all served in South Africa until the end of the war. Charlie and Bert's letters home describe their service.*

February 12, 1900, Charlie to Mother

My dear Mother,

I expect you have heard already that Bert and I are going to the Transvaal with Strathcona Horse. When this reaches you we will be well on our way to Ottawa, the first stay of our long journey. My only regret is that we were unable, owing to the short notice, to run up and see you all.

I suppose we'd have had an ovation if we had run up there, as we are the only Saltcoats fellows going to the front. Bert says he has given you all the particulars, so I will not repeat. I will write from Ottawa, where I hope to hear from you, as we will be there some days.

We are waiting now for the western men to come in, which will be about 5 o'clock. They will march up here, and we will have lunch in the Drill Hall, starting for Ottawa about 8 or 9 o'clock. Well, good bye and God bless you, dearest mother, & if we return, we will not be in Canada long before we make our way to Saltcoats.

Give my love to the boys. We have left a lot of things with Jim and Stan which you might as well make use of, as we may never need them again.

I saw George yesterday & he seems better, but we did not tell him we were going, as it might excite him. Good bye again & take care of yourself till we see you again.

Your affectionate son,

Charlie

June 1, 1900, Bert to Mother

Dear Mother,

We have moved a little nearer the front, after a long delay in Cape Town & I think it is going to be something the same, so I think your wish will be fulfilled & the war will be over before we get up there. We have been lying here outside the mouth of the harbour for 4 days, it being a week since we left Table Bay. The harbour here can only accommodate 2 or 3 ships at a time, & there were a lot lying waiting to get in & unload when we arrived, besides which, there is a bad bar across the mouth of the harbour. There has been a very heavy swell for the last few days, which has raised the bar several feet & consequently it is dangerous for large vessels going in rough weather. The news we got from the tug last night was that Roberts had entered Johannesburg, so it looks as if the end was near.

We have had about as bad luck as it was possible for us to have, ever since we started in the way of checks and delays of various kinds, that it looks as if we were never meant to get to the front. We came up here in three different ships, 430 horses and about 300 men on the

S.S. Maplemore; 1 troop and a large number of natives & pack mules, machine guns etc. on the S.S. Mohawk & 1 troop with niggers mules on the S.S. Chicago. One squadron of about 200 men with horses we left in Cape Town & as far as sound information, I think they are going up country by train to join us up there.

I was on the mounted patrol escorting a large number of Boer prisoners from the Green Point prison ground to the train, about two weeks ago & I tell you they are a rough looking lot for soldiers. They are just like a lot of German farmers you would see in some of the small towns in the Northwest, except that they nearly all wore the well-known slouch hat. They carried all their camping material along with them, bedding, bottles, mugs, etc.

I am beginning to get anxious about getting word of some sort from you or some of the rest as neither of us have had any letters from you since we left Ottawa which is a long time. I have had one letter from a friend in Ottawa & that is the only letter I have had from Canada. While I write, some of the ships in the harbour are decorating with flags and flying rockets so I will not close till we hear if there is any fresh news.

7 p.m.

The rumour that was brought in tonight is that Roberts is in Pretoria & Kruger has skipped so I guess that was what the hubbub was about this afternoon. It has likely no foundation however. I hope not, anyway, for our sakes. I must close now, hoping you will hear good news of us right along. I hope you are all keeping well & getting along good. Tell the boys to write me & give them my love. Remember me to all the people & with love & best wishes to yourself.

Your affectionate son,

Bert

January 1, 1901, Charlie to Mother

My dear Mother,

I have just received a letter from you to Bert dated Nov 16th, which I have of course opened & will keep until Bert comes in, which I think will not be very long now, although we do not know anything about the exact whereabouts of the regiment. I went to hospital in Potchefatrom with low fever, and the day after I went in, the regiment left for Bethulie in the north of Cape Colony. I was discharged after 2 days, & started to make my way down to join the regiment, but when I got as far as Johannesburg, I was done up, in fact about that time I was so weak I could scarcely carry my rifle. I paraded to No. 9 General Hospital & was admitted at once, & kept there a fortnight.

From there I was sent to the Convalescent Depot in Johannesburg where I stayed five days, being moved from there to the rest camp at Elandsfontein, which was a fine place, lots of good rations & nothing to do but play at cricket & football. I was there five days, when the Surgeon Major called for all colonials who felt fit to return to their regiments. I slipped out & the next day started down country. I had a nice journey down in the mail train, taking 1½ days to reach here.

This is the headquarters of our regiment & there are about 60 of us gathered here from the different hospitals and rest camps. The regiment is chasing DeWet & our men have no baggage with them at all, so they must be having a rough time. I hear that half of what are out there are dismounted & have scarcely any clothes but what they have commandeered, so that they are a motley crew. In fact, it is reported here that one British column trained their guns on them when they were seen approaching, under the impression that they were Boers. Under these circumstances it cannot be very long before they must come in to some base, so we expect to rejoin them shortly, & are in hopes that we will then start on our way home.

There is a report going that we are to sail about the 15th, but we have had so many similar reports & been disappointed each time that we do not take much notice of anything we hear & only believe half of what we see. The last I heard of Bert he was alright, & was in charge of the squadron stores, as Lambert Carson of Yorkton who is acting Q.M. Sergeant was left at Bethulie & has since come in here & gone to hospital. It is a curious thing that Bert has had no return of the rheumatism he had so much trouble with at Cape Town. . . .

We have just received a letter from one of our chums who was wounded & invalided home & is at his home in Devonshire, & his casual mention of strawberries & cream & other little dainties makes my mouth water—no easy thing to do, as we are camped on a sand plain, where the dust is everlastingly on the move.

Remember me to all my friends in your district,

Yours affectionately,

Charlie

April 4, 1902, Charlie to Mother

My dear Mother,

I suppose you will have read accounts of the engagement we had with the enemy the other day, but I hope you have not been anxious about us. It seems as if we weren't meant to be shot, as so far none of us have had a scratch. Bert & I were both in the thick of the fight, in fact, everyone in the column was. There was nowhere to get to for cover & we had just to take everything as it came.

We left Klerksdorp last Saturday, the whole division under Gen. Kitchener, with a big convoy. On Monday morning, Easter Monday, our brigade, under Colonel Cookson, moved on ahead of the other troops, which stayed with the heavy transport, & by daylight (we marched at 3 A.M.) our advance guard was in touch with the enemy. About 9 o'clock they had a bit of hard fighting with them, & lost a few men, but our guns going to their assistance, the Boers retired. The rest of the brigade then moved up (except the rearguard, which had to guard our baggage, wagons, etc.) & we formed camp close to a waterhole. We put our horse lines down, watered the horses & the tea was almost ready for our dinner, when the enemy suddenly appeared on the skyline, [?] towards us. Our two 12 pounders opened fire at once, when the Boers at once opened with theirs, & the battle commenced.

As soon as the guns got to work, the Boers just opened out, & in less than half an hour, they were completely around us. Our rearguard was cut off, & what were left had to fight their way in. Delarey, who was in command of the Boers, thought that with the assistance of his guns, he had nothing to do but walk in and take us, as they had 4000 men against our 1500, & both had the same guns, but he struck a snag, & after trying it for three hours, they drew off. Our losses were pretty heavy, but not nearly as heavy as that of the enemy, & considering the exposed position we were in, without the least cover, exposed to fire from all sides of the circle & in a camp not more than 200 yards across at any place, we got off light.

Our troop was the luckiest of all, as we hadn't a man hit, except one or two by spent bullets, & we only had one horse wounded, whereas some of the troops had 8 or 10 horses killed, the regiment losing over 150. The Boers did good work with their pompoms. The man next to me in the line got one, which laid him out, but somehow everything went past me, although I was covered with dust two or three times by shells bursting close to me.

That night we dug trenches & stayed in them, expecting another attack, until about noon, when Gen. Kitchener got in with 2000 men to our relief. At 2 P.M. we started for here, where the column is in camp, but about 8 miles from here we got word that our wagons were stuck 4 miles behind us, & we had to link our horses & wait without blankets or grub, until daylight.

The worst of it was that it rained almost all Monday night, all day Tuesday & a good deal of the night, so we were in a cheerful condition until the sun got up on Wednesday morning & we warmed up a bit. About 11 o'clock we got in here, & have been feeding up & getting rested since, ready for another trek as soon as our convoy gets back from Klerksdorp. Bert wasn't with us in the scrap, as he is attached to Colonel Cookson's headquarters Staff now, & was left in charge of their wagon with the transport. We are all in good shape & feeling like fighting cocks.

Probably by the time this reaches you, you will have read of other engagements, as we expect to be able to make a final roundup of the Boers about here this time. Delarey, DeWet, Botha & Rusterberg were all with the commands in our last fight. One of our wounded, who was left with the others at a farmhouse when we left, our ambulances being crowded, was asked by Delarey what supplies we had in the convoy, & answered that we had supplies for 15,000 men for 6 months. Then Delarey cursed, & swore he would shoot every one of his men that were with the guns, as he had given orders that they were to charge in on us under the artillery fire, & drive us out, when he would catch us on the other side. If they had managed that, & got our guns, they could have made a pretty good drive at the convoy & that is what they want just now. However, they haven't got it yet & I don't think they will.

What they got from Methven has kept them going for a while, but I think they are getting short again, & are likely to make desperate attempts to capture anything that comes in their way.

Those of the men who have seen Delarey say that you could not tell him from a British General. He even has the crossed swords & crown on his shoulder, some of Methven's clothes, probably. A great many of them are wearing khaki and any man captured with it are promptly court-martialed & shot.

The little mare I rode in Halifax is still in good shape & I hope to ride her right through. I wrote to Hannah from Volksrust & sent her 20 pounds, which I think will give her a comfortable trip out. I expect you will have heard from her, or possibly she will be with you, before this reaches you. We haven't had any letters for some time, but expect some when the convoy gets back. It may be a few days before this gets away, so goodness knows when you will get it.

I wrote Stan from Klerksdorp a week or ten days ago, & I expect he would send the letter on. I had a letter from him a few days before that & set down to answer it at once, when orders came to march that evening & we covered 100 miles by the next evening, & when one gets moving like that & going without sleep almost entirely, one doesn't feel like writing every day, even if there was time. I am out in charge of the herd today, so have managed to scribble this, but goodness knows when I will manage to write any more.

Yours affectionately,

Charlie

In the Militia, 1912–14

ARTHUR TURNER

1912

While homesteading between Munson & Morrin, and operating a Wheelright and Woodworking shop at Munson, one of my rancher friends, Chas. W. Robinson of Fox Coulee, and Munson, got me to join the 15th Light Horse. He was a Lieutenant and was trying to raise two Troops from the Munson district.

It was a nice pastime, and for two weeks each summer, we came into Calgary, at Sarcee Camp, for training. Each man took his own horse, some took more. I took two horses in 1912,—Bell, and Fanny— my driving team. Bell was my favorite saddle pony, part thoroughbred. She won several races at the Munson annual fairs.

While in camp in 1912, we were issued a Ross rifle, to go to the rifle range for rifle practice, which was 100 rounds at 100 yards. This rifle had a Sutherland Sight, but none of us knew how to manipulate it. To adjust the sight for 200 yards, it had to be lifted to an upright position, where it could be set anywhere from 100 to 1,000 yards, but lying flat on the rifle barrel, it was at 500 yards range, known as the Battle Sight. We didn't know that, so we were firing on a 200 yard range with sights at 500 yards.

After I had fired about 5 shots, an instructor crept up beside me, and told me to lower my sights, that I was hitting the top of the target every time. I asked him how he knew where I was hitting. He said, "Do you see that black spotting disk at the top of the target?" I said, "Yes, but I thought it was a hole in the target." He said, "No, that is where you are hitting every time." I showed him my sights, and he decided they could not be lowered, so he said, "Aim at the bottom of the target." I did, and finished up with a fair score, because the next shot was a bull's eye.

Well, any unit that does not make a good score, has a second chance to try again. When we went the next time, we had learned how to adjust the sights. My officer came to me all excited saying that I had won the Camp high score, a 94 out of a possible 100. However, because I had failed the first time, I was disqualified.

At Munson, the business men had formed a rifle association. There was a Crown Lumber trophy to be shot for each year. My officer, Charlie Robinson, got me to join the club because they would be shooting for the Cup in the fall. The day of the shoot came and I was about to leave for the rifle range, which was located in Fox Coulee, just below Charlie Robinson's ranch, when I saw a neighbour of mine who very

seldom came to town, Charlie Morgan. He invited me to have a beer
with him. I told him I couldn't today because I was going to shoot for a
cup. However he wouldn't take NO for an answer, so we had 2 beers.
I went down and won the Cup with a score of 94. It was won the year
before by Mr. Bowie, with a score of 92. Exactly one year later, I was
going down to shoot for the Cup the second time, I saw Charlie Morgan in town again. This time I told him I was going to have two beers
with him because I was going to shoot for the Cup again. I won the
Cup again.

1913

That winter I attended a school of Military Training conducted by the
Lord Strathcona Horse (RC) in Winnipeg, for Officers and N.C.O.'s.
It was a 6 weeks course.

Charlie Robinson wanted a Farrier Sgt., one Sgt., and two Corpo-
rals. Levi Bone, a Munson Liveryman, qualified for Farrier Sgt. George
Winters, later the Undertaker at Drumheller, qualified for Sgt., and
Fred Horn and myself, for Corporals.

During this 6 weeks course, Lord Strathcona died and we all had to
attend the Memorial Service conducted by the Reverend Dr. Gordon
(Ralph Connor) 26° below zero. I froze my ear going to church.

1914

About the end of July, Charlie Robinson and I attended a 3 weeks
Musketry course at the old 103rd Barracks in Calgary. We had only
completed 2 weeks training when the war broke out. The course was
discontinued.

HMCS Rainbow *Forces the* Komagata Maru
out of Vancouver Harbour, July 1914

REAR ADMIRAL WALTER HOSE

*Canada's immigration policy was a restrictive one; Asians were
unwanted in the Dominion. In the summer of 1914, just before
the outbreak of war, a boatload of Indians attempted to debark at
Vancouver, but the government called out HMCS Rainbow, one of*

the navy's two decrepit cruisers, to keep them away. This account by
Rainbow's *captain was written in 1936.*

HMCS *Rainbow*, the Canadian cruiser stationed on the Pacific Coast
went out of commission in March 1914 and was "laid up" with only a
"care & maintenance" party of 4 officers and a number of petty officers
and ratings who were pensioners and ex-ratings of the Royal Navy.

In the following June the Canadian Government decided to place
the ship in commission again in order to carry out a patrol of the pela-
gic seal fishery in the Behring Sea.

To supply the necessary complement the existing personnel were
to be augmented by as many ranks & ratings as could be spared from
HMCS *Niobe* then laid up at Halifax NS and the balance were to be
obtained on loan from the Royal Navy from England.

The work of preparing the ship for active service was carried on by
the existing ship's company of the *Rainbow* pending the arrival of the
balance of her crew.

While these preparations were in progress a Japanese ship, the
Komagata Maru arrived in Vancouver harbour in the beginning of July
with 365 Indians who demanded permission to land and settle in
British Columbia.

My recollection is that these Indians were under the leadership of
one Gurdit Singh who had chartered the *Komagata Maru* in Calcutta
for the purpose of transporting the Indians, also, I believe I am correct in saying that few, if any, of them embarked in India, but were
picked up at various ports en route and consisted of ne'er-do-wells
many of whom would have had attention from the police had they
returned to India.

Permission to land was refused by the BC Government on the
grounds of an Order-in-Council which had been passed earlier in the
year to check labour immigration on account of the increasing un-
employment situation in the Province.

On being informed of this refusal the Indians became obstreper-
ous & violent, attacking Customs and Immigration officials who came
alongside in a launch.

The situation became one of grave anxiety for the authorities in
Vancouver not only on account of the mutinous passengers but because

of the possibility of sympathetic demonstrations by their co-nationals already resident in the district.

Under these circumstances an urgent appeal for assistance was made by the Immigration authorities in Vancouver to the Commanding Officer of the *Rainbow* & to the DOC [District Officer Commanding] of the Military District.

The CO of *Rainbow* wired the Naval Dept at Ottawa for permission to comply with this request and to embark a detachment of Permanent Militia from Work Point [barracks in Esquimalt] to assist in suppressing the mutinous Indians.

The additional officers and men necessary to enable the *Rainbow* to put to sea had not, at the time of despatching the above telegram, arrived at Esquimalt, but were due the following day.

Special arrangements had been made with the Grand Trunk Pacific Steamships for their regular steamer running from Vancouver to Victoria, and in which the naval party from the East were to embark, to proceed on from Victoria with the naval contingent on board to Esquimalt harbour so as to steam alongside the *Rainbow* and discharge the naval officers and men straight on board the *Rainbow* with their baggage.

These duly arrived the following morning. Steam had been raised on board by the "care & maintenance" crew prior to the arrival of the new personnel so that all was in readiness to proceed to sea immediately the new crew had embarked on board *Rainbow*.

A reply, however, had not yet been received from Ottawa to the wire requesting permission to comply with the request of the Vancouver immigration authorities.

In order that there should be no delay and, being given to understand that the situation in Vancouver was urgent and critical, the CO of *Rainbow* put to sea in the afternoon and steamed slowly towards Vancouver having arranged for any telegrams from Ottawa to be passed by w/t [wireless telegraphy].

The detachment of Militia under Major Ogilvy was on board.

The expected permission to carry out this mission was duly received while on passage and was accompanied by instructions to avoid bloodshed.

The *Rainbow* steamed into Vancouver at 7:00 A.M. the following day—a glorious calm bright, summer's day.

It was a quaint sight that greeted the *Rainbow* on rounding Brough-ton Point. There was the *Komagata Maru* lying at anchor off the CPR Wharf, otherwise the anchorage was clear except for scores of boats of all sorts in which were Vancouver inhabitants who, in spite of the early hour, had come out "to see the fun." On shore, all wharves, roofs, and every vantage point which commanded a view of the harbour were crowded with thousands of interested sightseers.

As the *Rainbow* steamed past the *Komagata* to take an anchorage near her it could be seen that all her Indian passengers had crowded on to her upper deck, and one, at least, of them had a sense of humour. He was an old white bearded fellow who stood on her bridge and, sup-posedly, must have been at one time in the Indian army as he started making a semaphore signal to *Rainbow* which was perfectly executed. The message read:—"Our only ammunition is coal"!!

Immigration officials came on board *Rainbow* immediately she anchored and reported that the Indians were still truculent but the officials hoped the presence of the cruiser would reduce them to sub-mission. The Immigration officials also informed the CO of *Rainbow* that the Honourable Martin Burrell, Dominion Minister of Agricul-ture was in Vancouver and was acting as Dominion Govt representa-tive in the negotiations and arrangements.

On board the *Rainbow* everything had been prepared for taking possession of the *Komagata Maru* by force if that should prove neces-sary.

Broad gang-planks were in readiness to be thrown across to the *Komagata* directly *Rainbow* was placed alongside her, one forward and one aft.

The Militia detachment was divided into two parties to go at the double across the gang-planks. They were to have sword-bayonets fixed but no ammunition in their magazines. The ship's fire brigade were to be at the gang-planks and a full pressure of water was in readiness to be played in faces of anyone on board the *Komagata* who attempted to ob-struct the operations or the passage of the troops on board.

In this way it was considered that any possible resistance would be overcome without incurring bloodshed.

Conferences were held all that day by Dominion and Provincial au-thorities at the Immigration offices and negotiations went on backwards and forwards between them and Gurdit Singh until late at night.

Finally the Indians were made to realize that with the force at the disposal of the Government their case was hopeless and they agreed to let the captain of the *Komagata* take them to sea the following morning provided that there were no arrests and that sufficient food was put on board for the return journey to Calcutta.

The following morning these provisions were embarked and there was no further trouble; however, it was thought advisable that the pilot should not go on board the *Komagata* until she had steam raised and anchor weighed so he remained on board *Rainbow* until the last moment. The pilot was Barney Johnston, afterwards Lieut. Johnston RNR who distinguished himself in command of a submarine in the North Sea by navigating his ship stern-first back to port after she had been damaged by a depth charge off the German coast.

Rainbow put to sea with the *Komagata* in order to escort her clear of Canadian waters, but all excitement was not at an end with the departure of the vessels out of Vancouver harbour.

Rainbow followed the *Komagata* about 2 miles astern and when going through Active Pass the *Komagata* was out of sight for a time after she had rounded the point at the western end of the pass.

While out of sight the sound of continuous horn blowing was heard by *Rainbow* who put on full speed and, on rounding the point saw the *Komagata* stopped and flying an international code flag signal. This was to the effect—"Man over-board."

Rainbow's lifeboat was manned and lowered just above the water-line and a sharp lookout kept in all directions. In a few moments two heads were seen bobbing in the water about a hundred yards or so on the starboard bow.

Rainbow's engines were put at full speed astern, the lifeboat was slipped and in less than ten minutes after the signal from *Komagata* was sighted the two men were safely on board *Rainbow* almost exhausted as the tide rips were running strong at this point round Enterprise Rock.

The two men, one of whom was a mere boy, were members of the Japanese crew of the *Komagata*, they had deliberately jumped over-board, calculating on being picked up by *Rainbow*, or swimming ashore, and they beseeched not to be returned to the *Komagata* as they were terrified lest the Indians would mutiny on the voyage and take charge of the *Komagata*.

However, they had to be returned on board their own vessel at William Head where the pilot was dropped, and the *Komagata* continued on her voyage, escorted by *Rainbow* until she was clear of the Juan-de-Fuca Strait.

It is understood that on arrival at Calcutta the Indians eventually did mutiny and arrests were made by the Military at that port.

The Outbreak of War, 1914

ALBERT HERBERT JOHN ANDREWS

When war broke out on *August 4th, 1914*, I was spending holidays at Gimli, Manitoba. The papers were full of the "Calls for Men." I did not think very seriously of it, till a conference was held in the office at which it was pointed out that as I was Canadian born and had no ties, it was my duty to enlist. I was suffering from a rupture, sustained playing football, and gave that as an excuse for not enlisting. However, people kept asking me to enlist with them and others asked if I intended to go, until I couldn't stand it any longer and on *August 27th, 1914*, I made up my mind to enlist. I was at a party at Mrs. St. Louis' home that evening when someone made a statement about enlisting. Theo. Gunn said, "I'd enlist if anyone would go with me." I told him I was going to join the Fort Garry Horse in the morning and he said he'd come with me. I don't think he wanted to go but he was game and wouldn't back down.

On *August 28th* I went to the office and handed over my work to Sid Goldstine and together with Theo. Gunn went to the Headquarters of the Fort Garry Horse at Maryland Ave. opposite the Mulvey School and was sworn in. We were alloted to A squadron under Capt. Bedson. Claude Gadd of Willis' office was Squadron Sergeant Major and Henry Copeland of the County Court was a Corporal. No further duty was imposed on us that day but on the 29th I reported at 9 A.M. and ran up and down the Mulvey School ground till 11. At 2 we fell in again and took a long route march. My feet ached and in spite of the fact that I was in fairly good condition from football, I was tired.

We attended a further drill at 9 A.M. on Sunday and were ordered to report back at 6 P.M. to leave for Valcartier. I spent the day (*Aug 30*) visiting my friends saying goodbye. We had a rather heart breaking farewell at home but Mother and Father bore up well. We all felt that I wouldn't come back and I gave away a lot of my things. When I fell in at 6 P.M. I had on my oldest clothes and only took a gold wrist watch, given me by Uncle Fletcher, a Gillette safety razor, given me by the office and a change of sox and shirts. I drew my pay ($150.00) and had it changed into English gold and American gold. I put this in a belt round my waist.

At 6 P.M. we fell in on the Mulvey School grounds, watched by hundreds of friends and curious spectators. We certainly presented a bizarre appearance. Most of the men wore civies of varying vintage. The officers had everything from kilts to white helmets. After a lot of delay we marched down Portage Avenue and Main Street to the Union Depot. It seemed as if all my friends were on hand and as I was in the first file of fours they all spotted me. We marched down the street with chest out in what we believed the true military manner. Looked at from this distance (9 years after) all we can say is, "We knew not what we did." It was at once glorious and pathetic. Once on the train the next job was to find bunk mates. We rode in colonist cars and had blankets issued out to soften the boards. Theo. Gunn and I occupied the lower and Art McConnaghy and a chap named Heatherington shared the top bunk.

Breakfast (at 5 A.M.) consisted of ham, eggs, porridge and coffee. We did not take very kindly to the porridge as it had been burnt.

How good that same porridge would have tasted 2 years afterwards!

Gathering at Valcartier

LIEUTENANT ALEXANDER THOMAS THOMSON

> *The Canadian Contingent, summoned by militia minister Sam Hughes, concentrated at the new camp at Valcartier, Quebec. Alex Thomson of Port Credit, Ontario, described the sometimes chaotic scene in letters home.*

Aug 21/14
11:30 o'clock
Mrs Jno Thomson
Port Credit

Dear Mother

We got into Valcartier camp at 2 o'clock today P.M. and found our tents already pitched, it is a wonderful camp there are tents as far as you can see on a perfectly level plain, with a range of mountains all around in the distance. By tomorrow night there will be about 30,000 men on the plain. There is a train comes into Quebec every night at 6.30 to bring in the men working on the ground and goes out in the A.M. at 6 o'clock.

We came in that way and are going to stay at the above hotel and go out in the A.M. in time for parade, we have Geo. Cardoza with us as interpreter. Quebec is the quaintest old place imaginable, the streets are as crooked as a corkscrew and so narrow that 2 teams can barely pass each other, in fact one street you can shake hands across the street out of the upstairs window.

Since there is every possibility of our being in Valcartier 2 weeks you can send mail to

Lieut. A.T. Thomson

No 2 Co. 36th Regt.

Aug 28/14

Dear Doug

Received your letter. This is noon, have been drilling all morning very hot last night we found it comfortable. You know Capt. McGuire, Duncan and I are in one tent, so McGuire went up to Quebec last night and left us his 3 blankets that made nine blankets and a kid called Pearce from Cooksville is doing our work so he captured a bundle of straw that had been around glassware so that made it comparatively soft. We got to the ranges on the far end of the plain this afternoon about 4 miles, the ranges have just been put there and there are 1700 targets so you see if we had enough rifles we could soon shoot. Yesterday we had a bathing parade to above the dam on the Cartier River about 3 miles and the water was ice cold but every one got in and it was some sight, our whole Regiment or Battalion 1360 men went in at once. Our Battalion is called the 7th and is made up of the 10th Royal Grenadiers of Toronto, the 13th Regiment of Hamilton, the 12th York Rangers Toronto, the 19th regiment St Catherines [sic], the 34th of Whitby, the 35th of Barrie, the 36th of Peel and the 44th of Welland that makes 170 men to a company which will be cut down to 119 men and 3 officers which is war strength in each case. The three officers will be selected from about ten so some of us are going to get it in the neck, then it is wait for the second contingent or get my discharge and go home. There might never be a second contingent and then it is a wait here of perhaps a month after the first goes.

Col Sam Hughes is expected at any time to select the officers, he came here yesterday. . . .

We were at the ranges this afternoon I have been attached to Capt. Collins for drill while here, so Capt. Collins wife came down with Bill Blakeley's girl and they went up to Quebec with them and I took the company to the ranges. I learn more having command that way, than in a week as a Lieut. 170 men, worth being able to do, you know.

The Boys are having a whale of a time tonight, a procession has just passed with an accordian and a fife playing a march that the accordion player says a native band played when bringing him and 10 other soldier's to the station of Calcutta India some years ago. The Winnipeg Highlander piper band are playing and the 20th Border horse band of Calgary and other's.

I'm going to bed now goodnight . . . Alex.

Aug 31/14

Dear Margaret

Duncan and McGuire are using the only two pens so this will do I guess. The three of us just got in from the moving picture show, you see the Government put up a great high screen out in the open and they have their lantern in a tent 25 yards away (First post has just sounded 9:30 P.M. you know) there were about 10000 at the show and every picture they would criticize, it lasts about an hour and a half every night.

I was just over to the canteen and met Billie Bush he just got here yesterday with the second bunch of Royal Grenadiers.

Today, Col Sam Hughes sent out an order for all the Officers in camp to come up to Headquarters, so each Battalion marched its officers up, we circled around a little mound and he rode up the mound on horse back and lectured us, I couldn't help but think of the old reader I think on history about "on a little mound Napolean stood etc" there are about 1500 officers in camp he told us we were the finest bunch of men he ever saw and other hot air. He told us he would show no partiality in selecting the officers, the best men for the job would go, also he talked of three weeks more training. We are marching from 12 to 20 miles every day and are getting as hard as iron. Sam also told us that with the troops expected today there would be 30,000 men. Duncan and I have been in camp at night for three or four nights the nights are fairly warm and can sleep well.

Hope you had a good holiday things are running smoothly everybody seems happy tonight all singing.

Alex.

Sept 17/14

Dear Father,

. . . We are quite comfortable down here, I have got used to sleeping on the ground and we march ten, fifteen and sometimes twenty miles in a day and so at night we are so tired I could sleep in a tree and eat a man that had died of a . . . [?]. My appetite has increased 50%.

Col Sam Hughes inspected us today and I never saw a man make such an ass of himself, he insulted our Col. and [Sergeant?] Major and every Captain we have. I'm afraid Premier Borden will have to make a change or go out of power there are 33000 votes here in camp. . . .

Sept 18/14

Dear Doug,

Rec your letter.

This is noon and we have nothing to do for a while we were out on attack this A.M. and didn't get in till 1 o'clock and we just had dinner and I don't know whether there will be a parade this P.M. or not.

We are still waiting for the appointments for the first contingent to come out. I believe that the first will leave here very early next week. It is very hot here to day and has been for days now.

We had quite an exciting time last night, Duncan and I were walking home from the midway (that is the street on which there are about 75 cantinas) when I heard a noise like Niagara Falls and just then the word came up that the remount depot (this was in this case an oat field along the river open to the river) had stampeded there were about 1000 horses in it and about 150 took to the river, the balance kept the bank they swam down the river about a mile to the dam where a raft of logs were blocked and got in among the logs and they would get stuck then they would squeal with fright. Everyone that knew anything about horses got to work. I used a lantern and went down the steep bank about forty feet and found a place that they could climb up and called to them and they came out like rats, some of them would get stuck and almost give up and if you called them they would shove the logs and try again, then I went across the river and found that most of them were coming out there and couldn't get up the bank and couldn't land on the shore for raft mud so they had to be pulled up the bank with ropes. Well you couldn't hear yourself think for horses neighing and men bawling orders what to do. Then over this there was a ridge along the river and then a swamp of black mire, well the horses that kept the shore plunged across the swamp and they had to be taken out over a plank narrow bridge they made and every forth or fifth would shove the man leading him off into the mire and fall in himself then it would take 50 men to get him out. I went in on the ridge and caught the horses and put the rope on them and handed them over to the fellow leading over the bridge, every now and then we would think we had caught them all and you would feel hot breath on your neck and turn around and find another horse. I think we took 200 horses off that ridge. It was as dark as pitch and all undergrowth. They kept it quiet how many horses were drowned and legs broken but there must have been about thirty or so.

It's costing about $200,000 per day to run this camp and we have been here four weeks today.

We expect to hear almost any hour who are to go on the first and I don't think there will be any second. . . .

Sept 24/14

Dear Mother,

. . . We expect to move on board ship any hour now perhaps tomorrow the 4th battalion (our former battalion) started this A.M. It's five weeks tomorrow since I got here.

There will be about a half dozen cruisers or more convoy us over the bubbles, it will take twenty or more transport ships to take the whole division. They have been sending men home for the least provocation and they were medically unfit no matter what was wrong because they thought they had thousands too many, now our battalion was split up the day before yesterday because they couldn't agree (the 10th of Winnipeg and the 103rd of Calgary) and we want 200 men to complete our battalion but Col Sam said we could have men come from Calgary and continue to England. We will likely go into camp in England for a month or two or perhaps longer. You can't tell how long this war will last, and we are in no shape to go into action, we will surely be held and drilled until we arc soldiers in more than name. . . .

Sept 26/14

Dear Doug

Rec your letter, well we are still here, the Royal Horse Artillery embarked Wednesday, the other artillery went Thursday and the first brigade including the 36th regt. embarked yesterday and the second brigade and the third brigade should have gone today but we not being ready have delayed the third brigade in which we arc, rather they changed us to the fourth brigade and what was the fourth brigade and the second go to-day and we may go to-morrow, Sunday. It doesn't matter down here whether it's Sunday or Monday, all the same. The whole trouble with our Battalion is as follows, the 106th of Winnipeg and the 103rd of Calgary came down here thinking they were going as units, when they got here they were put together and called the 10th battalion, then it started the officers fighting for who should get the positions, then Col Sam heard of it and ordered the 106th out and the 103rd to recruit to full strength, which they found that they couldn't do, no men being left in camp, so many having been sent home for every little thing in order to thin them down, or they thought they had thousands too many. So last night the Col Sam came down and threw them to-gether again, they say the officers of the 103rd will hold their places, but are not sure we will hold them because there will be about fifteen officers of the 106th out of a job but the convoy of cruisers down the St Lawrence (seven in number) can't wait many more days, so it's off tomorrow or Monday or stay here, which would be a shame.

It's now 12:30 and pouring again. I just got it straight that the new commanding officer has cut off a few of us to put on some of the 106th officers and then left it to the Captains to select any one else they like, so Capt. Meikle (a Scotchman) asked em, just now, to go with him, so again I feel fairly safe, but you can't tell where I'll land yet.

There were 156 officers left over yesterday in the whole camp, the balance of the 1500 having gone away home during the last two weeks, so the 186 went up to Col Sam and asked him if they would be sent to Halifax, Quebec, or Vancouver, etc. to act as instructors, so most of them slipped away home, but there are about fifty left, all I hope is that I don't make it fifty one. . . .

Alex.

From Valcartier to Salisbury Plains

PRIVATE WILLIAM PEDEN

At the outbreak of World War 1, I was working for the Grand Trunk Pacific at Portage la Prairie. Four days later, which I think was August 14th, 1914 I enlisted with the local militia unit there, namely the 99th Manitoba Rangers. Other units throughout the district were raised under their various militia names from Brandon, Winnipeg, Fort Francis, Port Arthur and Fort William, which on reaching their quota were entrained together, and on reaching Val Cartier, Quebec, were amalgamated to form the 8th Battalion, 90th Winnipeg Rifles.

The make up of the unit, was composed mostly of men of Old Country extraction, many of whom like the P.P.C.L.I.'s, had seen service with the British Army in India and South Africa, and some with the Royal Navy. The others, like myself, had no previous military experience, but they had one thing in common, all were young and apart from the patriotic motive and the spirit of adventure, was the opportunity of visiting their home-land and of seeing again, the parents and relatives they had left behind, when emigrating to Canada. Whatever the reason they had for enlisting, they were second to none in the front line, and a great many were destined to never return.

Our brief training in Canada was done at Val Cartier Camp, where we were issued a leather harness named the Oliver equipment, the Ross rifle, of cursed memory, a new fitting uniform with the appropriate badges and insignia of our Regiment, putties for the legs, instead of the black leather leggings we had on arrival—so that we began to look like a combat unit, at least we were all dressed alike.

P.S. I should make mention here of the cute little winter coats provided by Sir Sam [Hughes], which were quietly and quickly removed on our arrival in France. The coats if I remember rightly had no sleeves, just arm-holes, so that they could be pulled over the tunic. They were made of bits and pieces of all the hair-growing animals and had just as many colours; the hair was still on and to the outside. God knows whose addled brain conceived them; when worn we looked like an army of cave men, out after a few heads.

Our training of course was very basic, as we had to start from scratch, the usual parade square drill, route marches and learning to handle our weapons, and shooting on the ranges.

In the meantime a great armada of ships was assembling at Quebec City, perhaps the greatest in history; consisting of thirty transports and ten battleships; then came the day: "Orders to embark" and we left Val Cartier for Quebec, and to the waiting ships. As the ships were loaded they moved out to Gaspe Bay and took up their assigned positions in three lines 400 yards apart each way, and with the arrival of the last transport, the whole fleet, guarded on all sides with cruisers, moved off for Britain.

The crossing took twenty-one days as the regular shipping lanes were avoided due to the fear of submarines, and also to the fact that we could only travel as fast as the slowest boat and some of those were pretty ancient. I have forgotten the exact date, but sometime towards the end of October we arrived in Plymouth.

From Plymouth we entrained for Salisbury Plains; what a surprise; due to the heavy rains the camp was just a sea of mud and it still continued to rain. It was impossible even to keep the inside of the tent dry. We tried ditching around and even through the inside of the tent to try and drain the water off, but, if successful, only passed it along to the neighbor next door who was not slow in letting you know what he thought of you, as he had more than he could handle of his own.

The whole camp was just a slithering mess of mud and our nice soft Canadian brown shoes quickly took on the appearance of soggy moccasins with turned up toes. In fact it was so bad that when I got my leave at New Year to go to Scotland, I walked out of camp with an old pair of shoes, exchanging them for a dry pair which I had in my kit bag after I got out of the mud. Here be it noted that while we were wallowing around in the mud, the British troops were in nice comfortable barracks—this of course was not due to prejudice or intent, but rather the lack of foresight on the part of Sir Sam.

How we fared for food I have little recollection, but I do remember one incident when the orderly officer came around one morning asking "Any Complaints." I told him the porridge was burned, sticking his finger into my mess tin and licking it off, smacking his lips, replied "I like that burned taste," after that I had no complaints.

We were however supplied with a generous amount of what was termed, "Iron Rations," bully beef and hard tack, this was well named and I suspect it also was left over from the South African War or the Riel Rebellion; the bully beef as it was named was good Fray Bentos, and came in handy when on the move, but when one got it everyday in the soup it began to loose its appeal. As to the hard tack, I have seen men with poor teeth putting it in their haversack and pounding hell out of it with the butt of their rifle then scooping the chips into their mouth. So much for the food: We survived. Added to the misery of the camp condition, in which we were practically imprisoned was the fact that on our arrival, the great military genius Sir Sam Hughes had placed all adjacent villages to the camp, "Out of Bounds" to the troops. As we had no wet canteens, all the soldier could do when off duty, was to try and keep warm, the comfort of a glass of beer and a chat with his buddies being denied him also. Sir Sam was opposed to wet canteens.

This stupid Bastard into whose care the Canadian people had entrusted the lives of some 30,000 men, must have had the idea that these were his personal contribution to the Great War, and as such were under his command to equip and manipulate as he saw fit, and in pursuing this idea, was continually at odds with the British.

I recall a muster parade, called by General Alderson who was in command at that time, addressing the troops in which he stated that he was leaving for London to request that unless canteens be granted, he would resign his command, as he had no wish to command an army of men which were being treated as school boys. This address and statement to the troops, is on official record. The outcome of his visit to headquarters, was that canteens were established. This must have upset the micro mind of Sir Sam, but it was an order and he had to carry it out, and this is how he did it. One small tent, the ordinary bell tent was set up, this was the canteen, it was open only at noon for an hour. The men lined up with their mess cans into which a pint was sloshed and had to be paid for, with the result, that when time was up, those at the end of the line did not get served and lost their dinner also.

This did not concern me too much, but at the request of the older buddies, who needed a drink, I would line up, and if lucky, turn it over to them. Sir Sam seemed to have the idea that this was his private army and hated the thought of having to conform to British standards, so that it could function smoothly as a unit within the Imperial forces.

Winter Training on the Prairies, 1915

ROBERT G. COMBE

> *Two-thirds of the men in the first contingent were British-born, and those from the Old Country continued to enlist in large numbers. This letter to a Scottish school magazine by a soldier who would win the Victoria Cross suggests a bit of the atmosphere on the Prairies.*

I hope to be able to call on you when the third Canadian contingent gets over in the spring and to become a Life Member. Training conditions here are sublime. I had fifty recruits out the other morning for a route march with the thermometer at 18° below zero. I froze my chin and one cheek. Several of the men had frozen noses and cheeks. We all feel very fit, however, and the cold is most invigorating. We are all very anxious to get over. Many men like myself have not been home for nine or ten years, while others have not even seen "the old country." We expect to concentrate at Regina or Winnipeg any day now, and after a short course there, hope to embark. I have a Lieutenancy in the 95th Saskatchewan Rifles. I have been trying to get back for a visit to the old country for two or three years, but being a married man now it is not so easy to pick up one's traps and march. My wife has never been in Scotland, and one of the things she is most anxious to see is "the old School." I hope it will come up to my boastful accounts. I just notice one of my old class in the first list of volunteers—Hugh F. Mackenzie, Glasgow. I hope I shall meet many more and that we have a chance to have a little reunion—preferably at Potsdam.

Trench Life, March 1915

PRIVATE WILLIAM PEDEN

Our introduction to the trenches was at Ploegsteert wood, going in a half battalion at a time (with the London Rifles) in order to get acquainted with conditions and procedure in the front line.

Leaving the chateau, where we were billeted, a rather fancy name for the bare bleak pile of stones which even in peace time would be a cold comfortless place in which to live, we arrived at the front line when it was quite dark. (We were detrained at St. Omer and inspected by Lord Roberts. The only man to hold two V.C.'s: His own and that of his son.)

After a slight delay in arranging for the disposition of the troops, I was assigned to the care of one of the "London Rifles" boys and with him detailed to take up our position at a listening post, a short distance out in front of the line.

This was the customary procedure on both sides as soon as it was dark, as those outposts were the eyes and ears of the army during the hours of darkness. It was a time of activity behind the lines; the bringing in of supplies, the rotation of troops, the working parties detailed to such activities as to filling sand bags, repairing wire and any other jobs which would make the trench safer and more comfortable and the general strengthening of the position.

The listening post to which I was assigned was simply a few sand bags head high, when one sat down. The ground was wet and cold and to keep my feet warm from freezing, wrapped my ground-sheet around them. Sometime later in the night an Officer and Sergeant, making their usual rounds of inspection paid us a visit and squatting down beside us we were interrogated in whispers as to what we had seen or heard; then the officer noting that my feet were covered with my ground-sheet, ordered the Sergeant to remove it, stating in no uncertain terms that, "this man is too comfortable."

It was well for me that he was not a mind reader, as I was mentally classifying him among the unmentionable lower order of things, otherwise I would still be doing time in some British prison, as in the British army at one time, one could be crimed for dumb insolence. (This night our rations failed to come up and the lad from the London Rifles shared his with me.)

From Ploegstrert we moved to Fleurbay or Fleurbeux. I don't know if those names are spelled right, but that is how they sounded.

Here we took over a sector of the front line to ourselves, our own responsibility. It was probably of no great importance in the general scheme of things and as a rule was pretty quiet, but to keep us on our toes, and when we least expected it, the Germans would open up with a barrage with sometimes disastrous effects. If they didn't open up, our battery of four light field pieces would and due to ammunition shortage, it was said, was limited to four rounds per day. For every round they sent over we would get a dozen back, so our boys at the guns were far from popular. However, sometimes we would have a bit of fun on our own. I can recall one time the Germans setting up a bit of a field kitchen, but they made the mistake of having one section of the stove pipe sticking up above the parapet. After it had been smoking away nicely for some time and we had figured that whatever they were cooking would be about ready to eat, we opened up with our rifles, cut down the stove pipe by grazing the top sandbags, so whatever he was cooking would be well seasoned with soot and sand, and judging by his immediate response I don't think he appreciated our efforts.

This I think was about the first we operated as a division; a self contained unit. The second brigade to which I was attached was composed of the 5th, 7th, 8th and 10th battalions and commanded by Brigadier Arthur Currie. When the brigade was in the line, two battalions would be up front, the other two lying back as immediate supports and getting a bit of rest. Sometimes however, the Germans would pay more attention to our supports than they did to the front line in order to disturb their rest as much as possible.

The 10th Battalion was our support when we were in the line and was our relief when we came out for a rest, and we rotated on a three in and three day out basis.

Our next move, and the last for me, along with hundreds of others, was to Ypres. We were moved from Fleurbeux to Ypres by truck and billeted in a non-operating coffee mill on the bank of the Ypres canal. I can't recall just how long we were there, only for a night or two, but long enough for our lads to become acquainted with the purveyors of wine and cognac. We were soon alerted however, for our trip into the line, and our company emerged from our coffee mill billet, sporting a fine light brown coffee tan.

Our part of the line was some few miles out of Ypres, traveling along what was to become known as the Graffenstafel Ridge to St. Julien and from there turning at right angles to the trenches.

Arriving at our rendezvous or contact point, we halted and pretty soon our guides appeared, followed shortly by the head of the column, whom we were to relieve and who were traveling in single file on one side of the road. We were then alerted, and resumed our march on the opposite side of the road, and in single file also, moved to take up the position in that part of the line which they had just vacated.

In the gathering darkness and in silence, the two lines shuttled past each other. The troops going out burdened with loaded stretchers of dead or wounded, and noting the number of them remarked to Fletcher that it looks like a hot spot, and its doubtful whether or not we will be coming out on our feet. Fletcher pooh-poohed this observation, asserting that we would both come out OK, his assertion however, sounded more like a smoke screen to cover up his own thoughts which were in agreement with mine. As it transpired, I was the one, largely due to his aid, that came out and he the one, destined to remain.

In the trenches one is only aware of that part which he can see, as the troops normally go in and out under cover of darkness. In front of him all that he can see is through a loophole or through a periscope. As to our contacts with our forces on either side of us, unless one is on the extreme flanks, as the trenches don't run in a straight line and are broken up with bays and traverses in order to give protection against infilade fire, ones view is restricted and very limited.

Arriving in the trenches the first order of business was the attending to the securing of our position. Listening posts had to be manned and each section or company assigned to their own particular part of the trench. In our case it was more of a wall or parapet of sand-bags than a trench, as the ground was low, to dig down was to get into water, but even to fill sand-bags had its problems. As this same part of the line "the Ypres Salient" in the early days of the war had been a burial ground for both sides, first one then the other side holding it, it was hard to fill a sand bag without disturbing the remains of someone buried a little too close to the surface.

Having got settled and allotted to our positions, our next concern was the parapet itself; to strengthen weak spots if any, working parties were assigned to this duty. About the parapet itself, which was a little better than head high, one could move about freely, but in the event of attack one had to be able to get up quickly and lie over the top, and in order to do this we had a firing step, which in most cases was merely a toe hold to get up, and the ability to get up quickly had to be demonstrated to the officer's satisfaction, in our case it was Colonel Lipsett himself who made the inspection.

Our listening post had been manned and as nothing could be expected during the night, part of our company had been withdrawn to a small support line about fifty yards behind, which was once a bit of a hedge, where if they were lucky, could snatch a bit of sleep.

Now in the line there were two exercises, which were performed twice daily; The Stand too, morning and evening. It was the generally accepted theory that if the enemy attacked in the morning, it would be in the period just before sunrise, just as it is beginning to lighten, a fake dawn, so that if their attack failed they could retire, without too much exposure, and if successful would have the coming daylight to press home their advantage, and as will be seen later, this was the theory the Germans put into practice.

The same theory applied to the evening, if an attack was contemplated it would be made sometime before sunset, if it failed they had the darkness to cover a withdrawal and if successful, all night to dig in and consolidate their gains.

Sometimes the nights in the trenches could be both interesting and beautiful, especially when there was no moon. On such nights I have leaned against the parapet and watched the powerful searchlights; like the fingers of God, sweep the darkness overhead, intersect with another, pause, then on with their probe of the heavens.

The dull boom of a gun in the distance, breaking the silence of the night, or some nervous sentry opening up setting off a chain reaction along the front. The very lights would be shot up, like giant firecrackers, hang in the sky for a moment, then slowly descending making an eerie glare and lighting up everything on the ground.

It was during those two critical periods of time that the order was given to Stand Too and which when passed, the order was given to Stand Down. Sentries could be posted and the others could relax.

It didn't take long for us to find out that this was an important part of the line: the following day, there was quite a bit of gun fire, mostly of the heavy variety, going far behind the lines, seeking out concentrations or ammunition dumps.

War in the Air, April 1915

ANONYMOUS

Eighth Battalion (Winnipeg Little Black Devils),
Somewhere in Belgium,
April 18th, 1915.

. . . Yesterday I witnessed my first aeroplane battle. All I can say is that after seeing it I am very sorry that I have not sufficient command of the English language to write a good description of it. It was actually the most thrilling event I have ever seen. Time, 5.30 A.M. Bright spring morning, hardly a breath of air.

1st round.—Two aeroplanes appear—first German, in all probability on a bomb-dropping expedition. The British 'plane beats it over to chase him.

2nd round.—Aeroplanes at a good height circling around each other, each trying to get above the other, and firing at each other. The manœuvring of the machines at this point is simply marvellous, almost beyond description.

3rd round.—The German has apparently had enough and starts to beat for home. Our machine is after him, they are going at a great dip, our machine is gaining and veering off to the left and above him, machines about 100 yards apart. He opens fire again, the German is hit and drops about 100 feet; he regains control. But his engine is not working. From here on this German is giving the finest exhibition of volplaning I have ever seen. He has taken several straight drops, but always somehow or other manages to right himself. At last he has gotten pretty close to the ground, when he turns over: exit one Gerboy, one Taube. One man badly wounded. These Germans certainly deserved a better fate, but the beggars have not done any acts to deserve any sympathy. In the meantime the British 'plane continued on with its job of observing as if nothing had happened.

The Canadian Battle of Ypres

ALBERT EDWARD ROSCOE

The Germans launched a massive attack on Ypres in April 1915, using gas against the French and Canadian lines with great effect. The Canadians reeled but held though the casualties were terrible. Roscoe, serving in the 5th Battalion, survived Ypres but was killed at Festubert eleven days after he wrote this letter.

Belgium
May 13, 1915

Mrs. Caleb Bateman
Stirling, Ont.

Dear Mrs. Bateman,

I hope you will forgive me in not writing home before now, as I have been very busy in our drill just before the great battle of Ypres. A few years ago, when I was home with the rest of your family, little did we think of what would happen between two great powers of the world. If Germany would fight like the British did the days that we were in the raging battle they would have been driven on their own soil, but they only checked us by using poisonous gases. We lost a great many men and also our company lost three officers. One of our officers, Major [?], died since of wounds. Major Sanderman and Lieut. Simpson severely wounded, Lieut. Mason killed in action, and man after man fell around me, a great many killed and a very large number wounded, although there will be a good number of the boys come back again shortly as they only have slight wounds. Our brigade you know is the second.

The Germans thought we Canadians would run because we were not like the English troops, but they found out to their sorrow we did run but the wrong way to their liking. Although they used gases to shift us we came back with such force that we mowed them down like a mowing machine mows down hay. I do not know how I came to be alive today, it is more than I can explain. I helped to carry our wounded soldiers out from the trenches into safety back about a mile on stretchers, then we would go back again under heavy shell fire which was fierce. My kit was blown clear off my back in which I lost my razor, comb, underwear, socks, towel and soap. Now I have not got any, and a good many other boys are like me, so we are letting our whiskers grow until we are issued with a razor. Well mother I will not say much more about the battle for I can't help but shed tears when I think of my close comrades that have been killed on the field of battle, you can get a better account of it when you read the papers of us in the second brigade. The brigade contains the following battalions, 5th, 7th, 8th, and tenth battalions under the command of General Currie of Vancouver, B.C.

Well, we were in the trenches 22 days, and the first nine days were terrible. After the battle we did not know just where to find our battalion, we were all mixed up with French and English soldiers, but when the roll came what was left in our battalion we had got mustered together fairly well, so now we are all pretty well lined up again and all the contingent made up in strength once more.

We are about 20 miles back of the firing line resting a bit, and we can still hear the roar of the big guns, and in the evening all the boys join in singing hymns and speaking of the boys which are dead and wounded, although there were about a dozen taken prisoners but got away again. We got a number of German prisoners as well.

In Flanders Fields

MAJOR JOHN MCRAE

> *A doctor then serving with the artillery, Major McRae was not yet famous for his poem "In Flanders Fields," when he wrote this letter after Ypres.*

N. France,
May 13, 1915

My dear Charley:

Thank you for your kind and interesting letter which reached me a few days ago. We have just got through the terrible battle of Ypres, which was not the brief affair you might judge from the papers.

We were going in on April 22, and were 3 miles behind the French line at the spot where and the time when it broke. We stood by in the mele and confusion all night from 6 P.M. and at 3.30 A.M. were sent in on the gallop to a spot on the canal north of the town, and there we stayed 17 days and nights: all the time we never even had our boots off; it was fight all the time. We were far up to the front, and to that we owe our effectiveness, as well as our losses which could not but be heavy.

The artillery fire was constant, heavy and from all sorts of guns. We were said to have 2 army corps reinforcements on our front—and it felt like it. The men behaved magnificently: and the labor was terribly hard. In one 30 hours we fired 3600 rounds: and at one time our brigade had only seven guns able to fire; two of these smoked at every joint and were too hot to touch with the unprotected hand. Throughout three nights they shelled us continuously: and the firing never ceased one consecutive minute, night or day; and yet the birds kept singing in the trees—what trees were not cut down by shells.

We were so close up to the trenches (for guns) that the rifle bullets came over us in clouds. We got the gas again and again. Of the 17 days the first 8 we were with the French army,—and all the time had French troops on our front: the anxiety was terrible, for we never knew if the French would hold on or give. Our part of the battle was to hold the German lines and allow the subsequent French and British advance to the south. And day after day it was firing to support French attack, or repel German attack. And we sometimes had 3 of these latter in a day. We got into them well again and again.

We lost very heavily (for artillery) but we have justified our existence. Of the "horrors of war" we saw them an 'undred fold—at close quarters. From some of my uniform I can't get the bloodstains clear yet.

My good old friend "Bonfire" got two light shrapnel wounds, but is quite fit again. It has been a terrible time, but we have been very mercifully preserved so far. My love to your family—

Yours very truly. JACK.

An Acadian Reports from Overseas, 1915

PRIVATE ATHANASE POIRIER

> *Francophones were much less likely than the British-born or Anglo-Canadians to enlist, their ties to Europe being much looser. But Athanase Poirier from Balmoral, New Brunswick, joined up in 1915, went overseas, served at the front, and was killed on March 27, 1916.*

East Sandling Camp, Angleterre
Le 4 sept 1915

Mes chers parents,

Avant de partir, je vais vous écrire encore un mot.

Les nouvelles sont un peu rares par ici. Inutile de vous parler de la guerre, vous en connaissez autant que moi. Nous recevons des nouvelles du front tous les jours: vous lisez le résumé sur les journaux.

Quant à la vie de soldat, je ne puis dire grand chose avant d'aller au feu. Mais ici la vie est agréable. Les deux mois que nous avons passés ici n'ont pas paru longs. Les Canadiens de la deuxième division sont tous ici, ainsi qu'un bataillon de la première et une grande partie de la troisième.

Le 2 septembre nous avons subi l'inspection finale par le roi George V lui-même et Lord Kitchener. La reine Marie était ici, ainsi que plusieurs grands personnages, entre autres le Prince de Galles. C'était un beau jour. Le roi et Lord Kitchener ont dit que c'était la plus belle division qu'ils n'avaient jamais vue. Honneur aux Canadiens! Nous devons partir très prochainement pour le front. Tous les soldats sont contents. Puissions-nous toujours être aussi braves!

Je crois que les petites Anglaises vont s'ennuyer, car elles aiment beaucoup les Canadiens. Il ne serait pas difficile de se trouver une femme ici.

Comment êtes-vous tous? Est-ce que c'est ennuyant à Balmoral? Parle-t-on de la guerre et y a-t-il bien des jeunes gens d'enrôlées? Jamais auront-ils une meilleure occasion de montrer au public avec quelle sorte "d'étoffe" ils sont faits. En Angleterre et en France on ne regarde pas du tout les jeunes gens qui sont trop lâches pour la cause de leur Empire. J'ai reçu une lettre de Soeur St. Victor contenant des médailles envoyées par la mère Supérieure pour Etienne et pour moi.

En terminant, je vous embrasse tous tendrement, et vous souhaite bien du bonheur. Ne priez pas pour notre retour, mais priez pour que nous battions les Allemands. Priez aussi pour le Roi, l'Empire et la paix du monde entier. Etienne vous présente ses bons souhaits.

Au plaisir de vous voir après la guerre. Votre enfant affectueux.

Athanase.

le 11 oct 1915

. . . Quoique je sois dans les tranchées pour la deuxième fois et que ce matin encore, on nous apportait la nouvelle qu'un sergent était tué et un officier blessé dans une autre compagnie du bataillon, je ne suis pas découragé. Déjà plusieurs des nôtres reposent sous la terre lavée de leur sang généreux, et d'autres moins heureux, peut-être, sont dans les hôpitaux. Mais, tout cela ne nous rend pas "down-hearted": le Français a trop de coeur pour se laisser abattre. Au contraire, nous sommes plus encouragés que jamais. C'est si beau de mourir pour sa patrie et d'être porté en terre vêtu de khaki, avec le "Union Jack" pour linceul.

Il est huit heures, lundi matin. Presque tous les soldats dorment, car comme d'habitude, nous avons veillé toute la nuit. Les tranchées des Allemands sont à deux cents verges de nous. Je crois qu'ils dorment tous, car ils sont bien tranquilles. A un endroit un peu éloigné, au nord, on entend un bruit sourd, comme une tempête de tonnerre: c'est un "duel d'artillerie." Autour de nous, de temps à autre, un coup de canon retentit; une aéroplane traverse les lignes de feu. Elle est très haute, parfois même au-dessus des nuages. Tiens, voilà que les Allemands l'attaquent, mais elle ne parait pas les craindre, et, comme d'habitude, elle échappera bien. A part cela et une détonation de carabine, ainsi qu'une balle qui siffle au-dessus de ma tête, tout semble plus mort que vivant. Regardant autour de moi, je ne vois plus qu'abandon, ruine, désolation. Je suis à la première ligne de feu. Entre les deux lignes, je vois les ruines d'un édifice en briques et une tombe où dort un héros. C'est une petite butte entourée de quatre piquets et d'une broche barbelée, ayant à la tête une planche avec une inscription. Voilà tout le monument de ce brave. Plus loin, et aussi loin que l'oeuil peut s'étendre, ce n'est que maisons, églises et autres édifices en ruine. Tout champ de grains, de patates, de navets, est abandonné, et présente un aspect capable d'arracher un soupir au coeur le plus endurci.

J'apprends avec douleur qu'un de mes amis de Montréal s'est noyé en se baignant. Cela me fait penser plus sérieusement à mes amis de là-bas. Tous, bien qu'ils ne sont pas soldats, sont exposés à une mort certaine. On la rencontre dans les collisions sur chemin de fer, dans les accidents de chantier, sur les "drives," dans les moulins, en un mot, partout. Oui, c'est encore nous les mieux partagés. [*sic*]

Certes, il faut l'avouer, il y a la guerre, un danger imminent. Nous le savons, et nous n'avons qu'à nous tenir sur nos gardes contre les balles, les boulets, la charge à la bayonnette, le gaz, le "bully-beef," les "hard tacks," etc. Cela prend tout notre temps, mais on s'y habitue vite et on devient indifférent.

J'apprends que . . . regrette de s'être enrôlé. Pourquoi craint-il? Les Allemands ne sont pas aussi malins qu'on le pense à Balmoral. Que l'on se tienne la tête basse et il n'y a pas de danger. Pour ma part, j'aime bien la vie de soldat. Lorsque nous sortons des tranchées, nous buvons du vin Français et mangeons du chocolat de Suisse. Il fait beau par ici, les tranchées sont bien sèches. Les nuits sont froides, mais nous avons de bons habillements.

Bien, je vous quitte à regret. Ecrivez souvent et longuement. Envoyez-nous des "snap-shots." Priez pour que je ne revienne pas avant d'avoir fait ma part. Etienne vous embrasse. Des baisers à tous.

Athanase

What an Officer Needs in the Trenches, 1915

LIEUTENANT ALEXANDER THOMAS THOMSON

10th Bn., 1st Canadian Division,
B.E.F. France.
Nov 28/15.

Dear Doug,

I got your letter of Nov. 10th last night and yesterday noon I wrote the Bank of Montreal London to remit to Will 30 pounds. I did that because he would be better known and easier found. He will give you all you need and keep the balance if there is any.

Speaking of reconnoitering patrol, I can't do that any more, a company commander isn't allowed to leave his trench, so my scouting days are over, for now anyway. There isn't any danger anyway why the Huns are just as badly frightened as we are. Each company keeps an officer on that duty, that is what I used to do quite a lot.

Yes, old Dr MacKay knows me darned well, he got half shot while under my tender care one time coming from camp, he is a good old scout.

No, I can't say much about the trench work, but I'll tell you on the side, that the novelty wears off in about two weeks and then you get down to mud and water and more or less discomfort.

According to the P.C. paper Frank Ott might not go back to England, but transfer to the Peel Regiment and I suppose get a commission. I know he was fed up last time I saw him, with his unit and the Colonel in particular.

I intended writing you before about what you should buy, they try to sell you useless articles. I will name a few that I can think of.

2 or 3 suits of underwear.

2 shirts.

1 sweater coat (like we used to get).

1 pair bedford cord breeches.

2 tunics whipcord.

2 pairs puttups.

2 pairs boots (ankle) (Slaters shoe store,
    don't buy a pair of riding boots).

1 cap (soft preferably) I wouldn't wear anything else.

1 great coat or a British warm.

1 slicker (not a burberry) I am throwing mine away.

1 pair of whipcord slacks (long trousers).

1 sou'wester hat (like we used to have at home).

4 pair socks.

1 pr binoculars (glasses) they may be on issue free.

1 Colt pistol (This ought to be issued).
    (With two extra magazines).

1 prismatic compass. (You can get along without this).

Bedding.

Some kind of sleeping kit with a sleeping bag, one of those padded kind, I have a jolger bag, but it cost some $15.00 and is not as warm as the cheaper padded kind. I have a Walseley kit, I carry everything I have in it, and sleep in it, inside the Jolger bag. I carry three issued blankets.

You also want a silk waterproof sheet, they cost 10 shillings, and only weigh a few oz's, the issue weigh 5lbs.

Now you can get along with ¼ of this stuff, so just buy it when you need it, but I think this covers most of the articles?

You can get them in England but not any cheaper or as cheap, as in Canada. I paid 4 pounds 4 shillings for my last tunic and 2 pounds 10 shillings for my bedford breeches. 6 pounds 14 shillings = $33.50 just the same as you paid, but mine are the best material.

You can always get the glasses and pistol in England if they aren't issued to you.

I just got a letter from Mrs Thomson and she says Bob went under an operation on his old wound.

I'll get this away tonight.

Alex.

Training Woes in Calgary, December 1915

PRIVATE S.E. ADAM

December 15, 1915

My dear Dad:—

I feel quite lost this week. They have divided the Draft Company up among all the other Companies in the battalion, which is a scandalous thing to do. Just imagine, we have all been together for practically 6 mos, and become well acquainted with each other; also our officers know us. Then suddenly we are all broken up and put among strangers. If you had been down at barracks this week you would have seen nothing but men staggering under huge loads, consisting of kit bags, straw mattresses, etc. and surrounded by a halo of straw from the said mattresses; trying to find a place to lay down their burdens. Of course the wildest confusion reigns in all the companies at present. I among others am put in D Company, which is composed mainly of recruits. This Company was recruited for the purpose of taking the place of the Draft, after it went away. Under the present circumstances, the 56th Battalion finds itself about 100 men over strength. These guilty ones are herded together in one of the buildings, preparatory to being either transferred or discharged.

Such is the condition of affairs at present. Austen May is in D Company also. Last night, our first in the new Company, the man in charge of the fires at night went to sleep and let them all go out. Consequently we were almost frozen in the morning, as there are about 5 broken windows in the building.

The only bright spot on the horizon is this; we are to be given 6 days leave for Xmas; two days being allowed for travelling. Please expect me then on *Thursday morning, December 23rd*, unless I write or 'phone to the contrary. If I cannot get off then I shall get 5 days at New Years. If I get Xmas leave I shall have to return on Tuesday evening, December 28th. Needless to say I shall try and come home for Xmas. I think this is very good leave, don't you.

Jack and I went to supper with the Grayburn's last night, and afterwards to a concert at Paget hall. I enjoyed myself very much. To-morrow evening I am invited to go out to the theatre with the Review Staff. Soldiering is not so bad in Calgary just now.

I hope you received my photographs safely.

There being no more news just now, I will close my letter. I shall be looking forward to next week, with great eagerness. I hope there are plenty of rabbits to shoot. Remember; the 10.40 A.M. train at Bowden on Thursday morning, December 23rd should contain

Your loving son

S.E. Adam.

I Was Frightened:
Dealing with Fear in the Trenches

LIEUTENANT JAMES THORPE

> *Born in Iowa in 1889, Thorpe emigrated to Canada. He enlisted when the war broke out and served in the Canadian Machine Gun Corps. He was killed three months after he wrote this letter to his family.*

Flanders 6th March 1916

Dear Ma and Tax:

By the time you read this the Battle of Verdun will be finished but the enclosed cutting from an English paper might be of interest to you as extraordinarily true to detail etc. We hear today that they are sending British troops there and it may be so but the French seem to be able to handle the situation. If the Germans lose this battle the war will be over by next fall.

Lately we have had a lot of cold and snowy weather but it can't last much longer and as I write the warm sun is on its way back and the snow is going fast. It is hell in the trenches for the men but the officers are able to make themselves more comfortable. We don't get anything from stores that the men don't get in fact not so much but we buy a lot of stuff. The men are hardened now and it is wonderful the way they stay cheerful under these conditions.

The machine guns are a little more interesting than ordinary infantry work and not so much drudgery to it. Its considered much safer too.

I have a friend in a howitzer battery near here and was over there yesterday. I fired the guns and also went up to the observation point to watch the effect on the German lines through my glasses. The guns were fired from behind hills and they fire by the map without seeing the target. (We do the same with machine guns sometimes.) We fired at any old thing we liked for a while. Our target was 3 miles away but the guns never missed a shot. Then we had tea down at the Battery Mess and after tea the chaplain came in and held a service. It was a funny church service. Almost every "amen" was followed by a cracking salvo from the guns which were only a few yards away. They were engaged with a German battery 5 miles away. Our billet is surrounded by batteries and they are banging away all day and night. We never notice them anymore.

I suppose you want to know how I felt the first time under fire. Well I'll tell you what every man will if he speaks the truth. I was frightened. Everyone is frightened under shell fire but the thing is not to show it. If an officer ducks and runs for cover he may as well quit because he's through so far as his men are concerned. They always look to their officer and if they trust him he can ask them to do anything and they'll do it.

It doesn't take long to show up a quitter out here. There aren't many though. I've got to go up and take a trench building party now so must quit and put on the high boots. Had a little sciatica and chilblains that's all so far.

With love,

Jim

P.S. Yours of the 14th Feb. came today thanks.

We All Shook As Though We Had the Ague:
A Bomber at the Front, March 1916

ERNEST M. TAYLOR

*Taylor, a private in the 1st Canadian Mounted Rifles, must have
terrified the folks at home with his graphic description of trench life.*

France
Friday March 24th, 1916

My dearest Nance,

Once more I am in a position to take up my pencil. The last four days
have been very strenuous ones. On Sunday night we marched from
our camp en route for the trenches. We had to pass through an historic
old town that has been blown to pieces. It was a never-to-be-forgotten
sight in the moonlight, and one I have no doubt tourists will travel
many miles to see when the war is over. It must have been a very pic-
turesque town, and though I don't suppose there was a single un-
wrecked building, most of the walls were standing, and the houses
looked like those dolls' houses whose front swings open and leaves the
interior exposed. On reaching the trenches half of us bombers went to
the front line and half stayed in supports. I was among the latter, and
we had the usual tedious hours wait before the taking over process was
finished and the men we were relieving got out of the way. I had my eye
on one dug out, but I overheard one of the previous occupants say
there were a main of dead rats under the floor, and it fair stank to beat
anything he had met in a long and varied existence. Fortunately Jack
called out to say he had discovered a little one he thought the two of us
could get into. It certainly was tiny. We could not stretch out at full
length or sit up. The most we could do was to recline on one elbow for
all the world like that picture of Alice in Wonderland when she drank
the contents of the little bottle. I woke up the next morning feeling
that I could tell all my bones. I think when the war is over I shall have
to start up as a contortionist. We had a fairly quiet time during our two
days here, then we took our turn in the front line. It was rather different to our previous experiences, the trenches only averaging about 60

yards apart. The part where we bombers held they were about 25 yards apart. It was fatal to even show a hand, and as the trench was only about shoulder high, it meant continual watchfulness. There was a short gap from the German trench from which they could throw bombs into ours. Jack and I and two others were told off to crawl out during the night among the debris of an old stable. We spent our nights lying prone on the wet ground seven yards from the Huns. The idea was to take them by surprise if they came out to throw, but principally to discover what they were up to. They were always at work, we could hear their footsteps on the wooden bath mats and hear them talking and coughing. A good deal of hammering and sawing went on and there was a continuous sound like pumping. I think they must have been mining under us. It drizzled incessantly during the two days and nights, and there was no place to lie down in the day time. From the time we went in to the time we came out we all shook as though we had the ague. You wonder at the time how you are going to live through it, but still you do, and I have never yet heard of a case of pneumonia. I was wishing I had got the chili paste as I had much trouble to keep my wet feet from freezing. We had a bit of fun the first morning. Just as we were going to have breakfast, the Germans threw a bomb over. We asked for nothing better and were soon returning the compliment with interest. We threw them in volleys and we threw them independently until they had their fill and stopped. We found several of their bombs that had failed to go off afterwards. They were ones we had been instructed on, and I took the explosive out of one that fell near me. It would have made a nice souvenir, but I did not bother with it, as I should have to carry it round so long before getting leave. We bombers had two casualties. One chap shattered his hand throwing a live bomb out of the trench that fell near another fellow. The other casualty happened whilst we were sitting close together having dinner. There was a piece of corrugated iron above our heads and a German sniper hit it. The bullet glanced off and struck the man that was next but one to me killing him instantly. We got back to reserve dugouts about midnight last night. I don't think I ever felt more exhausted as I had not slept five minutes during the 48 hours. I took off my wet clothes and socks and had just got into my blanket, when our sergeant

(God bless him) came round with a shot of rum. I lay down in a beautiful glow, went to sleep at once and woke up about 11 A.M. this morning, feeling stiff and sore but right as a trivet and ready for anything. There are quite a lot of hypocrites in Canada who would like to do away with the soldiers' rum ration. I should like to see them out here. I think they would alter their views considerably. We remain here four days and then go in again for four days. Dear Mother's letter arrived just as I started out for the trenches. Many thanks to her for it. Tell Olive I enjoyed reading the Bystander she sent. The silhouettes were very good, but they fail to reproduce the muddiness of everything. I have not got last week's parcel yet. I hear they are bringing them up tonight, so that will be jolly. It is snowing now. I do hope spring will return before our next tour. Leave started again yesterday and another of our men went. Well I must stop now old girl.

Much love to you all
Your affectionate brother

Ernest

Trench Life, April 1916

ARCHER TOOLE

Wednesday April 5/16

My dear own darling,

Here I am sitting in a dugout in the trenches with the pad on my knee. The dugout is a low one and I can just manage to sit on my bed and not bump my head. To get out I have to get on my knees, as there is a beam across, & crawl out. We came in the night I last wrote to you what an awful march getting here. We started at 5 I think it was about 11:00 before we got in. The men traveled light without packs but I brought mine and it weighed like a ton as I put my british warm in it as it was too hot to wear it. Since then, I have been thanking my lucky stars for bringing it as it is by no means warm. The sun is now shining which makes it a bit warmer but in the early morning about 3 or 4 o'clock it is chilly enough. We get quite a lot of sleep. Last night Ned and I turned in about 10 o'clock woke me at about 1.30 so I got up and wandered around, then went into the Coy H.Q. dugout and discovered a couple of letters from you. Needless to say I was tickled to death & if I had known would have been up sooner. At 5:00 I turned in again & slept until 5.30 when I got up & had breakfast. I watched the artillery (German) pounding away on our right for a long time, then went up and had a shave & wash & felt fine. Glad you got my letters OK. I was rather worrying that some had gone astray. Thanks for sending on your mother's letter. It certainly is good of her to send me the quid. I don't know what I will buy with it. Hang on to it until I get back & we'll blow it in together. Con seems to be enjoying life in the bank. Lumb still seems to be bent on joining. I hope if he does he gets the Paymasters job for Marjory's sake. Our Col. has just come back from leave & Doughtry resumes command of this company. Ernie is going on leave on Friday & should leave here tomorrow. We have all got steel helmets. There were some over after the men of this Coy were all issued so all the officers collared one. I feel very secure with it on. It . . . has padding inside it. It is green in colour but most of them put a sandbag over it which I think I will do. Can't think of any more news so will quit. Take good care of yourself my darling and get fat but not *too* fat. Am now looking forward to my leave. With love to all and ever so much for yourself

Your fond love,

Archer

Sea Sick, May 1916

PRIVATE MICHAEL DUGGAN

Arrived in Halifax in the dark, cannot see anything. Had our kits inspected . . . at 2 o'clock in the morning. All waiting to board our transports. Guards guarding the trains. Weather still unsettled yet. No water. Well good night. Back again after a lapse of nearly twelve hours. We are aboard the transport, Empress of Britain. Packed in like sheep. Our condition is only this way because of the war. Sleep in canvas hammocks over our tables that we eat on. We are still in Halifax harbour, probably we will leave tonight. Some life. Meals very good. Several transports in the port. All will be pleased I think when we land in England. Three battalions on board, besides the CMR and cavalry. Some crowd. Goodnight if we are ever torpedoed. Much difficulty in arranging hammocks. Posted some letters before arriving in Halifax. It will be a wonderful experience if I live to return. Similar circumstances exist only once in a century or two. Would not mind if I had the sporting page of some Toronto paper. Wonder how my friends are in Toronto and home sweet home. Well goodnight again. XXXXX

After first night's sleep. Enjoyed it—very good. We are now out in the M_____, liable to be here three or four days. Saw my first auxiliary cruiser (armed). Everybody helps to clean up after meals. All fall in at 10 o'clock. Deck shoes and life belts. Have the first life belt on that I ever wore. Well all are falling in so will have to adjourn soon. Met a St. Mike's boy on board this morning. My pen seems weak tonight.

Well back again. This page is some mess. My pen was somewhat in a deplorable condition. Monday morning at 5:30—so they say. Sun is shining brightly, it looks like a fine morning. Had some time going to sleep at night. Somebody falls out and the continuous music of nauseous odors (smells) make existence a pleasure. You have about a mile to go for your meals. Always have to wear life belts. Great numbers sleep on the decks at night. We are still lying in the river patiently waiting for our departure. Feeling hungry and thinking of former (beloved) acquaintances. Waking one of the boys by depositing boots on the floor anything but lightly. Water sometimes gets scarce. A person has no difficulty in feeling confused or lost.

Time I am writing this is 6 o'clock Monday morning, May 22, 1916. Depth of water where we are is about 300 ft. Large numbers have the effect of change of life. Up half the night with frequent visit to heads. Ship supposed to sail at 7 A.M. this morning. Started to raise anchors already. Indications point to an early departure now. Such is existence (life).

Well we departed all right. So did I to a land of bliss and sickness. Sea sick, sea puke, puke, sick, puke, sick,—sick rotten sea sick. We left

Monday morning. This is Friday and I am not over effects yet. Desire a good wash and shave. Do not feel like eating. Feel like nine cents worth of God help us. Slept out on the deck the last two nights. Rained considerably since we left. Sea calm—food good but our abode is poorly ventilated. Will have to subside for a while. Somebody ran away with my blankets and hammock.

This is one godforsaken voyage. One more trip and that is back home is enough for me. No more sea voyages packed in like sardines. Will be glad to inhabit land again.

Flying with the No. 7 Squadron, Royal Flying Corps, in France, May 1916

LIEUTENANT E.J. WATKINS

Watkins was posted to the No. 7 Squadron on May 17, 1916, and made his first patrol on May 20.

Saturday, May 20

My first trip on patrol. Ypres Salient. It was very misty & could hardly see ground. Left aerodrome 6.30 P.M. arrived 7.40 P.M.—9000 ft. Don was with me as escort in another machine but we lost each other & did not see each other till we arrived back here.

Sunday, May 21

. . . Long reconnaissance we got archied quite a lot over Lille & Menin—got back at 4.20 at No. 20 Squadron. One F.E. had engine trouble . . . and had to descend. 4 Fokkers circled over him to keep him well over the lines.

Monday, May 22

Up at 9 A.M. had breakfast & sat round till about 2.30 P.M. then took a walk into the town Bailleul & bought a pair of slippers it was very dull & cloudy so could not do my job of flash reconnaissance. Had tea and then dinner at 8.15 P.M. then to bed after copying a few notes.

Explaining War to the Home Folk, 1916: I

ARCHIE MACKINNON

Belgium,
May 13, 1916

Dear Sister,

Received your letters and 3 parcels OK and certainly was pleased to receive them. I have been very busy lately and had some experience. You say I am a lot fatter in the picture. Gee you ought to see me now. You seem to think I have an awful load to carry. But that is only 3 parts of it. I certainly can stand some awful knocking around. We were in trenches for 16 days counting Reserves and Front Line and am out for 16 days rest as they call it. I think when 58 comes back, Ray will be saying "My Archie isn't there." It only takes one small bullet. It is too bad about Ray being sick. I hope he never stutters. Too bad about Mrs. McArthur. Gee there seems to be a lot of fellows enlisting. I can tell them something and I hope from the bottom of my heart Ronnie never gets here. You want to know what to send me. Well biscuits or cake—anything to eat and all kinds Keatings. This is some place for lice! Good night! I have seen Percy Veale twice and Steve Mould once. You ask me if I were scared when I first went in trenches. Well no I wasn't. I thought nobody could wish for a better place until I seen wounded fellows and fellows getting killed along side of me and have to pick up pieces and put them in a blanket for to be buried. War is no joke. I have been hit 5 times but not serious. It was shrapnel. I was hit 4 times in a battle where your girl's friend was wounded. All Canadian battalions are here together. I was buried in, too, covered clean up once and my friends dug me out. So you can imagine how I like warfare but don't think I don't get back at them. They shelled us hard for 2 hours and tried to take our trench. When they come over the parapet believe me I put bullets and bombs into them as fast as I could but they didn't get our trench. We were only 35 yards apart so you know how quick we act. Poor old Fritz dead men lay in No Mans Land all that night and next day. We only got 15 prisoners. Two were officers. I went after them and I was so excited I didn't know what to do only give it to them. So you think 58 isn't in those battles? Well I am glad to be on this side of the firing line anyway but would sooner be at _____.

Your affec. bro. Archie

PS I received 2 letters from Pa last night. I met Ron Meek (cousin). I am sending his photo to Pa.

Explaining War to the Home Folk, 1916: II

HAROLD W. MCGILL

June 16/16

Dear Miss Griffis,—

You really owe me one or perhaps two letters but some swell stationary and one or two other very useful articles reached me today and I must really write at once and thank you. You send me so many parcels that I am always afraid that I shall forget to acknowledge one and incur the risk of being considered an ungrateful beast.

Our battalion has just come out of the trenches after 10 days of furious fighting at the front. The account of the fighting you will have read in the newspapers before this letter reaches you. Our battalion was in the trenches for the last German attack and also for our attack. I had a very busy time of it and passed a large number of wounded through my hands including some German prisoners. I had my aid post in an old mill. The place we were in was well sand bagged and comparatively safe although the Boches broke a large number of shells around it. Our artillery fire before our infantry advance took place was terrible. The Germans were plunking six inch shells around our aid post but although we could feel the building rock and shake with the concussion we could not hear the shells burst on account of the terrific noise picked up by our own artillery. To do them justice I do not think that the Boches were deliberately trying to hit our aid post or the dressing station of the field ambulance which was just across the road from us. They were searching for batteries in our neighborhood. During the last three days it rained almost constantly and the weather was cold enough for October. The wounded came in soaked to the skin and plastered with mud. In many cases we cut the clothes right off and wrapped the patients in blankets. The field ambulance ran a coffee and lunch stall in a dugout next door and we got hot chocolate for all our wounded which bucked them up wonderfully. Most of the cases were shell wounds and some of them were of terrible severity. We gave the German wounded the same treatment as we did our own men. I have not yet counted up the number of wounded I saw during the time we were in. We started one evening at dusk, worked all that night, all the next day and until 4 o'clock in the morning of the day following, except for an intermission of 3 hours when we had no wounded in.

My cousin who was medical officer with one of the units in the 3rd Division Canadians was killed on June 2 when the Germans opened their first attack on our lines. He was cut off in his aid post and made a fight for it until all his pistol cartridges were fired when the Germans killed him with bombs. The third division had 4 medical officers killed during the first week of fighting.

I am enclosing you a rose which I picked in a garden among the ruins of a famous and historic city.

There is a devilish bombardment going on now towards the front and I hope we are not called up during the night.

Sincerely Harold W McGill

The Newfoundland Regiment Is Wiped Out at Beaumont Hamel, July 1, 1916

CAPTAIN GEORGE HICKS

A separate dominion, not yet part of Canada, Newfoundland raised a regiment that served with the British army. On July 1, 1916, as part of the Battle of the Somme, this regiment attacked the German lines at Beaumont Hamel. Captain Hicks, wounded duing the battle, recounted the day.

I had participated in the Gallipoli Campaign for four months and was Sergeant of the rear Guard in the evacuation from Suvla Bay. After two months in the Suez we sailed for Marseilles, entrained there for Abbeyville where we rested for just a short while. Then we marched for 3 days to Louvencourt near the Somme River. For some two or three months we were involved in an intensive period of training in frontal attack, worked on digging trenches and did sentry duty at the front line lasting seven days at a time. Following this duty we would be brought back to the village of Louvencourt for short rest periods. This went on with no let up. The troops were aware that something big was being planned and all this training was preparation for the "BIG PUSH." Two days before the end of June the troops were brought up to the trenches which were 30 feet deep—narrow at the bottom, widening towards the top. Usually the men had to walk in mud but at this time the earth was baked hard from the sun and dry weather. There were dug out areas where men could sleep and get a meal. During the long night before the Battle I spent these hours in the company of four close friends from the Town of Grand Falls, Newfoundland. These were Roy Ferguson (*who was married and expecting their first child*), Bob Porter, Fred Wilcox and Mike O'Flynn. I remembered that we joked with each other but it was forced hilarity as we knew we were going out into No Man's Land and beyond. These four buddies were killed in that drive.

We were supposed to leave our trenches at 7:30 A.M. but the time was postponed to quarter to 9. We were told the reason for the delay was that the Brigadier and Colonel Haddow weren't able to get a clear picture of the situation. I believe now that they knew that the Germans were ready and waiting.

Prior to July 1st two raiding parties had been out to the German barbed wire and cut gaps which later proved to be not very effective. They did not capture any German prisoners which showed that the Germans were all ready and waiting for the attack. Rocks had been white washed and placed from the reserve trenches to the front line so that the men wouldn't make any mistakes in getting through the gaps in the barbed wire.

The order was given at quarter to nine that the Newfoundland Regiment will advance, a whistle sounded and the men climbed up from the trenches in single file. It is worth noting here that each soldier was burdened down with heavy equipment, consisting of mills bombs, shovels, pickaxes, ammunition, regulation kit, water bottles and even ladders. I remember my friends and I put Sherry Brandy in our water bottles. Each man was also issued with a tin star which he was to put on his back. The idea for this was that the British could trace the progress of the men by the glinting on these stars. Of course it backfired as they could be seen by the Germans and were clear targets. As the men marched off toward these gaps in the barbed wire in single file, they were picked off by the Germans machine gun fire and artillery. The gaps filled up with dead bodies. Those who did get through were mowed down on no man's land. There was NO British fire protection either. The impression given the men was that this push would be a quick walk over with no opposition. The Newfoundlanders were held up at the German barbed wire and were sitting ducks for the German with their field glasses the Germans could aim accurately on the advancing army.

I led my platoon toward a gap in the wire and knew nothing before I was shot in the shoulder, the bullet entering just above the lung and through the back. I was sitting down when my Sergeant rushed over to see if he could do anything. I told him I could make it on my own and to lead the men on. Of course he didn't survive.

I made my way along to one of our trenches, finally reached a communications trench, then down the line to a First Aid Post where a Doctor tended my wound, bandaged me and I walked on level ground, following the trench to Achieux Villers, a dressing station. There I was fortunate to get a ride in a Red Cross Car to Achieux, a village six miles away where I waited at the Railway station all day.

He Probably Won't Try to Lead Us Again: The RFC Stages a Bombing Raid, July 1916

SECOND LIEUTENANT JOHN B. BROPHY

Lieutenant Brophy's diary of his time as a pilot in the Royal Flying Corps is one of the better documents of the Great War. This account treats the period of the Battle of the Somme.

Thursday, July 6th, 1916

The weather is still holding us up, although our troops have been making a steady though slow advance. I stood by all day for a bomb-raid which didn't materialize. I was the joyful recipient of two parcels of eats from home today and indulged in same. In the evening Cox and I walked to the next village and back.

Friday, July 7th, 1916

I have a rooted conviction that it will rain for the duration of the war, as it is still at it. I got another box of candy today, and made inroads on same.

We took Contalmaison today and a strip of the front over 1,000 yards deep. Shadow of a 3:30 A.M. bomb-raid hung over me as I went peacefully to sleep.

Saturday, July 8th, 1916

It rained early in the morning, and so interfered with the bomb-raid. It was dull and cloudy all day, and it didn't come off.

The General [Trenchard] appeared on the scene today, and said that Sir Douglas Haig wanted him to congratulate us on our work in the big push, and that the Flying Corps was a big factor in the success, as the huns never came over our lines and our troops are free to move without being watched. The huns have had their trains and supplies blown up, and our machines watch their movements. The RFC bombed eleven hun observation balloons, and now the huns don't put them up, and can't observe what their artillery is doing. Our machines range battery after battery on to hun targets. One ammunition train was bombed, and the cars blew up one after another.

Sunday, July 9th, 1916

Got up at 3:30 and went out on a bomb-raid. Hewson and I were flying last. We crossed at Arras and went straight for Cambrai. The archies announced the fact that we had crossed the lines by a hail of shells. I didn't know we had crossed as I was following the one ahead, and there was a pretty thick mist. The archies came quite close, and we had to do some snake tricks to fool them. From the lines right into Cambrai we were shelled intermittently.

We turned south just beside Cambrai, and found our mark, Marcoing [railway] station. I let my bomb go and had to turn off quickly to dodge a bomb from another youth who was above me. I saw his bomb go down. Several lit on the tracks in the station yards, and probably ruined them. As soon as our bombs were dropped we turned and lit out for home, devil take the hindmost. He did, as poor old Hewson was picked off by a bunch of huns, who attacked us from behind, and fired at us and went away. We haven't heard what happened to him, and hope he landed safely.

We crossed at Peronne on the Somme coming back. In the morning I went over to 2 A[ircraft] D[epot] and got a new BE 2d for our flight. I flew it to the aerodrome. In the afternoon I took Street up in an RE for an hour and a half, and got up to 10,000 feet. We flew over Crécy Forest, and went to the coast, and could just see England in the distance.

We went for a walk in the village in the evening.

Monday, July 10th, 1916

I went up for 35 minutes to test an engine. It was very cloudy. Later I took a mechanic up to 10,000 feet to try a new scheme for giving the engine extra air at a height where the atmosphere is thin. It was a failure as it only choked the engine.

In the evening I went for a walk in Fienvillers.

Tuesday, July 11th, 1916

The chief kicks about our bomb-raids have been the poor formation, leaving us in danger of being separated, and "done in" by huns. The Colonel decided he'd lead us to show us how. He was to lead and Capt. Carr and I were next, and four others in pairs behind, and nine scouts [from 60 Squadron]. At 6,000 we met thick clouds, and when I came through I couldn't see anyone anywhere, so I just flew around and finally sighted three machines. I went over and found Carr and the Colonel, and two scouts, so I got into place and the Colonel went over to the lines, and kept circling to get higher for half an hour, right over the lines.

I thought this was a foolish stunt, as I knew the huns could see us, and would be waiting for us. I was very surprised that they didn't shell us, but there was a battle on, and they were probably too busy. We were right over Albert, as I recognized two huge mine craters that had been sprung July 1st.

When we did cross over with only two scouts, we hadn't been over more than a couple of minutes, before I saw three Fokkers coming towards us, and a couple of LVG's climbing up to us. Another Fokker was up above me, and behind, between our two scouts. I knew he was going to dive at one of us, but expected the scouts to see him and attack him, so I didn't bother about him, but began to get the stop-watch time of my bomb sight to set it for dropping.

While I was doing this I suddenly heard the pop-pop-pop's of machine guns, and knew the huns had arrived. I looked and saw them diving in amongst us, and firing. There were seven LVG's and three Fokkers as far as I could make out, but they went so fast I could hardly watch them. Our scouts went for them, and I saw the Colonel turn about.

My gun being behind me I couldn't get in a shot, and turned around after Carr and the Colonel. They fired some more as we went back but didn't hit me. The Colonel was hit and so the show was over. He had about a dozen bullets in his machine, and was hit in the hand. His gun was shot through, and his observer hit in the face. He probably won't try to lead us again.

There was a raid in the afternoon.

Explaining War to the Home Folk, 1916: III

HART LEECH

Lieutenant Leech of the 61st Battalion was killed in the attack, part of the terrible Battle of the Somme, much as he foresaw.

Sept. 13/16

Dear Mother

Just a wee note. I am "going over the parapet," and the chances of a "sub" getting back alive are abut nix. If I do get back, why you can give me the horse laugh. If not this'll let you know that I kicked out with my boots on.

So, cheer up, old dear, and don't let the newspapers use you as material for a Saturday magazine feature. You know the kind: where the "sweet-faced, grey-haired, little mother, clutching the last letter from her boy to her breast, sobbed, ' 'e was sich a fine lad,' as she furtively brushed the glistening tears from her eyes with a dish rag, etc. etc."

I'm going to tell you this in case my company commander forgets. Your son is a soldier, and a dog-gone good one, too, if he does say it himself as shouldn't. And if he gets pipped it'll be doing his blooming job.

In a way it's darned funny. All the gang are writing post mortem letters and kind of half ashamed of themselves for doing it. As one of our officers said: "If I mail it and come through the show, I'll be a joke. If I tear it up and get killed I'll be sorry I didn't send it." S'there y'are.

Shooting Down a Zeppelin over London, October 1916

SECOND LIEUTENANT W. J. TEMPEST

The war in the air underwent a quick technological revolution. By the autumn of 1916, the Germans were sending dirigibles to bomb London, and the Royal Flying Corps countered by sending night fighters up to attack the blimps. This account is by a Canadian pilot.

About 11:45 P.M. I found myself over S.W. London at an altitude of 14,500 feet. There was a heavy ground fog on and it was bitterly cold, otherwise the night was beautiful and star lit at the altitude at which I was flying.

I was gazing over towards the N.E. of London, where the fog was not quite so heavy, when I noticed all the searchlights in that quarter concentrated in an enormous "pyramid." Following them up to the apex I saw a small cigar shaped object, which I at once recognized as a Zeppelin about 15 miles away. . . .

At first I drew near to my objective very rapidly (as I was on one side of London and it was on the other and both heading for the centre of the town) all the time I was having an extremely unpleasant time, as to get to the Zepp I had to pass through a very inferno of bursting shells for the A.A. guns below. . . .

I therefore decided to dive at her, for though I held a slight advantage in speed, she was climbing like a rocket and leaving me standing. I accordingly gave a tremendous pump at my petrol tank, and dived straight at her, firing a burst straight into her as I came. I let her have another burst as I passed under her and then banking my machine over, sat under her tail, and flying along underneath her, pumped lead into her for all I was worth. I could see tracer bullets flying from her in all directions, but I was too close under her for her to concentrate on me.

As I was firing, I noticed her begin to go red inside like an enormous Chinese lantern and then a flame shot out of the front part of her and I realized she was on fire.

She then shot up about 200 feet, paused, and came roaring down straight on to me before I had time to get out of the way. I nose dived for all I was worth, with the Zepp tearing after me, and expected every minute to be engulfed in the flames. I put my machine into a spin and just managed to corkscrew out of the way as she shot past me, roaring like a furnace.

I righted my machine and watched her hit the ground with a shower of sparks. I then proceeded to fire off dozens of green Very's lights in the exuberance of my feelings.

I glanced at my watch and saw it was about ten minutes past twelve.

I then commenced to feel very sick and giddy and exhausted, and had considerable difficulty in finding my way to ground through the fog and landing, in doing which I crashed and cut my head on my machine gun.

An Amputee Breaks the News, 1917

JAMES HEPBURN

K Ward
Royal Hall War Hosp.
Huddersfield
Yorkshire
10th Jan'y 17

Dear Father,

I received your welcome letter which you sent to Uncle John. I was very glad to get it. I also got the wire which you sent with it which I wish to thank you for. I am still going on fine, and hope it won't be long before I am up. The doctor told me he would finish up my job one of these days so that will mean another little operation. You see the wound which is fairly large has to be closed up. When my arm was taken off there was a flap left for that purpose, so that has to [be] stitched to my shoulder. I have certainly made wonderful progress, so don't worry about me. After what I have been through I think I can go through anything now. I am sure it would be quite a shock to you all when you got the news, more so than it was to me. There are lots of little things I have been used [to] doing that I will miss, but I guess there is no use to worry myself as nothing can give me back my arm. There are thousands of others like me, and lots worse. My battalion must have had very heavy losses on the Somme, as I heard they had to get 700 to reinforce them. It is a terrible place and I am sure that is worse than the place they call Hell. I can't imagine how there possibly could be a place worse.

I have quite a few Canadians in this hospital, and I am in a bed next to one of my own battalion, so that makes it more cheerful.

The Hospital people in France most certainly did take an interest in me, especially Sister Shaw. I guess it was she who wrote you. I wrote her and thanked her for the kindness and attention she showed me. She wouldn't let me go until she was thoroughly satisfied that my wound was clean and out of danger. . . .

Well I think this is about all the news at present. I guess you have got some of the letters I wrote by this time. Tell Mother not to be worrying as I am getting on first rate and hope to be home in the spring or early summer. Well I think I will close now. Hoping this finds you all well. Best love to all.

I remain
Your Loving Son
Jim

PS Aunt Tina sent the potato scones they were fine.

The Terrible Poignancy of War, 1917

ARCHIBALD MACKINNON

The casualties at the front were huge in number, the mail to and from Canada slow. Archibald MacKinnon in Dundalk, Ontario, wrote overseas to his son, Ronald, in March and April, before and after Vimy Ridge, only to have the letters returned when the young man died at Vimy.

R.R.#1, Dundalk, Ont.,
March 20, 1917

My Dear Ronnie,

Yours of February 25th just received and pleased to hear that you are still able to do your bit and that everything is going well. Fritz seems to be on the run now but I guess he has some big wall he is going to lie down behind. You expect it will be over in three months. I hope so but I am afraid it will be a little longer. However, Fritz is beaten if only he had sense to lie down.

Just had word that Archie left England on March 12th so he ought to be at Toronto about the end of the month. I am going down to meet him. I do not know whether he will be allowed up here or not or whether he will be discharged or not. I will go up and see Lily and the children when down there. They are all well. We had a letter from

Jean today. We kept sending socks for fear that you were not getting them. Those in Scotland can stay till you are in need of them. Mother sent a parcel the other day containing nuts, dates, tobacco, bachelor buttons, mustard, candles, and soap. We will send some lice killer in the next; we hope you get it alright. If there is anything you would like, let me know.

They are going to raise 50,000 militia in Canada and put all the overseas men over. Men and women are making all sorts of money in Canada at present.

No more, Ronnie, my boy, and we hope and pray that you will get through it and that it won't be long till I am going down to Toronto to meet you coming home. Mother has not been well lately. Her rheumatics have been very painful. She has not been at the barn for months. Otherwise all are well. Let me have a postcard every week if possible and God be with you, my boy.

Your affectionate father

A. McK.

R.R.#1, Dundalk, Ont.,
April 5, 1917

My Dear Ronnie,

Just a line to say that Archie is home. Just got here. I met him at N. Toronto last Sunday morning. He is looking fine and not very lame but he is not the boy he was when he went away. However, he is in good spirits. He is here on pass. He has got to go back to the Hospital Monday morning for three months. Then he will pass another Medical Board. They are going to have a reception for him in Hopeville tomorrow night.

I called and saw Lily and the children. I intended to stay an afternoon with them but it rained nearly all the time I was down there so I splashed my way up there Monday evening. They are all looking fine. Archie is growing a big fine boy and Annie a big girl and a good talker. Archie knew me well but Annie was very shy. They are doing well and that is the main thing. Lily's mother seemed in good health but old Bill I don't think will last long. He seemed to be pretty shaky.

They met the Hospital Train with street cars and a band and took everybody to the Hospital. Then after they took the soldiers and their friends home in autos and you may be sure Toronto looked good to Archie. I would have liked to have seen you with him but we are looking forward to meeting you some day. So God be with you, my boy, till we do meet.

Your Father,

A. McK.

The Guns of Vimy

THOMAS EARL WALKER

Al Ward, Katesgrave Hosp.
Reading, Nov. 18

My Darling Vie.:

. . . I reached the 26th battery wagon lines which were then at Camblain L'Abbé just behind Vimy Ridge. I was at the lines until March 11 when I went to the guns. At that time we were building a forward position up at La Targette. About four days later we got word that the 26th battery was no more as we were being broken up to form six gun batteries instead of four. Two of our guns went to the seventeenth & two to the eighteenth. I was sent over there to the seventeenth battery in charge of the gun crew and we had our gun pit and dugout to make. It sure was a warm spot around there but fortunately we got away without anyone hit. We worked like slaves all the rest of March and first week of April. Apr. 8 was Easter Sunday. That night no traffic was allowed on the road and our guns were quieter than usual. But for some reason the German guns were working . . . harder than usual. We were busy until about ten o'clock then to bed. The tension was pretty high because we were to attack Vimy Ridge in the morning. We were up at three o'clock, had a last look over the gun, got our orders and a pile of ammunition at ready to fire—had a hot drink of tea and reported all guns ready at 5.15. I am just describing for one little gun.

Just think that at that same time those thousands of guns—eighteen pounders, 4.0 inch Howitzers, 60 pounders, 6 in. Howitzers, 6 in. navals; 8 in. Howitzers, 9.2 in. Howitzers, 12" Howitzers, 15 in. Howitzers—18 in. Howitzers etc. every one reported to their commanding officers who reported to brigade etc. until one general in charge knew all was ready. Also the reports from the infantry in the trenches were phoned in. Then came 5.27 A.M. when the officer called out three minutes to go when everyone got to his place and ready. That last three minutes before an attack dear always seems like an hour. However at 5.29 the word comes—one minute to go. Every artilleryman gets hold of whatever he is going to work. The man who is firing the gun sits with his hand on the firing lever. The infantry get ready to jump out of the trenches, then comes the fatal word "fire" and almost simultaneously all the guns open up and you cannot imagine the roar. The artillery opens up on the German front lines usually for two or three minutes to keep them down till our boys get out and ready to jump into them. Then infantry get out on top and creep up as close as they can to the barrage and then wait in shell holes etc. At the end of the time laid down every gun adds fifty or a hundred yards, according to the nature of the ground and infantry jump into the German front line and when it comes to hand to hand fighting our boys have Fritz beaten to a stand-still. Now just imagine this artillery barrage adding to its range and the infantry simply following behind it and dealing with what Germans there are left and you will know how Vimy Ridge was taken.

About nine o'clock in the forenoon an officer came in & told us our boys were on the ridge. We gave a good cheer and although we were dead tired we felt a lot better after that. The Germans had been taken absolutely by surprise and we got the whole ridge and practically every gun he had in front of us. Then came the work of getting the guns up on the ridge. We finally had to wait until the engineers got a light railway laid before we could get up at all. The mud was so soft & spongy it was absolutely impossible to take them up with horses. Then when we got on the ridge the Germans backed up about five miles & we had to pull out on the plain in front of the ridge.

The Best Show I Have Been In

HAROLD W. MCGILL

France, April 13, 1917

Dear Birdie,

I have your two letters of Feb 26 and March 10 respectively. And the night before last just after we came out of the big battle you have read about your parcel arrived. It could not have come at a more opportune time. We were all tired and hungry. My orderlies had had nothing to eat since the night before and I was just trying to rustle them some rations when your box arrived. I hope you will approve of my procedure when I tell you that I took nearly all the delicious eats with which the box was stuffed and added them to rations that the transport brought up for my boys. The cheese I kept to put in my haversack for our next fight, but the sardines, chocolate, wafers & chewing gum I took over to my orderlies who were in a dugout a couple of hundred yards away. It was snowing hard and the night was as black as a wolf's mouth. It would have done you good to have heard the remarks the boys made and to have seen their faces when they saw the feed that was brought them. They had been working for 3 days and nights almost with out any sleep and with wet feet all the time. I gave the socks to one of the orderlies whose own were soaking wet and who had his boots on his bare feet. You need have no fears that your parcel was not appreciated. The cigarettes I smoked myself and am busy on the box of tobacco. It came in very handy as I had lost my tobacco pouch and contents during the engagement. Thank you ever so much Birdie.

It was a wonderful battle, the best show I have been in. Our men trimmed the Boche in fine shape and our losses were not heavy. It was a wonderful sight when our artillery opened the show at 5:30 A.M. The guns all opened at the same moment with a roar like a terrible peal of thunder and for miles all along the German trenches there was the most wonderful display of fireworks caused by our bursting shells and Fritz's S.O.S. signals going up. Our troops advanced as cool and steady as when they had previously practiced the attack on ground behind the lines a few weeks ago. For of course we have been preparing for this attack for some time. After we got past the old German front line we reached some high ground and had a wonderful view of the battle. For miles we could see the artillery barrage sweeping like a blizzard across the German position and the whole country behind seemingly covered with our advancing troops. The sight must have struck a chill into the German hearts for the sight gave one the impression of irresistible power.

Our weather is of the most atrocious kind. It snows nearly every day and freezes every night. The mud is as bad as anything I have seen.

Narrow Escapes at Vimy

MAJOR PERCY MENZIES

In the field, April 17/17.

Dear Garnet—

As soon as we came out after the battle of Vimy Ridge, I sent a cable home that I was safe, and I knew that the word would very quickly get through to you. Now, however, I have time to write you a few words direct, about my doings and situation.

I cannot be too thankful to Providence for getting me out of it all so well. It was a wild show with that tremendous volume of artillery fire going both ways. At times it was very hard to know exactly where our barrage lines were and we officers had a hard time bringing back our men out of our own fire. The ground was so terribly chewed up that it was almost impossible to recognize the landmarks on which we had counted. However we were able to keep our proper direction and arrive at our proper objective. The Colonel praised us very warmly for getting everything so nearly right.

There is little use describing the operation in general, for you will get all that from the newspapers. I might mention a few of my own escapes for you have always been asking me to write that way.

(1). On the way over we got into our own barrage by mistake, but were able to extricate our men without getting hurt ourselves. All this time we were troubled by our own shells bursting short, but I was never touched. A special trial was our own fire bombs, for several of them broke over our own heads without doing me any damage.

(2). Just after we arrived at the final objective I was passing along inspecting the line, when one of our own shrapnel shells burst over me. I felt the concussion and was lightly hit on the shoulder, but when I picked myself up, I found that I was quite alright. However, a man had been standing a few feet ahead of me and he was killed by the same shell.

(3). I continue to walk along the trench and on the flank met Cliff Pierce, an officer in A Co'y, whom I knew at Queen's and whom I liked very much. I was shaking hands with him, when zip—a sniper's bullet shot through his heart and he fell without uttering a sound.

(4). Later I was standing against a wall watching a heavy bombardment of our line, when a shell hit the wall. Another officer was wounded, but my only injury was that my watch was smashed.

(5). A fresh officer came in the last night, and he was standing in a spot where I had spent about half my time, when a shell blew him to pieces.

(6). I was walking out with the Sgt. Major while Fritz was dropping shells sort of promiscuous over the landscape. Suddenly there came a swift whistle, a heavy thud, and a splash of mud six feet away. A dud had landed. If it had exploded we would be going yet.

These are some escapes which I noticed, though I have always contended, that the misses which one fails even to notice, may be the most dangerous. Further, I feel almost sinful in talking about my "luck," for there is a superstition among soldiers that the luck will change if you talk about it. They would cry instantly "touchwood" "touchwood." However I will try not to be superstitious.

It is an awful day for weather. It blew a cyclone of rain and snow all night, and has been carrying on intermittently all day. I don't think there has been a clear day in five weeks, and the wet and mud is a problem. We are at present bivouacked in an open field. The men are under tarpaulians; the officers in bell tents. The tents are no good, being old and British made, which always leak. Last night the pole of our tent sank about a foot under the strain, and the tent flapped and roared all night. However it was still standing this morning when we got up.

The batmen have since fixed it up for another struggle tonight.

Well I think I shall stop for now. Good-bye and all good luck.

Percy.

A "Reprisal" Bombing Raid on Freiburg, Germany, April 1917

SUB-LIEUTENANT WALTER P. FLETT

In retaliation for a German U-boat's sinking of a hospital ship, British fighters bombed the town of Freiburg. Walter Flett, a Royal Naval Air Service pilot, wrote this account of the raid three days later.

April 17th.17

Dear Sister Anne

I wrote you the day before yesterday telling you we had one more big raid to pull off + I would be back to England on leave, well it's all over little girl + I am o.k. I have a story to tell you would make your blood run cold. I had the luck of a Texas mule.

Well to begin with it was a raid on what we call an open city—that is the first reprisal of the wing for the sinking of a British hospital ship. You can realize what that would mean. The day broke clear as I predicted in my letter the night before it was to be mailed to you if I did not come back.

After a long wait we at last were sent off a strong front up top making it very difficult for us to get back. You will see in the papers where it was to.

My flight going first the fighters going up first to get height. The first Lieut, Lieut Colonel, a flight Sgt + myself with the fighters circling we soon were all in formation + off us [?] for the lines where we were very heavily shelled crossing but all came through ok. Then on for a long time to the objective away over the Rhine. Nothing happened all the Bombers let go there bombs. My gunlayer let go a big package of pamphlets explaining in German what we were doing this fore, + we turned [?]. Well all went well we came through very heavy shelling over the objective, but no [?] so far. I was just thinking well this is going to be pie when crack crack crack with the machine guns, + six Huns were at my tail, the Wing Commander Lieut Colonel—was on my left. The Huns came up from behind and under my right wing. He went in a loop over my tail and a roar from my gunlayers [?] brought my head around to see a [?] flash over not twenty feet off with our tracers (bullets) passing into the fuselage over went my machine in a [?] towards my wing Commander who was just on my right, in doing this my tail showed up a Fokker biplane under my tail down went the two [?] into him at point blank range two of them [?] firing 500 per minute each, he simply crumpled up + went down, but not before he riddled me with bullets cutting my tail almost off + cutting my elevator control wires. I was there practically helpless. On we went + back came two huns and [?] went the machine the machine guns again and Mr. Hun came on no more. On went little [?] just holding my height + sogging along with a big blow against me bound for France. My gunlayer then tapped me on the shoulder again that meant another Hun. Well I shook my head I had given up hope now of ever getting down 12 200 feet. Arround went my head I could see a machine wing diving for me. My flight was far off in the distance now. Well I gave up hope again but he did not come close. My gunlayer Kim got his glasses out. He tapped me off went the engine for a second. He yelled "French Newport" I said Thank God. On we went there whooff whoof we were in shell fire again that meant the lives + I slogged through it getting some [?] for my health.

Then came the job of landing with controls gone, it's all unpassable country all mountains + forests. I spotted a little Drome far below some 11000 feet there. I started to come down not knowing when my tail would fall off that meant instant death. I yelled to my gunlayer what is that drome, he got his glasses out but the machine was rolling so he could not get in it. Down we came I spotted the French marking on a plane again Thank God. In we came + landed her.

There was a rush of French flyers out to the machine. They dragged poor Kim out he was pretty well all in there, wounded in the leg + wrist with explosive bullets, I'm afraid. I just got out + cursed for fully five minutes, some of the French flyers could speak English. They took me for an American. I think it was the language. Poor Prince the American flyer was killed landing in this drome about 8 months ago. There is no use telling you the different parts where the machine was struck. I was simply riddled with bullets + shell or part of one had gone through my tail plane. . . .

I got back to my Drome by car, the captain was very good to me + packed me off to England on special leave, + I am not to go to the front any more, but stay in England. I think they figure I will never fly again + I am, so I am not putting up any argument.

I have just got a letter from the admiralty to say my application for leave to Canada cannot be considered, but all that will be changed now.

I was intending this letter for Eloise, sister but I think it is to strong and we might upset her so will send it to you instead [?] the opening. . . .

Lots of love, Pete . . .

P.S. The three other fighters with me are all missing. Lieut Col, Wing Commander, First Lieut of the station.

Learning to Fly, May 1917

CHARLES HENDERSHOT

> *Canada had no air force of its own in 1917 when Charles Hendershot enlisted to become a pilot. He trained at Toronto in the Royal Flying Corps and, in addition to encouraging his brother to enlist before he was conscripted into the army, wrote joyfully about the thrill of flight. Hendershot was later shot down and killed in action.*

Toronto Friday
May 1917

Dear Bro,

I hear that Canada has conscription. One of the boys said he saw an extra (Paper) and it said conscription. If it is true for the love of Peter get in the R.F.C. It is the only branch for a decent person.

We are going to try our exams a week from yesterday so will know for sure whether we pass or not I am going to get on a fighting machine, not one of these observing planes.

There is more excitement in a fighter and speed. They can go 140 per hr and on a nose dive a thousand feet in two seconds. This might sound fishy but when you get in the R.F.C. you will know.

We are going to get our officers uniform Friday and we are having an athletic meet the same day.

I tell you, one thing you have to learn when you join the R.F.C. is to keep a secret. Even the note books if lost you will get kicked out of the F.C. Every is strictly private.

I can send wireless at rate of 6 words per min. and receive at 5 so that isn't bad. I can also strip a machine gun. (that is take it all to pieces & put it together in 2 minutes.) I was out watching the fellows fly Sunday & they said to come out and they would take me up so I am going out soon. (The instructors.) Do you know Carson Linn & Lue Purdom—from London, well they are in the R.F.C. Well so long.

Your Bro.

The flying Bug.

The Call of Duty, 1917

PRIVATE THOMAS P. HARRIS

> *Many soldiers believed fervently in doing their duty, however horrid the conditions in which they served. Only rarely, however, has the pull of duty and comradeship against love and the possibility of future happiness been expressed so clearly as in Harris's letter to his fiancée. Harris survived the war to marry his sweetheart.*

May 24, 1917

Sweetheart,

It seems somehow fated that I shall always be causing you a certain amount of worry. It is two weeks since I wrote to you and in my last letter I said I would write soon. Two weeks have passed and all the time I knew you would be worrying as to how I was and yet I couldn't write. . . . But dearest, I must ask you to believe that if I could have written I would have done so. I have quite an interesting story to tell you when I next see you.

I suppose my health first. Well, I guess I am just about well now. The wound is all healed up and the arm OK. Occasionally, I feel a slight effect of the gas—nothing much. I have left hospital and am back with my outfit and I am hanging around our own hospital, although really I feel well enough for duty.

The poem enclosed with your letter is extremely good and makes one think. . . . May I repeat one or two lines. What truth in the words. *Her kiss, her tears, will haunt you in the strife*. It's too true, you try so hard not to think of her, as it would be better if you could forget for the moment, but always there comes back memories. . . .

Your next letter in which you say you have received the field service postcard, tells me quite plainly that it caused you an awful lot of worry. I think I have already explained that when I sent the card I was so dazed and half delirious that I couldn't think properly, much less write and it was the only way I could let you know. Once again dear I must tell you how sorry I now am that I sent it, as I now realize that it would have been far better to have waited until I was well enough to write and let you know I was OK. Always causing you worry. You say that you had prayed extra for my safety. Well sweetheart, the prayer was answered, as what happened to me could only occur once in a thousand times and me still here perfectly safe. The only bad luck I have had is going to hospital in France, as with even ordinary luck I would have gone to England—and England meant you.

I don't exactly know how to answer your last letter. I have never been in a harder situation in my life and I don't suppose I will again.

The girl whom I love more than anyone else and for whom I thought I would do anything she asked me to, has asked me for the first time to do something for her now, something that no doubt would stop her worrying and make her much happier and yet I don't know whether I can do it or not. For hours I have thought it over, many times before I received your letter, in fact ever since I came back from leave. I wonder if I can make you understand.

Let's suppose you were a big healthy boy. At the age of 17 or 18 a war broke out between you and some other country. You and your chums are all full of eagerness to enlist in the infantry. All of your chums do so, but through a defect in sight you are turned down. When you are sure you cannot get in the infantry with your chums, you manage to enlist in an ambulance as a stretcher-bearer. You meet a wonderful girl whom you worship. Eventually you go to the front to do your work as a stretcher-bearer. You take your share of the risks, but the risks you take are not nearly so great as those taken by the infantry. You have never really felt satisfied with yourself for being in an ambulance, until you have brought out some poor fellows wounded, maybe some of your own chums, and brought them out at risk to yourself. Well, you are in the firing for a long time, as you are extremely lucky. Always you have the satisfaction of knowing that you are doing good work and doing your share and you always remember the thanks the wounded men give you after you have managed to get them behind the lines safely. Well, your time comes for leave and you go to the girl. She asks you a lot of questions and for the first time you realize how hard it is for her, always to be in suspense and wondering if you are OK.

During your leave she tells you of this and asks you that as you have been out there so long if you do not think you could get a job further back from the line, out of danger, so as to stop her worrying. Of course you would do anything if it was possible to make her happier, but you explain to her why you would rather go back to your old job and you manage to make her understand your reasons.

Your leave finishes. You go back to the front after having had the most wonderful week of your life. After you have been back a few months it happens, but as usual you are lucky. Your companion is killed and you are knocked unconscious. You know nothing until you wake up on a stretcher. Then when you get full control of your senses, you think in earnest. Suppose you had been the other man and you had been the one killed? Well, as far as you yourself are concerned, it wouldn't have mattered, as there was no pain, no suspense or anything. But how about the people left behind. Your mother and father and the girl. It would have caused them an awful amount of grief. You guessed right away that you would hear from the girl, asking you for her sake and possibly for your mother's sake too to get, if possible, a safe job. How you dreaded to receive that letter, as you know that you would do anything else in the world for the girl.

Then the letter came. It was just as you thought. She said you had been at the front so long, been sick, wounded and gassed. You know that every reason she gives is correct and yet with all that, you somehow cannot give consent to do what she asks and what is worse you cannot exactly explain why you can't do it. And then there is always a kind of feeling that after the war is finished she would be far prouder of you and think much more of you if you do not do as she asks but stick through it, if possible to the end.

Dearest, perhaps it was unnecessary to tell you all this but I wanted you to try and understand how hard it is to say "no." You know dear, if it was anything else at all you asked me to do I would do it willingly for you.

What would the few chums I have left with me say if I quit now?

Dearest, there is no need to worry about me for some time—that's honest. I am and shall be perfectly safe for some weeks as I am still convalescent. As you know, I love you very, very much.

Tom.

The Hell of Passchendaele I: I Shivered Alongside Stephens, October 1917

PRIVATE JOHN P. SUDBURY

> *Almost a half-century after he was wounded at Passchendaele, Private Sudbury of the 9th Canadian Brigade Machine Gun Company set down his memories.*

October 25th 1917

The afternoon and night was spent by 27 of us carrying all our gun equipment and ourselves mile after mile from the rear of Ypres over the duckboards (often broken by shelling) and mud and more mud towards our positions from which we were to advance next morning towards the German Line. When the occasional rest came my friend "Curly" would persistently join me rather than stay in his allotted position in the single file line we maintained. He was particularly solemn and I did my best to cheer him up, for there seemed nothing else I could do, but inwardly I thought, "You, my friend, have a premonition[.]"

At last we were under enemy gunfire and I knew now that we had not much further to carry all this weight. We were soaked through with rain and perspiration from the efforts we had been making to get through the clinging mud, so that when we stopped we huddled down in the nearest shell hole and covered ourselves with a groundsheet, hoping for some sort of comfort out of the rain, and partly believed the sheet would also protect us from the rain of shells. I shivered alongside Stephens who was a quiet, kindly and refined lad having his first taste of the front line. Together we huddled in this hole when there was a great thump behind us, but mercifully that shell failed to explode. As the shelling grew worse it was decided we had better move on, so reloading ourselves we pushed through the mud again and amid the din of the bursting shells I called to Stephens, but got no response and just assumed he hadn't heard me. He was never seen or heard from again. He had not deserted. He had not been captured. One of those shells that fell behind me had burst and Stephens was no more. "Missing believed killed" would be the laconic message home.

The rest of us struggled on in pouring rain and complete darkness. We often fell over one another, for not being able to see we just listened for the groans and puffings of those ahead, at least when we could hear amid the din of artillery.

At last word came down our little line to lie down. Apparently we had reached our allotted position for the next morn's battle.

We waited in the mud. At 5.30am on Oct 26th our guns opened their barrage on "No man's land" and the enemy lines, or perhaps we thought they did. Whether we had gone too far forward or whether the guns had sunk further into the mud no-one will ever know, suffice it to say that their shells fell on us. One after another of my friends called out that they were hit and struggled back for help elsewhere. At last the whole barrage lifted and those of us left gathered ourselves and our equipment together, to go forward. A few paces ahead a shell hole on my right attracted my attention and horror. There was that curly head face downwards on one side of the shell hole and his body on the other. There was no time for grief or tenderness. On we went struggling with the mud step by step to the enemy barbed wire, and there in another shell hole were two live Germans—but only just alive. They were mere boys and could not have been more than 16 years of age—both bleeding profusely but the look in their eyes I have never been able to forget. A look of abject fear mingled somehow with pity. I remember I hastily grabbed my water bottle, drank a sip and threw it to within their reach for I had heard the call to hurry up with the gun I was carrying, and I had to move on. I caught up with our party and noticed that two other guns were unmanned already. I put mine down and with the help of my friend "Chips" we bent down to remove the gun from its "boot" (carrying cover). I felt a bang and toppled into a shell hole on my left, and Chips who was on my right side yelled "Oh, my wrist." Luckily my shell hole was new and had not had time to fill with water. I quickly realised that my left leg was useless and that we had both been hit by the same bullet and, what was more horrifying to me, was the realisation that from that direction the enemy must be behind me. So I decided that this was no place for "Suds" and that I'd try and get back from where we had started somehow or other. Glancing round I noted that all our Company were gone—at least no one was left there—and then I crawled forward and raised my head to see where I had to go. It was just one stretch of water interspersed with rings of earth here and there which I knew were the edges of shell holes and I must keep out of them or drown in the holes they enclosed. How I kept my bearings I shall never know as I dragged myself round half of this hole and half that, keeping my mind on direction but ever turning a bit this way and then that way. How long that quarter of a mile took me to traverse I do not know, but at last a friendly voice called "Suds!" Two of our company came from their hole and picked me up. They told me that they and five more were all that were left of our 27. Now they were to have a chance of respite by getting me out with the aid of two others who brought a stretcher.

Now the mud really came into its own. The only way to move that stretcher was to push it foot-by-foot, almost inch-by-inch, over the surface. Then for each to hang on to it and drag first one leg and then the other out of the mire to replace it with more mire, perhaps a foot or so further on our way. It continued to rain and the enemy artillery were now replying to our onslaught. Shells fell all around us and none of us expected to reach the dressing station, only 300 yards away. It was four hours before we did reach it. The stretcher was full of water, mud and blood and at one halting I managed to slap a field dressing, dragged from the lining of my tunic, on to my knee to try and stop the bleeding. At long last we made it, and to me the very worst kind of hell upon earth was over. There was, however, much more for me to go through, but at least the hopeless frustrations, desperations and the complete unreality of life on Passchendaele was over for I, like all my comrades, did not care one iota about fighting battles. The enemy and ourselves were in the selfsame muck, degradation and horror to such a point nobody cared any more about anything, only getting out of this, and the only way out was by death or wounding and we all of us welcomed either.

P.S. This filthy poisoned mud set up gangrene, and my left leg was amputated two months later after six operations to save it[.]

That was 46 years ago. I am now a retired schoolmaster.

The Hell of Passchendaele II: October 1917

ARTHUR TURNER

October 19th 1917. I was placed in the 10th. Platoon C Company 50th Batt'n.

Colonel Page, (our Colonel) called the Batt'n together for an instructive talk. He told us that he along with other Colonel's of the different Canadian Regiments had just returned from a Reconaisance of the Yepre front. And that something Big was about to happen there, and that the 50th Batt'n would be playing a big part in the operations.

"However" he said, "It is not going to be a picnic. The Belgians had distroyed the Dykes in an effort to slow up the German's, and the whole country was flooded."

The battle for the Passchendaele Ridge, and the Town itself was without doubt one of Muddy-est, Bloody-est, of the whole war.

Oct. 20. We climbed into Lorries, and were driven up to Yepres, right through the City, past the ruined Clothe Hall, and disembarked on the outskirts, in a field, and told to keep absolutely still till dark, (this was about noon.)

We did'nt know it at the time, but it turned out that the 46th Batt'n from Saskatchewan were to spearhead the attack, with the 50th Batt'n from Calgary. Alberta. in support.

All we were told was that we would be there for 7 days.

At dusk my Platoon Officer, Lt. Tommy Tweed, called us together, and we started the tramp through the mud to the front line, which was about 4 miles away.

There were no trench mats to walk on at that time, just had to find our way around the shell holes. Each step we took we had to reach down and pull the other leg up out of the mud. Besides our regular equipment and ammunition, each man was given an extra 50 rounds of ammunition, a shovel, and an extra days ration to carry, we were weighted down like Pack Mules, and all the time shells were dropping around us.

After going about 3 miles, our Officer told us to rest. 5 of us got into a hole that had been newly dug, about 6 feet deep, 2 feet wide, and 10 feet long. We got into it and sat on the bottom, each man sitting between the other mans legs, we filled up the hole.

We had hardly got settled when a screeching shell plowed threw one side of the hole over our heads, and into the other side, but it did'nt explode. Needless to say we got out of there in a hurry. We could have been buried alive *if* it had exploded, But it was a *Dud*.

I would like to mention here that hundreds of mens lives were saved at Passchendaele for this reason, either the German shells were poorly manufactured, or the ground was too soft to explode them. However there was a lot of *Duds*.

We went another Kilometre to a place called "Zonnebeck," to get there we followed a road covered with soft mud, about a foot deep, However, the roadway made good footing under the mud. One spot on this road was being shelled by a large heavy calibre gun every 3 minites. A lot of men on working parties used to get it here.

We relieved the Australians, and took up our positions in shell holes, 2 men in a shell hole 50 feet apart. The Germans were just across a ravine from us. on our left.

Well, we were told that we would be there for 7 days, We had to scrape a place to sit on in the side of the shell hole, but our feet were in water, over the tops of our boots all the time, We were given Whale Oil to rub on our feet, it was supposed to be done once a day. Imagine taking ones boots off under these conditions each day?

This was to prevent Trench feet. To solve it I took off my boots once, and poured half the oil into each foot, then slid my feet into it. It was a gummy mess, but I did not get trench feet. The other man with me was a boy 18 years old. His name was W. Scarr, from Bankhead, near Lake Minniwanka. His name is on the Cenotaph alongside the road at Bankhead, on the way from Banff to Minniwanka. He was killed on the 7th day, just before we were relieved.

We were on half rations, as the men carrying up the rations were being killed on the way up. One bad place was the spot on the road to "Zonnebeck."

Oct. 21st. I was detailed one day to hand out the water ration, half bottle, or one pint to each man. I had to go to Zonnebeck to pick it up, in two gallon gasoline cans, then go from shell hole to shell hole, half filling each mans water bottle. I was busy doing this when a voice behind me said, "Stoop down low, you are in full view of the enemy." It was our Colonel Page, a splendid man, well liked by all. I hadn't realized till now that we were that close, so when I went back to my shell hole, I fished out of my haversack, a small telescope that I had, and scanned the opposite slope of the ravine. Sure enough, there was two Germans, but they were carrying a stretcher, Thinking that they were Red Cross, of course I did'nt shoot, but I watched them till they put down the stretcher, Imagine my surprize when they lifted from it, a *Machine Gun.* Before I could get my rifle trained on them, they had jumped down into a shell hole, and all I could see was shovel-fulls of dirt being thrown out, but not another glimpse of the men.

Oct. 22 to 25. Well, for 6 days we sat in those shell holes, under continuous shell fire. Our own batteries were as troublesome as any, We did'nt know it at the time, but our own batteries were sending over heavy Lideite Shrapnel shells, that exploded right over our heads, The concussion was terrific, it made me feel as if my chest was being ripped open, The shells would explode over our heads, but the shrapnel would shoot forward onto the Germans.

One night, one of the chaps in the next shell hole to us, jumped into our hole almost frantic, a shell had plowed into their shell hole but had'nt exploded. We called them "Duds." We finaly convinced him that the next shell could just as easily drop in our hole as his, so he went back to his own hole.

Oct. 25th. This was the 6th day in the line, Just before dusk, the Sgt. came to our hole and said, "Be ready to move off in an hour." We knew we were to be there for 7 days, but there was the possibility that we might be relieved a day sooner[.]

Then it suddenly struck me that we might be going over the *Top*. As the Sgt. was moving away to the next hole, to warn the other men, I said "Which way are we going Sarge?" He said, "None of your damn bisiness," This hurt my feelings, and I blurted out, "Who the Hell cares which way we are going?"

This took the Sgt. by surprise. We stood glaring at each other, He did'nt know what to do,—No use putting a man on the "*Peg*" when in the "line," so he moved off to notify the other men. On his way back, he stopped and looked down at me. He said, "Have you been in the line before?" He himself had been wounded on three different occasions, and this was his third trip back to the Battalion after leaving Blighty, so he did'nt know me, and of course I didn't know him. I said, "You are damn right I have," He said, "Can you be ready in half an hour?"

I said, "I'm ready right now, What the Hell is there to get ready?"

He left me and came back in a few minites, and said for me to follow him to the Officers "Funk Hole." There was the Officer Lt. Tommy Tweed, and Cpl. Jimmy Law, sitting there, Sgt. Meyers just managed to sqeese in, but I could'nt get any further than the opening. I crouched down, expecting anything from a lecture, to being shot at sunrise. But instead, the Officer said to me, "Turner, the Sgt. tells me that you have been in the line before?" I said, "Yes, Sir."

Well, he said, "Confidentially, we are going over in the early hours in the morning, and before it gets too dark, we have to Reconnoitre the ground in front of us because we have to move the Plattoon up during the night as close as we can, ready to jump off. I will take the first Section, Sgt. Meyers, the 2nd Corporal Law, the 3rd and you will follow with the fourth.

(i.e.) Two Platoons of the 50th namely "10" and "11" Platoons. "C" Company had been detailed to act as "Imediate Support" to the "46" Battalion.

So the 4 of us went crawling along on our bellies. The Officer pointed out three pillbox's and told me to memorise them so that I could find them in the dark. One was Regimental Headquarters, the other, Company Head-qtrs. and the third the Dressing Station. He said I would be required to carry messages to Head-qtrs, and also take the wounded to the dressing station. The Officer picked out the place where we would dig in ready for jumping off, and then we made our way back to the men.

By this time, it was dark and so, as arrainged, we brought the men up, and told them to dig in, but not to dig deeper than 3 feet, as the ground here was a kind of quick sand and would not stand up. That is why we did not dig trenches at Passchendaele. We still stayed in pairs, each pair dug a hole 3 feet in diametre, and 3 feet deep, and got into it.

Oct. 26th 1917. Young Scarr and I did the same. The shelling was heavy, The Lad was not mature enough to stand this, but although frightened, he would drop off to sleep. Three times that night I dug him out with my bare hands when shells bored in our funk hole. One time during the night he gave me his mothers address so I could let her know if anything happened to him.

I took out several casualties. One of the casualties was named Millan, hit in the neck. Another went out with Trench feet, just before we went over, he afterwards lived in Noze Creek by the C.P.R. crossing.

As I was coming back to the platoon, after taking one man out, I heard the cries of a man in terrible pain, the Officer, and the Corporal, were working on him. A shell had made a direct hit on our Lewis gun, killing 2 men, and wounding this man in both feet. He was in dredful pain. I heard the Corporal say, "Here comes Turner now," The Officer looked up and said, "I hate to send you on another trip Turner, but we will have to get this man out," I told him that I would just as soon be doing this, as waiting for the next shell to get me. He said "I'll remember you Turner if we ever get out of this." . . .

These stretcher cases sure deplete a platoon, that is already depleted, through casualties, as it takes 4 men to a stretcher. We got back just before our Barrage opened up on the Germans. And the German Artilery opened up on us. We were moving forward at a walk. I had'nt seen a German yet. The 46th Battalion was doing all the fighting,

2 platoons of the 50th namely, 10 and 11 platoons, were following up in immedate support. Corp,'l Law and I were side by side when a heavy shell came over and exploded right behind our stretcher bearer, an old man of 45 years. We called him "Dad," his name was Milne. I saw the old man straighten up with a surprised look on his face, then he turned completely around before he fell. Cpl. Law called out, "Old Dad is hit."

We ran over to him, the blood was pouring from his chest. . . .

Oct. 26th 1917. By this time, our platoon was in danger of being annihalated, Our Officer ordered us to get down and dig in. We started to dig in but it was obvious that the German artilery had us spotted. We noticed a spot about 100 yards away where shells were dropping. The Officer ordered us to dash over there and dig in.

This is done by each man lying flat on his face, and scrapeing a hole (with his entrenching tool) about 6 inches deep on one side, and rolling into it, and then scrapeing the other side. This is continued without raising your head, until each man makes a hole for himself about 3 feet deep.

Another man got hit in the neck, I had to take him to the First Aid station.

When I got back, Lt. Tweed told me to take a verbal message to Company Head'qtrs. where Captain Pringle was in charge, It was that a Major Kennedy of the 46th Batt'n had sent for re-inforcement of 2 Platoons of men, and one Officer, and that Lt. Harrison had gone with his platoon, but that he (Tweed) refused to let his platoon go unless he went with them, and what was he to do?. (Lt. Harrison) was killed on arrival.

To get to Head'qtrs, now, I had to go through a German cemetry. I crawled into the pill Box, and gave Capt. Pringle the message. He asked me how Mr. Tweed was making out?.

I told him he had been having a harrowing time. Pringle reached under a blanket and brought out a water bottle, and told me to give it to Mr. Tweed. I smelt it, and it was whiskey. I said, "Is this for the Platoon, Sir?" He said, "No, it's for Mr. Tweed, But you can take a drink yourself."

While I was in the pill box, all the candles went out without a flicker. They told me that was what happens when a shell drops close.

I crawled out of the pill box with the Captain's reply. It was, "As Major Kennedy, of the 46th Batt'n is temporarily in command of 10 and 11 platoons, of the 50th you will do as he says."

Going back to Mr. Tweed with the message, I had reached the German cemetry. I felt played-out. My overcoat was wet through, and heavy as lead. I heard a heavy shell coming, I knew by the sound that it was headed my way, I looked up and saw what appeared to be a football coming straight at me, There was a terrific shriek as it struck the ground 6 or 8 feet in front of me, I instinctivly threw up my hands, expecting to go heavenwards, but nothing happened. It was a "Dud."

I had heard men say that the only time one could see a shell traveling was when standing behind the gun that fired it, or when it was coming straight at you, but those that saw it coming never lived to tell the tale. One thing I was surprised about through was, I felt no fear, Usually shell fire scared me stiff. Maybe it all happened so quickly, or maybe because I was too exhausted.

I got to Tweed's funk-hole and gave him the Captain's reply, and the bottle of whiskey, He reached into a gunny sack and brought out a can of Maconichie and gave it to me.

I went to my funk-hole and opened the can and began to eat. It was begining to get dusk, now the German Barrage started, The bursting shells filled my can with mud and sand and I had to throw it away. I knew what was coming, It was the German counter-attack.

I took off my overcoat and laid it on my ground sheet on the Parrapit and had to duck down below the parapit. We were right in the middle of his barrage. It would play on us for 3 minites, and then lift 25 yards, and the Germans would follow up behind their own barrage, and *Mop up.*

I had to keep my head down below the parapit, it would be suicide to look up, I saw steam raising up from my hand, there was a piece of hot schrapnel steaming on my wet hand I picked it off and dropped it into my haversack for a souveneer, A moment later another piece dropped on my hand in exactly the same place, It was the shrapnel striking my steel helmet and dropping down on my hand. But I did'nt want anymore souvenirs.

Oct. 26th 1917. All this time my rifle was ready with fixed bayonet, leaning against the parapit, the canvas breach cover was intentionally left snapped on around the mechanism, which acording to King's *rules* and *regulations* should be done till the last minute to keep the mechanisim clean, It only takes a flick of the hand to throw it off.

What I did'nt know was that as each shell burst and splashed mud onto the rifle barrel the rain was washing it down into the breach cover and forming a ball of mud all around trigger and bolt.

Now the barrage lifted 25 yards. *This* was *It.* I looked up and there was the 46th on our right, falling back in *Orderly Fashion*, One half of the men would rush back, while the other half opened a rapid fire, Then the other half would open a rapid fire so that the other half could get back. No Germans had shown themselves in front of us.

Young Scarr was badly scared, he thought the 46th were running away. He said, "What can we do?" (There was only about 4 of us privates left in our platoon, and the Officer and Corporal.) I said to young Scarr, "Keep your eyes on the front, and the first Hinnies you see let them have it."

Just then 3 Germans appeared about 50 yards away, I ripped off my breach cover. It was then that I discovered the Mechanisim of my rifle was caked in mud. I was amazed, this had never happened before. The Germans coming over and my rifle usless. Luckily for us these 3 Germans were a machine gun section, and instead of rushing us they were busy setting up their machine gun.

I scratched off the mud from around the trigger and bolt, One cartridge was in the breach, I fired this point blank and all 3 heads disappeared. I tried to reload for rapid fire, but the mud prevented the bolt from closeing. I looked to the Officers funk-hole, wondering why we

In 1866, Irish-American Fenians, seeking to free Ireland from Britain by attacking the Canadas, raided across the Niagara River. This train carried militia volunteers from St. Catharines to Port Colborne. National Archives of Canada

The new Dominion of Canada's first military expedition—under British command—was to deal with Louis Riel's rebellion at the Red River in 1869–70. Mrs F.A. Hopkins' painting shows the advance guard en route to the Red. National Archives of Canada

In 1885, Riel rose once more, and troops (the Halifax Garrison Artillery included, here at Swift Current in the North West Territories) moved west. National Archives of Canada

Canada dispatched troops to the South African War in 1899, all volunteers seeking adventure and to serve the Empire. These men were typical of their comrades.
Royal Canadian Military Institute

We are saving you
YOU save FOOD

Well fed Soldiers
WILL WIN the WAR

(TOP LEFT) The Great War stirred Canadians, not least those young men who aspired to fly. Billy Barker, one of the war's great aces, won a Victoria Cross and a chestful of medals for his skill and courage. National Archives of Canada/RE 17597

(TOP RIGHT) Women wanted to serve, and nursing overseas and at home beckoned. These Nursing Sisters in ward uniform gave extraordinary service to the wounded and ill. Canadian War Museum/19779477-001

(LEFT) At home, the government exhorted civilians to do their bit. Food was rationed by 1917. National Archives of Canada/c-095281

NOTHING is to be written on this side except the date and signature of the sender. Sentences not required may be erased. If anything else is added the post card will be destroyed.

I am quite well.

~~I have been admitted into hospital~~
{ ~~sick~~ } ~~and am going on well.~~
{ ~~wounded~~ } ~~and hope to be discharged soon.~~

~~I am being sent down to the base.~~

I have received your { letter dated 23-30 }
{ telegram „ _____ }
{ parcel „ _____ }

Letter follows at first opportunity.

~~I have received no letter from you~~
{ ~~lately.~~ }
{ ~~for a long time.~~ }

Signature)
only. } Willy

Date _____ 20/7/18

[Postage must be prepaid on any letter or post card addressed to the sender of this card.]

(25350) Wt.W458-591 1,500m. 4/15 M.R.Co.,Ltd.

(LEFT) Soldiers knew their folks worried about them, and cards like these let quick messages be sent when there was no chance to pen a letter. Canadian War Museum/19810649-028

(BELOW) Prime Minister Sir Robert Borden wanted Canada to sustain its troops overseas. After visits to hospitals, as here in March 1917, and the front, he called for conscription to maintain the Canadian Corps at strength. National Archives of Canada/PA000880

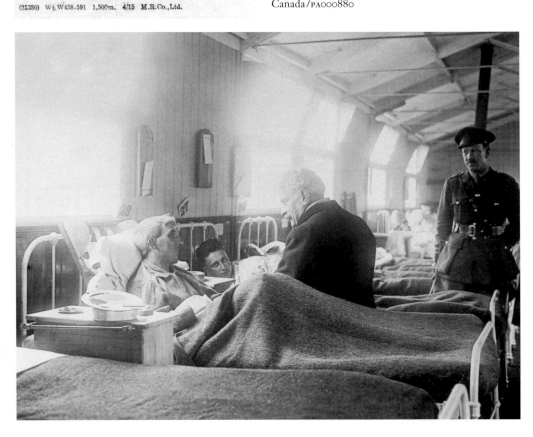

In April 1917, the Corps took Vimy Ridge, hitherto an impregnable German position. The blasted landscape after the fighting testified to its fierceness.

Canadian War Museum/19780067-004 p. 28c

In December 1917, two ships collided in Halifax harbour. The resulting explosion leveled much of the city and killed and wounded thousands.

National Archives of Canada/c-019945

Canada went to war again in September 1939. These troops of the Westminster
Regiment, training in England in April 1941, would not see action for
almost three years more. National Archives of Canada/PA132786

The first Canadian army operation in Europe was the disastrous raid on Dieppe
in August 1942. In this German photograph, the beaches are littered with
the dead, as well as wrecked equipment. National Archives of Canada/C14160

(LEFT) The Canadian contribution to the Royal Air Force's bomber offensive against Hitler was huge. This striking photograph shows an air gunner. Canadian War Museum/19940001-530

(BELOW) Air crew knew the odds against them were high. Many relied on lucky charms like this navigator with his stuffed lion cub.
National Archives of Canada

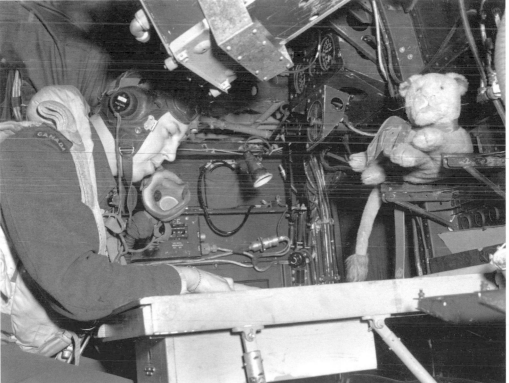

(ABOVE) The 1st Canadian Division and the 1st Canadian Armoured Brigade took part in the liberation of Sicily in July 1943. Two months later, these tanks of the brigade landed at Reggio di Calabria on the Italian mainland. National Archives of Canada/PA130247

(LEFT) A dental officer from Toronto, Captain Harry Jolley had this portrait taken in Sicily in 1943. He ended the war in the Netherlands as a major with an MBE and a Mention in Despatches. Courtesy Carol Geller Sures

hadn't had orders to retire. He probably had given it and we hadn't [heard] it in the noise of the barrage, Anyhow there was the Officer and Corp'l retreating. I said to young Scarr, "There goes the Officer, I guess we can go now,"

I tried to climb out of my funk hole, but everything was so wet and muddy, I slipped back in. I tried 2 or 3 times, but each time I slid back in. Eventually I clambered out, and started to run. I looked back to see if Scarr was coming, and there he was doing the same as I had been doing. Trying to clamber out, and sliding back in again.

I rushed back, grabbed his hand and hauled him out, I started to run again, but looked back to see if he was coming, and there he was stooping down to pick up his ground sheet. I yelled at him, "Leave that Damn thing alone and *Beat it*."

He started to run, but in the wrong direction, he was running half Left, I was running half Right. I yelled at him to follow me, but in the noise of the barrage he did'nt hear[.]

That was the last I saw of him. Our Red X men found his body 6 weeks later.

The way I ran took me over a knoll and I was safe from machine gun fire. . . .

The next thing I knew, I was almost into the German barrage again. I remembered the N.C.O.s training that I had had. i. e. "Stay 25 yards behind the barrage and you are fairly safe." I flopped down and waited for the barrage to lift. But it was a queer feeling following the Enemy barrage, and the Germans on my heels.

However, my one shot had made those 3 Germans take cover, I did'nt see them again.

As the German barrage lifted 25 yards each time, I would follow it up, and finally came to our Support trenches. I jumped down in, and who should I land beside ? but Sgt. Meyers. I got my rifle cleaned and felt much better. I had just got my rifle cleaned when a figure came towards us, from No Man's land. It was dark now, and Sgt. Meyers said, "Hold your fire, it may be one of our fellows," He went right past us and he was a Major of the 46th Batt'n wounded and holding his wrist.

The Hell of Passchendaele III: A Next-of-Kin Letter

LIEUTENANT ARTHUR G. STARKINGS

One of the tasks of platoon commanders was to write to the next of kin of those killed in action. After Passchendaele, there were many such letters to write, including this one to the mother of Private Clifford Shaver, age 21, killed on October 30, 1917.

Dear Mrs Shaver—

It is with sorrow that I write to say how deeply I sympathize with you in the sad loss of your son Clifford. I find it difficult to do this however first because I feel that words are so cheap at such a time and again because although we shall miss him, we know that you will miss him more. Believe me when I say that he was loved and respected by all. His comrades valued his friendship and mourn his loss while for myself I can only add that he was one of my best and bravest men. It was during a heavy barrage when we were expecting a counter attack that he met his death, nobly standing by his Lewis gun, coolly awaiting the expected attack. His conduct was an example to us all and it may comfort you to know that his death was a painless one. We buried him near the spot where he gallantly fell, which we could give you sometimes in the near future should you desire it. His personal effects, a testament, two fountain pens, a pair of scissors and a ring I have enclosed. His pay roll has been handed in to the orderly room. For us it remains to carry on, following his example and while we continue this struggle we trust that strength may come to you to help you in your bitter loss. May God be with you in your sad bereavement. On behalf of the platoon,

 Yours very sincerely,
 Arthur G. Starkings, Lieut

The Hell of Passchendaele IV: The Hardest Tour I Have Ever Made

KEITH MACGOWAN

Macgowan, an infantry officer, fought through the horror of Passchendaele and survived. His two letters, one very anodyne to his

mother, the other more graphic to his father, describe the battle and say much about social attitudes of 1917.

October 31 1917 — Belgium — (letter # 59)

Dearest Mother:

Am out of the line again and glad to be so. We have had the hardest tour I have ever made and are still bombed nightly. Our air service is very poor here and gave us no protection in the line. Raley and Jimmie Scott both got Blighties and so did Frank Clark who was with us. He was a fine little officer and I hope he won't have to come back. Poor old Hinkesman who was one of my chums and is one of the group I sent you was killed. We were in a bad hole and he and Allsopp and I had a consultation and they left me to return to their company. Poor old Hinck was shot through the head. I was very much cut up about him but had too much work on hand at that time to think of anything but the situation.

I have received two letters from you and one from Helen and was so glad to hear that you had had such a good trip to Victoria. I also had a letter from Father.

Leave has been extended to 14 days and is coming along well. With luck I should be due again in about a month. Anytime after 3 months and I came back hear Aug 25th.

The Italian situation certainly looks bad to me and I hope that it will be straightened out. We can't afford slaps like that.

I hope that we won't have another tour here but one can never tell.

Give my love to everyone and I will try and run over to see you all if an opportunity presents itself.

Lovingly yours,
Keith

October 31 1917—Belgium—(letter #59B to Father)

Dear Father:

I am going to give you a general description of our last tour. I can not give you any names of places etc. but will speak only of my own experiences which I believe is perfectly in order.

You know that we were billeted in a farm. It surely looked good to us after we had left it as it was the last we saw of comfort. On the morning of the 21st we had reveille at 3:30am and pulled out onto the road by 6. Thence by motor bus, again by foot, and finally through a town to our camp for that night. Fritz was slamming very heavy stuff into the town and we got mixed up with one of them. We were given an area and everyone dug a hole. We got an old tent and hoped for fine weather. It rained like blazes and at daybreak all tents had to be struck to avoid observation from the air. We existed that morning and in the afternoon moved forward. The area was one of the most desolate one I have seen. The wastage was frightful and the ground strewn with everything which moves into a battle area.

We got to our area in the evening and for the next two days we were there and the weather was frightful. Wind and rain.

Knowing that there would be trouble getting supplies forward I got everything well in hand and had all ammunition etc. correct and water bottles filled and managed to carry in 30 tins of water. All this time there was heavy artillery fire and our transport roads were being heavily shelled. The work went on steadily. Streams of men, horses, mules and motor transport and limbers moved up and back on the double. No trenches. Everything done overland. We moved further forward the evening of the 25th and it was quite clear and bright. There was to be a show early next morning so we dug ourselves in as we were support troops and Bailey and I dug a hole about 5 feet in diameter and put a tarpaulin over it. During the night the rain came on.

Nov.2nd.—Excuse the jump but orders came to move forward again so we entrained and are again in the confounded area though some six miles behind the lines. Now to resume—and of all the uncomfortable places and frozen chaps I ever saw that place and our boys were the worst. We were on high ground and could see well forward. The country was undulating and nothing on it save the "German Pill Boxes." Concrete emplacements and shelters constructed so as to cover the whole country. From the time we arrived in the country our artillery had kept up an incessant roar. Day and night. It became very tiresome as the vibration in our little place was a corker. The gunners were having their troubles. Pushing forward in the open. No emplacements or cover and the mud was bad.

We were both up by zero hour and I had just managed to get a little better than half rations for the men as our mule train had been hit by shells. We watched the show until the smoke hid all movement. Fritz of course filled the air with fireworks and his artillery and machine gun was beyond description.

I shall never forget the 26th, 27th, and 28th of Oct. if I live to be a hundred. At intervals the battle field would clear a bit and we could see our troops running here and there.

We waited for orders to go up. One by one our other companies stood to and silently moved over the ridge out of sight. We spent the day there eating a bit of cold bully and stuff full of mud and water. It was all most disgusting but one ate heartily. Funny things cropped up on all sides in spite of the uncomfortable conditions. I saw a chap standing in his mud hole, shaving. It made a queer picture in the rain and shell fire.

At 5pm we got orders to go forward and relieve a company of another battalion. We set out through the mud. As we went over the ridge an SOS went up in front of us and both artillery opened up to full speed again. We trudged on through the mud and the boys did well. We had trouble from one or two shells of course but the soft ground saved us considerably. Arriving at our destination we could find no one to relieve, they had gone forward. We got the company into a fighting position (as we did not know what the SOS meant) and sent runners to the nearest H.Q. to report and get orders and to find out who we were now under. About dark we were ordered to move up onto high ground on the right. We did so through heavy mud. We had one man mired, but got him out, and the odd casualty.

Arriving here Bailey got orders to push his company forward. About three different O.C.'s all had a crack at us I believe that day. He left me in charge and took guides, going forward to reconnoiter. In the course of an hour the guides were back to me. I was ordered to move the company forward in a wave. This appeared tommy rot and impossible but not knowing the situation I did it. The men were pretty well all in and I was carrying the load of one chap then. We got forward and connected up with our B.Co'y Bailey and the O.C. B.Co'y then pushed the line still farther out and we placed four posts to watch our left flank. The hun did not seem to be strong but he shot a couple of

flares very close. I learned that B.Co'y had no one on the right. Australians were on that side but patrols could find no one. Our left was
in the air by over 800 yards and we were a long way ahead of our other
troops.

An officer came up and said we would have to go back. There was
an argument between this chap and Bailey also the B.Co'y. The result
was that Bailey turned the Co'y over to me with orders to fight to a
finish and he and this other fellow went back to straighten the matter
out. The hun became stronger every minute and the rain had cleared
away leaving a bright moon behind me with a distinct skyline I could
not avoid.

Sniping machine gun fire became so that we had to jump from one
place to another. We had a few men killed and got a few huns. The
O.C. B. Hinckesman, his second, and I had a consultation and they left
me. Poor Hinckesman was killed going back to their company. Midnight came and the enemy getting stronger. I got a report that he was
coming over on one of my posts. I did not think this likely so issued
orders that they were to fight and, if forced to, to fall back on our line.
Everyone stood to and we waited for we knew not what. I had a hun
prisoner over whom I placed a man with orders to put a bullet through
his head upon the first sign of an engagement. The false alarm died
away and about 1am the O.C. Co'y came up and said he had orders to
me to retire. By this time retirement was a very difficult thing but the
men were too tired to dig in and I knew that by daylight we would be
picked off one by one. I got my officers together and arranged with
B.Co'y so that we could cover each other and we got back losing a few
but not many. Just before we started [the next part has been censored
but readable] Bailey came back to me and from that time until the end
of the tour he acted like a boy. It was the first time I was ever disgusted
with him in the line. I could not get him to attend to things and while
he was there I had no authority. . . . however, we got back to a trench
line behind a ridge but really too low on it to be of much use. I saw one
chap shot in the head on the way back. Lowe one of our company officers and I were both watching him go back and the bullet actually
sparked in the dark when it hit him on the head.

At 2am I found that our rations had not arrived I took a runner and
we started for advanced H.Q. After traveling for a time we arrived

back at our starting point. In a new area and not a landmark, also only a general idea as to where we wanted to go. Took a new runner and set out again. Fritz began to shell. We had to run and take shelter and run again. We were twisted about until it was impossible to say where you were. The moon had gone down and the country a sea of mud holes. We found piece of trench at 4:30am and slept under a ground sheet until 6 when I got my bearings and arrived at my destination at 7am, found my rations and made the front line again on the jump by daylight.

On the 27th he shelled us pretty hard and his planes were over us constantly. Our air service disgusted me absolutely. That night we pushed our men out to the top of the ridge and they dug in. Frank Clark left me to go on duty and got a bullet in the arm which broke it and entered the thigh. He started out after being dressed but it is an awful job to get out over six miles of that waste through fire. He made it the next day. Before we shoved our men forward Fritz gassed us. Threw the shells to our back area and the wind brought it to us. He was trying for the batteries I think. When the stuff struck me I gave the alarm and we all climbed into masks. Your eyes hurt and the nose runs badly, the throat and lungs also feel it if you get enough. We again had difficulty in getting our rations on the morning of the 28th and all my 30 tins of water had been lost. He commenced to shell us the night of the 27th but I slept fairly well except when we had to get out altogether. On the afternoon of the 28th he shelled us intensely. Our support was the only one he knew as his artillery had not yet found our front line. I thought I had seen shell fire but I know now I never had before. Very heavy stuff crashed in all afternoon. I got Bailey to make as many men as possible crawl from the support to the front line. We stayed with the remainder. It was simply hell. There was nothing to do and we just sat and talked each one wondering whether the next had our names on it. Lowe was partly buried and we had to dig a couple of others out but on the whole we were very lucky. No money could get me to go through such an afternoon again.

Our relief came in about 8pm and after the company had gone I took Lowe whose leg was very sore and we started on our tramp out. We were very thirsty and I finally salvaged a petrol tin half full of water but it tasted like turpentine. We had a good long drink and filled our bottles. It was a long hard six miles but we got to the duck walk and would have done well but Fritz shelled us with gas so we had to walk in respirators. You don't know what that means at night but take my word for it that next to being blinded it comes first. Twice we ran into heavy gas but came through without trouble. My lungs and stomach troubled me a bit afterwards but I think it is mostly cold as we were constantly wet and no fire. As we came to the transport lines a blooming gun fired just as we were approaching. It had a 20 ft. flash at least and slapped us on the chest nearly knocking us over by air alone. I called to the gunner to know what size he had there. He replied 9.2 and carried on.

I met Chic Robertson on the road as I got in. Their unit had not been up. We had something to eat and went to bed. Fritz dropped bombs around carelessly but I was looking for sleep and got it. The next morning we moved out by train and were supposed to be through here but after being bombed for two nights where we were we went back. We are at our old transport base. I have hopes of seeing the end of this place in two or three days.

This country is frightful. Everything gone and the people are worse than that French peasant by far. We pay enormous prices for everything and generally can't buy at any price.

The above is not written carefully and has been done as I could find time. It will not give you any idea of what the actual thing looked like I am afraid. Someday however, if you keep this for a reminder I shall describe the thing a little more clearly.

In a letter some time ago I mentioned an Englishman we have here who is the funniest thing out. He nearly shot a couple of pigeons the other day, and would have bagged them had he had a shotgun, before he realized that they were communication carriers. Oh he's some kid.

Must stop now. Hope to get leave in about a month and it is now 14 days instead of 10. Sloan is on leave now.

With love to all I am.

Your affectionate son,

Keith

A Stout Effort in the Air, 1917

WILBERT C. GILROY

4 Squadron R. F. C.
B. E. F. France
30/10/17

My Dear Mother:

Yesterday the parcel which was posted Oct 5th arrived in good shape. It was most welcome, too. It came just a couple of hours before I had to go up and so I had Joe make me a hot cup of cocoa. I had been up twice before during the morning and had missed my lunch so that it was doubly welcome. Then when I came down after my last trip (4th) it was quite dark and raining and, believe me, I was cold, so I had another bowl of it. . . .

I was surprised and delighted to see Alfred the other day. He rode into the acrodrome on horseback and I happened to be standing right at the entrance at the time. He looks very well but a little tired I thought. I had lunch served in my room so we had it together. We also had quite a nice chat. He was just resting a day while his battery were taking up a position nearby. I made him change his boots and socks, which were wet, and gave him fresh socks and a pair of good strong field boots that I had ready for him. So he will have a better chance to keep some of the wet out. It is his first turn in this part of the country and I hope he soon gets back to his own part again. He was feeling quite good, as his letters and etc were beginning to come after such a long delay while he was in various hospitals etc.

I felt quite a novice at flying yesterday. It was nearly two weeks since I had been up in a machine. About 12 days ago while I was on photography I ran into a bunch of three Huns. I missed my escort somehow, or else they failed to show up. Anyway, I had to go over alone. When I got over 3 scouts were there to greet me. Of course, I was scared stiff but it was too late to turn back so I did the unexpected and dived on the nearest one. I took him quite unawares, so I got my old machine going at about 100 or 110 m.p.h. and when within about

100 feet of him I pulled the trigger. But you can imagine how I felt when it didn't work. However, I don't think I felt any worse than he did. I saw his face and it was anything but pleasant. He saw at once that I was helpless so he got ready for a go at me, but just then a gust of wind got under one of his wings and before he had recovered I made a quick turn and my machine gunner in the rear seat got busy, and in less than 15 seconds he had 80 rounds into him and he went down. We saw no more of him. But the other two then came on and by attacking us from both sides at once, they gave us a busy time. My gunner was splendid and kept them off but they certainly got a few shots into the bus. I guess I turned the old machine upside down and into all shapes but it had the right effect anyway. Early in the scrap I got a bullet into my right leg, but it did not bother me much, and it was not until I was nearly home that my leg felt numb. At any rate we got our photos and landed alright, which are the main things. My gunner worked the camera with his feet while he kept the Huns off with the gun. Quite a stout effort on his part, don't you think? After I had finished lunch I got a tender and went to the Hospital (Canadian) where I knew all the doctors and had leg dressed and X-rayed. It was in there alright but pretty deep into the flesh so I decided not to have it cut open, so it is still there. I did not stay at hospital but they insisted on my going to bed, so I came home to my own bed and stayed there for 3 or 4 days. Since then I have been getting around with a cane. But I am O.K. again now, and flying as usual.

If I had stayed at hospital you should probably have received one of those tactless cables from the W[ar] O[ffice]. So as it is you have nothing to worry about now. Of course, I have lots of every-day experiences which I sometimes don't mention because there is no need to worry about things which are past. When I get back I will tell you all about it if you like. That is if there is anything worth telling.

We are all quite depressed tonight as one of our best pilots was brought down today by one of our own shells. It is hard luck to be hit by our own, isn't it? I had a similar experience about two weeks ago. A 6" shell went thru my planes, cutting away my flying wires on one side but it did not explode, so I got down alright. It certainly puts the wind up one at the time, though.

Must close now and have dinner. I am in the pink & feel absolutely fit. Lots of love for Father, Em & self.

Loving son,

Wilbert

Until You Hear from Me Again

JOHN ALLEN HUNTER
CHAPLAIN J.S. DARCEY

General Hospital No. 18
B.E.F. France
Nov. 10 — 1917

Dear George:—

Just a few lines. I'm feeling alright but thought I would write you. I have written to Dad, Lill, and Mag.

I'm hit in legs, left arm and back and will be in Blighty soon.

So long until you hear from me again.

Your loving brother

JA

Per Chaplain J.S. Darcey

General Hospital No. 18
B.E.F. France
Nov. 10, 1917

886528 Pte. Geo. Hunter
28th Can. Co.

Dear Sir:—

I enclose a note dictated by your brother J.A. Hunter who came here as a patient yesterday. You will prize it for it was dictated by him when he was dying. I don't know whether he knew it or not. His breath was coming short. I repeated the 23rd Psalm and the Lord's Prayer & he said them after me word for word. His spine was injured and he had no chance. He was a fine boy. God comfort and keep you. Your brother will be buried in the Etaples Military Cemetery.

Yours Sincerely,

J.S. Darcey W.S.A. Chaplain

A Hot Fight, November 1917

LIEUTENANT ANDREW WILSON

> *Wilson's letter to his wife in Rosetown, Saskatchewan, is unusually graphic in its details of casualties at Passchendaele. Being an officer, he was ordinarily not subject to censorship.*

Somewhere . . . Nov. 14, 1917

This is Tuesday afternoon, and the first moment I have had to myself for six days. I am glad to say I am alive and feeling physically as fit as ever. We went up into the danger zone on Thursday afternoon last and from 8 P.M. that night, until Monday noon, we were in constant danger. We had to dig ourselves into holes on Thursday night, but fortunately got well dug in before Fritz began shelling us. He piled over some odd thousands of shells that night, and we lost a few men. I had six of my platoon buried, but four of them got out. Then on Friday morning our guns opened, and Fritz came back with the worst artillery duel ever put on this front, so they tell us. We lay flat in our holes, until 9 A.M. when we had to pull out to support the front line, and it was some little hell getting up through a foot of mud and water. I lost two boys going up. We dug in again, in bunches, and I worked like a miner to get lower down. I lost my Major about 10 A.M. and lay in a shell hole with his body for six hours. It rained half the time too, and we had to keep digging to keep warm. That night was miserable. We had to stand in mud and water up to our knees, and I surely thought I would die from exposure, but it is surprising what a person can stand when he has to. That was the longest night I ever put in. Had to stand still in this hole and shiver with cold and wet. Saturday morning Fritz let up a little on shelling, but for 24 hours it was a living hell.

Throughout Saturday it was not so bad, and I moved around a little and got something to eat. We were all too miserable to eat on Friday. On Saturday evening, I had to pull my platoon out to the front line— or rather the new advance line—and hold a post for two hours, until relieved by the incoming Battalion. I only had nine men and I carried the machine gun myself. We were not bothered at all, here, although only about 300 yards from Fritz. I found a Scotch man and a Canadian of another battalion, and brought them with me. Also found a Welsh boy badly wounded and fixed him up the best we could and reported him to the dressing station. I cannot begin to describe the awfulness of war and wouldn't if I could. The most pitiable scenes I noticed were the wounded men, one of my own boys got hit in the leg and he made a fierce "how-do-you-do." I rolled him into a shell hole and told him to lie still until the shelling let up a bit. He got out later. Little Clyde Machan of Rosetown, was hit in the throat by a chunk of shell, and buried. They dug him out but found him dead. Jim Castle was taken out badly shell shocked, and Silmarie of Herschel was wounded. I think that is all of my old Rosetown Platoon, that was in the show. We were relieved Saturday night, and pulled out. Had to walk six miles in mud and water, and our feet were almost gone. We slept in tents that night, or what remained of it, and were roused up Sunday morning, to move further back. While fussing around a Hun plane came over and dropped a bomb, and wounded four men, and one of my company officers. This made eleven officers wounded and three killed out of 20 who went in, so only six of us came out without a scratch. I felt safe throughout the show. Somehow I felt sure I was coming through it alright, but just the same I believe the earnest prayers of relatives and friends were heard, and answered, and I don't deny I uttered many a humble prayer myself, throughout the long hours. I cannot tell you w[h]ere we were, but ask Will Van Allen where he lost his arm. We were in this vicinity, but further advanced probably six miles. This morning the battalion has gone by busses further back. I am orderly officer of the day, and am left to clean up and load baggage. Have one Sgt. and nine men also three prisoners. We may get away today, but it may be tomorrow. Anyway, we are out of danger and comfortable. The men are as cheerful as can be, but only half of them here. The death list is not as heavy as usual, though. The mud was so deep that shells did not have the usual danger zone. I had several shells burst within 20 feet of me and nothing more than mud or tiny bits of steel hit me. My Major was hit by a sniper, and only lived a few minutes. I took his pocket book, revolver, and other valuables and carried them for three days with me. You may remember Pringle, the colonel's chauffeur at N. B. He was killed by a shell. Only a few of the 232nd boys were killed.

I firmly believe that the Almighty will guard me throughout this struggle, and that I am to be spared to return.

General Currie on Conscription, November 1917

LIEUTENANT-GENERAL SIR ARTHUR CURRIE

> *In the summer of 1917, Parliament passed the Military Service Act, and soon an election, to be fought largely on this measure, was called for December 17. The commander of the Canadian Corps offered his thoughts on the necessity of compulsory service.*

30 November 1917

I am glad to hear you say that in your opinion the opponents of the Military Service Act will not have an opportunity of upsetting it. I feel that any interference with its provisions, or any delay in its operation will mean the death of this Corps. I feel that months have already been wasted, and even if the men who are being called up now are got into training at once we shall need them very badly before they will be fit to send. If they don't come at all within three months I feel that this Corps may still consist of four Divisions, but of probably only nine Battalions each; in six months, it would probably consist of only two Divisions, and in a year from now not more than one. It would suffer not only by reason of its loss in numbers but in the loss of morale of those remaining. The men who are here now are committed until peace is declared. If no others are sent to help them they can look forward to nothing else but to be killed or permanently maimed. Many of our men have already been wounded three or four times, yet the exigencies of the service demand that they be again sent to the firing line.

The death struggle is approaching, and if Canada neglects to put forth her full strength in that struggle such an action can be considered not only a desertion of the men in the trenches, but a desertion of the Empire as well. The Empire is fighting for its life, and must see this thing through. If we do not play our part, we cannot hold up our heads in honour at its conclusion, no matter what that conclusion is. Furthermore, I believe the withholding of men at the present time might have a great influence on the situation in Australia and South Africa. I believe the fate of the Empire is at stake, and I cannot believe that the people of Canada for one minute understand the true situation. I know that they have been deceived. They have been constantly told that Canada has raised 450,000 men; they assume that these men are capable of taking their places in the firing line; they have all studied arithmetic, and when they add the number who are serving in France to the number who have become casualties, and subtract that total from this 450,000, they naturally conclude that there must still be a couple of hundred thousand available for service. What they have not been told is that out of that 450,000 probably 100,000 were no use. If they add to that 100,000 the number who disappear through sickness and what we call the normal wastage, they will find that there are at present time very, very few available for reinforcements.

Not a Window Anywhere: The Halifax Explosion, December 1917

LAMBERT GRIFFITH

A sailor stationed at HMCS Niobe in Halifax harbour, Griffith survived the great explosion on December 6, and in this letter to his wife in Esquimalt, British Columbia, he recounts his wartime tale.

Sunday 16 Dec
HMCS Niobe
Mess No 9.

My darling;

I am just writing you . . . to let you know I am all right. Your letter of Dec the 2nd arrived all right. I am very anxious to get a letter from you, letting me know how the news of the great explosion was received in

Victoria. You poor old love, you must have had a scare. Never mind a miss is as good as a mile, & by this time you will have got my letter, written a couple of days after. We have been worked half dead ever since & have only had shore leave for the last three days & that only, from five P.M. I got special leave to go up town on Thurs the 14 at 2:30 & have only been up once since. What a sight it is. Not a window anywhere. All the theatres closed & used for hospitals. Y.M.C.A. and Union Jack Club the same. There is no place now to write letters, so we are better off on board. I wrote to father & told him that I was safe. We have been on the *Niobe* now for two weeks. Tomorrow Mon we are going back on the boom & will quite likely be left there for two weeks. I shall be glad to get out of all the work & be able to do some washing & c. We have hardly had time to wash ourselves, let alone clothes. From ships coming in I am told that the explosion was felt *60 miles* away. Fancy me on the *Niobe* only about 300 yds having such a wonderful escape. The devil looks after his own as they say. Talking about escapes, I have just had another letter from father. He had word that Will had been wounded badly. After waiting two weeks, he had a letter from Will himself saying that he had come thru a big charge & was the *only* officer not killed or badly wounded in his battalion. He is now going to be made Pay master with the rank of Captain. He will now have a bomb proof job & I hope now be out of all danger & will not have any more trenches to go in. I am very glad & am sure that you will be as well. He is now a big man. I will write you again from the boom I am trying to write this on the mess deck & it is very hard with all the row & shaking. The terrible accident has quite taken my mind off the great disappointment of getting turned down from Ottawa. Of course the *Niobe* has been badly smashed, but she saved our lives. Just the greatest luck. Hundreds were killed in their houses miles away. Even poor little children in their schools. No doubt you will read all about it in the papers. Hundreds of coffins in the streets. There is to be a big funeral tomorrow about 400 unidentified bodies to be buried. Thank God a hundred times that you & the dear little girls were not here. I wrote to the H. Office of the Sun Life in Montreal about the loan on the Policy. I will look after that. I expect that they will be glad to know that I am alive. There will be no Xmas here as it is a city of sorrow. Poor children without parents & c. We will get no leave. Do what you can old love &

I will try & send some thing later on. If I pay the int on the loan & $8 on principal (Life have not been thru' anything so awful in my life). We have been working so hard that I for one have not had time to realize what I have escaped. The dead are just laid out anywhere. I saw a basket on the jetty this morning & in it was a little baby, quite dead. Next to it was a stoker with his face all crushed in. I need not say any more. I have never seen death in this form before. I am sure that for ten minutes we have all been thru' worse than in the trenches. The whole town is a wreck even the roof off the station. A German fleet could not have done so much damage. An Imperial cruiser was just on the other side of us in the stream & they have lost their Commander & about 45 men. All the wood work on board the *Niobe* has been shattered & water cut off. The day after the accident it blew a blizzard & made rescue more difficult, but kept down the fire. Lots of ships have been sunk. The Belgian boat that caused the explosion is lying on her side on the opposite shore. The new YMCA in the yard of course is a complete wreck like everything else. I don't suppose I shall go up town till I return from the boom. Well darling, we have lots to be thankful for after all. There will be no Xmas leave now. Unless one went away there would be no where to go. Even the theatres are wrecked. Well love there are lots more details I could go on to but just as well not to.

Write soon to your lucky old Lofty. Every minute I thought I was dead.

Ever your loving hubby

Bert

xxxx

We'll be working pretty near night & day for a long time yet.

It Was the End of the World: Halifax Destroyed, December 1917

FRED LONGLAND

> *Longland, who was a junior officer posted on HMCS* Niobe, *wrote his account of events years later. The sense of immediacy remains strong, the details vivid.*

In due course I found myself back in Halifax at the end of October 1917, reporting to the "Niobe" for draft again. . . .

So here I was . . . reporting to the Drafting Officer. "Chippy" Carpenter was an old shipmate of mine and the next few minutes were happily spent in reminiscences and light-hearted conversation. Happening to glance through a porthole I noticed a ship inbound for the anchorage at Bedford Basin, and remarked to "Chippy," "There's no doubt about the nationality of that vessel; look at the size of her flag." I left him and found my way up to the boat deck to take another look at the ship with the large flag at her stern. She was "Mont Blanc," a French vessel arriving from Galveston, Texas with a load of explosives, 3,500 tons of T.N.T. and 3,000 tons of lyddite, as well as a deck cargo of benzol contained in steel drums, a very dangerous cargo. By this time I had returned to the upper deck to take another look and found "Mont Blanc" well advanced towards the Narrows, the entrance to Bedford Basin, and at the same time a Belgian Relief ship in ballast outward bound was coming out. Maybe it was due to the latter being in ballast and so not answering her helm, but she appeared to lose steerage-way, and I could see at once, unless some miracle intervened, there would be a collision, and so it happened.

This was serious, and I moved to the forecastle deck for a better view. The next thing was a series of minor explosions as the benzol drums ignited and exploded. By this time the fire had begun to get a serious hold, and a large column of black smoke rose from the deck of the stricken ship. I stepped on a bollard and placed my hands on the shoulders of a chief petty officer to steady myself.

Practically the whole ship's company had assembled on the forecastle as the word "ship on fire" got around, and I thought "There's going to be trouble here before long unless I am very much mistaken." I turned to Jock standing next to me and said "They'll never put that fire out" and I had hardly spoken the words when there was a blinding flash, an awful shudder, and a bang which made me think it was the end of the world. I felt as though I had been hit in the face with a big flat board. There was a momentary stillness, and then boiler tubes, rivets, and jagged steel plate from the hull were flying all around us. I saw a large piece hit the foremost funnel of our ship and completely flatten it; flying debris destroyed our other three funnels. It was imperative to take cover quickly but I could find none as the crowd on the forecastle deck must have thought the same. Every conceivable hole and corner was occupied; some were even hanging down ventilators. There was nothing else for me to do but to run the whole length of the deck to reach the after companion-way when I would be behind armour and safe. But the explosion had caused a large tidal wave to sweep across the harbour, lifting our ship to an acute angle and throwing me down violently on the steel deck. I had to crawl the rest of the way and thankfully reached the shelter of the after deck badly bruised.

What an unholy mess the main deck was in; 19 men lay dead without a mark of any kind on them and the wounded crowded the sick bay for attention. One poor fellow was bleeding to death and nothing could save him. It seems he suffered from that condition known as haemophilia when even a cut finger can be serious.

By noon the ship was on an even keel but adrift from her moorings. Willing hands rectified this, and a little order began to appear out of complete chaos. The scene in the harbour was unbelievable. Cargo ships partially wrecked, drifted about out of control; the Belgian Relief ship "Imo" involved in the collision, had been flung so far up on the Dartmouth beach that it took expert engineering to get her back in the sea again. A large tug-boat was reposing on No. 2 Pier dropped there by the tidal wave. Four large cargo ships were complete wrecks with their middles cut out as though by a giant scythe.

I was detailed now to take a platoon and look for dead sailors on the streets, and in the schools which had been turned into morgues. The bodies just as they were picked up, were in the boy's side of the school, and when cleaned up a bit were laid out in the girl's side for identification. It was my job to go into the streets and wherever I saw a pair of bell-bottomed pants, to heave out the remainder and lay it on one side.

At the end of this gruesome task, I returned to the ship and had a much needed brandy in the wrecked wardroom. Then in walked a Commander who said "Does anyone know of an officer called Longland?" I stood up and said "Yes Sir, that is my name." Then he said "There is a man in Victoria Hospital Emergency ward, badly hurt and in his extremity keeps on calling out your name. Have you any idea who it is?" I replied "No Sir, but I will go along and see." On reaching the hospital I was taken to where this man lay but could not recognise him at all. He was pitted all over with what looked like bits of cinder, and was a nasty yellow colour. I was very puzzled when he started repeating my name, and could not make head or tail of it and had to go away. For three weeks he was in a state of coma but when he became conscious, the hospital advised me and I went down there again. He was sitting up in bed and nearly normal. He said to me "Hello Fred" and I found him to be a youthful friend of mine, the son of the Post-master at Waterloo. He had remembered where I was serving and in his extremity had called my name. This man caused a real sensation in Halifax. He was the chief officer of the cargo ship just moored ahead of us but I had no idea at all he was anywhere near, else I would have gone to see him. The force of the explosion disembowelled his ship, killed most of the crew and the Captain and blew him 150 yards on to a grass plot in the dockyard, where he landed naked except for one boot and a sock.

On my way back to the ship I was hailed by an undertaker and asked if I could identify an officer he had collected on the road. I found it was Rod Burnett the carpenter, without a mark of any kind on him. It seems that a concussion of this kind causes a bubble to form in the blood stream with fatal consequences.

I had hardly returned to the ship, when news was received that the ammunition dump in the dockyard was ringed with fire and in great danger. Volunteers were called for and practically everyone who could respond, including myself did so, and all the ammunition was removed by hand to safety.

By now it was evening, and the sky looked overcast and ominous. Soon it began to snow, becoming worse as the wind rose to a gale. By the time it was dark, we were in the middle of the worst gale I have ever lived through, a real Canadian blizzard. There was further danger now in the harbour. Ships out of control were drifting about with the ebb and flow of the tide; I have never experienced anything like it. Halifax has a large harbour and now it was just like a wild sea. Particularly dan-gerous were two partially wrecked vessels on fire, one with a cargo of black gunpowder. We simply had to secure this ship, wandering up and down and from side to side in the middle of the harbour, as there was the possibility of another explosion. In such a crowded area, it would have been another disaster.

Eventually, she was secured. When we went aboard we found that only one bulkhead door separated the fire door from the explosive cargo.

The cruiser "Highflyer" anchored in the middle of the harbour and just back from convoy escort, was in a bad way. Her funnels and part of the upper deck were stove in and her casualties were 25 men killed and many wounded. The Lieut-Commander was on the bridge watching "Mont Blanc" burning when the explosion happened and was decapitated. The lower part of his body was shielded by armour but his head was exposed to the blast. Her picket boat carrying fire-fighting apparatus, must have reached the doomed ship just as the explosion occurred. Our own picket boat under Boatswain Mattison left with the same object in view; both have never been seen since. The two crews were awarded posthumously Royal Albert Medals.

The French 75 mm gun on the stern of "Mont Blanc" was found six miles away, on the other side of the North West Arm, and the anchor three miles away. . . .

When the hard weather set in, stray dogs became a problem which the naval patrol keeping order in the ravaged city had to tackle. The dogs were living on human carrion and were as savage as wolves. Volunteers to shoot them were called for and many were destroyed.

A Nursing Sister Near the Front, May 1918

NURSING SISTER KATHERINE MACDONALD

This brief letter home was Nursing Sister MacDonald's last. She was killed in a German bombing raid on her hospital the next day.

May 18, 1918

Dear Mums & Sis:

How are you all to-day say this paper belongs to someone very nice dont you think, here it is Saturday again and another nice day my the weather is grand hope it continues because it is so nice.

I suppose we will have another big push again hope they make one grand one and finish but dont worry we are far from harm.

Listen do you know that canned meat you sent me do you think you could get any more I cannot get any here it is just splendid I forget what it was called in fact destroyed the can's.

So far have not had any more word about the transfer of course it may not come for a month but am looking for it any day now.

Everything must be so nice when it is all out but that grass is another question. Can you not get a boy to cut it every week for you.

I expect to get another bunch of letters from you soon because there was a big bunch of Canadian mail in last night and mine always comes in later because it goes to Calais first but am looking for it any-day now hope a lot comes.

Now my dear this means one every day for weeks surely you get my letters now should get a lot no letter from Tom last night again I wonder what is wrong.

I went over to the cemetary last night they have millions burried some Canadians but did not know any of them at all lots of officers and 2—V.A.D.s & the officers have graves to themselves but the privates are two in a grave, each have a wodden cross at the head & all are fixed up nicely.

With love
Katherine

Cracking the Hindenburg Line, August 1918

IVAN CLARK MAHARG

This superb letter by a young officer describes his unit's efforts in the Battle of Arras, one of the decisive blows struck by the Canadian Corps. Its author was killed one month later.

"Behind the lines"
France, Friday
August 30th/18.

Dear Folks:—

According to my diary it is ten days since I last wrote you (Aug. 20th). Since then I have been as a man in one long dream, days of which were pleasant others not so pleasant. It is now 8:45 P.M. & we are visiting in a small village about ten miles behind our front line. We marched twelve kilometres since two o'clock this afternoon & we are all pretty tired. Our Coy. Left the front line at 3 A.M. on 29th (yesterday) & marched back over the country which we had taken from the Hun in our rush of Aug. 26th–28th gee we were all in but kept going with only one rest until we landed in a big city on the western front about 8:30 A.M. Had breakfast & tumbled into our rolls & I slept right thru till they ordered me up to go on a billeting party at 6 P.M. It was an awful rush & I piled out & went billeting & I hadn't had so much as a wash, let alone a shave, for a whole week. We stayed in cellars last night on account of the usual long range shelling out the town we were in.

I guess by now you will have gleaned from my letter that I have been in a scrap. Well you are right & a real scrap it was too. Not a case of into the line to hold the trench, but rather, over the top after only one hour in the front line & a rush in the dark & on into daylight right through until noon. In this time we found we had reached our final objective & had pushed forward five miles. Gee but it was sure some initiation for me, but the hardest part of it all was that first single hour of waiting until our barage opened up at 3 A.M. and we jumped off. It was a grand advance & our barage was wonderful. The artillery gave us a gun for every 12 yards of our front so you can imagine that when they opened up on the hun front line it was too late to give instructions to anyone. If I had shouted in anyone's ear they wouldn't have known I was speaking at all. As well as our artillery barrage our Divisional Machine gun battalion put up their barrage too. They made so much noise whistling over our heads that the Boche shells bursting around us were hardly noticeable as regards their noise.

Well, I could go on for hours talking about the bally thing but I must mention our casualties. The Hun seemed to be depending upon the large number of his machine guns rather than his artillery to hold us back. About ⅓ of the distance to our objective we came under heavy machine gun fire just crossing a high ridge known as "Orange hill." The "Imperials" on our left (across the Scarpe river) were much slower in there advance than ourselves & the hun was firing from a wood across the river right into our left flank. We at once sized up the situation & hurried forward & down into the valley. It was on the top of this ridge that we had the only officer in our Coy. killed. It was a Mr. Shannon who was in charge of #4 Platoon. He was shot through the head with a machine gun bullet so never really knew what happened. The poor fellow had just returned from leave & was just aching to get into another scrap. I am sorry that I have to mention poor *Carey McKee was among the list of killed*. He went forward with "B" Coy. just ahead of us. They reached their first, second, & final objective (the town of Monchy) with only a few casualties. The hun by this time seemed absolutely up in the air & was evacuating & leaving everything behind in his endeavor to escape our . . . rush. The opposition seemed so slight that the company instead of stopping pushed on past the town & into the open. As far as I know Carey was still with them. In front of them there was another small wood & apparently the enemy had it full of machine guns. Here he made his stand, & opened up such a heavy fire that "B" Coy. had to retire at once to where they could get a line of trenches for cover. They suffered heavily coming back but soon got settled down in a bunch of shell holes. One of the officers (M. Wilson of "B" Coy.) told me that McKee, his Sergt. & two men got into a shell hole together. In another shell hole close bye they had seen a wounded R.C.R. soldier. The latter seemed to be suffering very much so Carey got up to move over & see if the fellow's wounds had been dressed just as a large shell burst right on top of his same shell hole. Carey, the Sergt. & the wounded man were killed outright so none of them had any suffering to hear. The other two men were badly wounded. I know about where he was buried the same day & I think our Padre has erected a cross over his resting place. It is about two hundred yards to the north west of the Village of "Monchy." McKee was doing fine work here. It was his third time over the top & I guess he saw as much fighting as any man out here for the length of time that he was at it. His platoon had grown to look upon him as a chum & a leader & his Coy. officers respected him as a gentleman & a conscientious officer. I have thought of writing his people but perhaps if you showed them this it would do just as well. Use your own judgment about the matter.

We had seven officers killed & four wounded in all. I dont know how many N.C.O's & men we had casualties but not over 75 or 100 I think. I had #2 Platoon throughout & they did splendid work & respected every order given by myself even though it was my first fight. I had only three casualties in my platoon but they meant quite a loss as you will see. On the A.M. of 26th one of my men by name of Burgis was wounded while working as a stretcher bearer on Batt. Hqrs. On 27th I had no casuals & we took a breathing spell & kept the men in deep dugouts except for a post here & there along the trench just to watch the enemy's movements. On the afternoon of the 28th the batt. moved over to a position on the south side of Monchy to support an attack by the 43rd Camerons & 58th batt's. About 6 P.M. we advanced in artillery formation under a rather heavy high explosive and gas shell bombardment. I was at the head of the platoon with the Sgt. in rear. A N.E. shrapnel shell exploded just in rear of us & pieces of it wounded my Sgt. in the right forearm & my #1 man of my second Lewis gun crew just in the left shoulder blade. My senior corporal automatically became platoon Sgt. & #2 of the gun took charge of the Lewis gun. Our open formation certainly kept down our casualties.

Ralph West went out wounded but I guess he's allright as his brother Percy says he was a "walking" case. Russ Ferrier came through it O.K. & in the final stages was put on some important patrol work in no man's land. You can tell his people that he's "making good" here fast.

Well I'm pretty tired & footsore so will roll in. Hope to get time to finish this & get it off in the morning. "Bon Soir."

1 P.M. Saturday Aug. 31st.

Well I've just finished a good lunch of Pork & Beans, Tomatoes & potatoes, also sago pudding bread & tea. Even with that the officers are kicking at me for not feeding them fresh meat. Mr McKenzie is leaving at any time to take charge of our re-enforcements at the wing & I have been made Mess President. I have just given our "caterer" 20 francs to see if he cant find us some eats in this village. I doubt if he can, there's not much here. I had a dandy sleep last night & am feeling pretty well rested after our trip in the field.

We got 75 reinforcements in yesterday & among them was the lad who used to be Major Chenoweth's batman when we were in Quebec. He went to "C" Coy. but I am having him transferred today as the batman I have had is no "bonne." He can't even read or write. Sixty more men came in today so we are again filled up. Also six more officers came in, and one of them to my coy. so that puts me up a wee step higher as I am no longer the junior sub of the coy. Our seniority dates from time of joining the unit.

I had my platoon on parade for a couple of hours this A.M. We are putting through some promotions & my only Corporal is to become platoon Sergeant. An old 196th (#7 Platoon) boy who is a Lance Corporal with me will be made corporal & I am sending another old 196th boy down to take an N.C.O's course at the wing. I have three old 196th "B" Coy. lads in my platoon. One of them was in #8 with me but not for long. He joined up late in the summer at camp Hughes.

Mr. Young got a bunch of Bdn. Suns this morning so I will look them over as soon as I finish this letter. My last letter from you arrived . . . before I went into the line. I am looking for more any day now. I am keeping up my diary as best I can but I can't take it into the line so have to write it up from memory when I come out.

I have been wishing lately that some of my lost parcels would reach me. The ground was so badly cut up with shell holes after our advance that it was hard to get the rations up to us, the result that we went pretty hungry for a day or two. Now I'm trying to make up but can't even get filled up back here. I know that Eva sent me some parcels that never reached me. There may be some others too.

I was wishing that you could have seen my poor servant trying to get me a meal under fire. For a day & a half it was easy as we were down a dry dug-out & he could cook with ease. At other times he'd try to get me a pot of tea where we happened to pause in some trench or shell hole. Once he had a pretty fair looking meal ready to give me when a big shell burst so close that he kicked over the tea & spilt some bacon he was trying to fry. On another occasion he was all ready when the order suddenly came in to move forward. We had to move at once so no meal was had that time either.

I have a couple of little souvenirs here that a fine big Hun handed over "Tout de suite" on demand, such as a cap, shoulder strap of the 23rd (Skidoo) gunman battalion & his personal cigar case. In the next push I'll try & get you a real gunman watch or a compass. I may have a chance at a little revolver. The hard part is getting things out to you from here. If I could ship the things any way I'd furnish the den in my future home with Bosche helmets, guns, bayonets, machine guns, uniforms, respirators & dear knows what not. I think I'll drop a line to Geo. McL. Brown & see if he'll handle my goods. Ha! Ha! I'll try & find a hop this afternoon & send you the tunic cap & cigar case. The base censor may throw them away, there's no telling if he examines them.

Bye the way I wish you'd put me straight as to my assigned pay from February to August inclusive. They have been over-paying me and now I have to forfeit over $100 I expect, to make good the over-payment. It doesn't make much difference however as I need very little money to keep me going out here. The only thing is I'll need a surplus to see me through my leave when it comes.

One of our Capts went on leave yesterday & Capt. Petherick is likely to go any day now. If we make another try into the line it will likely be with Major Bradbrooke [?] the Coy. My first leave will hardly come before the new year. If I'm lucky it may come at Xmas but the old men will be given the foriference at Xmas I expect.

I still have your letters of July 29th or 31st written at Kenora. They are the last I have received. I have read them & find nothing in particular to answer. I have been busy this forenoon trying to get a pair of Tommies breeches from our Q.M. I have a pair on now but are too large. I'll have to try another pair. My first pair of officers breeches that I got with my uniform in Wpg. in Jan. 1917 I wore for the last time this trip in the line. They certainly lasted wonderfully. When I came out they were torn to pieces about the knees & I was about to fall right out of them at the seat. I discarded them yesterday in arras. I wore my tommies tunic through it all & some of the officers remarked as we were advancing "There's no chance of them sniping you as being an officer Maharg you're the toughest looking nut in the coy." I guess they were right too. It rained hard all through our advance & I was mud from tin lid to the studs on my boots. My maps got so wet that the paper surfaces rubbed off & made the features on the map unrecogniseable. I finally threw them away, they got so mussy. I carried a heavy pack with my trench coat in it & a bunch of rations & S.O.S flares as well as extra rounds of ammunition for my "gat." I thought it would be heavy but I never even knew I was carrying anything after we got moving.

There were other things more important to occupy my attention.

Well I think I'll ring off now or I'll never get finished. Heaps of love to all & if you have the necessaries send me a couple of nut loafs & do them up in a strong tin box.

M. XXXXXXXX Son Ivan

Oh, For Three Months' Leave . . .

LIEUTENANT LEWIS HONEY

> *Even the brave were tired of the war by September 1918. Honey's letters make clear his need for a respite, but eleven days after his last letter home, he died of wounds. Three days earlier he had won a Victoria Cross for knocking out machine guns, organizing his company's defences, and repelling four German counterattacks at Bourlon Wood.*

September 11, 1918

As you see, I haven't got away on leave yet, but I assure you that every day it is postponed only makes the thing more certain of coming in the end and I'll enjoy it all the more thoroughly.

I wish I could manage to get about three months leave to Canada but scarcely see how it's going to be managed. I've made a few inquiries on the side and about the only way of managing it is to have the application come from the Canadian end. It seems that if three or four influential citizens in Canada consider that it's time some soldier whom they know had leave they make statements of the reasons for said soldier getting leave and I suppose submit them to H.Q. at Ottawa or wherever that place may be and if the authorities consider these reasons sufficient, why the leave comes through. I believe quite a few are getting away on the grounds of business affairs requiring their attention, but, rack my brains as I may, I can't figure out any business proposition that requires my presence in Canada.

Of course I have a notion that nearly four years in the army, three of which have been spent overseas and the fact that I haven't been a dud should count for something, but it's not enough I fear.

I hope Dad's holiday did him good and I think mother should arrange something of the sort for herself now. There isn't much in the way of news. This is simply to let you know that I'm going strong. Will write again in a few days.

Love to all

Lew

September 19, 1918

There is very little in the way of news these days. We are working hard perfecting our organization which has been slightly shaken since the early part of August.

I don't blame you for giving up reading the casualty lists. It isn't pleasant reading and I don't see there is any advantage in it. If I get hurt you'll hear about it long before you see the lists and anyway I don't anticipate my luck changing. I dare say that I'll be going strong for the duration unless my job is finished before then and we never can tell when that time comes.

No leave has come through yet, but I've heard a rumour tonight that there's a large allotment in for the end of the month, so it's very likely that my next letter will be from Blighty.

Provided I have fine weather, its my intention to spend a couple days in London then move on to Edinburgh for a day; then up to Stirling; from there to Glasgow via Scott's country taking about five days for the trip; then a few days in Carlisle and then back to "la belle France."

I'm afraid I won't have any use for my skates this winter but just wait till the year after. I'll be skating all the time, to make up for the winters I've missed.

Love to all

Lew

My First Aerial Scrap, September 1918

WARREN HENDERSHOT

> *We met Hendershot's brother Charles earlier when he was in training in Toronto. Warren took his brother's advice to join the Royal Flying Corps. Unlike Charles, who died in training in England, Warren survived his few months in the air over France.*

19 Sqdn. France.
Mon. Sept 16/18

Dear Father & all,

Well how go things with you these days. I am sitting here in the mess all by myself. The rest of the chaps are away over the hun lines on a patrol. I should be there myself, but just at the last minute the oil pressure on my flight commanders bus went dud so he took mine, consequently I am here. "Thank the Lord."

Yesterday I saw my first aerial scrap. We were flying about fifteen or twenty miles over Hunland when five Hun "Pfalz" scouts came out of "no-where" and dived on two of our chaps that were lagging behind and am sorry to say that they got one of us tho in a way it was the chaps own fault. Contradictory to all laws of aerial fighting, he put his nose straight down and dived away from us. Of course being so far over the German side, the Huns followed him right down and we could do nothing at all. One of the flight commanders tried to help him out, but got a few bullets in his machine for the trouble.

Just about the time the scrap was on, my petrol gave out in the bottom tank. Well I immediately turned on the top tank and pumped up my pressure and started for the scrap. All at once I realized I had only fifteen minutes supply left and I was a long way over so I turned about and beat it for home. I was a little afraid to come home so far alone but I took the chance and as soon as I crossed the lines I landed at a Belgian drome & filled up with petrol.

Oh Boy! but this is a great life. It cannot be beaten, no matter how hard you try. While you are more or less afraid all the time, yet you are not what you would call "frightened." When you see the Huns, all you think about is getting at the devils. You always think you are better than they are.

Well to make matters just a wee bit better, I will tell you of a compliment I had payed me last night. (tho do not spread it around as it looks too much like bragging on my part.) After dinner was over last night and we were just about to leave the mess, the C.O. said "Hendershot, Moore & Davies" you stay behind. Well I wondered what was up. I thought we must be in for a straff for something. Well after the rest had left he said, "you chaps are doing wonderfully well, especially you

Hendershot, you are a marvel" and then he told us to just take things easy for a while and not to be too anxious that soon we would be the back-bone of the squadron. I do not know what I ever did to deserve that. I know I fly pretty good formation and all that, but I have never done anything yet that is very wonderful.

What do you think of your son, now anyway? Gee but I hope I have luck with me and can get a few Huns without them getting me. Don't worry, I never will run into any unnecessary dangers, not if I can help it. You know when you first start flying over here, you may run into a dozen Huns and never see one. You will wonder what your flight commander is diving and split-diving so much for. It takes experience to get so you can see things like that. I am now just getting to see them. Yesterday, I was the only one in our flight except our flight commander that saw the Huns at all. It is easy to distinguish them from our machines. You can never mistake that long stream lined body and the funny looking fish tail. Gee you can even see it in your sleep. The other night one of the chaps that sleeps near me said I yelled out "here come the buggers, they are diving on us."

How is everyone at home these days? How is business with you, is it up to last year?

I have had all the papers in regard to Charlie's Estate fixed up and sent them to the war office, so expect before very long to be sending you the £50.

Well it is nearly time for the patrol to be back so must close now and go out to the drome and see them all come in. Write.

Love to all
Your Son
Warren

Following Fritz, October 1918

JOHN MENZIES

Following Fritz,
Oct. 18, 1918.

I want to write to you and the dear little Scout about my experience of the last two days, while they are still fresh in my mind. Without a doubt they are the most interesting days in my War experiences, and I only wish I could tell you all my feelings in going through them.

I wrote you a short hurried note from the place where I stopped for lunch on the way up. That was really the beggining of the trip through the War-zone, for the city I was in then was just on the fringe of the fighting, and marked the high tide of the old German advance in that sector. After lunch that day (there were four of us) we boarded the first motor lorrie that came along, bound for the Front Line. It happened to be full of turnips and cabbages and we made quite an ultra-rural picture perched up on top and gradually sinking down amongst the vegetables. It was not as uncomfortable as you might think and the best part of it was that I had an observation post in the rear, from which I had a perfect view of the surrounding country. Right from the time we started we were covering country over which Fritz had retreated during the past few weeks and the first eight or ten miles had been very hotly contested, right up to the famous Hindenburg Line. It was the typical shell-torn trench area about which I have told you many times, lined in the most intricate way with trench systems, dotted all the way up with graveyards, with their long rows of little crosses, looking very much like whole battalions on parade and speaking in dumb eloquence of the price that had been paid for the freedom of this little part of France. The dozens of villages we passed through were only piles of ruins, levelled to the ground, the only clean parts of them being the roads, which had been cleared up by our Army in their passage up. The most remarkable thing I saw was the heavy belts of wire protecting the Hindenburg Line, so numerous and so deep that it made one wonder how our fellows ever got through them. After we passed the H— Line it was quite evident that he had retreated very fast, for the country was again open, with green fields, torn here and there with our shells, the trees green and brown and yellow—all the Fall colors, the roads good and the sun shining over it all. But the villages were still wrecked, for he still had time to blow them up and burn them as he passed through. The road we followed was perfectly straight for over 16 miles, until we came to the place where we had to branch off to the place where our transport lines were SUPPOSED to be. We finally had to get off and walk, as the lorrie could go no further. Fritz had flooded the country ahead of us by blowing up the canal and we had quite a time finding the little bridge the Engineers had built across the stream. Whole fields were inundated in this area, but of course it did not interfere with our heavy transport and artillery moving up, for there are plenty of parallel roads. We walked straight across country, through camps and horselines right out in the open, for about five miles and finally found our own rear headquarters. They were in the middle of a field and looked for all the world like a small circus or gipsy camp, just two small tents, the remainder, little bivouacs of canvas and oil sheets, anything at all for cover. We were all pretty tired, for we had a long hard day behind us and we were hungry and footsore. It was six o'clock then and we had supper (a good one too), and then prepared to dig ourselves in for the night. But no such luck. Word was received at 7:30 that Fritz was retreating so fast that our front-line people had lost touch with him entirely, and that we would immediately move the rear headquarters up about FIVE miles. It is a tribute to the speed with which our arrangements are made, that we were all packed up, all the wagons and limbers and cook-kitchens loaded up and the horses harnessed in half an hour and we were on the way again. By this time it was dark, the roads were not good, and the route to be followed was very tricky. A great many other battalions were moving up on parallel and we had to go slowly and carefully. All these roads lead to one pontoon bridge across the canal that Fritz had been holding up to a few hours before. He had blown up all the bridges as he left on his way to the Rhine. It took us five hours to get to our destination, just on the other side of a nice village, practically untouched by shell-fire and which he had fortunately not had time to damage in any way. We made our camp there, in a field on the far side of the town, and after a short search the officers found a billet in a very comfortable shed, that had been used by the Boche as a carpenter shop, in connection with a small detention camp. The heaps of clean shavings on the floor made excellent beds, and we had a much needed sleep till nine o'clock the next morning. At breakfast we got orders to move on again and we were on our way in half an hour. By this time the road was covered for miles with transport of all kinds, and guns of all sizes, a wonderful sight at anytime, and a most heartening sight when they are all going the right way. One of the best features of the whole thing is that there is not the usual string of ambulances coming back from the line, in fact, I have only seen two wounded so far.

Our next move, mentioned above, brought us to another village about five miles East and we were billited right in the houses. It was one of the industrial suburbs of a city which has just been entered by the Canadians within the last few days—a splendidly built and well laid out village. There were no civilians left in the town, and all the signs pointed to their evacuation some time ago. We went through many of the houses, and I only found ONE that by some mistake had not been visited by the filthy Boche. This one house, by its clean rooms and generally domestic comfort (all the clothing and furniture and dishes etc., were still there) only emphasized the wanton destruction in the other houses. All of them had been thoroughly plundered, anything of value that could be carried, taken away, and everything else totally destroyed. Beautiful furniture smashed, mirrors and dishes broken, mattresses and pictures cut up, the paper torn off the walls, sewing machines broken—everything done with a devilish thoroughness only equal to the Hun, and to crown his wickedness and reveal what a real swine he is, he had filthed nearly every room and even the children's cradles. God in His Heaven could never look down on this and allow such devils to prosper.

This morning we were up at five and on his heels for another few miles. And now, where I am finishing this letter (Oct. 19), we are in the first village where he has left any civilians. The first thing we saw was the Tri-color of France, floating proudly and thankfully once more, over the first little cottage—and as we entered the village, the women and children and old men came out and greeted us with happy faces and tears in their eyes. "La von deliverance" was all they could say just then, but I have since been talking with some of them and have heard stories which one could not believe of any people except dirty Germans. He only left this village yesterday and before he left he blew a mine up under the church, so as to block the road to our advance, and last night well knowing there were civilians here, he shelled the village with gas. One of the shells hit the house I am in now, and the two little kiddies, pretty little girls, were deathly sick from the fumes. Can you imagine it?

There are many more things I would like to tell you now, but this letter must get off tonight. You cannot imagine what an experience it is being with a victorious army in an advance of this kind. Everybody is just as happy as though we were on a picnic.

At 11 a.m. It Went Quiet

CLARENCE ELDER

Promptly at 11 A.M. it went quiet and seemed out of place, the French civies came running out on street all yelling "La guerre finis" but about then a land mine up ahead or close by would go up and they'd yell "Ah non finis" and tear back indoors.

These land mines were still going off every 10 or 15 min. for next day or so, as they were triggered by a timer or some device in a roadway and it took a while before either they all went off or were located and cut off.

We were still wondering what next when a H.Q. motor cycle came and picked up Sgt. Mills and off to H.Q. somewhere near by. He came back in 15 minutes with orders to get his platoon slicked up a bit, fed and off to a victory parade in Mons. The slick-up was chiefly a brush up of shoes and dust off spots on uniform, straighten out webb equipment and eliminate odd man with worn elbows or too sloppy uniform. All lined up at ease, ready to move off; likely a Lieutenant to lead us though I cannot place exactly who but do recollect while waiting in the street a gun limbre went by and a P.P.C.L.I. firing party with two rough wood coffins, the last burial party of the war that I saw, though half an hour later as we passed through a bit of park area on outskirts of city I saw my last dead Germans. Three or four were laying in the open park in shadow of few trees and had been caught that morning I guess.

The odd stone or brick house facing the park showed some M.G. chips on corners, so can only assume the firing up front that Am. may have been the German rear guard holding up the 42nd and R.C.R.'s who had taken over from the Princess Pat's and 49th, I think early before daybreak, and I think it was the 42nd that made it to the City Hall Square before 11 A.M.

When we reached the city centre about 1:30 P.M., we entered by the R.H. corner entrance towards Jemappes and were guided to our place, rear platoon representing 9th Battalion Engineers with same number ahead for 8th Battalion and 7th Battalion and H.Q. in front.

As usual in army precadence the artillery were finally lined up in similar formation on our right. To left was similar platoons for 7th, 8th, 9th brigades of infantry, P.P.C.L.I., R.C.R., 42nd and 49th Battalions for 7th brigade, the four mounted Rifle Battalions for 8th brigade, 1st, 2nd, 4th and 5th and the 9th brigades, the 43rd, 52nd, 116th and 58th; they pretty well filled the square in front of Hotel de Ville (City Hall) and a flank reviewing platform extended out a bit from City Hall steps.

At 2 P.M. the band struck up the Belgium National anthem and the crowd that filled all space on sidewalks, windows and balconies of 3 and 4-storey stone buildings roared out the anthem; we were first called to attention from the rest easy position and had to stand at attention for quite a while before we got a present arms, after a few odd speeches by Mayor, etc., and Gen. Currie representing the Canadian Corps as he and his staff, including the Prince of Wales, were on the platform.

Anyway, after the odd this and that and stand at ease, etc., we were due to get a march past the reviewing stand in column of fours, and our eyes right, etc., previously we had fixed bayonets for the first present arms and I remember having to be careful not to slip on the cobblestone paving as the long British bayonet at the slope extends back near the head of man behind, and he is bit leary of a clip on the ear due to a slip.

The crowd was so dense we departed by another road exit at opposite corner we came in at, and had to march at slope and bayonets fixed for quite a piece before had a chance to halt and unfix bayonets and sling rifles in regular marching order. The dress for the parade had been battle order and no greatcoats or large pack; weather fair, no rain.

The next day I think we did very little, but were due to move by route march through Mons to Nimy the following day. We as lowly privates only got most of our news by the cook house, rumor handouts while waiting to get our usual dish-out, but it was surprising how accurate most would turn out to be, leaks via the orderly room clerks and big ears of someone in H.Q. for some reason or other could pick up news pretty fast. . . .

Anyway, the Colonel had intended to make it his first peace time battalion march and orders called for a general smartening up of all personnel and equipment as he intended to "show em."

Alas, it fell apart due to an accident; the night before a Flemish civie pulled his cart, covered with straw, into a barn beside the H.Q. cook kitchen. He had just come back from rear with a big supply of wines, etc., for local pubs. Trust an army cook to smell a bottle. A cook up to get fires going etc., got nosy and located this gold mine and after caching away a goodly supply he let all other cooks and drivers etc., in on his find.

In a short time before the officer of the day got wise the whole surrounding billets were in on it and even a few civies close by, as this particular owner of cart was unpopular with neighbors it was found out later.

By the time the O.C. got to the courtyard the sampling of the assortment had got quite a few very hilarious and when the R.S.M. finally got some order restored and had them lined up, the odd dozen had to be carted away to a temporary clink nearby and of the rest, the O.C. ordered them to march in line across the courtyard and any who couldn't make it in good shape were placed in the coop to sober up.

Our B. Company was not too close and only got the news when breakfast was called and while standing round the kitchen waiting. The cooks no doubt elaborated on the amount of Cognac, etc., that had faded away.

As the Colonel had his orders to route march the odd 5 miles to other side of Mons, he had to move off on schedule, but he sure took a round about way to get there.

His transport was necessary to handle the limbres etc., and they were gay and noisy. We as ordinary foot sloggers got a big kick out of the noisy drivers in rear, sounded like a bunch of cowboys that hit town after a dry spell.

After we halted for first break, about halfway, the battalion fell out in a park area and the Colonel knew then there was more hidden somewhere, so he had a search made by the R.S.M. and some N.C.O.'s of all water bottles, packs and especially the cooks' dixies and kettles; sure enough it was said that they had filled all containers and wept to see it poured out on the ground.

We finally reached Nimy on the far side of Mons and B. Company were billeted along the canal bank and even across the only bridge left up. The cook house and H.Q. were on the other side of the canal, the farthest north of all the Canadian Corps as far as I know. There was some sort of a light railway got going in a few days and it came as far as our H.Q. area. Civies were returning on it and it was said to run as far as Brussels, but I don't know about that as none of our troops were allowed any leave or to use it.

One of the drawbacks that now came into effect due to end of war was guarding against pilfering, etc. All troops are bit slap happy about making a few fast dollars by lifting anything saleable from some other outfit.

Right away it was back to guard duties over the limbres, horses and the clink; about 30 were held in a school house, sleeping under and on desks and benches.

Back to 2 hours on and 4 hours off on a 24 hour guard plus less arduous horse picket where one also put in 2 hrs. on and 4 off, but could sit around as long as watched no one stole a nag, as you signed for so many when came on and had your relief count and sign same deal.

A horse or mule immediately became valuable as the butchers paid handsomely for one and no questions asked. So if the R.C.A.S.C. lost a couple it was easier for an O.C. to let it be known he'd quietly pay well for them to be replaced and no questions asked, so the artillery would lose two maybe and same repeat performance went on again; this was the reason for horse pickets.

While a war is on one can write off to shell fire most losses and no question raised, but with no action or excuse, all at once everything had to be accounted for, after four years of easy come, easy go and what a fast change that was.

The cooks and Quarter Master stores had to all at once watch for odd pilfering, as soap, clothing, leather plus canned goods were worth their weight in gold, and due to sudden let down the crown and anchor boards etc., were out in full strength plus local pubs and money again would buy plenty of local favors, etc., so it had value again not just something to gamble easy come and go. Also about then the Xmas pay was issued, about 40 francs I think for a buck private, and a franc was 20¢ then, so for a bit everyone had same extra funds.

Also bath parades got going again weekly and with soap and colder weather, I remember we finally got pretty free of the louse problem.

The stay at Nimy was supposed to be short as we knew the 1st and 2nd Divisions had left a week after armistice to route march to the Rhine for duty, and it was rumored the 3rd and 4th Divisions would replace them.

It turned out that due to rails and roads not being ready, that to keep the occupation forces supplied was a big job and eventually it was decided to get the Canadian Corps settled in near Brussels and let the 3rd Division come home (had as many early units as 1st Div.) first and be followed by the 1st, 2nd and 4th, who would take over the quarters and billets near Brussels as others left for British base camps and home.

We knew very little of all this but rumors proved correct and it worked out that way. We marched slowly by middle of December towards Brussels and spent Xmas at Rixensart, about 10 miles out and maybe 5 miles from Waterloo, marched by Waterloo the last afternoon on way to Rixensart.

Brussels was to be a leave area and I was down for New Year's, 2 days leave but not to be; two days after Xmas we left our dandy billet, a 3-storey big mansion in a park area, too good to last and were back route marching to the French border and ended up staying a month in a flat broken up war torn village near Tournai. Headed to Le Havre in early February and across to Weymouth and Bramshott camp, headed home on the Olympic in late March and got home end of March on 2nd troop train into Calgary, turned in rifle and equipment at Stampede grounds and mother met me and home on street car in uniform.

The Last .303 Cartridge I Will Ever Fire

JOHN GAITZ

Nov 13th 1918

Dear Mother

I have just unloaded my rifle, I guess the last .303 cartridge I will ever fire was fired the day before yesterday when we had a hard days encounter with "his" rear guard that night "he" retired and just as we were getting ready to push forward again next morning the official news of the *armistice* came through the signal station. Even yet although every thing is peaceful and quiet except for the enthusiastic civilians, one can't realize that the fighting is over. I am so used of surprises and disappointment that I don't believe I would bat an eye. If they told us to stand too, hiene was counter attacking. I guess I would utter the odd oath though.

I suppose we will be following him up now. . . . Just at present we are taking it easy I have been in Mons a couple of times its a fine place.

Well I was just where I wanted to be when the end came right in the most forward position.

I'll write and tell you more later when the bonds of the censor have eased. I must just make the remark that I have greeted more civilians in the last three days than in a good many years. They were very enthusiastic on seeing us coming through the villages. This is a scribble but there are many interruptions and jokes going around so that the uniformity is somewhat blighted.

Best regards to All,
John

Veterans and the Political Mood in Winnipeg, 1919

**OFFICER COMMANDING,
MILITARY DISTRICT NO. 10**

> *Canada was in a tense political condition after the end of the war, with high inflation and political agitation roiling the waters. "Returned men" without jobs took out their resentment against those who, they believed, had profited during their absence overseas, in this case "foreigners" and socialists.*

At 2.00 P.M. on Sunday the 26th of January, some 1500 to 2000 Veterans assembled in the City Hall Square and the Socialist Meeting was not held, but some of the Socialist fraternity in the neighbourhood were rounded up by the Veterans and made to kiss the Union Jack, and roughly handled. The Veterans then split up into three different columns and visited the various known Socialist headquarters, which they wrecked. . . . One of these [columns] visited the Alien Quarter in the North End of the City, another proceeded to Elmwood, paying a visit to the Edleweis Brewery, the proprietor of which is a naturalised German. This place was badly smashed up. The third party of Veterans visited the establishment of S. Blumenburg, the . . . noted anti-conscriptionist and Socialist. . . .

On Monday the 27th of January, three large parties of Returned men again assembled, and the situation began to look somewhat serious. The feeling of the Returned soldiers against aliens and firms employing them was running high, and some irresponsibles amongst the Returned soldiers attempted to inflame the others by proposal that all establishments, such as the Swift Canadian Company, the Canadian Pacific Rlwy., Shops, and the Canadian National Rlwy., Shops, should be raided and wrecked and the aliens employed thereat beaten up and chased out of town.

About 2.00 P.M. I was informed . . . that this had actually been determined on by the Veterans and that a large body of them were on the way to the Swift Canadian plant, to carry out these intentions. I was shortly afterwards telephoned by the Mayor of Winnipeg, asking if I would go down to this mob and address them. . . . The Secretary of the Great War Veterans Association . . . called on the men and stated I had come to speak to them. I pointed out to them that they were destroying their hard earned record in the Field, and advised them to go about getting their aims brought about in a proper and constitutional manner, in which they would be given every possible assistance and support. . . . The result was that the Returned soldiers deciding to follow our advice, quietened down and began to disperse. . . .

Bush Pilots in Uniform, 1925

T.F. COOPER

The Royal Canadian Air Force, constituted after the end of the Great War, was scarcely a warlike organization. Much of its service consisted of bush flying, crop dusting, mercy flights, and photography and survey work. This account from 1925 portrays the problems of flying Avro Vipers in the bush.

Once when Flying Officer Bill Weaver, flying one of these contraptions, was forced down on tiny Stormy Lake in central Manitoba I was taken in to investigate the damage and found that the engine was a total wreck as two con rods had smashed through the crankcase.

It was a problem to land another aircraft as the lake was only a mile long and a little over 100 yards wide, surrounded by high trees. Flying Officer Frank Wait came in to find out what was required and stalled on take-off; that meant that we had two aircraft in this pothole and something had to be done about it. Joe Maskell was then flown in to Beresford Lake and hiked through the bush to give us a hand. The crashed aircraft was towed to shore by making a winch between two trees. The engine was removed and the mud and slime taken out, the serviceable mags and carburetor were removed from the wrecked engine. One engine was made out of two, installed in Flying Officer Weaver's aircraft, tested and flown out by Flying Officer Roy Slemon.

To fly the aircraft out the fuel was reduced to a minimum, the tail of the aircraft was tied to a tree and when the engine was at full throttle I cut the rope with a sharp axe and the aircraft just made it over the trees.

Strike Duty, Sydney, Nova Scotia, 1925

LIEUTENANT-GENERAL GUY G. SIMONDS

> *The interwar army, like the RCAF, performed a variety of duties, not the least of which was to provide aid to the civil power service. Sometimes, as in Sydney, this meant keeping the peace between strikers and bosses. Simonds, then a lieutenant, recalled the scene.*

I joined the . . . Brigade on strike duty in Sydney. There the regiment, organized as cavalry, had to provide mounted patrols, each under an officer, to circulate through the areas of mines and steelworks to suppress any riotous gathering and protect lives and property.

As part of our course in Military Law at the R.M.C. [Royal Military College] we had been instructed in the laws and regulations governing military intervention in aid to the Civil Power, but this was the first, though not the last, time that I participated in what is probably the most objectionable of all military duties. It seems inevitable that though the role of the military is neutral and solely that of protecting lives and property in face of threatened violence, the potential disturbers of the peace almost invariably earmark the troops as their "enemy," even though the latter are in no way involved in the causes of dispute. For the soldiery it is a high test of discipline and morale. The officer in charge of an anti-riot detachment or patrol bears the responsibility for ensuring that no more force is used than is necessary to maintain law and order and protect lives and property, and his actions are subject to judgement by the equivalent of the Monday morning quarterback who "wasn't there," in the atmosphere of wisdom after the event. If he fails to take determined action, and loss of life or serious damage to property results, he can be adjudged culpable. If it is judged that he used more force than was necessary to bring a mob under control, he may be accused of brutality and may equally be judged culpable. In many potential riot situations a fine hair-line separates the reactions of a crowd where emotions may be charged by fanatical leaders. Confronted by determined and obvious resolution on the part of a body of troops to maintain order, they may cool and quietly disperse. But if they detect cowering and irresolution on the part of the forces of law and order, a crowd can quickly turn into a frenzied mob, and spend their pent up energies in wholesale destruction.

In the early stages of the 1925 strike in the Cape Breton mines, the strikers regarded the troops as stooges of the owners. We were subjected to every verbal and a good many physical abuses. Mounted patrols were assaulted by stones being thrown down upon them from upper storey windows in villages and the many railway overpasses which intersected the area. We always wore tin hats on patrol which gave a good degree of protection. Gradually the point was established with the miners that we weren't on anybody's "side" in the dispute, but were there only to protect lives and property against violence. Someone had noticed some of the strikers kicking a soccer ball around a field. We had a good regimental soccer team—I had played on the first soccer team at the R.M.C. and was given a place as forward when I joined the regiment—and we challenged the miners to a match. A large crowd, wives and families of the miners, turned out to see the event. It was a good close match. I can't recall who won and it wasn't important.

What was important was that it led to regular weekly games, and the abuse of our mounted patrols diminished, then ceased. When the strike was over and we rode out of Sydney Mines to entrain for Petawawa, the miners and their families lined the streets and cheered us on our way. A very gratifying outcome to an unpleasant duty, during which our men had behaved admirably.

The Chief of Staff Resigns, 1927

CHARLES VINING

> *An able soldier, General J.H. MacBrien was chief of staff of Canada's tiny armed forces until he gave up his post in 1927. With disarming frankness, MacBrien told journalist Vining his reason: money.*

"What do you think is the greatest thing in life?"

"To know that you've accomplished in your work what you started out to do. If it's to study certain things, to know you've mastered them. Whatever you set yourself to do, to know you've done it properly."

It is a good soldier's creed. It means to take one's objective. It appears from General MacBrien that going on leave is not the most important event in a soldier's life. To be a soldier is to serve and he must be willing to adjust all habits and pleasure to being always at the top of physical fitness and in possession of mental self-control in order that there may be no flaw in his effectiveness. A soldier like that places himself and his comfort, in peace as well as in war, secondary to the fellow citizens whom he defends. It means honest living and an unselfish heart.

To a man like that, it is not pleasant to give up being a soldier:

"You must feel badly about resigning?"

"Yes," simply.

Why He Is Resigning

There were no complaints in the explanation which later followed. General MacBrien's resignation is after all an application of the code by which he has lived and it probably does not occur to him to complain. He is resigning in order to take care of those most closely dependent upon him and the sacrifice of his own habits and inclinations is perhaps too bad but it does not matter.

He is resigning because he has not enough money. His salary as chief of staff is nine thousand dollars a year. This, he thinks, seems like a fairly good salary but as chief of staff he is obliged to maintain a suitable establishment, to entertain, to keep up his uniforms, and in Ottawa this is not simple. On the personal side he has five children to educate and they are now reaching an age where the process becomes expensive. He has promised that they shall be well educated and it is to him an obligation. There are three boys. They all have decided to be soldiers.

"I took up the question two years ago with Mr. McDonald, who was then minister of defence," said General MacBrien, "and there were indications that something might be done. Nothing has happened however, and in the meantime I have come to the end of my resources. I have submitted all my expenses and bank books for examination. They show that to be chief of staff and to care for my family costs three thousand a year above my present salary. I have already economized. I do not belong to any clubs. I have given up polo and golf during the last two years. My house is as moderate as possible because I have secured it through the kindness of my friend Admiral Kingsmill. My only approach to extravagance is two polo ponies which I keep to ride for exercise. They were given to me by a friend in Montreal and I can not part with them."

"How have you managed during the last few years?"

"A dear friend of mine, Colonel Bart McLennan, of the 42nd, left me ten thousand dollars when he died. I was fortunate enough to increase it and I have spent it all to supplement my salary. But I can not go any longer without running into debt and soldiers are not supposed to go into debt. If they can not manage they must stop and that is what I am doing."

"Is there no way to cut your expenses?"

"Yes. I can take my children out of school or I can change our house and ask my wife to do the work. . . ."

We were at his house and Mrs. MacBrien was listening to the conversation, a charming young woman with a direct manner of thinking and speaking. I turned to her:

"How do you like the idea of a back country farm after Ottawa?"

"I do not mind. I have been on the farm and I like it. It is better than going into debt. And it is a relief to have it all settled anyway. We have been uncertain for months."

"Yes," agreed the general, "uncertainty is not a pleasant thing."

From inquiries made, it appears that things are not so difficult for soldiers in England. Major-Generals are frequently allowed a house and servants and horses while the chief of the general staff, which though a position of higher responsibility is the English equivalent of the Canadian chief of staff has a salary of approximately twenty-five thousand dollars a year in addition to living establishment. At Ottawa we have other public officials drawing salaries much higher than nine thousand a year and without the responsibility for the lives of his countrymen which attaches to the chief of staff. But in such apparent peculiarities there is never any explanation. It just is, and what is, usually does not change.

"Are you sorry that you have been a soldier, General MacBrien?"

"No. I would do it all over again. I am glad that my sons want to be soldiers."

"What gave you the idea of being a soldier?"

"I think it was my uncle Australia."

"Your Uncle Australia?"

"Yes. My grandfather went out from Ireland to Australia and found the first gold there. He helped survey Melbourne, and then was able to return to Ireland and live on income from Australian land he owned. He called one of his sons 'Australia'—my uncle. Uncle Australia was a soldier, and he inspired me to be one."

General MacBrien left the room and came back with a package.

"Here are his medals. He gave them to me."

There were three, two for service in China and the other a Turkish medal. Then the general unwrapped a sword, a short affair with a long hilt and elaborate scabbard.

"It is a Japanese sword," he said. "They gave it to me over there. It is three hundred years old, and it is two-handed, because the Japs are not very big. Be careful that you don't cut yourself. It is very sharp."

Yes. It was.

"You know," he continued, "the Japs are proud of their sharp swords and their skill in handling them. They like the story in Japan of the Jap soldier who met the big Russian soldier. The Jap made a swift slash with his keen two-handed sword. It was so swift that the big Russian soldier did not even feel it. 'Hoho,' said the big Russian, 'you never touched me.' 'Is that so?' replied the little Jap, 'well, just try to nod your head.'"

Queer old wars those, swords and flags and prancing horses. Is war getting worse or better?

"Was this war worse than South Africa, General MacBrien?"

"There was more danger of being killed in this war. In South Africa I think there was greater hardship. Food was often scarce, and clothing and blankets. All that was marvelously organized in this war."

"Will there be another war?"

"There is almost certain to be another war. The most careful study gives no reason for believing that war will not recur. We do not know how soon."

"Where is the most likely place for it to break?"

"At present the most likely combatants are Japan and Russia with Manchuria as the cause."

"Would it involve Britain?"

"We do not think so. But when war starts who knows its limits?"

Militarism in the Nation's Schools, 1927

AGNES MACPHAIL, MP

> *In the interwar years, pacifism was strong in Canada, and the government's (tiny) support for cadet training regularly came under fire in Parliament.*

National Defence—cadet services, $500,000.

MISS MACPHAIL: What reason will the minister give for the increase in the cadet vote from $400,000 to $500,000?

HON J.L. RALSTON (Minister of National Defence): The reason of the increase is that there have been actually organized, but not authorized, some forty-nine cadet units which have been functioning without any assistance from the department, and the amount of

$100,000 will not very much more than take care of them. I will give the hon. member the number of these units and the provinces in which they are located.

MISS MACPHAIL: We shall be very glad to have that.

MR. RALSTON Four in Alberta, four in British Columbia, two in Manitoba, one in New Brunswick, five in Nova Scotia, fifteen in Ontario, sixteen in Quebec and two in Saskatchewan.

MISS MACPHAIL: I understand they are having province-wide shooting contests. Someone was telling me that where one boy won a contest he was chosen to compete against a boy from another town, and finally it came to be a province-wide contest. What does the minister know about these contests?

MR. RALSTON There is a contest in which these teams participate. Scores are kept, and the contest is for a trophy presented by His Majesty. The South African boys won the contest for the last two years, and I think the Canadian boys were second.

MISS MACPHAIL: I have always been opposed to the military authorities having any influence on the educational system of the different provinces. Other Dominion departments do not interfere with the matter of education in the provinces. The provinces themselves are supposed to control education, and I am therefore opposed to the increase of $100,000 in the cadet vote, which increase is evidently due to the number of units that are being asked for. I believe cadet training is military training. It is supervised by the Department of National Defence and is paid for by that department. It certainly was the idea of the founder, Sir Frederick Borden, to build up a citizen soldiery. Up till now, as I said a moment ago, the vote has been $400,000. To-day $100,000 is to be added, and the total of $500,000 I believe will be supplemented by the Strathcona trust fund. Possibly the minister could tell us what will be contributed by that trust fund.

MR. RALSTON The Strathcona trust fund is $500,000, the interest on which is available for the giving of prizes to cadets in the various provinces. The money is distributed on the basis of the school population.

MISS MACPHAIL: In its issue of February 24, 1927, the Ottawa Journal very clearly pointed out that cadet training is military in character.

It said:

> If Agnes Macphail M.P., doesn't understand the purpose of high school cadets, and the need of men of courage who can shoot straight the white women in Shanghai do.

I thank the Journal for that item. I think the newspaper is right and that cadet training is military training. I have always maintained this because I cannot imagine the Department of National Defence asking for a vote of half a million dollars and going to the trouble of having provincial contests, training officers, and providing uniforms and arms unless the organization was entirely military in character.

MR. QUINN: To defend the women of Canada and every other country.

MISS MACPHAIL: That is an old joke. Nobody believes that any more.

MR. QUINN: It is no joke, it is an absolute fact.

MISS MACPHAIL: The purpose of cadets, then, is to produce men who can shoot straight; or to state it more brutally, to teach the boys of Canada to be "killers of men." I think anyone who has watched cadets training before these buildings could hardly deny the fact that cadet training is military training. Every time the militia troops parade, to receive military visitors or at military funerals and displays, the cadets take part, clearly identifying themselves with the military machine. Military men train them. The Department of National Defence pays the bill. We can safely conclude that cadet training is military training.

The Teachers' Journal in an issue of a few years ago told of cadet reviews in military barracks in Winnipeg at which winning teams of school cadets took 28 to 34 seconds respectively to bring machine guns into action. The same journal states that teachers in military district No. 10 would get free transportation and subsistence while taking the cadet officers' training course in Tuxedo barracks, Winnipeg. Two years ago the Minister of National Defence assured us it was true that the instructor of cadets received two dollars per head for each cadet up to fifty, and one dollar per head for each cadet over that number. It is easy to see how the larger salary paid the instructor will make him a good recruiting officer, and how a boycott against boys not in the corps can be effectively used, and I believe is used, to swell the number of cadets.

There are many people whose boys are taking cadet training who say: It's just physical training. This, I believe, is an error, and if to-day I can but establish in the minds of even some Canadian parents that cadet training is not physical but military training, I shall think it worth while to make this effort. The development of a healthy body, if considered at all, is considered only as a means to an end in military training, not as an end in itself. The aim is to make soldiers out of boys. Men who have specialized in physical training affirm that military drill is not good physical training. Dudley A. Sargent, physical instructor of Harvard, physical instructor and medical doctor, has said:

> Taking the most favourable view possible of military drill as a physical exercise, we are led to conclude that its strained positions and closely localized movements do not afford the essential requisites for developing the muscles and improving respiration and circulation, thereby improving the general health and condition of the system.

Let me quote now from an extract taken from the Boston Medical and Surgical Journal:

> This defect, we are pleased to state, is recognized by the great military nations of Europe, and measures are taken to give all the recruits from three to twelve months gymnastic training to develop them as men before they are expected to conform to the requirements of the soldier.

I could quote many other authorities to the same effect, but I will give only one more. Mr. Claxton, former United States Commissioner of Education, said:

> All schools should provide such means of physical culture through outdoor games and exercises as will result in the best

possible control of the body and all its members. I do not believe that military drill in our public schools is the best means to this end and I feel quite certain that rifle practice in the schools is undesirable. There is so much else that is better for all purposes that can be provided at much less cost.

During the war "setting up" exercises were freely used to counteract the bad results of military drill. I believe all military schools employ physical training in order to keep their men fit. In games, in the gymnasium and on the track boys and girls dress for vigorous exercise. They aim, one might say, to get up a sweat; but cadets go out in stiff-looking, warm clothing and carry heavy guns, and they have all the appearance of trying to keep cool. I believe that our youth, both boys and girls, need physical training, but that training should be of the kind that is pleasing to them. To be good physical training it should be something which in itself is so pleasing that those engaged in it become intensely interested. Let me quote John Langdon-Davies of England on this point. In his book, A Public School in War Time, I find the following at page nine:

> Physical training which is to form character must appeal to the child as a pleasure. A pleasant thing is one which appeals to healthy instincts, and this can never be the case of routine drill. This last has to rely on something else than healthy pleasure for its incentives, thus proving itself to be the bending of human nature out of its natural course for the sake of an external object, and is therefore the antithesis of education.

I should like to make it clear that it is not the sum of money involved that I am objecting to. I would favour a sum exceeding the amount now in the estimates, to be paid by the Department of Health to the Department of Education in the various provinces for them to use for physical training, but not for military training. I think we could safely model our physical training on the Swedish system. We should use the beauty of colour, music and form in training youth physically, but all military forms should be eliminated.

We know Sweden heads the world in physical training. As a matter of fact, in no other country have results been so striking, and she sticks to her athletic sports and games and does not indulge at all in military training. Is it not strange that Canada is increasing the military training of cadets at this time? I see no cause for it. I fail to understand why a department of the Dominion government is inducing the boys of Canada to take military training. France, after the crushing defeat of 1871 began to train her school boys to the practice of arms, but in 1890, after fifteen years experience, she abandoned the cadet system, not because the problem of defence was less urgent, but because military training was arresting the physical development of her secondary schoolboys. Australia tried the military system of training, but previous to the war her director general, after a thorough study of the problem in Switzerland, Sweden, Germany, France and England, recommended a system of games and organized athletic sports as the best training for schoolboys. I might quote other countries, but I will leave it there.

John Stuart Mill has said that all attempts by the state to bias the conclusions of its subjects on disputed points are evil. And that is just what the state is doing by influencing the education of the provinces. Education is being used as a political institution to form habits of thought and to circumscribe knowledge in such a way as to make one set of opinions inevitable. That is my greatest objection to military training. The thing it does to the boy's mind is far more disastrous than the injury it does to his body. A great educationist, Mr. J. L. Paton, headmaster of Manchester grammar school writes:

> The people who instil military training permanently into our schools seem to me to be closing the gates of hope upon mankind.

These are very strong words coming from a great educationist. When in Canada not long ago he said practically the same thing. Bertrand Russell has said:

> I think it would be a real gain if men could be made to see that militarism is a form of cowardice. It is a desire for security that

makes the common man acquiesce in the schemes of the militarists. Armaments are the most foolish method imaginable for seeking security, but fear makes men unable to think clearly and so they cling to old absurdities.

In our own families, as every one of us knows, active goodwill is the central principle that keeps the unit together, and that is true of our schools and of every form of government. It is true of every form of group life. If we have not active goodwill there can be no real progress. The world stands today in need of that spirit and, laugh me to scorn if you will, I think it is the only road to security. We cannot find security by arming ourselves to the very limit. I do not believe that preparedness for war will bring peace. What we carefully prepare for we usually get. If we prepare for war we get war; if we prepare for peace we shall get peace.

The American Enemy, 1927

COLONEL J. SUTHERLAND BROWN

As director of military operations and intelligence at the army's headquarters in Ottawa, Colonel Brown had the duty of preparing plans for all eventualities. Defence Scheme No. 1 dealt with the possibility of war with the United States, and this memo set the stage for his work.

November 11, 1927

It will be argued by many people who know about International affairs that war between United States and the British Empire is unthinkable.

I have studied the United States and the United States' citizens since I was a youth and I flatter myself that I know something about them. I am firmly convinced that it is from no humanitarian point of view that the United States has not had war with Great Britain. Great Britain has borne patiently insults from the United States on many occasions. She has taken these insults I am fully convinced on account of the weakness of the Canadian frontier.

The United States has forced the hand of Canada on many occasions and is now attempting to force her hand with reference to the development of the St. Lawrence.

The day may come when the United States may think she is strong enough to bluff the British Empire with a threat of war. It is necessary then for the Empire to be in a strong position to meet this threat.

Canada is slowly, but surely, molding a national feeling which stands for looking after her interests and she will show a strong front to any demands from the United States. If the United States knows that the Canadian Military Forces are a factor that cannot be lightly considered and that the whole Empire is behind us they will think before they take any action against us.

This all above is not only an argument that the United States may be a possible enemy, but also to look at it from the academic point of view. A defence scheme that provides for the defence of our frontiers will cover, with but slight variations, every military problem with which we will be faced. All the great soldiers that have ever considered Canadian defence have laid that down as an axiom on which to base Canadian defence.

I think it desirable that we should pursue the very sound course of organizing the Canadian Militia for the primary duty of Home Defence and I therefore recommend that as soon as you can get the Honourable the Minister's concurrence Defence Scheme No. 1 should be rewritten and brought up to-date. It should be divided into two parts:—

Part I being a general appreciation of Canadian Defence dealing with Canada's position within the Empire; topographical descriptions of the frontiers or areas in which operations may take place; arguments on which to base a sound war organization.

Part II should consist of the definite proposals for defence, that this—the Preface of the Defence Scheme; the War Organization; and a definite statement for Mobilization, Concentration, Strategical and Grand Tactical projects.

J. Sutherland Brown
Colonel,
D.M.O. and I.

The Navy Deals with Revolution
in Latin America, 1932

REAR-ADMIRAL FRANK HOUGHTON

Canada's tiny navy happened to be sailing off Central America when a revolution broke out in El Salvador. To maintain order and to protect British interests, the RCN intervened. Houghton's account tells the story.

In January 1932 we set out on what was to become the annual Southern Cruise. Calling in at San Diego, where we were guests of the U.S. Navy, we then visited Manzanillo, Mexico, where we painted ship in preparation for our rendezvouz with the East Coast destroyers in the Caribbean. As it happened, we got no further than Balboa, the Pacific entrance to the Panama Canal. . . .

On the 22nd of January, not quite halfway to the Canal, we intercepted a wireless message addressed to Naval Service Headquarters from the Commander-in-Chief, America and West Indies Squadron. It stated the British Foreign Office had reported that British lives and property in the Central American Republic of El Salvador were in danger owing to the imminent possibility of a Communist-inspired uprising in that country; and would it be possible to divert *Skeena* and *Vancouver* to the ports of Acajutla and La Libertad respectively? We immediately altered course for Acajutla and ordered *Vancouver* to La Libertad, actions which N.S.H.Q. approved by signal soon afterwards. We arrived at Acajutla at noon the following day. . . .

Canadian warships were on the spot, and on this occasion we made headlines all over the world. As one newspaper writer put it, "After spending several years in virtual oblivion, the Royal Canadian Navy has suddenly emerged into the full glare of the international limelight." While this statement was slightly tinged with journalistic exaggeration, the fact remains that our presence in El Salvador on this occasion certainly increased the number of people who now knew that there really was such a thing as the R.C.N., even if certain English dailies referred to us as H.M.C.S. *Schuyler*, and the Secretary for Foreign Affairs in the British House of Commons was unable to enlighten the members as to the meaning of the "C" in H.M.C.S. It took another war to clear that one up! . . .

Anchoring one mile off the only pier, we found Acajutla to be little more than a native village, a collection of low huts on the flat, sandy littoral with three more or less prominent buildings—the British Consulate, the Railway Station and the headquarters of the Port Commandant. Acajutla's importance lay in the fact that it was—and still is—the terminus of the British-owned railway connecting with San Salvador, the capital of the Republic. . . .

In order to ascertain the actual state of affairs the Captain sent me ashore in the ship's motorboat with two armed men hidden under the engineroom canopy—just in case. I was met by the British Vice Consul, the Port Commandant and the Port Doctor. I learned from the Consul that so far all was quiet locally, but there had been several disturbances up-country; and that at Sonsonate only fifteen miles up the line, the Customs House had been attacked, five Customs police killed and their bodies dragged into the street and mutilated. The attacking Indians all wore red armbands with the letters "S.R.I."—"Socorro Rojo Internationale," "Red International Aid." This certainly seemed to confirm that the uprising was Communist-inspired. The Railway offices in Sonsonate were close to the Customs House and the railway officials, fearing further trouble had brought their wives to Acajutla and we were asked if we could accommodate them on board *Skeena* until the situation cleared up. This we managed to do with some dislocation to the junior officers' accommodation, and we had five ladies on board for eight days. We heard later that the newspapers had made great copy out of this knightly gesture of ours; one report went so far as to say that ". . . there are five lady refugees now on board *Skeena* but the Commanding Officer reports they are in no immediate danger"!

It happened that one of our "refugees," a very pretty young Spanish lady, was very obviously pregnant; in fact, we were given to understand that she was quite liable to present us with an additional refugee at any moment. Our Medical Officer at that time was the late Major J. Earl Hunter, R.C.A.M.C. . . . As an Army doctor, obstetrics was certainly not his *forte*, and for those eight days Doc Hunter was the most nervous man on board. We organised a sweep in the wardroom as to whether it would be a boy or a girl, with the "field" in case it was twins.

However, in the end we were able to put the young lady ashore before anything happened, and Doc breathed a heartfelt sigh of relief.

The Captain went ashore and spoke to the British Charge d'Affaires in San Salvador by telephone. He was requested to visit the capital to judge the situation for himself. The Consul suggested it would be advisable that his party be armed in case of trouble on the line. The Captain decided to take me with him, and we were accompanied by the Gunner's Mate, Petty Officer Priske, who carried a Lewis gun and a couple of drums of ammunition in his lashed-up hammock. . . .

Arriving at Sonsonate, our driver refused to go any further, apparently having been persuaded by his friends that he would be most unlikely to get through alive. This wasn't particularly encouraging for us, but someone found a volunteer for the job and we passed safely through the so-called "danger area," reaching San Salvador without incident. . . .

The government of President Araujo came into power in the normal way in 1931. Despite many public utterances and voluble protestations to the contrary, it appears that the President (well-educated, married to an English wife and with two charming daughters) not only failed to carry out his election promises of higher wages and better living conditions for the workers; he soon amassed a private fortune said to be at least half a million dollars.

As a result there was a revolution in December 1931, led by General Maximilian Hernandez Martinez and a group of young military officers, supported by the Army which President Araujo had rashly omitted to pay. The Government was overthrown, the President and his family escaped to Guatemala and General Martinez took over the reins of government. His government had not been recognized by the United States, Great Britain or the other Central American Republics by the time we arrived. It also appeared that in the two months during which the General had been in power, no changes had taken place in Government policy and conditions in the country were as bad as ever. . . .

In the circumstances, it is hardly to be wondered at that Communism made many converts. Organised by experienced agitators, the workers were soon ready for decisive action of the "oppressed classes" against "capitalism." Finally, on the night of January 22nd 1932, disturbances broke out simultaneously in several of the larger towns in the Republic. This was the situation which prompted the British Consul to report to the Foreign Office.

On our arrival in the city of San Salvador, we were surprised to find that the Consul had sent a message requesting *Skeena* to ". . . land an armed party immediately" without having consulted the Salvador Government though this was obviously correct procedure under International Law. An armed party was in fact sent ashore but was not allowed to land; whereupon the Consul repeated his message. This time the party was allowed to form up on the pier but to go no further. They were therefore employed filling sandbags as a form of protection for railway cars in case they should be ordered to proceed up-country.

It very soon appeared that the British Consul, egged on by the Railway authorities, had panicked unduly. This was confirmed when the Captain and I were given an audience by General Martinez himself. He stated quite definitely that he had the situation well in hand and was adamant in his refusal to allow our party to land as he could see no reason whatsoever for foreign intervention. Commander Brodeur assured the President that we were only trying to help, but that we must insist on immediate and thorough protection of British lives and interests. This was at once promised, and by the next morning the whole of the Railway and all British property were under the protection of the National Guard; a picked body of men who were well trained, better armed than the ordinary troops and with a reputation for fearlessness. It soon became clear that General Martinez was as good as his word.

As it was considered too risky for us to return to Acajutla at night, we were accommodated in the residence of one of the railway officials who had moved his family, together with those of other British residents, to the Station Building, where it was considered they would have some protection. The Captain and I slept in a double bed, sharing the only pair of pajamas we could find and the one and only sheet which was meant for a single bed. It wasn't a particularly comfortable night, and we were disturbed at intervals by sporadic gunfire, which we strongly suspected was probably bored soldiers shooting at stray cats as the curfew which the General had instituted appeared to be completely successful. We returned to the ship the following day.

For the next few days the General's troops were busy rooting out the disaffected Indians, shooting them after a brief interrogation, then soaking their bodies in gasoline and burning them. The ringleaders were hanged on the nearest tree. We were informed that to date 4,800 had been executed and that the situation was rapidly "returning to normal."

On our last day in El Salvador, Generals Calderon and Chatore arrived in Acajutla and invited the Commanding Officers of *Skeena* and *Vancouver* to lunch in Sonsonate and ". . . to witness a few executions." They reported the lunch as excellent, but while they were shown the five prisoners, they felt it inadvisable to be present at the executions.

So ended our Salvador adventure.

The Non-Permanent Active Militia in the Great Depression

MAJOR J. MURRAY SAVAGE

We've always had pacifist advocates of disarmament, some related to our potential enemies, others simply the victims of woolly thinking, and we still have them, particularly in times of economic stress. A particularly virulent strain was headed by an M.P. named Agnes McPhail who distinguished herself annually by a motion that Canada's expenditure on National Defense be reduced to one dollar. She had appreciable support from voters reduced to desperation by no work, no welfare, no insurance and no improvement in sight.

The result of pressure on government was disgraceful neglect of all of our armed forces including the NPAM. Militia pay was meagre and for commissioned ranks non-existent as all of it was usually turned over to the mess. Equipment was inadequate and replacement of it almost non-existent. The state of our Naval and Air Force reserve units was no better than that of the Army.

In these difficult conditions the units managed to carry on mainly because of the unfailing efforts of a solid core of dedicated individuals. Most of these leaders were or became senior officers, but in the successful units there was a similar basic structure among the ORs [other ranks], and a strong Sergeants Mess also a vital factor in their survival. Somehow at both levels recruits were found to replace those who finished their tours of duty.

The most reliable source of junior officers continued to be RMC, whence at that time a very small proportion of graduates were joining the permanent forces. There was no compulsory full-time service for ex-cadets, but in repayment for an almost free education there was an understood and almost completely observed obligation to serve at least three years in the NPAM, including of course Naval and Air Force units. The result was an input of about three dozen new officers each year, many of whom served for many more than three years. Other new officers came less regularly from universities. . . .

Annual training in the 'thirties amounted to weekly evening parades and exercises during the winter months, full time summer camp for a week or so, and occasional parades for special occasions. . . .

As economic activity continued to drop in the early 'thirties so did weekly parade attendance and general interest. At the same time it seemed that some unemployed young men were joining up partly to acquire warm trousers and a good pair of boots. This was acceptable of course as long as they attended parades, but when they did not there was no way of replacing this clothing. It had to be returned and most of it was, but the process of getting it back was often tiresome. Many a long evening was spent by senior as well as junior officers, generally in pairs, driving around the areas of Point St. Charles, Goose Village, Verdun and St. Henri, and applying a blend of firmness and cajolery, usually to the culprit's mothers, in order to recover the missing government property.

The highlight of each year's activity was of course the period at training camp, which meant firing practice at Petawawa. An interesting item here was that militia batteries were sometimes short of junior officers because some could not be released, or did not dare ask for release, from precarious civilian occupations. Such vacancies could be filled by serving cadets on summer leave with benefit to all concerned, not only at the time but in establishing connections for post-graduate service.

Opportunities of this kind had also occurred before the Depression Period and the writer once managed to attend camp in Petawawa with the Toronto Regiment in the middle 'twenties. This was an unusual experience and an interesting one because at that time Petawawa represented an oasis for the desert folk of Ontario . . . The flow of fluids from the land of plenty across the Ottawa River was a wondrous thing, and by evening time "Old King Cole" was a "Jolly Old Soul indeed."

Unfortunately but inevitably Training Camp activity also suffered as the depression deepened. Time was cut down, numbers of personnel were cut to skeleton proportions, and in some cases Camp was suspended entirely. In effect the NPAM units were left to get along as best they could until prospects of war provided stimulation. Their survival was amply demonstrated in 1939. Had they not been there, ready and able to expand by recruiting up to strength and with trained reserves available, 1 Cdn Div would not have been in the U.K. by the year-end.

Cadet Life at the Royal Military College in the 1930s

BRIGADIER-GENERAL ROBERT BENNETT

Date—the mid-1930s
Location—mainly, but not exclusively, a "flat" in the Stone Frigate
Time—0555 to 2215 hrs, any day in late October.
In pre-dawn darkness the flat-orderly rouses each recruit, and draped in FS cap, towel and soft slippers (hard heels are sleep-disturbing) we twelve line up by the clock to "sound" a hoarsely-whispered, "Reveillé, Reveillé, Reveillé" at precisely 0600 hrs. in unison with Trumpeter Fox as he signals from in front of the faceless Clock Tower the official start of another day. En masse, we jostle into the "bogs" for the sadistic cold-bath ritual and then to report our bedewed bodies before the slumbering form of the appointed Senior. For those on Defaulters it is then a tantivy to get on parade before the BOS (Battalion Orderly Sergeant) calls a Marker and then the Roll. After a cursory inspection by the BOS, or occasionally by a disgruntled Orderly Officer, the defaulters begin their dreary, mindless circuits of the Square in full marching kit until dismissal at 0645. (Throughout this, one catches glimpses

of furtive figures dressed in riding kit crossing the Square—seniors fulfilling their local punishment of "Breeks").

For the recruit-defaulter such timing means a breathless return to your room moments after the remaining recruits "sound" the second flat-call of the day—this a full-throated "Dress, Dress, Dress" to signify to the lie-a-beds that Breakfast Parade is but 15 minutes away. Hopefully, seniors appear on their own, but many have to be awakened, and each to be presented with the appropriate uniform items, buttons polished and trousers creased—the latter accomplished by yourself having slept on (NOT in) them throughout the night. Five minutes later, again from in front of the Clock, comes the Flat-Orderly's rendition of "Ten More Minutes," sometimes described as sounding not unlike a heifer in heat!

With luck, you and your room-mate can usually count on a few very brief minutes to put the finishing touches to your room, and mutual whisking before lining up for the last group call of "Turn-Out, Turn-Out, Turn-Out"! Chaos then reigns while Seniors are accoutred and whisked, upper classmen begin to move onto the company assembly area of the Square (or in foul and winter weather, in the hallways of the Administration Building where the Upper and Lower Dining-rooms and basement kitchen are located). "Three Minutes More" from the Flat Orderly alone signals a scurry of late-risers to vacate the dormitory for the morning ritual of Breakfast Parade—roll call, inspection, and finally the march into breakfast. Except for a slightly more human routine on Sundays, each day begins in identical fashion, the only diversion for a recruit being through the acquisition of periods of "ex-recruiting"—or medical "light duty." The former is awarded in numbers of days as recognition for some commendable endeavour, usually athletic in nature.

Whether in the old dining-rooms, or the new dining-room (opened in mid-1936) the meal begins with a rather irreverent (and perhaps irrelevant) "For what we are about to receive, thank God" and chairs are occupied. The BSM [Battalion Sergeant-Major] and six CSM's sit in awesome isolation, whereas the remaining Seniors are seated at either end of each table flanked by several recruits, and with the remaining places taken by 3rd and 2nd Classmen. Throughout the meal

Seniors are uninhibited; 2nd and 3rd Classmen sit erectly but are allowed to converse quietly; and recruits—existing on but 2 inches of their chairs—sit at rigid attention, staring straight ahead, usually directly into a pair of eyes on the opposite side of the table. This in itself is not entirely conducive to good digestion, or to appreciation of the gastronomic delights of the food! Nevertheless, most recruits manage to stow away more than enough as indicated by solid gains in weight over the months.

Once the Mess has been dismissed by the Senior Cadet present, one is free to leave the table, provided permission is sought from and granted by the Senior Cadet remaining at the table. Such is done by "proving"—a rigorously executed extension of the right arm to shoulder height, and, when queried, an unintelligible staccato "permission-toleavethetableplease?" (Indeed, "proving" is an essential part of a recruit's existence. As he never speaks until spoken to, it is mandatory to attract initial attential silently by "proving." When standing one does so by smartly raising the right forearm elbow high and then to pose the request or question in the form "permission-to———?") Back on the company flat each recruit "stands by" in his room for room inspection with bed made according to an unvarying daily format, floor swept, uniforms hanging in pre-ordained arrangement, windows open at prescribed levels, and overall—everything free of dust and polished! Immediately that ordeal is concluded the room of your personal Senior is similarly "repaired" and put to rights, for all rooms may be inspected by the Company Officer during the day.

At 0745 the already described "sounding" is repeated at the appropriate intervals to alert everyone to the commencement of the daily academic programme when the "C" in RMC comes into its own! After all, Gentlemen Cadets are there primarily to gain an education despite the many unofficial distractions and impediments to the contrary. Classes continue until 1230 hrs., except for a 30 minute "Milk and Biscuits" break halfway through the morning, and even then the unfortunate Flat Orderly is required to return to his flat in order to once more "sound" the four calls for the benefit of anyone temporarily on the flat for whatever reason! Of course the inconvenience of returning to the "flat" at that hour can also provide a flash of quiet amusement by witnessing the garrulous flat-servants characterised by Alf 'inks and Nuts Nuttal as they argue the relative merits of the "'ome and away" football opportunity to instant wealth. This half-hour break is also used for Company Orderly Room should any miscreant have to be paraded to his Company Commander for official reasons of discipline when the punishment can be as high as 28 days CB [confined to barracks]. For truly heinous crimes one is paraded in an atmosphere of absolute automation before the awful majesty of the Commandant—a semi-deity seldom seen, but whose distant and omnipotent presence overwhelms every facet of college life. And he can award that worst of all punishments—a protracted period of "rustication"!

Lunch parade is repetitive of breakfast, except that Seniors are now much more alert—and unpredictable, depending upon the course of the morning. Recruits have always to be in possession of two things: a bundle of ten matches, and a joke. The former is for the benefit of a Senior's cigarette, while the latter is for his entertainment. When a recruit is ordered to "shoot" a joke, his instant response invariably must begin "permissiontosay, once there was a bugger 'n a bitch." No other form is acceptable, regardless of the substance of the joke to be "shot." Subtle aspects of sex are encouraged, and once told, a joke is repeated only at peril! And a recruit must never lapse from a stoney-faced delivery—self-appreciation is taboo. One's repertoire and memory develop to truly remarkable proportions which is more than can be said for moral tone. The matches, too, present a constant hazard, for the friction from straight arms swung at unnatural height and speed not infrequently result in a minor conflagration in the pocket where the bundle (cardboard covers are not permitted) is carried. . . .

Later, as the playing fields begin to fall into shadow, everything suddenly comes to an instant stop as Trumpeter Fox's pure notes of "retreat" signal that the Flag is being lowered. Though it occurs daily, it remains a poignant moment as every College activity within earshot halts to pay homage to a colourful bit of bunting slowly descending the flag pole—an act that occurs unchanging throughout every reach of the British Empire at the setting of the sun.

Soon the trek back to the flat begins in preparation for dinner parade, though the footballers always seem to remain at practice until the field is enveloped in darkness. Then, the dash to remove mud-caked gear and festoon radiators in the Frigate with sodden clothing—drying rooms are non-existent—a quick shower, and "Dress, Dress, Dress." Dinner Parade inspections are always times of tension, especially on Thursdays when "Staff Inspection" is the particular trauma as one Company in ordered rotation is subjected to the coldly impersonal but highly critical eye of the BSM. Lucky the recruit who escapes with no more than one D.D.—Defaulter's Drill—regardless of the impeccability of his pre-parade preparation, for the credo of the BSM is that by his very nature and the low estate a recruit is forever culpable of some infraction, detected or otherwise.

Very soon after arriving at RMC the necessary acceptance of your own inadequacy, at least as it concerns relationships with anyone your senior, manifests itself in the reflexive retort "No excuse" to all accusations. No matter the justification for your action, the degree of your knowledge, the extent of your effort or the effect of your experience, when you are challenged it is mandatory—sine qua non—to offer no excuse or explanation other than covered by "No excuse," "Yes," or "No." Under some circumstances this can denigrate the very meaning of the first word of the College motto—Truth. And unfortunately, such unthinking responses result in an expressionless, unresponsive facade when confronting authority in its various guises.

The scene soon shifts back to the flat and an hour of utter silence as enforced study takes over at 1915 hrs. A recruit's door must remain open so that he can be seen to be at his desk, regardless of where his mind may be. All too soon the blessed hour of peace is roughly shattered by a call for all recruits to appear in three minutes, dressed in sweaters, toques and fatigue clothing to participate in a battalion or flat "bender," or even for some specialized individual ministrations! At other less cantankerous evenings the Seniors may desire the rude, uninhibited amusement produced by a "flat show," or recruit participation in a variety of games such as "Burnt Meat" (who can sit longest on an over-heated radiator), "Sliding Jesus," removing the fuzz from new flannelette pyjamas by a Senior holding matches at the bottom of each leg (and watch your eyebrows!), or pushing an open can of shoe polish with your nose the length of the hallway. Boisterous, to say the least!!!

However, even the less pleasant antics must end, usually at the bugle notes of "First Post," so that all may prepare for the nightly announcement of the next morning's Defaulter, the staccato summons "Roll Call this flat, stand by in front of your doors!", the last scramble to collect your senior's gear to prepare it for the morrow—and at 2215 hrs. the sadly sweet haunting sound of "Lights Out." Though others may be working later, for the recruit the trials and tribulations of 17 hours have ended.

We Owed It to Our Country, 1936, 1938

W.L. MACKENZIE KING

> *Prime Minister King is usually thought to have been uninterested in defence questions. These diary entries from 1936 and 1938 make clear that the Liberal cabinet as a whole was largely antagonistic to military spending, but that King could see the weaknesses in Canada's preparations for another war.*

September 10, 1936

The afternoon was taken up with many minor matters, and with an interesting discussion on defence. I found the Cabinet very much divided, all the French Members, excepting Lapointe, pretty well content to leave matters as they are. Some of the English Members rather fearful of doing very much. Gardiner made a first class presentation of the need of protecting Canada's Commerce with Britain through the St. Lawrence if we were to hope for trade with Britain. Lapointe and Dunning were both prepared to go a considerable length on coast defence, though Dunning stressed pretty strongly the costs. I was surprised that Ilsley saw little or no need for safeguarding Atlantic coasts. Excepting Mackenzie, I myself presented, I think, the strongest case for immediate coast defence, taking the ground that as a Canadian citizen, I thought we owed it to our country to protect it in a mad world, at least to the extent of police service, both on sea and in the air, alike on the Atlantic and Pacific coasts. I stated it was humiliating to accept protection from Britain without sharing on the costs, or to rely on the United States without being willing to at least protect our neutrality.

That we had no enemies, but owed it to ourselves and subsequent generations to lay foundations on which they would have to build. I told Mackenzie he might have to extend his five year programme to ten years. Got agreement on having Departmental Committee gather information re war supply materials, food transportation facilities, munitions, and facilities for producing such. I drafted this order pretty much in my own way this morning. I spoke very earnestly of the unsettled conditions of the world, and the danger of class struggle extending to Canada. . . .

Owing to the wet, the men were not paraded at Barriefield. I found the buildings interesting and apparently suitable except that the officers' mess seemed to me quite overdone being much finer, in some of its rooms, than any part of the Chateau Laurier. I was told that the Officers themselves had contributed to the expense. It shocked me a bit to find young men being put into buildings filled with gas, so as to prepare them for gas attacks, but such is modern warfare. I thought that a great deal more might have been done towards improving the grounds than has thus far been done. Indeed around the Military College and approaches to and from, there is room for a great deal of improvement in which men who are unemployed might be set to work.

In the Military College, it was interesting to reflect that had I been a year older at the time, I might myself have received a training at the Military College. I recall father was very anxious I should take a course there, and was impressed by the value of the training. I was, however, a year too young at the time of being prepared to enter. I thought of the prospect of young Harry Lay going to the Military College, and am now inclined to think it is wise that he should do so, though, at first, I viewed the matter somewhat differently. He no doubt inherits a love of military life through his father, and would probably make a success of the opportunities that would grow out of a training there.

I was impressed in visiting the College, at seeing a statue—a gift of the French Government to the College—in recognition of the services to France in the Great War, of graduates of the College. The statue, small in size, is appropriately placed on a pedestal, at the top of a stair-case, on either side of which are portraits of Wolfe and Montcalm. It was interesting too to recall that Alexander Mackenzie had laid the corner-stone of the Military College. He also was employed as a stonemason at one or more of the Martello Towers in connection with Fort Henry. . . .

August 1, 1938

One could not but feel how great an ideal of service men must carry in their breast, who devote their lives to the military career, especially one to be lived in the Spartan simplicity of early colonial days. . . .

August 19, 1938

At Camp Borden, Brigadier Elkins drove me over the fields in search of the infantry. We were unable to discover them but came across the mechanical transport and saw them go through part of their operations. Returning to headquarters, we passed the tanks manoeuvring and saw the cavalry returning. The different services were brought together for a review at the saluting base where I took the salute. Before this, however, I went over part of the airport with Air Vice Marshal Croil. The day was very warm and the driving over the ground, which was very rough, quite an exertion; also standing for the saluting at the base. I shall always remember a dog running in front of the horses at the head of the procession. The London band played just opposite the base. McCuaig, M.P., and his wife, and MacLean, M.P., and his wife, along with Jennie, Jean and Rosabel were with me at the saluting base. Later we were given tea in the Officers' Mess. Met the Officers and some of their wives, and later had a special inspection of one of the new tanks recently arrived from England.

I confess the effect of the visit was on the whole depressing. To begin with, such buildings as there are, are very dilapidated and out of date; fire traps, primitive kind of sanitary arrangements. The ground is overgrown with poison ivy; except a muddy stream, there is no water for bathing, and there is little in the way of interest for the men at the Camp.

On arrival, I have been greeted by the guard of honour—French Canadian Regiment from Montreal. An exchange officer, a young lad from India, was among the number of Officers. It seemed to me the life was excessively hard for the young men, as it expressed only privation. Life itself, I should think, would be hardly endurable in the tanks.

Men must have some great ideal of service or heroism in their breasts to engage in the work of the kind to enable them to go on.

The Army Goes to War, 1939

MAJOR E.G. WEEKS

Major Weeks was the assistant director of organization at National Defence Headquarters. His diary conveys the ebb and flow of opinion as Canada made its decision for war in August and September 1939.

1939
23 Aug.

The A.G. (Maj. Gen. Matthews) called me at 10.00 P.M. and said there would be a meeting of Defence Council at 10.00 A.M. tomorrow. He wanted me to have ready for the meeting a submission to Council seeking authority to bring the P[ermanent] F[orce] up to Peace establishment.

24 Aug.

Everybody busy at the office before 9.00 A.M. Vokes and I prepared two submissions. One to bring P.F. up to establishment, the other for increasing key specialists to Peace establishment. After meeting of Council, the A.G. told me the key specialists submission was agreed upon and would be included in first Gov. Gen. Warrant. All P.F. leave cancelled. Mil. Secy. (Clyde Scott) told me the Minister was of the opinion there was little hope for peace. Working tonight on authorization for increases in P.F. units; wires, etc., will go out first thing in morning. C.G.S. on leave, expected back tonight.

25 Aug.

C.G.S. back late last night, remainder Military Members of Council waiting for him. They had late meeting. Decided to send, in code, wires re increases in Arty personnel at Coasts and AA Bty.—More delay. Orders went out for 4 AA Bty to return to Kingston from

Petawawa at once and be at 12 hrs notice move by train to Halifax. "Precautionary period" telegram sent at 2315 hrs. Cabinet meeting today, but nothing announced in press.

26 Aug.

Minister approved G.O. calling out NPAM units on service. Kept staff here all day up to 10:00 P.M. G.S. ordered 4 AA Bty to Halifax, leaving Kingston after 8:00 P.M. DOsC 6 and 11 reported difficulty in obtaining Arty recruits quickly. Tried to get Col. Stockwell, O.A., R.C.A., on phone, but could not locate. Col. Stuart, DMO & I, stated good progress in turning out NPAM reported. MD 2 reports Irish Regt of Toronto unable to obtain sufficient recruits. Therefore decided to add York (1st American Regt) to list of units. . . .

31 Aug.

Woke up at 6.30 A.M. and decided to turn on radio. Heard Hitler's speech. Knew it was war. At 7.00 A.M. A.G. phoned me and I left for office at once. We worked hard getting submissions to Council ready.

1 Sep.

Gov. decided to place Militia on active service in Canada (Mobile Force). Although all submissions to Council were ready and all plans made, we were horrified to hear the Cabinet decided at last minute to change the name of the Mobile Force from "Canadian Field Force" to "Canadian Active Service Force." The result being many changes, torn up stencils, and $65,000.00 worth of Mobilization forms almost useless. Very hectic day—but we managed to get the General Order 135/1939 issued and in the mail to all Districts. . . .

3 Sep.

At 0730 hrs. Cpl. Goss (Orderly) woke me up. He said "Good Morning, Sir, it is 7.30—War is declared." Turned on radio and heard Chamberlain's speech. France is expected to follow with her declaration in a few minutes. France is in. Heard the King's speech—very good. Mackenzie King, Lapointe (in French), Rogers, Power (in French) on radio this afternoon. I gather from their speeches nothing will be decided till Parliament opens on 7 Sep. Lt. Smith (my assistant) wrote military Orders for the Opening of Parliament. It will be a service dress affair as in 1914. Writing Orders for the Opening of Parliament rather amused me, when we were so very busy on mobilization problems....

6 Sep.

Heard today that Gov. has decided not to send any land troops out of Canada, but might consider sending 18 Bomber Squadrons on the say-so of C.A.S. I doubt very much whether such a number could be equipped or maintained from Canadian resources for some time. In any event Orders were sent out to DOsC stopping mobilization of 45 units, provided recruiting had not commenced. It was also decided not to adopt the original plan of moving troops to Concentration Camps on M+21 day. This change possibly because of weather and isolated location of camps. Troops to be billeted and Q.M.G. is now arranging. There is a continual stream of "A" problems coming in from Districts. The mob. machinery is creaking, but it is going! ...

7 Sep.

House of Commons opened today. ...

8 Sep.

This was a very disappointing day. The House of Commons heard a long three hours speech by the P.M., which was to the effect that it was up to Parliament to decide whether to declare war or not. It appears the Gov. has decided not to send a Field Force but rather to send individuals to serve in the R.A.F. This would mean loss of Canadian recognition. Recruiting returns show that approximately 30,000 have been attested to date in the C.A.S.F. Had to phone D.O.D. 13 (Calgary) re stopping mobilization of certain units, but as enlistment had commenced told him to carry on. Was told I would not be able to take up my appointment in C.A.S.F. for some months. Saw Col. Earnshaw, who is going to see what he could do. Meeting Earnshaw, Genet, MacPherson, re C.A.S.F. (Signals).

9 Sep.

Routine work. Kicks are beginning to come in as to why such and such a unit has not been ordered to mobilize. House of Commons still sitting. Heard on radio that debate on Throne Speech had been concluded without division and that the Government was preparing a proclamation declaring a state of war between Canada and Germany.

10 Sep.

At 1243 hours today Department of National Defence received a copy of Proclamation of War Canada/Germany. The G.S. sent out the "War Telegram," and I note the date of war in Canada's case is 10 Sep, whereas G. Britain is 3 Sep. This will be meat for the constitutional lawyers. The Proclamation was not announced on the radio till 1310 hrs. One hears there is little chance of an Expeditionary Force for the time being at any rate. Q.M.G. Branch very busy working out details for winter accommodation.

Creating the 1st Canadian Division, 1939

LIEUTENANT-GENERAL GUY SIMONDS

On reporting to Headquarters in Ottawa I was informed that the "special duties" to which I had been assigned were a cover for the appointment G1 S.S.O 2 (Operations) of 1 Canadian Division. The division was being formed but was not as yet so designated, and its formation was to be kept secret until officially announced. Maj.Gen. McNaughton, nominally appointed "Inspector General" of the units selected to mobilize to war strength was to be the Divisional Commander, Col. Guy. Turner his S.S.O 1. and Col E.W. Sansom the A.A. and Q.M.G.—the senior general and administrative staff officers. Maj. A.E. (Ernie) Walford had been appointed D.A.Q.M.G. (Supplies, movements and quartering) and Maj Darell Laing D.A.A.G. (Personnel Administration). Both these officers were from the Non-Permanent Active Militia. Ernie Walford, by misrepresenting his age, had served as an artillery signaller in the field in World War I and had been awarded the M.M. Between the wars he had continued part time military service as a conscientious and able officer with the Montreal Militia Artillery Regiment and had passed the Senior Militia Staff Course with Distinction. Darell Laing was a Rhodes Scholar, had been serving with a Halifax Militia Regiment and had also passed the Senior Militia Staff Course. In the war years ahead both these officers were to establish enviable reputations as exceptionally capable administrators. Capt Churchill Mann, who had been a classmate at R.M.C. in our recruit year, and had just completed the course at the Staff College, Camberley was G.S.O.3. (Intelligence) and Lord Tweedsmuir, son of the Governor General and working in Canada at the outbreak of war had immediately joined the Canadian Army, and was appointed divisional intelligence officer. This staff team of 1 Canadian Division remained substantially the same until after Dunkirk and regroupings of higher formations for defence of U.K. started a wave of new postings. Though probably not unique, to play a major part in the raising of a division from the status of civilian recruits off the street, to a highly battle worthy formation was not an experience shared by many officers.

I was delighted with my posting, for the duties of G.S.O.2. embraced operations and training—subjects which my studies and work in recent years equipped me to tackle with confidence and enthusiasm, though during the weeks in Ottawa, before moving overseas my work was in the sphere of what in military language was called "staff duties"—concerned with organization and equipment.

As appointees to divisional headquarters arrived in Ottawa we set up shop in two stories of an old red brick office building on Queen Street which had been rented for the purpose. Whilst General McNaughton and Guy Turner travelled across the country inspecting and signing-up regiments and battalions as recruits streamed in, the rest of the divisional staff worked on organization and equipment tables to put together and arm a division for war. In Canada we had literally nothing in the way of modern weapons and negotiations were in train between the Canadian government and National Defence Headquarters on the one hand and the British government and war office on the other as to the equipment of a Canadian Division if and when it was dispatched overseas. In the interest of demonstrating Commonwealth solidarity in the war crisis, it was desirable to have the leading Canadian formation transferred across the Atlantic to the European theatres as early as possible, and this in turn was dictated more by the availability and assembly of shipping, to which other considerations had to be subordinated, rather than the state of readiness of the troops. Canadian cloth and clothing manufacturers rose to the occasion and provided the new pattern battledress quickly, of good quality and well made, and nearly all troops were outfitted with it before we embarked in December. But proper boots were a serious deficiency. Not only were our available supplies negligible, but I was informed by General McNaughton that production could not proceed in Canada because of lack of stocks of flax linen thread which had to be imported from Northern Ireland. Military and heavy duty boots had to be stitched with linen thread for cotton, then the only available alternative, would not stand up to rough usage and a cycle of alternate wetting and drying. The shortage of boots was a serious handicap to even elementary training. Though General McNaughton got authority for units to purchase footwear locally through retail stores, it was an expedient that only partially solved the problem and some men went overseas still wearing the footwear they were wearing on enlistment.

The worst shortcoming during the time we spent in Canada was failure to send our staff officers out to visit the mobilizing troops and their officers and commanders. I believe this was a result of exaggerated secrecy about Canada raising a division for overseas service and to avoid any action which implied that our mobilized troops comprised in fact a divisional order of battle. I considered this exaggerated secrecy more a Canadian political issue than anything closely related to the risks of war, and military efficiency was the loser. It was not until regiments settled into quarters in Aldershot that the staff officers who were largely to chart their destiny met the troops that they were serving, and then in an atmosphere confused with many other and new problems. General McNaughton, Colonels Turner and Sansom had frequently visited units in Canada, but they had been the only ones permitted to do so.

General McNaughton Talks to
the Prime Minister, 1939

W.L. MACKENZIE KING

*A former chief of the general staff and head of the National Research
Council, McNaughton took command of the 1st Canadian Division.
Just before departure for England in December 1939, he met the
prime minister, who quickly saw that the general was under strain.*

December 7, 1939

After lunch I had a short rest. At 2.45 Gen. McNaughton called to say
goodbye. He talked till a quarter past 3. He said to me that he was
"absolutely content" with everything pertaining to the First Division.
The right men had been appointed as officers. He had inspected the
different regiments; looked at almost every man. They were in good
condition—the medical examination had been very strict because of
the many seeking to enlist. They had been well out-fitted. Everything
was as complete as it could be, except the equipment which they were
to secure in England. He could not wish for a finer body of men.

He expressed his strong admiration and affection for Rogers, who,
he said, had done excellent work as Minister; had gained the confidence of the army.

He spoke of there being a feeling among manufacturers that orders
were not being placed for equipment and more in the way of munitions. I encouraged him to tell me anything that he had in mind. He
then went on to say that the fault he had was not with the Ministers but
with the bureaucracy of the Treasury Board. He thought Campbell of
the War Supply Board should be given a free hand to mobilize industry
as he thought best, and in a way which would take account of the possibility of the war going on for two or three years, placing orders immediately to meet situations as far ahead as that. He believed the moment
would come when a terrible onslaught would be made upon Britain
and many of her industrial plants might be put out of business. She
would have to look to us to supply her with equipment, munitions, etc.
He said the manufacturers had secured tools and skilled men, antici-
pating large orders. The latter, at Massey-Harris, were washing windows, having nothing else to do.

I asked him if the Defence Department were to blame. He said on the contrary, that some of their men were very discouraged at not being able to get what they thought should be supplied. I asked if Ralston was at fault. He said he had found Ralston most agreeable in first conversations, but thought he had come lately under the influence of Finance officials. He spoke rather strongly against Clark as being too much of a bureaucrat; thinking only of the fiscal year, not understanding war conditions. He thought Campbell of the Supply Board might resign some day. Said he and Campbell were very close friends. That he (McNaughton) had really been the one who had worked up all the plans for industrial mobilization. They had been ready when the war broke out but had not been put into execution as yet. He spoke about Simard's plant at Sorel. Described it as an amazing concern. Thought Simard was a real patriot, was not concerned about profits. Spoke of the old ships he had bought and which were being converted into guns; referred to it as a marvel of industry.

I thanked him for giving me his views and said I would go into the matter at once. In saying goodbye he thanked me again for the way in which I had backed him and the sympathy I had shown him in everything and said that it was what I had said to him that had made him accept the position. I told him he would find me and the government at his back. I then asked him if he would give a message to the officers and men of the First Division, telling them how greatly I admired their bravery, how much they were in the thoughts of the country, and to emphasize to them the nature of their part in the war as a crusade— defenders of the faith and of civilization against the domination of free countries by barbarism.

The last word I said to him was to remember that in quietness and confidence was strength, and that God was on his side. We both felt the emotion of the situation. I gave him as well messages for his boys. They as well as he are in war. Mrs. McNaughton is going to England to help in work of mercy.

As I talked with McNaughton I felt a little concern about his being able to see this war through without a break-down. I felt he was too far on in years to be taking on so great a job. Having been through the strain of a previous war that he and many others like him might find they had not the endurance that they believed they had. I am even more convinced that the Canadian public would not have listened to anyone else as Commander of the Expeditionary Force.

A Small Boat Captain at Dunkirk, May 1940

REAR ADMIRAL R.W. TIMBRELL

The German blitzkrieg rolled over the borders of the Low Countries and into France, cutting off the British Expeditionary Force. A flotilla of small boats set out to rescue the army; on board one of them was a then junior officer in the Royal Canadian Navy.

On the 26th May the evacuation named "Operation Dynamo" was implemented as ordered with the first ships leaving Dover. During the next nine days, 931 allied ships and yachts were employed in the evacuation, of which 236 were lost. 338,226 allied troops were successfully evacuated to the United Kingdom. Every form of craft was employed i.e. Destroyers, Ferries, Trawlers/Drifters, Skoots, ML's, and yachts including one fire fighting boat from London.

My part in the evacuation started on the 29th May while I was under training at the Gunnery School, Whale Island (not a naval summer holiday camp!) when about 20 of us Acting Sub-Lieutenants were detailed off, ordered to collect our gas masks and shaving gear, and then embarked in a lorry to the Dockyard where we were assigned various craft, yachts and ferries and even mud hoppers.

My assignment was the yacht "Llanthony," located at Kings Stairs, 77 feet long, it was owned by Lord Astor and in every respect a luxury yacht. Here also were my crew members consisting of 6 Newfoundlanders newly recruited into the Royal Navy (all woodsmen, not fishermen); 2 civilians who were diesel engineers from the London Bus Depot (volunteers) and 1 Petty Officer (supply branch). With this "experienced" and "well trained" crew we sailed within the hour to arrive at Ramsgate the next morning—I might mention here that in addition to all this talent onboard I had the pleasure of navigating with an uncorrected magnetic compass! On arrival at Ramsgate I was met by a Captain Royal Navy, who had been appointed as Naval Officer in charge, together with a small staff to receive and dispatch the yachts to and from Dunkirk. An additional task was processing all returning Allied forces. We were handed a chart of the channel with the minefields marked and were given instructions to proceed to Dunkirk, avoiding the minefields on route. Then we were to load off the beaches keeping clear of the MOLES where the larger ships were loading. Barrels of fresh water for the troops on the French beaches were taken on board and each time we returned to Ramsgate we had to restock with water as there was none available to the waiting soldiers over the two weeks except that which we and others transported. The English and French coastlines are flanked by sandbars through which one must sail to reach one's destination: the approach to Dunkirk was alerted by a heavy black cloud over the town from the burning oil tanks; on further approach one witnessed the destruction of the town by German artillery (the German army then was about 10 miles inland) and finally the beaches where 400,000 soldiers (about half the population of Nova Scotia) were crowded in awaiting evacuation. The beach is of white sand, stretches for miles up the coast and is of shallow depth out to a half mile, making it very difficult to close because of the draught. This will increase the loading times with one's own boats from the davits as one endeavours to board soldiers, scrambling to be taken back to England.

It was during this first trip with about 50 soldiers loaded that a near-by explosion off the port bow caused the loss of the anchor, ruptured the fuel lines to both twin screw engines rendering them unserviceable and resulting in the yacht drifting up on the beach. We unloaded (the soldiers not all that keen to return whence they had come!) then dug out the propellers and rudder to avoid damage. My first command! High and dry and not to their Lordships' wishes or expectations! It was from a backdrop of thousands of soldiers, seated on the beach, disciplined, under shell fire and bombs that a Sergeant with 8 Guardsmen appeared at the yacht to inquire if they could be of use as they also wished to return to England.

I asked the Sergeant to go back into the town and bring down a tank (this equipment was then being destroyed to avoid it falling into the hands of the Germans.) This he did, and on my further direction drove it out into the water until it stopped. We used the tank as an anchor and fulcrum (good use of army equipment!) to pull ourselves off the beach as the yacht was fitted with an after capstan. No time to pause, loading recommenced and after 4 hours with about 100 soldiers on board we returned to Ramsgate through heavy traffic. Reporting to the NOIC he then assigned 5 drifters/trawlers to my command— before sailing for the second trip I briefed the 5 skippers capturing their full attention when I came to describe the minefields and how we would be and where we would be on loading. Of course on this pleas- ant sunny day in Ramsgate with the quiet green hills in the back- ground I noticed how old the skippers appeared—at least 35 to 40— I at the doubtful age of 20!

We sailed, night passage—unfortunately on the final approach to Dunkirk one of the drifters ran over a mine and disappeared with no survivors. We anchored and loaded from the beach using my small rowboat and the power boat with a total carrying capacity of 16 to load all five ships!

There was no rushing the boats, never-the-less there were many dead floating near the beach from various reasons—yachts on loading being swamped or shelled. To load the five ships was very time- consuming and required a great deal of patience on everyone's part especially the boatmen and it was here where the guardsmen were able to control the embarkation. Envision my Sergeant on the beach yelling orders such as "step lively—don't rush—carry your rifle and keep quiet—no smoking" it worked. The yacht could carry 100 sol- diers and each drifter 75.

My third trip was fairly routine until leaving the beach for the return night passage. On clearing the French coast an "E-Boat" closed for ripe pickings of a white yacht with a yellow funnel and 4 Scottish drifters but we were fortunate to have loaded 8 Bren guns and 2 anti- tank guns— small—on wheels, firing a 40 mm shell. The drifters moved on the inside away from the E Boat and what looked like ripe plums for the picking turned into a prickly opponent as we held fire until the last possible moment and then fired with all 10 guns—the E Boat being close at hand veered off, startled, into the darkness and we continued on to Ramsgate. One of the many fears I had at that moment was if my passengers started to move from one side to another as we were over- loaded but discipline held fast and no problems of imminent capsize occurred.

The fourth trip was cancelled as we were about to return—Dunkirk had fallen but we had evacuated 900 soldiers. . . .

I then returned to Portsmouth with my mixed crew of sailors, civilians and guardsmen. We marched out of the dockyard pulling the anti-tank guns to the main gate near the harbour; this is also where the local buses turn around to resume their routes. I approached the nearest bus to inquire which one would I take for Whale Island. The conductor observing a rather dishevelled Sub Lieutenant backed up by a mixture of unshaven and dirty sailors, soldiers and civilians inquired "Are you just back from Dunkirk Sir?" I said yes and with that he went around to the driver returning in a few seconds to say "Get aboard Sir we will take you there." I then confessed that I had no money, to which he replied "No problem."

The Canadians Go to France—After Dunkirk, 1940

MAJOR-GENERAL HARRY FOSTER

> *After the miraculous evacuation, the British scrambled to re-create a defence line, and elements of the 1st Canadian Division were dispatched to Brest and sent inland. This diary account by Captain Harry Foster, then a junior staff officer, tells the tale of an almost unremembered expedition.*

24 May [1940] Arrived Dover Marine 0630 unable to detrain for 45 minutes place congested by arrival of thousands of refugee civilians and French soldiers rescued by the 20 G[uar]ds B[riga]de and a destroyer force during the night from Boulogne. The refugees were a sight to make your blood boil. . . .

We were given a filthy breakfast at the customs shed and then embarked on the Canterbury. Spent the day loading ammunition and stores. . . . It is quite obvious Calais is now out of the question, why don't we get going for Dunkirk while its still free. At 1800 hrs . . . a liaison officer from Div[ision] arrived to tell us we would entrain for Aldershot at 2000 hrs—how to tell the troops, their blood is up. . . .

26 May At 0230 hrs received warning order to be prepared to move

overseas from the same ports under same arrangements. . . . At 1215 the move was cancelled. We slept the balance of the day. . . .

27 May Vehicles loaded, everyone standing to ready to move. . . . The news in the papers is not so hot. . . . At 1545 received warning order. We do not go to France but will be mobile reserve for defence of G[reat] B[ritain]. . . .

6 June Was hauled out of bed at 0330 hrs by Div. . . . We are to return to Aldershot . . .

8 June All our transport and baggage left for Falmouth at 0800 today—We are to join the re-organized Second Corps under Lt. Gen. Brooke. Thank heaven we are to be just another British Division and not a fancy bunch of pampered colonials. . . .

13 June Arrived Plymouth 0830. . . . Embarked on French ship EL MANSUR congestion terrific. . . .

14 June Arrived Brest 0430 hrs disembarked by 0730 hrs. Heard the most alarming stories of our transport drivers beating up on the town. . . .

15 June At 0430 hrs as dawn broke we arrived at our destination SABLE—two hours late. We were greeted by a rather upset R[ail]way].T[ransport].O[fficer]. who announced that the French were folding up, the Bosch were only 25 kilos away last night, that we were to return to Brest and he was off immediately—he then disappeared. Doubts immediately—was he Fifth Column? What to do? . . . The French railway men say "la guerre est fini." . . .

We detrain ST MALO at 1700 hrs and embark on SS BIAR-RITZ—a British ship, thank God. We are mixed up with R[oyal] E[ngineers], Naval Expeditionary Force and odds and sods, all are full of fight; the French have let us down . . . but we are all cheerful and everyone seems to feel we've a tough job ahead but there's no doubt we can take him—will fight our own battle from now on. This of course all based on no news.

19 June We hear for the first time that the whole of our precious new transport was wrecked at Brest and all our kits burned.

Prejudice Against Aboriginals in the Navy

MAX BASQUE

> *Max Basque, a veteran of the Merchant Navy, tried to join the Royal Canadian Navy. He failed because of a navy policy against recruiting aboriginal Canadians.*

The Navy recruiting officer looked at me. He said, "Are you an Indian?" I said, "Yes, sir." "Sorry we don't take Indians in the Navy. But . . . you're not a full-blooded Indian." "No I'm not," I said. "I don't think there's any full-blooded Indians east of Winnipeg! . . . But on the books I'm an Indian. Here's my border-crossing card." You know, we used to carry those cards, that I'm an Indian, this and that. Didn't have any pictures, like. "Well," he said, "you got a French name: B-a-s-q-u-e. We'll sign you as a Frenchman." I said "No, you won't. . . . That's not a French name, anyway. It's Basque—it's from northern Spain." "Well," he said, "we'll sign you on as Basque." I said, "No. On the books, I was born on the Indian reservation and I've always gone as an Indian all my life. . . . What in the world? Disown my own race, just to get into the Navy?" I said, "I'm a Canadian, even if I am an Indian. Same as you are. . . . I was born here in Canada."

A Nursing Sister in Britain, February 1941

NURSING SISTER ELAINE WRIGHT

One of our nurses is going home & I am asking her to take this with her & mail it in Canada. It will get there much quicker & I might be able to tell you a few things I otherwise couldn't.

I received another letter from you to-day, Mom, & was very glad to get it. Expect some more will arrive to-morrow.

To begin at the beginning, we were on the "Pasteur" & it is a lovely boat. There were three other boats with us, all troop ships, one Dutch battleship the Revenge, & 2 cruisers. The war cruisers were the sinister looking boats! Our escort left us about ½ way over & the convoy (Do not mention this to many people as it is very important.) from this side was to meet us in a day or two but we missed it & came in alone. Our last day out we met a convoy going to Canada & it was a wonderful sight—right on the horizon. Four planes came swooping down on us & kept circling & dipping over us. We were thrilled. They were a bit worried about us one day as a boat was hit 25 mins. sailing distance behind us but we knew nothing about it till later.

The Camerons of Canada was the Scotch Regiment on board, also Artillery, Engineers, Forestry. I have sent you the pictures they took on board. Pick out Brg. Phelan, he is Scotty's Uncle, the one who took us to dinner & he has been up visiting here several times & takes a great interest in all of us. He is stationed in London.

We went up the Clyde as far as Gaurrock & the whole river is filled with boats from canoes to ocean liners. I don't know how they all got in.

We couldn't see anything coming down as it was dark & I think I told you everything anyway.

We are stationed at Marston Green but *do not* put that in any letters. We are really just outside the village.

There are planes flying around all day long from early in the morning, as there are about 4–5 airdromes within a very small radius of us—say 6 miles, one is a training centre. There is also some bomber factories & other factories I don't know just what they are. You see, if you ask any questions, nobody knows anything. Did I tell you that one afternoon Sister Kennedy-Reid & I were cycling along this road & a plane dropped down, for a minute we thought it was going to land, but went over our heads with I'm sure less than 2 yards to spare.

Yes the people talk with quite an English accent & they find some of our expressions amusing. I will never get used to hearing a big well-built man saying "Ta, ta." & "oh my deah!" It sounds so sissified.

The Chaplain on the ship was with the Forestry Corps, I believe, & his name was Bennetts or something like that, that was all I could find out, but I liked him very much.

Rev. Mr. Jones, Captain Jones now, from Calvary Church, Montreal was up here on a visit. He was on the ward & when he left he asked if I had ever been at his church so I told him I went all the time for the year & 3 months I worked at the Western. He was quite pleased; he knew several of the girls here.

No, I wasn't much impressed with the country at first but it was about the worst time of year to see it. I am beginning to appreciate it now & am sure it is going to be beautiful in the summer.

No I haven't been in an air raid shelter yet but haven't had any need to. The girls that arrived here first had raids every night but we haven't had any since we came. An incendiary went through the roof of one of the huts but did no damage. We have heard them in the distance & heard the guns & one bomb landed about 3 mi. away once, made things on the table jump around a bit, but didn't bother me at all.

I had better tell you about the hospital. It is built in an oval with the huts opening into the centre. There are 18 huts altogether, one is the Orderly Room & one the kitchen. Some of the others are being used temporarily as the men's quarters, men's mess, dispensary, quarter master stores, laboratory, sergeants quarters & mess. We have [patients] in 6 huts at present. Each hut has 36 beds but can hold 40 & more easily—we are supposed to be a 600 bed hospital. We are really well equipped, have good operating room & X-Ray department. . . .

I have been getting a daily paper & so I have got the news that way. The wards have radios now, given by the Red Cross, & so we hear it on the radio too. The paper only costs a penny a day & I think is worth it.

We are well organized here for air raids & the wards are well equipped for incendiary bombs. We are going through the gas chamber to-morrow & have had a couple of more lectures on it. Nothing is being left to chance. There are several gas detectors around & well watched.

The general impression just now is preparedness for the invasion attempt very shortly. Whether or not it will really come no one knows, but the whole country is being prepared. With the system of spotters, fire watchers, home guards, etc. it is hard to imagine they would get far if they did try to invade.

Now for the food questions. Some foods are hard to get, others not too bad. In the village we can buy ¼ lb. of biscuits only, *when* they have them which is not always. Fruit is practically impossible to get, I have occasionally bought apples but they taste half-frozen & its only sometimes they are in stock. The stores here have canned goods but they say when their stock runs out they can get no more. But they have managed this long, so I suppose they will get along somehow. Milk & eggs are hard to get. Cream is unheard of. Chocolates are scarce.

We are rationed of course but our meals are not too bad tho' very much alike. It is always beef in some form, stew very often, & the vegetable almost always carrots. Desserts are bread pudding, rice pudding or jam pie. Occasionally we have had apple pie from canned apples. For breakfast we can have porridge or corn-flakes (which is extra, bought with our mess fees) toast, tea, sausage some days, very fat bacon other days, & jam. Sometimes we have prunes & apricots with custard for dessert. But in Birmingham the other day I had roast chicken—and paid for it, but it was good. The only thing I really miss a lot is my breakfast with fruit, coffee & egg.

You asked about the patients but there is not much to say about them, I haven't been looking after any but sick officers & am now with the nurses & a couple of English girls who had their appendixes out. Almost all the patients get up & about half are to be boarded back to Canada, a lot of lead swingers among them. A lead-swinger is one who complains of something he hasn't got, in other words there is nothing wrong with them except the desire to get out of the army.

I come off night duty March 8th & am going to London, & further south to see Paul. He is at Brighton now but might be back in Cheam by then.

Well I think I have told you all the things I shouldn't, & hope you get this safely. I haven't said what I've been doing lately but will write another letter & mail it.

Love to all

Elaine.

P.S. Am very glad to get any letters, even if it is about ordinary every day things.

Training Seamen, 1941

LIEUTENANT WILLIAM H. PUGSLEY

This account was written during and just after the war by an officer who secured permission to give up his commission so that he could serve with and write about the lives of naval ratings.

The next thing we knew we were taking gun drill. This is intended to shake you to the core, and at first acquaintance it certainly does. The Gunnery School is littered with the last traces of civilian ways that have been knocked out of luckless new entries being made over into naval ratings.

"Don't run, don't jump—FLY!" we were told by a beetle-browed Gunner's Mate on our first morning. We'd learn to do our drills smartly, or else! The Gunnery School, it seemed, had its own special version of a fate worse than death, and we'd find out all about it if we didn't "smack it about" at the gun. Thoroughly intimidated, we moved as if we'd been unleashed.

Our Instructor was a permanent force Leading Seaman who knew his stuff backwards and forwards. He was plenty tough. He didn't like people leaning against the wall while he was instructing, and he had strong views about those who chewed gum in class.

The first time he caught someone leaning against the wall, he'd drop everything, dash over and push at the wall dramatically as if it were about to collapse.

"It's all right," he'd tell the offender, to the latter's embarrassment, "you can stand up now. I'll hold it for a while."

The next time a man failed to stand up straight he'd get a six-inch projectile to hold in his arms. This is 98 pounds of solid steel, with no handles. It wasn't just the P.O.'s authority that made him hold on to it. There was the class. They'd be watching him closely—to see what sort of guts he had. He'd hold on to that "projie" no matter what it cost him, and it cost one of the lads in my class plenty.

He was chewing gum, second offence. That was just asking for trouble. So there he was, clutching a six-inch "projie" that got heavier every second. The Instructor turned away and went on unconcernedly explaining mis-fire drill. We watched the offender out of the corners of our eyes till he wasn't smiling any longer. His brow began to glisten, and the shell started to slip lower and lower.

No matter how hard he tried he didn't seem to be able to raise it. We could see he was getting pretty exhausted. Suddenly the shell slipped and landed on the toecap of his boot. It must have hurt: we could see the tears spurt into his eyes. He just stood there, his lips trembling.

The Instructor strode over and stood right in front of him. He knew exactly how the culprit felt—he'd been through the same mill himself. We all knew him to be a thoroughly white guy—absolutely white, but hard as nails.

"What do you mean by dropping that projectile? Pick it up at once."

"I—I won't."

"What's that?"

"I—I—." The kid's face was an agony of indecision.

"Are you going to pick up that shell, or aren't you?"

The youngster just stood there for a moment or two, his watering eyes first meeting the Instructor's cold stare, then sliding over to where we watched in silence.

Slowly he bent down, groping almost blindly for the shell. He got his hands around the awkward bulk, straightened up, and with a final heave brought the "projie" to chest level. His eyes were no longer blurred. They stared right back at the "Killick," and gave as good as they got. In that moment we felt the whole atmosphere change. The boy had been on the point of giving in, but he hadn't quit and that was what mattered.

The Leading Seaman turned again and resumed instructing. The youngster bit his lip once or twice, but that "projie" stayed up. It must have felt like 200 pounds by now. Then suddenly the "Killick" told him he could put it down.

When the lad did so, he found he was trembling, but it was his round and he knew it. The class knew it too, and thereafter he was definitely "one of the boys." He had no grudge against the Instructor, whom the class frankly admired. If challenged, we knew he'd promptly have held that "projie" just to show us how soft we were. Anyway, you expected Gunnery to be tough for people who wouldn't obey orders. . . .

As regards the food, I really don't know quite what to say. It certainly wasn't what Mother used to make. All that can be said has, I think, already been said—in the privacy of the mess decks. I do know, however, that I'm feudin' for the fellow who thinks weiners and sauerkraut is a meal for matelots, and I'm sharpening up my sheath knife to use on the man who invented "red lead and bacon." Anybody who really likes disembowelled tomatoes in a lot of warm water with a few slashes of discouraged-looking, undercooked bacon, well, he needs a discharge.

Each class held the odd one who'd be made to stand up, red to the ears, before the rest of us at table, while a "Killick" gave him a great blast: "Just because you're a matelot doesn't mean you needn't have any manners. In the Navy we don't drink milk right out of the mess pitcher, and you're not going to either." The culprit was mortified, but in two or three years, when he was a "Killick," he'd be just as indignant in turn with some other new entry. . . .

There hadn't been much "crime" in the class. We learned in due course that ignorance of the law (naval) was no excuse, and that knowledge of it could be equally dangerous. Generations of ratings have been brought up to understand that you can't quote "K.R. & A.I." (King's Rules and Admiralty Instructions) in self-defense against a charge. I've never been able to find any legal basis for this—all senior authorities repudiate it—but even officers, who've been ratings, tell of Regulating P.O.'s jealously letting men see only single sections of the Regulations at a time and warning that trying to quote from them as a Defaulter would be a punishable offence.

Our misdemeanors were fairly innocent, and for these, now that we had our full kit, there was a very suitable punishment, Kit Muster. I didn't like it at all. You had to move all your gear out of your locker and into your kit-bag, carry the bag miles to the Officer of the Day's cabin, and there lay everything out in a very special order for his inspection. Each item had to be turned so as to show your name on it.

The O.O.D. then came out, checked it all with a glance, and left you to get the whole works back into your locker again. It all had to be done, of course, in your time—and when there wasn't much of it at that. As a punishment, the Kit Muster is particularly exasperating. . . .

The last part of our training was our week at sea. My group went to the *Ambler*, formerly some millionaire's yacht. It might have been palatial enough down in Florida, but not in the Halifax North West Arm in winter. We slept fully dressed in our hammocks, and there was snow over our blankets in the morning.

Then, too, being "trainees," which is a polite term meaning anybody's drudge, we did not only our own dishes but those of all the regular crew as well. That was for practice! We also scrubbed out their mess as well as our own. Likewise for practice.

It was so cold outside that ice gathered on the ship's dinghy till it looked like a floating birthday cake. But the cold needn't dismay the regular crew: a couple of trainees would gladly row them ashore for liberty. What's that? They wouldn't be glad to? Well, no matter, they'd do it whether they liked it or not. And do it we did!

Sometimes after all the trouble we'd had getting warm, we'd have to climb out of our 'micks in the middle of the night, get all bundled up in heavy clothing, and row an officer either in to shore or back to the ship. It's tough, chum.

Each day the ship went to sea, and we were examined in compass and helm, bends and hitches, lowering boats, and heaving the lead. There was also the very important business of how a look-out should report what he sees, so as to tell the most in the least time, and that accurately.

HMCS Chambly *Boards a U-Boat, September 1941*

LIEUTENANT E.T. SIMMONS

> *In September 1941, the corvettes* Chambly *and* Moose Jaw *left St. John's on a training cruise. The two ships encountered a U-boat on the surface, stalking convoy SC-42, and they damaged it severely with gunfire and by ramming.* Chambly *sent a boarding party to investigate the sub's condition.*

REPORT OF BOARDING PARTY

Submitted the following detailed account of the boarding party from CHAMBLY to the surfaced submarine on 10th September, 1941.

. . .

2. In the boat I took away I had eight men: 1 E.R.A., 1 Leading Stoker, 2 Stokers, 2 Seamen, 1 S.T., and 1 Signalman.

3. I approached the submarine on her port quarter to within twenty feet. With my flashlight I noticed a large hole on this quarter of the submarine approximately ten feet from the stern. It was about four feet in diameter and centred at the point where the ship's casing joins the hull. It looked to me as if the submarine's port hydroplane had been blown off. As it was apparent there was better lee on the starboard side of the submarine I crossed her stern. Whilst doing so, I noticed the smell of burning oil, the occasional puff of smoke and the submarine's screws turning over slowly giving her slight way.

4. I counted eleven men still standing on the submarine's casing, well aft, in a group. As I came alongside, several of the men attempted to board our boat and with some difficulty we kept them clear, made the boat fast, and I boarded the submarine.

5. I noticed that she was well down at the stern, the casing aft being practically awash. I had all the men searched, meanwhile finding one of them who appeared to be an officer and who could speak a little English. I told him I needed two of his men to go forward with me as I intended to inspect below. He advised me not to, the reason apparently being the submarine was about to blow up, also that the seacocks had been opened and she was filling rapidly. He refused to go with me as ordered, claiming he had a hip injury and could not walk. It was only at the point of a pistol and a certain amount of assistance from behind that I made two of the crew understand where I wished to go. I left the Signalman with Lewis Gun covering the remainder, two Seamen beside the boat and took my E.R.A., Leading Stoker and two Stokers forward with me.

6. We stopped at a hatch roughly midway between the conning tower and stern and opened it. Below was apparently completely flooded as the water was level with the deck. I carried on up to the conning tower. This hatch was open and I could see below into two compartments. The lower compartment lights were lit and water was just beginning to come in, running from aft forward.

7. At this point, my two prisoners refused to go below. I told them I would shoot, which they appeared to understand but still would

not move. I noticed the stern was now well under water and the crew, held in charge by my Signalman, had moved closer to the conning tower. As the swell was pounding my boat badly against the submarine's side, I ordered my two Seamen into the boat, to cast off and lie off as close as possible to the submarine. As I could do nothing further with my prisoners, I decided to go below myself, having to remove my gas mask to enter.

8. At this point, I heard water rushing in below me, looked down, the lights had gone out. With my flashlight, which because of the wet was burning dimly by this time, I could just see the water. It appeared to have suddenly rushed into the compartment as if some door or bulkhead had given way. As the water was coming in very quickly, I realized it was useless for me to continue. I ordered my men on the submarine to quickly make for the boat. I remained on the conning tower until I saw all of my men swimming off for the boat.

9. The submarine was now only at conning tower depth. My two prisoners followed my men and then the submarine went down with a rush. I then swam off and joined our boat.

10. When I gained the boat, I mustered my men and found all were aboard except one Stoker, Brown, W.I., R.C.N.V.R. We called his name for some time, pulling around searching, but without success. As the boat appeared to be filling and we were surrounded by the Germans swimming in the water, I considered that we should discontinue the search and return to the ship.

11. I made the following observations whilst aboard the submarine: As well as the missing hydroplane and rent side at this spot, there was a large dent in the casing abaft the conning tower. The submarine I would judge to be 175 feet long. She looked very new, camouflaged with brown and green mottling. She had three guns, one large gun mounted forward, one A/A on the conning tower and one H/A Gun aft. MOOSE JAW's round had put a hole about six inches in diameter in the conning tower cowling. This apparently was the cause of the injury to the German Officer. The crew in general were not belligerent, in fact, were more than willing to be taken prisoner.

The Hong Kong Disaster, 1941

BRIGADIER JOHN H. PRICE

> *Ottawa dispatched two battalions and a brigade headquarters to Hong Kong in the autumn of 1941, and after vicious fighting from December 8 to 25 the island surrendered and the surviving Canadians became prisoners. There was much effort to fix blame for the disaster and much—justly or not—fell on the Canadians. This British account is followed by a Canadian officer's rebuttal.*

Extracts from the Report of the Historical Section, Cabinet Office, London

21 Dec. At 2200 hours at Stone Hill headquarters Lieut.-Colonel Home informed Brigadier Wallis that he wished to see the Governor: his battalion was exhausted; further resistance would only result in the wastage of valuable Canadian lives; as senior Canadian officer he felt a grave responsibility. This unprecedented request came as a great shock to the brigadier who pointed out that the G.O.C. could not be ignored in such a fashion. Eventually Colonel Home was persuaded to await what counsel a night's sleep might bring and Brigadier Wallis reported the matter to General Maltby by telephone.

The attitude of Lieut.-Colonel Home, who had consulted Lieut.-Colonel Sutcliffe of the Winnipeg Grenadiers, is not to be regarded as that of an ordinary battalion commander. He was, indeed, the senior surviving Canadian officer and as such felt himself answerable to the Canadian Chief of the General Staff, to the Dominion Government, to the Canadian people.

22 Dec. At 1030 hours the brigadier (Wallis) conferred over the telephone with General Maltby, after reporting that Lieut.-Colonel Home's attitude had not changed: he was more than ever convinced of the futility of continued resistance.

23 Dec. At night Brigadier Wallis telephoned to Fortress Command a request from Colonel Home to speak both to General Maltby and to Sir Mark Young. The Canadian commander had again urged that his men were unfit to continue the struggle which had become a useless waste of lives, and the arguments and persuasions of the brigadier had no effect: all he required was an assurance that the Canadians would continue to resist.

In the early morning of the 24th Brigadier Wallis held a discussion with Colonel Home and the senior officers of the Royal Rifles of Canada who were all firmly convinced that their men could do no more. For five days and nights the Royal Rifles, the only infantry battalion remaining under Brigadier Wallis' command, had borne the brunt of the attack and counter-attack; they had had little opportunity to rest and for long intervals had gone without food. Untrained, they had bought their knowledge at a heavy price, their hardships and casualties being the greater for their total lack of battle experience. Discussions over the telephone between the brigadier and General Maltby followed. Eventually it was understood that the Canadians would be withdrawn into reserve at Stanley Fort, but that the defence of the Stanley Peninsula would continue.

Brig. John Price to Lt. Col. G.W.L. Nicholson, January 27, 1948

I must apologize for not having answered your letter of the 13th of January.

This account is written in such a manner as to create a wrong impression as to intent and motive.

There were plenty of Canadian officers who had battle experience in the first war and who were competent to judge as to the possibility of a successful outcome of the defence of the island. Consider the facts— The Island had been split in two by vastly superior Japanese forces. On the eastern brigade front, which included the Stanley Peninsula, the Royal Rifles and one company of the Hong Kong Volunteer Defence Force were the only troops who had fought continuously day and night, without rest, since the landing on the 17th and were still carrying all the fighting. By the 21st they had been greatly reduced in fighting strength and by the 23rd to a strength of around 500 all ranks. (It might be interesting to note that when troops in this sector were marched out of Stanley fort as Prisoners of War, they numbered over 2000).

The enemy controlled the sea and the air. 3" Mortar ammunition had run out. Only one battery of 18 pdr. guns were available for artillery support. Only L.M.G.'s and rifles were left to fight with.

The men had been fighting without much food and practically no sleep and were dead tired. They were obviously in no condition to put up a spirited defence without some rest. A request that they be given 24 hours rest was a reasonable one particularly as it was judged that there were ample troops available who had participated up to date only to a comparatively small degree in the battle and also as the plan then was to contract the front held by a retirement to the Stanley Peninsula itself.

This is part of the story.

The other part casts a reflection on Brig. Home and senior Canadian officers which I greatly resent and about which I protested to General Maltby when I was with him at Argyle St. Officers P.O.W. Camp, Kowloon, in 1942–1943.

In my opinion Brig. Wallis' report is not to be relied upon. He was then in such a state of great nervous excitement and I believe his mental state was such that he was incapable of collected judgement or of efficient leadership. The insinuation in his report is that Brig. Home suggested a complete and final withdrawal of the Canadian force from the fighting. This is untrue and I so told General Maltby.

What happened was this. It was known definitely by December 21st that Brig. Lawson and Col. Hennessy had been killed and that consequently, Brig. Home became the senior Canadian officer in the Colony. As such he inherited responsibilities which he took very seriously and which caused him great anxiety.

It required no great military genius to predict the outcome of the battle once the Japanese had landed on the island with their control of sea and air and great superiority in weapons and men. He felt, I think rightly, that he would be derelict in his duty to his men and to the Canadian Government if he did not communicate his conclusions to the highest authority. Also neither Brig. Home nor his officers had any faith in Brig. Wallis' judgement or in his conduct of operations. And who had better right than he had? He and his men were bearing the brunt of the fighting and knew from first hand knowledge the strength and armament of the forces against them. The Higher Command had consistently shown an inability to grasp the realities of the situation and to pursue tactics which might have prolonged the struggle but could not have altered the final result.

At the meeting on the morning of the 24th, reported by Brig. Wallis, the question of capitulation of the Colony was discussed but never was any suggestion made of a separate final withdrawal of the Canadian forces.

It was after this meeting that the Royal Rifles were withdrawn and came into action again on Christmas day after some six hours rest only.

Generally speaking, there are certain inaccuracies which should be corrected:—

1) Brig. Home on the 21st was called by Lt. Col. Sutcliffe who informed him that he had received and answered a cable from the Minister of National Defence and also that Brig. Lawson and Col. Hennessy had been killed. Lt. Col. Sutcliffe reported that his battalion had been terribly decimated and also that he had had some argument with Higher Command about useless attacks which his regiment was ordered to make. He asked Brig. Home if he could not do something to stop what he considered was a useless waste of lives.

2) I cannot believe that Brig. Home asked Brig. Wallis to see the Governor. This does not make sense as we were cut off from the other sector and there was no practical way of carrying this out.

3) So far as I can remember, Brig. Home and I were the only two Canadian officers present at the meeting with Brig. Wallis on the 24th.

If there are any further details you think might serve to clarify the situation, I will be glad to let you have them if I can furnish the information.

Sincerely yours,
John H. Price

"Studied Brutality" in Hong Kong, 1942–43

GEORGE S. MACDONELL

On the 30th of December [1941], we were marched across the island from Stanley to North Point, on the northeastern shore of the island. North Point had been a Chinese refugee centre before the war and now was to serve as our prison camp. Nearly four years of starvation, maltreatment and torture were about to begin.

North Point Camp had been a battleground where the Japanese had initially landed and was littered with the dead and decomposing bodies of men and pack animals. The litter, filth and stench of the dead were awful and it was a perfect breeding place for millions of flies. The huts were riddled with shrapnel and there was no running water, no latrines, no cooking facilities and no food or water for the prisoners. The ground was ploughed up by shellfire and covered with the wreckage of the battle.

Upon arrival, the men, many of them walking wounded and all of them exhausted, simply lay on the ground or on the cement floor of the shattered, windowless huts. The crowding of the facilities, such as they were, made for hopeless congestion. Lice, fleas and bedbugs were rampant. There was no soap and not even simple items of hygiene, such as toothbrushes, were available.

The men were filthy and battle-strained. Within a short time, many were infected by the cloud of disease-carrying flies and began to succumb to a virulent form of amoebic dysentery. There were no medical supplies, no hospital and no provisions for the sick and the wounded. My bayonet wound had become infected and my left arm was badly swollen. The seriously wounded and the dysentery cases lay on their stretchers where we had carried them. They were now covered with their own blood and filth and crawling with flies. This was our introduction to a Japanese camp and to how the Japanese treated their prisoners.

When food was finally issued the next day, it consisted of mouldy rice full of rat droppings and worms. Our rations were two bowls of rice per day, one in the morning and one in the evening, and one sourdough bun per man, at noon. Nutritionists have calculated that in order to maintain his health and weight, a soldier or an average male engaged in manual labour requires 3,500 calories per day. It is estimated that at North Point Camp, where the diet consisted almost entirely of rice and chrysanthemum tops, the caloric intake for the individual prisoner was about 1,200 calories. Added to the lack of calories in the daily diet was the severe deficiency of essential vitamins such as B complex, so essential to maintaining health. Lt. Col. Sutcliffe, Commanding Officer of the Grenadiers, was the first to die of malnutrition in these appalling conditions. He was soon followed by many others.

Escape seemed impossible because of our inability to speak Chinese, our inability to merge with the population and our lack of water transportation. Despite these obstacles, on August 19, 1942, a sergeant and four riflemen escaped from the camp. They were quickly recaptured and summarily beheaded.

In September of 1942, after nine months in this hellhole, we were moved from North Point on the island to Shamshuipo Camp on the mainland. Here the crowding was less of a problem, but now we were forced to work every day with pick and shovel at lengthening the runways of the Kai Tai Airport, with no improvement in rations. It was here that we were exposed to the notorious "Kamloops Kid." He was an interpreter for the Japanese, who had been born in Kamloops, British Columbia of Japanese parents and moved to Japan before the war. He was a sadistic maniac who vented his sickness in the deliberate torture, abuse and even murder of his Canadian countrymen. By now I had been promoted to Warrant Officer II, and I stood by in helpless fury as I watched him abuse my men. At the end of the war, he was captured at Hong Kong, tried and executed by an Allied court for his conduct at Shamshuipo.

It was at Shamshuipo that the outbreak of diphtheria added to the scourge of dysentery, malaria and malnutrition. In October of 1942, diphtheria raged amongst the prisoners in an epidemic that lasted for six months. At its height, three or four men died every day and, by the end of this period, another 115 men in our regiment had needlessly died of a combination of malnutrition and diphtheria. The Japanese refused to supply serum to fight the disease and showed a callous indifference to our doctors' repeated pleas for some, or any, form of medication for those afflicted. Instead of providing serum or some form of assistance to our doctors, Dr. Saito, the ranking Japanese medical officer, accused our doctors and orderlies of neglecting their patients, for which they were severely beaten.

By now, after more than 16 months of captivity, almost every prisoner suffered from beriberi, dysentery, partial blindness, pellagra, tropical ulcers and serious skin infections. Added to these afflictions was "electric feet," caused by malnutrition, that exposed the victim's feet to constant sensations of multiple needles plunged into his flesh night and day, without relief. Those who could not stand the psychological and emotional shock of these conditions and the starvation tactics and studied brutality of our captors soon died to escape what, for them, was intolerable. They were a small minority. For the rest, we maintained strict discipline. Daily orders and crime sheets for disobedience of any orders were in effect. We were an organized military unit, with its formal structure and ranks intact and fully operational. No unit was left outside this formal, regimented organization and each individual was constantly reminded that he was a Canadian soldier who was only temporarily under the control of the Japanese. I have no doubt that this structure and philosophy saved countless lives and provided concrete support for the survival of many who would otherwise have died. The will to live is very strong. The desire not to disgrace your uniform or to let your officers and comrades down through personal weakness is just as strong.

Requests for Special Privileges "Simply Not Done"

LIEUTENANT-GENERAL MAURICE POPE

> *General Pope, a professional soldier, was serving in Ottawa when his son Harry, a cadet at the Royal Military College, wrote him for help. His reply was firm.*

Ottawa, 27th January, 1942.

My dear Harry,

On my return from Washington yesterday afternoon, I found your two letters of the 20th and 24th January.

It will be quite impossible for me to write the Commandant to let you get off duty earlier than has been arranged. One simply does not do such things. Imagine yourself at Saint Cyr or the Kriege Academie where to such a request the commandant would reply with a stroke of apoplexy. The R.M.C. is, as its name implies, a military college and requests for special privileges are simply not done. Sorry.

As for my new job, I am not quite sure what to think of it. My friends describe themselves as being thrilled. For my part, I think the old watch-word "wait and see" is still a pretty safe rule.

Believe me,

Always my dear boy
Your affectionate father
Maurice Pope

Recruiting CWACs

CATHRYNE BLACKLEY ARMSTRONG

In 1941, the army created the Canadian Women's Army Corps to free men for combatant service. Kay Blackley was a recruiter in Hamilton, Ontario.

After basic training, while I was waiting for my posting, the authorities interviewed me and decided that I had an empathy with people. They felt I should be on the recruitment team, so I was told to pack my bags and take the train to Hamilton. I wound up recruiting in Brantford and Niagara Falls for about a year and a half. That was quite an experience, taking command of a small unit of recruiting personnel like that!

I was prepared for my work by a RCMP officer, who taught me some methods of interviewing and the secret of how to establish common ground. He said: "When the potential recruit comes in, the first thing you do is comment on something she's wearing. Tell her it looks nice and you want to know where she got it." That way, you completely disarm them.

Our recruiting office in Hamilton was at 2 King St. West, upstairs from a drugstore—the regular army was on one side, and the women's division on the other. There was a ton of paperwork—you always had all these papers in front of you. (Everything was done in triplicate everywhere in the armed forces. You had to have that third piece of paper! If you didn't, we used to say, "Bay Street is after you." Bay Street, in Toronto, was where recruiting HQ was located then.)

The criteria for enlisting were quite strict. You could apply anywhere in the country, but you had to be at least eighteen. (At first the minimum age was twenty-one, but it was lowered in 1943.) You had to fill in an extensive questionnaire. You had to have references, and the references were checked. And you had to be in really good health. Before being accepted, you were taken to hospital and given a very thorough medical check-up for contagious diseases, or to see if your system was prone to illness. If so, then you were rejected.

I had quite a few interesting interviews: some girls would come up from the United States to try and join the Canadian army. Nine times out of ten, they were trying to avoid problems at home or some sort of theft charge.

But one of the most memorable interviews concerns a young lady who came bouncing up the stairs into the recruiting office one day. I began to interview her and fill out the questionnaires but she was quite aggressive and I didn't take to her that well. I found her very demanding. When we got to her age, it turned out that she was only seventeen.

I said, "I'm sorry, I can't do anything for you," and she stood up and stamped her feet.

"Your only alternative is for your father or mother to come in and attest that they realize what you're doing, and that they give their support," I said.

She said, "I'll be back tomorrow—and I will get in!"

The next day she came back with this older, white-haired gentleman and said, "This is my father, and he agrees to me going into the service."

I asked him if this was all right with him, and he said: "If this is what she wants, then let her go in."

Well, as it happened, I knew of this gentleman: he was a judge, and there was a rumour in the Niagara peninsula that he had many contacts —who were not all favoured by many people. I was concerned, and I thought, "What do I do now? Here I've got this volunteer standing in front of me demanding her rights."

So I fixed his signature to her papers and said that I would be in touch. As soon as they left, I phoned Bay Street and said, "I've got a problem here. I've got this girl . . ."

But when I told them who her father was, they just said to send her on down. Her name was Judy LaMarsh, and . . . she was just as aggressive in her political life as she was in her private life. I guess it worked out for her.

Another recruiting incident never sat right with me. One day a Japanese girl, born in Canada, came in to join up. She was a primary-school teacher in British Columbia, but she and her family had come to Hamilton because they were moving the Japanese away from the West Coast at that time. She was a delightful person, soft-spoken and very feminine, and would have made an ideal worker in many positions in the army. I was sure that she could do quite well, and wrote a personal note on the interview form saying: "This girl is Canadian, born in Canada, and she deserves recognition for what she is trying to do."

But when the application came back, they had turned her down. So I appealed it. I said I couldn't understand this: The girl was a primary school teacher, good enough to teach children, she was born in Canada —she ought to be good enough to put on the uniform! Could they not place her in a position that wasn't related to security, yet would still recognize her Canadian citizenship?

They never did let her join, though, and I often wondered what happened to her. She was turned down by her fellow Canadians out of fear. That was one of the things I didn't like about the army—this was a case where they could have righted a real wrong. There was so much of that in the war.

In general, the types of girls who came to join up depended on their background. There was a strong military connection from the eastern provinces, but many from the West didn't have that connection—they were mainly of Ukrainian or Polish backgrounds, and from farming communities. I found that people were more oriented toward serving the empire in central Canada. The main reason I joined up was that in our family, my brother was younger than I was and no one else was old enough to serve the Empire. That term was used quite widely: it was felt that you had an obligation, a responsibility.

Monty on Canada's Senior Officers, 1942

FIELD MARSHAL MONTGOMERY OF ALAMEIN

McNaughton's Canadian Corps served under Montgomery in Britain, and the then Lieutenant-General Montgomery observed training exercises. His report on "Beaver III" in April 1942 was damning.

1.

1 Division has very fine material and should be a first class Division. But it was very badly handled on this exercise and, in consequence, failed badly.

Pearkes is unable to appreciate the essentials of a military problem and to formulate a sound plan. His mind works in a groove and he gets the bit between his teeth, puts on blinkers, and drives ahead blindly. He is a gallant soldier without doubt; but he has no brains.

I consider he is unfit to command a Division in the field.

Two of the Brigadiers, Potts and Ganong, made a very poor showing in this mobile operation. In my opinion they are both too old, and too set and rigid in their ways, to command Inf Bdes in modern war.

2.

It was not the fault of the regimental officers and men that *1 Division* failed badly.

It was the fault of the Divisional Commander.

If *1 Division* is to do well in its battles, it must have a new Divisional Commander.

Potts and Ganong should also go back to Canada, and be replaced by two good Brigadiers of the younger and more receptive vintage.

There is good material to hand. Salmon would command a Division well. Mann and Snow would make good Brigadiers.

3.

2 Division did well in the exercise. This was because it was well handled.

I would put Roberts down as the best Divisional Commander in the Corps. He is very sound, but he is not in any way brilliant; he would always do very well if he has a good G.S.O.1.

I watched *2 Division* carefully and there is no doubt that Mann is a very big influence in that Division. If he is removed to command a Brigade then I consider that he should be replaced as G.S.O.1 by a really good officer.

Wright (the G.S.O.2) is a very good lad, but he lacks experience at present and requires a good G.S.O.1 over him to bring him on.

4.

As a result of this exercise, *2 Division* has gained a high morale, and we want the show to crack along now, to make progress, and not to become unsettled.

If therefore Mann is removed, for any reason whatsoever, I would suggest it is important that he be replaced by a really first class officer.

   2 Division has certain weak links which will gradually get stronger; until they *do* get stronger the Division requires a really good top piece.

5.

If it is decided to make the changes indicated in para 2, then I suggest they should be made at once.

   It is important that *1 Division* should settle down and become a first class weapon as soon as possible.

Striking Against Germany, 1942

DENNIS JOHN QUINLAN

August 3, 1942

Dearest Mums

Once again here I am in your famous London and as usual I am staying at Auntie Lilly's in Earl's Court. Since arriving yesterday afternoon I have done very little but laze about, sleep for yesterday marked the first break in two or three weeks of rather intense flying.

   Tony and I and the rest of the Crew just finished our training together in time to go on the last two raids over Germany. They really were successful ones and though the thought of what we are doing sometimes appals me, one derives a terrific sense of satisfaction from playing such a part in striking these devastating blows at our enemy. The R.A.F. is really & truly pounding the Hun with ever-increasing ferocity and accuracy.

   We did have an amazingly busy time lately what with training & finally going on Ops and of course the inevitable number of times one would prepare to fly and then find it all cancelled. One got used to going to bed at breakfast time and getting up for lunch & preparing all over again for the same business.

   Tony, as my new Pilot, pleases me immensely the two trips we have done together have proved to me that I will receive the same co-operation as from Johnny—in fact our whole Crew is running very smoothly indeed and that really counts for a lot.

The last week on the Station was therefore much the same as ever —with the odd "flick" seen early on in the evening sometimes before a trip. This is my first time off since when I saw Bryan in Grantham a month ago.

From Alberta to Camp Borden, 1942

KEN HUTCHINSON

Camp Borden Aug 14 1942

Dear Folks,

Well here we are at last. It certainly took a long time, although it wasn't a bad trip. Really it was a privilege to get a trip like that for no money at all. We got off the train about 7:30 this morning.

The only thing that is wrong is that we are in quarantine for two weeks. There were two fellows on the train got the mumps. Boy are we ever mad . . . it will be awhile until we are able to see what is about us. So far all we've seen is tanks, cars, motorcycles & sand. Really it's just like one big sand pit.

There are about twenty of us in this hut today, and there were four others in before.

Say was I ever dirty when I got here. That old car we were in was terrible. Every time we hit a bump there would be a cloud of dust come up & then we didn't have a change of clothes with us. I wrote down some of the happenings on our way so will give them to you. We didn't go to Edmonton at all. We took the line out through Round Hill & East from there.

Our first stop was Wainwright for 5 or 10 minutes, just enough for an ice cream cone or something.

Then we had a 15 min. stop at Biggar Sask. of course all the boys ran over to a hotel for some beer.

Then we stopped an hour at Saskatoon. The fellows in charge of us marched us through town & back to the station which was very nice.

Then we went to bed. Maybe I should say to sleep cause really there was no bed to it just the hard seats to sleep on. All the way, when we woke up we were at Marmorton Sask.

Then there was a ten min stop at Kipling. Then Brandon was our next stop and 30 or so men got off there.

Then Shilo was next stop and all the 85th Battery got off.

Then the best of all they stopped 3 hours at Winnipeg. We were taken up to the Y.M.C.A. for a shower & a swim, and boy was it ever nice. Then they turned us loose for two hours. I thought that was good of them. Then we were on our way again about 7:30. Got into Ontario about 1:30 P.M.

There was a ten min stop at Redditt a very pretty place, and the people all seemed as nice. The young girls even picked flowers for us.

Aug

7:00 A.M.. Armstrong first station stopped at 816 miles to Toronto.

Honest I never saw such a country before we came to the more civilized parts. All it is is rocks & bush & swamps. That's about all we saw for 36 hours. Then we stopped at one place for coal & water so three of us ran up to a place where it said "light lunches." We asked if they had any ice cream, but no they didn't. Then we went to a Café but they didn't have any there. Finally we got some up in a so called Pool Hall.

The heck of it was the most beautiful spots we passed at nights & couldn't see them.

Golly Charley Matthews should be here if he wants to see planes. They are just going over here all the time. It seems just as they get over this but they seem to give her the gun.

One thing in this dump I will be able to get caught up in some letters.

I still don't know my directions down here, but I can use my watch & find out. Well I guess this is all for this time, although there is lots more news but will save some for next time.

Well I guess I'll close for now & hope to hear from you real soon.
Your loving son
Ken

This is a continuation from yesterday. Well we've moved again. The bunch of us are over in tents now. Boy Scouts you know. There are four of us to a tent. But there is one good thing we are being fed darn good.

If the fellows in Camrose saw this they would fall over backwards.

I think I'll drop a line to Gerald and just find out exactly where he is. Then soon as I can get a week-end I'll go down & see him. By the sounds of things we won't be in Camp Borden very long. One fellow asked an officer about harvest leave & he said no cause it won't be long until you will be going overseas, so heres hoping.

Well must go now

Love

Ken

August 22/42

Dear Folks (this means everybody),

I haven't received your letter as yet, although I've received the one you sent on the 13th. I haven't anything else to do just now so will sit down & write.

There has been lots of things happened since the last time I wrote you.

We are still in quarantine, but I don't mind much cause this is a big camp with lots to do. There are three places with shows & two of them are free & the other is 15¢. Although I tell you I've only got 60¢ left from my $14 I had when I left Camrose so I have to go kind of careful how I spend it. The other night one of the fellows & I went to a show at the 15¢ place. It showed on the screen that the "Jungle Book" was coming on . . . Friday & Saturday. . . . He was bound & determined that it was on Sunday. So we argued for quite some time & then I said, "Well listen Jack, if it's on Friday & Sat. you pay my way & if not I'll pay yours." Naturally I got a free show out of it.

They haven't been working us very hard as yet. It's mostly *school* here. I thought I was out of it once. But really you know I seem to get along O.K. with most of the stuff. In fact I've had to explain to some of the fellows how to figure out the gradients of a hill. Maybe you in civilian life haven't heard anything about these, but it is the degree of slope of the hill. To see if it is too steep for a truck to go up.

They have got me slated for a Driver I.C. Gunner in a tank. Isn't that nice of them. I don't mind though, the sooner we get over there to help the rest the better I'll like it.

I've received about 4 letters altogether now. But I'm still waiting to get an answer from Gerald. Say mother will you send me Ian's address. I'd like to write him too. Maybe you could send this letter all through the family & save me writing so many eh. By the way what is Helen's & Doris's address. I have great ambitions you know but its sure nice to get letters.

Next week we start in the gunnery school, some that are taking it say its awful tiresome, but I don't mind sitting around you know.

There certainly a nice bunch of instructors up here. The sergeants aren't anymore than 26 & some of the Lt. aren't that old.

I had a letter from Liz. Nelson, he is at Barrifield & he hates it there. I guess the eats aren't as good. He said one morning after the milk jug was empty there was a piece of dairy soap in the bottom of it. That doesn't go so good.

But we are really getting fed here. I believe I've gained another four pounds already.

The Captain was telling us the other day that if all the rest of the boys that were in the Regiment were as trustworthy as the bunch that came from Camrose they wouldn't have anything to worry about. Something for us eh what.

There was a fellow killed up here on Thursday night. He was riding in a convoy on a motorcycle & a civilian car came along just as this fellow was going to pass a truck. He was going about 60 miles per. & he saw that he couldn't make it & he got rattled & hit the smash fence along the road you know those posts along the road. He broke his neck. It's kind of funny he was eating with the rest of the guys at 5 o'clock & at 5:45 he was dead. One never knows when it will happen. The other night when I was in the wash room this fellow came in & gosh I thought I knew him. So I went up & asked him if he wasn't Jacobs from Lloyd. Sure enough he was. Then we had a great old talk. He is a cousin to Doris Simmons, at Lloyd, I guess you know who that is. You will sooner or later any how. *Maybe*.

One thing here we have a very good church parade on Sunday's. They have the big band & they play the hymns although it was the same except for one hymn as last Sunday. It's different though when there is a band playing.

Today is Civy day. Boy there are a lot of the other sex around here but they can't compare with the West.

I certainly wish that I could get a week-end at last before we leave & then I could spend it with Gerald & Min. I found Algonquin Park on the map & they are about 100 miles north of here. That's approx.

Just made another 6¢, sold two stamps.

Well I guess this will have to be all for this time so will close & hope to hear from you as soon as possible.

Lots & lots of love

Your son & brother

Ken

A Padre on the Tragedy of Dieppe, August 1942

MAJOR THE REVEREND MIKE DALTON

On August 19, 1942, some 5000 Canadians raided Dieppe. Everything that could go wrong did, and the casualties were horrendous. The Essex Scottish's Roman Catholic padre, Dalton, was not on the raid, but his diary account of those days in August is powerful.

August 18, 1942

6 p.m.—T.L.C.'s seen from our windows going east. We had a hunch it was France. I had practiced for Dieppe and knew the town from maps and air photos. Lieutenant Jim Palms told me it was a land manoeuvre. He was killed.

August 19, 1942

8 o'clock: Radio confirms our susupicions.
Noon: Down to beach to find wounded and returning—no luck at Chicester canal and beach.
5 o'clock: Saw bomber attacked by 3 Spitfires. He jettisoned 2 bombs. They look like 2 men falling in turnip field. I didn't have time to view craters in neighbouring field.

August 20, 1942

Small groups come home with tragic story of fierce opposition but gallant action. Major Chas. Turnbul makes me Colonel for afternoon. His brother Russ missing. Out of 550 Essex Scottish only 44 accounted for

including only 1 attached officer McRae. Morning—Requiem Mass
for fallen and wounded. R.I.P.

August 21, 1942

7:30: Another Mass at Littlehampton Convent for dead. Visited R.Reg
C and R.H.L.I. to get locations of wounded.

Noon: Row upon row, ward after ward of Battle casualties. Only a
few Essex men and Captain McRae among wounded and many dozens
of others of Brigade at No. 1 Hospital Horsham.

18:00 hrs. to No. 14 G. H. Horley—many wounded. Brought cigarettes, beads, etc. to wounded.

Eve: notified all Regiments R.C.A. and 8th Recce of times of Sunday Masses.

9:30 Home for supper. Col Mothersill new O.C.

The Tragedy of Dieppe

No Essex officer returned . . . Out of 30 officers who lived together at
Aldershot and previously. *I am the only original.* Others had been transferred or shot down in France. Remnant of one proud and gallant outfit
are quietly solemn, but morale is high. Lads say they are glad I didn't
go. I couldn't have done much good. In plan of United Nations, Dieppe
may be no tragedy, but blessing. I was Colonel for a day but forgot to
collect a colonels pay.

August 22, 1942

All morning in Bramshot No. 15 Hospital to see wounded. Identified
Ray Belcourt in morgue, accompanied by Jim his brother.

Afternoon: To No. 8 Can. Hospital Aldershot. All have some stories
of heroism unparalleled in history of human relations, officers leading.
Their parents must have been genuine to produce such men.

Sunday, August 23, 1942

I preached shortest sermon. It was one short story as follows. It was
hard to face lads, so many empty seats, so many old reliables missing,
but I asked co-operation from remnant to build up new spirit, *to close
in the ranks and carry on* and to pray for fallen. When we enlisted we
bargained for hardships of war, *but didn't realize we would* miss our pals

so much after almost 3 years of friendship. Through "Communion of Saints" they are still with us in spirit. Although only 44 out of 550 Essex Scottish who invaded returned, personal loss is nations gain, (we hope).

The Calgarys at Dieppe, 1942

GRANT ODUM PHILLIP

n.d. [August 1942]

Dear Dad:

These lines are addressed to you for only you could appreciate what has happened to me this past week or so. I turn for sympathy and under-standing. By the time this note reaches you the Dieppe raid will have been forgotten by most people but we never shall. The scars will be livid in Prairie towns for generations to come. So now that the final casualty list is ruled off as finished as well as those heart breaking jobs of searching kits to be sent home. The full story must wait a happier day's telling but to you who knows all the sorrow of missing faces at the mess table I need say little more except our last memories of those giants are tales of stark heroism that you would scarcely credit unless you knew the calibre of the men who made this regiment the pride of the Canadian army in one short year. I also hope my wire arrived in time to spare you any anxiety on my behalf for in my rather thoughtless way I neglected to let my English friends know and if any thing good can be gleaned from that ghastly day it was the flood of mail expressing hope for my good luck and well being for I had doubted that the units involved would be named and my identity connected in any way with the raid but by noon all England knew that the Calgarys were in.

My own minor part nearly turned into a major one but a slight acci-dent left me high but mighty wet on the landing beaches from a barge that failed to return so the clumsy feet that have shamed me for a life-time sure kept me safe that night. I felt dreadful at the time for after months of heart breaking work to get those guns perfect I would fall overboard at the last minute. Not only that but this is the second time and if it happens to me again I think I shall just stay there in pure cha-grin. This much at least those guns fired until the last cartridge. In a previous letter I mentioned a lad who is engaged to a young lady living over Mrs. Stewart's old store well poor Tanner didn't make the trip home and if you think it might help a little you might tell her she picked a real man. He was the Gunner for the adjutant crew who will always be the pride of this regiment for having gained their objective they went off in the smoke never to be seen again yet their wireless wild with excitement told of encounter after encounter taking on a whole German regiment single handed batteries and pill boxes in their stride never thought of turning back just of more ammunition and a chance to go on. The whole day was episodes like that but because his tank was HQ we take more than special pride in him and therefore even deeper regret at his loss. Dad since this note seems rather emotional, perhaps I had better cut it short and write again when time has healed some of these scars we carry in our mind so please excuse me. Jo's last letter brought poor news of mother that leaves me a little more than upset but I hope the next mail brings the best from her and the rest of you dear people. At least the reinforcements are led by old friends we said goodbye to in the spring and once more Charley Norman is back here with me which helps a whole lot.

Yours as ever
Grant

I Am a Prisoner, August 1942

LIEUTENANT H.W. HOCKIN

Lieutenant Hockin, an officer with the Essex Scottish, was captured at Dieppe. Just five days later, his captors permitted him to write a postcard to his brother, serving in England.

France, 24 Aug. 42

Dear John: Today is the first chance we have had to write, I think it is phoney, but worth a try.

This is to let you know that I am a prisoner along with a number of my pals and many others, and not killed. However, you will probably have an official report before you get this, if you get it at all.

I won't tell you much about what has happened [Paragraph deleted by censor].

Please let dad and mother know and tell them I am O.K. and not wounded. Also look after my kit and uniform. Better store them in England, I think.

Hope to be able to give you the full story some day. Until then we are counting on you fellows. Good luck.

As ever, Bill

The Men Belittled Us at Every Turn, 1942

NEVA BAYLISS

Neva Bayliss joined the WDs, the Women's Detachment of the RCAF, in 1942. Her account of her training and service says much about wartime attitudes.

After two months, I went down to the office to see why I hadn't heard. They put me through the motions of questioning and a quick eye test and medical. Here the men seemed to be trying to see who could embarrass us the most. I can remember wishing the floor would open up and swallow me when the man at the desk bellowed down the hall, "Here's another eighteen-year-old," meaning me. Another eighteen-year-old, two or three recruits ahead of me in the line, and I have been the closest of friends ever since. Until recently, the age limit had been 21 years so the two of us were considered "oddities" worth bellowing about.

We spent four days on the train from Vancouver to Ottawa picking up a third recruit in Kamloops. The three of us still try to visit at the reunions. We were the third Women's Division Air Force squadron to train in Ottawa and, like so many things during the war, the place was still getting set up while in use. The parade square was leveled but was really like a big muddy field. Until we got our service shoes and uniforms, we were constantly in a mess. For one month we learned drill and marching and quick change from uniforms to fatigues and back. Once the Sergeant felt safe with us, he took us on route marches.

We got used to having our bed and area perfectly tidy before breakfast at 7:00 am and on the parade square by 8:00 am. Lights out was 10:00 pm and if you weren't in bed by then, you fumbled around quietly in the dark. You also got used to showering with 20 other women and hoped you were properly attired when the day officer came to inspect the barracks.

It was very embarrassing if your shift was the one caught in the showers! We had gray blankets with a black stripe, which was to be down the middle of the bunk bed. We used to think sometimes they brought a ruler. If anything wasn't just right, you got some extra work like waxing floors.

The men belittled us at every turn and spread some nasty and untrue rumours about our reason for being in the Services. They made fun of our awkwardness on the parade square but they had been no better when they started. Getting fitted out for uniforms was a total embarrassment as the men in charge of fitting us took one look, decided what size you were and gave you one. Even if we knew it wasn't the right size, we weren't sure we should complain and didn't. If it fit too badly, we were sent from the parade square to have another issued to us.

The only ones that really appreciated our efforts were those who had lowly jobs like peeling vegetables and washing dishes. They were only too glad to see us come. Finally we were accepted and we held some very responsible positions by the end of the war. Many were sent overseas—some at the very end—to let the men that were there get home earlier.

A Jolly Good Chance:
Trying to Escape, Hong Kong, 1942

SERGEANT JOHN PAYNE

Conditions in the Japanese POW camps were appalling, so much so that soldiers contemplated escape, even though it was all but impossible for whites to be swallowed up in Japanese-controlled China. Sergeant Payne wrote this letter for his mother just before he went over the wire. He was caught and executed by the Japanese.

19.8.42
North Point Camp
China

Dear Mater,

I have decided, either fortunately or unfortunately as the case may be, to take a chance on getting through to Chungking. I've investigated as much as possible and feel sure we stand a jolly good chance of getting there. There are numerous reasons for this step the chief being that the Cholera season & fly season is starting, Dysentry & Beri Beri are high in Camp, and anyway I'm ruddy sick of Japanese hospitality.

You share, I know, my own views on fatalism, so for that reason I know you won't condemn my judgement. So just in case I shouldn't make it you must remember that according to our beliefs I have departed for a much nicer place (I hope) although it will grieve me to exchange the Guitar for a harp even though there is a higher percentage of gold in the latter. But that's enough of this drivel, I'll be able to destroy this note myself I'm sure so bye bye for now . . .

Your devoted Son

John

P.S. Best regards to Di & Yvonne.
Tell Ben to join the Air Force next war.

The Sinking of the SS Caribou, October 1942

ALEX BATEMAN

> *A steward on the SS* Caribou, *Bateman was aboard when the Cape Breton–Newfoundland ferry was sunk by a U-boat on its regular run. The Royal Canadian Navy discounted Bateman's account of Germans firing on survivors and sinking rafts.*

I was a member of the crew of the S/S *Caribou* since February 15th 1942, I remember well the last voyage from North Sydney.

Before sailing that night Captain Taverner gave orders to acquaint the passengers with their life boats, some passengers accompanied me, but the greater portion scoffed at the idea and refused to come.

As far as I know and I believe, the ship received her death blow about three forty A.M., I was in bed at the time and immediately rushed to the deck, and the first man I saw was the Bosun Elias Coffin trying to cut the boats clear. I assisted him and cut No. 4 boat clear.

That boat at the time was full of people. I was instructed by the bosun to get aboard this boat as there was no Officer to take charge of her. We lowered away and in a few minutes we were clear of the ship which was rapidly sinking, and in a few minutes the boat capsized and the whole occupants were thrown in the water.

I estimate there were about sixty persons in this boat. I swam back to the boat and clung to the bow hoping to upright her, but before that happened most of the people were drowned. I then swam and got on a raft which was between fifteen and twenty yards away from the boat. I figure I was on the raft about thirty seconds when the submarine came up alongside this raft about ten feet away. I again jumped overboard being afraid this submarine would shell my raft. He then proceeded and rammed another raft which was loaded with people which I estimate was either killed or drowned as this raft was completely demolished and the barrels of same floated away. The submarine then flashed a light over the water, evidently looking for more boats or rafts. He then fired several shots with apparently a swinging gun, spraying bullets in all directions.

I then saw a life boat about forty yards away, and swam for it. This was No. 2 boat occupying 25 persons. The condition of this boat when I got alongside was half full of water and the occupants refused to allow me on board, until after some time Trimmer Charles Ford, Jr., discovered my identity and assisted me into the boat.

I immediately inquired what was the trouble with the boat, as no effort was being made to bale her out. I discovered in the darkness James Spencer, Able Seaman, was in the boat and I told him he should know if the plug was in, being on deck. Spencer discovered the rubber flash light in the life boat and we found the plug was in position, and then I inquired for buckets and was informed there was two which I instructed to be put working immediately, which we did, and I figure in fifteen minutes or less we had the boat dry.

I then decided it better to run the boat before the wind, and I arranged for Seaman Spencer to handle the rudder while I looked after the crew who were rowing. We ranged on this course until daylight, and I figure we made four miles from that position, and then I decided to head the boat to the wind and keep her up.

We saw the Corvette shortly after daylight, and saw two planes which then circled and steered towards the Corvette which rescued us approximately nine thirty A.M. During this time I never saw Captain Taverner or any of his Officers.

This Can't Last Forever: A Dieppe POW at Christmas, 1942

PRIVATE JACK GRISS

After being taken prisoner at Dieppe, Jack Griss of the Royal Hamilton Light Infantry wrote his wife from Stalag VIII B.

Stalag VIII B
Dec 19th/42

Dear Olga—Here we are, a few days for Xmas. Well dear I hope that you are all well, and enjoy your Christmas. I expect we POWs shall enjoy the Red Cross parcel of food next Friday. We shall all be thinking of our loved ones, not to say that our thoughts aren't always towards home. The weather is nice at present. I read your dear letters every night before retiring, and we retire early. Have received two letters from England one from Freda, one from sister agnes. I am getting used to being a "gefanyaner" but always thinking of that day when I shall return to the woman I love, who is so brave and does her part so well. I hope that will not be very long. I keep very well and the only thing I lost in action was a tooth. Very lucky eh. The boys are trying to decorate the hut for Xmas and they are putting on a pantomime "Alladin" also other entertainments. There are some good soccer games here. I am still with the Colonial troops. Jimmy McGhee is in the next compound, and I chum up with a Aussie from Melbourne. I would like you to send me the means of keeping respectable like needles thread shoe polish, toothpaste, etc. but hope that I am out of here before it arrives. My love to Mother & Elsie and all our friends in good old Canada. Keep smiling honey. This can't last forever. Cheerio.

Love Jack

A Day on a Bomber Squadron and a Last Letter

FLIGHT LIEUTENANT F. LAWRENCE PARKER

Parker, an RCAF bomber pilot, wrote this account of an operation against an enemy target. He also prepared a "last letter" to be mailed to his family if he was shot down. Regrettably, he was.

The list of crows who were "on" was just coming over the 'phone from the Squadron Leader. Everyone was listening intently as the names were repeated—"Brown, A—Apple; Gardiner, C—Charlie; Leitch, D—Donald; Parker, F—Freddie; ——." That was all I wanted to know, I didn't wait to hear the rest of the list, but set off to the mess for lunch. As I walked, I thought how insipid life would be, were it not for the pleasure of eating three or four times a day.

Back at the mess the first thought was mail, and everyone was eagerly looking for the white of an envelope showing in the top of his letter-box. If there were none visible, he would always feel inside before giving up hope. Surprising how important a letter is. I was lucky, and took mine into the dining room to read while waiting in the soup queue.

There was time after lunch for a game of snooker and perusal of the London dailies—or possibly a few rounds of "hearts" or "knock rummey." Nobody discussed the coming operation, the only mention of it being a casual "Are you working to-night?" and the nod or monosyllable in reply. The ones who were not "on" would be off on the afternoon bus to town, or possibly out to the golf course or into the hills on bicycles. Many would spend the evening in the murky but convivial atmosphere of the "Black Bull."

The navigator had to be at the "hive" by 1400 hours to be told the target and the route to be taken, so leaving the rest to enjoy another hour's relaxation, we toddled off. Then followed a busy time when tracks and distances were worked out, approximate magnetic courses and estimated times of arrival at the turning points were computated, and various other bits of secret "gen" were put to use. Even after dozens of trips, the thrill of drawing those route lines on the charts never lessened, and we showed as much enthusiasm as a family planning its summer motoring tour with the aid of coloured "gasoline" maps.

At 1500 hours, all the crews had to be in the main lecture room for the "briefing"—that is where the general instruction takes place. So a few minutes before time we left the hive and headed for the main building.

Promptly on time the Wing Commander called out the names of the captains who answered for their crews. Then quite unemotionally he announced "The target for tonight is Dieselburg—and its a very large effort, 850 altogether. We'll hear from Intelligence first." Then the Intelligence Officer, a quiet, inoffensive little man with horn rimmed glasses, spoke his piece. He told us what we were to aim at, the importance of the target and the need for definite identification and accurate bombing. He told us our time on the target, the colour and position of the indicator flares to be dropped by the Pathfinders, where to expect enemy fighters, and the locations of ack ack concentrations. He gave us a lot of other useful information which might be valuable in an emergency.

Next came the "met" man. From him we got a complete description of the weather conditions on the way out, at the target, and coming back. He warned us of icing conditions and dangerous cloud formations over which we should have to fly. He told us the estimated winds, temperatures and atmospheric pressures, and showed us the synoptic chart—that maze of coloured lines which reveals so much to the meteorologist.

We heard from the Navigation officer and the Bombing and Signals leaders, and when all had been told, the Wing Commander spoke again. "All crews to be at the crew room by 2130, at the aircraft by 2215 and take-off starts at 2300. Good luck." That was all.

The crews then went into separate huddles to discuss the effort among themselves. Pilots and navigators had to decide on rates of climb, heights and airspeed, bomb-aimers and wireless operators had their contributions to make, and even the gunners were chiming in. It was very much like a football team talking over its strategy—only this time the game was being played for life itself—the visiting team just had to win.

There was still quite a lot to be done, especially by the poor, overworked Navigators, so off we went to complete the many details of the flight plan. When this was done, we packed our maps and charts, instruments, computators, books of tables and other accessories in our green canvas "sacks," and set course for the mess.

"Operational Supper" was to be served at 1945, so there was plenty of time. Some of the boys wrote letters, some played billiards or table tennis, while others just dozed in the easy chairs. As soon as the big clock gave us the signal we trooped off to the dining hall for our egg and bacon. That is the standard diet served at pre-operational meals; it is the great contribution of the British hen to the Bomber Command offensive.

After supper we left our thermos flasks to be filled with hot coffee and went to our rooms to start the lengthy process of getting ready. First of all we changed into our heavy woollen underwear and then our blue battle dress. Everything in the pockets had to be cleared out—letters, bus tickets, pocket books, everything—for such innocent articles might give the Germans some surprisingly useful information. Then into the pockets went the amulets, the love tokens, the religious trinkets—the little "bits of stuff" to be found on the person of every operational flier. It might be a ring, a rabbit's foot, a baby's shoe, a lock of hair, a tiny bible, a St. Christopher medal or a crucifix, but certainly there was something in every man's pocket. It was not that many believed the mere presence of some such article would fend off a jagged piece of white hot steel from an exploding shell. No, for most it was just the tangible evidence of the thoughts and love and prayers of someone back at home. The knowledge of that "someone's devotion" would be a source OF GREAT STRENGTH in moments of grave danger. So, fortified in body and spirit we went off to the crew room, collecting our navigator's paraphernalia on the way.

Here we began to gird ourselves with the multitudinous articles of flying clothing which high altitudes demand—thick woollen sweaters, heavy leather fur-lined trousers, and jackets, flying boots, gauntlets, helmets, oxygen equipment—then the Mae West, and finally, the parachute harness. When the costume was complete, the effect was gargantuan.

We hadn't long to wait in the crew room before the transports rumbled to a halt outside. We lugged our parachutes, our thermos flasks and rations, our navigational bags and sextants, and our unwieldy selves out to the truck, and somehow managed to clamber aboard. It was pretty dark, but we all had our flashlights, and with four or five crews crowded into each transport, we started off for the dispersals. Soon we could see the rows of tiny red and green lights which indicated where the aircraft were marshalled. In with us was the Padre, and as each crew was dropped off beside its plane he had a cheery word and some chewing gum for every member—and a silent prayer too, I believe. F—Freddie was near the end of the line-up, so we were the last crew to unload from the van. Then away it went, leaving us standing under the stars with our mighty bomber. In a few minutes we should be pounding through the night in its spacious interior.

It looked rather awesome—the huge black wings seemed to stretch too far, and the body with its load of destruction assumed such an impossible size—that we, who but a few minutes before had been the giants now seemed to have shrunk into insignificance. On the side of the "nose" we could just make out the rows of tiny painted bombs which showed that F—Freddie was a veteran of no mean experience.

We still had some time before we were due to start up the engines, but there were certain things each had to do. So, one by one we climbed up the ladder through the hatch, and made our way to the various positions. First of all, the "intercom"—that is the telephone system, which like a party line, connects everyone in the plane, had to be tested. This was the responsibility of the Wireless Operator, so Hughie called up each one in turn, "Hear me O. K.?" and the answers all being satisfactory he went on with the routine check of his radio equipment. Wally the bomb aimer, was looking over the leads to the camera, and seeing that the photo-flash and flares were installed properly. Larry was testing the rudder, elevators and ailerons, and the thousand and one things which pilots check before take-off. Even Smitty was back there in his little cage making noises like a rear gunner, and I was spreading maps and charts on the table, putting the various instruments and computors in their proper niches, and generally getting things ship-shape in my cabin.

Still being too early when all this was done, we climbed down the ladder and stood talking and smoking a little distance from the plane.

This was the worst time of all—nothing to do but wait. It's just like the boxer before his turn in the ring, or the actor standing in the wings awaiting his cue. Conversation and laughter were forced, a trifle brittle. There was an unnatural calm, an unrealness, a feeling that this was all a horrible dream. Then, suddenly a green rocket shot up from the control tower—the signal to start the engines. That was better, now there was something to do.

So back into the plane again—and Wally being the last one—pulled in the ladder and closed the hatch. I went back to the astro-dome where I could get a good view of all that was happening.

"Switches off!" from the ground crew, and the echo came back, "Switches off!" from Larry.

"Contact port!"—and the reply, "Contact port!" There was a labouring sound as the electric starting motor ground away, then an uncertain shuddering as the engine responded, unwillingly at first—but almost immediately came the strong throated roar as it leapt into vibrant life. Soon after, the starboard engine joined in and for several minutes they sang a contented duet. After they were properly warm, each engine in turn was "run up"—tested at full power—the plane meanwhile being held by the brakes and the chocks. The terrific air blast shook the whole plane so violently that every rivet shuddered—but held firm.

"Everything's O. K." said Larry through the intercom, and we knew we could rely on his judgement. He signalled the ground crew to take away the chocks—and a moment later another green rocket was fired. This was the signal for the take-off to start.

From the astro-dome I could see the red and green lights of the other planes, and the first one started moving on to the end of the runway. It had a white light on the tail, and it was fascinating to watch it move down along the stretch, gradually increasing speed—and then slowly rise into the air.

Its roar was drowned in the general chorus, most of which happily was kept out by the snug fitting helmets we wore.

As each plane took off, the rest moved up one in the queue. At last there was only one ahead of us and we watched as it sped down between the rows of lights which bordered the runway, and became airborne.

Now it was our turn. We moved on to the runway and waited for the green aldis lamp signal from the controller. There were a number of figures standing beside the flare path, and as we started forward, they all waved. We waved back. In a few seconds we were moving along at full throttle. I watched the lights flash by at ever increasing speeds. The pull of the many thousand "horses" in our engines soon had us tearing madly down the flare path, ever faster and faster—90—100—110 miles an hour—and then the earth could hold us no longer and we were free. There is an indescribable feeling of relief when the wheels have made their last contact with the ground, and the furious charging motion gives way to the steady lift of the airstream. The take-off with a heavily loaded bomber is an anxious time for the crew and continues to be so until a certain height has been reached.

London, England
May 17, 1943.

To My Family:

It has long been my intention to write a "last" letter to you—but for one reason or another, it has always been postponed. I am leaving instructions that in case of my being listed as "Killed" or "Missing, believed killed" which amounts to the same thing—this shall be sent to you by registered mail.

Although it is still my sincere hope and expectation to be reunited with you after the war—nevertheless, the type of work I am called upon to do, makes it quite obvious that life may be terminated very quickly, and without warning. Indeed, I have no more right to live—rather, much less right to live—than many of those fine chaps now gone, whom I was proud to count as my pals. When I consider that out of the twelve of our G.R. course who came across together, only five of them are still alive, it brings home, all too clearly, the uncertainty of life. I know that there is nothing I can do to reduce that uncertainty—and I am content to leave it in God's hands.

If my life is spared, I shall try to live in such a way as to justify that sparing. If I am called upon to die, it shall be with the knowledge that I have served a just cause, and helped to prepare the world for the time when force shall be subjugated to reason, and the welfare of mankind as a whole, shall be placed above the welfare of individuals or nations. National pride must give way to international understanding.

It is going to be very hard, after this struggle is over, to expel from our minds the bitterness and hatred which has developed towards those who were our enemies. But that is the prerequisite to any sort of international amity. We must consider our vanquished enemies as potential friends—only thus can the foundation be laid for a world federation.

I do not hate Germans—I do not hate Italians. Yet I have done my best to destroy them, and their works—and God knows they have done their best to destroy me. But, after this is over, I must be ready to look upon the individual German, who with liberal education and meted justice, strongly tempered with mercy, will be able to take his place in a world brotherhood. Hitler's children must learn that they are God's children,—and we, too, must not forget that.

It is hard to say farewell to life—especially to a life that has been so pleasant. There is so much to live for—but thank God, there is much to die for, too.

I thank God that I have grown up in a Christian family—that I have been taught the worth of a wholesome belief in God, and the faith in a life after this one has ended. I thank God that I have learned the value of temperance—that I have been privileged to have so many good friends —that I have learned to appreciate the beauties of nature, and the goodness of an outdoor life—that I have had the benefit of a good and noble father, a generous and understanding mother, and two kind and loving sisters. I have always had the most tender fondness and affection and sincere admiration for my family.

My greatest regret is that I may not have the privilege of taking any part in building that fine new world which must rise from the ruins left by this conflict. If, however, my sacrifice, and that of the hosts of other young men and women who have died, will help to bring about the desire and determination for international understanding which alone will guarantee a lasting peace—then I am content.

And so "farewell"—be brave and keep the faith that God will bring us all together again. I am grateful to you all for your devotion, loving thoughts and prayers. May God bless and keep you all—

Lawrence,
Son & brother

The Three Rivers Regiment Lands in Sicily, July 1943

JACK WALLACE

> *The army finally went into sustained action in July 1943, when the 1st Canadian Division and the 1st Canadian Armoured Brigade formed part of the force that invaded Sicily. Wallace was a squadron commander in the Three Rivers Regiment, equipped with new Sherman tanks.*

July 10, 1943

We had been on an LST (landing ship tank) for weeks en route from Scotland. Early that morning we dropped anchor about a mile and a half off the Sicilian coast. There were trucks secured by ropes and chains on deck and stowed below were most of our squadron's tanks and motorcycles. The night before, the ship's commander gave orders for the ballast to be released so the ship would rise when we beached for the landing. There were heavy swells in the evening and our vessel bobbed around like a cork. We were ordered to be ready at 6 am as part of the reserves so after reveille, I went up on deck to see what was going on. It was still quite dark, but I could make out the grey forms of ships all around us.

We expected to run into defences similar to Dieppe on the beach, but up to that point everything had been unusually quiet. By noon, we still hadn't landed and the men were getting very restless. The only news we'd received was a BBC broadcast that said the Canadians had landed. At 2 P.M. our orders finally arrived. The tanks plunged into the waves like water beetles and were soon ashore. When I arrived in the de-water-proofing area, I found our tanks, but there were no signs of my men around. After some initial inquiries, I found them in a watermelon patch feasting on the first melons they'd had since leaving home three years ago. Nearby some infantrymen were passing the time in a vegetable garden throwing tomatoes at each other.

Around 5 pm we were ordered to support the Carleton and York Regiment in an attack on a hamlet called Burgio. Zero hour arrived and the attack rumbled forward with 35 tanks and a regiment of infantry. We advanced steadily—200, 300, 500, 800 yards, but there was no sign of the enemy. We approached the objective ready for all hell to break loose until we saw a tiny white flag at the first house. Inside it we found four very poor Sicilian peasants.

Doubts About General McNaughton's Abilities, 1943

VINCENT MASSEY

> *Massey was Canada's High Commissioner in London, and he knew everyone. In his diary he recounted a conversation with the chief of the imperial general staff, General Sir Alan Brooke, when serious doubts about the First Canadian Army commander's abilities were raised.*

July 14, 1943

Sat between Southwood (*Daily Herald*) and Alan Brooke, (C.I.G.S.). With the latter I had a very interesting conversation. The name of Harry Crerar came up and Brooke observed that he was a better Corps commander than "Andy" as he called McNaughton, and went to say that the latter, although a genius in connection with applied science and the development of weapons, lacked many of the qualities of a military leader. I mentioned the exercise "Spartan" in which he had taken part as the leader of one of the two opposing forces. He suggested that McN.'s part in that exercise provided evidence in support of his view. He gave me an example. During the course of the "Spartan" exercise he went to McN.'s headquarters and found him at work on a bridging problem which he said he found of the deepest interest. McN. discussed his attempts to solve it but Brooke said that he had no very clear idea of what the particular bridging plans were for in terms of the larger tactical problem. We discussed the future of the Canadian army. I said that a good many people from what I could gather were worried about McN.'s future in relation to his present command. If the Canadian army does not move abroad as an army McN. will be left without a command. His expectation naturally is that he will command the army in the field. Brooke then said that would mean that he would be an army commander with Canadian forces under him, probably with the addition of British troops. I asked "What do you feel about it?" He, in answering my question, used the word "nervous." He said the problem could be solved by McN. being given another kind of job in which his own very distinguished abilities would have full play. He asked me whether there was anything in Canada. I said that, in my view definitely no. For one thing his removal from his present post would be a great disappointment and humiliation to him, but quite apart from that it would be a tremendous shock to the Canadian public with whom he has very great prestige. I said that the only sort of job to which he could be moved would be one in the widest possible sphere which would preserve his personal prestige. Brooke agreed. I then told him that [Defence Minister] Ralston was coming over very shortly and suggested he should talk to him confidentially about the problem. He asked whether I really thought this would be all right for him to do. I said the importance of the question is so great that I thought he would be quite justified in taking it up very personally and informally with Ralston; that after all there were tremendous issues involved, first of all the lives of the men under his command. Brooke then said, "also the success of the operations concerned." Brooke expressed himself as very glad to have had the talk and I am sure it was useful.

Ike on McNaughton, Canada, and the Empire, 1943

CAPTAIN HARRY BUTCHER

General Dwight D. Eisenhower had to drive a sometimes balky team of generals in Sicily. One problem he faced occurred when General Bernard Montgomery forbade General Andy McNaughton to visit Canadian troops. Ike's US Navy aide recounted in his diary how Eisenhower, at his headquarters in Tunisia, tried to deal with the Canadian general and the British. McNaughton eventually made it to Sicily.

Amilcar, Tunisia, (Advance C. P. AFHQ), Sunday, July 18, 1943—Last evening we went to General George Clark's villa for a swim. General McNaughton, the Canadian Commander-in-Chief, was there. He spoke to Ike about the refusal of General Alexander to permit him and his immediate staff to visit the Canadian Division in Sicily. Ike had already arranged for McNaughton to go as far as Malta but had told him he would have to get permission of the 15th Army Group to proceed to Sicily. When this permission was firmly declined by Alexander, McNaughton's pride obviously was hurt and he claimed that no matter how quiet he kept the affair it was bound eventually to come out and had already reached the importance of a "governmental matter" between Britain and Canada. Ike has no authority over the British commanders in such matters which are classed as "operational."

When Ike related this conversation to me on the beach I told him I thought it was a gross insult to Canada, that he would get the blame, that the affront to Canada would be picked up by the anti-British press in America and there would be all hell to pay. I suggested that we get McNaughton a C-47, load a jeep in it and send him to the American sector and let him make his way to the Canadians, telling Alexander and Montgomery what we are doing. They have control of who comes and goes in their sector just as Americans have the same control in our sector. Further, he felt it was an issue between the British Empire and one of its Commonwealths. He felt disinclined to intrude in such a "family matter." However, General Alexander appeared for a swim and Ike immediately swam out to discuss with him the incipient revolution. He found Alexander adamant. Said McNaughton had no business coming here during an operation and that while he had treated McNaughton politely, if he had been a junior officer he would have placed him under arrest. Said that when he was ashore in Sicily there was no transportation, that he had thumbed a ride on a lorry carrying rations, and that he knew Montgomery's Eighth Army headquarters had only one car. In view of the critical shortage of transportation and the nuisance to busy staff officers to look after the Canadian Commander-in-Chief, he positively would not grant McNaughton's request.

Ike pointed out the danger involved, the apparent weakness of Canadian morale, and cited the incident of the Prime Minister Mackenzie King making a public statement to the House of Commons in Ottawa claiming the British government and Ike had intended to present release of the fact the Canadians were in the Sicilian invasion as indicative of a "chip-on-the-shoulder" attitude. But since Alexander was so insistent, Ike felt constrained to support his subordinate commander.

Consequently, he trundled up the long steps to the villa and informed McNaughton that his intervention on behalf of the Canadians had been of no avail, repeating Alexander's reasons in diplomatic language.

Last night with General Whiteley we discussed this ominous situation. I had already made clear my fear about the psychological reaction of the bombing of the Rome marshaling yards near the Vatican which is to start Monday at 11 A.M. I told Ike that when he recognized Darlan he had offended the Jews, now he will be blamed for the "insult" to the Canadians and is running the grave risk of an unfortunate Italian and world-wide reaction from the bombing of Rome. He is likely to be as unpopular as a skunk at a husking bee.

Whiteley sided with Alexander but Ike said he felt Alexander was not giving sufficient weight to the problem of a democracy conducting a war. It is obvious he said, the Canadian public needs inspiration and some means should be worked out for accommodating McNaughton. Said he might be told that we would put him ashore in Sicily on the Canadian beach with rations and let him thumb a ride to the divisional headquarters, now some 50 miles from the beach, but Whiteley thought McNaughton would be just a damned nuisance. Said the Canadian was being "naughty."

I ventured the query as to how in the hell the British had ever succeeded in holding together an empire when they treat the respected military representative of its most important Commonwealth so rudely. Whiteley replied that if McNaughton is the military figure he is supposed to be he will understand the situation and will accept the inevitable like a soldier.

It is my guess that when Mackenzie King hears his Commander-in-Chief has not been permitted to visit the Canadians there will be all hell to pay and I hope Ike will take affirmative action and override Alexander's short-sighted decision.

The Fears of German POWs, Sicily, July 1943

MAJOR ROY DURNFORD

> *Durnford was the padre of the Seaforth Highlanders of Canada.*

We got back to our Battalion Headquarters and managed to get hardtack & bully beef. Perspiring and weary with worn out energy we slept. Young German prisoners came in later in the day. One of them limped up to me with a bullet wound in his foot. It had ripped the leather of the toecap and had torn its way across his instep. I did my best for him. How he had walked down a half mile to our base I could not think. He begged me to help him by signs & a beseeching look in his tired & dirty young face. How marvelously easy it is to interpret the meaning of eyes—of whatever race or nationality! These were appealing, frightened & tired to the point of exhaustion. I gave him a cigarette, took off his boots, bandaged him up & gave him some of my "dog-biscuits" & some cheese. He was ravenous. In his own way he managed to tell me that he had been flown in from Italy two days before. He had been stationed near Rome. On the day of his landing he was sent up the line & was wounded very shortly afterwards. White of face & on the verge of tears he lay down at my instruction. I left him to interview other prisoners coming in. One very young German officer—quite a boy actually—expressed his relief and gladness at being out of the war. "My mother will be glad to know I am a prisoner & safe," he said, and that in the main was the feeling of most of our very young captives—some thirty of them. I was able to let them know that I was a Padre, which to them meant Pastor. The information was happily received. It seemed to reassure them, for many had been told frightful things about our cruelty to prisoners. Later on, when some were ordered to dig the graves for fallen German comrades they mistook our intentions & told us afterwards that they thought we were asking them to dig their own graves prior to facing a shooting party! What agony of mind they had endured could only be imagined.

Characteristics of Canadian Soldiers, Sicily, 1943

MAJOR A.T. SESIA

Major Sesia was a field historian, a trained researcher sent to Sicily with the Canadian troops to gather historical information. These diary entries would not make it into the army's official history.

Mon. 9 Aug (SICILY)

Just across the valley from here there is a small stone hut in which live a woman and her daughter. The woman is said to be six months pregnant.

Her 15-year old daughter is the mother of a child. Both are doing lucrative business taking on the troops from Advance and Rear Div for one shilling. It seems that they are doing a land-office business and the troops are queueing up for what must be one of Life's necessities if they go to all that trouble to get it. It's hard to believe, yet I've heard of stranger stories.

Tues 10 Aug (SICILY)

There are numerous cases of sickness among the troops throughout the Division. Most of the trouble seems to be dysentery with vomiting and bouts of cold sweats. Jack Slayter says that the main cause for this are the flies with which the country abounds and which must carry every germ imaginable since sanitary facilities are practically non-existent on this island. In areas which we occupy the Field Hygiene Section makes every effort to ensure that sanitary measures are taken for the prevention of flies and the spread of infection but one cannot control flies that leave the civilian areas to enjoy our more palatable army rations. . . .

To some extent looting by civilians is still prevalent, nor are our troops entirely innocent of this crime. Instructions were issued this evening from this H.Q. reminding all ranks that looting is a serious offence. In order that there would be no misunderstanding, these instructions also included a clear definition of what is meant by "looting." This was to be made known to all troops. According to Arnold, civilians have been robbed at the point of a gun of their personal effects such as rings, watches, jewelry, etc., by some of our troops. A very serious view is being taken of this since, obviously, our behaviour in Italy will determine the extent of the resistance of people in occupied territory against the Germans. We cannot continue to preach to the rest of the world that we are the liberators of oppressed peoples, if we ourselves rob them indiscriminately.

I was later told by Thrupp (who acted as interpreter) that General Bologna complained to General Simonds that only this morning the car in which he was riding was stopped on the road by Canadian soldiers who demanded, and took from its mast the insignia of his rank and dignity. General Simonds expressed sincere regret at the incident and said that while the act was in bad taste and to be deplored, it was undoubtedly due to the fact that our forward troops had not yet been informed that the Italians were no longer our enemy. He would make it a very serious crime, continued General Simonds, for any of our troops to interfere with, molest, or disarm Italian soldiers. After his interview with General Simonds, General Bologna was met by a group of his staff officers who with much shouting and waving of arms, told him that while he was in conference with General Simonds, one of our officers had relieved a Carabinieri Outrider of his pistol. According to Thrupp, Bologna threw up his hands in despair and said, "Come, let us go from here quickly before they steal the very shirts from our backs!"

There Is Great Hope That He Is Alive: Caring for Those at Home, 1943

VARIOUS

In July 1943, William Ivan Mouat was shot down in a bombing raid over Belgium. These letters detail the response from his squadron commander, an unofficial POW association, and the Canadian Red Cross. Blessedly for Mouat's family, a postcard from Pilot Officer Mouat, sent from a POW camp in Germany, arrived in September.

S/Ldr. J. M. ——
R.A.F. Martlesham Heath
Suffolk, England

13th August 1943

Dear Mr. Mouat

Before you receive this letter you will have had a telegram informing you that your son Pilot Officer W. I. Mouat has been reported missing. Please receive on behalf of myself as his commanding officer and his many friends in the squadron the great sympathy which all of us feel with you in your great anxiety.

In my opinion there is a great hope that he is alive. On the afternoon of July 11th, 1943 he went with his Flight Commander to

Belgium to attack locomotives and barges. When they were attacking some barges two enemy aircraft came behind them and fired at great distance. His Flight Commander gave the order to climb into the clouds and last saw your son entering the cloud. Whilst in the clouds, your son gave a reply to his Flight Commander's call but this could not be understood. That is all we know.

There is a possibility that he is a prisoner of war, in which case you will either hear from him direct or through the Air Ministry who will receive advice from the International Red Cross Society. Your son's effects have been gathered together and forwarded to the R.A.F. Central Depository, where they will be held until further news is received, or in any event for a period of at least six months before being forwarded to you through the Administrator of Estates, Ottawa.

Your son was very popular in the squadron and was Deputy Flight Commander. He was always very keen to have a crack at the Hun and to help, far from his home, the fight in the cause of Freedom and humanity.

If you should require any further information, please do not hesitate to communicate with me.

Canadian Prisoners-of-War Relatives' Association
Victoria Headquarters
1013 Government Street, Victoria, B.C.

August 23rd. 1943

Dear Mrs Mouat:—

I am sure that you must be greatly relieved to learn that your son is a prisoner-of-war. I wonder if there is anything that we could do to help you with your next-of-kin parcels etc. There are certain foods that may now be included in the parcels which we are able to obtain, such as chocolate, chipped beef.

We also send cigarettes and books to the boys, cigarettes have already gone to your son from British Columbia House in London.

The enclosed information may be of help to you.

Yours truly,

Violet A. Thistle
Sec-Treas.
Phone. E.4164.

This is the contents of a parcel that I sent to a prisoner on Friday
It weighed 10 lbs. 12 ½ oz. which left 3 ½ oz. for wrapping etc.
There is no postage. Weight when packed 11 lbs.

2. Shirts (fleece lined)
2. pr. Draws " "
1. Shirt (grey flannel)
1. Suit Pyjamas. (flannelette) striped
1. Towel (white)
1. Wash cloth
4. Handkerchiefs (blue)
2. pr Grey woolen socks.
2. pr Shoe laces.
1. Shoe brush
    Shaving soap
    Toilet soap
    Razor and blades
    Tooth brush
    Tooth powder
    Shoe polish
    Comb.
6. chocolate bars
    1.lb. Chocolate plain.

This parcel cost $16.00
We could not include food in this parcel as there was not room.
The Red Cross cable had asked for warm clothing as he had just
come out of hospital.
The Red Cross supply each prisoner with a parcel every week, also
a capture parcel which includes some clothing.

The Canadian Red Cross Society
August 27th, 1943.

Dear Mrs. Mouat:

We were very pleased to note in the Press that your son, who had pre-viously been listed as missing, is now reported a prisoner of war. We are entering your name on our mailing list to receive the "Prisoner of War" magazine; this is a monthly publication giving reports on the prisoner of war camps visited by the International Red Cross repre-sentative, as well as excerpts from prisoners' letters.

We are forwarding to you under separate cover a Red Cross pam-phlet giving a very full account of the work of our Society with the prisoners of war, a map showing the location of the prisoner of war camps, and also a booklet issued by the Postmaster General concern-ing communication with prisoners. Full particulars of the next-of-kin parcel are contained in this book, and you will note on page 8 that labels for these parcels will be issued by the National War Services, Ottawa, on receipt of the prisoner's address. It is possible that you will receive the camp address direct from your son before it is received through official channels.

Letters to Air Force prisoners in Germany should be sent to Stalag Luft 3 (as this is the censor point for all airforce mail in Germany) with the addition in brackets of camp where the prisoner is actually in-terned. This does not apply to parcels which should be sent direct to the actual internment camp.

It is the sincere desire of our Society to be of assistance to Next-of-Kin at all times and we trust you will avail yourself of this service.

Yours sincerely,
F. W. Tuffrey
Provincial Commissioner.

Kreigsgefangenenlager Datum: Sept. 22/43.

Dear Mother & Dad:

It's so hard to write these short cards, but I'm feeling fine and my leg has healed up completely. I'm going to write to Allie at the address I used to have of his. I've received no mail yet, but expect none from you until another month. Give my love to everybody at home, tell Grace I'll write her soon.

Your loving son Ivan.

Washing Out of Pilot Training, 1943

JAMES KESHEN

Virden, Man.,
Thurs., Oct. 21, 1943

Dear Harry:

I'm a no good shit for not answering you sooner, but the only letters I've had time to write are one home every few days, and even they are pretty short. But now, things are really going piss-poor with me. I'm waiting for my wash-out tests as a pilot, and I have plenty of time to write. Who told you about my crack-up? I hope it wasn't my Mom or Dad. I don't want them to know or they'll worry themselves sick—and I'm in the best of health.

Well, here's the score about my wash-out tests. I haven't got what the RCAF calls "depth perception." That means I can't judge how far I am from the ground when I'm landing. And that's one thing they can't teach you. Either you've got it or you haven't got it, and they don't think I've got it. That's how I had that crack-up. I was bringing her in for a landing, and I started to level her out when I thought she was 5 feet off the ground. Well, anyhow, later on my instructor told me we were actually 50 feet off the ground. Well, at that height with my throttle off, I didn't have much airspeed, and I started losing height fast. Anyhow, I had the presence of mind to throttle her up, and I'd just got my motor racing when she hit the ground, so it deadened the bounce a hell-of-a-lot. But now I was racing along the ground at a hell of a speed, and my tail was away up. I cut my motor again but it was too late—the wind caught my tail and we flipped right over on our back. I was left dangling upside down in my harness, but I didn't have a scratch, and I was none-the-worse for my experience, but I think that's what cooked my goose.

Well, if I flunk as a pilot, I'm going through for an air bomber, which is a pretty nice course too. . . .

Your devoted friend,

Jimmy

Tank Training in England, 1943

BRIGADIER-GENERAL CHRISTOPHER DE L. KIRBY

Re: 2 Canadian Armoured Corps Reinforcement Unit (2 CACRU)

. . . It was late 1943 when I got to 2 CACRU, ie, after some Canadian armour had been committed to battle, as all of its fighting components would be within a few months. There was no shortage of reinforcements at that juncture: they were piled up in England in thousands, the unluckiest among them in 2 CACRU, Aldershot, Hants.

Never mind accommodation in obsolete cavalry barracks, designed for the cool comfort of horses in India.

2 CACRU was big enough to be commanded by a colonel, at this time the stout Colonel Perry, never glimpsed outside his office by his soldiers. . . . He had given up on his command and no bloody wonder!

It was overseen by the scum of the Armoured Corps, spat out by regiments, but not returned to Canada for the menial labour to which they were so patently suited. They wreaked their bile instead on massed reinforcements, trained to some degree in Canada . . . but robbed by 2 CACRU of any enthusiasm for the cause, military skill they may have acquired, or respect for the Army. . . .

As a desperately keen reinforcement, I spent weeks alone in a closed bay, pounding tin cans flat for salvage . . .

Hundreds of reinforcements on the verge of battle lined up on the parade square every Saturday morning in the winter rain, with their gallant leaders—commissioned, warranted and non-commissioned—dry on the covered second-storey balcony above them. We laid out the prescribed contents of our small packs in the muddy puddles at our feet: "Toothbrush in the right hand, housewife in the left," some oaf would yell as we squatted, "Up!", which was our Armoured training for that half-day. . . .

I was charged by a warrant officer for stripping a breechblock on my own on a tea break; no one was going to learn anything on his watch. . . .

The Strains of High Command, 1943

LIEUTENANT-GENERAL GUY SIMONDS

> *Guy Simonds, then a major-general, successfully commanded the 1st Canadian Division in Sicily and then took over the 5th Canadian Armoured Division under corps commander General Harry Crerar. The relationship between the two artillery officers was taut and difficult, full of slights imagined and real.*

In regard to your request for self-examination, I know I have a hot and quick temper. It is a characteristic of which I am not in the least proud. It is a fault I know, but it has always been with me and I am afraid always will be. I believe I have improved it somewhat, but I am afraid, though I try to exercise restraint, it will always be there. I am impatient of stupidity, dullness and indifference—or gaucheness, and I know I sometimes lose my temper when I shouldn't. But the same fault has been characteristic of commanders who have risen to far greater heights than I ever expect to reach.

I consider it most unjust to suggest that the incident about which you have written is in any sense an indication that my decisions are influenced or based upon impulse. You have suggested that same thing before now but I would like to say, that though things may "burst out" suddenly, there has been a lot of very deep thought behind them. You might consider the way I dealt with the recent personnel question, about which I wrote to you, to have been impulsive. It might have appeared so to the officer concerned. But I had weighed the question very carefully since the first day he arrived here and I discussed his C.Os with him. I got a bad impression then. This bad impression was reinforced as further evidence came to light. I weighed the evidence carefully and it was sufficient to satisfy me that he was not good enough for his job and I decided he would go, immediately I had discussed the question with Brownie. The following morning I sent for the officer concerned and told him in the first sentence that he would not do for me and the reasons why. He may well have got the impression it was an "impulsive" decision but I think my letter to you, written two or three days before, is sufficient evidence that it was not.

I believe my judgment both of personalities and things in general to be as sound as anyone's and I do not make decisions on impulse. I have also satisfied myself that I can keep a level head and still make sound decisions, under considerable stress and I believe I could produce highly responsible witnesses to bear me out in that.

Physically, I think I can claim with accuracy that, since the outbreak of war, I have had fewer days away from duty for sickness or rest (weekends, leaves etc) than any commander in the Canadian Army. I have had more sudden changes and demands placed on my stamina than any other. I know you think I should carry more weight, but after all surely that is a matter of opinion? Some have prejudices for fat men and some for thin, but I honestly cannot see how that affects mental capacity or judgment—both kinds have it and both kinds haven't.

You say you appreciate that I have been under very heavy mental strain for some months. I did not find it so, but I would not be honest if I did not confess that two things of recent occurrence left a very strong feeling of resentment.

The first was that whilst "Timberwolf" was actually under weigh, no word was sent to me. Regardless of my rank or seniority I was the senior Canadian officer in this theatre. It became obvious to me that both the Army and Corps Commander under whom I was serving were in possession of knowledge of impending changes about which I knew nothing. It was obvious they expected a change of command in the division, for what reason I had no idea until some ten days later. It made my own position most difficult for I did not know whether I had lost their confidence or not, yet was charged with the responsibility for conducting operations. It is my opinion that I was entitled to be informed. I feel General McNaughton ought to have informed me, and considering the previous occasions on which I have worked for you, I would have expected you to have asked him to so inform me. Loyalty is not a one way street, though I am afraid that in our service it is frequently regarded as one.

Secondly, during the first evening's talk in my caravan, you accused me of "Thinking of nothing but myself" and "wanting to go home to bask in my newly won glory." I thought the remarks and the sense of others, unjust and uncalled for. You have referred in your letter to discourtesy as between senior and junior officers. Taking into consideration our relationship, it was quite impossible for me to reply to the remarks you made. The conversation left me with the impression that the principal purpose of your visit was to administer a rebuke to me—for what reason or purpose I did not, nor do I yet understand.

When I was eventually informed of the impending changes I asked to see General Montgomery and suggested I should hand over 1 Canadian Division at once. Chris had been commanding, the 2 Bde was in the middle of an operation under Hoffmeister and doing well. Forin was doing well in command of the Seaforths. To shift all back to their original posts and bring them out again within about a week, seemed to me a stupid thing to do. It was far better to leave things as they were with the new arrangement working well. General Montgomery agreed and suggested I should fly to England at once. I told him I could not go until you arrived as there were powers attached to my rank that could not be exercised by anyone else. He then suggested in a cable, I should go back immediately when you arrived. I had told him I would enjoy a few days leave and as the information then given to me by Tow indicated the first flight would not arrive until the third week in November, it would give me a chance to make what I might consider necessary changes in the division before it sailed. It would have avoided my being without a C.R.A. now. Though, as things turned out, that could not have been avoided, over six weeks have now passed and my "new division" is not yet assembled and much of its equipment not even in sight. It looks very much as if I shall have little opportunity of influencing the training of the armoured brigade. You have pointed out that such things were inevitable taking into account the circumstances in which the division was mobilized and despatched. I do not think my own appreciation of the problem as at the end of October was unsound or very wide of the mark. Your remarks, during our first conversation left me with an impression I had not had from you before and not a little resentment.

Your reference to "brilliance" I do not understand. I have made a point of paying no attention to press "bally-hoo" or the public statements of politicians. I think I can correctly assess the value of both.

I have been perfectly frank in telling you of my feelings about being kept in ignorance of "Timberwolf" and as a result of our first conversation. I would like to make it clear however that I have not allowed nor do I intend to allow personal feelings of mine to influence my judgment nor my attitude to my senior commander. It had nothing whatever to do with the Kirk episode which arose solely from annoyance with a junior officer who, I consider, acted in a most impertinent manner.

I can assure you quite honestly also, that you can rely upon my loyalty in carrying out your policies. I have worked for senior officers whom I neither personally liked nor respected, but I have never had one complain of my loyalty, honesty or usefulness of the service rendered.

I have worked for you on three occasions, and I do not think that you can honestly say that I have not served you well and represented my views honestly even when I knew they differed from your own.

I was not happy at Corps, I had been told before you took over (and I cannot tell you by whom without betraying a confidence) that you had strongly opposed my appointment as B.G.S., that you disapproved of me being there and that I could expect to be removed very shortly after you took over. What I had been told seemed to be confirmed in our first interview when you told me you did not think it was the place for me and that you intended to post me to a brigade just as soon as you were in the saddle. I knew Guy Turner was knocking me behind my back. I was delighted at the prospect of getting a show of my own. I was kept on and on at Corps with the unhappy feeling that you really wanted someone else there and were only waiting for a suitable opportunity to change. But I do not think you can say that my own feelings influenced my loyalty or service I gave to you. At least you have never suggested it to me. If you felt I "thought too much about myself" then, I certainly was not happy considering the false position I felt I had landed into.

I would welcome an opportunity for a perfectly frank talk with you. Your letter reinforces the feeling that you are looking for an opportunity to "take a crack" at me.

I do not believe you can quote any reasonable evidence for assuming my judgment to be faulty. Everyone makes mistakes and I don't claim that I do not make my share though I think that is probably below the average.

I am quite certain of one thing, I will not take troops into battle under your command if I have lost your confidence. It would be unfair to the troops and would prejudice a reasonable chance of a successful result. When that time comes, if you cannot express full confidence in my judgment and ability to handle my command in battle, I shall have to ask to be relieved.

As Tough a Go as Anything We've Encountered: Italy, December 1943

CAPTAIN HARRY JOLLEY

Captain Jolley, a dental officer, served in Canada, Britain, Italy, and northwest Europe. His comments on the Moro River fighting would be echoed by every Canadian serving in Italy.

December 17, 1943

Even if this reaches you in an unusually short time, it will be a couple of weeks before you get it. By that time any war news I report will seem ancient. Then there is always the problem of censorship. I don't want to disclose anything accidentally. . . . I can tell you this that I am on a front of which Canadian veterans of this war will speak in the future in awesome tones. Imagine this is about as tough a go as anything we've encountered. If any Canadian soldiers ever had any doubts about the Germans' abilities as soldiers his experience here has undoubtedly set them at rest. Not only is he a good soldier in the defensive & offensive phases of that profession, but he is a master of destruction of anything that may be of value to his opponents. I hope for the day when he'll be practising that aspect of his art on his own territories will not be far distant. He's got a powerful lot to answer for. I've seen towns so completely & thoroughly destroyed that you could hardly believe what you saw. We're well-led by what I consider a very humane general—that will have to await explanation. War is certainly as awful & horrible as anyone can imagine. . . .

Let me hasten to reassure you. I'm eating regularly & working not too hard . . .

There Are No Trenches: At Ortona, December 1943

GREGORY CLARK

> *Toronto journalist Greg Clark, who had served in the Great War, compared the terrible struggle for Ortona to his experiences in the trenches.*

With the Canadians in Italy, Jan. 10—Capt. John Heller, Toronto doctor who served as medical officer of the Royal Canadian Regiment from the landing in Sicily up to the outset of the Ortona battle, through which he served with a field ambulance, says the Canadians' recent battle only adds to the unexplored realm of human endurance, as recorded at Hannibal's crossing of the Alps and Napoleon's retreat from Moscow. It is impossible to put limits, he says, to human endurance.

In the old war there were deep, dry trenches, kept so by engineers and endless working parties. There were deep, dry dugouts, or in the worst cases, funkholes in the trenches, shielded by ground sheets, where men could rest. The routine was that men working in teams of two stood duty two hours on and four hours off. The four hours off they spent in the dugouts or funkholes, where they could rest, if not sleep, and be reasonably dry under blankets. In the worst battles, they fought two or three days at the most and then were brought well to the rear to rest. These were the days of four Canadian divisions in the corps, to rest one another.

At Ortona, our Canadian battalions were in on each other's heels day after day. They had slit trenches which filled with water. In the approaches to Ortona were scattered Italian farms, rapidly ruined by the shell and mortar fire of both sides. These ruins afforded the only shelter.

Endurance Is Remarkable

Yet in the opinion of Captain Heller there is not recorded a more remarkable example of human endurance, physical and mental, than this month-long struggle by men never really rested or withdrawn from the body wrack and nerve wrack of battle. Cases of what they now call "exhaustion" instead of the old war phrase "shell shock" were very rare.

"There has always been," says Captain Heller, "a proper understanding by the medical profession of ordinary exposure. We realize, of course, that soldiers are better able to withstand exposure by reason of their long training than men in ordinary circumstances. But after days and nights of constant exposure to temperatures just above freezing, in self-built slit trenches half full of water, with cold rations and unremitting nerve strain, the cases of exposure that passed through our hands were extraordinarily few.

"After the first few went through our hands in the field ambulance I decided to hold one and observe his recovery, to see if there were anything else we might do before sending them further back. He was a young westerner, big and strong. He had been in battle four days and was completely helpless from exposure and exhaustion. He had been fighting continuously from slit trenches in rain, sleet and cold wind and had had no proper rest. He came in on a stretcher, unable to move a limb or a finger. He was semi-conscious, shaking in every muscle. We put him under 10 blankets, with hot water bottles, and gave him normal treatment for exposure. He could not even hold a cup or bring his hand to his lips."

Thawed Out in 10 Hours

"In 10 hours," Capt. Heller went on, "he was thoroughly thawed out and in complete control of his muscles. He was up and about the ambulance, bellowing that he wanted to get back to his company. We ordered him to remain until we were ready to let him go. Thirty hours after he had been admitted a helpless exhausted body, he was back to his unit, as fit by every test as a man can be. This has been a common experience of Canadians throughout the battle. Much of it has been handled by the companies and platoons themselves. In the platoon there grows a family feeling that looks out for its own."

In the Ortona fighting and beyond there are no trenches in which officers and sergeants can organize a sort of domestic economy of hours and relief. One platoon goes on patrol ahead, while the others hole up in a ruined house or sunken road or just self-made slit trenches dug almost automatically now by men who never used a shovel seriously before in their lives. But in every man is a basic instinct to do his share, providing the others do theirs. Two hours on and four off, as in the last war, appears to be about the system now adopted by Canadians fighting in these winter conditions.

Carry on by Memory

Besides Capt. Heller I talked to several men who had been through the toughest experiences around and beyond Ortona, including Pte. Dick Wright of Bowmanville, who experienced exhaustion after day after day of slit trenches, and who says that however hot the shell and mortar fire and however pinned down you may be in a slit trench half full of ice water, you reach a stage where the shells no longer bother you at all, a sort of semi-consciousness in which you carry on your job by memory almost.

Wright was the picture of health when I saw him, but what he had been through he thinks would have finished him back home around Bowmanville if he had not been patiently toughened up by his army training and his adventures in Sicily and Italy.

There was a sort of West Toronto gathering at the same place on the road, with Corporal Nyle MacKenzie, of Pacific Ave., Lance-Corporal Bill Hall, of Indian Rd., and Lance-Corporal Bill Morris, of West York, all of whom had experiences and stories to tell of plain human endurance among their comrades. The opinion is the Canadians have no nerves except physical nerves, like telephone wires, strung through their bodies and unless these wires get damaged or crossed by physical shock or injury, a man can go 10 miles farther than he thinks he can.

Hall, who was servicing a tank and had no business taking part in the fight, was involved in a counter attack in which he found himself digging a slit trench on one side of a gully, with Germans clearly audible talking on the opposite side of the gully digging their slit trenches three or four doors away in pitch black winter rainy night. Yet, though untrained for this emergency, Hall said he was fairly lifted by the spirit of the men around him.

One of the German prisoners taken at point 59 was like most of

The pace of training for the attack on Hitler's Europe stepped up in 1944. Soldiers from the 3rd Canadian Division's North Nova Scotia Highlanders, selected to spearhead the invasion, trained hard. Here they debark from a landing craft on an English beach in May 1944. National Archives of Canada/PA132859

The D-Day invasion of Normandy on June 6, 1944, put the men of the First Canadian Army into heavy fighting that lasted for eleven months until V-E Day. These soldiers of Le Régiment de la Chaudière seem surprisingly calm as they head toward Juno Beach.

National Archives of Canada/PA131498

(TOP LEFT) The fighting in Normandy was vicious. This Sherman tank rolling through the ruins of Caen would find itself outgunned by German panzers. National Archives of Canada/PA132859

(TOP RIGHT) General Maurice Pope had served in the Great War and in the Permanent Force. During the 1939–45 war his service culminated as Prime Minister King's military adviser. National Archives of Canada/PA188985

(LEFT) The Royal Canadian Navy grew fifty-fold during the war and served in every theatre. Here the destroyer *St Laurent* is tied up alongside the armed merchant cruiser *Prince David* in 1944. National Archives of Canada DND/PA132787

(LEFT) V-E Day was May 8, 1945. Over the next year, Canadian servicemen returned home. These officers and men of the Royal Regiment of Canada arrived in Toronto on November 22, 1945. City of Toronto Archives/100378

(BELOW) War in Korea erupted in June 1950, and Canada joined in the first United Nations war. These infantrymen of the 2nd Battalion, Princess Patricia's Canadian Light Infantry, were ferried across the Imjin River in June 1951 by American troops. National Archives of Canada/PA132638

(ABOVE) The terrain in South Korea was tough country to fight in. These soldiers of 2PPCLI moving through a valley in March 1951 received help in fording a stream from a Korean farmer.
National Archives of Canada/PA114888

(LEFT) Canadian battalion commanders in Korea were tough, experienced vets of the Second World War. LCol Jim Stone of 2 PPCLI, here reflectively eating a cold supper, was one such.
National Archives of Canada/PA142233

(ABOVE) Korea was not good tank country, and Canada's Shermans were primarily used as artillery. This tank from the Lord Strathcona's Horse was on patrol in June 1951. National Archives of Canada/PA129109

(LEFT) This famous photograph shows the strain of combat. Private Bob Macpherson of the 2nd Battalion, Royal Canadian Regiment, was reloading Bren gun magazines after a Chinese night attack on November 3, 1951. National Archives of Canada/PA131761

The Korean commitment lasted more than three years. These soldiers of 3PPCLI were cleaning their weapons in July 1953, one a long-obsolete Sten gun.
National Archives of Canada/PA132637

Canada committed its troops to United Nations peacekeeping operations all around the world. These soldiers in Egypt with UN Emergency Force II played tourist in their off-duty hours. DND REC79-279

Canadians went into the chaos of the Congo in 1960 and remained there
for four years. Here a Canadian colonel (centre) talks to his polyglot
staff during one of many crises in 1964. DND UNC64-009-6

Duty in Cyprus stretched for almost thirty years, long years of boredom interrupted
by moments of terror. This armoured personnel carrier, painted in UN colours, was
on the Green Line between Greek- and Turkish-Cypriots in 1984. DND ISC84-351

(LEFT) Canada sent a small contingent to a United Nations operation in East Timor, a breakaway territory claimed by Indonesia, in 1999. Here Canadian infantry come ashore from a landing craft.

DND ISC99-433A

(BELOW) Peacekeeping duty put Canadians in contact with different cultures, as this soldier in East Timor found.

DND ISC99-438A

them, fairly near finished with exhaustion and exposure. By the time he reached the hands of an intelligence officer, through whose hands they have to pass, he was thawed out and told the officer the only reason he was captured was his finger would no longer bend on the trigger.

"And what is more," he said, "I don't like Canadians, because they took advantage of us because their fingers would still bend."

Dining with Colonel Zabotin in Halifax

LEO HAMSON

> *The Soviet Union was Canada's ally, and for much of the war it bore the heaviest burden in the war against Hitler. But the Soviets thought of the alliance with the West as temporary and actively spied against nations like Canada. Colonel Nikolai Zabotin, based at the embassy in Ottawa, ran the GRU, or Red Army, networks that were exposed when cipher officer Igor Gouzenko defected in September 1945. Hamson's account suggests that Zabotin was a formidable figure.*

Along with many others, I was not sent overseas until the threat to our own shores had abated. Remote radar stations from Greenland to New England fed their plots into a central Filter Operations Room at Eastern Air Command H.Q. in Halifax. Much of the Lord Nelson Hotel had been altered and taken over to house this, with Naval Operations North Atlantic in an adjoining room. In that room, on a huge wall map, we could watch the agonizing Battle of the Atlantic unfold as W.R.E.N.'s on ladders moved the symbols representing convoys and U-Boat wolf packs.

I found myself posted to these top-secret rooms with an appointment as Army Liaison Officer to Eastern Air Command with a desk on a balcony looking down on the huge map displaying the radar plots of all aircraft movements on the East Coast Approaches. My job was to co-ordinate the anti-aircraft batteries around the Defended Ports with the squadron of Hurricane fighters based at Dartmouth. I felt that such a heavy responsibility warranted a rank promotion . . . but that didn't happen. It wasn't in the "job description"! But then again, nothing else happened to break the boredom, aside from a few heart-stopping false alarms. On one dark night we nearly shot down an aircraft carrying Bob Hope, Betty Grable, and a troop of other entertainers returning from a tour of American bases in England . . . but that's another story!

In Halifax, we Garrison Officers had membership in the mess of Royal Artillery Park bestowed upon us. They claimed it was the oldest officers' mess in Canada, dating from the British conquest of 1754. It was a somber old place, with two brass cannons flanking the entrance, overstuffed arm-chairs, and old etchings of long-ago battles on the walls. It was some time before we learned from a casual remark that one of the tables we ate our breakfast on was claimed to have been the funeral bier of General Montcalm when he lay in state in the cathedral in Quebec City after the valiant old commander of the French forces died of his wounds after the Battle of the Plains of Abraham in 1759. It was said that the British brought it to Halifax as a trophy. I cannot vouch for the veracity of that story, nor can I dispute it.

A handful of elderly Permanent Force officers with chests full of ribbons and red tabs on their collars ran the place as if they owned it. When they settled in behind their newspapers they wanted it as quiet as an undiscovered tomb. These newspapers would be lowered just enough to glare over when a troop of brash young subalterns would come bursting through the door at meal time, beer in hand, and hob-nails scratching the polished floor. The old guys retaliated by fixing messing dues (from which they exempted themselves) so horrendously high that we young upstarts avoided the place except on compulsory regimental dinner nights.

This was the setting and the atmosphere for what happened next. I cannot remember the date—1943 or early 1944. The G.O.C. Atlantic Command sent orders that a select group of officers that included me were to attend the mess at R.A. Park for a very special dinner for a number of high-ranking guests that included some American generals, Col. Ralston, Canada's Minister of National Defence, and the Guest of Honour, the Soviet Military Attache, Col. Nikolai Zabotin. We were ordered sternly to ensure that our batmen had our best uniforms neatly pressed, to review the manual on mess etiquette, and to be on our best behaviour. Obviously the old boy had heard about us!

This made me quake with apprehension, as it was my turn for the rotating duty of Messing Officer, whose function it was to ensure that the kitchen of the Officers' Mess and everything and everybody related to it were up to snuff. As my ignorance of such things is to this day absolutely total, this periodic appointment was for me a pointless exercise, but it never bothered me. All I ever did was walk quickly through the kitchen while the cooks and men on fatigue duty snapped to attention, lift a pot lid or two on the stove and peer inside with an air of knowledgeable authority, nod at the men with an "As you were" and walk out. I did not have to worry about negative remarks from my fellow-officers at the dining table, because we were fortunate to have a superb sergeant-cook who had been head chef at the Chateau Laurier, and, so it was said, had cooked for the King and Queen when they visited Canada in 1939. But there was a problem. He was an alcoholic with a penchant for going off on monumental benders that lasted for days. This was tolerated because a chef with his skills was irreplaceable in the Army.

The Mess President summoned me to address this potentially disastrous problem. He advised me to place our cook under open arrest immediately with confinement to barracks but full duties until the banquet was behind us. I was astonished. "On what charge, sir?"

"Use your bloody imagination and get on with it!" he snapped and walked away. I racked my brains and then remembered Section 40 of the Army Act—a broad section that is very useful when you can't think of a specific charge that will stick. I don't recall the misdemeanor I dreamed up when I accosted the cook, but I was struck by the fact that he did not protest or seem at all surprised by my fictitious allegation. It was almost as though he expected it. He just said "Yes, Sir" meekly and went on with his work.

The evening of the great event came, and there was an undercurrent of subdued excitement as we assembled in the ornate mess anteroom. I had made a worried check in the kitchen and found our chef in his finest whites with towering white chef's hat, in complete command of the situation. He had created a marvellous tableau on a huge backing—the Royal Artillery Crest in fruits, vegetables, and smoked salmon, and his men were carrying it to the dining room wall. I was immensely relieved, and the sergeant-cook winked at me as he passed by. I returned to the ante-room to join the waiting group of about a hundred officers. It was then I noticed that the white-coated stewards scurrying about were not our staff. We had never seen them before.

There was a commotion at the door as a limousine pulled up. A group of American generals came up the short flight of steps between the two polished brass cannons. We stood to attention while they regarded us with puzzled frowns. They probably did not realize that unlike Americans, British and Commonwealth troops do not salute when their heads are uncovered. We juniors stood aside while the generals, brigadiers and colonels were introducing each other and accepting cocktails from the trays of the stewards. Then there was another commotion, and the solemn Colonel Ralston, in civilian clothes, entered with his aides. But all this did not diminish the faint, uncertain air of anticipation. We had a feeling that the main event was yet to occur.

Then it happened. There wasn't exactly a fanfare, but it had all the elements of a Grand Entrance. A hush fell over the group and we all stared in astonished wonder at the magnificent sight before us. A tall figure was striding down the hall toward us such as we had never seen before. The head steward (obviously brought in for the occasion, as he was not one of ours) announced "Colonel Nikolai Zabotin, Military Attache to the Government of Canada from the Government of the Union of Soviet Socialist Republics." He was obviously intended to be the star of the show, and on cue from our colonel, we all broke into applause. Col. Zabotin bowed slightly and broke into a dazzling smile. He looked as elegant as a prince in an Austrian operetta.

He was dressed in a crisp white tunic with gold epaulets, tan breeches with a red stripe, and knee-length black riding boots polished until they shone. He had wavy blonde hair, penetrating blue eyes, and radiated a remarkable charisma that was quite overpowering. Within minutes, we had all fallen under his spell.

He was accompanied by another officer who was always silently by his side. This man was short, barely up to the shoulders of his superior, powerfully built, square-headed, with dark scowling jowls—the very image of what we had imagined Russians to look like. In the conversation that followed, Col. Zabotin would occasionally glance down at him, as though seeking confirmation or approval of what he had just said. A subaltern noted for his wisecracks and standing behind me whispered in my ear "He is the NKVD agent sent to watch *HIM!*"

Very shortly, the two Russians were standing encircled by us as we stood sipping our cocktails. Col. Zabotin spoke quite good English, and we learned that he also was an artillery officer, and had participated in some of the epic battles on the Eastern Front, including Stalingrad. We eagerly plied him with technical questions about artillery—such things as deployment, ranging and fire control methods, breech block mechanisms etc. He seemed particularly interested in our experiments with radar control for heavy coast artillery, in which I was never involved, but some senior officers readily answered his questions about this new and secret technology.

It was not until the following day in our "post mortem" of the event, that we realized to our chagrin that we had answered all his questions and he had answered none of ours. He had turned all our questions against ourselves with such amazing skill that we failed to notice it. We felt sheepish about being fooled but . . . after all, the Soviets were our valiant, noble allies in our desperate war against the evil Nazis, were they not? In any event, there was little they could learn from us. They made massive use of artillery and were masters of that art and science. If only we had known the awful truth about Col. Zabotin that was not revealed until war's end!

Our cocktails and conversation were interrupted when dinner was announced, and we all trooped into the dining room. The tables were arranged in an "E" pattern, and we were dazzled by the gleaming silverware and candelabra that we had not seen before. It was whispered that these R.A. Park treasures had been put in storage by the old Permanent Force guys who resented their peaceful world being invaded by us rude and unworthy young fellows when World War II broke out. The polished tables shone in the candlelight except where they were covered by the long linen strips under the dinnerware at our places. I was near the head table where those powerful dignitaries sat, and had a good view of them. There were speeches—predictable rhetoric on the only subject that mattered, but I paid little attention. Like everyone else, I could not take my eyes off the magnificent spectacle of Col. Zabotin.

At the end of the meal that was indeed a tour de force of our extraordinary chef, the stewards put on an amazing performance. After removing the meal dishes, they went up and down moving the wine glasses from the cloth to the bare wood in the center between the candelabra, while we put our hands in our laps wondering what was going on. Then stewards stationed themselves at each end of the table, grasped the ends of the cloths and twisted them into a rope. One began pulling on his end while the other held his under tension, then suddenly let go. The cloth shot down the table like a snake, not hitting a single glass, into the arms of the man at the other end, who then walked out with it. They did this flawlessly with all seven cloths. It was a breath-taking stunt and the two Russians rose to their feet and led us all in applause. Then the stewards solemnly went up and down replacing all the glasses before us.

This was the appropriate time for our colonel to rise and propose the ritual toast to the King. As decreed in the rules of mess etiquette, we said simply "The King," sipped our wine, and sat down. No clinking of glasses or "God Bless Him." Then Col. Zabotin surprised us by rising to propose a toast "To the Glorious Canadian Army." Then an American general rose to propose a toast "To the Valiant Red Army." Col. Zabotin responded with one to Churchill. There was then a bewildering succession of toasts, mostly proposed by Col. Zabotin, to just about all the peoples, forces, and leaders involved in the war on our side. We then realized that the legendary gusto of the Russians for drinking endless toasts was no myth. White-sleeved arms kept appearing over our shoulders to refill our glasses. We young fellows were not accustomed to drinking on that scale. Feeling alarmed, and not knowing if it would go on all night, we cut back to mere sips. I noticed that Col. Ralston, our Minister of Defence, drank hardly at all, and I had the impression that he did not approve of the Soviet Military Attache seated next to him.

When we had toasted just about everybody in the world, Col. Zabotin suddenly rose, showing no signs of impairment (unlike the bleary-eyed rest of us), reached into his hip pocket and produced a silver flask. Unscrewing the cap, he handed it to our Col. Craig, a very short, bald old veteran whom we referred to as "Shorty" (out of range of his hearing, of course). A hush fell over the room. "My God!" we thought, "Vodka!"

At that time vodka was largely unknown in Canada, but we had all heard of the Russian fondness for what we believed to be liquid dynamite. Our beloved colonel rose unsteadily to his feet, staring at the flask in his hand while Zabotin gazed at him intently. "Come on Shorty!" we whispered anxiously to ourselves. "The honour of the Canadian Army is in your hands!" Shorty croaked out a toast to Joseph Stalin, and drank from the flask. His eyes seemed to rotate in his head. He recovered quickly, smiled, and handed the flask back to Zabotin, who joined in the thunderous applause that followed. We were sure that Zabotin was putting him to the test.

Then Zabotin rose and expressed his appreciation for the quality of the dinner, and wished to thank the chef personally. Colonel Hart nodded to me, and this was my cue to go to the kitchen door and fetch the chef to accept the compliments of our guests. When I went into the kitchen I was puzzled to see no-one in sight. As I turned to leave, I spotted a pair of feet on the floor sticking out from behind the counter. There lay our celebrated sergeant-cook, out cold with a nearly empty bottle beside him. He probably had it hidden in the kitchen all the time, untouched until his duty was done. "You're a good soldier" I whispered as I left him.

I returned to the dining room and announced to the assembly—"I regret that the chef is indisposed and is unable to come to his door to accept your compliments" and sat down. Col. Hart glared at me and scribbled a note on a napkin that he passed down the table to me. "I'll see you in my office at 0900 tomorrow." My heart sank. I knew I was in for it. Why hadn't I looked for that bottle?

As it turned out, Col. Hart was still in bed at 0900, according to his batman, and when I did see him near noon he was very genial, made no mention of the deplorable finale in the kitchen, rubbed his hands and exclaimed, "By Jove, Hamson, wasn't that a splendid dinner last night!"

The Problem of Home Defence Conscripts, 1943

LIEUTENANT-GENERAL MAURICE A. POPE

In 1940, Canada's government implemented conscription for home defence service but, despite a plebiscite in 1942, refused to force the conscripts to fight overseas until the conscription crisis of late

1944. General Pope's tolerant views towards the National Resources Mobilization Act (NRMA) conscripts were not widely shared in the military or the country.

27 *December 1943*

When I came back from C.M.H.Q., now nearly three years ago, I was saddened by the evidence at every hand that the then so called R Recruits were being subjected to every form of moral blackmail. The treatment they experienced in the training centres seemed to me to be wrong from several points of view and certainly from that of the national interest. During that year of 1941, which I spent in Ottawa, I found few men who did not give at least superficial assent to the proposition that any Commanding Officer who drew the slightest distinction between G.S. [General Service] and N.R.M.A. personnel was an unwise Canadian. But they all seemed to persist in practices which were not less than baneful in their effect.

In those days the G.S. man was allowed to put up "Canada" shoulder badges on being warned for overseas duty. Then after a while the true light came into our minds, if only for a moment, and the same privilege was accorded the R Recruit. But shortly afterwards we re-created the invidious distinction by allowing the G.S. man to wear the "G.S." badge on his sleeve. This put us back precisely where we had been before. And now once more C.A.R.O. 3929, which, if it does not make for confusion worse confounded, drives a wedge between the several elements of our army at a time when, surely, cohesion should be our watchword.

The N.R.M.A. man is simply exercising a freedom of judgment allowed him by the Government. He is carrying out a duty required of him by our elected representatives and, at a time when we never weary of proclaiming that we are fighting for the preservation of freedom, we penalize him for exercising what I would go so far as to say is a God-given right. Surely it is for our Government to tell the man where and how he is to serve. There is no moral obligation that I know of worthy of the name which throws this responsibility upon the man himself. Actually he is serving his country faithfully and well in Petawawa, in Rupert, at St. Johns, at Goose and in the islands to the south. Why should we deny him the symbol of service we freely grant the runner at N.D.H.Q.?

And to cap all, some months ago a Canadian force of five or six thousand men left our shores on a military expedition to recapture Kiska, as far from home as is Dieppe from Halifax. Those men set out, as you so well know, in good heart, prepared to carry out a ruder task than any that has yet fallen to us in this war. That they found the island deserted by the enemy has no bearing on the question. In so serving these men have become eligible for an American decoration, an honour that is denied them by their own country. Surely this must be repugnant to every principle and feeling of moral justice. And as surely this must be the reaction of every man who gives the matter a moment's thought.

Service in Italy Behind the Front, 1943

JACK AINSWORTH

> *Ainsworth served with a transport company of the Royal Canadian Army Service Corps. His job was to haul supplies forward to the front.*

December 9, 1943

Just finished off the last of the jam, it was a real treat. Most of the jam we get is a mixture of fig and whatever other fruit it happens to be. We were hauling some men and it was one of the trips that start in the morning and last till night and only go 30 miles with no official stops so that we were unable to cook up anything. That was the day we ate most of the can.

We have had plenty of rain and I'm sure glad they have taken our bikes away, it is more comfortable to sit in a truck and let it pour down.

The truck behind us just made tea so now I have a mug of it on the floor. A few days ago, we went on a ration draw and as it was the first time there, they didn't watch our boys very closely, so now all the trucks are well supplied with this canned bacon. It's good fried right and bean and milk. We can usually get all the tea and sugar we want from our kitchen, so we are the best fed branch of the army, I guess. Never eat bulley beef anymore and we have been able to run down the odd can of spam.

December 15, 1943

The monotony of our roads here is broken by some of the signs the Provost put up. It is a very winding road, so after 5 miles of "S Bends," "Bad Corner," we came across one "Monotonous As Hell, Isn't It." Then "Rita Hayworth Has Curves, So Has This Road." Other signs read "Go Ahead Cut Right In. We'll Inform The Next Of Kin." I've forgotten some of the good ones, but that makes it less tiresome for us.

It makes me laugh to think of the rigid enforcement of black outs in England and out here we can see fires all over the countryside; brew fires for tea.

We had a show the other night, projector on a bank and a screen about 4' by 4' hung up on the bush. It was alright but the show itself was really old.

December 23, 1943

The army are doing the best they can for us out here, going to quite a bit of trouble to provide cake, beer, cigs, oranges, apples and nuts, so we aren't forgotten men.

March 9, 1944

You mentioned about the Jerry soldier being fed up but talking to some of our infantry boys, they say different. A Sgt. told us about one he brought in that could speak English and as far as he was concerned or knew, London was no more, only a pile of rubble. They knew nothing of the Russian advance and said it was just propaganda when told. When asked about the shortage of German planes here, he said that if the Furher wanted planes here there would be planes and that was all there was to it. I don't believe half these stories of their morale cracking, they are fighting too well for that.

July 1944

We are not being overworked these days, on the road about every other day. Just handling supplies now and eating very well. We haul fresh meat, all frozen, and where we draw it from the rail head or dump, we always get an extra quarter and divide it up amongst our-selves and have lovely thick steaks before going to bed. Yesterday, we had pork, first since X-mas so you can imagine how we enjoyed that. When no meat is available, we go to work on the canned goods, spam and steak and kidney pudding are my favorites, but we always have something if we aren't too lazy to get it.

My work consists of looking after 6 trucks and 11 men. I have a good L/Cpl. and all my men are good drivers and take good care of their trucks so really I have very little to do. According to plan, I would ride a motorcycle but the roads are so bad we have done away with them.

Politics and Food in the Navy, February 1944

FRASER MCKEE

The war saw a rise in the popularity of the Co-operative Common-wealth Federation, or CCF, Canada's democratic socialist party.

Cornwallis, N.S.
Feb. 20, 1944

Dear Mum:

I'll take a little while this Sunday morning to drop you a line. Sunday is pretty much a free day, as we can't get into divisions, and we get any church over the radio. So we rest, write and discuss various topics.

You would be surprised at the tone of our talk—for instance we have long "table talks" on the C.C.F., socialism, small enterprise, cattle ranches, and so on. I have learned a lot by just listening in on these dis-cussions, and throwing in my own comments and opinions. There is sort of one going on now on co-op farming, and I am listening out of one ear as I write. . . .

I get lots to eat here, and I think we have one of the best cooks in the navy. He really turns out good food, appetizingly prepared, which makes a terrific difference. . . .

You should have seen it. 8 of us at a tiny table. Morch supplied some tomato juice each. Then soup then the main course—large helping of chicken, green peas, mashed potatoes, dressing & gravy. 2 kinds of ice cream for dessert, & tea. Not bad, eh, for an ordinary Sunday dinner.

. . .

Love,
Fraser

Young Officers Emerge in Battle, 1944

MAJOR-GENERAL CHRIS VOKES

> *At the beginning of 1944, Vokes was the commander of 1st Canadian Division. He had fought through the Sicilian and Italian campaigns, initially as a brigade commander.*

I had learned a great deal from my experiences in command of an infantry brigade and an infantry division in action. The important lesson I had learned was the vital need to delegate responsibility and at the same time accept full responsibility if the results were bad. I had seen too many instances where commanders blamed their subordinates for their own shortcomings.

I had developed confidence in my own ability to command in battle. I disliked any senior officer breathing down my neck in battle either when a brigadier or as a divisional commander. If I failed to deliver the goods requested, I expected to be taken apart verbally, but I resented any butting in before results were apparent. I treated my subordinate commanders in the same way I wished to be treated by my senior commander. I told them what I wanted done and let them get on with it within the scope of the instruction given. This developed their independence and initiative. Where any officer failed to measure up to the responsibility thrust upon him, steps were taken to have him replaced. The occasions on which this was necessary were very rare.

When the division had been mobilized in the autumn of 1939, all officers holding the rank of lieutenant colonel and above, and many other officers and senior nco's, had seen service in the 1914–18 War. Now in January 1944, the number of persons in the division who had seen service in that war were very few in number. None of these held unit command or above. I was 39, the brigade commanders were below

35, and the battalion commanders all below 30 years. As far as the 1st Division was concerned it had become a young man's war.

I had been first posted to the division in September 1940. In England, I had served in both the senior staff appointments at divisional headquarters, had commanded a battalion for several months and the second brigade for a year. Now after 3 years and 5 months continuous service in the division, there was little I did not know about it.

All the lieutenant colonels now in command of battalions or equivalent sized units, all the brigadiers, and all the senior staff officers and myself, had been of major's rank or below on the outbreak of war. They had risen in rank through ability. I knew well the capabilities and shortcomings of each including my own. I had complete confidence in each of them to perform his duties in an efficient and humane manner. I sensed they had this same confidence in me.

The Rise of the Militia Officer, 1944

BRIGADIER WILLIAM MURPHY

> *A militia officer, Murphy rose to command the 1st Canadian Armoured Brigade in Italy. He was always conscious of the divide between the regulars and the militia.*

February 20, 1944

Dearest family—

I know you will be glad to hear that your eldest son is now a Brigadier. I'm rather proud of the fact that I have received this promotion "at the front" and that the armoured brigade I will command has fought since the first day in Sicily. I take them over "in the line" as it were and don't go back to command one in England. So all in all my tail is up a bit. As I wrote Esther I am now resplendent in red tabs and red hat band— altho the latter I intend to overlook and cling to my beret. I'm a little premature to say I am now so dressed. I don't take over until a week today and in the meantime have to scurry around and try and raise the necessary finery. They have travelling officers shops out here and I hope to find what I need in one of them. At the moment I am somewhat overwhelmed at the responsibility that I am assuming. I'll have something over 3000 all ranks under my command and equipment worth I don't know how many millions. However no doubt I'll get over it—to a certain extent anyway. Its very nice to get away from the desk work once more and go back to commanding men. If there ever was a next step after this it would be to command a Division, or possibly go Brigadier General Staff on a Corps or Army HQ. Neither is in the least likely and I feel I have got about as far as a militiaman can in this war. It will mean an increase in income of course—altho I must confess that I don't know how much. Esther will get an automatic increase of something in her wife's allowance and I think I get $2.00 a day more. That should further assist in the nest egg we are gathering to re-establish ourselves, as I certainly haven't need for any money to speak of out here. So all in all everything is OK, except that I still want this blasted war to get finished—with the right ending of course—as soon as possible. We have had no mail now for some weeks but as one plane was lost—or at least its cargo—that is understandable. I hope another mail gets in shortly. You weren't getting mine very speedily last I heard. I think my letters of 26 Dec were the last you had got the last I heard from you. You should have had quite a few since then. Well darlings, I'm still disgustingly fit and healthy and sincerely hope you both suffer from the same complaint. Don't forget to send Cameron's address and give my best to the Killorans. I guess their holiday will be almost up when you get this. All my love and take care of yourselves.

Bill

The Generals Ready for D-Day, 1944

LIEUTENANT-COLONEL G.S. CURRIE

A key aide to defence minister J.L. Ralston, Currie visited Britain in April 1944 and talked with senior Canadian commanders readying their troops for the invasion of France.

6 April 1944

Had Generals Stuart, Crerar and Simonds to dinner and we had a most interesting talk. Was deeply impressed with the feeling of almost supreme confidence they have in the success of operations. Morale has never been higher. Again most important thing to watch in that connection is regular mail. Crerar remained after the other two left and we had a long discussion.

General Simonds is our very best technical commander but he needs guidance politically. He must be ridden like a temperamental racehorse—with safe but firm hands. We discussed the McNaughton episode. Crerar expressed himself personally sorry for General Mc-Naughton, but the change was inevitable, and absolutely necessary. Discussed the Military Mission as proposed in External's wires 34 and 35. Crerar agrees with tactical phase of the cables but not the strategic—to have a further discussion with General Stuart. Crerar's analysis of the war situation was most impressive. His analysis of General Montgomery and the stories of his relationship with him were most interesting. General Montgomery plays for publicity but is absolutely sound tactically. Before General Simonds left he gave a good example of this, when General Montgomery refused to rashly commit his Army when the Americans were in trouble at Salerno. Crerar, however, feels that the public and the intermediate commanders will turn upon Montgomery and slay him at his first failure. General Crerar said that he was the person responsible for the condition of training and the morale of the Canadian Army. McNaughton had steadily neglected training and Crerar found the situation in a "hell of a state" when he came from Canada to take over. In all the time that he served under McNaughton, the latter took almost no interest whatever in training and, in fact, seldom visited him at all.

Crerar developed and invented the assault detail which is to be used in the first assault. Crerar forecasts that if the first assault succeeds the remainder of the Canadian Army will not see action as the Germans will fold up. If the first assault fails the remainder of the Canadian Army will not be committed for some time thereafter. Crerar has supreme confidence that the first assault will succeed, provided the timing is right, i.e., this will be the Balkans, the air bombing and the Russian offensive. Germany will invite British and American Army to go into Germany to save them from Russia. The German Army in France, with her inland lines of communication as against our sea lines, can bring to bear about five military tons to our one and, for this reason, in order that the assault may be successful a great deal depends upon the action of the French people, of the French underground. We depend upon their sabotage and interruption of German lines of communication to make the assault a success. For this reason also bombing will from now on be centred to a great extent upon German lines of communication. Crerar did not leave until between one and two in the morning.

The Opening of the Hitler Line Battle, Italy, May 1944

BRIGADIER WILLIAM MURPHY

In May 1944, when the Allies attacked the Hitler Line, which was blocking the path to Rome, the Canadians played a major role. The 1st Canadian Armoured Brigade was supporting British troops.

May 17, 1944

Don't worry about miles on a map. Our job is to kill Germans, pin his divisions in Italy and we are doing just that and incidentally going steadily forward. This was a powerful line, built over five months and which has successfully withstood two major attacks. Of course when the Eighth Army got to work thats all there was to it. The line was busted. My tanks were the first over the river and put up a very gallant display indeed. Naturally I am terribly proud of the Bde. Our losses in both tanks and personnel have been astoundingly light thank God and we are still full of fight. The weather has remained fine throughout and getting very hot. You should see the dust. I rush about in a jeep mostly—you get there faster and its pretty quiet compared to an armoured vehicle so you can always take off for a ditch if you hear anything unpleasant coming. We don't have a windshield—they have a nasty habit of splintering when Jerry gets busy. So the dust you collect on your person is a caution. You are white from head to foot. We rather fooled Jerry on this one. We collected forward before the battle by night—carefully hiding ourselves in every fold of ground and clump of bush and tree. Driving thro a day or two before the show you never would have realized that there were thousands of men, vehicles, guns and tanks all around you. Everybodies tails are away up because we know we have had a tough job and it has been done. We shall keep hammering away and already he is groping in all directions for reserves. We have 'em but he hasn't. He has some, I should say, but he is drawing on them steadily and still he hasn't stopped us. I can't say too much about my regiments. All fought very gallantly indeed and we have shot up many more Jerry tanks and anti tank guns (our mortal enemies) than he has of ours. I'm sure he never expected to have tanks get into the Liri Valley, so he didn't put down many mines. That was terribly fortunate. They can be a bloody nuisance. So to have commanded the Bde that first got its tanks into him is very pleasant. For a whole day we were the only ones that were able to get over and believe me we shook him to the roots. We have many prisoners and more are reported this morning. Don't worry about me. If its dangerous anywhere I stay home and read a nice book, altho I have seen Jerries being taken. We have the bit firmly in our mouths and we're on our way. Please forgive the bad writing—its due to my trembling with fear and also our guns are shaking my caravan to beat hell. A letter from Dad and two from Mother—the latest the 6 May. So we get our mail even in battle. All my love for the moment. I'll write when I can.

Bill

We Are Going In Tomorrow Morning, D-Day, 1944

SERGEANT EDWARD WORDEN

> *On June 6, 1944, the 3rd Canadian Infantry Division and the 2nd Canadian Armoured Brigade landed on Juno Beach. Rifleman Worden of the Regina Rifles wrote his wife on board ship the night before. Worden survived the landing, only to be killed on April 8, 1945.*

To my darling wife:

How are you to-night? fine I hope. Lee darling I find it very hard to write this to you. I only wish I could have seen you but I can say this. I am fine and feel a 100 percent for I know I have someone waiting for me, who is very brave and knows how to smile.

We are going in to-morrow morning, as I write this we are out on the water so the big day has come. I often had wondered how I would feel but I don't feel any difference, as I ever did before. Thanks to you. I know I can truthfully say if it was not for you I would feel different but it is the love and trust I have for you, and that will help me over many a rough spot.

I am glad in away that it has come, for it means you and I can be together sooner, something I have always prayed for, and I know you have to. So promise darling you will not worry for I'll be alright and home before you know it.

Just you and mum look after each other, and time will pass swiftly.

Now before I close I want to say again that I love you very much and you mean the world to me. So now darling I'll say good-night and God bless you till we meet again soon.

Yours forever,

Love.

Ted.

P.S. Tell Mum that I am thinking of her too, and not to worry but look after you. I am enclosing a message they gave us. Good-night I'll write as soon as I get a chance.

Beach Head Taken: A Journalist Lands in Normandy, June 6, 1944

ROSS MUNRO

> *By this point a veteran of the Dieppe and Sicily landings, the 30-year-old Ross Munro of the Canadian Press sent this dispatch to Canada from the D-Day invasion fleet.*

WITH CANADIAN FORCES LANDING IN FRANCE, June 6— (CP Cable)—In two hours and 45 minutes of fighting on the beaches here, the Canadian invasion force won its beach-head and shoved on inland.

At 10:45 this morning the Canadian Commander (Gen. Keller) sent this message to Gen. Crerar, G.O.C. 1st Canadian Army: "Beach head taken. Well on way to intermediate objective."

The strip of coast won by the Canadians in this initial assault was quite narrow, but it gave them the beaches and provided a base for further penetration.

There was some stiff street fighting in the little coast towns and the Canadians also met considerable enemy fire on the beaches and as they worked their way into the defences. They had to overcome numerous steel and wooden obstacles which were placed out on the tidal part of the beach and which were covered at high tide to trap landing craft. However, the assault went in at 7:15 A.M. just as the tide began to rise and many of these obstacles were cleared away by the engineers before the water covered them, thus enabling follow-up craft to beach and unload.

Some casualties were suffered in the assault by the Canadians from enemy machine-guns, mortars and artillery fire.

By 10:00 A.M. the Canadians were about 1,000 yards inland and going strong, meeting only small pockets of Germans. The first prisoners were taken and identified as belonging to a coastal unit. On other parts of the front near us the operation is moving along. Canadian and British airborne troops did a good job when they dropped and came in by gliders at 3:30 this morning. They captured several bridges and held them.

Cruisers provided very effective support to the Canadians and one cruiser knocked out a troublesome battery about a mile and a half from the coast with six direct hits.

Enemy tanks are reported about 10 or 15 miles south of the beach-head and some enemy transport is also moving.

Up to noon the German air force has not shown up. It is estimated to have 2,350 aircraft in Western Europe but it looks as if the air attack will come tonight.

The French coast is still wreathed in smoke driving far down the Channel. In some of the bombarded towns fires are burning and destroyers and support craft are still prowling up and down the coast to finish off anything else that may show up.

The Allied air cover over the fleet and the beach-head is complete. Every few minutes Spitfires or Lightnings sweep past in the sunshine. The wind shows signs of abating.

The assault in this sector saw our troops bounce through a stormy sea in landing craft and in broad daylight storm the beaches and battle their way inland. An hour and a half after the landing, reports of successes began to come in rapidly to the Headquarters ship.

The big surprise in the Second Front attack was that it went in in daylight. A heavy sea was running and small assault craft plunged headlong through six-foot waves to reach the beaches and land troops. For miles along the coast the invasion fleet is lying offshore shoving in men, supplies and vehicles.

As we crossed the Channel and the fleets mustered from ports all over Britain, R.A.F. heavy bombers struck at beach defences and specific targets up and down the long coastline. As daylight came, United States medium bombers took over the bombing and sent hundreds of planes over the beaches dropping high explosives all along the beaches. Then Fortresses and Liberators went in, with a roar that drowned out the naval gunfire, and struck other targets. Cruisers started off the naval bombardment, which was by far the heaviest coastal shelling of the war. For 40 minutes, hundreds of guns fired without a let-up.

Under cover of this colossal barrage, Canadian infantry and engineers in the first assault waves plunged through the white-capped waves in their landing craft, and the first regiment touched down on this sector at 8 A.M.

Other units followed in rapid succession. Some came under heavy machine-gun fire and shelling but they fought their way forward and gained their first objectives on scheduled time.

Allied tanks also landed with the assault force and went into action with the infantry. The deliberation with which this huge fleet stopped off the coast after dawn and formed up for the assault was astounding. The Navy had everything under control and there was not the slightest interference in the early morning from enemy surface craft.

Fighter patrols were over the fleet from daylight on, Spitfires and Lightnings. In mid-morning the sea began to calm, and the black rain clouds and high wind which had threatened to upset the operation in its early stages changed for clearing skies and a falling wind.

All the way across the Channel, there was no interception of our particular Canadian convoy in which landing craft of the Royal Canadian Navy carried Canadian infantry.

So far the operation seems to have gone as well as could be expected. Destroyers and gunboats are cruising up and down the coastline banging away at last coastal points of resistance on our beach.

Now the rest of the assault troops are going in. I am going ashore with them.

We French Canadians Are in
No Way Subordinate, 1944

MAJOR T.L. BULLOCK

June 12, 1944

The situation is that French-Canadian officers in the Canadian army are not being given an equal opportunity with English-Canadian officers. Harvey says that is the fault of the Nationalists at home, who have made the English-Canadians mistrust us all. Perhaps others share his opinion. But that is the short view, a dangerous view which will have serious repercussions after the war when our men go home with a sense of grievance.

I think that in viewing this problem we must begin with the realization that the French-Canadians who have volunteered for active service overseas are those among our young men who, generally speaking, have the broadest minds, the most tolerant views and the greatest aptitudes to become leaders. Because of the political atmosphere in French Canada for a whole generation, it takes more courage for a French-Canadian to enlist than for an English-Canadian. Boys in the other provinces live in a mental neighborhood which tends to force them into the army as the easiest way of pleasing public opinion. Our boys have to defy public opinion to enlist, and that, in a young man, takes great moral courage.

If you agree with me so far, you will agree that, in the main, our young men begin their army careers with a strong disposition to favour national unity at all costs and a desire to become good soldiers and good officers which deserves to be encouraged. English-Canadians, if they are wise, will seek to cultivate these boys, not to drive them back into the shell from which they have had the guts to break out. It is not sensible to say: "Oh, you French-Canadians don't enlist because you are slackers," and then, when we do enlist, treat us as inferiors. You may be sure that the people back home in Quebec are not unaware of the situation over here, and if the whole thing is becoming a vicious circle, shutting us in, then the fault is certainly not with the French-Canadians.

After many Battalion Commanders, some of them inferior, had been put ahead of him, and after a great deal of very blunt speaking in many quarters, Bernatchez, C.O. of the R 22e R, was finally made a Brigadier. He was the first French-Canadian since early in the war to hold a higher rank in the Field than Lieutenant-Colonel. The appointment, when it did come, was made so late and so reluctantly as to be almost an insult. But he and Allard between them have done a glorious job in the last month. Military security will not allow me to give the details, but they are known to the English-Canadian command.

We remained silent a long time while officer after officer was pushed ahead of Bernatchez and of other competent French-Canadian Bn. commanders. Our effort to be patient, to preserve the unity of the Canadian army at all costs, was apparently taken as a confession of inefficiency and timidity. Men were given command of Divisions who have shown themselves not half the commanders Bernatchez has proved to be. There have been English-Canadian Brigadiers who were children beside Allard. Now we are waiting to see how long Bernatchez will have to wait to get a Division, and how long it will take for Allard to be given a Brigade.

The excuse which has always been given for excluding French-Canadians from posts of authority in the Field has been Harvey's plea that we were not technically or temperamentally equipped to hold them. But when this war began, in 1939, French- and English-Canadians started together from scratch and for five long years we have learned our business together. And although, from the very beginning, French-Canadians have been differentiated against in the Field, we know now that they are just as competent, just as level-headed, just as reliable, just as brave as any other Canadians. In the profession of arms we are fully equal in all respects.

His Majesty's French-Canadian officers have now lived abroad for a long time. No men in our army are more anxious than they have become to see prejudice and mistrust disappear in Canada. If they are given half a chance, there will be no stouter champions of national unity in the Dominion after the war. Therefore, it must be clear to all sensible people that they are the men who must be shown that English-Canadians are not riding race and religion against them in the Field. We know that we, better than any other French-Canadians, perhaps better than any other Canadians, will be in a position after the war to smooth away the tragic prejudices that make Canada in so many ways an internal battle-ground. But if we are to be forced into a defensive attitude while the war is on, then our ability and our desire to help afterwards will be nullified. We came to war to fight against Hitler's theory that there is a master race in the world. It is not amusing to find that the Canadian command feels there is a master race in the Canadian army. . . .

Something must be done about this problem right away, and it must be done here, in the Field, before the soreness goes any deeper. In the Field, with rather less than equal opportunities, French Canadians have proved themselves. And they must be given full and equal recognition *in the Field*. That means they must command Divisions and, before the war is over, a Corps, on an equality of footing. We have one Brigade, that is all, and, as I have told you, we got it only when it was no longer possible for it to be withheld another day.

There is a big issue at stake in this situation, my friend. Canada is a Dominion, a sovereign state, in no way subordinate to any other part of the British Commonwealth. Within that Dominion we French-Canadians are in no way subordinate to any master race. . . .

I feel that the Canadian government of the day, on the party side, has a grave responsibility for the fissure which divided Canadians at home. And I feel that if the Government is sincere in its professed desire to promote national unity, it must act as a Government to force the Army to remove the disabilities under which French-Canadians labour. In the summer of 1941 I heard Ernest Lapointe promise us, in a broadcast, that this would be done. But it has not been done. Instead, we had a referendum which drove the wedge deeper, and made our position overseas worse. Any child could have told before that tragic blunder was made how the referendum would be interpreted in all parts of Canada and what the result would be.

So Long Without Eat & Sleep:
In the Normandy Beachhead

TROOPER KEN HUTCHINSON

Hutchinson served with an armoured regiment. His letter from France eight days after the invasion said nothing about the overall military situation, but his fatigue showed through the simple sentences.

June 14, 1944

Dear Folks,

Well here I am again, in a new country altogether, though. Been pretty busy for a few days but has quietened down quite a bit now. All you can hear is a few guns blazing away and the odd whistle of a bomb.

Didn't know one could go so long without eat & sleep, but seemed to do it with two hours a day.

At present I'm sitting in our dugout underneath "Smasher" our tank. There are five of us living in it & there is quite a bit of room too. Of course we all have our bed rolls made into sleeping bags. The operator & I spell off at cooking and do a pretty good job of it too. We have all our own rations, so get plenty to eat. The other night we had steak & kidney and vegetables and date pudding. Of course its all in cans & all we do is warm it up.

Received your May 26th letter on the 12th and was real glad to get it. So Byron thinks he was hard on me eh. To tell you the truth I'd forgotten all my school days & don't want to remember them very bad.

So we are raised with a sarcastic tongue eh. Say if anyone is sarcastic its those two. But let them go their way eh.

I was going to have you pass this letter around to the whole family but I guess it's kind of impossible now eh. Oh well it won't hurt I guess.

Say you haven't forgotten to send some more smokes have you. Am getting pretty low and they really went fast for the first eight days.

Well I guess this will be all for this time as it's getting pretty dark and there are no lights allowed.

Sent a telegram today but don't know when it will get there.

God Bless you all and will be back one of these days.

Lots of love
Ken

I Saw French Women Throwing Roses: Liberation, June 1944

MATTHEW HALTON

> *Journalist Halton wrote this article ten days after D-Day to describe the joy of the liberated French.*

The welcome we all got in France touched our hearts. Right in the battle a few hundred yards beyond the beaches with shells striking both ways I saw French women throwing roses at Canadian soldiers as they passed and putting garlands of roses around the necks of marching infantry. We had to destroy some of their homes and villages and some of their ancient Norman churches and, of course, some of the French civilians were killed in their own homes and fields.

They welcomed us with tears and their hearts and with everything they had. They showered gifts on us, not us on them.

A young priest, the curé in one village, brought me a bottle of French cognac—Vin Champagne. I said, "I thought the Germans had stolen everything." He replied, "They stole everything they could, even some of our rations. They could not find everything. You understand every family along this coast has saved a few bottles of their finest wine to celebrate this very day."

An old woman said, "Monsieur, we waited and waited and sometimes we thought you would never come. These last few days we had known it would not be long. We have little news because the Germans have taken away all the radios in the coastal area and we could no longer listen to the English news. But we knew you were coming this morning when your bombs and shells started blowing our houses to pieces. I ran to my deep trench and I was very content. I shook my fist at the Germans as they retreated past my house."

Imagine that if you don't think we were welcome in France. Put that on the ledger of greatness. An old woman, Madame Dorelle, in the little village of X, in the province of Normandy saying, "I knew you were coming when your bombs and shells were blowing our houses to pieces. And I went to my deep trench and was very happy." Right after getting ashore I had found a house in which I could start writing. There was a handsome old couple there—a sailor and his wife—taking shelter in the cellar. They came out when I arrived, and hovered over me as I worked, like hens with chicks. I had had to swim to shore, and was soaking wet. They gave me dry clothes—the woman dried my face as I worked and brought me socks and felt slippers. She brought me fried eggs, and strawberries. At first I positively refused to touch her food, because their need is greater than ours, until at last she said, "Monsieur, you would make me very happy if you would eat the eggs." So I did. As I ate, we talked a blue streak. She and her husband had a thousand questions to ask and so had I, with battle raging around us, enemy shells falling a few hundred yards behind and a few hundred yards ahead, and every ten minutes a couple of German fighter-bombers screaming, unloading their bombs and then strafing the roads with their cannon, bombs, and machine guns.

The Germans and French quislings are trying hard enough to make the French hate us. My friends showed me a copy of a district newspaper, *L'Ouest Eclaire*, with the headline "The Anglo-American Murderers are drowning France in blood." I asked my host how many Frenchmen disliked us because of our bombings—how many believed the German-controlled papers. He said, "I honestly think that not five per cent of the French people are against you. Naturally, people are always bound to resent it when their own loved ones are killed, but as you saw here, Monsieur, you are welcomed by people who have lost their relatives. There may be some French who are so sick of war and so desperate to have their sons back from the war that they don't care who wins, but at least ninety per cent will weep tears of joy this day."

As we talked, another Frenchman came in—a man who had lost an arm in the last war at Verdun. He had a bottle of wine as a present—a bottle of fine Bourgelais. He said he had saved it for me. "For me?" I demanded. "Yes," he said, "for you, the first British officer I saw."

I told him he should give it to one of the fighting officers but he said, "No, Monsieur, it is for you."

I went outside wrapped in a blanket when I heard ack-ack start chattering. A German fighter-bomber moaned down at us, dropped a bomb and then machine-gunned us, and then at last I begged the young priest to make his people lie down on the floor in their houses. Then I heard a French child shout "Regardez les sales Boches." Around the corner came two Canadians with forty German prisoners. One soldier led the procession, another rode behind on a fine horse he had borrowed and the priest said, "Monsieur, look at those types—those offensive types—a few hours ago they were our masters, now they are prisoners."

It was hard to make the people believe that the victory was not won just because the landing had been made, and that in the next few days there would be ferocious and critical battles. They all believed we would be in Paris in a few days. When I had written my story, I put on my half-dried clothes and went forward down the roads of France looking for the battle. How often in peacetime had I driven down those long avenues with Lombardy poplars. How strange it was to go down them now. I got a ride on a tank destroyer and made my way to the headquarters of a Canadian unit. Two of its regiments had had a tough time on the beaches but now they were on their objective and one company of them was attacking a clump of farm houses held by the enemy in some strength.

The enemy had field guns there as well as machine guns. A bombardment officer sent a signal back to the Navy asking for concentration of fire. Watching from the second story of a house I saw two shells hit a hundred yards from the German positions. Another signal went out and two more shells came falling fifty yards beyond. The third time the shells were square on the target and, on receiving the signal, the destroyer, five miles away, put down a salvo from all its guns. Fifteen minutes later, the Canadians had taken the position.

Once I dived into the ditch at the side of the road as seven planes came screaming down but they were our aircraft and we watched them strafe another German position half a mile away.

The weather was good now and the sky was full of our planes—medium and heavy bombers and fighters—and I thought of four years ago when all the planes were German. As dark was falling on that first day, we saw our planes coming in with more paratroopers to drop behind the German lines. One of them was brought down by the German ack-ack. Before dark, I walked back to my little village to spend the night.

The great war engines which we had not had when we were last here were clanking down the roads. There are more German prisoners going back and Frenchmen sitting beside the ditch are staring at them and staring. I spoke to a young German and asked him what he thought of the war now. He said at some length, "You should win because the world is against us but you haven't won yet. We knew we couldn't stop you from making a landing somewhere—after all, you can't hold 2000 miles of coast in strength, but you haven't won yet. The real west wall is a few miles away and you will know about it to-morrow when Rommel strikes. You may not be on the beaches very long."

Except for the last line, it was a pretty true summing up of the position. The next few days are as crucial as any in our history. Try to imagine the immense problem of getting enough reserves, arms and ammunition ashore in these first few days. The supply problem is complicated enough when you are land-based but we are still based on the sea—remember that. For the first few days we face a superiority in numbers but thanks to the air force and to the wonderful weapons, even in these first days, the Germans have not got as much fire-power as we have. It will be two weeks or so before we can be sure of victory and absolutely sure of the end. In the meantime, Frenchmen all over France are getting ready not only their hidden bottles of wine to toast their liberated friends but also their daggers and bombs.

Night Flying Training in Wales, July 1944

PILOT OFFICER WILLIAM WATSON

Navigator William Watson wrote this letter just as he began night flying training on Wellington bombers. He and his crew were killed when they crashed into Cardigan Bay, Wales, on July 23, 1944.

July 11th, 1944

Well, it seems a long time since I wrote last—about a week in fact, but it seems about twice that time since I heard from you last. It hasn't been that long because I got that letter from Dad with the photographs of Skipper and in the same mail got Paud's letter written four days later. Apparently the surface letter just caught a boat, and was more than welcome. I don't know what's got into you Dad. Believe it or not that's three letters this year. If you only knew how much they're appreciated, you'd make it 3 a week. However, I'm lousy at getting down to write too, so I guess I'll have to forgive you.

Since I wrote last, we've finished our day flying and are just starting on nights. It's just past noon now, and I just got up and had dinner, and here I am back at the hut trying to overcome the urge to crawl back into bed. However, I don't fly tonight, so I can sleep as long as I like later.

There's really nothing just yet about night flying except the nuisance of staying up. Larry's just on circuits & landings, and we have to go along to see he doesn't get lost. Wally (the bombaimer) and I take alternate nights, but I don't see why we need to go at all because we never go further than 10–15 miles away. However, it won't be long until [Larry] solos at night, and then off we go on night cross countries. I imagine about another three weeks or a month we'll be all through here.

Well, then there is the rumour about going to India or the near East someplace, but I'm afraid we're not lucky enough for that. However, it would be wonderful.

Between day and night flying they gave us another 48 and again we went to Birmingham for a rest. We got the same hotel room as last time and slept almost one complete day. We did absolutely nothing except go to a dance, saw "For Whom the Bell Tolls" and did some more shopping.

I don't know what possessed Larry and I to do it, but we both bought some leather jackets. They're really wonderful though, the same on the outside as Dad's old one and leather-lined with a zipper up the front. Boy, they're really swell, but I don't know when we'll be able to wear them. They cost us the equivalent of about $23.30 and ten clothing coupons, but really they're more than worth it. When they say 5 pound 5, it doesn't sound nearly so much. That's the trouble with this darn English money. It inclines to make a person extravagant.

I also got a letter from Ralph and Helen which I must answer too, so it seems I'm going to have plenty of correspondence to catch up on.

Paud was asking in her correspondence just what a Nissen hut was. Well, first of all, they're the grimmest places possible, and yet could be worse. They have a cement floor, and from there up are covered with a curved corrugated metal, so they appear to be semicircular in shape, and have two windows in the front. As soon as I get some film, I'll send some pictures. Six-twenty is the size (hint).

Well, anyway it seems I'm always asking for something, and usually every week along comes a parcel with something wonderful. About a week ago I got that parcel with the grapefruit, pencils, socks, shampoo, bars cookies & chocolate mix. Boy, everything was wonderful. Then yesterday along comes another carton of cigarettes. So you [see] the name "Mama's Baby Boy" is justified. Well, must sign off now, but will write again shortly.

Thanks for everything.

Write Often and Send Grub

JACQUES GOUIN

> For French-Canadians, military service in Europe highlighted kinships and gulfs between French, British, and Québécois culture. Comfortable with the French and the British but distinct from both, Quebecois soldiers such as Jacques Gouin looked forward to victory and a return home after the Normandy landing.

France, le 17 juillet 1944
[Vaucelles, au sud de Caen]

Cher mon oncle,

J'espère que mes lettres écrites de France se sont bien rendues. J'ai bien pensé à toi dans ton jeune temps, ces quelques jours, alors que je fouillais les caves à vin. Actuellement, le mess des officiers est bien garni, je t'assure. La vie n'est pas trop difficile encore. Après deux jours et deux nuits de tir, nos canons se reposent, et j'en profite pour écrire.

Mon batman m'a creusé un bon "dug-out" où je suis à l'abri de tout. Je n'aurais jamais cru qu'un jour je verrais le front; eh! bien j'y suis et ce n'est pas si mal; j'ai vu des casques allemands sur des croix de bois, des uniformes abandonnés près de canons détruits, des tanks démantibulés et des petits villages entièrement rasés par les bombes; il n'y a rien de bien joli et de bien gai à voir mais le moral est bon; les quelques civils que j'ai rencontrés sont courtois et contents d'être débarrassés du «sale boche». Mais la misère est grande et il faudra des années pour remettre l'Europe sur pied. . . .

Ma moustache progresse toujours et prend les proportions d'un «handle-bar» assez imposant. La campagne française ressemble beaucoup à nos paysages canadiens. Le paysan français, de même, rappelle beaucoup «l'habitant» de chez nous. Il ne faut pas s'imaginer que la France, ce n'est que Paris. Et même, de Paris malheureusement, les étrangers ne connaissent que les lieux de plaisir louches, qui existent d'ailleurs aussi bien à Londres et à Montréal. Tu liras la petite brochure sur la France, que j'ai envoyée à Lucrèce, tu y verras des choses intéressantes et bien au point.

Il y a deux jours j'ai vu deux jeunes prisonniers allemands que notre police militaire avait ramassés dans un trou où ils étaient cachés depuis cinq jours; ils attendaient le moment propice pour se donner; l'un avait 18 ans et l'autre 20 ans. Ils avaient l'air fatigués, abattus et résignés. Notre médecin soigna la blessure que l'un d'eux avait à la jambe, tandis que l'autre se tenait bien raide, sans bouger, selon les ordres de notre M.P. qui parlait allemand couramment. En voyant ces deux jeunes spécimens des victimes qu'Hitler envoie à la boucherie, je n'ai pas douté un instant de notre victoire prochaine. Les événements vous paraissent peut-être languir mais ce n'est qu'un répit stratégique: Montgomery a plusieurs tours dans son sac, dont l'un sera une surprise qui ébahira tout le monde. En attendant, il faut être patient, ici au front et là-bas au Canada. Je sais que pour ceux qui attendent au loin c'est dur, car on ne sait pas au juste ce qui se passe et on s'inquiète inutilement. Je cours la même chance que les millions d'autres qui sont engagés dans la même tourmente. Je ne suis pas plus en danger qu'à travers la circulation d'une grande ville. Donc ne vous tracassez pas inutilement.

Écrivez souvent et envoyez de la «grub». Le soleil commence à percer les nuages et je vais en profiter pour prendre quelques photos.

Bonjour à tout le monde,
Cheer up
Ton Poucet

The Normandy Diary of Gunner Brady

GUNNER JAMES P. BRADY

> *Brady's diary talks frankly of French civilian attitudes and deals with the tragic accidental bombings of Canadian troops in August 1944.*

July 27, 1944—

Our echelon groups have moved back across the river in Caen. In P.M. went with Huot across Churchill Bridge into Caen and had tea in an English Naafi. While sitting in the street a heavy enemy shell landed in a brewery across the street. A heavy .255 calibre. A Frenchman claimed to have worked building the emplacement during April 1944 and says it is situated in a forest near Mezidon.

Had my first taste of Calvados. We helped a French woman remove rubble and debris from her *estaminet* (Le Cafe Normandie) and she treated us to this celebrated drink. She was frankly anti-British. This sentiment appears strong in Caen because of the terrific pre-invasion bombings. Twenty seven thousand inhabitants are reported to be buried in the ruins—a statement well supported by the all-pervading stench of death and decay.

The mistress of the establishment considered our troops barbarous and lacking the arts of civilized living. She reported the Germans were comparatively well behaved until their retreat began. German discipline was rigid and inflexible. She cited as an eye witness an incident which had occurred on this same street. In 1940 a German officer summarily executed with his own hand a German soldier who had attempted to rape a French girl in public. He had him placed under arrest and calmly emptied a pistol into him. In perfect French he told a German N.C.O., "Take this Carrion away," and apologized profusely to the proprietress of the establishment assuring her there would be no repetition of this behavior by any man under the garrison command.

This was during the period when the Nazis were making a studied effort to win over the French population politically and ideologically to support the war. The German temper has vastly changed since that time.

The Calvados proved potent and the good dame was sadly lamenting that none of her beauteous and chic barmaids, as she alleged, were on hand to cheer us on our way.

The rumour of Canadians being shot by the S.S. persists. Latest report alleges that 48 men from the Chaudieres were shot near Authie. Others say it happened to the Royal Winnipeg Rifles. Noted the first appearance of R.A.F. Typhoons on our sector and they certainly raise hell with German communication lines. . . .

Aug. 8—

At midnight I stand in our Command Post and listen to the thunderous roar of our barrage. I look at Jeff's face, visible in the narrow shaded circle of light on the artillery plotting table and I think of that other August 8th, 1918, Ludendorff's Black day, and wonder if history is repeating itself. Will we break through? Shortly after midnight the barrage is halted and we go on call to support infantry. At 2:45 we fire a Yoke target on a previously registered target which we identify as the stone quarry near Verrieres. Fire has been requested by the attacking Scottish infantry. At 4:30 a Sitrep comes through from Regimental Command Post informing us we had knocked out 28 German mortars and their crews who had retreated to the quarry and pinned down the 51st Highland Division infantry with accurate and deadly fire. When the Scottish troops advanced they found a scene of deadly carnage. Not a single German was found alive.

An area 4 kilometres wide and 6 kilometres in depth had been selected for the breakthrough. Into this zone moved the 4th Canadian Armoured Division and the First Polish Armoured Division, with the 2nd Canadian Infantry Division supporting. The 51st Highland Division attacked Tilly La Campagne. In this pre-selected zone of attack fell the full fury of the air bombing. Ordnance later reported an expenditure of ammunition as follows: 184,000—25 pdr., 87,000—5.5 Mediums—6,500 Heavies 9.2 Long Tons. This excludes anti-aircraft and armoured units.

This accumulated fire fell on that narrow frontage for its full depth. Its effectiveness is gauged by an Intelligence report that our attack was launched while a relief was under way. The 89th German Infantry Division which had been on garrison duty in Norway since 1940 had just arrived in France and were relieving the 12th S.S. Panzer Division.

The full fury of the attack fell on them. 800 men survived of the Division. All German Divisions numbered below 100 are considered first-class formations. The 89th Division, an all-German unit, contained no non-Germans, and had not fought elsewhere, having been on Garrison duty in Norway since 1940. It had not seen service on the Russian front.

The enemy have begun to retire. Returned to Caen and rested for a few hours. In P.M. we received order . . . Prepare to Move. The unit assembled in convoy.

About 1:30 P.M. I observed U.S. Fortresses approaching from north-east in line with the smelter chimneys of Colombelles. The leading formations passed overhead to the southwest. Then the front waves suddenly loosed an avalanche of heavy block-busters and anti-personnel fragmentation bombs. In a moment a huge orange-colored flame blossomed upward and the village of Cormelles erupted skyward. Blinding smoke and fumes enveloped us. Cries of the wounded could be heard amid the terrific concussion of the bursting bombs.

When the smoke cleared away and the bombers passed, the first person I saw was Sergeant E. Carpenter, Boston, Massachussetts, my immediate superior, almost cut in two by a bomb fragment. Casualties and damage were heavy. Our entire forward observation party were caught in the bombing and every man wounded. We suffered 19 men killed, 47 wounded, whilst 11 guns and 27 vehicles were destroyed. A violent day. . . .

Aug. 14—

Moved to a position north of Cauvicourt (Rouvres). About 2:00 P.M. a large force of R.A.F. and R.C.A.F. heavy bombers staged a daylight raid. Our position was deluged with bombs. Our unit escaped with the loss of 1 man killed and 4 wounded. Sergeant Pelletier, an old veteran of the 1940 blitz had joined our unit yesterday and was killed his first day in action. An English armoured division had a tank harbour to the south of our position. They lost over a hundred armoured vehicles. The Poles suffered grievous losses. Headquarters: 3rd Canadian Infantry Division was also hit and the Divisional Commander Major General R. F. L. Keller was wounded.

After the bombing we pushed on to Cauvicourt. The enemy had swiftly retired and we entered the village. However, the Chaudieres and Queen's Own Rifles arrived before dark and two young Nazis were flushed out of hiding. Before dark we turned out to search for a sniper. A Chaudiere brought him in.

On night duty with Lieutenant Geoffrion alone as situation was "Target out of range." At 11:20 P.M. enemy bombers passed north following the Louvres valley. It was an exceptionally dark night. For an inexplicable reason I found myself apprehensive and nervous. At 12:40 A.M. the bombers returned after a sweep toward the channel. I stood up to ensure the black outs were in order and noted that parachute flares lit up the entire valley. The whistle of falling bombs could be heard. The building rocked and I heard the tile roof of the kitchen collapse. I hugged the floor.

Later we discovered a huge crater outside the building. The 4-foot-thick wall of the old Norman medieval building had resisted the blast. Lieutenant Scheur called on phone and was greatly relieved to hear we were safe. From their point of view it appeared our Command Post had sustained a direct hit. Polish Light Anti-Aircraft put up a terrific barrage without results.

We had no casualties but one of our boys took shelter in a narrow tunnel. In the darkness he noticed another occupant. He offered him a cigarette which was accepted. Upon striking a match he discovered a German as badly scared as himself. The German surrendered. He was in the same orchard as the Polish Ack Ack and had hidden himself as the Poles have the unpleasant habit of killing their prisoners occasionally.

Our unit suffered no casualties but some of Queen's Own were hit.

Falaise Is at Last Ours:
The Closing of the Gap, August 1944

FREDERICK GRIFFIN

The Toronto Daily Star's Frederick Griffin reported on First Canadian Army's success in sealing the Falaise Gap in mid-August 1944. The long, bloody struggle cost thousands of Canadian casualties, but it ended the battle of Normandy and sped up the liberation of France.

With the First Canadian Army in France, Aug. 18—The last clean-up of Falaise was going on Thursday afternoon when I reached the edge of this lovely medieval town towards which the Canadians have fought for the past month. Twenty miles in a month from Caen, a long month that cost a good many Canadian lives—and yet in a jeep today I drove back up the straight road from Falaise to Caen through military traffic in exactly 45 minutes.

Falaise is at last ours, except for at the moment, one pesky German bazooka or portable mortar and a few fanatical snipers. Many times in the past months as our troops fought grimly down the corridor from Caen, which the Germans held so desperately, it seemed as distant as Paris.

As I stood on the hill within a kilometre of the town on the north road it lay below, gray, old and beautiful, with many trees, in a valley cup of the river Ante, which trickles through its northwest edge. It looked peaceful enough, but shots sounded and the ruins of St. Gervais church were still smoking. The Church of the Trinity, another medieval shrine, seemed not too badly damaged. The fine chateau high up on the west side of it was seemingly untouched.

So this small market town lying so snugly in the hills was the objective for which the Canadians have fought for so long and so hard because it is a road centre. Now some of our units are dug in on those hills yonder to the south.

Falaise, perhaps one-tenth the size of Caen, has not suffered as badly as Caen. It suffered, as a road junction, considerable bombing earlier, but has since taken no such punishment as Caen, so that the quaint and lovely pattern of it remains and much of its Norman form survives.

But when the Canadians took it they took a dead town. Up to the time I write only some 30 or 40 of its former 5,000 citizens have come out of holes and hiding places to greet the liberating Canadians. The others were all gone somewhere, driven out by the Germans when they regarded it as the last bastion of the corridor, indeed of the bridgehead.

Where its people went nobody yet seems to know. This afternoon the road to the south toward Argentan had many refugees moving along it and latest reports showed some 500 flocking into Falaise.

This morning an elderly Falaise couple, man and wife, came creeping out of a basement where they had hidden and greeted the incoming Canadians with information about the Germans. As they talked to our men a sniper fired at them and killed the woman. This was told to me by the officer commanding the troops who took Falaise and have since been mopping it up.

Incidentally one of the few citizens who stayed in Falaise as the Canadians drove down the corridor and into the town as the Germans sullenly pulled out was the mayor. He is already working with officers of civil affairs branch on plans to restore life to it.

The unpopulated state of Falaise is matched by the whole Caen-Falaise corridor. This stretch of French countryside, some 20 miles long with a width of from three to perhaps 10 miles, does not contain a living soul except Canadian soldiers. All its people are gone heaven knows where, driven forth by the Germans from their villages and farms. Going down to Falaise with my companions, Dick Sanburn of the Southam papers, and Bill Stewart of the Canadian Press, I took a route along back roads to the west of the main highway between Caen and Falaise from Bretteville Sur Laize south. This was partly to follow the Laize river valley, which had marked the west axis of the Canadians' recent advance.

It was also partly to get away from whatever danger there might be on the main highway, although we came back that way.

Driving south and driving north again, I did not see, except soldiers, a single human being. I did not see a horse or a cow, a pig or a chicken. I saw one lonesome black dog loping along a road, and at one Canadian unit headquarters, I saw a small red calf lying in some straw in a corner of a farmyard.

Otherwise the land, this fruitful land, was as deserted as a land of plague. No child romped, no cock crew in this countryside plowed and harrowed by the fearful juggernaut of modern war. Crops stood uncut, orchards untended. Dahlias bloomed in gardens and there was none to view their beauty but tired, dusty men from Canada. There were no cows to milk and no one to milk them. Homes, yards and barns were untenanted. From this rich and vibrant stretch of Normandy, the cradle of many generations of men, every living thing was gone.

On all sides might be seen the gashes, the ruins, the dreadful bric-a-brac of war in the form of smashed and burnt-out tanks and carrier vehicles. Wednesday eve I had made a briefer visit down as far as the quarry at Haute Mesnil and seen the scarred, tortured remains of what had been Tilly La Campagne, one of the villages for which the Canadians had fought so long. Even its Lombardy poplars were smashed into jagged sticks.

Perhaps the most dreadful sight of all was Quesnay wood, which R.A.F. heavy bombers had literally blasted yard by yard to aid the Canadian advance toward Falaise. The riven trees were in many cases uprooted. The topsoil was completely gone and the gray underneath was pocked with overlapping craters in a horrible chaos. In that wood nothing could have lived, nothing. That bombing dug deep into German shelters and strewed misshapen vehicles about like bits of old tin cans.

As I drove down south in from Haute Mesnil through Gouvix, St. Gervais la Vasson, Clair Tizon, Ussy and Villers-Cateret to Falaise I saw varying fearful effects of war's passing. And one village, St. Gervais la Vasson, stood out as a symbol of how lovely some of the villages had been before they became in whole or in part rubble heaps.

St. Gervais lay virtually unhurt on a peaceful back road like a Sussex road in a winding silence. For all its people too were gone. But, unlike the other villages its homes with their curtains and their geraniums awaited their return. It was merely as if everyone, man, woman and child was away at mass and would soon be back. How happy will be their return by contrast with their neighbors of these many other villages to whom return will bring great grief.

There were many things I might have noted but actually in this panorama of a countryside from which all life had gone except the life of the soil I noted particularly only one thing. That was a graveyard of German SS troops by the roadside near Ussy.

We got out for a moment and viewed curiously this French resting place of 100 Nazis. It was neat and ordered and exact. Unlike the simple crosses over our soldiers it had over each an iron cross. At the head of the cemetery was a larger cross on a cairn of stones.

This was no ordinary hasty burial place such as may be seen so often on these battlefields of the world. It had an air of occupancy, of permanency which mocked the Germans, who had left so fast this land they had conquered and ravaged. Each plot had a neat square of stones around it. On each was planted a matching plant. Paths were covered with red pebbles. Tiny firs like the trees of Kris Kringle had been planted with mathematical care around and across.

But to return to Falaise itself. At a forward command post we met the officer commanding the forces in the attack and cleanup. He told us how men of western Canadian units had gone through the town Wednesday evening and night and how French-speaking Canadians had been all day cleaning it up in ugly street fighting.

The toughest part, he said, had been getting into the town. It had had a strong crust of the usual German defences, 88-m.m. guns, self-propelled guns, machine-guns and snipers. Then there was the river to cross, with the main roads to the bridges barricaded with rubble and other obstacles. On the southwest side craters from bombing attacks made another kind of obstacle to the Canadians in their attack on the town.

The southwest part of the town is high and there the Germans had considerable light artillery. They were using churches as strong points and sniping from the spires.

Canadian tanks supporting our infantry had to strike at these infested spires. One church evidently used as a gasoline pump caught fire and blazed furiously and was still smouldering.

Many houses also burned. It was by the light of these fires that the Canadians fought their way through the town and by dawn were in positions above high ground to the west and south.

French-Canadians went in to do the nasty job of "winkling" the remaining German desperadoes out of cellars, churches and heavy buildings. These shadow forces, flitting from spot to spot, from building to building, from street to street by picked passages and even tunnels, had a strong and vicious fire power.

They had over 50 machine-gun posts at points of vantage to sweep streets, plus three tanks or self-propelled 88's and eight or 10 easily carried infantry guns. These had been all cleaned up by later afternoon except for the bazooka I have mentioned, which is a kind of German Piat gun, and a few fleeting snipers.

By nightfall all this last wasplike nuisance fighting had been silenced and Falaise was a silent city without people. Beyond it Canadians held the high ground down toward the gap to Argentan, poised lest the Germans stage either a counter-attack or an attempt to break out. They were ready for either.

A Nursing Sister on German POWs and Canadian Slackers, September 1944

NURSING SISTER JEAN M. ELLIS

When patients finally arrived, they included many German prisoners sent down from the huge P.O.W. cage near Dieppe. Among them was a Major-General, no less. He had an Iron Cross around his fat neck, and brought his own medical orderly and batman to look after him. We longed to swipe his beautiful German boots, but nobody made the grade.

Just why he was a patient was never clear. For two days he went through various tests aimed at diagnosis, but the most any doctor could find wrong with the man was a cut finger. He was promptly sent back to prison camp, protesting loudly.

German patients were kept in separate wards if possible, but often they overflowed into our own men's wards. Stories we had heard about Germans being physical cowards were abundantly proved. I wouldn't have believed grown men could ever make so much fuss. It was partly because they had been told over and over that they would be used as guinea pigs if captured—and they knew perfectly well that their own doctors were experimenting on prisoners. So the first time a nurse would come near to change a dressing or give a hypo, agonized shrieks would go up, and cries of "Nein! Nein!"

They cringed, wept, and let out howls which literally could have been heard for blocks, before anyone had ever touched them. One even spat at a nurse. She couldn't do anything, not even spit back, but she went for a medical officer who told the man in no uncertain terms that if he didn't undergo treatment he would be shipped right back to camp.

All this was very hard on our own patients, but one section was played against another. Our boys would be told, "This patient thinks he belongs to the 'Master Race,' and see how he carries on when he has a dressing changed or gets a needle. You show him how a real man takes it." Then German-speaking personnel would say to the prisoners, "You think you belong to the 'Master Race,' but you make a lot of noise, while these Canadian boys don't even whimper. Do you want them to laugh at you?" I must admit it wasn't long before the Germans caught on.

As Red Cross workers, we visited Germans as well as other patients, but we didn't give them cigarettes or chocolate bars. They got wash cloths, toilet articles, and all other necessities, but not luxuries. We had been told these orders resulted from Germans doing the same to our prisoners. However, while a package of cigarettes could not be left, we often gave them a couple of loose ones or left extra with the boy in the next bed, who would share.

Another group of problem patients was composed of S.I.W.'s. These were boys accused of having deliberately injured themselves, usually by firing a gun into their legs or hands, in order to get out of combat. They were under guard, but were considered innocent until proved guilty. Trials were going on all the time and a section of the Canadian Army legal department was attached to us. Frequently they went to the front lines and crawled around on hands and knees for hours trying to get evidence.

If convicted, the boys got two years at hard labour, but some were acquitted. If acquitted, they were seldom sent back to the front, and instead were given jobs behind the lines. We always felt that even when they were guilty, these boys should not be judged harshly. Some men are cut out to be soldiers, others are not. The Canadian Army was still a volunteer army and all soldiers had enlisted of their own free will, yet even so, they weren't all capable of "taking" combat experience. It was awful up at the front . . . living in slit trenches, enduring wet, cold, and discomfort in addition to constant fear of death . . . no wonder some men cracked up. Just the same, their conduct could not be condoned, because they did desert their comrades, and they had to go through court-martial. In our work we treated them like any other patients and gave them the benefit of the doubt.

The patients who really made us hostile were the V.D.'s. They were deserters just as much as the S.I.W.'s because in a great many cases they had acquired infection deliberately in order to get out of action for a while. According to medical officers there was absolutely no need to become infected even if they were unable to resist temptation, because preventive measures were available for the asking. Many men admitted they had intentionally "got a dose" and would say, "You haven't seen the last of us, girls. We'll be back." Sure enough they would be back, two and three times. The first time they might get only forty-eight-hour treatment, but afterwards they were sometimes kept for two or three weeks. They were "up-patients," of course, and used to be a great nuisance in the Red Cross tent, swaggering around and being very rude. We tried not to let them have any books.

Outarmoured and Outgunned by the German Panthers: Tanks in Italy, 1944

BRIGADIER WILLIAM MURPHY

17/8/44

Dearest family—

. . . I have no doubt we shall continue to spread alarm and despondency within the German army in Italy before long and thus play our part in the cutting up process that seems to have commenced. It will be interesting to see if [Hitler] is miracle man enough to stabilize that left flank of his in France particularly after the new landings. Dad mentioned a point in one of his letters that surprised me. It showed me how much that we take for granted is really not known outside the army, so there will be even more to talk to you about when I get home than I thought. He mentioned reading a despatch in one of the papers that the German tanks are better than ours. That is quite true and has been true since 1939. At the same time it is quite understandable. Jerry had plenty of tanks when he started and we had practically none. He had improved models on the drawing boards and we had none. He decided to produce new models as he went along, but we had to decide on a good solid sort of tank that we could produce in vast numbers. We had so far to catch up that we couldn't afford to retool and slow down production by getting out a new model every few months. So we chose the Sherman. It is a damn good tank but as we thought everyone knew it is outarmoured and outgunned by the German Panthers and Tigers that we meet these days. That was serious in the desert, not so serious here. This country is what we call "close" country—lots of trees, vineyards, olive trees, ridges, gullies etc. Visibility is good from the many hills but the close nature of the country hides detail in the valleys. Thus we can use ground and creep up on him—manoeuvering until we can bring our guns to bear on a weak spot on his tank—all of which are known to us. Of course if he sees us first it is too bad. But we have secured our original object—we invariably heavily outnumber him. So we engage him from hull down positions with some tanks and creep up on him from the side with others. This Bde has the system pretty well worked out and that is one reason why we receive so many compliments from higher command. We've knocked out many and many a Panther and Tiger and are prepared to take them on at any time. Dad should join the intelligence service the way he tracks us around. Its remarkable. I can't say how close he comes to the truth but its a hard job because we may pack up overnight, track 50 miles, and be fighting with another Div altogether the next day. We certainly see life and the country. I think we have now been in action longer than any armoured Bde in 8 Army and are very proud of that record. We feel we can't be spared. At the same time a rest will be much appreciated if operations will ever permit it. Haven't been able to get particulars of just how the pay off scheme just passed affects Brigs on demobilization. Has Dad any particulars that were published in the papers. I don't know if the 7.50 per month for service in Canada and the 15.00 per month for service outside is basic for any rank or whether its graded by rank. Also on demob is it correct we get 7 days pay & allowances of rank on discharge for each six months service—covered by granting one leave before discharge for the necessary time. Even if the monthly figures are basic and apply to me, and the leave pay is based on rank at discharge, I figure I'll be due for over $2000.00 by the time I get home. Tough on the taxpayer but a big help in settling down again and making up to my family for my long absence. All my love

    Bill

The Loyal Edmonton Regiment at the Gothic Line, September 1944

BILL BOSS

Canadian Press reporter Bill Boss watched the Loyal Eddies take on the Germans' Gothic Line near Rimini, Italy.

With the Canadian Corps on the Adriatic, Oct. 18 (CP)—Short shots on highlights of the Loyal Edmonton Regiment's campaign around and about the Gothic Line:

At Monte Marino men of a company under Capt. J. Harper Prouse, Edmonton, who had infiltrated after dark past the German positions, were complimenting themselves on smart work, when an enemy light mortar detachment of six horse-drawn carts, mortars and personnel aboard, hove into view. They were apparently coming to establish mortar positions somewhere south of Monte Marino.

Without casualties Capt. Prouse's men took one prisoner, then seven more at dawn, together with all the horses, carts and weapons. There was general glee as horses and carts were divided between platoons under Lt. John Laudrum, Vancouver; Sgt. N. E. Olsen, Evansburg, Alta., and Capt. Prouse himself. But to the disgust of the boys, and the delight of local Italians, the horses couldn't tug the carts over the stiff countryside, so they had to unload them and carry the weapons themselves. The horses were turned loose.

A company resting outside Monteciccardo was being sniped at from a hill 300 yards to the southwest. Major Frank McDougall, company commander, Weyburn, Sask; Capt. A. M. Johnson, Edmonton, and CSM R. N. Craven, Peace River, made their own recce to the hill and discovered no one. Major McDougall then ordered a platoon to occupy the hill, advancing under covering fire from Capt. J. Harper Prouse, Edmonton; CSM R. W. Ulmer, Castor, Alta.; Cpl. R. C. Cull, Hardy, Sask., and Pte. L. J. Gallinger, Cornwall, Ont. These four drew enemy attention to themselves while the others went forward. They accounted for two Nazis, and the rest when they saw the little force approach, made a quick escape.

Directions at Fault

Lieut. John Laudrum, Vancouver, went on a fighting patrol, told to "kill as many Germans as you can." Trouble was the intelligence officer sent him in a wrong direction. When recalled for new orders he protested: "But you might just as well have let me go on. We'd already killed two, had chased five from one spot, and were well on the way to another."

Pte. Wilbur B. Aberdeen, Edmonton, company runner, took nine Germans prisoner one evening when he brought them from their hole with a burst from his tommy gun. . . . On another occasion he carried wounded Pte. Melbourne I. Gibson, Barrie, Ont., 100 yards under shell and small-arms fire to a regimental aid post.

Attacking one position, a platoon under Lieut. Keith MacGregor, Calgary, went up right under our own barrage, captured several Nazis as they tried to escape. An enemy section which chose to give them fight was whipped by a section under L.-Cpl. Robert Wilson, Denman, Alta. Four were taken prisoner, one was killed, one escaped.

Two company signallers were detailed to go into a house and set up signals for a headquarters. Ptes. Stan Doyle, Nelson, B.C., and Neil Thompson, Goderich, Ont., went in, came out a few minutes later with seven happy prisoners, taken persuasively, without a shot.

Letters from the Mud, November–December 1944

LIEUTENANT J.E. BOULET

> *After First Canadian Army drew the duty of clearing the Scheldt estuary so that the port of Antwerp could be used, the Canadian divisions had a respite. But no one said the conditions were good, as Lieutenant Boulet of the Royal Hamilton Light Infantry told his wife. He was killed in action early in 1945.*

November 12/44

Well now as you can see I am fighting troops and I don't mean perhaps at all. Things are going fairly well tho regardless and I won't stick my neck out any more than is absolutely necessary, you can count on that.

You asked me if I had planned on going to Japan when this is all finished. At this time the answer is no. If I come out of this with a fairly whole skin I think I will be ready to settle down to the quietest life possible and maybe drink the odd bottle of good beer which is something we can't get under any circumstances.

At the moment we are living in the basement of a building which I think is fairly bomb proof but the greatest trick of all has been the improvising of lights to carry on with. Any kind of oil and a piece of string will make a light of sorts until now we have had two coal oil lamps one without a glass and a fairly good stock of coal oil. One small quart which is enough for 24 hours if we are careful and don't use both lamps at once and don't turn up the wicks too high.

And cold. I appreciate now what the last war must have been like in the mud and the rain and the slush. It must have been a son of a gun to say the least.

November 19/44

Well we shifted position slightly since that last letter and the move was all for the better as now we can move around a little during the day. . . .

We also have a fire going in a pail to get dried out and warm for a while and right now I am waiting for a big kettle of water to heat and then I am going to shave and have a sponge bath as it is all of two weeks now since I had a good wash. Ain't life hell.

November 22/44

The war seems to be continuing on but maybe it will stop one of these days and then Johnny will come sailing home again.

I have come to the conclusion in the past two weeks that the actual front is the best place to be excepting when there is an attack on as Jerry lobs his heavy stuff into the rear areas trying to break up the supply routes and communications. Well this is all for now and I will stir my stew. I hope the parcel gets home safely and that you like the contents even if they don't look very fancy.

December 3/44

A few lines this evening. Am stuck as duty officer tonight so will have to stay up all night. It wouldn't be so bad but I have been up since before daylight digging and cutting logs all day for a master trench to keep a roof over my head and keep the rain off. It is good exercise after being in areas where you have to keep your head down all the time and never make a sound either day or night. Now tho it is all different work all day and am quite tired at night.

December 12/44

You should see my present home. Made it myself, 6' x 8 1/2' inside measurements and about 5' ceiling. Log roof, of course it is underground. Yesterday we installed a stove of sorts. A biscuit tin for a stove. A nine foot sewer pipe is part of the chimney. The only trouble is that when you light the fire you have to move out because it gets too hot. That is a poor fault, but it will be rectified.

What the Hell Is the Matter with Everything?: Manpower Bungles, November 1944

FLIGHT LIEUTENANT ALEX GRAHAM

As the army went through the wringer in its efforts to find reinforcements, the RCAF released fit men into civil life. Serving with the RAF in Italy, Graham commented acerbically on the situation.

November 23, 1944

When we were in S[outh]. A[frica]. we used to laugh very loudly about the situation down there. They had their so-called "famous" 6th Armoured Division situated up at Cairo "in training" and howling for recruits to get its strength up and the recruits just weren't coming in, that was all. And what is more, they never will! And now I suddenly discover that things are the same way at home for the overseas army. Just what the hell is the matter with everything anyway? I was talking to some chaps before I left Cairo, who were saying that the R.C.A.F. is discharging a lot of men because they don't need them. What happens to them? Instead of discharging them, they should just transfer them to the army, the same as they did in England. These chaps were telling me that the boys who were discharged were rather upset about the whole thing. Apparently by joining the air force they thought they were in on a good thing. As any sane person would figure, by the time they had finished their training there would be nothing else doing in the war line, so they would just go back into civvies having had a darn good time and worn a uniform and learned to fly at the expense of someone else. It seems they were quite put out when it didn't come off for some of them.

What is the general opinion of the plans for demobilization? I don't know a great deal about it except that every man is going to be a millionaire and be given a home and a cushy job. Somehow, or other, that doesn't sound right to me, but then I'm not genned up on these things. I'll know more about it when I get time to study it. I also got a pamphlet on the Veteran's Land Act. What is your opinion on that?

Bye now, and Merry Christmas to you all. Loads of Love.
Alex

A First Christmas in Stalag Luft III, 1944

IAN H. FOWLER

> *Fowler was shot down in February 1944 and taken prisoner in the Netherlands. He was held at a POW camp at Sagan, Poland.*

Dec. 22, 1944

My own darling Pem. This has indeed been a red letter day for me dear for I got four letters this A.M. two of them from Pem, an air letter of

September 28 & one of Oct. 2nd containing a snap taken in Banff this summer and gee its absolutely wizzard dear—its boosted the old moral no end. You know dear I've been longing for such a photo for ages it seems & I might say you can't send too many for my liking darling. Reckon the boys in the room are really envious of me now & I can well understand for I'm a very lucky lad. Glad to hear about the coffee spoon too dear for I hope we two will be setting up house shortly after I get back. We must lay our plans together though dear & oh what a time that'll be! There are 3 small ice rinks in use around the camp now & the 4th, a much larger job is to be ready to-morrow. So I borrowed Eski's skates this afternoon & really enjoyed myself for ¾s of an hour. Then the first hockey match is planned for Xmas day & boy I'll be right in the thick of things. Be the best thing that happened to me for months. We got our Xmas parcels today (½ per man) & they contain turkey, pudding, sausages, sweets, etc.—which will make for a grand bash on Monday. Fondest love dearest,

Your Ian

The Luftwaffe's Last Throw, New Year's Day, 1945

SERGEANT W.L. LARGE

By the end of 1944, the Luftwaffe had largely been driven from the skies over the battlefields, as most of the German air force was devoted to increasingly vain efforts to shoot down bombers over the Reich's cities. But on January 1, 1945, the Luftwaffe mustered its resources for a surprise attack on Allied airfields in Holland. An RCAF sergeant of No. 438 Squadron at Eindhoven fought back.

I was down the road from dispersal waiting to see the Sqn take off when I saw a number of e[nemy]/a[ircraft] making an attack on the airfield. I first thought this was a hit and run raid, but after the second and third wave had passed over and I saw e[nemy]/a[ircraft] circle the field and continue their attacks from out of the sun, I figured they were playing for keeps and therefore hurried back to dispersal where our Bren guns were kept. There I saw F/Sgt McGee and we decided to take a whack at anything flying over the dispersal. We each took a Bren gun and two boxes of clips and stood outside the dispersal door and waited for any Jerry who came within range. . . . One aircraft coming from the south turned off the runway and made a steep climbing turn about 120 yards away from us at a height of not more than forty feet. We both fired, each emptying a full magazine at him. We saw strikes down the engine cowling in the direction of the cockpit and saw small pieces fall off.

Battle Fatigue, February 1945

BURTON FITCH

> *Lieutenant Burton Fitch, a platoon commander with the North Nova Scotia Highlanders, was in action in France, Belgium, the Netherlands, and Germany for over five months continuously. His comments on battle fatigue and on the humanity of his regiment's medical officer are powerful.*

It was my impression . . . that being shot at, was less stressful than expecting to be shot at. In the first case, I can usually cover myself, at least from view. In the second case, the attack can come from 360 degrees making protection from fire virtually impossible, and hence that much more stressful.

I bring to mind two of my men, who succumbed to battle fatigue. The first was a man of some 40 years of age, who was about 6'2 in height, and well over 200 pounds in weight. He had been wounded twice before and finally in January 1945, I was sitting on the ground with his head and shoulders in my arms, and he was crying like a baby. What would it have taken to diagnose this man's condition before he broke down completely? In another case, on the day we landed on the Scheldt, just East of Hoofdplaat, we were subjected to three hours of heavy shelling. I was visiting my men in their slit trenches and came upon one of them reading his bible, and his companion was very dead. It seemed to me, that this man should have gotten the dead soldier out of the slit trench, even if he needed help to do so. I felt that he was exhibiting a lack of stability and sent him out as a casualty.

On or about the 20th of February 1945, I had been in a house sleeping in an easy chair, with my revolver and web belt on a table beside me, when I heard some unfamiliar noises coming from the street. I went outside and found a Canadian soldier, somewhat in his cups and fraternizing with the young Germans, contrary to an Anti-Fraternization Order. While telling him that he was under arrest, he threw a punch at me. I should have been able to easily block his punch, had I only raised either one of my arms. But I failed to react at all, and ended up with a cut to my maxillary facial nerve, because of his ring. I ordered two men, whose Regimental numbers I took for the record, to deliver this man, under close arrest, to the Regimental Sergeant-Major. . . .

When Lieut.-Colonel Forbes asked why I didn't shoot the man, I remember saying that I wasn't being paid to shoot our own people. (I avoided telling him that I hadn't been armed; my revolver was still back on an end table, beside a chair I had been sleeping on).

A day or two later, having experienced a loss of feeling in my cheek, I went to see Captain Ken Campbell, our medical officer. It was his decision to send me to the hospital. Many years later, when I met Dr. Campbell in Canada, I mentioned the incident. He said that he remembered it, and was fully aware that the cut on my cheek would have healed itself without any medical attention. His decision to send me out, was based on the fact that I had served five and a half consecutive months as a Rifle Platoon Commander, and he had decided that I had had enough. My own experience was that such a lucky platoon commander should not be asked to serve, under similar conditions, for more than three months consecutively, in any one Battalion.

Tough as I was, after four months, which included a relatively easy month around Njimegen, I could feel my value diminishing. I was still officially fit to continue as a Platoon Commander, but I assessed myself to be stressed enough to voluntarily stay in Europe, once I was released from hospital. I remained for almost six months, rather than go back to England. In England, as the war was winding down, I would have had little or nothing to do. In Europe, I was posted to a military trade school and was in charge of physical training and discipline at a school that taught civilian trades to people who would be resuming these trades on their return to Canada. I needed to do what I felt was necessary so that I could go home feeling my old stable self.

A Passover Seder at Cleve, Germany, March 1945

CHAPLAIN SAM CASS

Supplies—The basic religious supplies for Passover . . . included matzah (unleavened bread), wine, and a kosher tinned meat preparation . . . tinned vegetables, fruit, tea and sugar . . . from formation supply points . . . I obtained paper plates and wine cups in Belgium, and also the green vegetables and bitter herbs required in the seder. Cutlery and dixies were loaned to me by 2 Canadian Corps.

Location of Celebrations—Because of the uncertainties of the operational picture on Passover, it was advisable to postpone definite plans . . . as late as possible . . . Two locations were finally chosen in forward areas—at Cleve, Germany, for 2 Canadian Corps, and at Greve, Holland, for 1 Canadian Corps . . .

A work gang of German labor was provided at Cleve. The Provost Corps signed all routes for both locations.

Distribution of Matzah—U.K. Jewish Welfare sources permitted approximately two (2) pounds per man . . . Troops were also able to get it at the celebrations, if supplies did not reach them in time . . . Troops actively engaged in operations who could not attend services had the unleavened bread with them in the field.

Notification of Services—Through First Canadian Army routine orders, by signal to Headquarters of all formations and individual circular letters to all affected personnel.

The Celebrations—I conducted four (4) celebrations on the 28th and 29th of March at Cleve, Germany . . . More than 225 men, Canadian and British, assembled round the tables. There was no doubt at their joy at being able to commemorate the Festival of Freedom on the soil of the enemy of all human freedom. The recitation of the Hagaddah took on new meaning, for in truth, the struggle they were engaged in was the freeing of the whole world from the threat of enslavement and bondage . . . Many present on the first day were already across the Rhine and in action when we reassembled for the second celebration ... The same evening I held celebrations at Grave, in Holland ... 159 Canadian and British personnel, including RAF, attended each evening.

On the afternoon of the 30th of March, I conducted a seder at Nijmegan for the civilian community and about 35 troops. This was the first Passover these surviving remnants of Jewry enjoyed in the past five years. We met in the vestry of the synagogue, formerly the home of the rabbi, who had been deported by the Nazis. The synagogue itself, once a beautiful sanctuary, had been desecrated and stripped by foul vandal hands.

The chairman of the group in addressing them said that the passage of the Hagaddah which reads "This year we are in bondage; next year may we be free" may well be amended for them to read "In the past year, we were in bondage; but this year we are free." This was a dramatic gathering, and its impressions will not be forgotten by all personnel, British and Canadian, who attended.

Free at Last: An RCAF POW Writes Home, April 1945

WARRANT OFFICER DON SCOWEN

April 3, 1945

Dear Folks:

This is the letter I've been waiting a long time to write and now I don't seem to know where to start. We've been released now for four days but are still in a camp but hope to be on our way to England in a few days. The Americans are treating us first class and most of us are beginning to feel our oats again after that long march. This will be hard for you to believe but from the 22nd of January to 13th of March we were walking from Lamsdorf to here—just over 500 miles. After the first 15 days we stopped at a Stalag but Joe Stalin was too fast for the Hun and we had to move off again and then we were just over four weeks on the road before we got here. I carried a Martin tenor sax all the way. When we got here there was no Red Cross so we had to live on

German rations till the Yanks came and they have helped us out quite a bit even tho their Army is moving so fast that the supply columns find it difficult to keep up. Strange to relate it was Good Friday afternoon when the Yanks got here and if you ever saw a mad house this place was it. It was one of the greatest sights of my life to see that old white star. Most of us are in pretty bad shape at present but will soon buck up on good rations. We had a lot of deaths from dysentery & exhaustion but I'll bore you to death with the details in a few weeks time. God, does it feel good to *know* it won't be long now Before I see all of you again. I can hardly wait. God bless you & Gen Patton.

V-E Day in Germany, May 1945

GUNNER JAMES P. BRADY

May 7

At Marx. Germany is in collapse. Hundreds of civilian refugees and German soldiers on the loose. Here we roust out a German farm family from their house and take it over as our billets. We gave them 15 minutes to vacate which they did with the utmost alacrity.

The interior of the farm house presented a scene of kulak splendor. These people really had it good. With Bethke of Gaylord, Minnesota who speaks fluent German, we hold converse with a Russian tankist captured at Bialystok in 1941 and an Ukrainian peasant girl who were employed as slave labor on the farm. We permit them to use the bedroom of their former master, which gratifies our ironic spirit of revenge.

May 8

At last the wondrous day. Victory in Europe. Our crew however are silent and thoughtful. Anti-climax. There is no feeling of exultation, nothing but a quiet satisfaction that the job has been done and we can see Canada again.

We assemble in convoy before noon and await for "Prepare to Move." Shortly before our departure our new found Russian friend beckons silently and we follow him to the cellar which we had meticulously ransacked yesterday evening without success. Here he indicates to us the secret liquor stock of his former master. What a find. Our troop have a glorious binge.

For a while I retire and remain inert under a hedge. Evening approaches as I return to the convoy. Movement orders having been postponed. Orientation is a difficult problem but I manage to load our Gun Position Officer into the jeep when the order "Mount" comes down the line.

We pass through Meppen to a concentration area at Hemsen and bivouac in a farm house. Our troop kitchen burner exploded and burnt the building to the ground. I could not help but feel pity for this poor peasant family.

May 9

At Hemsen. We assemble and parade before our Officer Commanding, Colonel Gagnon, and march to a memorial service in the little rural church nearby to commemorate those of our regiment who fell in the campaign. The Colonel begins to read the 36 names of our fallen. Tears are in his eyes. He falters and hands the paper to the Adjutant who calmly folds the paper and puts it in his pocket and quietly says, "It is not necessary. They were comrades. We remember."

V-E Day in London, May 1945

EDNA WILSON

May 9, 1945

Dear Blanche,

Well this is what we've been waiting for, and what a commotion. It was really something to see cold, mind-my-own-business Londoners prancing around with paper hats on, wearing ribbons and carrying flags— some of them even forgot themselves so far as to carry noisemakers and went whistling or rattling along the Strand. People went around in gangs, singing down the street. They'd throw their arms around other people's shoulders and they'd all join in. I heard the greatest variety of songs, from *Tipperary* to the *Volga Boatman*.

Monday night they announced VE Day would be Tuesday, but people didn't wait to start celebrating. None of us went to work. We have two days off—one to celebrate, one to recover. Tuesday we relaxed and didn't do anything of note. About 7 o'clock, Art and I and Mac and Mabel started down town. We gave up on the idea of going through Piccadilly and went to Charing Cross and walked down the Strand to Trafalgar Square. This is where the mob was. People were all over the lions and the steps of poor old Nelson's monument. The tide was going down the Mall, so we went down. Here is where people were really singing. Gangs arm-in-arm across the road took everything in their stride. We ended up with thousands of others on the steps of Victoria's monument in front of the Palace. What a squash! We listened to the King's speech on the loudspeakers. Then, we started to think about how dry we were and decided to come home.

It was a beautiful night, and warm. As we left, they turned the floodlights on the Palace. Quite a few buildings were flood-lit, signs were lit up, windows, car lights were on—it sure looked odd. We reached one pub that was open. All they had was lemonade, but it was wet. We finally made it to Holland Road about 11:30 to discover our own pub was still open. Mac ordered pints with no arguments from us. All the local characters were there. About six middle-aged women did a conga up and down the floor. People were singing like mad. French Bert, who used to live here, had a flag draped around him. The place had its usual quota of Canadians. The Horvath family was there. One old boy had a glass of about two-gallon capacity and made great inroads on it. At closing time Bert conducted patriotic songs, standing on the bar. Finally we got home and went to Mabel's room for coffee. I stumbled to bed and hardly remember hitting the pillow.

It's almost worth the year over here to be in London on VE night. Maybe it didn't make thousands of people consoled to their losses, but in spite of it everybody was happy. It made one feel good to be in uniform. I expect to work darn hard for the rest of the week. So long for now.

Love, Edna

The End of the War in London and Toronto

CAPTAIN PAT BATES AND PEGGY BATES

> *By May 1945, Canadians were tired but looking forward to the future. These letters, exchanged between a wounded officer recovering overseas and his wife in Toronto, suggest that looking backward was part of going forward.*

Pat Bates to Peggy Bates, 2 May 1945

My Dearest,

Its been a grand week so far in many ways. Monday brought your two letters of Apr 17. Tuesday the news of Mussolini's death, and to-day Hitler's. But to-night brought the greatest piece of war news—the capitulation of the German army in Italy. The announcement by Churchill filled me not only with pride at having been there, but also regret that I had not been enabled to fight to the end of the campaign. I hope that the writing of the Italian war will some day be done by one who can combine the grafic portrayal of war with the truth. It will require much more than the normal war historian's gifts to make people realise how difficult fighting in Italy was and how brilliant the campaign was against almost insuperable difficulties. Certainly if the armies in NW europe had had to fight under the same conditions of enemy, ground and equipment we would not now be on the threshold of complete victory. Italy was fought by a first rate army against first rate troops in superior numbers and often we fought short of equipment and it of second rate quality. We had none of the new weapons until the second front was established and much of what we had had seen years service in the desert. We were a subsidiary front and achieved almost miraculous victories. We made mistakes. Even [General] Alexander made them. Sometimes he was forced to make them and when he did it was always because for some reason or another Jerry decided to hold on when reason dictated that he should not. Often we felt that the next smack we dealt him would be a knock out blow only to find that he was so resilient that he came up almost as strong as he was before. A man who has fought in Italy can be as proud as any who has fought in NWE [Northwest Europe].

I am glad too that the arch fiends have met their death as they have. True Hitler by dying as he has done, may have given birth to a Hitler legend which he might not have done had he been captured intact. But they have met their end as they have so long deserved to and who knows that in the exhultation of peace we might have pardoned them. I fear that the task of executing all those who should be executed will be so great that we will revolt against it as we have revolted against the prison camps.

I did not comment on [U.S. President] Roosevelt's death, because I felt that my comments would be too mundane. I very often feel that he was the greatest man that this war has brought forth. He led the States better than anyone else could have done and what is more he made them into a fighting entity. His greatness is shown by the very insignificance of the criticisms levelled against him. There has been very little real and constructive criticism of him. That some of his acts have not been more criticized shows the paucity of his opponents, for truly some of his acts have been strange and worthy of criticism, and some of those which at the time seemed worthy of criticism have later proved the wisdom of his planning. It is often said that a country only gets leaders who are worthy of itself. He, alas was not one of those. He was infinitely greater than his country. He was perhaps worthy of the States as they should be with all their huge resources and potential greatness as a leader of the world into the ways it should go. But the internal acts of the states were often most unworthy of him. Politically he was so far ahead of the average American that they took his calls for sacrifice and the acts he passed to implement those calls as a betrayal of their fundamental rights. What a indictment of the people it is when it is said by the mayor of New York that 90% of meat sold in NY city is Black Market. He will be loved by many for years to come and will unlike Washington and Lincoln never sleep undisturbed in his lofty memorial for unlike them too many of his acts hurt certain classes of the people. . . . Roosevelt too often appeared to be disloyal to his principles for what people thought should be principles, were to him selfish and unearned privileges which had to be sacrificed for the nation and in fact for the benefit of the whole world. . . . No man was more sure that the States would play its correct part in it. Thanks to him perhaps more than to any one else the states find themselves in the same but better position than they were after the last war. It is a pity for the world that he is not here now to see that they do not again throw it away and help to plunge the world into international anarchy again.

I have left myself little space to tell you how grateful I was to get your letters and once more read that you love me and above all else want me home again. I have missed your letters and in that I have missed you. For such is my condition now that I often feel life is without purpose. Your letters reassure me.

All my love

Peggy Bates to Pat Bates, May 18, 1945

My Darling, . . . VE Day burst upon us upon a rising tide of excitement & expectation. We had had the radio going practically all day during that last week & as CBL was staying awake all night too, on account of the expected news, I *nearly* made a date with the alarm clock to get up & listen. However, the news (courtesy of Kennedy of A.P.) came over about 9 o'clock am on the Monday, & I awoke the Edisons upstairs to tell them & phoned Mary downtown to see what she was going to do. . . . I felt like walking on my hands & dreadfully wanted to go downtown with Jock but was afraid he might be crushed. Bells rang all over the place & sirens whined & flights of planes zoomed over & all sorts of jaloppies strangely decorated whizzed through the streets filled with shouting kids. Racks of flags broke out everywhere & Mary brought home what she could find downtown, namely a Canadian & a British one, which we stuck into the tub on the balcony rail in which chives are growing. That afternoon Mary & I concocted some punch out of some reserves of rum & other peculiar ingredients & people began to splash in & out. I dressed Jock up in pink linen with his B[lack]W[atch] pin & he caught the excitement & ran around charming the dropped-in people. That evening after Jock was tucked away, a sort of drifting al fresco party took place with a sort of rough buffet spread dreamed up by me, several contributed bottles and our own reserves. . . . The next morning Mary very kindly took care of Jock while I went to church—Church of the Redeemer at the corner, where there was a small congregation & a Communion Service, but unhappily

no music. Toronto celebrated in a glad & orderly way, quite sponta-
neously, I believe, without the embarrassment of the New York
crowds & certainly none of the Halifax hooliganism. I personally felt
waves of exhilaration & depression all day, the latter because you
weren't here too. But I listened to London celebrating over the B.B.C
& hoped you felt as happy as they all sounded.

I still can't believe it & it will take a long time to become accustomed to it. Before it happened I had the firmest sort of confidence
that it *would* end *soon*, but now that it's here I can't grasp it. It will be
easier when you get home. I realized from the first that if you weren't
home by VE that it would certainly not be a question of jumping onto
the first ship. I am resigned to your not getting home immediately but
I do hope it will be soon soon soon. The papers here have carefully told
us in just what order everybody will be sent home & all about the point
system, & as far as I can see it, your usefulness there may probably cancel out your eligibility for return. But I am aware that miracles do happen & I look daily for a miracle.

Yes, I heard Churchill; he sounded so tired, but if possible outdid
himself in eloquence & sheer skill of statesmanship. It seems that
he even moved [Irish leader] de Valera into taking his (Churchill's)
remarks with good grace. What a great man! But what an unspeakable
tragedy that Roosevelt had to go when he did. I feel that he would have
continued in his peerless role of buffer between Churchill & Stalin,
something we could certainly use now. I don't know whether you may
express an opinion or even an intention about the coming Canadian
elections, Federal & Provincial, but I hope our votes don't cancel each
other. I believe I shall vote CCF. Will carry on in another of these, darling, in the meantime all love from both.

Occupying Germany, May–June 1945

STANLEY WINFIELD

We arrived at Bienfeld at about 1:00 o'clock and decided we should
halt and have our dinner. We picked a little clearing just outside the

town, took the rations off the tender and Rostock, the self appointed chef went to work. While we were eating, a couple of young German boys stopped by the side of the road and watched us and by the time we finished the meal there were over a dozen Germans of all ages also standing and watching. We were all a bit concerned about our audience at first, but it became quite obvious from the look on their faces that they were all damn hungry and were just waiting for us to leave in the hope that we might leave something behind. I got a definite satisfaction out of their hunger and when we were finished and packing the utensils back in the tender, a couple of the boys tossed the Germans what was left of the butter, canned milk, etc. When I noticed this I told them to cease and even if we have to throw it away, the Germans were definitely not to have any of the food. After all, why should we be feeding these people and on top of that it was contrary to the non-fraternization regulations. Naturally, my name immediately became mud with everyone concerned and at this point Squadron Leader Aplin appeared on the scene, rescinded my order and told me that inasmuch as they are Germans, it is still a greater sin to waste the food. I had to agree with that and on thinking it over when we resumed the journey I realized what a damn fool I was. . . .

The weeks rolled by and things still remained chaotic, a handful of us were working, the remainder had nothing to do but lay around in the sun, go swimming, barter cigarettes on the black market which brings up an interesting point to be discussed later. Also, a few whose will power and ideas of continence were very poor, made the acquaintance of some of the village frauleins. They were sticking their necks out for a Court Martial but I guess they figured a little female companionship was worth the risk. Fortunately they were Canadians and therefore smart and none were ever caught. One might gather from all this that here is the perfect vacation: swimming, sunbathing, acquiring great quantities of loot for practically nothing, and love affairs with virile, healthy, blond German frauleins. However, such is not the case and with a little explanation my meaning will be clear. Most of the fellows like myself, have some job to return to and have just been waiting for the day when the war would be over and we would be back at our jobs. Then there were the others who have no jobs or want to change

from their present line to something else. Well, if this Roman Holiday
was to last maybe six months or so, o.k., lets take advantage of a good
thing—but, this little effort is expected to last two years! Thats what
the Intelligence Officer told us last week when the "tin gods" decided
they had better appease the airmen and try and convince them that
they had an important job to do. It goes without saying that any fellow
with a spark of ambition would not be content to fritter away two good
years laying in the sun. And thats why the morale was so low.

However, my position is very different from that of the other fellows. Outside of being purely disgusted with the attitudes of our senior
officers and the apparent importance of a job that was not being done,
I was definitely enjoying my presence in Germany and could see a very
interesting time ahead of me for even two years and had many reasons
for feeling this way. Here I am, only 21, and fortunately not afflicted
with the pangs of homesickness as so many of my comrades suffered
from and in the best possible position to see for myself if I made any
attempt to do so, events and conditions that the whole world was getting second hand via the radio and the press.

I took a great interest in the Germans and their attitudes towards
the occupation forces. They were still bowing and scraping, doffing
their hats and saluting every private just to be sure of not making any
mistakes but were definitely amazed and I am sure could not understand why we were not allowed to have anything to do with them. The
frauleins took definite advantage of this order and saw only the wonderful opportunity of "getting even." They would go for a stroll where
they knew Allied soldiers would be, such as the park, the river, and
appear as vivacious and desirable as they possibly could. They knew if
a soldier was caught talking or even smiling at them it would mean a
heavy fine or imprisonment for the soldier involved. It is said that what
you can't have you want most and in this case it sure was true. However
plenty of fellows were foolish enough to let their emotions get the better of their judgment and conscience and ended up in trouble. Our own
troops were smart since they never seemed to be caught. The two
theatres in town were originally put into operation and opened up for
the troops. George MacMurray and I went down and while standing
in the inevitable queue, I saw just what kind of a perverted sense of

humour some English soldiers have, to say nothing of our own airmen. We were lined up on one side of the street and on the other side were dozens of displaced persons, mostly Jews evacuated from Belsen because of the typhus epidemic, waiting and watching for a soldier to throw a cigarette butt away and then dash after it. If a cigarette has that hold on a person—O.K.—but I cannot see any civilized person getting such satisfaction and enjoyment out of purposely tossing a butt into a dirty gutter or down a shallow drain so that the poor displaced persons must fish for it. I couldn't see myself even giving a butt to them so I just didn't smoke when they were around. However, after a couple of weeks I got used to having about three men or children scramble after my cigarette butt. After the show that night we went for a stroll in the park and were approached by two men who asked for a cigarette. They both looked definitely Jewish but according to the regulations I asked them for their identity cards and they both turned out to be Polish refugees. We gave them each a couple of cigarettes and then one who spoke a little english mentioned that he had been in Belsen, and that it was "nicht gut." We walked on and I remember George saying; "You know, that's the trouble with these guys, they immediately tell you that they've been in Belsen and they expect you to empty your pockets." I was coming to the conclusion that George had a mean tongue, but this statement was the payoff and I told him so on no uncertain terms. This was the first time we had ever had an argument, but certainly our friendship was not quite the same from that point onwards. George meant no harm by the remark I am sure, but he simply was a man who had contempt for anyone who capitalized on his misery, whether past or present. I thought it was a pretty narrow-minded point of view in the case of these people and I told him so.

The black market on cigarettes is really booming. Most of the deals are being made with the Yugoslavian displaced persons who are camped down the road. Our boys are acquiring articles worth hundreds and hundreds of dollars for practically nothing. Not being much of a businessman, plus the fact that I have been smoking most of the cigarettes I get, is putting me in the position of an onlooker. Here are the latest black market quotations:

Camera: (Zeiss, Leica or Agfa) from 500 to 1500 cigarettes

Watches: 500 to 800 cigarettes

Binoculars: 300 to 500 cigarettes

Silk: 10 cigarettes per metre

Jewellery and precious stones: 100 to 500 cigarettes

Of course, in addition to the above, you can get all kinds of Nazi sou-venirs such as swords, swastikas, flags, etc., etc., etc. Where the Yugo-slavians get their stock, no one knows, but there have been many cases of German homes being raided so that is the answer I guess. . . .

The first leave allocations have finally come in—for Amsterdam. Since I had been observing the non-fraternization ban, I could hardly wait to get to Amsterdam and some female companionship. The beau-tiful German girls working our Mess as waitresses were not helping our morale any. So, after an uncomfortable fourteen hour truck jour-ney, we finally arrived in Amsterdam and were taken to the Red Lion Hotel. What a change—soft beds with sheets, hot and cold running water, telephones (but we didn't know anyone to phone). After a won-derful dinner (it is amazing what a good cook can do with straight Army rations), we went downstairs to the bar, fortified ourselves with a couple of glasses of gin, and set out to see what Amsterdam had to offer. According to the map supplied by the Canadian Army, there were clubs, cabarets, dances all over town, laid on especially for the troops, with entertainment assured. We went to a place called Polmans which was just across the street. Armed with a Dutch-English dictionary, we surveyed the assortment of Dutch girls who had volunteered to act as hostesses that night. We decided on two—one very good looking in a Dutch sort of way and the other not so bad. We both figured on danc-ing with the good-looker but I got there first and so began a beautiful friendship with Greet Van Lanser. Unfortunately she didn't speak a word of english and I don't speak dutch, so we had to depend upon George's girlfriend Corry who spoke a "leedle" english to translate when necessary, which was not too often. The girls became our com-panions for the entire three days, and we partook of movies, swim-ming, dancing and even horseback riding. Expenses for the whole time cost us 1,000 cigarettes a piece, which we sold on arrival at two guilder per cigarette.

I Have Just Seen Belsen, June 1945

SQUADRON LEADER TED APLIN

June 17, 1945

Dear Lil,

I have just seen Belsen and am ashamed. Ashamed that Gentiles all over the world have not risen in one vast crusade to erase forever this evil mark on their record. For responsibility for such deeds as were perpetrated here cannot belong alone to the masters of the Nazi creed. This is Anti-Semitism carried to its final extreme.

The camp itself is situated in a beautiful part of the country, extraordinary in its resemblance to parts of Ontario around Barrie and Camp Borden. It is concealed from view by thick pine woods, and all roads around it were "Verboten." Adjacent to it is a permanent Panzer Grenadier Division location, with magnificent buildings, barracks, hospital, roads, grounds and lake. Into these quarters have now been moved the remaining survivors, totalling several thousand. The majority of these appear to be females, mainly under thirty, mostly Jewish, of all European nationalities.

Admission to this and the original site of horror has been prohibited as from midnight last night, due I believe, to unfortunate incidents of an intimate nature between visiting soldiers and some of the girls. Permission has now to be obtained (i.e. to enter the camp) from high Army authority. However, we managed to talk our way in.

The patients are mostly convalescent, and are living quite freely in the former Army barracks, and roam about the camp at will. They bear the marks of their experiences with them, on their faces and their gestures, in their furtiveness and their physical condition. At first glance all the women and girls appear to be about six months pregnant, but it soon becomes obvious that such a universal condition would be extremely unlikely. Investigation reveals that during their incarceration, almost all their nourishment was obtained from drinking a very weak soup. In order to survive, some of them consumed incredible quantities—say 12 quarts a day. Persisted in over a long period this has resulted in dilated stomachs, and a change in position which will possibly remain with them for ever. The men are this way also, but the condition is not so apparent to the eye. Having survived at all however, would indicate generally a relatively short term of suffering, although I gathered that some had survived as long as four years. The hospital is filled, but I did not venture in. Typhus still is present in the camp, and danger signs abound. The death rate has fallen off considerably due no doubt to medical control as well as to the vastly reduced numbers of patients as a result of its former intensity.

Today was moving day. Patients or inmates are being segregated into barrack blocks according to nationality. It seems that actual fighting has taken place between certain groups recently. What a tragic sequel to such an experience as theirs!

The horror of camp itself of course has been burned down and presents a picture of complete desolation. Bull dozers have been to work, scraped out the remaining embers of the vile wooden brick buildings. But all the essential features are there—the thick barbed wire fences dotted with guard towers, the incinerator, the mass graves, the piles of burned and broken shoes and bits of clothing, the bones, identification tags, and so on.

Over the whole place is the still of death, and the sweet sickly scent of human flesh. When the Army arrived here there were 10,000 unburied bodies on the ground and 13,000 more have died since then. This of course only represents the toll of recent months—the camp was in operation prior to the war. Most of these deaths resulted from typhus and starvation.

These dead have been buried by the British authorities in huge rectangular graves, giving the date and numbers. They read: May 12, 5000—5000—1000—800—and so on. No one will ever know the true numbers that this fiendish place has really accounted for.

There are some fresh individual graves there also, several hundred of them. I stood by while a young Jugoslav officer conducted a short ceremony over one of these for two young, distracted girls who had survived after 12 months imprisonment. It was the grave of a sister.

We talked afterwards, and he gave me some of the story. He himself had been a prisoner of the Germans elsewhere for four years, and was released by the British. His own treatment had not been too bad.

He arrived with the British Army when they first reached Belsen, and his description of the place was almost inconceivable. Children he saw, and most women were put to death by gas practically on arrival. Some survived, how cannot be explained. Our Medical Officer here has carried on some investigations on his own, and while I am not aware of his actual findings, I know of some. He speaks German and has talked patiently and lengthily with many of the inmates. The shocking experience which they have been through makes this very difficult, especially to attempt to get a coherent story of dates and times and numbers. However, it seems as if recently at any rate, the place has been a gruesome experimental station for poison gases. Considerable care was taken in the daily selection of victims—as to size, age, physical conditions, muscle tone and so on, and each one was given a careful bath before being placed in the gas chamber. It is probably that the effects were measured and recorded after which the body was disposed of in the incinerator. There is evidence that they were often merely paralysed at this point, and were conscious of what was going on. There is also evidence that the doctors on duty were usually drunk at the time.

There is only one incinerator, and as the camp population was usually 40,000 it would indicate that mere extermination in quantity was not the only goal. I believe Lublin was much more a mass execution ground than this. (You probably know far more about this place already than I, because I have not had regular access to newspapers for a long time, and British newspapers are pretty slim now anyway.

I am not trying to make a gruesome story, but I feel I must get this thing off my mind, and do not intend to write to anybody else about it just yet. So, would you be good enough to pass this on, especially to Max & Vera Morris?)

The camp area is only approximately one quarter of a mile wide, and maybe half a mile long. You can hardly imagine the living conditions of 40,000 people in such an area, denied as they were the most primitive conveniences or sufficient food and water.

The Jugoslav I mentioned previously was Jewish, with a fine, sensitive, intelligent face. He told me that places like this account for the fact that one sees no Jewish children in Germany today—which is quite true in my experience. In fact, I have scarcely seen anyone of any age who would be considered at all "semitic" in appearance. He said his whole family, mother, father, brothers and sisters, had been wiped out.

The existence and real history of places like Belsen to my knowledge have not been identified in the public's mind with the true nature of Fascism. Allied propaganda has painted them as a product of the German character.

I am convinced now that this is dangerous. Bombard the German people with this story. Utilize whatever Anti-Nazi forces remain for the purpose. Insist on them seeing movies of the scenes here. Make them accept their share of responsibility for their leader's degeneration. But let us not fail to identify all this with Fascism itself. Our own people must also learn that Anti-Semitism leads to Belsen! Let us put truth in our own laws, and stamp out the Anti-Semite who, even if unwittingly, is condoning Belsen.

The suffering of the German people has been, is and will be great. The stupidity which was responsible for giving the green light to Belsen was also responsible for their own condition today. The two are inexorably related. The rest of the world must be forced to see this relationship, and then maybe it will decide it cannot afford the risk.

In London recently, a Communist told me he felt so strongly on the Jewish question that he had often wished he could become converted or naturalized into a Jew if that were possible, so as to share the burden. I feel that way today.

There have been spearheads in every battle. In this war against Fascism, the Jews have paid in blood the biggest price of all. This the Gentile people can never repay. We can however, pledge ourselves to eradicate vigourously from our midst every sign of ingratitude to, or lack of solidarity with our Jewish brothers in our common fight against Fascism.

Fascism will not be defeated until the inter-relationship of its fundamental, social and economic concepts, and the war, are recognised by everybody. "Matters should not be restricted to the military defeat of the Fascist forces. It is necessary to complete the moral and political defeat of Fascism as well."

The responsibility for ensuring this as far as Canada is concerned rests on you people back home. If you do your job I don't mind staying here and doing mine. But lets not have our boys crushing Germany here, while even a single remnant of Fascism flourishes in Canada.

Think it over!

A Soldier's Suicide

CAPTAIN KEN CALDER

Men overseas returned to Canada full of hopes and expectations. Sometimes the reality was different, with alienated spouses looking to end relationships. Captain Calder's suicide note to a friend overseas tells a terrible, depressing story.

6 July 45
Vancouver

My Dear John,

Wish I weren't writing this tonight but you dared me to tell you how things are back here. You being, in my opinion, the best friend I've got, here it is: the whole shot with nothing held back. By the time this gets to you I will already be rotting in my grave but then, what does it matter after all?

After a week of "don't touch me" when all I wanted was a little love and affection, my wife Margaret whom I idolized finally summoned up courage to tell me that she had been unfaithful. I took that like a good soldier, I think, but then she put over the belly punch. She told me that she had never loved me and that she had lived with several men all the time I had been away. One in my own home town shortly after I went overseas. She won't say who he is but said I'd never reach him so something clicked into place and I asked her if he was dead. She couldn't answer that so I presume that I was right. Salute to the R.A.F!

She has told me, John that her affair with Dr. Boyd Story has lasted for a year and only quit when I wired from Halifax. She also says that she had far more experience with the one in M. Jaw. Let me tell you about Story. Married, two sons, one in the navy. His wife is supposed to know all about it, also the navy son. The both of them told me that he couldn't get along with her so she, Mrs. Story, sleeps with some other guy and Story himself takes Margaret. That's the Canada I came home to, John. For some sadistic reason Margaret gave me the supreme insult by telling me she was not a virgin when we married. Claimed all kinds of previous experience.

John, believe me, I cried and pleaded with that girl all day to give me another chance to start over but she turned me down. I still love her, God dammit, so I'm licked. Tomorrow afternoon when she is out I'm going to put on my serge, seal up the very small kitchen and turn the gas stove on. I want it that way, John, because I still love that girl and she killed me two days ago. Please don't feel bad, it was nice to know you because you were my buddy even if it was for only a short while. You very ably took the place of another, Fred Cooper, who died a year ago last September.

Please don't feel that I'm doing the wrong thing. I want release, not maggots in my brain for the rest of my life. I'm sane, John, in spite of what the coroner's jury will say but I'll be out of this rotten world. I forgot to tell you that 9 out of 10 returned men are coming back to the same thing. This is the only victory the German Army ever had.

I'm putting a condensed version in the mail for the Commish. of Police so they'll know why. Had to say goodbye, John, and this is it. I'll never find happiness so I'm checking out. Nothing can hurt me now. Goodbye old pal, good luck, may you never know sorrow like mine. This is my farewell to you John, you and I and perhaps Juliette if you wish. This dirty bitch I married and still love isn't fit to clean Juliette's shoes.

FAREWELL DEAR FRIENDS.

The Difficult Re-adjustment to Peace

RODOLPHE CORMIER

> *An Acadian, Cormier fought in Italy. He served for five years in the army and felt the war exposed him to a lifetime of trials. Seeing his youth swallowed by the demands of war, he left the army forever marked.*

Après la guerre, même le tonnerre me faisait coucher par terre. Il y avait des choses que je ne comprenais pas. J'avais joint l'armée à 18 ans et j'y avais passé cinq années qui étaient pour moi toute une vie. Je suis sorti de l'armée à 23 ans, mais j'avais l'expérience d'une personne qui avait vécu 25 ans de plus. J'avais des questions auxquelles je ne pouvais pas répondre. Il y en avait d'autres que je n'osais pas poser.

J'avais perdu la meilleure partie de ma jeunesse et je pensais à mes jeunes amis qui s'étaient fait tuer, qui étaient restés là.

Je me suis tourné vers la bouteille et j'ai bu pour 12 ans afin d'oublier. En buvant, je pensais oublier, mais je n'oubliais pas parce que le lendemain ça recommençait.

Mes cinq années au combat ont été moins difficiles pour moi que les années après la guerre. Je ne pouvais pas trouver de réponses.

Our Grandchildren Will Ask Us Who Liberated Us

EDITOR, *OUR FREE HOLLAND*

> *In March 1946, Canadian headquarters in the Netherlands closed down, bringing to an end the friendly occupation. The Dutch were sorry to see the Canadians go and somewhat relieved as well, but unshakeably thankful. That gratitude remains strong.*

Good-bye, Canada!

Open letter to the Canadian soldiers!

To Jimmy, Jack, Harold, Reggie, Tom, Bill and Harry and the thousands of other battle-dressed boys of the Canadian Army!

Old Boy! With the farewells that finally you, too, had to take from your Dutch friends, now you return to your country. You will permit me to give you a few words in a heart-to-heart talk.

When you, eight months ago, on a, for us, historical day, entered the capital of our country, from all skies the boys and girls jumped on your jeeps, then you found a nation of grateful and moved people, who hardly knew their happiness.

First you didn't understand the tear you saw in many eyes and you couldn't understand that, because you didn't know the sufferings which we had to bear during five years, the sufferings from which thousands of men, women and children went to rack and ruin and that we all, when you got acquainted with us, bore in despair.

Your first impression gave you a wrong idea of the reality. That wasn't your fault. You thought that the cigarette was the principal thing that we had done without, we hailed you with the "classic question": "Have you got a cigarette for me?" Just as if that was our national greeting. And the cigarette that you used to dole out, sometimes it was your last one; at that moment it was a benefaction, we recovered our sick nerves when we smoked your "real" cigarette. We revived, but your cigarette—you were astonished on account of the gratitude they showed— was an emblem, for you gave us every time the same, the confirmation of our liberty, and it took us some time, dear boy, to demonstrate our great happiness.

We knew that our capital, Amsterdam, became a "leave centre" under the guidance of your chief, Lieut.-Col. G. Weir. It wasn't the least result of the circumstance that you and your comrades took care of, that it isn't a heap of rubbish now. During the time you stayed in our country, you saw something of our manners and morals, of our habitudes and unmannerliness, learned something of our history and our nature, our traditions and our temper, and many other things. You will take them with you like a memory to your country, so far away in the north of America.

　　Between the very old history of our country, with its civilization and cultivation, and the still young history of your country, is a world of difference. You and your family don't know about the Middle Ages and the Renaissance, but something else you didn't know, too, the torment of the German occupation during five years, that was finished when you came. The German yoke of bondage, the Jerries, as you used to call them, gave themselves the name of "nation of gentlemen," and when I think now—excuse me—that you Canadian boys often brought us the memories of the cowboys from the American Wild West pictures, then, I must say, that the acquaintance with the "boys," in spite of all, was much better than that one with the "gentlemen."

I said, in spite of all, for you know as well as I know you sometimes gave us reason for uneasiness and worry. You see, sometimes you were a little bit too spontaneous and too tempestuous. You were a little bit too rough with your vehicles on our roads and "a little bit" too tempestuous with our girls.

As we, free Dutchmen, were fit again after our "struggle for life," you and your friends started your "struggle for love," and be sure that you presented troubles to many Dutch mothers. They spoke and wrote much about you, and I don't like to be severe on you for that, for the carelessness with which you threw yourself into the reckless love affairs was an understandable result of the hard war, with its privation, solitude and want, that you hadn't wanted any more than we.

How can I reproach you at all, when you showed courage, when five years ago they asked you with emphasis to join the army, because the leadership of a country, of which you hardly knew its existence, so bestially broke bounds?

Dear boy, of course your action sometimes was a little bit more rough and unpolished than we in the "old west" are accustomed to. But we shall never forget, boys, that with that same rough indifference your comrades fought to death near Nijmegen and Arnhem, while we still were suffering under the "bad Jerries."

And do you know our dear Queen, her child and grandchildren are safely in our midst again? That was your work. We can say again what we like to say, we can write everything and we don't spare our statesmen our criticism, thanks to you. We are no more hungry, since we started to eat your biscuits and now eat tarts again; our trains and street cars go again, we have coals for our stoves and food for our children. That was your work.

And now, take to your Canadian country a good lasting memory of us, the gratitude of a nation that was itself again by your co-operation.

Once our grandchildren will ask us who liberated us and then we will say, many brave, gay boys with caps on their heads; we shall tell them all—much and much more than that Montreal and Ottawa are two big cities in Canada!

Godspeed, boys, and welcome home!

Maybe you will see a tear in the eyes of your mother, your wife, your girl or your sister, but don't forget that a tear is a smile of the heart, and that same heart is beating in the small low-lying country near the sea, Holland, that will set down your name in the chronicles of its history.

In the name of thousands,

The Editorship of a Dutch Illustrated Weekly, *Our Free Holland*

A Commander for Korea, August 1950

MAJOR-GENERAL JOHN M. ROCKINGHAM

> *On June 25, 1950, North Korea invaded South Korea. The United States rallied the United Nations to resist the aggression, and Canada soon dispatched ships and aircraft. By August the decision had been made to raise a brigade for service in Korea. A very successful battalion and brigade commander during the Second World War, Rockingham was asked to take command.*

About 6:30 P.M. on August 17, 1950 I was sitting in my office talking to the Executive of the Amalgamated Union of Transit Employees. I was Superintendent of Pacific Stage Lines, then a subsidiary of the British Columbia Electric Company. Pacific Stage Lines was responsible for the long line bus transit system operating between Vancouver, Seattle and parts of the B.C. Interior.

The subject of the conversation was a request from the union to have all bus drivers presently employed given an hour off (12 noon to 1 P.M.) when they could all have lunch. I asked the Business Agent if he thought I would close the system for that hour; he suggested that I could hire enough extra men to drive over the lunch break. I explained that we already catered to that by our shift system covering all runs which could be selected by the drivers on a seniority basis. It was intended, I explained, that these shifts together with layovers at the end of the trips would take care of time for meals for all drivers.

At this point the telephone rang. I answered it rather brusquely because the operator had been instructed not to ring until the meeting was over. She explained that the Minister of National Defence, the

Honourable Brooke Claxton, was on the line; he had insisted on talking to me. He said that the Canadian Cabinet had just decided to send a Brigade Group to Korea, and they wanted me to organize, train and lead the Group in battle. He was supposed to tell the Cabinet that night whether I would accept. . . .

While talking to the Minister of National Defence on the telephone, I had to be a little cautious in my conversation because he emphasized the need for absolute security until the release was made from Ottawa. Remember, the Union Officers were listening to me intently and that could put the security in jeopardy.

Although it was not clear to me at the time, the reason for my selection rather than one of the regular Brigadiers was that it was hoped that there would be many ex-soldiers and civilians in the force, and it was thought that a "civilian soldier" could handle a situation of this sort better.

As soon as the telephone conversation finished with my saying that I would have to consult my wife and my boss, Dal Grauer, the President of B.C. Electric, I told the Union officials that their proposal was not acceptable. They then said that they would go to the President with the proposal. To their surprise, I expect, I said to go ahead. It was not usual to let a labour dispute go to the President until all means had been tried to settle it at a lower level.

I went to the parking lot for my car without being able to decide what to do next. However, I went home where my wife was preparing dinner and suggested that we have a drink. She expressed some surprise at this as it was not usual for us to have a drink if we were alone. I said that I wanted to talk to her without the children present. She then said that she knew what I wanted to talk to her about, as the Minister's call had first come to the house, and she had just heard over the radio that Canada intended to send a Brigade Group to Korea. She supposed that the Cabinet wanted me to lead it. Thus the first obstacle had been overcome without undue strain.

However, I had to face up to the President next. I telephoned his house and although he and his wife had guests for dinner, he invited me over straight away. His observations after my explanation were that the company would be very proud that I had been selected; moreover, I could come back to the B.C. Electric any time I wanted to do so. This was very important to me as it gave me freedom from undesirable pressure throughout the war.

Very shortly after my return call to the Minister accepting the appointment, it was announced in newspaper headlines. The B.C. Electric Public Relations Officer, Ted Fox, a very old friend whom I had hired several years before, came to see me in the office. He thought it the greatest thing in public relations that B.C. Electric had ever experienced, and proceeded to feed the papers and other media with stories, pictures and all the rest.

That night I was a little surprised to see my batman from the Second World War (he lived in Hamilton) appear at the door with a brush sticking out of his pocket. "Well, here we go again!" he said without even uttering a greeting, but looking somewhat critically at my shoes. Someone somewhere along the line had added a personal piper to my retinue. He was a fine piper, and stayed with or near me throughout the campaign.

The Chinese Intervene in Korea, December 1950

MAJOR RODERIC BRIAN MEREDITH

A Canadian, Meredith was the chief information officer for the United Nations Commission for the Unification and Rehabilitation of Korea. His letters capture the panic that swept Seoul when the Chinese seemed to be taking all before them.

Seoul, Korea, 12 Dec, '50

My dearest People:

It seems only yesterday that I heard your voices on the phone, and I am bad not to have written you before this about it, particularly as letters have been fluttering in from you, and you have been keeping me cheered and well posted.

These are exciting times here as you can imagine, but they are thoroughly secure so far as we are concerned, and from being very worried about the general safety of the city of Seoul itself, we have now passed into a peculiar period of not knowing where we stand, there having been no real contact with the enemy in some time. It is all really a remarkable example of the ineffectiveness of a modern army with all the gadgets against an army working along primative lines, and based on superiority of numbers and simplicity of equipment and operation.

There will be many explanations for the debacle, the basic one being that we were outnumbered; but history will never forget the turn of events that two days brought when a UN attack brought a counter attack that pushed us back, and how and why the numbers against us were not known, and why reconnaissance and intelligence were not better, no one will ever know, I suppose. The US high command has been peculiar to say the least, they . . . themselves are highly aware of this; but most notable danger being the division between 10th Corps on the east coast and 8th Army on the west, the two working independently of each other, commanded separately, and working not independently but almost in competition and with much evident jealousy between. There should have been a field headquarters and complete cohesion, and there wasn't. On a minor level their handling of their PR arrangements were bad and added to the alarm and despondency when the going got rough; but bad PR doesn't lose a war as this did for a time, and the fault must lie deeper than that.

I have been feeding back a great deal of material for broadcast, and I am only sorry that more of it does not become audible to you. UN Today is the most faithful consumer, but there is also a new network at 6pm in the east, the Liberty Network, that takes a number of my items, I believe; and perhaps you can hear that in Ottawa. Anyway I gather you have had some reports, and any reactions you do get are of course cheering for me to get.

The whole course of our work has of course changed, and just now I don't know what will happen, or how our plans will shape up. Manifestly the original concept for a large PR set up here to inform Korea about the UN and what UN was trying to do for them will have to go by the board, that is unless we are in fact going to work above the 38th parallel, which seems unlikely at the moment.

I am thoroughly comfortable, well fed, warm, and otherwise spoilt. The main thing is that I am frantically busy as all the others with me have been sent back to Tokyo, and I am liking it very much. The most depressing thing is not having enough to do, as was the case in India; and this is quite the reverse. The situation generally, of course is depressing. One gets to know and like the Koreans, and its horrible to think of pulling out and leaving them to what is certain death for so many. They are sturdy, tough people and should be given a break.

Pusan, 4 January /51

My dearest Family, and I mean you all, Elizabeth and Mark and Ann and Mother and Father, and I should like you to pass this letter on as I am limited in my energies and resources and can't write all the individual letters that I should like about the last two unpleasantly unforgettable days. There was nothing about evacuation that was dangerous, difficult, or even very inconvenient. It was easy and orderly enough. We got everything out that I wanted save three inches in the bottom of a whiskey bottle that sadly I had to leave on the shelf of my cupboard. But it was depressing, it was shaming, humiliating even. To clear out, be cleared out, while others remained, Koreans one had known, soldiers who were going to carry on; to leave places one had come to know, had seen repaired and made habitable again, and to know they will be smashed up, was not an uplifting experience. And then tonight scarcely thirty six hours after leaving Seoul, no about 2 hours, to hear by radio that the place is completely abandoned, that the enemy is in the outskirts, that much of the city is said to be in flames; that is not pleasant either. What happened was this. Our commission had been whittled away in the face of mounting realities: two delegates remained, plus the principal secretary, a couple of field service drivers and your very faithfully. We had just kissed the last lot goodbye with the view that we should be holding on for a few days at least. But a few hours later we were on their heels. We gathered to compare notes in the Chosen Hotel in the morning, one of the senior officers of the American Embassy came. The signal had come: the last civilians were to be out forthwith, planes would be available early in the afternoon, the exact time would be made known soon. It was. An hour later I was told we should be ready to leave in about three quarters of an hour. I was in the midst of talking to a Korean who was thanking me for trying unsuccessfully to aid him in getting a job as an interpreter. The UN field service officer came in and interrupted our pleasantries. The Korean and I parted, both subdued and I thoroughly embarrassed, and I proceeded to go through the final motions of packing. It was simple enough as I had been tied up for some time. I carried my bags down into the lobby. Joined the others, and in a few minutes was being ferried by car to the American embassy mess for lunch. And after lunch we left in a convoy of civilian jeeps and sedans for the airfield. The streets were almost deserted, except as we approached the south outskirts when refugees, all headed out became more numerous. Across the pontoon bridge the military traffic moved solidly. The refugees streamed across the ice, just strong enough to hold them, and there were two or three columns of them within sight from the bridge; they straggled across the flatlands beyond the stream itself, gathered in conjested knots where they crossed the road traffic, and paused in crowds along the high slope overlooking Seoul. There some waited to see what was going to happen. The convoy dropped us by the airfield, and we waited there for two hours of uncertainty in the midst of much equipment, jet engines awaiting shipment, all the gadgets for loading and transport peculiar to an airfield, helicopters, everything. And now I know that that airfield is abandoned, that much, very much must have been lost. The rest was simple enough: a four engined military transport with bucket seats, ie a shelf along either side, and the luggage piled along the middle between the rows of passengers facing each other. We were forty, and a mixed lot of state department officials, some Koreans, a family of Czechs or some nationality I couldn't place, and a small Korean child beside me who was air sick just before we landed. And so, on to Pusan airfield, with a UN station wagon to take me to our new quarters, ended my inglorious, depressing journey to safety, the end to an assignment that promised so much for so many, the beginning of another journey for many more from which there can be no turning back. Believe me, I am glad to be here in Korea, and I don't want any more of this evacuation business. I am being quite useful in my own peculiar way, and I don't want to quit this affair unless it promises to be in better order. So be patient, keep your fingers crossed, and rest assured that providence will likely continue to give me the special and undeserved treatment I have had in the past.

Hands Off Korea: Captain Pope and
the Trotskyist Blonde, April 1951

HARRY POPE

> *Harry Pope was an officer with the Royal 22e Régiment, training*
> *in Washington State with the brigade destined for Korean service.*
> *He was a troublesome but brave and intelligent officer, though his*
> *encounter with the blonde Trotskyite came close to getting him*
> *cashiered. He went on to win the Military Cross in Korea.*

I should at least have spent an hour or so in church on Good Friday
1951. Instead, I spent a good part of the day in a Seattle Rathskeller.
On re-entering my hotel (a second-class one, the first-class hotels
were full of automobile conventioneers), I passed a meeting room with
about 50 people in it and with a big sign up on the wall: "HANDS
OFF KOREA." Being slated for Korea in about three weeks, I asked
the man at the door if this was a Republican meeting, the Republicans
being very critical of Truman's war.

"No," he replied. "It's Socialist Workers Party of America, Trotskyist." Not having had a good political discussion in a long time, I
asked: "May I sit down with the proletariat?" "Yes, for thirty-five cents."

After about two hours of Comrade Joe Hansen's speech—he being
the leader and a secretary to Trotsky when the latter got a Stalinist
icepick in the back of the head in Mexico a decade earlier, I turned and
noticed a very young blonde with glasses sitting at the back of the
room. "A beauty with brains!" By now having had more than my fill of
Comrade Joe, I switched all my attention to the young beauty. The
only way to get to know her was to stick around.

At midnight, sitting in a restaurant with about a dozen Trotskyists,
all of them seemingly a little uncomfortable at having a soldier in uniform in their midst, I was not able to get Colleen's address and could
not do better than find out where the Trotskyists would be meeting
the next evening: a Saturday-night social in a black woman's house.

For the Trotskyist social, I polished the buttons of my service dress
and turned up, Sam Browne belt and all. As the evening wore on Colleen
and I were in the pantry looking sufficiently happy with each other

that our hostess suggested that we might be yet happier upstairs. Agreeing, we had hardly got there before we heard a loud voice downstairs asking for Colleen. "My fiancé!" It seems that the wretched band in which her fiancé played the drums quit at 0100 hours. Hearing his footsteps on the stairs, Colleen got behind the door while I sat at the window as though I had just come up for a breath of fresh air. "Have you seen Colleen?" he asked. I replied, "Who's Colleen?" "Beautiful blonde with glasses and long hair." "Oh, yes, I've seen her around." The lad shoved off to continue his search, followed, at a discreet interval, by his fiancée.

Of course, with all this, I still had not obtained Colleen's address. Nothing for it but to go to a Unitarian church next morning, Sunday, to hear Comrade Joe's lecture, "The Agrarian Reform Movement in China," this being Mao Tse-tung's takeover. This paid off: Colleen agreed to a date the next Saturday evening, when her fiancé's band had another gig.

Next morning, back in Fort Lewis, I said to the CO, Colonel Dextraze, "I'd better tell you what I've been doing over the weekend before the FBI tells the Adjutant-General. Ha-Ha." The most prophetic joke that I ever made in my life.

Two days later, Colonel called a mess meeting and told the officers that the mess would throw a thank-you party on Saturday for our American hosts in view of 2R22eR's imminent departure for Korea. "All officers will attend," concluded the CO. *"Tous les officiers?"* (*"All officers?"*) I asked, horrified. "No, no, all except those that have a date with a Trotskyist blonde." . . .

The date went well. But I never saw Colleen again. I had her address, of course, but I had no wish to tell her of the events of the next few weeks and months.

Two or three days after my date with Colleen, Dextraze told me that he had been told by Brigadier Rockingham, Commander of 25 CIB, to parade me to him immediately. "I think you're in trouble."

Although most of 2R22eR—all the officers certainly—had heard of my two Trotskyist week ends, Rockingham was learning of it for the first time. "I think you've been a little indiscreet," he said, "I'll phone the Adjutant-General and see what can be done." However, the

AG had not yet heard of it either: it had been handled at ministerial level.

I was ordered back to Ottawa to become adjutant of No.1 Army Administrative Unit, the clerks who handled the personnel adminis-tration of the AHQ staff. Before I left, Dextraze and I agreed that the affair would probably cost me my commission. "Come back as a pri-vate," Dextraze said, "and I'll keep a Company-Sergeant-Major's vacancy open to which I'll promote you as soon as you get back." Years later, General Dextraze told me the Americans really were not con-cerned by my Trotskyist episode. Maybe he was joking, maybe not. If not, it seems that the FBI has more of a sense of humour than it is usu-ally given credit for.

With the Guns in Korea, 1951

LIEUTENANT DON DALKE

On May 17, 1951, 2 RCHA fired its first shots in action as part of the Commonwealth Divisional Artillery.

The terrain in Korea presented various deployment problems, especially for the artillery. For one thing, the landscape was a continu-ous succession of hills and mountains, ranging in height from 50 to 800 metres. There were also rice paddies that had no firm footing for our heavy vehicles and guns.

When we arrived at our battle positions we had very little protec-tive gear. Our groundsheets were the only personal cover we had from the elements that went from one extreme to another. Fortunately, we had an excellent supply of liquor, and an even greater quantity of good old Canadian ingenuity. With a case of Canadian Club, it was amazing what we could acquire from our American comrades.

It did not take long to obtain tents, vehicles and weapons that were far superior to our vintage WW II equipment. For example, our Sten gun—a type of lightweight submachine gun—could best be described as a "pipefitter's spare parts all screwed together." It was often referred to as a plumber's nightmare. Sometimes the gun worked, sometimes it did not. It certainly was not the best thing to have as your survival tool. Consequently, we were well equipped for the rest of our time in Korea.

Another example of our weapons woes was the 25-pounder artillery ammunition we received shortly after arriving in theatre. Most of it had been recovered out of Hong Kong Bay after WW II. When the Japanese invaded Hong Kong in 1941, Allied ships—loaded with ammunition and military equipment—were sunk in the bay. Between 1947 and 1949, the British recovered most of the equipment, including the 25-pounders.

This ammunition helped fill a major need in the first year of the Korean War, but we literally had to hammer the sand and silt off of it before we could load and fire it. Another major problem had to do with the timing fuses on the air-burst shells. These shells were designed to inflict maximum casualties by exploding above the ground and creating a large pattern of shrapnel. However, the shells did not always function because they had been underwater for so long. As a result, we had a good number of premature bursts just outside the muzzle of our guns. Fortunately, we suffered very few casualties because we had well-prepared gun pits.

The ammunition was also not as effective at the target end because with the faulty timing fuses the air bursts were not at the right height above the enemy for the best effect. . . .

The first thing we did when the infantry moved into a new defensive position was to register defensive-fire targets.

This was necessary in order to cover every possible line of attack. While working as FOO, I discovered that the Chinese and North Koreans consistently made three major assaults on a position. The first wave was made up of raw recruits, many of them civilians who had been gathered from villages and forced by bayonet point to charge our positions. Many of these people were not armed.

The enemy would use the first wave to identify our major fire positions. They would then send in the second wave made up of more raw recruits and some seasoned troops. The enemy's thinking was that we would expend much of our ammunition on the first and second waves, and that the bodies would fall onto the barbed wire in front of our position. The more seasoned soldiers in the third wave would then run over the bodies on the wire to get into our position.

We always held the high ground with well-prepared dug-in positions of good cover so that when the enemy finally started to overrun our position we could bring our guns to bear on our own position, killing off the majority of the enemy. This left our infantry in a position to clean up what was left.

The defensive-fire targets were the real key to cutting down the overwhelming numbers of the Chinese. While they were identifying our positions for their third-wave attack, we were identifying their lines of attack so that by the time they were pushing for the final assault, our divisional artillery had established a wall of hot steel for them to come through.

We were able to listen in to their communications and could hear commanders saying they were receiving very heavy casualties and could not get through the artillery shield to support the attack.

On one occasion, while supporting the infantry on Hill 227, the Chinese put a heavy concentration of fire on my observation post. The fire was making it very tough to effectively control our artillery fire. They finally were successful in putting a round into my post. All I remember from that is that when the dust cleared, I was lying on the back of the hill with the telephone in my hand and about a foot of wire attached to it. I was looking at the phone trying to remember what order I wanted to give to the guns. In order to carry out the rest of the battle, I had to find a portable radio and move to a flank position. I ended up in a trench with an infantry section.

Crossing the Imjin River, 1951

MAJOR-GENERAL JOHN M. ROCKINGHAM

As part of the preliminary to the Commonwealth Division offensive operations, a "raid in strength" was made by 25 Canadian Brigade Group across the Imjin River. "In strength" is a most appropriate way to describe it, as the raiding force was made up of two Infantry Battalions, nearly the whole Tank Squadron, a Battery of artillery, plus a portion of my tactical HQ made up of about eight people. We crossed the Imjin River easily as it was only about 18 inches deep, making it quite easy for the whole force to ford. But no sooner had we crossed than the monsoon broke and the river rose rapidly. The operation was designed to swing left after we had penetrated a certain distance. I designated 2 PPCLI to hold the pivot and protect the flanks while the other Battalion did the left wheel.

One hill I pointed out to the CO, Jim Stone, was essential to hold at all costs. As I approached, I could see the mad turmoil of battle going on for possession of the critical hill. Just as I arrived at Stone's HQ, a breathless Company Commander who had been told to capture the hill which was the pivot, reported over the radio, "My company has captured the hill, but I cannot live here." Stone replied shortly over the radio, "Well, die there." (The expression when used in battle does not really mean I can't live here, but can mean anything from discomfort to a critical situation.) It was always said that Stone's troops feared him more than they did the enemy. He has very big hands which he uses freely to illustrate a point he is making, and I have often thought that his subordinates might imagine themselves in his grasp if they exhibited any lack of soldier-like qualities.

Anyway, the operation went well and we had to return with quite a few prisoners we had captured when the left wheel effectively cut off the retreat of the enemy. The Imjin, now swollen to about 14 feet deep, had defied tremendous efforts by our engineers to get a bridge across. We were getting short of ammunition and food and other supplies. Somewhere we had acquired some powerful motor boats to help keep us supplied. We went to the river bank to watch them unloading their supplies. It was a spooky night, very dark, but the sky was filled with the light of searchlights, flares and tracer bullets. The sound of battle was everywhere. It was a truly scary situation. The following story and others illustrate that the Canadian soldier has a wonderful sense of humour even under the most adverse circumstances. A Corporal was in a boat which had just crossed the river and was fully loaded. He was handing boxes of ammunition to one of our privates on the enemy bank. There was a temporary silence in the black night.

"Hey, Corporal," whispered the Private in a hoarse voice. "Don't call me Corporal," came the reply out of the night, "Don't you know that the Chinese are looking for us leaders?" How could one doubt the outcome of a battle when such men were serving on our side?

After a couple of days being counter-attacked and generally living a pretty uncomfortable life, we had most of the force back to the other side of the river on a cable raft which the engineers had managed to build. I was on the last ferry which was being shelled and machine gunned. I believed that no one knew it was my fortieth birthday and that even if they had known, it would have meant nothing—the lack of sleep and the strain had made me a bit sorry for myself! As the ferry beached on our side of the river, we cut the cable and scrambled over the dyke-like bank where I was greeted by my piper playing "Blue Bonnets over the Border" (The Canadian Scottish Regimental March) and the chef marching behind him with a large cake. On it was enscribed "Life begins at 40" in different coloured icings. The cake was washed down with some champagne which the staff had acquired somewhere. When we left the river bank, I felt much better and not at all neglected.

There Sure Isn't Much News: Private Roy Dooley Writes Home from Korea, 1951

PRIVATE ROY DOOLEY

Nov/2/51

Dear folks

Just a few lines to let you know how everything is getting along up here in Korea. The weather up here is not bad it has snowed in other parts of the front but not here. The days are warm but at night it really gets cold. And that's when we do all our fighting. The first night up in the line I was sure scared. The Chinese sure gave us a warm welcome. We are on top of a hill and all around the hill is barb wire. We wait till the enemy gets caught in the barb wire. Then we go into action. The first morning after we went down and pulled out one hundred and twenty nine Chinese that were dead out of the barb wire and buried them.

Well, there sure isn't much news to talk about. . . . the meals are good here so is the clothing. We were on a couple of patrols behind the lines last nights. The first night it was rough. Last night I got hit in the wrist by a bullet it cut it up pretty good but not enough to bother about says the doctor. Well it is starting to get dark and we can't have no lights after dark so will have to close for now. . . .

Roy

Problems in the NATO Brigade, 1953

LIONEL SHAPIRO

Shapiro, a former Second World War correspondent, visited the army's contribution to NATO. He was not impressed by the 27th Infantry Brigade's standards.

The 27th Brigade is composed mostly of unhappy restless men. Since the brigade's arrival in Hanover in November 1951 the Canadian people and parliament have intermittently received reports about poor morale and occasionally of mass rioting in the city itself. As for the brigade's military mission, which is to become an efficient defense force, the most sanguine judgment this reporter has been able to draw out of high officers is a meaningful shrug and the comment, "Well, I suppose they'll pass."

Here then is the supreme paradox. The six thousand troops—"the cream of Canadian youth" as we are accustomed to call our Canadian volunteers—are failing as ambassadors and as soldiers. A collection of indifferent, morose, restless characters bear Canada's banners in the heart of Europe.

There is of course an explanation for this extraordinary state of affairs, but it must be painfully arrived at. And when it finally comes into focus it poses an acute problem for the Canadian people as well as for the military high command and the government in Ottawa.

The correspondent who arrives here for a visit with the brigade encounters a chronic reluctance on the part of the officers to talk to any outsider about the fundamental weaknesses of the brigade. This is an inbred characteristic of military men and it's especially stubborn when they have something to conceal. Besides, this has been an election year in Canada . . .

There is, for example, a jailhouse in the Hanover encampment. I asked half a dozen officers, who would be expected to know, what the capacity of this detention barracks was and whether it was filled. Not one of them seemed to know. They pleaded loss of memory, being out of touch, not having seen the latest figures and so on. Was the capacity about twenty or fifty or a hundred? I persisted. Even an approximate round figure seemed to elude their memories; they just couldn't say.

On the other hand, it was a simple matter for me to obtain permission to visit the detention barracks. I walked through the corridors and counted the cells and the inmates therein. There are forty-seven cells and forty-seven detainees fill them to capacity. There was also a long list of men condemned to detention and awaiting vacant cells to begin a term of punishment for a variety of crimes ranging from theft and assault to chronic incorrigibility and long absence without leave. In addition, the battalions have makeshift cells in their own quarters for men found guilty of lesser infractions.

How many men are awaiting detention, how many are confined to battalion barracks, how many are incarcerated in cells of small Canadian units strewn across Western Germany—these figures are effectively denied a reporter. What is not denied is that for a community of 5,499 "other ranks," the total for the brigade, the military crime rate is "high."

One morning at ten o'clock, the hour for the coffee break, a young medical officer walked into his mess and sank heavily into a chair.

"I'm bushed," he mumbled to his companions, "haven't been to bed yet. What a night of work this one was!"

What had happened? An outbreak of infectious disease? An accident? A riot? The medical officer looked blandly at his questioner. "Nothing extraordinary," he replied. "Yesterday was payday. The men sure went to town last night."

I asked a sergeant, a good solid-looking citizen, a career soldier, about the men in his outfit. He said, "I suppose if we got into a shooting war this bunch would do okay. Anyway they're tough enough . . ." He shook his head decisively. "But this peacetime business is something else again. I guess it's the guys' own fault. What are you going to do with a bunch that's got two things on their mind twenty-four hours a day—liquor and women? . . . Sure, there're some good guys here, damn good guys and damn good soldiers, but—well take a guy I've got in my outfit. Doesn't drink, doesn't go downtown, saves his dough. And he's the lonesomest private in Germany."

The point was made more succinctly by one of the eight padres attached to the brigade. He said, "I've been in the army many years now. I knew the army after the war when we had the veterans in, later when we had a small permanent force" . . . he added sadly—"We have some good men here, but mostly it's an abyss of immorality."

When a community of men is consistently at odds with the conditions of its existence, either the conditions are at fault or the men are inadequate.

Let's look at the conditions. In a military community these depend partly on the facilities for living, partly on the nature of the command. The physical layout in Hanover is as good as this reporter has seen in Europe and superior in most respects to any military encampment in Canada. Built before the war to house an elite German cavalry regiment, it is generously designed. The barracks buildings are widely spaced, well heated and well ventilated. There are huge training squares and sports fields and, when the weather is good (which, unfortunately, it usually isn't), the country is altogether pleasant. Five miles from the camp, a fifteen-minute bus ride, Hanover is a lively city of five hundred thousand inhabitants and offers everything from excellent grand opera to the lowest kind of dive this side of the Casbah.

Food, which was a source of lively complaint in the first months after the brigade's arrival, has been stepped up to adequate Canadian standards and the men appear to be satisfied with the rations. . . .

To put it bluntly the representative recruit in the 27th is, statistically, of a lower standard than the average Canadian young man. We are trying to build a better-than-average brigade with lower-than-average human material.

It is impossible to indict a whole community of Canadians—the good with the indifferent and the bad—but judged as a community the 27th is not an accurate reflection of the whole community of Canada.

Take the evidence of an experienced padre: "In the years 1946 to 1950 we had a small permanent army in Canada—about twenty-two thousand men—but it was a good army. We took the average in education and intelligence of the Canadian wartime soldier and set up the top half as the minimum requirement for recruitment into the permanent force. The army then was an average, even better than average, Canadian community.

"Then," he continued, "the bars were let down. After the 25th was recruited for Korea we recruited the 27th for Germany. We took in everybody.

"I've talked to hundreds of these men who've been in one trouble after another. I've asked them why they came into the army and it's nearly always the same story. They were the kind that drifted, couldn't hold a job or didn't want to hold a job, so they figured they'd try something new—the army. Most of them didn't realize that you can't drift in and out of the army if you get tired of it. That kind of man makes a bad peacetime soldier."

What the padre said is confirmed by statistics. The average education of the private soldier in the 27th is between fifth and sixth grade. Even this figure is likely to be high. On recruitment the men were given no examination; their own words were accepted for their educational standards. One officer recalled that a private in his outfit, presumably of fifth-grade education, couldn't write his own name; he drew out the individual letters that formed it.

Even if the estimate of between fifth and sixth grade is accepted it means that the average recruit in the 27th left school at a time when he had barely mastered reading and writing. This is the *average*. If it is balanced off against the men who went as high as seventh or eighth grade (there are forty-six soldiers now writing their senior matriculation examinations) then we are left with a substantial number of men who are practically illiterate.

Chary as they are about making comparisons or revealing statistics, responsible officers in the brigade admit that Canada's force in Europe has a lower educational average than that of the British and American formations on its flanks. With this educational standard as a signpost there is only one direction for other statistics—and it is not a direction of which Canadians can be proud.

The venereal-disease rate of the 27th is, for instance, inordinately high. It is officially admitted that it is higher than in the British or American armies. The VD rate of the 27th is one hundred and eighty-three per thousand per year. Some months it goes as high as two hundred and seventy-five per thousand. The VD rate among soldiers in Canada during the last war, using October, 1942 as a sample, was forty-eight per thousand. But obviously a soldier serving at home is not as likely to contract venereal disease.

Evidence of the drastic lowering of recruiting standards is seen in the number of hopelessly inept men who managed to join the 27th and be transported to Germany. There are men who, in the opinion of their unit officers, cannot possibly be made into soldiers. They are turned back to headquarters and in most cases eventually returned to Canada for discharge. The number of these is also a brigade secret, but in one six-week period this spring between twenty-five and thirty men were returned to Canada by the Highland Battalion of the 27th. . . .

The facts, therefore, dissipate the mystery of the 27th. When the educational standard is dismal, the crime and VD rate high, and the human material lower than average, it is hardly possible for the brigade to be anything except second-class.

The task of building an operational defense force out of this reservoir of human material is one that gnaws at the morale of the officers no less than the other ranks. It is difficult, for instance, to make an artilleryman out of a youth who has never learned simple arithmetic, or a sentry out of someone who can't read the writing on a worksheet. The brigade, therefore, has been saddled with the added task of running a primary school to bring all soldiers up to eighth-grade standard. These classes take four to five hours out of training time each week and are attended by sixteen hundred soldiers out of a total of 5,499 in the brigade. This doesn't mean that the remainder have the requisite education. Classes are compulsory for all men who failed to reach eighth grade in school, but the education officer estimates that "a good many" have one way or another evaded taking the classes.

The teaching is done by junior infantry officers who don't like being schoolteachers so the whole program is more lip-service than learning. The attitude of the men was summed up for me by one of them: "The whole thing is a lotta baloney. If I wanted school I woulda gone when I was a kid. Whad'ya godda know to fire a rifle?"

What Problems in the NATO Brigade?

COLONEL CHARLES P. STACEY

> *The army reaction to Shapiro's piece was shock. Army historian*
> *Colonel C.P. Stacey sent this memo offering suggestions on ways to*
> *counter the bad publicity.*

Military Efficiency, etc.

2. It occurs to me that the most convincing evidence on the efficiency
    of the Brigade, would be *unpublished* reports by British inspecting
    officers or formation commanders, if any such documents exist in
    AHQ files and can be cleared for publication. I have not searched
    the files. . . .

Discipline, etc.

4. Attached is a compilation of cases investigated by 27 Provost De-
    tachment during five months early in the present year. Although
    these statistics include accidents as well as crimes, the totals are
    really not particularly large. The source is the War Diary of the
    Detachment and the records of Provost Marshal, AHQ.

5. I note in a report of a visit by Canadian Army Historical Liaison
    Officer, London, to 27 Cdn Inf Bde in the summer of 1952 the fol-
    lowing reference to 1 Cdn Rifle Bn:

    > 21. Discipline within the unit is good and is evidenced by the
    > bearing and turn-out of unit guards, etc., and the smartness of
    > its men off duty. The Rifles have been particularly fortunate
    > in that many of its officers and N.C.Os. are regular soldiers. A
    > recent examination of the conduct sheets revealed that most of
    > the unit crime was the work of about 50 habitual offenders, and
    > drunkenness accounted for large proportion of the remaining
    > entries.

It may be that HQ 27 Cdn Inf Bde can provide statistics on habitual offenders and the extent to which they are responsible for the crime rate. I understand these have been requested.

Health

6. The V.D. rate is undoubtedly very high, but Mr. Shapiro's comparison with the rate in Canada during the Second World is irrelevant, as indeed he admits.

7. Mr. Shapiro makes no reference whatever to the special circumstances of the Hanover area, and the particular prevalence of prostitution there. However, in the interest of good relations with the German population it might be undesirable to refer to this in an official statement. The availability of cheap liquor is another point perhaps worth mentioning.

Educational Standards

8. Mr. Shapiro says, "The average education of the private soldier in the 27th is between fifth and sixth grade." This is interesting; since no official statistics are available on this point, where did Mr. Shapiro get his? I have obtained the following figures from Org 3. They represent the educational standing of Men in 27 Cdn Inf Bde in the summer of 1952:

Below Grade 8	38.5%
Grade 8	32.3%
Grade 9	13.9%
Grade 10	8.7%
Grade 11	3.6%
Grade 12	2.2%
Grade 13	.4%
University	.2%

There is no break-down of education below Grade 8. These figures seem to indicate that Mr. Shapiro has exaggerated the lowness of the educational standard. But our figures are a year old, and the probability is that the standard in the Brigade today is lower than it was a year ago. Org 3 informs me that of enrollees from September 1951 to April 1952 inclusive 46 per cent had education below Grade 8, while 31 per cent had Grade 8 education.

Keeping the Peace in Suez, UNEF, 1959

CAPTAIN G.R. TOMALIN

Initially Canada was uninterested in United Nations peacekeeping, but after Lester Pearson won the Nobel Peace Prize for his efforts in cobbling together the UN Emergency Force that separated Egypt from its Israeli, British, and French attackers in November 1956, Canadians decided that they had a special aptitude for the endeavour. This letter from an army captain discusses life with UNEF in 1959.

Despite the precautions of UNEF drivers, many goats, sheep and camels are struck and killed. UNEF makes reparations on a sliding scale. A goat, for example, is usually valued at ten Egyptian pounds, a sheep at fifteen pounds, and a camel at twenty or twenty-five. One wise shepherd complained that his goat was worth at least fifteen pounds since it was pregnant. This was allowed. Since that time, only pregnant animals have been involved in accidents.

Black marketing is an ever-present problem and UNEF goods, including Canadian tax-free cigarettes, are to be seen publicly displayed on the streets of Gaza town. Recently the author attended the public court in Gaza town. While there a ragged Arab peddlar passed through the court selling a well-known brand of Canadian cigarettes. Complaints against black marketing seem to be confined to the Egyptian cigarette companies. . . . Egyptian officials consistently refused to prosecute the shopkeepers for selling UNEF goods and materials openly.

Members of UNEF are subject to the exclusive jurisdiction of the national state to which they belong in respect of any offence they commit while in Egypt. . . . The Military Police cells have been used only once in three years. . . .

From time to time the Military Police company is called upon to help with tasks such as tracking down hashish peddlers. Under Egyptian law the sentence for being in possession of, or even being involved in the hashish trade, is life imprisonment. . . .

At Christmas 1958 during the visit of the [UN] secretary-general, the author was assigned as a personal guard. . . . The visit through the refugee-clogged villages of over 216,000 displaced persons was an exciting and arduous task. The crowds of Arabs chanted slogans such as: "Give us back our land. . . ." One curly-headed youth who shouted "Down with Eisenhower" was whisked away by the secret police. . . . The omnipotent police are everywhere and . . . have a surfeit of power.

Governor General Vanier on His Beloved Vandoos

MAJOR-GENERAL GEORGES P. VANIER

> *Vanier was a member of the Royal 22e Regiment, the famed Vandoos, in the Great War and into the 1920s. He became a diplomat and, in 1959, Governor-General of Canada.*

10th July 1959

My dear Brooke,

Your letter, which gave me much pleasure, reached me a few days before our sailing. . . .

Yes, dear Brooke, I was proud—and gave thanks to God for the pride—of the "Vandoos." You see it's forty-five years that I've been associated—sometimes more and sometimes less—with the Regiment. It and my family fill the larger part of my heart. The troops were magnificent—much better than at rehearsal. The presence of their Colonel in Chief gave them a rush of blood to the heart and wings to their feet. It was a great day.

Two hundred years after a certain defeat the sovereign of the same nation which was victorious—she is sovereign also of Canada—came back to the scene of battle and presented colours to a French Canadian Regiment which proclaims a two fold pride—that of its French ancestry and that of its allegiance to the Queen of Canada. Her Majesty's address, the reply of the Officer commanding the parade and all the commands were given in French. Oh defeat, where is thy sting! . . .

    Georges

The World's Most Provincial Animal: Canadian Peacekeepers Abroad, 1962

ANONYMOUS

January 3, 1962

The attitude of GI Canadians over here [in Egypt] is a subject for much discourse. Before filling in the details I might say that the Canadian appears to be the world's most provincial animal. Straight from the farm. Compared to the average Swede, Dane, or even Indian Canadians rank as clots. Closed minds, complete ignorance or even desire to learn or accept another's point of view marks the *average* Canadian. Needless to say I am the epitome of cosmopolitanism. The average European here speaks at least 3 and sometimes more languages.

    Suprisingly enough the mixed contingents got along better with other nationalities than they do their own. I suppose it is much like fighting with your own wife or family. A civilized human would never think of fighting with some one else's family or wife. Even the Canadians have the good grace to accept this and generally get along with everyone else but other Canadians.

    [UN Secretary General] Dag [Hammarskjold]'s death produced a great deal of sincere grief and I am not being too hypocritical to say that I shared it. Whatever else this force may be it does foster the belief that the UN is a working reality and that editorialists are both wrong and foolish to forecast its demise. Gaza HQ is a hodge podge is more than 2 dozen representative countries although not all countries are here officially. Its quite a sight on sunday nights to see Saris, turbans, business suits, fezes etc. A very good feeling. The brotherhood of Man is a possibility although a remote one these days. . . .

April 29, 1962

Greetings from Wogland. I find myself in the midst of intrigue and espionage, belly dancers and secret police etc. In other words I am in Port Said. A very dull place although a vast improvement over Rafah. You are really quite fortunate in your selection of religions. I think you hold onto your faith (for the records only of course) because you realize that it exempts you from service in the Middle East. Very "clifty." Is it difficult to enter the Jewish faith? I am thinking seriously of it.

I am Commander (Dig that!) of the Port Said Garrison. This includes my own Movement Control Detachment, a frozen food storage depot and a 25 man Indian Guard Platoon to keep Jimmy Nasser [president of Egypt] and his 30 million thieves away from the UNEF stores. We handle about 35 thousand tons of freight a year most of it beer and canteen stores. Not a bad job at that. I am my own boss, work my own hours and am free from the multiplicity of chiefs that bugged me in Gaza. I am Senior UN officer in the Port so I am also sort of a mild "big efendi" which does'nt hurt the old ego any.

The Port itself is dull as sand but I play a little tennis, take piano lessons, paint water colours, have considered starting a novel (That's about as far as I will likely get on that one) and am designing a massively complicated tactics game for Canadian Army officers which I will patent and make a million.

The Port used to be one of the main havens for Europeans, shipping agents etc . . . but Nasser's restrictive policies on all non-Egyptians is driving them out en masse. In one way I cannot blame Nasser. The European has lived the "Dolce Vita" in Egypt for a long time. Big money, no taxes and a cost of living that must have been one of the world's cheapest a few years back. However many of these Europeans have lived all their lives in Egypt and now find themselves without a country of their own. Nasser's socialism can't really be called a bad thing but pragmatically it may be ruinous to Egypt. He is driving what administrative and technical assistance the country has away and has nothing to replace it. The US Consul tells me that the USA is feeding about 40% of the country with free food from the States. Nasser's hard currency situation is so severe (reported at about 20 millions) that Egypt pays for all its movie imports (this is virtually the only item that is being imported) with potatoes.

Getting Out of Egypt Ahead of
the Six Day War, May 1967

FLIGHT LIEUTENANT MICHAEL BELCHER

The Canadian contingent in the United Nations Emergency Force in Egypt was ordered out of the country by President Nasser in late May 1967. This account by an RCAF officer at the airfield at El Arish centres on the chaos in the days before the war between Israel and Egypt began.

The Six Day War in the Middle East was less than a week away. The RCAF at 115 ATU El Arish and the Canadian Army at Raffa were given 48 hours to leave Egypt by Col. Nasser, after which we were "persona non grata."

Monday morning, 29 May 67 had, as usual, a beautiful sunrise. The first C-130 from Trenton whistled over our Camp at dawn toward El Arish Airport, eight miles in the desert, to begin shuttling personnel to Pisa, where the Yukons were waiting to take our people to Trenton. As adjutant, all ranks started to ask me if it was okay to go to the airport to see the action taking place there. Little did I know that as soon as they got to the airport they were hustled aboard a C-130 and departed forthwith for Pisa and Trenton. Even my CO (W/C James Fitzsimmons) said he was heading for the airport to meet the first C-130 and that I was to see that the Marina was evacuated in an orderly manner. He told me he would be back by 1000 hours to ensure everything was made ready to abandon the Marina, which had been the home of the RCAF for nearly ten years with UNEF.

I kept myself busy, destroying files, papers, code & cypher books, classified documents, etc. I never realized that as the Canadians poured out, the "Gypos" poured in. The Marina became a bedlam and nightmare. As the buildings became vacant, the house boys and laborers looted them. Fights broke out all over the camp. I saw our Egyptian workers carrying away rations, chairs, tables, and anything that could be moved. The mess hall staff had so much stuff piled in their arms that it kept falling off. I remember seeing a frozen turkey awkwardly juggled like a basketball, being dropped and picked up in an endless cycle. They were merely enacting a typical desert scene—when a camel dies on the Caravan Road, the hyenas are first on the spot and take what they want, and vultures have to wait, but immediately the hyenas withdraw, the vultures rush in, and after this, the disintegration of the carcass is rapid.

I went to the Officers' Mess, where, over the entrance door was a sign reading "Welcome to 1000 B.C.," at about 1100 hours, and although Mess Regs. stated I should not partake of drink before noon, I thought—what the hell! As the temperature was getting into the 90's I may as well enjoy myself, and have a beer. As I approached, I could hear the clatter and loud shouting in Arabic, when I opened the door, the place was choked with our former servants, laborers, house boys, etc.

These people who would have never entered this "Sanctum Sanctorum" under any circumstances, were helping themselves to our "hospitality" bar. The word was out! The Canadians are leaving—fast! and as I said before, according to their laws of survival, everything and everyplace was fair game for looting. A few fled when they saw me, but many stayed, just to defy me. One had our Christmas decorations strung around his neck—my expression was answered!— "they would," he said, "make a nice decoration for his Bedouin wife,"—A Muslim! with Christian symbols? I agreed, but snickered to myself, what would the Israelis think when they saw this walking Christmas tree. That is, if they ever got this far!

Little did I realize, that only five percent of the Egyptian Army was literate, and could handle the sparkling new Russian equipment they were entrusted with. I was always fascinated when I used to watch how the Egyptian mechanics removed MIG-17 Main Spars with a sledgehammer. I always joked with our EO about one sledgehammer is just as good as a whole box of tools.

On the way to the Mess, I wondered—where the hell are all of my buddies? No Canadians in sight—what the hell was going on? Where the hell was the CO? The road outside the gate was clogged with long lines of military traffic. From Cairo came the ponderous T-34 and T-54 Russian tanks, clanking down the only road in the Sinai, and up to Gaza to join the billion dollars worth of equipment already arrayed along our camp perimeter road. Flat cars of confidently waving troops, shouting "Tel Aviv in three days," chugged by.

The grass shack outside our gate which sold souvenirs to new "Pinkies," (new arrivals who sunburned easily), appropriately named "Simpson Sears," had a new sign, "Going out of business." The Egyptian, who was the proprietor, and who could not read English, wondered as well as I what was happening.

I got myself a beer and waited with my entourage of tattered "Gypos," I smiled, and they smiled—we were all having a wonderful time! Just like the "Mad Hatters Tea Party." 1300 hours—and no CO! Where the hell was he? Not a Canadian anywhere in sight on the camp! It was then I realized I was the only one left at this God damn Marina, eight miles from the airport.

The C-130's were still flying overhead, heading for Pisa with happy time expired RCAF personnel on board—and maybe even my CO, who had, I thought, completely forgotten me.

Finally at 1330 hours, the CO burst into the Mess, and wanted to know, what the hell was going on? I said that I was having an early TGIF and do you care to join me, Sir! I mentioned we had a few extra Mess guests, and that I couldn't vouch for their conduct!

After several beers, suddenly the electric power was shut off. The CO instructed me to go and check the power house, and get the power on. "Christ," I was never in the power house in my life.

I made my way towards the power shack, watching beds being thrown out second story windows, looting and screaming, it was a shambles. The Egyptians were everywhere, picking the bones of our once spotless little camp clean.

The power house contained two large diesels, the operators were having a discussion, chattering in Arabic, and when I ordered them to turn the generators on, they replied "you turn them on," to which I made a 180° and headed back to the Mess.

Things were getting a little hot and the natives, not being used to alcoholic drinks, were really getting restless. The CO and I realized at once, that although we were supposed to stay till 1630 hours—remaining any longer would only have been foolhardy, so with my one suitcase, and the clothes on my back, we headed for the airport. It was like a grade "B" movie, the CO driving like a lunatic, I had all my nails bit down to the quick before the first mile. The name of the game was blow the horn and step on the gas! Half way there, an Egyptian MP waved us to stop. The CO told me to hold on, and we flew off the road and over a sand dune, I thought I was back with "Lawrence of Arabia." On the other side was a large Russian T54 tank manned by an Egyptian crew, who had lost control and ran over one of their scout cars, the two occupants were squashed like "bugs in a rug."

We finally got to the airport, and there, waiting for us was one of our Caribou's, flown by F/O Reb Edgar, and, I believe, F/O Dave Lamb. The starboard engine was shut down, but the port was still running. They had been waiting for us for at least an hour, and didn't know if we would ever "show" or not!

As we drove up and stopped under the starboard wing, the CO took the keys from our white UN staff car and threw them into the desert. We were airborne in minutes. As we flew over the Marina at about 50 feet, the CO in the right seat called me forward, and said with a smile, "I just looked down at our Headquarters building, and 'YOU' forgot to lower the ensign!"

Keeping Peace in a Troubled Cyprus, 1975

ROBERT BURNS

> *Canadian troops went to Cyprus in 1964 and remained there for almost 30 years. Ordinarily the duty was boring, but at times, as in 1974, tensions exploded between Turkey and Greece over the future of the island.*

In December 1974, my unit, 1st Battalion, Royal Canadian Regiment, was sent on its third, six-month tour to the troubled island. Very quickly, we found ourselves in the heat of the problem, manning the infamous buffer zone between the Turks and Greeks. We were located in the heart of Nicosia where the Green Line followed a typical European style street not much more than 30 feet wide.

Both sides had strongpoints, mainly sandbagged bunkers with firing slits. These defensive positions looked like ancient fortifications. Occasionally we would see an armed sentry. The Turks seemed to be more serious, but both sides would usually respond to us with a wave or a salute.

My time in Cyprus proved to me that soldiering can indeed be described as long periods of boredom followed by short periods of intense activity and excitement. During January and February 1975, my battalion experienced several serious incidents that involved the exchange of gunfire between the opposing sides. It was very obvious that the events of the previous summer were still fresh in the minds of people on both sides. Clearly, the Greek Cypriots were not happy about the loss of the northern part of the island.

I was employed as company operations officer of B Company, and on the night of March 31, 1975, I was duty officer in the company command post situated in an old British army barracks, called Wolseley Barracks, just outside the ancient walls of Nicosia. The battalion headquarters and the rest of B Co. were located in the same area. East of the barracks was the Ledra Palace Hotel which in its former glory had been a five-star hotel. I use the term former because from 1974 onward it was to become a barracks for the Canadian contingent.

Although the hotel was a rather solidly constructed concrete building, it was located between two armed and hostile forces and had collected its share of bullet holes, some of a rather large calibre. Roughly 300 metres north of Wolseley Barracks and less than 10 metres south of the Turkish forward defence line was a modern-style house. The house, which was nicknamed the Casa, was the temporary home of B Company's officers.

The duty officer was responsible for manning the company operations centre, ensuring that information to and from the observation posts was maintained and that any and all situations were properly actioned. This wasn't a difficult task when it was calm, and quite often it presented the opportunity to get caught up on letters home. That is exactly what I was doing on the night of March 31. In fact, I remember I had just closed my letter to my wife with the remarks that all was quiet and that I was going to turn in early.

I went to bed and it seemed like I had only closed my eyes when I was jarred by the sound of heavy machine-gunfire coming from somewhere not far from my location. This was soon followed by shooting across our entire company sector.

By the time my feet hit the floor, the phones and radios were blaring away and it seemed all hell had broken loose. One of my first callers was my company commander demanding to know what was going on. I couldn't tell him much except that I was sending out the duty driver with the standby section to bring in the company officers from the Casa. The company commander arrived a short time later and quickly took charge by sending the platoon commanders down the Green Line in their jeeps. He followed shortly after in his own vehicle and left me to man the communication nets in the command post.

The company commander and I were roughly the same vintage, but had come from two different regiments to meet in the RCR. I had not served with him before, but we thought and acted in much the same manner. I must admit that I was not envious of his job that night; travelling down the narrow streets of the Green Line between two opposing sides intent on killing each other. And all the while making the journey in an open jeep, with headlights on and the UN flag fully illuminated, and announcing over a loud hailer that they were to stop shooting.

Although I was kept busy talking to people at our observation posts and trying to make contact with the local Turk and Greek headquarters, I was very grateful to be in the command post behind very thick stone walls. However, my personal situation changed rapidly once I received a call from the company commander who ordered me to pass over control of the communications to the operations warrant officer and proceed immediately to the Casa. It had been reported that firing was coming from the area of the Casa and I was to determine if it was occupied and where the fire was originating from. All of a sudden this battle took on a very personal aspect.

The duty driver had been standing by with a jeep and so he and I drove off to find out what was happening. The Casa was only 300 yards down the road from the barracks, but it was between the opposing forces.

It was around 1 A.M. and dark, but the street lights were still on. In fact, every light was on in the Casa, just as my fellow officers had left them. As soon as the jeep pulled up to the front door, I ordered the driver to get out and take cover in the Casa. I ran into the same building and turned off the lights as I proceeded to the second-floor balcony at the back of the house.

A sandbagged, unmanned observation point on the balcony afforded a view north into the Turkish held area. My plan was to try to determine where the small arms fire was coming from, but all was quiet immediately to my front for a few moments until I heard a loud snap. My first thought was that someone had thrown a grenade because the snap reminded me of the noise that comes from a 36-Grenade, once the firing lever flies free. I ducked behind the sandbagged wall and started to count. One, two, three. . . . Nothing happened so I stuck my helmeted head up again and heard another snap. I repeated the same movement, but by the time I reached the count of three, it became obvious that someone was shooting at me.

Just then a machine-gun opened up from the northwest, immediately in front of our other company area. With this information, the driver and I beat a hasty retreat back to the jeep. The news was passed on to my company commander who then ordered me to check out the Greek Cypriot positions just south of the Ledra Palace Hotel. It seemed that I was not going to get back to the safety of the command post quite as soon as I had hoped to.

While driving up Shakespeare Avenue—the main north-south street in front of Wolseley Barracks—I spotted someone lurking behind a stone pillar that marked the entrance to the Ledra Palace Hotel parking lot. I ordered the driver to stop and immediately recognized the person to be our unit padre who was waiting for an opportunity to cross the street to get to the battalion operations centre.

The padre told me that there was shooting down the street, but I insisted it was safe to cross the road since we were stopped in the middle of it and hadn't been shot yet.

This explanation must have sounded convincing because the padre very quickly darted behind our jeep and then ran into the operations centre. The driver and I both laughed at this and then made some disparaging remarks about prayer merchants. However, both of us soon changed our opinion when we noticed the leaves and branches lying on the ground in the hotel parking lot, and then started hearing those damn snapping sounds again.

We soon spotted muzzle flashes coming from the rear of an old house immediately south of us. I knew this was a Greek Cypriot National Guard position and we had earlier suspected it was a platoon headquarters location.

After telling the operations centre what we had observed, I instructed my driver to stop in front of the house. It was my intention to do whatever I could to have the occupants stop shooting. I knocked loudly on the huge front door and almost immediately it was opened just a crack, allowing me to see the biggest set of eyeballs I have ever seen.

In my best parade square voice, I told the eyeballs that I was a UN officer and that their command had issued a ceasefire order and they were to stop shooting immediately. I pushed the door wide open and was confronted with about 20 very young, very scared Greek Cypriot soldiers led by an equally frightened second lieutenant. All the soldiers were seated on the floor of a long hallway with their backs against the walls and holding their weapons between their knees. After a short pause I ordered all of them, rather forcefully, to stand to attention and clear their weapons. I then inspected their guns and told them to remove the magazines.

I repeated my explanation that their headquarters had ordered a ceasefire. The young Greek Cypriot officer responded by giving me his solemn promise to keep his men on the floor until someone from his headquarters arrived to give him further instructions.

It was only after we got back to our operations centre that my driver asked me when I had received word about a ceasefire because he had been listening to the vehicle's radio all the time and had heard nothing to that effect. I had to admit that I had pulled a bluff and it worked. However, I knew that our battalion headquarters had been working towards that end as a standard operating procedure.

At War in the Gulf, January 1991

LIEUTENANT (N) RICHARD GIMBLETT

In the summer of 1990, Canada dispatched a naval task force to the Gulf as a response to Iraq's invasion of Kuwait. The navy was in disrepair and had to scramble to find crews and ships. Gimblett was aboard HMCS Protecteur *as combat officer, part of a new crew flown in from Halifax on New Year's Day. These letters were written to his family in Halifax.*

Jan 9 / 91
Dubai, UAE

My dear girls,

Just another quick note before I head off to bed. I intend to call you again in the morning, so this will help me collect my thoughts.

Another little gift for you [Muriel] is enclosed. I hope it will make an acceptable Valentine Birthday present until I get home and can give you something in person. Hopefully this will all be over soon and it won't be as long as we had planned.

Things are going quite well. My people are really coming together quickly and I have even fewer hesitations as regards our abilities. Sea Training and Workups will not be easy, however, and the next two weeks will be tiring. Saw J.Y. [Forcier, Chief of Staff for Operations to Commodore Summers in the CF Joint Headquarters in Bahrain]. I wouldn't want to be where he is—thank God to be at sea. Not nearly as stressful.

I must get to bed now—I'm very tired. . . . If I don't get a chance to write any more in this letter, do take care of yourselves, know that I love you very, very much, and that you are always in my thoughts. Can't wait to be with you again.

Jan 28 / 91
At Sea

My dearest Muriel Anne,

Just got the news that a helo is going ashore to Sharjah at noon and that mail will close at 10:00 to go on it, so I'll take a quick minute to remind you how much I love you. Rather appropriate that I should be writing now—it's 08:00 and I've just come off the Long Mids; my "long sleep" (4 hours) is in the evening, and this is my "short sleep" coming up. I find I'm out solid for the long one, but dream during the short, and invariably my dreams are of you, my dear, as I am sure you can well imagine. . . .

I found Dubai this time around to actually be somewhat friendlier, what with all of the Americans and Brits being out of town [*Protecteur* returned regularly to Dubai about every 10–12 days to pick up fresh stores to pass to the destroyers which remained at sea]. I really only got ashore to call you the one morning (your time), but I finally did get my stamps. Haven't started the carpet search, but hopefully end-February will be quiet enough that we can get in for more than just 2 days, and I can get a full day off to go up to Sharjah, which is, as you recall we were told in Toronto, reputedly the carpet-smuggling capital. There are several others who want to go, so I won't be wandering the bazaars alone.

Just a few unconnected thoughts to close: mail is really irregular and the papers have dried up. Can we re-activate the plan to send me the interesting portions of the Friday & Saturday *Globe*? We get *Maclean's* but my *Saturday Night*, when you are done, would be appreciated. *Slow Boats to China* is going slowly. That reminds me—if you get a chance to pass by Nautica or any used bookstore, can you try to dig up a copy of *The Sinbad Voyage* by Tim Severin to mail out? . . .

While I was thinking of it, I just took time out to write to Meaghan. I sure miss my girls, almost as much as I miss you. You will always be first in my heart, but they each have their special place too. I hope Meg is being a good help. . . . She must be terribly cute in her ballet outfit. Sounds like little Beth is growing so fast, too. Do send lots of pictures so I don't miss too much; a video would be great. I'll bring them all home, promise.

More random thoughts: during a RAS [replenishment at sea] yesterday we went within a mile of *Missouri* and *Wisconsin*, two [USN] battleships (with 16-inch guns and lots of Tomahawks) at anchor. A lot of impressive naval hardware around the Gulf. Before this letter gets to you, I hope they will have had a chance to use it some more. Immediately after that, we RAS'd the USNS *Mercy*, a hospital ship; her first ever RAS at sea, it went well. 1200 medical staff on board, but only 7 patients to date. They are very bored. Hope they stay that way. We've been incredibly busy: in the past 9 days (2 of them alongside in Dubai) we have RAS'd 21 ships from 7 different countries. The Argies [Argentinians] are our most frequent customers, because the Brits refuse to give them gas. Coalition warfare is such a lovely concept.

Alas, I must sign off because the mailman is knocking. . . . Please keep thinking loving thoughts of me, as I do of you, til we are together again.

Jan 31 / 91

Just heard a helo is coming in a half-hour, so just a short time to tell you how much I love you. . . .

I was going to write a proper letter on watch tonight because it looks like it will be quiet, but not knowing when the mail will go, I have to seize the opportunity to get a letter off. I think you should be getting them at regular intervals.

Not much new in the war, in fact a lot of "same shit, different day." Good news—Iraq's surface navy (for all it was worth) has been just about destroyed, and their better aircraft are being effectively neutralized by internment in Iran. Just hope we don't have to come back in 5 years to clean them out in Round 2. Bad news—the oil slick & burning wells in the north of the Gulf. The slick is still a ways off, & should break up by the time it gets here [in the southern Gulf], but the haze is darker and thicker than it was a week ago. . . .

Have to go now. You (and the girls) are in my thoughts constantly

The Canadian Airborne Regiment in Somalia, 1993

ROBERT PROUSE

> *Robert Prouse served in the army for ten years and was in 3 Commando in Somalia. He was on leave when the torture and killing of a Somali youth occurred, but his journal of events before and after the murder reflects the troubles faced by and within the Canadian Airborne Regiment.*

9 January 93

The fever hit last night during the patrol. I wandered dazed through the shadows of town like in a half dream. Most of the time the pistol in my hand hung limply by my side instead of chasing movements in the shadows. Hallucinations haunted me like some surreal drug trip and my mind reeled at the horror that surrounds me.

Last night after the patrol, as we were going to ground, two para-flares went up and we stood-to. 20 men had been advancing on 32's position, but the light of the flares scared them away. Then this morning during stand-to, five shots were fired in rapid succession across the field from us. It is such a common occurrence now, nobody even really took notice.

After stand-to this morning, still in fever, I passed out in my trench for a few hours. The rest did me good, it is the most I've had in awhile.

Most of the refugees live in small huts made with sticks and covered with animal hides or sheets of plastic. They cook and sleep outside. The huts are surrounded by a fence made of thistle bushes like the ones we have erected around our perimeter in place of barbed wire. These fences are used to pen in their few goats, donkeys or sheep.

The farmers on the outskirts of town live in a more typical African hut made of interwoven sticks with a thatched roof. These are then sometimes plastered with mud or dung.

In town, the people live in the few remaining buildings, in the many ruins, in small shanties built up against the sides of walls, or just in the street. The whole town is littered with feces, garbage and the carcasses of dead animals. The stench of death and disease is overpowering at times, forcing you to gag.

The only sources of water in the town are the well and the muddy river water. Both are contaminated and a long walk for most of the people.

The temperature is well over 50° C (120° F) today and there is little wind. The sweat evaporates as fast as I produce it, yet everything I touch is soaked. My body is stained with the salt I sweat out, my head hurts from dehydration, we crawl into the shade and move as little as possible. It has been abnormally hot the past few days, too hot to sleep on this quiet afternoon. So instead I washed my underwear and socks with the bit of extra water we have been given and stripped down to my shorts to air out my tired body.

Tonight, after the sun goes down, we will fill sandbags to re-enforce our position. I only have one, two hour shift tonight. Maybe I can sleep for once.

11 January 93

What a rough couple of days. The *"cold"* led to heat exhaustion and I felt like I would die. I had all the symptoms, headache, exhaustion, dizziness, muscle cramps, nausea, diarrhea, loss of appetite and hot and cold spells. I'm staying in the shade for the entire day today, if I can, and am starting to feel better.

Jacob is going back to Canada. He was returned to his platoon, but he soon lost it again, so they are taking no more chances. [One man] is another stress casualty. He got married just before he came over to a woman he'd only known a few weeks. He is now having marital problems and stress has taken its toll. We also have many heat and diarrhea related casualties, but most of us are staying in the field.

One of the Somali kids snuck past the thorn barriers and stole Lt Webb's carry on bag with his CD player. We got the bag back and a couple of the things in it, but the CD player is missing. Womack's wallet has also been stolen. $100 and credit cards also missing. People are starting to get pissed off at the kids. Someone has already shot a Somali who came at him with a knife. It won't be the last as tensions are rising between us and the villagers.

12 January 93

Whatever I have, it won't leave me alone. The diarrhea has gotten severe and is quickly draining me of energy. I am losing fluids faster than I can replace them, it is keeping me up all night and I still can't eat. I'm exhausted. I am barely strong enough to walk to the latrine, having to sit and rest numerous times on the trip. Usually I have to turn around and head back again before I even get back to my trench. Often I don't make it and am living in my own filth. The medics gave me pills to slow up the shits. If it hasn't gone away by tomorrow they will evacuate me to the med-station. It is one in the afternoon, I have taken all the pills the medics gave me and it has not helped one bit. I've already shit myself three times. I'm miserable.

13 January 93

I have lost a noticeable amount of weight in the past few days. My fingers are so much smaller that my once tight ring falls right off and the flab on my stomach is gone. The medics think I have dysentery. I don't even really know what that is or how bad it is. Maybe I'll find out more tomorrow. I have been going to the washroom less frequently today, but the cramps have been bad. I still have no appetite even though I am wasting away. The pills did some measure of good in that they reduced the frequency of my shits enough that I could get a few hours of sleep last night. The sleep did me good and I feel a bit better today. The main difference is that I am not so weak which in itself is a world of difference. . . .

Okerlund had a bag stolen from his trench today. He lost his camcorder, tapes, beret, passport, camera, etc. All that has been returned so far is his passport.

An old man brought his sick young child to us the other day. The child has TB, but there is nothing any of us can do. The child will be dead soon.

News from this evening's O'group: C/S 8 is no longer allowed to have mags on their weapons because they've had so many accidental discharges. A few days ago an RCD officer shot himself in the arm while cleaning his pistol. A marine was killed in an ambush in Mogadishu today or yesterday. Also we have been informed that the bandits have moved back into Beled Weyne.

14 January 93

We are moving to the main camp this morning, filling in nearly all of our trenches and only leaving one platoon to secure the airstrip.

There was a great deal of gunfire in the village all through the night. Maybe they are right about the return of the bandits. I wonder what it could mean for us.

17 February 93

We headed out on patrol early this morning exploring the many small villages in the hilly region east of the highway. I am standing in for Tim on the radio so I get to ride in the crew commanders hatch.

I saw a strange animal today. It was grey with black spots like a hyena, but had the body of a large cat. It passed fairly close, but I did not get a good look at it as it disappeared in an instant.

We spent most of the afternoon resting in the shade as I talked to the interpreter about Somalia. He argued strongly in favour of female circumcision, the oppression of women and about how every other race was inferior to the Somalis. Most of his arguments were just based on a "because that's the way it is," but occasionally he would venture further and state that women have a sexual power over men that must be repressed and that women's sex drives are so high that circumcision is the only way they can remain faithful. We are both so far apart in our beliefs that in the end we just had to agree to disagree.

. . . Shots rang out in the dark, somewhere a grenade went off. The radios sparked to life as reports went out and people tried to find out what was going on. In the dark street, illuminated only by the searchlights on our carriers, the crowds surrounding us were close, much too close.

We had been setting up a roadblock on the Mogadishu highway to search for weapons when the call came over the radio. Things were turning violent in Beled Weyne and Two Commando needed some help. There have been many fatalities and demonstrations over the past few days, things are heating up. Soon we found ourselves in the market, trying to set up a position on one of the two bridges in Beled Weyne. As darkness fell, we moved back the crowds, laid concertina wire to our flanks and began to picket the bridge. Earlier the crowds had turned on some of the troops. The result was one Somali killed and three others wounded. We did not expect the night to pass without incident.

Out of the dark and the crowds came the rocks. They winged off our carriers, helmets and flak jackets. We responded quickly and decisively, moving the crowds back and singling out the culprits. Speed and discipline won out over violence, apparently they didn't want to tempt fate as they had earlier in the day. Then came the shots and the grenade blast. The radios buzzed as everyone tried to piece together what was going on. With a shot report from one callsign and a sighting from another, eventually the pieces began to fall into place. For once the violence wasn't directed at us. It turned out to be a failed attack on the Red Cross compound nearby. Luckily no-one was injured and the situation ended as quickly as it had started.

We settled down to wait out the night, peering into the darkness and the crowd. We watched for the kid with the grenade instead of a rock, or the sniper in the shadows. You never know when it will happen. You must always be on guard. . . .

Later, a local police constable came to us for help. Fifteen armed bandits were robbing stores on the main street and the police were powerless to do anything. We sent out a small patrol to assist, backed by the carriers of another callsign. The bandits heard the carriers coming though and fled. We didn't capture any of them, but at least they were stopped.

Eventually the crowds drifted away and we were able to spell each other off. I curled up in the filth at the edge of the street with the asses and dogs, pistol in hand, and slept.

7 March 93

Our open fire policies and rules for confiscating weapons have changed again, very effectively tying our hands. We are no longer allowed to shoot people breaching our wire unless they have a weapon or are stealing weapons, ammunition or communications equipment. This is crazy, at night, all you know is that the person breaking into your compound *may* have a grenade or weapon and *could* do you harm. At night you cannot see well enough to make subtle distinctions.

This is all because the media is blowing the killing of the Somali all out of proportion. Once again we are letting our policies be set by public opinion which is shaped by the media coverage and slant they decide to put on the news.

As for weapons confiscation, the sweep of Beled Weyne has been called off. We are no longer allowed to confiscate weapons we find during the day. At night we can confiscate weapons at the platoon commander's discretion (which is questionable). Now the bandits will adapt again and start moving in the day. Just the other day bandits shot up a relief convoy killing five people and injuring a score of others. What good are we doing?

They tell us in O-groups that they know where the bandits are, but the intelligence is never acted upon. It is as if higher is just doing their time here and is afraid of actually committing their troops for fear someone may get hurt. That would be a bad career move. They would rather pretend the problems are solved and ignore the evidence to the contrary. Coalition troops are dying, will their deaths be meaningless?

427 Squadron has been arriving over the past couple of days. Hopefully they will be used to give us the mobility we need to chase

down the bandits, instead of just to get some flyboys another medal.

We have firm word on redeployment now. The first troops will be leaving on the 15th of May with the last troops out by the end of June. The longer the better.

9 March 93

We were relieved from garrison duty at six this morning and were out on patrol by seven. It was an extremely boring day, two five kilometer sweeps for weapons caches along the river. It ended up being a hot walk in Somalia. We did see some interesting things though. Three boys were copying the Koran onto long planks shaped like tombstones, two large 4 foot long lizards swam in the river (possibly camens), vultures standing over 4 feet high and large cranes almost as big that left footprints about 6 inches long.

In the afternoon we came across a tunnel dug in the side of a bank. We thought that it might contain weapons, so Daren grabbed my pistol and a flashlight and crawled in like a tunnel rat. He came backing out swearing as quickly as he went in, it was a porcupine den. The 13 inch long quills around the hole attested to its size, but no-one else was willing to go in and look for themselves.

We returned to camp before dinner to find more beer in the canteen. Happy day.

Orders tonight were interesting. All sweeps have been called off because coalition forces in other sectors are not keeping up with disarmament, leaving the people in our area open to bandits raiding from other areas. Bandit activity is on the rise on the border of the Italian sector. We are also allowed to confiscate weapons again.

12 March 93

The last couple of days have been busy. I have been taking the classroom portion of a scuba course which I will finish on R & R in Mombasa. I'm really enjoying the course and may take the advanced and rescue courses next month. It is rather strange though, sitting in the middle of the desert, without water in sight, learning to scuba dive. . . .

Last night we went on an all night patrol with full blackout drive.

We patrolled the eastern part of our sector down to Yesouman returning to camp at close to 3 A.M.

13 March 93

I spent most of yesterday catching up on my sleep and writing letters.
The days are becoming unbearably hot. The average temperature is
over 50 degrees celsius in the shade, Ugh!

   In the past couple of days we have killed two camel spiders in our
tent. They are huge beasts, the colour of sand and the size of my hand.
It makes me nervous sleeping with them running around.

   We guarded 1 commando's compound last night then took over
garrison duty here this morning. I am on canteen duty again. Once
again I am running on 4 hours of sleep and will get the same tonight.
I'm on empty and getting lower. I spend the day reading *Old Path
White Cloud* about the life of Buhdda. It is a great book, a nice change.

   This evening as the sun set, the camp filled with birds like starlings
flying all around our heads. What beauty, these birds filling the orange
sunset sky. . . .

The Killing of Shidane Arone, Somalia, 1993

COURT MARTIAL TESTIMONY

> *The murder under torture of Shidane Arone led to court martials
> and to the Somalia Inquiry. In the process, amidst charges of brutal-
> ity, racism, and cover-up, the Canadian army came perilously close
> to losing the support of the government and the people of Canada.
> This excerpt from a court martial suggests why.*

Testimony of Master Warrant Officer Mills:

Q. Now, when you saw the photograph, you immediately formed the
   opinion that the prisoner had been beaten, is that correct?

A. Yes, sir.

Q. And you related this in no uncertain terms to Major Seward, is that
   correct?

A. Yes, sir.

Q. And this wasn't the prisoner . . . it wasn't the condition the prisoner had been in the night before when you observed him in the bunker?

A. To the best of my of my knowledge, that's correct, sir.

Q. If and when you saw him in the bunker the night before he had any of those injuries that you saw on the photograph, would you have reported it to Major Seward?

A. I believe I would have. Yes, sir.

Q. And you would have gotten that prisoner medical attention, isn't that correct?

A. I certainly would have, sir.

Q. In fact when you went back to the compound, you felt so strongly about this that you raised the issue again with Major Seward at 1100 hours approximately, is that correct?

A. That's correct, sir.

Q. In fact subsequent to that, you raised it again at about 1245, isn't that correct?

A. I believe I brought it up again, I think so, sir.

Q. And would you say that you put your position forcedly to Major Seward during all those times that you . . . ?

A. I told him what my opinion was. Yes, sir.

Q. And your opinion was that the prisoner had been beaten and that he had died as a result of the beating?

A. I told him that's what I thought. Yes, sir.

Q. And this would be on the 17th of March 1993?

A. Yes, sir.

Testimony of Sergeant Hillier:

Q. OK, all right, can you describe what happened to you at the gate?

A. At the 2 Commando gate, sir?

Q. Yes, please.

A. OK, just as we're . . . myself and MacGillivray we were going to come into the gate, Trooper Glass, who was the sentry on duty at the time, he recognized me and he called me over to the weapon's pit. I could tell something was bothering him because of the tone of his voice. He told me to look in the pit. I took my flashlight, again it was a white light. I shined it into the pit and I seen the prisoner.

Q. And what was the prisoner's condition?

A. He was facing the entrance into the pit. His hands were still secured behind his back. His jacket or shirt there had been used as a blindfold. From basically the cheek bones down to his chin was covered in bright red blood. He was breathing at the time forcibly, real labouriously. The body was physically . . . he was rocking against the side of the pit. I asked who was responsible and Trooper Glass told me.

Q. As a result of that. . . .

A. I then went into the CP. Warrant Murphy was on duty. I asked him if he was aware of the condition of the prisoner in the pit. He looked at me surprised and he told me that he didn't even know that there was a prisoner there. I informed him there was and he was in a pretty bad shape. I then left the CP and I went to the 4 Platoon weapon's section tent. I went in it and I told Master Corporal Matchee to get out to the weapon's pit and clean up the prisoner and he did. I then left the weapon's section tent and I made my way to the platoon commander's tent. I woke up Captain Sox. First, I had informed him that patrol was back in and after I told him that I then asked him if he had seen the prisoner lately and he said "No." I said, "Well . . ." I said, "Maybe you should, sir, because he is up in the pit and he is in a pretty bad shape." I then left the platoon commander's tent and I was making my way back towards the CP when roughly in line with the same tent where I had received the orders, the TV tent, if you want to call it . . . I was intercepted by Master Corporal Matchee. He told me . . .

Q. Without indicating the words . . .?

A. OK. I told him to go back to his tent and I would talk to him later. I got a little bit further towards the CP and I was intercepted by Trooper Brown. He came up to me and he asked me if he could talk to me and I . . . first I brushed him off. I told him I was pretty busy. I didn't have time to talk to him. He said it was very important. I said, "All right Brown . . ." Brown told me what he had to tell me. I told him to go back to his tent and wait and I would talk to him later. I then went into the CP. I started to fill out a patrol report which was an SOP within the Commando. A commander, regardless at what level, after a tasking or a patrol upon the completion of it, he would fill out a report whether it be a patrol report or whatever type of report it was on the tasking that you had carried out. I did that in the CP. Just as I was completing my report, Sergeant Skipton came up to the side of the CP. He said, "Joe, can I talk to you for a minute." . . .

Anyways, he told me what he had to tell me. At that point Trooper Glass yelled up from the pit. We went down to the pit. I got into the pit. The prisoner wasn't breathing. He didn't appear to be breathing. I started feeling for a pulse. I couldn't find one. I was checking the area of the . . . up in the shoulder, the collar bone up by the neck there, whatever that artery is called. I couldn't check . . . the pulse in the wrist because his hands were still secured behind his back.

At that point Sergeant Skipton, he went to wake Captain Sox, to get Captain Sox up at the pit and also to try to get medical attention over to 2 Commando. Trooper Glass, he was pretty upset. I had to get his mind off of what was going on. I told him to go in the CP and see if he could find a blanket. I said maybe the prisoner is in a shock. He is just cold from being in a shock. He went to the CP trying to find a blanket or something. . . . I couldn't find a pulse.

I took my compass out of my pocket. I opened up the mirror portion. I held it up close, not right against, but up close to the prisoner's nose and mouth area. I held it there for a good minute. I pulled it away and it wasn't fogged up. Also upon taking a look I could smell, the prisoner's bowels had released. His legs were all fouled. I was pretty sure at that point that the prisoner had passed away. I was moving his head around and I am still hanging on him where the arteries are up here in the neck area and I felt a pulse or something.

At that point, Sergeant Skipton and Captain Sox were approaching the pit and I hollered out of the pit, "I think I might have a weak pulse here" or words to that effect. Anyways, we got the 5/4 [a truck]. . . . Sergeant Skipton got a 5/4. We started to move the prisoner out of the pit. At that point we discovered his hands weren't plasticuffed anymore. The plasticuffs had been replaced with metal handcuffs. The key was available in the weapon's pit there. We took the handcuffs off the prisoner.

Sergeant Skipton grabbed his upper body. I grabbed his legs. We put him into the back of the 5/4. I got in the back of the 5/4 with the prisoner. Sergeant Skipton drove . . . us over to call-sign 8 to the field hospital. We took the body inside. We put him up on the table. There was a medic there. The medic started to dress the body, clean the body, whatever you want to call it and at that point, Captain Gibson, the MO, came in with Major Seward and Captain Sox. At that point we weren't needed anymore so myself and Sergeant Skipton made our way back to 2 Commando lines. Captain Sox came back and he asked us who was responsible. . . .

Q. As a result of that, what did you do?

A. As a result of that, Trooper Brown and Master Corporal Matchee were brought forward. Sergeant Skipton went and got them. Captain Sox talked to them. He talked to them, himself to them. I don't know what was said and then shortly after that Sergeant Skipton, Trooper Glass, Master Corporal Matchee, Trooper Brown, they picked up the body from the field hospital in an MLVW and took it downtown to the civilian hospital in Belet Huen where it was, I guess, given to his relatives.

Testimony of Acting Sergeant Skipton:

Q. OK, after you secured the detainee in the bunker what did you do then?

A. After that I asked if the patrol was going to end there or carry on and I was told that the patrol would carry on until approximately 2400 where I moved back out to the observation point and remained there until 2400.

Q. OK. At 2400 hours what did you do at that time?

A. At 2400 hours we were contacted by radio and told to stand down the patrol. I then cleaned up the position where the wire had been opened, closed the wire and moved back to the bunker position, sir.

Q. When you arrived back at the bunker, can you describe what you did, what you saw?

A. When I arrived at the bunker, Trooper Glass was there as well as Master Corporal Matchee. I looked at the prisoner. I noticed that the plasticuffs had been replaced on his ankles. They looked tight this time from swelling. I moved into the bunker to cut off the plasticuffs. I had to be a little rough when I did that and there was no squirming that I assumed would accompany that. I looked back to see if there was a rise and fall of the chest. I found none. So I checked for a pulse, did not find a pulse. I also had two other people check for a pulse, sir.

Q. OK. At this time did you have an occasion to have a conversation with Master Corporal Matchee?

A. I did not have an actual conversation with him but he had made a couple of comments.

Q. And could you describe for the court what those comments were?

A. The first comment was, "Look at his feet, I think we broke some bones." And the second comment was, "We've got some great pictures."

Q. And can you describe the tone that he used when he made these comments to you?

A. He seemed almost pleased with himself when he said that, sir.

Q. After you examined the prisoner, what did you do then?

A. I then decided to go and get the platoon commander. As I walked past the CP I noticed Sergeant Hillier was in there filling out a patrol report. I went in and had three or four words with him and then I told him I was going to get the platoon commander and that's where I went next to wake up the platoon commander.

Q. And what did you say to him when you woke him up?

A. I told him that I think that they beat him and I think they killed the prisoner.

Q. And following that meeting where did you go?

A. Following that I went back out to the bunker. At that time Sergeant Hillier was in with the prisoner and he stated that he may have found a pulse.

Q. OK. What happened from that point on?

A. From there we elected to take him over to the MIR (Medical Inspection Room) which was at call-sign 8. So I moved the truck over and we moved over to call-sign 8.

Q. OK. And once you arrived at call-sign 8 what happened after that?

A. Once we arrived to call-sign 8 he was taken out of the back of the

truck and put in an examination room and I moved outside after
that so I didn't really see what went on inside.

Squaring Off with Serbian Forces in Croatia, 1993

SERGEANT PAUL GÉLINAS

> *Yugoslavia fractured into mutually hostile countries after the end of
> the Cold War, and the UN sent in UNPROFOR, its Protection
> Force, in which Canadian troops served. This incident is recounted
> by a reservist serving with the 2nd Battalion of the Princess Patri-
> cia's Canadian Light Infantry.*

There are many incidents that occur during a United Nations peacekeeping tour that go by unreported. One such event happened in 1993
when our platoon-size UN patrol arrived in the village of Okucani,
roughly 120 kilometres southeast of Zagreb, Croatia. At the time, I was
a sergeant in the reserves, serving with 2nd Battalion, Princess Patricia's Canadian Light Infantry.

It was May 28th and extremely hot; there was no wind and the sun
was blazing down on us without mercy. We were heading north—en
route to our camp at Daruvar—when our young platoon commander
decided we should stop in the village for a short break. Little did we
know how close we would come that afternoon to being involved in a
violent situation that could have ended in bloodshed.

One of my main responsibilities in Croatia was company transport.
The job involved assisting with the control and use of all company
vehicles and their maintenance. This included the task of making sure
we had a steady supply of fuel and oil. My second major job involved
the more dangerous side of peacekeeping. It had me commanding a
pioneer section comprised of six highly trained men from across
Canada. Two of them were infantry and four were engineers. Our task
was to destroy arms caches, mines and other weapons of war found by
us or by other infantry platoons in the company.

Each platoon was ordered to search specific areas within no-man's
land for hidden weapons and other ammunition, and it was while

returning to camp from one of these missions that our patrol encountered the trouble in Okucani. In fact, we had just finished our tasking south of the village, in an area characterized by rolling hills, small hamlets and farms.

Our small convoy was comprised of four armoured personnel carriers, an armoured personnel carrier ambulance and a 2½-ton truck. I was the lone passenger in the truck's cab. The back of the vehicle, which was covered with a tarp, contained four engineers and a private as well as an assortment of explosives—minus their detonators—and other items needed to destroy any unauthorized ordnance found by the platoon.

Within minutes of stopping in the village, several civilians appeared from their homes and began surrounding our vehicles. At first we thought they were just coming out to look at the carriers and perhaps ask for goodies. There were several children as well as women and old people. Everyone seemed quite friendly, and some of the kids enjoyed climbing on our vehicles, but when we tried to move forward after saying goodbye, the crowd didn't move. We decided to stay put because the risk of running over somebody was too great.

The crowd successfully detained us until about 30 Serb soldiers arrived. They, too, seemed friendly until they parked civilian cars in front and behind our convoy and told us there were snipers in the nearby bush. Within seconds my platoon commander contacted me by two-way radio with instructions to move our personnel from the back of my covered truck to the ambulance in front of our truck. The rationale behind this, I suppose, was to get these people out from under the tarp to a more protected area.

Our platoon commander also told me not to allow anyone into the back of the truck. But as soon as our personnel were out of the vehicle, the Serbs decided to go in and remove the explosives. They posted soldiers on the left and right side of the truck to prevent us from exiting and making any attempt to interrupt their plan.

The heat in the truck's cab was stifling. Nevertheless, I had to make a quick decision on how to stop the Serbs from removing the explosives, and I had to do that without anybody getting killed. The tension, which was compounded by the intense heat, was unbelievable. My quick decision was to bluff the Serbs. I locked my door and told the driver to do the same. He wanted to close the driver's window, but I told him to keep it open because part of the bluff was to make sure the Serb soldiers could hear what was going on inside the cab.

A small window in the back of the cab allowed us to see into the back of the truck. I placed the barrel of my rifle through this opening and shouted at the Serb soldiers to get out immediately. I then cocked my weapon which ejected a cartridge. To this day, I will never forget the sound that small cartridge made when it came in contact with the cab's metal floor.

Indeed, the sound of metal on metal did the trick. The Serb noncommissioned officer immediately started to shout at his men to get off the back of the truck. It was now a matter of survival for me and my driver. On the driver's side, a Serb soldier had managed to unlock the door by reaching in through the open window. Now, with his body leaning into the cab, he was trying to wrestle the rifle from my driver's hand. My driver, meanwhile, was leaning his back against me and pushing on the steering column with his right foot and kicking at the Serb with his left foot.

On my side of the cab, I had one Serb soldier punching me with sledgehammer blows to the face and head. Another Serb soldier was trying to pull my rifle out of my hands, while a third was trying to open the locked door, an action he couldn't complete because my elbow was pushing down on the lock. Fortunately, one of our personnel on the ambulance had by this time swung the carrier's machine-gun around and had it trained on the Serb soldiers.

The noise and confusion continued as two Canadian soldiers jumped from the ambulance to the hood of our truck. They started yelling and kicking at the Serbs who were trying to get at me. This was when the Serb non-commissioned officer realized things were getting out of hand and that these UN peacekeepers were not going to back down. A lone Serbian police officer also joined the fray and was trying to get the crowd to back off.

Finally, the Serb non-commissioned officer ordered his soldiers to back away. The old sergeant was red in the face and very furious to say the least because his decision was not looked upon favourably by his men. However, in our view he made the right decision because we certainly had no intention of letting them have their way.

Our vehicles remained surrounded by Serb soldiers and civilians until a local politician and a general arrived roughly 45 minutes later. The latter ordered photographs to be taken of the platoon's vehicles and we in turn trained our cameras on the Serbs, an act that infuriated the general who immediately ordered the Serb police—accompanied by an interpreter—to collect all film from our cameras.

Our platoon signalman quickly took his film out of his camera and inserted a fresh roll. He then quietly hid the roll he'd been using. The Serb police ended up with his unexposed film.

It wasn't long before our battalion commander arrived on the scene and proceeded to resolve the situation with the Serb general. What was said between the general, the politician and our commanding officer is unknown to me, but the general finally released our vehicles.

The battalion, we were told, was in place on the heights above the village and was ready to attack and rescue our platoon by force if necessary. I was not surprised by how quickly the battalion moved into position to help us. Indeed, Canadian soldiers have a reputation for moving quickly when they have to.

The incident didn't last that long and I don't remember being frightened. Perhaps there was just too much adrenaline running through my system for me to feel that way. Although I do remember the tremendous sense of relief when it ended.

Just before we moved out, a fighter aircraft, which had been sent from Italy, flew in low over the village. All of us were very impressed by the sudden appearance and loud noise of the jet.

Our convoy moved out very, very slowly because we didn't want to re-excite the locals or the Serb soldiers. Back at our base camp we learned the reasons behind the incident. Apparently, some property had been damaged by a previous UN patrol and so the civilians thought the only way to get reimbursed for the damages was to attract some attention.

The following day our company returned to Okucani with more than 14 armoured personnel carriers. The objective was to show the United Nations blue flag and demonstrate that we were still there and would keep the UN mandate in effect.

The platoon's warrant officer and I could not participate in the excursion because rumour had it there was a reward placed on us for our capture on Serb territory. I suspect this was just a rumour, but our company commander decided not to take any chances and left us in camp which was fine by me because I had my regular transport duties to attend to.

Medical Risks in Croatia, 1994

DR. ERIC SMITH

I was the senior medical officer for the First Princess Patricia's Canadian Light Infantry Battalion Group that was deployed to Croatia in 1994. As soon as we arrived, the mandate shifted from observing the Zone of Separation (ZOS) from the Serb side to occupying the area and under- taking mine-clearing operations. It was a dangerous undertaking. We had our first casualties within three days.

As part of the reconnaissance team assessing a site for a new head- quarters, I and a number of soldiers explored a bauxite plant that had been destroyed. There was a reddish dustlike material everywhere. In the bombed-out building where the transformers were kept there was a tenacious oily black material on the ground. The plants' labs were also destroyed, with various processing chemicals pooled together on the floors of the main building.

Samples of materials from all these areas were sent to the United Nations Protection Force headquarters in Zagreb. We recommended against using the site for a new main camp, though some personnel were deployed in the immediate area.

That, in a nutshell, is the background to the events that have raised calls . . . for an independent inquiry examining the health of military personnel on duty in Croatia. I sincerely hope that as a result of the attention that has been drawn to this issue, the Canadian Forces adopts a hard-and-fast policy of evaluating potential risks in all areas in which soldiers are deployed. This must be standard operating procedure. When someone voices concern, resources need to be provided to get answers. Members of the forces—like me, like the soldiers I worked with—need reassurance that their requests for clarity will not lead to reprisals. That did not happen in this instance.

After my inspection of the bauxite plant, I started preparing a medical intelligence report. I said I was concerned about the possible bauxite and PCBs we might have been exposed to.

I am a jack of all trades; I can deal with trauma, fire a weapon, run with the troops and jump out of an airplane. But this situation called for specialists in occupational and environmental medicine. None was sent.

The soldiers were also concerned about the health risks they faced. I assured them I would deal with the matter appropriately so they would be protected for pension purposes if their health ever became affected and it could be related to exposure to materials they encountered on duty in Croatia. But I was unable to answer the central question: Was there sufficient reason to suspect health risks?

I did not get the impression that the soldiers were scared, but they wanted to know for sure whether and to what extent they were exposed, and what the potential risks were.

When we returned to Canada, in October 1994, many of us were very tired. I was diagnosed with post-traumatic stress disorder, a result of my experiences in Croatia. After a short leave, I returned to duty in Calgary in January 1995, and once again tried to do something about our possible exposure to dangerous substances.

First, I drafted a memorandum, which is the most efficient way to get action in the Canadian Forces, stating that the soldiers might have undergone exposure to bauxite and PCBs. This went to the commanding officer; he approved it, and the memos were put in each soldier's file. My concern was that we had not received the results of the analysis of the samples—and I was beginning to think we never would, because my initial calls for an expert appraisal had received no response.

After I returned from a course in Toronto, several officers discussed my memo with me. There was concern that it had apparently "fallen" into the hands of some of the soldiers—not surprising, given that soldiers have access to their medical records. I was told that the families were asking questions and that some soldiers were experiencing medical problems. My superiors told me that I shouldn't be alarmist, particularly since there was no conclusive evidence that the soldiers had been exposed to hazardous materials.

It was then, in May 1995 that I wrote the second memo, downscaling my original assessment, and instructed my staff to put it in each soldier's file. This was as a direct result of pressure on me from the people in command. I compromised to deal with the pressures I felt from the military bureaucracy.

Interestingly, when I asked for my own medical file a year later, the memo wasn't in my records. I don't know when or at what level the decision was made to remove it.

I know I became complicit with Canadian Forces authority when I agreed to redraft the memos. I was extremely stressed from my experiences in Croatia, and found it difficult to get answers to the bauxite and PCB issue and thus bring closure to my tour of duty.

The fact is that I also felt personal fear of reprisal for raising the issue of hazardous exposure in the first place. My ambivalence was understandable. I wanted to do the right thing. But I also worried about speaking up.

As children we are taught to respect authority and, for many, to fear it. It's fear of reprisal that influences children's decisions on how they will view their environment. The most frequent adaptations are polarized to either compliance or rebellion. We have a good idea of what a rebellious attitude can do to a child in a dysfunctional home. Compliance leads to a smoother course but damages the child's identity and self-esteem.

There is a parallel in military life. The military itself is attractive to people with traumatic or dysfunctional pasts. Ironically, these people are drawn to an organization that will parent them in a similar way. Our superiors structure our lives, and in return we get a strong degree of dependency and security.

Your career becomes your identity. This leaves little time for individual exploration, expression and growth. This also means that you may follow orders or comply with superiors' requests when you shouldn't.

So what can be done? There are many experts on organizational psychology who can help the military come to terms with the dysfunction within its framework. Awareness of these issues is paramount. Other organizations and families have recovered from dysfunction. I believe the military can.

I don't know conclusively whether soldiers were exposed to bauxite and PCBs and, if they were, whether soldiers are becoming ill because of that exposure. I do know that the stress of not knowing their health status has not helped them. And the military itself needs to change, so that officers who raise an alarm do not live in fear of reprisal. The soldiers who risk their lives for their country deserve nothing less.

Dealing with Serbs and Croats, 1994

ANONYMOUS

July 26, 1944

The Serbs are really and truly becoming a royal pain in the behind! They don't keep their word, they steal, lie and generally impede our actions every chance they get. It is becoming more and more difficult to do the job we were originally tasked for. The Croats are slowly catching up though as I can attest. They have now closed all the entry points into the UN area of operations, effectively cutting our system of overland resupply. I was guiding a convoy with one of my sections of troops this past week. We were supposed to go to our new battalion headquarters in Rastevic. The convoy was 47 trucks filled with food, fuel and our mail. The Croatians stopped us at a bridge and refused to let us pass. We spent five days in a stand off. In the end, the convoy turned around and returned to Split on the coast. It was very tense the very first day as the Croats made all sorts of threats and on one occasion, even cocked a weapon. Of course, as Canadians we told them to "bugger-off" and we were ready to shoot it out. Fortunately, it didn't get to that point, but I can tell you, many of my soldiers are frustrated; they are just waiting for either side to provoke us in the legal sense!

The Nightmare of Rwanda—and After

ANONYMOUS

> *In 1993, the UN created a small "assistance mission" to try to prevent a war between the Hutus and Tutsis of Rwanda. But UN Headquarters paid no attention to warnings of trouble, and genocide resulted, forever scarring some of those Canadians who served there.*

My first week in Rwanda was spent sleeping in an abandoned building in downtown Kigali amongst hundreds of Rwandan refugees, injured people, corpses, dead rats and across the street from where the battle for Kigali was taking place.

On Day 2 of our visit, I was providing the headquarters in Ottawa with a situation report by satellite phone from the United Nations HQ in Kigali. As I was talking to XYZ in Ottawa, an RPG round (antitank rocket) was fired at the building. The round impacted on the wall of the room next to the one I was in.

The impact was extremely loud. It threw me off my feet and I lost the handset of the phone. When I took the phone back, XYZ was still at the other end, yelling my name; he thought I had been killed.

One day in Kigali near a refugee camp, I was subjected to machine-gun and rifle fire. Crowds of refugees poured into the building nearby. As I turned to follow the crowd and seek protection, an 8- to 10-year-old boy standing next to me was shot in the leg. I remember him flipping over and collapsing on the ground yelling in pain for help.

On another occasion, my vehicle was stopped by a Hutu militia group (Interahamwe) at a checkpoint. The soldiers did not want to let us through the checkpoint. One of the soldiers reached in through the window of the vehicle and placed a machete in front of my face and asked me in Swahili or Keni-Rwandan something to the effect of "Are you Belge?" and kept insisting that I was from Belgium [the former colonial power] and that I get out of the car.

After 20 to 30 seconds of this, the driver hit the gas and our convoy broke through the barricades. As we were accelerating, some soldiers opened fire on our four-vehicle convoy. Although we made it back to the HQ, two of the vehicles had been hit by small-arms fire in the rear bumper area and one of the spare tires had been punctured.

On another day, I was arrested by a teenaged soldier of the Tutsi-led Rwandan Patriotic Army. As I was attempting to figure out the reason for my arrest, he became extremely agitated and pointed his AK-47 in my face and pressed the barrel of the weapon in my nose. When I backed up, he pressed harder. One of the civilians I was with spoke Swahili and eventually defused the situation. . . .

At the Centre Christus in Kigali, which had become a haven for non-governmental organizations and other civilians during and shortly after the war, a Rwandan man I knew called me into the back of the yard one day.

He was very agitated and spoke of a terrible incident. I followed him down a trail, asking him what was going on. At the end of the trail was a large crater surrounded by blood and the debris of skin and clothes.

He then told me that I had to help him remove the young boy who had stepped on a land mine. I then realized that he had brought both of us into a heavily mined field.

We screamed for help, but no one came. After standing still for what seemed like 15 to 20 minutes, I decided to simply walk out of the minefield.

Later that day, I returned to the scene with Canadian engineers. I walked back to the area with an engineer, we slowly walked on the trail. He suddenly stopped me before my left foot set down on the ground. I stepped back and he dug out a TS-50 mine from where I was to set foot. The engineers uncovered a dozen TS-50 antipersonnel land mines in the 50-metre-long trail I had twice walked earlier that day.

Life after Rwanda

Upon my return from Rwanda, some of my peers and superiors at work noticed some changes in my behaviour. I had little patience, I was tense and was often visibly angry at superiors.

By then, I started having nightmares. Some nights my wife would have to wake me and shake me out of the nightmares.

I was not happy at work. I found my job back in Ottawa irrelevant and did not find any of my past hobbies interesting. I eventually closed down my woodworking business, which I had started before my departure for Rwanda.

The nightmares are to this day pretty standard—lots of killing, lots of dead bodies, I relive the shooting incident and see the boy suffering and many other scenes too often.

One particular night, however, I had a nightmare in which I could see myself killing people as opposed to only witnessing the horrors being committed by others.

The next day I had a harder time than usual getting through the workday. I came back home for dinner, but had to go back to work in the evening. As I was driving back to work, I had pretty much made my mind up to commit suicide.

I remember aligning a specific telephone pole on my way back in to work that night and I started accelerating toward it. In a moment of lucidity, I shook off the feeling and drove to work, got my job done and came back home. The next morning I reported to the hospital and demanded to see a specialist.

I met twice with a psychiatrist, but did not feel like he understood or believed the stories I was telling him. He kept asking about my family, which in my opinion was not the source of my problem. He convinced me that I only had a mild case of stress, or something to that effect, and I remember him suggesting medication. I had little confidence in him and decided to cope with my problem by myself.

For several months, I tried to cope the best I could. Mostly, I always tried to play down the reasons for my nightmares, emotional reactions to events at work, or flashbacks triggered by sounds, scenes, smells.

After several months, I became closely involved in problems at work. Severe disciplinary actions were taken against me and I was ordered to seek therapy, as my behaviour was seen as once more out of sorts and unreasonable. I was put on formal warning.

I began to see a psychiatrist, but deliberately told her what she needed to hear in order for her to file a favourable report to salvage my career. I was diagnosed with minor PTSD [Post Traumatic Stress Disorder] and I then authorized her to inform my superiors that I was better and ready to resume work. My file was cleared of the warning and I resumed work as if nothing had ever happened.

Following this incident, I deliberately kept myself extremely busy at work and began travelling extensively around the world from January, 1997, to the summer of 1998.

The pace of my job then slowed down significantly. I noticed I had to struggle to remember what my subordinates told me. I often tuned people out when they talked to me if I was suddenly reminded of Rwanda. I would lose track of time and on occasion got off at the wrong bus stop on my way to work or home.

Finally, I realized I needed help again in November, 1998, and have been in therapy since the winter of 1999. So I have again, for the third time now, started therapy. . . .

I have now lived with my condition for over four years. Living with PTSD is not as obvious as living with a missing arm or another part of one's body. PTSD affects one's soul, it drains you, it prevents you from enjoying life the way you used to enjoy it and in my opinion cannot be measured in an accurate, quantifiable way.

The best way I can think of characterizing how PTSD has affected my life is to compare it to how rape or sexual abuse would affect a young child.

It also feels as if you have lost your taste buds for life. You know how you should feel and how life should taste, but there is no flavour any more.

I try to avoid as much as possible situations that I know will trigger a reaction, but as a husband and father of two, it is difficult to isolate myself sometimes and I find it very difficult to cope with situations that others deem very normal.

One thing is certain, I am not the same person who departed for Rwanda in 1994. Every day now brings uncertainty. "What am I going to forget?" "Am I going to break down?" "Will I have a flashback?" "Am I going to make a fool of myself by forgetting what I was told yesterday by my superiors or subordinates?"

I am very uncomfortable in large crowds (especially if there are many Africans). I avoid going to museums, cinema and amusement parks to avoid being put in a crowded situation.

I lost interest in lifetime hobbies after coming back from Africa—rappelling and mountain climbing. I completely stopped all my past hobbies.

For no apparent reason, I start daydreaming about what I could have done differently in Africa that might have changed things and saved a couple more people. I wonder how come I was never injured or killed, given all that happened to me.

I have difficulty concentrating: Reading long complex documents at work is almost impossible now. By the time I get to Page 2, I forget what was on Page 1.

I snap very easily at my children and spouse for reasons that I find trivial after the fact. I have no tolerance toward others and have lost the ability to make and keep close friends. This has put great strain on my relationship with my wife. I often find the company of others trivial and pointless and don't like socializing any more.

I am always very tired and have little energy left at the end of each day for family activities.

Serving in Kosovo, 1999

CAPTAIN PAUL DE GRANDPRÉ

> *The Serb regime based in Belgrade wanted to extend its control in the province of Kosovo in 1999 and used brutal methods to get its way with the population of Albanian descent. NATO, including Canadian troops, intervened and drove out the Serbs. Captain de Grandpré was serving with a European observer group when he sent this letter.*

Decane, Kosovo / À 10 km de la frontière albanaise

Chers amis,

Le soir est calme, pour l'instant, à Decane. Ces derniers jours, on a vu le massacre de plus de 45 albanais à Racak: des affrontements entre la police et l'Armée de libération du Kosovo (ALK) ont causé 30 morts au cours des trois dernières journées dont 24 lors d'une intense fusillade. Il y a quatre jours, un père et son fils furent piégés dans leur véhicule. Le père est mort sur le champ et son fils gravement blessé et hospitalisé. Ce dernier attentat s'est produit dans mon secteur à 2 km d'ici et nous avons pu sauver le fils en le transportant en toute urgence à l'hôpital. Nos brancardiers ont pu prodiguer les premiers soins qui lui ont sauvé la vie. Quant au père, il était trop tard. Il avait le corps criblé de balles d'un AK-47.

Au cours des trois dernières semaines dans la région de Decane, la police de l'état (MUP), l'armée yougoslave (VJ) et l'ALK se sont affrontés à quelques reprises. Une batterie d'artillerie de 122 mm située sur une butte à environ 600m des bureaux de l'O.S.C.E. (Organisation pour la sécurité et la coopération en Europe) faisait feu sur l'ALK vers l'est. On avait déployé des chars T-55, des canons anti-avions 30mm, des véhicules blindés avec canons 20mm, des mortiers, des mitrailleuses lourdes et un bataillon entier d'infanterie contre les positions de l'ALK, à 4km de là. L'ALK a réussi à faire sauter trois véhicules blindés de la police avec des mines, prendre quelques camions en embuscade (y compris deux membres du personnel de l'O.S.C.E. qui avaient tardé à s'éloigner, malgré des exhortions à cet effet). L'on ne peut parler de guerre au sens militaire du mot, mais celà dépasse les simples patrouilles policières du voisinage. Par ici, une patrouille policière typique comprend deux camions blindés avec une vingtaine de policiers en tenue de combat (AK-47, 5 mags, grenades à fusil, vestes anti-balles et au moins une mitrailleuse). Bien entendu, leur adversaire typique est équipé de mitrailleuses RPG-7, de fusils de haute précision de calibre .50 et de mines anti-chars.

Les villageois en ont marre des combats et ils sont épuisés. Il y a suffisamment de nourriture pour tous, grâce au concours de plusieurs organismes d'aide humanitaire; cependant la pénurie de soins médicaux inquiète. La plupart des habitants craignent de se déplacer trop loin, de peur d'être interceptés lors de contrôles policiers. De plus, bon nombre d'entre eux n'ont pu renouveler leur carte d'identité à cause du conflit et ils doivent à leur risque et péril se rendre au poste de police pour la renouveler. Dès que la fusillade commence, les gens enfourchent leurs chevaux ou leurs tracteurs et prennent la fuite, mais ils ne peuvent vraiment aller nulle part. L'armée VJ et la police MUP contrôlent les routes et les lieux stratégiques au moyen de leurs postes d'observation et de contrôle qui isolent les villages. Les habitants doivent donc trouver refuge dans la forêt avoisinante lorsque les obus éclatent.

Une tactique caractéristique de la police d'état (MUP) consiste à encercler un village avec de l'artillerie légère 30 mm et des mitrailleuses 12.7 mm et à simplement ouvrir le feu. Compte tenu du récent massacre d'une famille de cinq personnes qui se déplaçait en charrette tirée par un tracteur, il se peut fort bien que les villageois choisissent désormais de subir les attaques près de leurs maisons plutôt que de s'aventurer sur la route. Les habitants mieux nantis tentent de s'échapper furtivement vers l'Albanie ou le Monténégro. Un tel comportement débouche sur de nombreuses arrestations, car la police tente d'enrayer l'immigration "illégale."

Mes fonctions consistent à diriger le groupe des opérations rattaché au centre administratif de l'O.S.C.E. à Decane. Je dirige cinq patrouilles dans mon secteur avec l'aide d'une équipe internationale de 25 personnes et d'une équipe locale de 21 personnes. Je peux déployer 5 camions blindés et 3 véhicules du type Mitsubushi Pajeros (non blindé). Tous sont recouverts d'une peinture orange-citrouille qui accroît leur visibilité. Je dois surveiller les actions de chaque individu ainsi que l'utilisation de chaque pièce d'équipement. L'écart dans les compétences professionnelles et linguistiques du personnel international requiert des instructions claires et explicites pour les tâches les plus simples. Mes ordres de patrouille doivent inclure des listes de contrôle détaillées (cartes, essence, radio, etc.), et mes instructions répétées 3 ou 4 fois afin d'être bien sur qu'au moins une personne par équipe a tout compris. (Comme les soldats canadiens me manquent.)

Ma journée débute vers 0700h avec la planification des patrouilles et autres tâches quotidiennes, une réunion avec mes équipes à 0800h; les patrouilles quittent vers 0900h et ensuite je parcours le secteur une partie de la journée afin de contrôler les patrouilles et vérifier tout incident qui a pu survenir. De plus, je me tiens au courant des communications par radio et des déplacements de mes patrouilles et je m'efforce de régler les problèmes de logistique et de personnel (tous veulent être embauchés par l'O.S.C.E.). Heureusement, le directeur de la logistique, le directeur des opérations et bon nombre de militaires à mon quartier-général à Pec sont des canadiens. Ceci facilite la tâche lorsque des urgences surviennent. Je termine la journée par une rencontre des patrouilleurs à 1600h et ensuite je compile les rapports quotidiens du centre administratif de Decane. Je transmets le tout par télécopieur satellite à mon quartier-général vers 1900h et je délègue mes tâches à l'officier de service de nuit qui, je l'espère, peut se débrouiller en anglais. Dieu merci, la plupart des nuits sont tranquilles.

Les patrouilles effectuées au cours des dernières semaines m'ont permis de constater les souffrances de la population locale résultant de la maladie, de blessures, de l'inconfort de logements avariés et de la violence pure et simple. Il est courant de voir 20 ou 30 personnes réunies autour d'un poêle dans une seul pièce d'une maison ravagée. Les albanais ont souvent des familles de 8 à 12 enfants et ceux-ci sont très vulnérables face à la maladie et aux intempéries. Plusieurs jeunes enfants sont morts lorsque les familles ont dû s'enfuir. Les réfugiés serbes sont aussi victimes d'un sort semblable, entassés dans de petits campements près des bases militaires ou des villes afin de se protéger contre l'ALK. Plusieurs sont retournés à leur village depuis l'automne, il y ont vu des lieux calcinés et ils ont ni les matériaux ni l'énergie pour reconstruire, du moins à ce moment-ci. Le bétail et les récoltes ont subi la destruction dans ces régions, ce qui n'encourage pas le renouveau. Pour assombrir d'avantage ce tableau lugubre, les escarmouches se font plus fréquentes et plus sanglantes d'une semaine à l'autre.

À ce jour, l'O.S.C.E. est bien perçue par les habitants du Kosovo. Alors qu'une majorité d'entre eux doute de sa véritable utilité à long terme, ils apprécient le répit que leur procurent les véhicules "Citrouille." Les albanais nous invitent pour des collations et nous demandent de visiter leur village chaque jour. Les civils serbes feignent de nous ignorer ou nous font la grimace. La police MUP et les troupes VJ sont des professionnels et savent faire preuve de courtoisie dans les bonnes circonstances. Certains petits gestes d'intimidation tels que commencer à foncer sur les véhicules de l'O.S.C.E. ou tenter de stopper les véhicules aux postes de contrôle sont chose courante mais il y a peu de menaces graves exprimées à notre endroit. Les plus grands dangers qui menacent les inspecteurs demeurent les mines, les erreurs sur la personne et les balles perdues. J'ai dirigé des opérations nocturnes ici, mais elles sont rarement nécessaires. Lorsqu'il faut patrouiller la nuit, j'utilise 2 véhicules blindés et au moins 4 patrouilleurs. Le premier véhicule est illuminé par les phares du véhicule arrière, ce qui nous permet de mieux identifier nos véhicules et de ne pas être confondus avec l'ennemi.

Les conditions de vie ne sont pas si difficiles, compte-tenu de la conjoncture. Decane fut lourdement endommagé l'été dernier et plus de 75% des bâtisses ont été détruites par le feu ou bombardées. Je partage une petite maison albanaise avec un capitaine de l'armée italienne (infanterie) et un lieutenant-colonel de l'armée française (infanterie). Ils sont tous deux de commerce facile, et l'italien se charge de faire la cuisine, ce qui me convient tout a fait. Le pain et les pâtes alimentaires sont omniprésents. La bière et le vin du pays sont excellents et peu coûteux. Le fromage, les jus, les boissons gazeuses et les aliments préparés coûtent plus cher qu'au Canada, et les habitants n'ont pas tous les moyens de se les procurer. La maison est pourvue d'eau chaude, d'électricité et d'un minimum de chauffage. Nous avons la télévision par satellite et les émission Euro-News et BBC News nous tiennent au courant des actualités. Nous devons débourser un montant considérable pour louer la maison (1,000 DM par mois + les frais connexes et la subsistance), mais le propriétaire est empressé de voir à notre confort. Un salaire moyen pour un professeur d'école secondaire, par exemple, est inférieur à 200 DM par mois. L'O.S.C.E. paie ses interprètes 50 DM par jour et ses gardiens de sécurité 35 DM par jour. Autrement dit, nous sommes des clients fort recherchés.

Nous vivons sous une menace d'évacuation depuis environs deux semaines, maintenant. Bien que ce ne soit pas un énorme problème, ceci ajoute au stress de nos activités quotidiennes. Cette mission est en quelque sorte à la merci du jeu diplomatique qui s'improvise. Espérons que les officiers d'état-major préposés aux plans, quelque part dans les labyrinthes du Q.G. de l'O.T.A.N. penseront à rappeler les inspecteurs de l'O.S.C.E. avant que les frappes aériennes ne soient autorisées ici. Qui vivra verra. Tous mes véhicules ont le réservoir toujours plein d'essence, sont prêts à démarrer et l'on se tient au courant des allées et venues de chaque membre du personnel.

Quelque soit le positionnement des acteurs de la politique et de la diplomatie internationale, la Mission de vérification du Kosovo est tout à fait valable. Nous avons sauvé plusieurs vies au cours des deux derniers mois en abaissant le niveau d'intensité des conflits locaux. En patrouillant la région nous facilitons le travail des organismes d'aide humanitaire qui ont une plus grande liberté d'action et nous leurs transmettons des rapports complets sur les besoins de chaque village. Le cessez-le-feu d'octobre 1998 n'a pas duré, mais il est à souhaiter que notre présence contribue à réduire la gravité et la fréquence des agressions, ne serait-ce qu'un peu. Il revient à la République Yougoslave (FRY) et à l'armée de libération du Kosovo (ALK) de dénouer le sort de la province du Kosovo dans ce grand drame balkanique.

Making a Difference in Kosovo

LIEUTENANT ELEANOR TAYLOR

> *Lieutenant Taylor served with the 1st Battalion of the Royal Canadian Regiment in Kosovo in late 1999.*

Bravo Company complete has been in theatre in Kosovo for a little over a full month now and we are starting to establish a routine. Improvements are being made around the camp everyday to make life more comfortable for all of us. The Pioneers have redone the mess area; the floor is almost completely done and they are working on finishing the walls. The gym is a work in progress. We have increased the number of weights that are available and are waiting for a stereo to improve the workout experience.

Currently, 5 PL is the company's patrolling platoon. Patrols platoon has two primary objectives. The first is to provide security to the various communities in our Area of Operations (AO) and the second is to gather information. The information that is gathered is generally used to paint a clear picture of the communities that we are responsible for, and to establish who needs humanitarian aid. Much of the information that is gathered is forwarded to Aid Agencies who then go and try to provide for those in need. Everyday the section commanders take their sections to various villages in our AO and talk to them about everything from the number of wells that exist in their village to the method by which they dispose of their garbage.

Patrolling is, without a doubt, the most interesting of all the company tasks. It is the only task where you get to get out and see the people who live in the surrounding villages. Being able to see the state of the people in this country can be both inspiring and discouraging. The people here have a tremendous resilience. They have endured things that we Canadians can only imagine, and yet they manage to carry on with their lives despite some deplorable conditions. Such perseverance must be admired. Many are kind and generous, and most are happy to have us in their country. However, the ethnic mistrust and hatred that is so deeply engrained in the hearts of so many of these people certainly will not be resolved in the near future.

Most of the people are now simply trying to survive the winter. Temperatures here in Kosovo have dropped well below zero and there are still many people without adequate shelter and heat.

Patrolling becomes truly rewarding when you see peoples lives improved as a result of your presence. For example, Sgt Eric Simms was patrolling the town of Banjica when he came upon a family that was living in a tent with inadequate food, clothing and firewood.

He assessed the situation as urgent and the next day he dropped off 5 bags of clothing for the family. He also passed up to the chain of command that the family required assistance from an Aid Agency and within two days it was decided that a roofing kit would be delivered to this family so that they could move out of their tent and into a house.

Soon 5 PL will change from patrolling to Vehicle Check Points (VCPs), and our patrolling tasks will be taken over by 4 PL. It will be a welcome change for 4 PL as they will be able to get out of the camp with a bit more regularity; however, we are not so excited about leaving our current task for VCP's. After our stint on the VCPs everyone will be ready for a good R&R.

Stopping Smugglers in the Straits of Hormuz, 2002

ANONYMOUS

> *As part of the War on Terrorism, Canada sent naval vessels into the Arabian Sea and the Straits of Hormuz, off Iran. HMCS* Ottawa, *a frigate, intercepted an oil tanker suspected of smuggling. The team on* Ottawa *told the story.*

The full story of the mission started days before the ensuing excitement commenced, as intelligence was received that a contact of interest was weighing anchor in the gulf and proceeding to destinations unknown.

Ottawa was tasked to track down the *Roaa* south of the Straits of Hormuz, a fairly narrow choke-point entrance to the gulf. Hemmed in by the territorial waters of Oman and Iran, the Canadian ship's surveillance options were a little limited. For three days the naval communicators in HMCS *Ottawa* queried a multitude of vessels passing through the strait in order to get an identity and voyage information for each ship.

"The area was a big bottleneck, so the traffic was heavy and the hailings were fast and furious," said Leading Seaman Ian Vanderswan, one of the naval communicators working on the bridge. "We were just all anxious to find the guy and get the job done."

The data collected was tested for legitimacy by the acoustic section, who checked the vessel against its destination.

Three days and hundreds of vessels passed, with no sign of the MV *Roaa*. Further intelligence indicated that the *Roaa* had anchored in the approaches to a nearby port—an area known affectionately as "The Parking Lot."

Hiding amongst 100 anchored vessels proved to be insufficient cover to elude the sharp eye of the Canadian Aurora maritime patrol aircraft that was working with the Canadian Task Group. The Aurora spotted the *Roaa*, compared digital imagery with a photo, and passed her position to a coalition helicopter that was working only a few kilometres away.

In the early morning of April 18, one of the other ships in the multinational task group reported sighting the MV *Roaa*. She was about 65 kilometres to the south of *Ottawa*, at anchor. Under the cover of darkness, *Ottawa* closed in to apprehend the vessel. Once *Ottawa* was in close enough to gain a positive identification of *Roaa*, the frigate took over the surveillance.

A naval communicator, Able Seaman Alex Kiraly, was on the bridge as *Ottawa* approached the vessel. "Everyone was up on the bridge looking for the *Roaa*," she explained. "We had to weave through about 20 ships anchored close together just to find her." The game of cat and mouse began.

Ottawa needed to maintain contact, without being spotted, and wait for the *Roaa* to make the error that would allow the boarding party to move into position. The navy vessel started her close observations during the night. With all lights off, and panther-like stealth, she closed and began to take video footage with the infrared camera fitted on her own helicopter. From the helicopter's position on deck, *Ottawa* could tell she had definitely found her mark. All that remained was to wait. As day light broke, it was confirmed that this was, in fact, the suspect vessel. However, it was travelling under a new name and flag.

A day and a half of patience soon paid off. *Ottawa*'s radar operators spotted movement amongst the field of contacts. The bridge lookouts focused on her lights, and captured her slow departure. Not wanting to tip her hand, *Ottawa* waited as she passed by, still inside territorial waters and outside of her reach, and took up a slow chase. *Roaa* was heading back to the gulf.

Naval Combat Information Operator Able Seaman Jon Colbon was responsible for maintaining continuous tracking on the *Roaa*. "From the time she weighed anchor and headed north, we were tracking her for over 12 hours," he said.

Attempting to get back to Iraq, *Roaa* would have to choose between a long transit following the safety of Iranian waters, hiding out in Omani waters, or taking the direct route through international waters. Each option has its appeal, but the fastest transit, and most cost effective, is the latter.

With the boarding party waiting astern of the *Roaa* in the RHIB (rigid hulled inflatable boat), *Ottawa* went to full speed ahead and stopped very close to the *Roaa*. After the captain announced his intentions to board her, the boarding party stealthily scaled the side of the *Roaa* en route to what would be Canada's first night time noncompliant boarding. Before the crew of the *Roaa* had any indication that they were being overtaken, the bridge and engine room were secured, and *Ottawa* had control of the ship.

"We'd been on two minutes standby since quarter to six. The ship came to boarding stations at about 10 P.M." explained Master Seaman Bob Sackett, a member of *Ottawa's* boarding team. As soon as the *Roaa* had made her way into international waters, *Ottawa* quickly positioned herself on the *Roaa's* port side.

The alpha wave of *Ottawa's* naval boarding party climbed into the RHIB in the dark. Leading Seaman Patrick Moulden was the RHIB coxswain. "*Ottawa* screamed in at 30 knots," he recalled. "It was intimidatingly fast. Then they illuminated the *Roaa* with the xenon (the ship's high power search light). The guys on (*Roaa's*) bridge must have been stunned."

Before the *Roaa* could take any evasive actions, the naval boarding party was on board. The first person up the ladder was Leading Seaman Chet Horne. When asked what it was like to be the first person to go on board, he replied, "No real worries. We're always ready for whatever might happen. You trust the other members of your team."

The team had trained for this situation so many times that it had become a habit for them. "Besides. . . . If they can't see you coming, it doesn't make you a target," Horne noted. He described the crew's reaction to the sudden arrival of an armed boarding team. "At first, the crew were really stunned, but when they realized that we would take care of them they relaxed a bit."

It was a beautiful thing, a seamless insertion, a block that would have NFL scouts drooling two seasons from now. Control was established before the crew could affix the anti-boarding devices. Lying in wait at every door, hatch, and window were sheets of steel ready to be welded on at the hint of a boarding. Training and a little creativity paid off. This was what *Ottawa* came to do.

Throughout the remainder of the evening *Ottawa* escorted the vessel, under the temporary command of Lt. (N) Peter Sproule and the protection of the boarding team. "What an experience," Sproule said. "It was a nice change from the routine of the ops room."

Given the call-sign "Horn-blower," Sproule took direction from *Ottawa* over the radio and drove the *Roaa* to the detention area. When asked how he liked his first ship he replied, "The ship was absolutely filthy, but fortunately I only had to stand on the bridge and didn't have to search through the galley or the heads. Eight hours was long enough."

The vessel was diverted into the southern Arabian Gulf to a holding area where the *Roaa* would be held until local authorities could begin the legal process. The vigilance of the boarding party's security rounds ensured that none of the crew of the *Roaa* would have the opportunity to destroy any evidence or do the unthinkable, scuttle the ship.

Once all of the evidence was collected it was decided to set the *Roaa* on her way. Although this somewhat anticlimactic ending to *Ottawa*'s story may cause some to say, "What was the point?," her crew would argue it was twofold. First, *Ottawa*'s teams got a firsthand opportunity to test out their readiness in this new battlefield in which she now finds herself. Second, the evidence that was gathered may contain links that could eventually be used to capture a bigger foe. Any small step towards a successful ending to this campaign is worth the effort.

Fighting in Afghanistan, 2002

STEPHEN J. THORNE

Canada deployed infantry to Afghanistan to fight with US troops against al Qaeda and Taliban forces. Stephen Thorne, a journalist, marched with the 3rd Battalion, Princess Patricia's Canadian Light Infantry, in their action at Tora Bora.

It was the first weekend of May 2002. We'd flown into Bagram eight long days before aboard an American C-17 transport aircraft loaded with more than 100 troops and two ambulances. I'd spent the entire 90-minute trip staring at a chain holding one of the vehicles in place. It was inches from my right leg and, as we made our rapid descent into the mountain-rimmed airfield at Bagram, the weight of that armoured ambulance jerked at the chain repeatedly. I had resigned myself to the fact the chain was going to snap and take out at least half my leg. Of course, the massive aircraft landed without incident.

We spent the next eight days in miserable wind and dust, waiting for the troops' American superiors to make a decision on what to do. It was a frustrating time for me, a reporter-photographer with The Canadian Press, Canada's national news cooperative. Due to operational security, I couldn't file a word, not a picture. I couldn't even tell my bosses where I was, though they figured it out easily enough. But at least I could talk to my wife semi-regularly on my satellite telephone. The troops didn't have that luxury. They had been denied telephone privileges since some time before we departed Kandahar. Many didn't have the chance to tell loved ones that something was up. Back home, the silence spoke volumes.

The troops spent those eight days getting ready for what by all accounts was going to be a very challenging mission, complete with rappelling, caving and, possibly, combat. There was simmering frustration among some, particularly the reconnaissance platoon, because the Americans insisted on inserting their own Special Forces to conduct the mission recce—finding suitable landing zones, assessing enemy threats and scouting potential cave complexes. It was a classic case of the Americans not knowing the Canadians' potential. The American forces are well equipped and seem to have an endless supply of troops, but they are not necessarily well trained.

The thing that makes the regular U.S. Army work is its leadership—bold, decisive, rock-hard senior officers with years of rich combat experience behind them. They know how to motivate troops. They weren't particularly good diplomats, however. And in Afghanistan—at that point, at least—they didn't know that Canada's army, while small and ill-equipped, is among the best-trained in the world. Canadian reconnaissance troops are highly qualified with a challenging 10-week reconnaissance patrolman's course, for example. Many had patrol pathfinder and other specialized qualifications. All of this enabled them to perform a myriad of tasks an American commander wouldn't dream of entrusting to his own scout platoon, much less his regulars.

The Canadians spent days and nights at Bagram, training for the mission ahead by rappelling off rooftops, crawling around the darkened hallways of an abandoned building as if they were tunnels, marching the dusty roads around the base in full kit. . . .

Finally, on the morning of Saturday, May 4, we lifted off aboard American Chinook helicopters destined for a mountainside in Tora Bora. The Afghan countryside is a study in contrasts, from lush green valleys to barren desert to snow-covered peaks. It seemed we saw it all during the 55-minute flight to our tiny landing zone. Flying low, we raced across open plains and rocked and turned through valleys and up ravines.

My Operation Torii, as it was called, began with an uneventful drop-off about 7,500 feet up the side of the mountain known as Towr Ghar. The landing zone overlooked the site where the terrorist mastermind [Osama] bin Laden was supposed to have staged his last defence. Just a few kilometres to the east were the snow-covered peaks of Pakistan. The Alpha Company boys were up top, a couple of thousand feet above us.

Canadian filmmaker Garth Pritchard and I were to spend three days with U.S. Special Forces and Charlie Company, 3 PPCLI, halfway down the mountain. About 600 feet above us was the command post of Lieutenant-Colonel Pat Stogran, commander of Canadian Forces in Afghanistan. In the ravine far below were the C-4 explosives experts from 1 Combat Engineer Regiment. They didn't know it at the time, but this would turn out to be engineer heaven.

My immediate concern was to reach the engineers. Back in December, U.S. air crew had reported smoke emerging from the mountaintop after hitting what they believed was a cave entrance in the ravine. This incident and, no doubt, other evidence led American commanders to believe this was the main entrance to a vast cave-and-tunnel network. Problem was, the suspected entrance itself was now obliterated by a massive rock fall. While Canadian snipers and reconnaissance troops kept an eye on things from surrounding peaks, two companies of PPCLI scoured the area for hidden caves and bunkers. It was the engineers' job to clear caves, including the ravine site, where they were to reopen the entrance if, indeed, that's what it was. Already, we were hearing explosions echoing upwards from the ravine floor.

I set out with a small section of troops. Assuming I'd likely end up spending the night below, I carried my full kit—helmet, flak jacket and backpack with 24 hours' water and rations. My laptop computer and satellite telephone had been seized back in Bagram by a Canadian military public affairs officer, who wanted to make sure I couldn't file during the operation. And so my story and pictures would have to wait until the operation was over—a blessing and a curse.

The 2,000-foot descent was relatively easy, winding along steep goat trails and across ledges, past a shepherd's hut nestled into the mountainside, and on down. We reached the engineers by early afternoon, only to find them in problem-solving mode. A morning's worth of blasting hadn't produced much in the way of results. Using explosives to do the work of backhoes may appear untechnical and brutish but, in fact, it is conducted with surgical precision. The engineers use charges called beehives, specially designed to lift rock and debris. They use a special granular explosive that can be mixed with water to compound its effect. They use hundreds of feet of explosive primacord to set them off, and they mix and match these materials like mad scientists until they get the effect they are looking for. Tora Bora was the laboratory of laboratories for this crew, the home of massive explosions—first from the B-52s when Osama was here back in December, now from the Canadian engineers trying to determine what happened to him. They would trigger some monstrous blasts over the next few days. . . .

Up top, the pioneers were facing their own demons. Pioneers are light engineers and the only guys other than Special Forces who are allowed to grow beards on deployments. The tradition dates to Roman times when pioneers would rise early and be the first ones out to lay roads ahead of the army. The top pioneer was Sergeant Tom Duke, a clever, confident 49-year-old veteran who had an insightful, if not cynical, opinion about just about everything. Deployed with Alpha Company, the California-born Duke and three other Pioneers—Cpl. John Reynolds, Cpl. Aaron Bygrove and Master Corporal Dave Bibby—destroyed eight bunkers and a vertical shaft that was initially believed to lead to tunnels. Duke had the unenviable job of being the first one down the shaft—less than a metre wide and about five metres deep. He carried only a flashlight, a makeshift ladder and a safety line. "There wasn't room to take a gun," said Duke. He seemed unfazed by the experience. "I had six guys to pull me out if I needed it. Hell, I was armed—I'm a freakin' weapon." The shaft, however, appeared to lead nowhere.

All the while, blasting could be heard from below. The main concentration of engineers was still working that supposed cave entrance in the ravine. A helicopter arrived with dozens of wooden crates filled with C-4 plastic explosives, beehives and other tools of the trade. They formed a chain line and stacked the whole business right next to our tree. This was comforting. "What's it take to set this stuff off?" I asked some soldiers. An intense flash, one suggested. "Like a mortar round?" I asked. More like a lightning flash, I was told. Just then, lightning lit up the sky a few kilometres to the north. A few seconds later, the engineers let off another one—a big one—in the ravine. I nearly jumped out of my pants. Everyone cracked up. The cases of explosives came in handy, though, as Pritchard and I used some—still full—to build a little dining room, complete with coffee tables, next to our abode. . . .

The next day, Pritchard and I joined Nicholson and 40 men, this time with their own shovels, and we set out for Ali Khayl. The four-hour trip could have inspired a Tolkien novel. We descended steep mountain slopes, snaked our way along the length of that walled ravine and followed winding goat trails beneath a canopy of fruit trees.

We emerged into another world: an idyllic river valley surrounded by terraces of poppies and wheat, houses built into the sides of cliffs and an elaborate electrical system that was rumoured to have been paid for by bin Laden himself. The lush green and white terraces, including

80 hectares of flowers used in the preparation of opium, heroin and morphine, couldn't have stood in greater contrast to the Canadians' desert base in Kandahar, hundreds of kilometres to the south. Our procession wound its way around huge white boulders along a dry and open riverbed before coming to the village centre and a wedge-shaped rock formation that dominated one side of the valley. The feature bore an uncanny resemblance to Gibraltar on a small scale and was covered in graves, their colourful martyr flags flying stiffly in the breeze.

The troops wasted no time in proceeding with their grisly task. There were 23 graves, in all. Some of them had been here to unearth the three the day before. Now they had 20 more to finish in time to get back to camp before dark.

The job was labourious. Each plot was covered by a mound of rocks that had to be removed by hand. Beneath was almost a metre of dirt and stones ending at a floor—a roof, actually—of wood planking or sheet rock. As the digging got deeper, the stench grew stronger. Teams of infantrymen from Charlie Company took turns along with engineers. Using a penlight on a rifle barrel and a compass mirror, the engineers looked beneath the planks for booby traps before removing them, exposing shroud-wrapped bodies inside walled sarcophagi. The remains, clad in battle dress and with their heads enshrouded in a ghostly white mould, were pulled out by rope and scanned with metal detectors before the forensic guys took hair or tissue samples. Each body was then carefully reburied.

Canadian infantrymen had a perimeter set up around the site. Snipers and reconnaissance troops provided overwatch from high on nearby peaks as their comrades worked. And all the while, villagers watched from patios and rooftops on the hillsides around us. The snipers notwithstanding, the gravediggers appeared to be sitting ducks. Nicholson and the others maintained their cool, however. "These people were rabid al-Qaida/Taliban fans when they were around," said Nicholson. "Now, of course, they're 'not and never were.' They're very pro-coalition, as long as we let them grow their opium." . . .

The Canadians were careful to reassemble the plots much as they found them. When it was over, the soldiers appeared emotionally and physically exhausted, and they still had a long hike ahead of them. The sight of those ghostly white cadavers, with every facial feature still intact, would no doubt haunt some of these kids the rest of their days. "It sucked," Cpl. Shaun Seaton said after the last grave was excavated. "I don't ever want to do it again. I realize it's part of the mission and it had to be done, but it's not something I really signed up for. The smell, the shape of them and just actually having to dig up a grave. . . . I'm glad it's done and over with."

They made the trek back the way they came, all the while keeping their eyes cast upward at the cliffs surrounding them. Word was, the al-Qaida had moved over to the next valley soon after the first Special Forces had appeared a week or two earlier. It often seemed the case— the enemy would mysteriously disappear before an operation was launched.

On the way back, we passed the site where the engineers were still blasting away at that suspected cave entrance. They were wrapping up. After humping tonnes of explosives down the mountain and triggering more than a dozen detonations, they had found nothing.

In fact, no major cave complexes were found at all.

Stogran was doubtful the multi-storeyed complexes existed, at least in Tora Bora. "We've been chasing around a lot of country looking for these cave complexes," he told me. "There must be something lost in the translation. Maybe the indigenous word for 'bunker' or 'trench' translates as 'cave.'"

There may not have been labyrinthine cave complexes, but there certainly were lots of places to hide in bin Laden's last known locale. Besides two grave sites, Alpha Company had found a complex network of bunkers. There were many smaller caves and overhangs. Intelligence officers suspected Osama was wounded at the non-cave entrance in the ravine. Locals claimed he was evacuated to Pakistan by helicopter that same December day his 25 bodyguards were killed.

Operating in Kabul, December 2003

MAJOR KEITH CAMERON

In the summer of 2003, Canada sent 2,000 troops to operate with the International Security Assistance Force (ISAF) in Afghanistan. Much of the burden was borne by small patrols. Two Canadians died when a mine blew up their patrol vehicle, as an engineering officer recounts.

Preliminary results from the minestrike have been released. We think it was deliberate (90% certain, says the investigative team). We found fragments of a TM57 AT (anti-tank) mine in the crater, found two additional fuzes and mine shipping plugs on the scene. The threat for the area had indicated AP (anti-personnel) mines only (the valley had been cleared in 1998 but the demining agencies are known to miss areas, and you cannot discount washout from the hills). A former mujahideen soldier has since pointed out that AT mines may have been laid during the civil war fighting following the withdrawal of the Russians. However, the mine placement was right on the vehicle track in an area easy to bury a mine, the demining agencies had used the road when they were clearing the valley and we had sent 12 vehicles down that road over the previous 24 hrs. We'll see . . . it'll be hard to get final determination unless we catch someone, somehow. Plans afoot to re-work some aspects of how we do business to lessen risk—no plans afoot to change the "doing business" bit!

It's now mid-morning Friday, our "weekend" here—we've matched the battalion patrol plan to the Muslim holy day. That means reduced traffic on the roads, and serves to avoid making us a target on what can be a good bombing day. Nights here are now becoming a bit chillier—need a fleece. Days are still warm (shirt sleeves) with the ever-present sun warming up the morning quite quickly. With the cool nights, the dust and smog seems to clear (or settle) over Kabul. We're on the southern outskirts and can see the city spread out to our north. The last few mornings, the closest, dusty range of jagged mountains has been etched on the skyline, quite clear, and very close-looking. Until the air warms, and the view is obscured by haze, you can see the snow-covered peaks of the Hindu Kush to our far north.

Our camp is quite luxurious by deployed standards, even if it is still being built. All my troops are now moved into our "permanent" quarters—Weatherhaven arched tent, 8 soldiers to a tent about the same size as four modular tent sections. These have cloth floors and zip-up doors, power and heat. Every bedspace has its own lamp (clip on type) and some have fans. We're sleeping on army cots, but have been issued foam mattresses to go on top. Loads of civilian workers here, contracted for welfare support, kitchens, cleaning, maintenance. Once the Nepalese kitchen help figured out how to cook Western food, it has been mostly very good (though someone made up "meatloaf" sandwiches the other day, neglecting to ensure that you actually cook the hamburger first!—a less than popular option . . .).

We have Canadian civilian staff that runs the gym, clubs, CANEX, leave flight bookings and supervise maintenance. The CANEX management initially stocked the store with over the counter medication (available free at the hospital) and boot polish—neither are needed here. There's not a lot of deployed experience on the civilian staff, but they are coming along. The civilians follow the same rules as we, the Nepalese are paid a pittance, Canadians make upwards of what a Cpl (with theatre allowances) makes—pretty good considering they spend all their time on the protected camp. No real complaints for a first rotation!

Camp infrastructure is quite interesting from an engineer view (even if we have nothing to do with that type of engineering)—it's a small town being built here. Our water is from three deep wells (80 m deep) drilled here during the camp construction. The water purification system is not yet 100%, so we shower in it, but drink bottled water from Pakistan for now. While "safe to drink" (I brush my teeth in it and have had no problems), it will not meet standards for residual chlorine, etc right now. Shower units are Weatherhaven pre-plumbed MECC shelters (like a fold-out sea container)—somewhat of a line at peak times, but lots of hot water. We will eventually have a sewage treatment plant (the only one in Kabul?), but there is still work ongoing on the digester tank. For now, a company called Ecolog comes along daily with a pumper truck. No idea where they dump the gray/black water . . . Ecolog does our laundry too—drop it off before noon, it (mostly) comes back folded and in a plastic bag the next afternoon. I've had no problems, though several people have lost kit.

My squadron here continues to be busy—never a dull moment for engineers, especially in a new theatre. We continue with route and area proving, clearances if required, construction of bunkers for gun pits, OP construction, route reconnaissance, routine and high readiness explosive ordnance disposal tasks (lots of work here from the detritus of war to employ people here for decades!), etc . . . The reactions of my sappers following the minestrike make me (and indeed the Engineer Branch) proud—they responded professionally with skill and perseverance as many of my soldiers have in other theatres (Somalia, Bosnia, Croatia, Ethiopia). Responding with the infantry quick reaction force, combat engineers secured the scene and proceeded to manually breach into the incident area (took over 12 hours on their stomachs, physically prodding each centimeter of ground to ascertain that there were no more mines to injure anyone else).

There are two different responses—a more risky quick extraction to evacuate casualties, a very deliberate clearance to retrieve kit, the bodies of Sgt Short and Cpl Beerenfenger and allow for investigation. The quick extraction was done by those first responding; it took the next day to fully complete the clearance for the investigation. Four other soldiers (including one engineer) have been repatriated, one stress, PTSD, or shock (not all caused by this one incident, for my soldiers it is an old mental wound re-opened). Both the memorial service here and the one in Pembroke struck me as fitting send-offs, and a tribute to the reason why soldiers are here, running the risks called for by soldiering.

SOURCE ACKNOWLEDGMENTS

The authors have conscientiously sought out copyright holders. If there are omissions or errors, they will correct them in future editions. They gratefully acknowledge the following for their contribution to this volume: "Wolfe Takes Quebec, 1759," anonymous, from *An Accurate and Authentic Journal of the Siege of Quebec 1759* (London: J. Robinson, 1759); "The Battle on the Plains of Abraham," Captain John Knox, "The Battle of Quebec," *Old South Leaflets*, No. 73; "The Assault on Detroit, 1763," Major Duncan to Sir William Johnson, July 31, 1763, National Archives of Canada, Indian Papers, 1761–1763; "The Americans Fail to Take Quebec, 1775–76," National Archives of Canada, Sir Guy Carleton Papers, Carleton to Germain, May 14, 1776; "The Indian Way of War," Thomas Anburey, *Travels Through the Interior Parts of North America* (London: William Lane, 1791); "Fighting with Brock," W.H. Merritt, "Personal Narrative," in E. Cruikshank, ed., *Campaigns of 1812–14: Contemporary Narratives* (Niagara: Niagara Historical Society, 1902); "Honour and Glory," Anne Prevost, "Recollections & Extracts from the Journals of Miss Anne Prevost," at www.galafilm.com/1812/e/people/anneprevost.html; "Corporal Chrétien Fights off the Invaders, May 1813," from J.L.H. Neilson, ed., "Diary of an Officer [Captain Jacques Viger] in the War of 1812–14," Kingston Historical Society [Canadian Institute for Historical Microreproduction, No. 159626]; "The Difficult British–Indian Alliance, 1813," from "A Letter from Lieut.-Colonel Matthew Elliott to Colonel Wm. Claus," in E. Cruikshank, ed., *Campaigns of 1812–14: Contemporary Narratives* (Niagara: Niagara Historical Society, 1902); "An Officer's Wife on a Campaign in Upper Canada, 1814," from National Archives of Canada, William Dunlop

Papers, extracts; "Seizing the *Caroline*, 1837," from Andrew Drew, *A Narrative of the Capture and Destruction of the Steamer "Caroline" and Her Descent over the Falls of Niagara on the Night of 29th of December, 1837* (London: Spottiswoode, 1864); "The Battle of the Windmill, 1838," from Scott McLean, "The Battle of the Windmill Revisited As Recounted by Lieutenant Andrew Agnew, 93rd Highland Regiment of Foot, 8 December 1838," *Canadian Military History*, IX (Autumn 2000), by permission of *Canadian Military History*; "Fighting the Fenians at Ridgeway, 1866," from "Otter's Official Account," in Captain Ernest J. Chambers, *History of the Queen's Own Rifles of Canada* (Toronto: E.L. Ruddy, 1901); "They Could Teach a Lesson to Many: French Canadians in the Militia, 1871," from "Report of the Adjutant-General," in *Militia Report 1871* (Ottawa, 1872); "Aboriginal Boatmen on the Nile, 1884," from Colonel Sir William F. Butler, *The Campaign of the Cataracts Being a Personal Narrative of the Great Nile Expedition of 1884–5* (London: Sampson Low, 1887); "The Midland Battalion Moves to Battle, 1885," from Walter F. Stewart diary at web.mala.bc.ca/davies/letters. images/W.F.Stewart/diary.1.htm; "The Trek Around Lake Superior, 1885," from Lt.-Col. George T. Denison, *Soldiering in Canada: Recollections and Experiences* (Toronto: Morang, 1900); "Letters Home from Battleford, 1885," from Glenbow Museum and Archives, Henry Brock Fonds, M136, Harry Brock to his Mother, May 18 and June 2, 1885; "Fighting the Cree at Frenchman's Butte, 1885," from Glenbow Museum and Archives, William Parker Fonds, M934, "History of Captain William Parker, Life in the NWMP, 1874–1912"; "A Gentleman Cadet at the Royal Military College, 1898," from Brig. F.H. Maynard, "Reminiscences of the RMC, Kingston, Canada from 1898–1901," in R.G.C. Smith, ed., *As You Were: Ex-Cadets Remember*, vol. I, *1876–1918* (Kingston: RMC Club, 1984), by permission of the RMC Club of Canada; "Going to War in South Africa, 1899–1900," Tom Wallace papers, letters of October 29 and November 26, 1899, and March 16, 1900, by permission of Dr William R. Young; "Plenty of Fighting to Suit Everybody: The RCR at Paardeberg," from Douglas McPherson to Mamie, March 3, 1900, printed in the *Dutton Advance*, April 19, 1900, at web.mala.bc.ca/davies/letters.images/Dutton.Advance/Dutton. Advance/ letter.April19.00.htm; "A Journalist Reports on Paardeberg, February 1900," from Stanley M. Brown, *With the Royal Canadians* (Toronto: Publishers' Syndicate, 1900); "We Have to Do or Die: A Strathcona in South Africa, April 1900," from J.C. Walker to C. Witherden, April 16, 1900, printed in *Dutton Advance*, July 26, 1900, at web.mala.bc.ca/davies/letters.images/ Dutton.Advance/Dutton.Advance/letter. July26.00.htm; "The Volunteers Melt Away, 1900," National Archives of Canada, J.S. Willison Papers, C.F. Hamilton to Willison, May 25, 1900; "Cavalry in South Africa," Charlie Rooke to Mother, February 12 and June 1, 1900, January 1, 1901, April 4,

1902, at web.mala.bc.ca/davies/letters.images/Rooke/rooke.collection. htm; "In the Militia, 1912–14," Museum of the Regiments, Lord Strathcona's Horse Regimental Archives, "The Memoirs of Arthur Turner," by permission of the LSH Regimental Archives; "HMCS *Rainbow* Forces the *Komagata Maru* out of Vancouver Harbour, July 1914," Rear Admiral Walter Hose, "Personal Recollections of the 'Komagata Maru' Incident at Vancouver, BC, in July 1914," n.d. [1936], National Archives of Canada, Eric Morse Papers; "The Outbreak of War, 1914," Albert Herbert John Andrews diary, at web.mala.bc.ca/davies/letters.images/Herbert. Andrews/ diary1.htm; "Gathering at Valcartier," Museum of the Regiments, Calgary Highlanders Museum and Archives, Alexander Thomas Thomson letters, August 21, 28, 31, and September 17, 18, 24, 26, 1914, by permission of the Board of Directors of the Calgary Highlanders Regimental Funds Foundation; "From Valcartier to Salisbury Plains," "Recollections of Private William Peden, 8th Battalion, Canadian Expeditionary Force," from www.pacific-pages.com/hpeden/histo02.htm, by permission of Mr. H. Peden; "Trench Life, March 1915," "Recollections of Private William Peden, 8th Battalion Canadian Expeditionary Force," from www.pacific pages.com/hpeden/histo03.htm, by permission of Mr. H. Peden; "War in the Air, April 1915," Anonymous, "A Soldier of the 8th Battalion, April 18, 1915," in *With the First Canadian Contingent* (Toronto: Hodder and Stoughton, 1915); "The Canadian Battle of Ypres," The Albert Edward Roscoe Collection, Roscoe to Mrs. Caleb Bateman, May 13, 1915, at web. mala.bc.ca/davies/letters.images/A.E.Roscoe/letter. Roscoe.May13.1915. htm; "In Flanders Fields," Yale University Archives, Harvey Cushing Papers, McRae to Dr. Charles Martin, May 13, 1915, by permission of Dr. Michael Bliss; "An Acadian Reports from Overseas, 1915," Athanase Poirier to his parents, September 4, October 11, 1915, published in *L'Acadien*, 30 septembre, 30 novembre 1915; "What an Officer Needs in the Trenches, 1915," Museum of the Regiments, Calgary Highlanders Museum and Archives, Alexander Thomas Thomson Letters, Lieut. Alexander Thomson to his brother Doug, November 28, 1915, by permission of the Board of Directors of the Calgary Highlanders Regimental Funds Foundation; "Training Woes in Calgary, December 1915," Glenbow Museum and Archives, Lynch-Staunton, Adam Family Fonds, S.E. Adam to Father, December 15, 1915; "I Was Frightened: Dealing with Fear in the Trenches," James Thorpe to his family, March 6, 1916, at web.mala.bc.ca/davies/ letters.images/Thorpe.Nailen/letter.March6.1916.htm; "We All Shook As Though We Had the Ague: A Bomber at the Front, March 1916," Ernest M. Taylor to his sister, March 24, 1916, at web.mala.bc.ca/davies/letters. images/Taylor.Bury/letter.March24.1916.htm; "Trench Life, April 1916," Glenbow Museum and Archives, Toole Family Fonds, Archer Toole to

Phoebe Toole, April 5, 1916; "Sea Sick, May 1916," "Diary of Michael Duggan 1916–17," by permission of John Fulford, Toronto; "Flying with the No. 7 Squadron, Royal Flying Corps, in France, May 1916," Canadian War Museum, #1985-166/19, Lieut. E.J. Watkins, "A Soldier's Diary"; "Explaining War to the Home Folk, 1916: I," Archie MacKinnon letters, MacKinnon to his sister, May 13, 1916, by permission of Gordon MacKinnon, Toronto; "Explaining War to the Home Folk, 1916: II," Glenbow Museum and Archives, McGill Fonds, Harold McGill to Miss Griffis, June 16, 1916; "The Newfoundland Regiment Is Wiped Out at Beaumont Hamel, July 1, 1916," George Hicks, "Memories of the Battle of Beaumont Hamel," at collections.ic.gc.ca/legion/caphicks.htm; "He Probably Won't Try to Lead Us Again: The RFC Stages a Bombing Raid, July 1916," Brereton Greenhous, ed., *A Rattle of Pebbles: The First World War Diaries of Two Canadian Airmen* (Ottawa: Directorate of History and Heritage, 1986), "The Brophy Diary," by permission of Directorate of History and Heritage, National Defence Headquarters, Ottawa; "Explaining War to the Home Folks, 1916: III," The Hart Leech Collection, Hart Leech to his mother, September 13, 1916, at web.mala.bc.ca/davies/letters.images/H.Leech/letter.Sept13.1916.htm; "Shooting Down a Zeppelin over London, October 1916," Second Lieutenant W.J. Tempest, Directorate of History and Heritage, National Defence Headquarters, Lieutenant W.J. Tempest file, accounts of October 2, 1916 and September 15, 1920; "An Amputee Breaks the News, 1917," James Hepburn, The James Hepburn Collection, James Hepburn to his Father, January 10, 1917, at web.mala.bc.ca/davies/letters.images/Hepburn/collection.htm; "The Terrible Poignancy of War, 1917," Archibald MacKinnon Letters, MacKinnon to his son Ronald, March 20, April 5, 24, 1917, by permission of Gordon MacKinnon, Toronto; "The Guns of Vimy," Canadian War Museum #2000030, Thomas Earl Walker to Vienna Patterson, November 1918; "The Best Show I Have Been In," Glenbow Museum and Archives, Harold W. McGill and Emma Gillis McGill Fonds, Harold McGill to Emma, April 13, 1917; "Narrow Escapes at Vimy," York University Archives, #1989-036/006 (95), J.L. Granatstein Papers, Percy Menzies to Garnet Menzies, April 17, 1917; "A 'Reprisal' Bombing Raid on Freiburg, Germany, April 1917," Sub Lieutenant Walter Flett to Mrs. C.R. Hopper, April 17, 1917, by permission of the Dominion Institute's Memory Project (www.dominion.ca); "Learning to Fly, May 1917," Canadian War Museum, #20010240001, Charles Hendershot to Warren Hendershot, May 1917; "The Call of Duty, 1917," Thomas Harris to Gladys Gillett, May 24, 1917, in Jennifer Trewartha, "The Sweet Escape," *Legion Magazine*, May/June 2001, by permission of Jennifer Trewartha; "The Hell of Passchendaele I: I Shivered Alongside Stephens, October 1917," John Sudbury memoir letter, October 1963, at web.mala.

bc.ca/davies/letters.images/Sudbury/Memoir2.htm; "The Hell of Passchendaele II: October 1917," Glenbow Museum and Archives, Arthur Turner Fonds, Diary 1917 to 1919; "The Hell of Passchendaele III: A Next-of-Kin Letter," Arthur Starkings to Mrs. Shaver, n.d., at web.mala.bc.ca/davies/letters.images/Shaver.C/newspaper.letter2.nd.htm; "The Hell of Passchendaele: IV," Museum of the Regiments, Daniel Dancocks Fonds, K.C. Macgowan World War I letters, Macgowan to mother, October 31, and father, October 31, 1917, by permission of the Archives, Museum of the Regiments; "A Stout Effort in the Air, 1917," Wilbert C. Gilroy Collection, Wilbert C. Gilroy to Mother, October 30, 1917, at web.mala.bc.ca/davies/letters.images/Gilroy/letter.October30.1917.htm; "Until You Hear from Me Again," The John Allen Hunter Collection, J.A. Hunter to Private George Hunter, November 10, 1917, and Chaplain J.S. Darcey to Private George Hunter, November 10, 1917, at web.mala.bc.ca/davies/letters.images/Hunter/letters.htm; "A Hot Fight, November 1917," The Andrew Wilson Collection, Andrew Wilson to Monica Wilson, November 14, 1917, at web.mala.bc.ca/davies/letters.images/Wilson.Andrew/letter.Nov14.1917.htm; "General Currie on Conscription, November 1917," National Archives of Canada, Sir Arthur Currie Papers, Currie to J.J. Creelman, November 30, 1917; "Not a Window Anywhere: The Halifax Explosion, December 1917," Lambert B. Griffith, RCNVR, to Dorothy Helen Griffith, December 16, 1917, by permission of John Griffith Armstrong; "It Was the End of the World: Halifax Destroyed, December 1917," National Archives of Canada, Norman Ellison Papers, Fred Longland, "The Great Halifax Disaster of December 1917"; "A Nursing Sister Near the Front, May 1918," Canadian War Museum, #19950037-014, N/S Katherine MacDonald to her family, May 18, 1918; "Cracking the Hindenburg Line, August 1918," The Ivan Clark Maharg Collection, Ivan Maharg to his parents, August 30, 1918, at web.mala.bc.ca/davies/letters.images/Maharg/letter.Aug30.1918.htm; "Oh, For Three Months Leave . . . ," Canadian War Museum, #19950008-014, Lewis Honey to his parents, September 11, 19, 1918; "My First Aerial Scrap, September 1918," Canadian War Museum, #20010240-005 (104), Warren Hendershot to his family, September 16, 1918; "Following Fritz, October 1918," York University Archives, J.L. Granatstein Papers, #1989-036/006 (95), John Menzies to his family, October 18, 1918; "At 11 a.m. It Went Quiet," Clarence Elder, Glenbow Museum and Archives, Clarence John Elder Fonds, "Experiences of M Clarence Elder in World War I"; "The Last .303 Cartridge I Will Ever Fire," Glenbow Museum and Archives, Gaitz Family Fonds, John Gaitz to his mother, November 13, 1918; "Veterans and the Political Mood in Winnipeg, 1919," Officer Commanding, Military District No. 10, National Archives, Department of National Defence Records, HQC 2514, OC M.D.

10 to Militia Council, January 1919; "Bush Pilots in Uniform, 1925," T.F. Cooper, "Trials and Tribulations," *Roundel*, XI (January–February, 1959); "Strike Duty, Sydney, Nova Scotia, 1925," Lieutenant-General Guy Simonds, "Unpublished Memoirs," by permission of Colonel Charles Simonds; "The Chief of Staff Resigns, 1927," Charles Vining, "The General Packs His Kit Bag," [Vancouver] *Sunday Province*, February 20, 1927; "Militarism in the Nation's Schools, 1927," House of Commons Debates, April 9, 1927; "The American Enemy, 1927," Queen's University Archives, J. Sutherland Brown Papers, Col. Brown to Chief of the General Staff, November 11, 1927; "The Navy Deals with Revolution in Latin America, 1932," Directorate of History and Heritage, National Defence Headquarters, "A Sailor's Life for Me, 1913–1951"; "The Non-Permanent Active Militia in the Great Depression," Major J. Murray Savage, "The N.P.A.M. Between the Wars," in R.G.C. Smith, ed., *As You Were: Ex-Cadets Remember*, Vol. II: *1919–84* (Kingston: RMC Club, 1984), by permission of the RMC Club of Canada; "Cadet Life at the Royal Military College in the 1930s," Brigadier-General Robert Bennett, "A Recruit Recalls," in R.G.C. Smith, ed., *As You Were: Ex-Cadets Remember*, Vol. II: *1919–84* (Kingston: RMC Club, 1984), by permission of the RMC Club of Canada; "We Owed It to Our Country," W.L. Mackenzie King, National Archives of Canada, W.L. Mackenzie King Papers, Diary, September 10, 1936 and August 1 and 19, 1938; "The Army Goes to War, Ottawa, 1939," Directorate of History, National Defence Headquarters, #113.302041, Personal Diary of Major E.G. Weeks; "Creating the 1st Canadian Division," Lieutenant-General Guy Simonds, "Draft Memoirs," by permission of Colonel C.R. Simonds; "General McNaughton Talks to the Prime Minister, 1939," National Archives of Canada, W.L.M. King Papers, Diary, December 7, 1939; "A Small Boat Captain at Dunkirk, May 1940," Rear-Admiral R.W. Timbrell, "Dunkirk-Return-2000," unpublished mss., by permission of Admiral R.W. Timbrell; "The Canadians Go to France—After Dunkirk, 1940," Major-General Harry Foster, Diary, May–June, 1940, by permission of Tony Foster; "Prejudice Against Aboriginals in the Navy," Max Basque, Untitled Recollection, at collections.ic.gc.ca/courage/nativeveterans.html; "A Nursing Sister Reports on Conditions in Britain, February 1941," Canadian War Museum, #19970015-037, N/S Elaine Wright to her parents, February 24, 1941; "Training Seamen, 1941," Lieutenant William H. Pugsley, *Saints, Devils and Ordinary Seamen: Life on the Royal Canadian Navy's Lower Deck* (Toronto: Collins, 1946); "HMCS *Chambly* Boards a U-Boat, September 1941," National Archives, Department of National Defence Records, vol. 6901, file NSS8910-339/21, Lieut. E.T. Simmons, "Report of Boarding Party," n.d.; "The Hong Kong Disaster, December 1941," Extracts from the Report of the Historical Section, Cabinet Office, London and Brig. J.H. Price to Lieutenant-Colonel

G.W.L. Nicholson, January 27, 1948, National Archives, R.G. 24, file HQC 5393-13 (DDHS); "Studied Brutality" in Hong Kong, George S. Mac-Donell, *This Soldier's Story, 1939–1945* (Ottawa: Hong Kong Veterans Association, 2000), by permission of the Hong Kong Veterans Association; "Requests for Special Privileges Are 'Simply Not Done,'" Harry Pope Papers, Uxbridge, ON, General Maurice Pope to Gentleman Cadet Harry Pope, January 27, 1942; "Recruiting CWACs," Cathryne Blackley Armstrong in *Equal to the Challenge: An Anthology of Women's Experiences During World War II* (Ottawa, Department of National Defence, 2001); "Monty on Canada's Senior Officers, 1942," National Archives of Canada, General H.D.G. Crerar Papers, "Notes on Commanders," April 25, 1942; "Striking Against Germany, 1942," The Dennis John Quinlan Collection, Dennis Quinlan to his mother, August 3, 1942, at web.mala.bc.ca/davies/letters.images/D.Quinlan/letter.August3.1942.htm; "From Alberta to Camp Borden, 1942," Glenbow Museum and Archives, Ken Hutchinson Fonds, Ken Hutchinson to his folks, August 14, 22, 1942; "A Padre on the Tragedy of Dieppe, August 1942," York University Archives, J.L. Granatstein Papers, Major the Rev. Mike Dalton Diary; "The Calgarys at Dieppe, 1942," Museum of the Regiments, Grant Odum Phillip Fonds, Phillip to his father, n.d. [August 1942], by permission of the Archives, Museum of the Regiments; "I Am a Prisoner, August 1942," H.W. Hockin to Captain J.M. Hockin, August 24, 1942, printed in the *Dutton Advance*, November 12, 1942, at web.mala.bc.ca/davies/letters.images/Dutton.Advance/Dutton.Advance/letter.Nov12.1942.htm; "The Men Belittled Us at Every Turn," Neva Bayliss in Margaret Galloway, ed., *Women of the War Years: Stories of Determination and Indomitable Courage* (Gladstone, MB, 2000); "A Jolly Good Chance: Trying to Escape, Hong Kong, 1942," Canadian War Museum, #19950077-001, Sergeant John Payne to his mother, August 19, 1942; "The Sinking of the SS *Caribou*, October 1942," National Archives, Department of National Defence Records, vol. 11939, file 8871-3986, "Statement of Alex Bateman, Steerage Steward, S/S *Caribou*," October 21, 1942; "This Can't Last Forever: A Dieppe POW at Christmas, 1942," Canadian War Museum, Private Jack Griss Papers, CWM 19750217-006, Griss to Olga, December 19, 1942; "A Day on a Bomber Squadron and a Last Letter," Glenbow Museum and Archives, F. Lawrence Parker Fonds, "Between Two Dawns: An Account of a Day on a Canadian Bomber Squadron," n.d., and Parker to "My Family," May 17, 1943; "The Three Rivers Regiment Lands in Sicily, July 1943," National Archives of Canada, Jack F. Wallace Papers, Diary; "Doubts About General McNaughton's Abilities, 1943," University of Toronto Archives, Vincent Massey Papers, Diary; "Ike on McNaughton, Canada, and the Empire, 1943," Dwight Eisenhower Library, Pre-Presidential Records, Captain Harry Butcher Diary; "The Fears of

German POWs, Sicily, July 1943," Diary of Major Roy Durnford, Seaforth Highlanders of Canada; "Characteristics of Canadian Soldiers, Sicily, 1943," National Archives of Canada, Department of National Defence Records, Major A.T. Sesia Diary; "There Is Great Hope That He Is Alive: Caring for Those at Home, 1943," various letters from the William Ivan Mouat Collection, at web.mala.bc.ca/davies/letters.images/Mouat/Mouat. collection.htm; "Washing Out of Pilot Training, 1943," Dr. Jeffrey Keshen Papers, James Keshen to Harry Lazarus, October 21, 1943, by permission of Dr. Jeff Keshen; "Tank Training in England, 1943," Memorandum, Brigadier-General C. de L. Kirby to John Marteinson et al., January 15, 2003, by permission of General Kirby; "The Strains of High Command, 1943," National Archives of Canada, Harry Crerar Papers, Simonds to Crerar, December 15, 1943; "As Tough a Go As Anything We've Encountered: Italy, December 1943," Canadian War Museum, Major Harry Jolley Papers, Jolley to Eva Geller, December 17, 1943; "There Are No Trenches: At Ortona, December 1943," Gregory Clark, "Old Trench War Was Easy Beside Ortona, Says Clark," *Toronto Daily Star*, January 10, 1944, at "Democracy at War: Canadian Newspapers and the Second World War," www.warmuseum.ca; "Dining with Colonel Zabotin in Halifax," Leo Hamson, "A Personal Memory," unpublished account, by permission of Leo Hamson; "The Problem of Home Defence Conscripts, 1943," National Archives of Canada, General Maurice Pope Papers, Pope Diary; "Service in Italy Behind the Front, 1943," Jack Ainsworth, York University Archives, J.L. Granatstein papers, #1989-036/007 (109), Jack Ainsworth Papers, excerpts from letters to his parents; "Politics and Food in the Navy, February 1944," York University Archives, J.L. Granatstein Papers, #1989-036/006 (88), Fraser McKee Letters, McKee to his mother, February 20, 1944; "Young Officers Emerge in Battle, 1944," Royal Military College, Christopher Vokes Diary, "The Adriatic Front—Winter 1944"; "The Rise of the Militia Officer, 1944," York University Archives, J.L. Granatstein Papers, #1989-036/006 (96), Brigadier William Murphy Papers, Murphy to his parents, February 20, 1944; "The Generals Ready for D-Day, 1944," National Archives of Canada, J.L. Ralston Papers, "Memorandum of Notes Made by Lieut.-Colonel G.S. Currie During Visit to England"; "The Opening of the Hitler Line Battle, Italy, May 1944," York University Archives, J.L. Granatstein Papers, #1989-036/006, Brigadier William Murphy Papers, Murphy to his family, May 17, 1944; "We Are Going In Tomorrow Morning, D-Day, 1944," Canadian War Museum, #19800396, Rifleman Edward Worden to his wife, June 5, 1944; "Beach Head Taken: A Journalist Lands in Normandy, June 6, 1944," Ross Munro, Canadian Press despatch, June 6, 1944, at "Democracy at War: Canadian Newspapers and the Second World War, www.warmuseum.ca; "We French Canadians Are in No Way Subordinate, 1944," Directorate of History and Heritage, National Defence Headquarters, #312.009 (D52), Major T.L. Bullock to C. Papineau-Couture, June 12, 1944; "So Long Without Eat & Sleep: In the Normandy Beachhead," Glenbow Museum and Archives, Ken Hutchinson Papers, Hutchinson to his Folks, June 14, 1944; "I Saw French Women Throwing Roses: Liberation, June 1944," Matthew Halton, "'The Welcome We All Got Touched Our Hearts . . .,'" *Saturday Night*, June 16, 1944, by permission of David Halton; "Night Flying Training in Wales, July 1944," William Watson to his family, July 11, 1944, at web.mala.bc.ca/davies/letters.images/William%20Watson/letter.July11.1944.htm; "Write Often and Send Grub," Captain Jacques Gouin to his uncle, 17 juillet 1944, University of Ottawa, Centre de recherche en civilization canadienne-française, Gouin fonds; "The Normandy Diary of Gunner Brady," Glenbow Museum and Archives, James Brady Fonds, War Diary; "Falaise Is at Last Ours: The Closing of the Gap, August 1944," Frederick Griffin, despatch to *Toronto Daily Star*, August 18, 1944, at "Democracy at War: Canadian Newspapers and the Second World War," www.warmuseum.ca; "A Nursing Sister on German POWs and Canadian Slackers, September 1944," Jean M. Ellis, *Face Powder and Gunpowder* (Toronto: S.J. Reginald Saunders, 1947); "Outarmoured and Outgunned by the German Panthers: Tanks in Italy, 1944," York University Archives, J.L. Granatstein Papers, #1989-036/006, Brigadier William Murphy Papers, Murphy to his family, August 17, 1944; "The Loyal Edmonton Regiment at the Gothic Line, September 1944," Bill Boss, "Nazis Routed by Edmontons in Gothic Line," Canadian Press despatch in *Globe and Mail*, October 19, 1944, at "Democracy at War: Canadian Newspapers and the Second World War," www.warmuseum.ca; "Letters from the Mud, November–December 1944," J.E. Boulet to his wife, at collections.gc.ca/courage/j.e.bouletpart2.html;"What the Hell Is the Matter with Everything?: Manpower Bungles, November 1944," Alex Graham to his parents, November 23, 1944, published in the *Dutton Advance*, February 1, 1945, at web.mala.bc.ca/davies/letters.images/Dutton.Advance/Dutton.Advance/letter.Feb1.1945.htm; "A First Christmas in Stalag Luft III, 1944," Glenbow Museum and Archives, Ian H. Fowler Fonds, Fowler to Dorothy Pemberton, December 22, 1944; "The Luftwaffe's Last Throw, New Year's Day, 1945," Directorate of History and Heritage, National Defence Headquarters, 73/847, Statement by Sergeant W.L. Large on Combat Reports; "Battle Fatigue, February 1945," Burton Fitch, *A Toast to the Survivors* (privately published, 2001), by permission of Burton Fitch; "A Passover Seder at Cleve, Germany, March 1945," National Archives of Canada, Sam Cass Papers, Monthly Report, March 1945; "Free at Last: An RCAF POW Writes Home, April 1945," Canadian War Museum, #19840297-001, WO Don Scowen to his folks, April 3, 1945; "V-E Day in Germany, May 1945,"

Glenbow Museum and Archives, James Brady Fonds, War Diary; "V-E Day in London, May 1945," Dominion Institute, the Memory Project, Veteran's Archive, Edna Wilson to her sister, May 9, 1945, at www.thememory project.com; "The End of the War in London and Toronto," Pat Bates to Peggy Bates, May 2, 1945, and Peggy Bates to Pat Bates, May 18, 1945, by permission of Jock Bates, Hilary Bates Neary, and Rosemary Bates Terry; "Occupying Germany, May–June 1945," the Stanley Winfield Collection, Memoir, Summer 1945, at web.mala.bc.ca/davies/letters.images/Winfield/ memoir.1945.htm; "I Have Just Seen Belsen, June 1945," York University Archives, Nick Aplin Papers, #1997-044-001, Ted Aplin to Lil, June 17, 1945; "A Soldier's Suicide," from Robert Calder, *A Richer Dust: Family, Memory and the Second World War* (Toronto: Penguin Canada, 2004), reprinted by permission of Penguin Group (Canada); "The Difficult Re-adjustment to Peace," Rodolphe Cormier, *J'ai vécu la guerre* (Moncton: Les Editions d'Acadie, 1988); "Our Grandchildren Will Ask Us Who Liberated Us, Editor, *Our Free Holland*," March 10, 1946, "Democracy at War," at www.warmuseum.ca; "A Commander for Korea, August 1950," National Archives of Canada, General John M. Rockingham Papers, "Recollections of Korea," August 1975; "The Chinese Intervene in Korea, December 1950," Canadian War Museum, #19950074-043, Major R.B. Meredith to his family, December 12, 1950, January 4, 1951; "Hands Off Korea: Captain Pope and the Trotskyist Blonde, April 1951," William Henry Pope, *Leading from the Front: The War Memoirs of Harry Pope* (Waterloo: Laurier Centre for Military Strategic and Disarmament Studies, 2002), by permission of Laurier Centre for Military Strategic and Disarmament Studies; "With the Guns in Korea, 1951," Don Dalke, "With the Guns in Korea," *Legion Magazine*, July/August 2003, by permission of Don Dalke; "Crossing the Imjin River, 1951," National Archives of Canada, General John M. Rockingham Papers, "Recollections of Korea," August 1975; "There Sure Isn't Much News: Private Roy Dooley Writes Home from Korea, 1951," Museum of the Regiments, Princess Patricia's Canadian Light Infantry Archives, #114(14)-1, Private Roy Dooley to his Folks, November 2, 1951; "Problems in the NATO Brigade, 1953," Lionel Shapiro, "The Failure of the 27th," *Maclean's*, August 15, 1953; "What Problems in the NATO Brigade?" Directorate of History and Heritage, National Defence Headquarters, 410 B27.061 (D2), Stacey to Vice Adjutant-General, August 7, 1953; "Keeping the Peace in Suez, UNEF, 1959," National Archives of Canada, Department of External Affairs Records, file 50366-40, vol. 15, letter by Capt. G.R. Tomalin, 1959; "Governor General Vanier on His Beloved Vandoos," National Archives of Canada, Brooke Claxton Papers, Vanier to Claxton, July 10, 1959; "The World's Most Provincial Animal: Canadian Soldiers Abroad, 1962," Canadian War Museum, J.L. Granatstein Letters, a Royal

Canadian Army Service Corps captain to J.L. Granatstein, January 3, April 29, 1962; "Getting Out of Egypt Ahead of the Six Day War, May 1967," Michael Belcher, "Exodus El Arish," *Airforce* VII (September 1983), by permission of Michael Belcher; "Keeping Peace in a Troubled Cyprus, 1975," Robert Burns, "A Hot Night in the Zone," *Legion Magazine*, May/June 2001, by permission of Robert Burns; "At War in the Gulf, January 1991," Richard Gimblett to his wife and family, January 9, 28, 31, 1991, by permission of LCdr (ret.) Richard Gimblett; "The Canadian Airborne Regiment in Somalia, 1993," "The Canadian Airborne Regiment in Somalia," at www. commando.org/somalia, by permission of Robert Prouse; "The Killing of Shidane Arone, Somalia, 1993," Court Martial Testimony, Testimony of MWO Mills, Sgt Hillier, A/Sgt Skipton, Court-Martial of Major Seward, Exhibits P33-P33.6, Inquiry into the Deployment of Canadian Forces to Somalia; "Squaring Off With Serbian Forces in Croatia, 1993," Paul Gélinas, "Close Call in Croatia," *Legion Magazine*, September/October 2001, by permission of Paul Gélinas; "Medical Risks in Croatia, 1994," Eric Smith, "A Dysfunctional Family Called Our Military," *Globe and Mail*, July 29, 1999; "Dealing with Serbs and Croats, 1994," anonymous to Jane Snailham, July 26, 1994, in Jane Snailham (ed. By Alex Morrison and Steve Torrisi), *Eyewitnesses to Peace: Letters from Canadian Peacekeepers* (Cornwallis Park, Nova Scotia: The Canadian Peacekeeping Press, 1998), by permission of Canadian Peacekeeping Press, Pearson Peacekeeping Centre, Cornwallis Park, Nova Scotia; "The Nightmare of Rwanda—and After," "Dave, I could see myself killing people," *Globe and Mail*, July 8, 2000; "Serving in Kosovo, 1999," Captain Paul de Grandpré, Captain Paul de Grandpré, "Lettre de Kosovo," *Veritas*, December 1999, by permission of the RMC Club of Canada; "Making a Difference in Kosovo," Lt Eleanor Taylor, "Making a Difference in Magura," *Vanguard*, #1, 2000, by permission of *Vanguard*; "Stopping Smugglers in the Straits of Hormuz, 2002," Anonymous, "HMCS *Ottawa* Captures Suspected Oil Smuggler," *Trident*, June 3, 2002; "Fighting in Afghanistan, 2002," Stephen J. Thorne, "The Caves and Graves of Tora Bora," *Legion Magazine*, July/August 2003, by permission of Stephen J. Thorne; "Operating in Kabul, December 2003," Major Keith Cameron, "Afghanistan Diary," *Veritas*, December 2003, by permission of the RMC Club of Canada.

INDEX

Abbot, Lieutenant, 27
Aberdeen, Wilbur B., 359
Aboriginal peoples
  and British Army, 24–27, 28–30,
    38–41, 55–57
  in Latin America, 226, 229
  at Quebec, 15, 18, 21–22
  in Red River Rebellion, 68, 71–74
  in Second World War, 252
  in War of 1812, 31, 33, 38–41
Adam, S.F., 127–28
Afghanistan, 1, 2, 457–65
Agnew, Andrew, 50–52
Ainsworth, Jack, 323–25
Akers, R.E., 52
AK-47 rifle, 447
Albanians, 447, 448–49, 450
Alberta, 96–98
Alberta Mounted Rifles, 71, 72
Albert (France), 143
Aldershot, 244
Alderson, Edwin A., 113
Alexander (of Tunis), Harold, 296–97,
    371
Ali Khayl, 460–62
Amalgamated Union of Transit
  Employees, 388–89
Ambler, 259
American Revolution, 1, 28–30
Amherst, Jeffrey, 17, 20
Amherstburg, 38–39
Amherst's Regiment, 14, 15
Amsterdam, 378, 386

Anburey, Thomas, 28–30
Andrews, Albert Herbert John, 103–4
Anstruther's Regiment, 16
Aplin, Ted, 375, 379–83
Arabian Sea, 453
Araujo, Arturo, 227
Argentina, 421
Armstrong, Cathryne Blackley "Kay,"
    269–71
Armstrong (ON), 275
Army Act, 317
Arnold, Benedict, 27
Arone, Shidane, 429–35
Arras, 192–98
Astor, John Jacob, 247
Atlantic, Battle of the, 315–16
Aurora aircraft, 454
Australian Army, 176, 222
Avro Viper aircraft, 211–12

Bagram, 457, 459
Banjica, 452–53
Barrie, 106
Barriefield, 237, 277
Basque, Max, 252
Bateman, Alex, 284–86
Bates, Pat, 371–73
Bates, Peggy, 373–74
Bayliss, Neva, 282–83
Bean, Lieutenant, 24, 26
Beaumont Hamel, 138–40
Beauport (QC), 13–14
Bedson, Captain, 103

Beerenfenger, Robbie, 462, 465
Belcher, Michael, 412–15
Belcourt, Jim, 279
Belcourt, Ray, 279
Beled Weyne, 425, 426–27
Belgium, 360–61, 364
Belleville (ON), 58
Belsen, 377, 379–83
Bennett, Robert, 231–36
Berthulie, 93
Biarritz, 251
Bibby, Dave, 460
Bienfeld, 374–75
Big Bear, 69, 73–74
bin Laden, Osama, 458, 459, 460
Birmingham (UK), 343
Biscotasing, 59, 65–66
Blakeley, William, 106
Bloemfontein, 81–82
Boers, 82, 84, 85, 86–88, 92, 94
Bologna, General, 300–301
Bone, Levi, 98
Booker, Alfred, 53
Borden, Frederick, 218
Borden, Robert, 3, 107
Boss, Bill, 358–59
Botha, Louis, 95
Bougainville, Louis-Antoine de, 22
Boulet, J.E., 360–61
Boulogne, 250
Boulton, Charles, 64
Bourlamaque, François-Charles de, 20
Bourlon Wood, 198
Bowmanville, 58
Boy's Own Paper, 78
Bradbrooke, Major, 197
Brady, James P., 346–49, 368–69
Bragg's Regiment, 16, 23
Brandon, 61
Brantford, 269
Bremm, Lieutenant, 27
Brest (France), 251, 252
British Army. *See also specific units;*
    Revolutionary War
  and Aboriginal peoples, 24–27,
    28–30, 38–41, 55–57
  in First World War, 122
  in Middle East, 421
  on the Nile, 57
  at Quebec, 21
  in Rebellions of 1837–38, 50–52
  in Red River Rebellion, 61, 64,
    70–71, 72, 74
  in Second World War, 362, 377
  in War of 1812, 30–46

British Broadcasting Corporation
    (BBC), 374, 451
British Columbia, 99–100, 302
British Columbia Electric Company,
    388–90
Brock, Harry, 68–71
Brock, Isaac, 31–34, 35
Brodeur, Commander, 228
Brooke, Alan (Lord Alanbrooke), 251,
    295–96
Brophy, John B., 140–43
Brown, Buster, 5
Brown, J. Sutherland, 223–24
Brown, Kyle, 431, 433
Brown, Lieutenant, 25, 26–27
Brown, Stanley M., 79, 80, 84–89
Brown, W.I., 261
Buchan, Major, 85–86, 90
Bullock, Captain, 33
Bullock, T.L., 335–37
Burgio, 294–95
Burnett, Rod, 190
Burns, Robert, 415–19
Burrell, Martin, 101
Burton, Ralph, 21
Bush, William, 107
Butcher, Harry, 296–98
Butler, William, 55–57
Bygrove, Aaron, 460

Caen, 346
C-17 aircraft, 457
Cairo, 362
Calder, Ken, 3, 383–84
Calder, Margaret, 383–84
Calderon, General, 229
Caledonia, 32
Caledonia Rifle Company, 52–53
Calgary, 97, 98, 127–28, 209
  units from, 106, 163–71, 280–81
  103rd (Calgary Rifles) Regiment,
    109–10
Cambrai, 141–42
Cameron, Keith, 462–65
Cameron, W.B., 73
Cameron Highlanders, 195, 253
Campbell, Ken, 365
Camp Borden, 238, 274–78
Canada, Government of. *See also*
    Department of National Defence;
    House of Commons
  and *Komagata Maru*, 100–102
  in Second World War, 239, 243–44,
    245
Canadian Airborne Regiment, 422–35
  1st Canadian Armoured Brigade,

294–95, 327–28, 330–31
2nd Canadian Armoured Brigade, 331
4th Canadian Armoured Division,
    347–48
5th Canadian Armoured Division,
    307–11
Canadian Army, 355–56, 396, 401–8,
    410–11, 412, 420. *See also specific
    units;* Canadian Expeditionary
    Force
  1st Canadian Division, 2, 242–47,
    250–52, 294–95, 307–8, 326–27
  25th Canadian Brigade Group,
    398–400
  9th Canadian Brigade Machine Gun
    Company, 160–63
Canadian Broadcasting Corporation
    (CBC), 373
Canadian Corps, 271–73, 366
Canadian Expeditionary Force (CEF)
  4th Battalion, 109
  5th Battalion, 119–21
  7th Battalion, 106, 116, 206
  8th Battalion, 206
  9th Battalion Engineers, 206
  10th Battalion, 109, 116, 125
  46th Battalion (Saskatchewan), 164,
    167, 168–69, 170, 171
  50th Battalion (Calgary), 163–71
  56th Battalion, 127
  58th Battalion, 195
  61st Battalion, 143–44
  1st Brigade, 109
  3rd Brigade, 109
  4th Brigade, 109
  1st Division, 123, 125, 209
  2nd Division, 123, 209
  3rd Division, 123, 138, 209
  4th Division, 209
Canadian Forestry Corps, 253
  25th Canadian Infantry Battalion, 395
  2nd Canadian Infantry Division,
    347–48
  3rd Canadian Infantry Division, 331,
    349
Canadian Letters and Images Project, 7
Canadian Machine Gun Corps, 128–29
Canadian Mounted Rifles, 90, 94–96,
    130–32
Canadian Pacific Railway, 59–61, 65
Canadian Press, 457
Canadian Prisoners-of-War Relatives'
    Association, 302–3
Canadian Provost Corps, 366
1st Canadian Rifle Battalion, 406
Canadian Scottish Regiment, 400

Canadian War Museum, 7–8
Canadian Women's Army Corps
    (CWACs), 269–71
Cananocoui. *See* Gananoque
CANEX, 464
Cape Breton Island, 212–14
Cardoza, George, 105
Caribou, 284–86
Carleton, Guy, 27
Carleton and York Regiment, 294–95
Caroline, 46–49
Carpenter, "Chippy," 188
Carpenter, E., 348
Carr, Captain, 142–43
Carson, Lambert, 93
CASF (Canadian Active Service Force),
    240, 241
Cass, Sam, 366–67
Castle, Jim, 183
Cauvicourt, 349
CCF (Co-operative Commonwealth
    Federation), 325–26, 374
Centurion, 14, 16
Chamberlain, Neville, 240
Chambers, Major, 31
Chambly, 259–61
Chatham (ON), 39–40
Chatore, General, 229
Chicago, 92
China, Republic of, 390–93, 397–98,
    400
Chippewas, 39
Chrétien, Corporal, 36–38
Churchill, Winston, 374
Clark, Clifford, 246
Clark, Colonel, 33
Clark, Frank, 173, 177
Clark, George, 296
Clark, Gregory, 312–15
Clarke's Crossing, 64
Claxton, Brooke, 388–89
Cleve, 366–67
Coffin, Elias, 285
Colbon, Jon, 455
Collins, Captain, 106
1 Combat Engineer Regiment, 458–60
Combe, Robert G., 113–14
Commonwealth Division, 396–400
Communists, 226–27, 382
Contalmaison, 141
Cookson, Colonel, 94, 95
Cooper, Fred, 384
Cooper, T.F., 211–12
Co-operative Commonwealth
    Federation (CCF), 325–26, 374
Copeland, Henry, 103

Cormelles, 348
Cormier, Rodolphe, 5, 384–85
Cornwalls and Shropshires, 82
Craig, Colonel, 320–21
Craven, R.N., 359
Cree people, 56, 71–74
Crerar, H.D.G. (Harry), 295, 307–11, 328–30, 332
Crimean War, 57
Croatia, 435–42
Croil, George M., 238
Cronje, Piet, 82, 86–88
Cull, R.C., 359
Currie, Arthur, 116, 120, 184–85, 206
Currie, G.S., 328–30
Cut Knife, 70
Cuyler, Lieutenant, 26
Cyprus, 415–19

Dalke, Don, 396–98
Dalton, Mike, 278–80
Dalyell, Captain, 24–26
Darcey, J.S., 181–82
Darlan, Jean Louis, 298
Davies, Stephen, 7
D-Day, 328–30, 331–35
Dearborn, Henry, 35
Defence Scheme No. 1, 223–24
Delarey, J.H., 94, 95–96
Denison, George T., 60, 65–67
Dennis, Captain, 34, 61–62
Department of National Defence (DND), 215, 217–20, 222, 239–40, 242, 246
Directorate of History and Heritage, 7
National War Services, 304
Detroit, 24–27, 31–32, 35
Detroit, 32
de Valera, Eamon, 374
DeWet, Christiaan, 93, 95–96
Dextraze, Jacques A., 396
Dieppe, 278–81, 286
Dieselburg, 288
Dooley, Roy, 400–401
Dorelle, Mme, 339–40
Doyle, Stan, 359
Drew, Andrew, 46–49
Dubai, 420–22
Duggan, Michael, 133–35
Duke, Tom, 460
Duncan, Major, 24–27
Dundas, Henry, 50, 51–52
Dunkirk, 247–50
Dunning, Charles A., 236
Durell, Philip, 13

Durnford, Roy, 298–99
Dutton Advance, 83–84

Earnshaw, Colonel, 241
E-boats, 249
Ecolog, 464
Edgar, Reb, 415
Edward, Prince of Wales, 123, 206
Egypt, 362, 408–15. See also Nile River
Eindhoven, 363–64
Eisenhower, Dwight D., 296–98
El Arish, 412–15
Elder, Clarence, 205–9
Elizabeth II, 409–10
Elkins, W.H.P., 238
Elliott, Matthew, 38–41
Elliott, William, 40
Ellis, Jean M., 354–56
El Mansur, 251
Elmsley, Lieutenant, 48
El Salvador, 225–29
Empress of Britain, 134
1 Combat Engineer Regiment, 458–60
England. See British Army; Great Britain
Essex Scottish Regiment, 278–80, 281
Euro-News, 451

Falaise Gap, 350–54
Fascists, 382–83
Fenians, 6, 52–54
Ferguson, Roy, 139
First World War, 3, 6, 103–210, 217. See also Canadian Expeditionary Force
Fish Creek, 64
Fisher, Ensign, 26
Fitch, Burton, 364–65
Fitch, Lieutenant, 69
Fitzsimmons, James, 412
Flett, Walter P., 154–56
Fokker aircraft, 143, 155
Forbes, Donald F., 365
Forcier, J.Y., 420
Ford, Charles, Jr., 285
Fort Detroit. See Detroit
Fort Garry Horse, 103
Fort George, 32
Fort Niagara, 20
Fortress bomber, 334, 348
Fort Schlosser, 47–49
Fort Wellington, 50
Fort William Henry, 23
Foster, Harry, 250–52
Fowler, Ian H., 362–63
Fox, Ted, 390

Fox, Trumpeter, 231, 234
France. *See also* French Army
    cadets in, 222
    in First World War, 237
    in Second World War, 240, 339–42,
        344–54, 356–57
    vs. Great Britain, 1, 13–19
Frazier's Regiment, 16
Freiburg, 154–56
French Army, 22, 122, 128, 450. *See also*
    France
French-Canadians, 54–55, 56
    in Second World War, 335–37,
        344–46, 353–54
Frenchman's Butte, 71–74

Gadd, Claude, 103
Gaitz, John, 209–10
Gallinger, L.J., 359
Gananoque, 36, 37
Ganong, H.N., 272
Gardiner, James G., 236
Gardner, Captain, 63
Gaza, 408, 411, 412
Gélinas, Paul, 435–39
Geoffrion, Lieutenant, 349
George V, 123
George VI, 240, 370
German Army, 379
    in First World War, 115–18, 124,
        131, 136–38, 162, 165, 170,
        204–5
    as POWs, 196, 298–99, 314–15,
        341–42, 345, 349, 354–56
    in Second World War, 311, 324,
        346–47, 348
Germans, 365, 375
Germany. *See also* German army;
    Germans; Luftwaffe
    Canadian Army in, 374–83, 401–8
    in First World War, 120
    and Second World War, 371, 374–78
    V-E Day in, 368–69
Gibson, Captain, 433
Gibson, Melbourne I., 359
Gilroy, Wilbert C., 179–81
Gimblett, Richard, 419–22
Gladwin, Major, 24
Glass, Trooper, 430–31, 432, 433
Globe, 79, 89–90
Gordon, Charles (Ralph Connor), 98
Gordon Highlanders, 82, 85, 87
Goss, Corporal, 240
Gothic Line, 358–59
Gouin, Jacques, 344–46
Gouzenko, Igor, 315

Grable, Betty, 316
Graffenstafel Ridge, 116
Graham, Alex, 361–62
Grandpré, Paul de, 447–51
Grand Trunk Pacific Steamships, 100
Grant, Captain, 25–27
Graspaan, 82, 83
Grauer, Dal, 389
Gravelly Point, 37
Grave (Netherlands), 367
Gray, Captain, 25–26, 27
Great Britain. *See also* British Army;
    Royal Air Force; Royal Navy
    and Canada, 243–44
    vs. France, 1, 13–19
Great Depression, 229–31
Great War Veterans Association, 211
Griffin, Frederick, 350–54
Griffith, Lambert, 185–87
Griss, Jack, 286
20th Guards Brigade, 250
Gulf War, 1, 419–22
Gunn, Theo, 103, 104

Haddow, Colonel, 139
Haig, Douglas, 141
Hale, Colonel, 22
Halifax, 256–59, 315–21, 374
Halifax Explosion, 185–91
Hall, Bill, 314
Halton, Matthew, 339–42
Hamilton, C.F., 79, 80, 89–90
Hamilton, G., 31, 32
Hamilton, General, 90
Hamilton (ON), 106, 269
13th (Hamilton) Royal Regiment, 106
Hamilton Spectator, 8
Hammarskjöld, Dag, 409, 410
Hamson, Leo, 315–21
Hanover, 401–8
Hansen, Joe, 394, 395
Harris, Thomas P., 157–60
Harrison, Lieutenant, 168
Harrison, William Henry, 39
Hart, Colonel, 321
Hatt, Captain, 31
Heath, William, 58
Heller, John, 312–13
Hellfire Bay, 60
Hendershot, Charles, 156–57, 201
Hendershot, Warren, 199–201
Hennessy, P., 264, 265
Hepburn, James, 146–47
Hicks, George, 138–40
Highflyer, 191
51st Highland Division, 347–48

Highland regiments, 50–52, 85. *See also specific regiments*
  at Quebec, 14, 21, 22
Hillier, Joe, 430–33, 434
Hindenburg Line, 192–98, 202
Hitler, Adolf, 240, 371, 372
Hitler Line, 330–31
Hockin, H.W., 281
Hoffmeister, Bertram, 309
Holcroft, Captain, 33
Holland. *See* Netherlands
Holmes, Charles, 16
Home, W.J., 262–63, 264–65
Home Defence, 321–23
Honey, Lewis, 198–99
Hong Kong, 262–68, 283–84, 397
Hong Kong Volunteer Defence Force, 263
Hooper, Sergeant Major, 64
Hope, Bob, 316
Hopkins, Captain, 25
Hormuz, Straits of, 453–56
Horn, Fred, 98
Horne, Chet, 455
Hose, Walter, 5, 98–103
Houghton, Frank, 225–29
House of Commons, 217–23, 241–42, 297
Howe, William, 14–15, 20
Hughes, Captain, 68, 69
Hughes, Sam, 80, 104, 106, 107, 109–12
Hughes, Sergeant, 64
Hull, William, 31–32
Hume Blake, Samuel[?], 68, 70
Hunter, J. Earl, 226–27
Hunter, John Allen, 181–82
Hunt Walsh, Colonel, 23
Hurons, 39
Hutchinson, Ken, 338–39
Hutchison, Ken, 274–78
Hutton, Edward T.H., 80

Ilsley, James L., 236
Imjin River, 398–400
Imo, 187, 188, 189
Indians. *See* Aboriginal peoples
infantry, 54–55, 55. *See also specific units*
25th Infantry Brigade, 404
27th Infantry Brigade, 401–8
Intelligence Scouts, 61–62
Interahamwe, 443
International Security Assistance Force (ISAF), 462–65
Iran, 453
Iraq, 419, 422
Irish Regiment (Toronto), 240
Iroquois, 56

Israel, 412–15
Italian Army, 450
Italians, 300–301, 358–59
Italy, 311–12, 323–25, 327–28, 330–31, 356–59, 371. *See also* Italian Army; Italians; Sicily

Jackfish Bay, 60, 67
Japanese, 216–17
Japanese Army, 263, 264, 266–68, 397
Japanese-Canadians, 270–71
Jefferson, Thomas, 30
Jewish Welfare, 366
Jews, 298, 366–67, 377, 379–83
Johnson, A.M., 359
Johnston, Barney, 102
Johnstone, William, 51
Jolley, Harry, 311–12
Jones, Captain (chaplain), 254
Jones, Lieutenant, 89
Juliana, Queen of the Netherlands, 387
Juno Beach, 331, 333–34

Kabul, 462–65
"Kamloops Kid," 267
Kaye, Lieutenant, 88
Keller, R.F.L., 332, 349
Kennedy, Major, 168–69
Kennedy-Reid, Nursing Sister, 253
Kennedy's Regiment, 16, 23
Keshen, James, 305–6
Khartoum Relief Expedition, 55–57
Kigali, 443–44
Kildonan Redcoats, 71
King, William Lyon Mackenzie, 3, 236–39, 240, 245–47, 297, 298
Kingsmill, Charles, 215
Kingston (ON), 41–46, 58–59. *See also* Barriefield; Royal Military College
Kiraly, Alex(andra), 454
Kirby, Christopher de L., 306–7
Kiska, 323
Kitchener, Horatio H., Lord, 93, 94, 95, 123
Knox, John, 19–24
Komagata Maru, 98–103
Korea, 1, 388–401
Kosovo, 1, 447–53
Kosovo Liberation Army (KLA), 447–48, 450, 451
Kowloon, 264
Kruger, Paul, 92
Kuwait, 419

Laing, Darell, 242, 243
Lake Superior, 60, 65–67

LaMarsh, Judy, 270
Lamb, Dave, 415
Langdon-Davies, John, 221
Lapointe, Ernest, 236, 240, 337
Laprairie (QC), 54–55
Large, W.L., 363–64
Lascelles' Regiment, 16
Laudrum, John, 358–59
Laurie, General, 69
Law, Jimmy, 166–67, 168, 171
Lawson, J.K., 264, 265
Lay, Harry, 237
Leech, Hart, 143–44
Levis, François de, 20
Liberator bomber, 334
Liberty Network, 391
Lightning aircraft, 333, 334
Lindsay (ON), 58
Linn, Carson, 157
Lipsett, Colonel, 117
Liri Valley, 331
Llanthony, 247
London Rifles, 114–15
London (UK), 369–70
Longland, Fred, 187–91
Lord Strathcona's Horse (Royal
    Canadians), 89, 90–94, 98
Louisbourg Grenadiers, 20
Louvencourt, 139
Loyal Edmonton Regiment, 358–59
Lublin, 381
Luftwaffe, 118–19, 363–64
Luke, Lieutenant, 26
LVG aircraft, 143

Macbean, Major, 50, 51
MacBrien, J.H., 214–17
MacCormick, Lieutenant, 48
Macdonald, Edward M., 215
MacDonald, Katherine, 191–92
Macdonell, George S., 265–68
Macdonnell, Lieutenant, 87–88
Macdougald, Lou, 60
Macgowan, Keith, 172–78
MacGregor, Keith, 359
Machan, Clyde, 183
MacKay, Dr., 123
Mackenzie, Alexander, 237–38
Mackenzie, Hugh F., 114
Mackenzie, Ian A., 236, 237
MacKenzie, Nyle, 314
Mackenzie, William Lyon, 46–47
Mackinnon, Archibald, 147–49
Mackinnon, Archie, 136–37
Mackinnon, Ronald, 147
MacMurray, George, 376–77

Macnab, Allan, 49
Macphail, Agnes, 217–23, 229
Magersfontein, 85
Maharg, Ivan Clark, 192–98
Mail and Empire, 79
Major, Pell, 32
Maltby, C.M., 262–63, 264
Manchuria, 217
99th Manitoba Rangers, 111
Mann, Churchill, 243
Mao Tse-tung, 395
Maplemore, 91–92
Marjoribanks, Lieutenant, 36–38
Marston Green, 253
Martinez, Maximilian Hernandez, 227,
    228–29
Maskell, Joe, 212
Mason, Lieutenant, 120
Massey, Vincent, 295–96
Massey-Harris, 245
Matchee, Clayton, 431, 433–34
Matthews, A.B., 239–40
Matthews, Bruce, 2–3
Mattison, Boatswain, 191
Maund, Captain and Mrs. Charles,
    41–46
May, Austen, 127
Maynard, F.H., 74–79
McConnaghy, Art, 104
McCrae, Constable, 72–73
McCrae, John, 121–22
McDonald, Colonel, 32, 34
McDougall, Frank, 359
McDougall, Louis, 64
McDugal, Lieutenant, 25–26
McEachren, Ensign, 53
McGee, Flight Sergeant, 363–64
McGhee, Jimmy, 286
McGill, Harold Wigmore, 137–38,
    151–52
McGill, Major, 76
McGuire, Captain, 105, 106
McKee, Carey, 194
McKee, Colonel, 39
McKee, Fraser, 325–26
McKellar's Bay, 65
McKenney, Lieutenant[?], 33
McKenzie, Lieutenant, 195
McLennan, Bart, 215
McNaughton, Andrew G.L., 242, 243,
    244
    as commander, 245–47, 271–73,
    295–98, 308, 329
McPherson, Douglas, 83–84
McRae, Captain, 279
Meek, Ron, 137

Meikle, Captain, 110
Menzies, John, 201–5
Menzies, Percy, 152–54
Merchant Navy of Canada, 252
Mercy, 421
Meredith, Roderic Brian, 390–93
Merritt, W.H., 30–34
Merritt, William Hamilton, 67
Methven, 95
Métis, 56–57. *See also* Red River
 Rebellion
Meyers, Sergeant, 166–67, 171
Miami people, 39
Middleton, Frederick D., 63, 64, 69–70,
 73
Midland Provisional Batallion, 58–65, 67
MIG-17 aircraft, 413
Military Police, 408–9
Military Service Act (1917), 184–85
militia, 96–98, 327–28. *See also specific
 regiments and places;* Canadian
 Expeditionary Force
 in *Komagata Maru* incident, 100, 101
 non-permanent active (NPAM),
 229–31, 240
3rd Militia Brigade (1871), 54–55
Mill, John Stuart, 222
Millbrook (ON), 58
Mills, Master Warrant Officer, 429–30
Mills, Sergeant, 205
Minto, Gilbert Elliot, Earl of, 80
Missouri, 421
Mitsubishi Pajero, 449
Mogadishu, 425
Mohawk, 92
Monchy, 194–95
Monckton, Robert, 16, 20, 21–22, 23
Mons, 205–7, 210
Mont Blanc, 188–89, 191
Montcalm, Louis-Joseph de, 19, 20, 22,
 23–24, 316
Monteciccardo, 359
Monte Marino, 358–59
Montgomery, Bernard, 271–73,
 296–98, 309, 329, 345
Montmorency Falls, 14–16
Moose Jaw, 259, 261
Morgan, Charles, 97–98
Moro River, 311–12
Morris, Bill, 314
Mothersill, Colonel, 279
Mouat, William Ivan, 301–5
Mould, Steve, 136
Moulden, Patrick, 455
Munro, Ross, 332–35
Munson (AB), 96–97

Murphy, Warrant Officer, 430–31
Murphy, William, 327–28, 330–31,
 356–58
Murray, James, 16, 20, 21, 23
Mussolini, Benito, 371, 372

Nasser, Gamal Abdel, 411, 412
National Resources Mobilization Act
 (NRMA), 321–23
NATO. *See* North Atlantic Treaty
 Organization
Navy Island, 49
Nelson, "Liz," 277
Nepalese, 464
Netherlands, 363–64, 365, 378, 385–88
New France, 13–19. *See also* Quebec
 City
New York City, 374
Niagara Falls, 49
Niagara Falls (ON), 269
Nicosia, 415–19
Nijmegan, 365, 367
Nile River, 55–57
Nimy, 208–9
Niobe, 99, 185–89
Norman, Charley, 281
Normandy, 338–42, 344–54. *See also*
 D-Day
North Atlantic Treaty Organization
 (NATO), 1, 401–8, 447–51, 451
Northcote, 61, 62, 64–65
North Korea, 397–98. *See also* Korea
North Nova Scotia Highlanders,
 364–65
North Point Camp, 265–67, 283–84
North-West Mounted Police, 71–74
Northwest Rebellion. *See* Red River
 Rebellion
Norton, Captain, 33
Norway, 348
nurses, 146, 191–92, 252–55, 354–56

O'Flynn, Mike, 139
Ogilvy, Lieutenant, 86, 90
Ogilvy, Major, 100
Okucani, 435–39
Olsen, N.E., 358–59
Olympic, 209
O'Neill, John, 54
Organization for Security and
 Cooperation in Europe (OSCE),
 447–48, 449, 450
Ortona, 312–15
Osborne Smith, Lieutenant-Colonel,
 55
Ott, Frank, 123

Ottawa, 453–56
Ottawa Journal, 218–19
Ottawa people, 39
Otter, William D., 6, 52–54, 68, 69–70
  in South African War, 81, 86, 90
L'Ouest Eclaire, 340
Our Free Holland, 385–88

Paardeberg, 82, 83–89
Page, Colonel, 163, 165
Palms, Jim, 278
Panther tank, 357
Paris, 345
Parker, F. Lawrence, 287–93
Parker, William, 71–74
Passchendaele, 160–78, 182–84
Pasteur, 253
Paton, J.L., 222
Pawly, Ensign, 26
Payne, John, 282–83
Peacock, H.M., 52
Pearkes, George R., 272
Pearson, Lester, 408
Peden, William, 111–13, 114–18
36th Peel Regiment, 104–10
Pelletier, Major, 86, 90
Pelletier, Sergeant, 348–49
Perrin, Herbert, 63
Perry, Colonel, 306
Petawawa, 230–31
Peterborough (ON), 58
Petherick, Captain, 197
Pfalz aircraft, 200
Phelan, Frederick R., 253
Phillip, Grant Odum, 280–81
Pierce, Cliff, 153
Plains of Abraham, 18–19, 21, 316
Ploegsteert Wood, 114–15
Poirier, Athanase, 122–25
Poles, 377
1st Polish Armoured Division, 347–48,
  349
Pontiac, 24
Poole, Cadet Sergeant, 76
Pope, Harry, 268, 394–96
Pope, Maurice A., 268, 321–23
Porter, Bob, 139
Port Hope, 58
Port Said, 410–11
Potawatomis, 39
Potts, A.E., 272
Poundmaker, 68, 70
Power, Charles G., 240
Prescott (ON), 50–51
Prevost, Anne, 34–35
Prevost, George, 35, 38

Price, John H., 262, 263–65
Prince, William, 56–57
Princess Patricia's Canadian Light
  Infantry (PPCLI), 205, 206, 399,
  435–42, 458–59, 460–62
Pringle, Captain, 168–69
Priske, Petty Officer, 227
Pritchard, Garth, 458, 460–62
Proctor, Henry, 38–40
Protecteur, 419–22
Prouse, J. Harper, 358–59
Prouse, Robert, 422–29
Pugsley, William H., 256–59
Purdom, Lue, 157
Pusan, 392–93

Quebec City, 13–24, 27, 105
Queen's Independent Regiment, 24
Queen's Own Rifles of Canada, 52–54,
  58, 68–71, 349
Queenston, 32–34, 35
Queen's York Rangers (1st American
  Regiment), 61, 106, 240
Quesnay Wood, 352
Quinlan, Dennis John, 273–74
Quinney, Reverend, 73

Rafah, 411, 412
Rainbow, 5, 98–103
Ralston, James L., 217–18, 246, 296,
  316, 318, 320, 328
Rangers, 16, 61, 106, 111
Rat Portage, 61
Rebellions of 1837–38, 46–47, 50–52
Red Army, 315, 316
Red Cross, 302–4, 355, 426
Redditt, 275
Red River Expedition (1870), 56
Red River Rebellion (1885), 1, 6, 58–74
Régiment de la Chaudière, 347, 349
Regina Rifle Regiment, 331
Revenge, 253
Revolutionary War, 1, 28–30
Reynolds, John, 460
Ridgeway, 6, 52–54
Riel, Louis, 58, 64, 69
Rixensart, 209
Roaa, 453–56
Roberts, Frederick S., Lord, 82, 88, 92,
  114
Robertson, Chic, 178
Robertson, Peter, 63
Robertson-Ross, P., 54–55
Robinson, Charles W., 97, 98
Rockingham, John M., 388–90, 395–96,
  398–400

Rogers, Captain, 25–26
Rogers, Major, 25
Rogers, Norman M., 239–40, 245
Rome, 298
Rommel, Erwin, 342
Rooke, Bert, 90, 91–92, 93, 94, 95
Rooke, Charles, 90–91, 92–96
Roosevelt, Franklin Delano, 372–73, 374
Rorke, H.V., 80
Roscoe, Albert Edward, 119–21
Ross rifle, 97, 111
Rouvres, 348–49
Rowland, Alec, 71, 74
Royal Air Force, 241, 253, 273–74, 301–2, 361–62. See also Royal Flying Corps
  and Normandy invasion, 333, 334, 347, 348–49
Royal Albert medal, 191
Royal American Regiment, 14, 15, 20, 22, 23
Royal Canadian Air Force, 211–12, 305–6, 341–42, 348–49, 361–62
  Bomber Command, 287–92
  Eastern Command, 315–16
  in Egypt, 412–15
  in Germany, 374–78
  Pathfinder group, 288
  POWs from, 367–68
  No. 427 Squadron, 427–28
  No. 438 Squadron, 363–64
  Women's Detachment, 282–83
Royal Canadian Armoured Corps, 306–7
Royal Canadian Army Cadet Corps, 217–23
Royal Canadian Army Service Corps, 208, 323–25
Royal Canadian Artillery, 240, 279
Royal Canadian Horse Artillery, 396–98
Royal Canadian Mounted Police, 269
Royal Canadian Navy, 225–29, 252, 256–61, 325–26, 419–22
  and Normandy invasion, 334, 341
Royal Canadian Regiment, 79–90, 415–19, 451–53
  in world wars, 194, 205, 206, 312–13
Royal 22e Régiment ("Van Doos"), 336, 394, 395, 409–10
Royal Flying Corps, 118–19, 135, 140–45, 156, 199–201
  No. 4 Squadron, 179–81
  No. 7 Squadron, 135
  No. 20 Squadron, 135
  No. 60 Squadron, 142

Royal Grenadiers, 106, 107
Royal Hamilton Light Infantry, 52–53, 106, 279, 286, 360–61
Royal Horse Artillery, 109
Royal Military College, 74–79, 212, 213, 230–37, 268
Royal Naval Air Service, 154–56
Royal Navy, 36–38, 47–49, 99, 247–48, 249
Royal Newfoundland Regiment, 138–40
Royal Regiment of Canada, 279
Royal Rifles of Canada, 263–64, 265
Royal Winnipeg Rifles, 111, 118, 347
Russell, Bertrand, 222–23
Russia, 217, 413. See also Soviet Union
Russians, 368–69
Rusterberg, 95
Rwanda, 442–47

Sable (France), 251
Sackett, Bob, 455
St. Catharines, 106
St. Gervais la Vasson, 352
St. Julien, 116–18
St. Lawrence River, 37, 224
St. Martin, Mr., 26
Saito, Shunkichi, 267
Salerno, 329
Salisbury Plain, 112–13
Sanburn, Dick, 351
Sanderman, Major, 120
Sansom, E.W., 242, 244
Sargent, Dudley A., 220
95th Saskatchewan Rifles, 114
Saskatoon, 63
Saunders, Charles, 14
Savage, J. Murray, 229–31
Scarr, W., 165, 167, 170, 171
Scheldt River, 360–61, 364
Scheur, Lieutenant, 349
Scotland, 253–55
Scott, Clyde, 239
Scott, Colonel, 61
Scott, Jimmy, 173
Scowen, Don, 367–68
Seaforth Highlanders of Canada, 298–99, 309
Second World War, 2–3, 6, 239–383
  8th Army in, 330, 357–58
  British Army in, 362, 377
  1st Canadian Army in, 350–54, 360–61
  French-Canadians in, 335–37, 344–46, 353–54
  U.S. Army in, 318, 320, 329

Seoul, 390–92
Serbs, 436–39, 442, 447–51
Sesia, A.T., 299–301
Seven Years' War, 13–27
Seward, Anthony, 429–30, 433
Shamshuipo Camp, 267
Shannon, Lieutenant, 194
Shapiro, Lionel, 401–5, 407
Sharjah, 421
Shaver, Clifford, 172
Shaw, Nursing Sister, 146
Shawnees, 39
Sheaffe, Roger Hale, 33
Shepherd, William, 64
Sherman tank, 294–95
Sherritt, Alfred, 80
Short, Robert, 462, 465
Shropshires, 82, 85
Sicily, 294–95, 296–301, 307–11
Sillery, 21
Simmons, E.T., 259–61
Simms, Eric, 452–53
Simonds, Guy G., 212–14, 242–44,
    300–301, 307–11, 328–29
Simpson, Lieutenant, 120
Singh, Gurdit, 99, 102
Six-Day War, 412–15
Skeena, 225–29
Skipton, Sergeant, 432–35
Slemon, Roy, 212
Smart, Wal., 61
Smith, Eric, 439–42
Smith, Lieutenant, 240–41
Socialist Workers Party of America,
    394–96
Somalia, 422–35
Somme, 138–44, 146
South African War, 1, 2, 6, 79–96, 217
South Battleford, 69
South Saskatchewan River, 62–64
Soviet Union, 315, 316, 318–21
Sox, Michael, 431, 432, 433
Spencer, James, 285
Spitfire aircraft, 333, 334
Sproule, Peter, 456
Sproule, Sergeant Major, 64
SS (Schutzstaffel), 347, 348, 353
Stacey, Charles P., 406–8
Stairs, Captain, 87
Stalag Luft III, 304, 362–63
Stalag VIII, 286
Stalin, Joseph, 374
Stanley Fort, 263
Starkings, Arthur G., 172
Starnes, Lieutenant, 74
Steele, Major, 72

Steele's Scouts, 71–74
Sten gun, 396–97
Stewart, Bill, 351
Stewart, Sandy, 64
Stewart, Walter F., 58–65
Stockwell, Colonel, 240
Stogran, Pat, 458
Stone, Colonel, 36
Stone, Jim, 399
Story, Boyd, 383–84
Strange, Thomas B., 70, 71–72, 73
Strathcona, Donald Smith, Lord, 98,
    218
Stuart, Kenneth, 240, 328–29
Sudbury, John P., 160–63
Suez, 408–9
Summers, Kenneth J., 420
Superior, Lake, 60, 65–67
Sutcliffe, J.L.R., 262, 265, 266
Sweden, 221–22
Swift Current, 61–62
Sydney (NS), 212–14

Talbot, Thomas, 31
Taverner, Ben, 284, 286
Taylor, Eleanor, 451–53
Taylor, Ernest M., 130–32
Tecumseh, 31, 38
Tempest, W.J., 144–45
13th (Hamilton) Battalion, 52–53
Thistle, Violet A., 302–3
Thompson, Neil, 359
Thomson, Alexander Thomas, 104–10,
    125–27
Thorne, Stephen J., 457–62
Thorpe, James, 128–29
Three Rivers Regiment, 294–95
Tiger tank, 357
Tilly La Campagne, 347–48, 352
Timbrell, R.W., 247–50
TM-57 mine, 463
Tomalin, G.R., 408–9
Toole, Archer, 132–33
Tora Bora, 458–62
Toronto, 61, 106, 231, 373–74
Toronto Daily Star, 350–54
Toronto Regiment, 231
Townshend, George, 14, 15, 21, 22, 23
Trenchard, Hugh, 141
TS-50 mine, 444
T-34 tank, 413
T-54 tank, 413, 415
T-55 tank, 447
Tuffrey, F.W., 304
Turnbull, Charles, 278
Turnbull, Russ, 278

Turner, Arthur, 96–98, 163–71
Turner, Guy, 242, 243, 244, 310
Tweed, Tommy, 164, 166–69, 170–71
Tweedsmuir, Lord, 243
Typhoon aircraft, 347

U-boats, 259–61, 284–86
Ulmer, W., 359
United Nations, 1, 388, 410–11, 442–44
United Nations Commission for the
    Unification and Rehabilitation of
    Korea, 390–93
United Nations Emergency Force,
    408–9, 410–15
United Nations Protection Force
    (UNPROFOR), 435–42
United States, 372–73, 388, 391, 411.
    See also U.S. Air Force; U.S. Army;
    U.S. Navy
    and Canada, 5, 27, 30–46, 223–24
UN Today, 391
Upper Canada, 41–46
U.S. Air Force, 334
U.S. Army, 39, 368, 391, 396, 457–58
U.S. Navy, 421
USSR. See Soviet Union

Valcartier, 104–10, 111
Van Allen, Will, 183
Vancouver, 225, 229
Vanderswan, Ian, 453
Vanier, Georges P., 409–10
Van Lanser, Greet, 378
Van Rensselaer, Stephen, 32
Vaudreuil, Pierre de Rigaud de, 13
Veale, Percy, 136
V-E Day, 368–70, 373–74
Verdun, 128–29
Veteran's Land Act, 362
Victoria Cross, 198
Viger, Jacques, 36–38
Vimy Ridge, 147, 149–54
Vining, Charles, 214–17
Virden, 305–6
Vokes, Christopher, 239, 309, 326–27
Les Voltigeurs Canadiens, 36–37

Wait, Frank, 212
Wales, 342–44
Walford, A.E. (Ernie), 242–43
Walker, J.C., 89
Walker, Thomas Earl, 149–50
Wallace, Jack, 294–95
Wallace, Thomas, 79–82

Wallis, C., 262–63, 264–65
Warburton, Colonel, 39–40
War of 1812, 1, 30–46
Watkins, E.J., 135
Watson, William, 342–44
Wauchop[e], Andrew, 85
Weaver, Bill, 212
Webb, Lieutenant, 424
Weeks, E.G., 239–40
Weir, G., 386
Welland (ON), 106
Wellington bomber, 342–44
West, Ralph, 195
West Germany, 401–8
Whitby (ON), 106
Whiteley, John, 298
Wilcox, Fred, 139
Williams, Arthur, 58, 61, 63, 64, 67
Williams, Captain, 34
Willison, J.S., 89
Wilson, Andrew, 182–84
Wilson, Edna, 369–70
Wilson, M., 194
Wilson, Robert, 359
Windmill, Battle of the, 50–52
Winfield, Stanley, 374–78
Winnipeg Grenadiers, 262, 265–68
Winnipeg Light Infantry, 109–10
Winnipeg (MB), 61, 103–4, 210–11,
    219, 275
Winters, George, 98
Wisconsin, 421
Wolfe, James, 14, 15, 17, 18–21, 23–24
Wolseley, Garnet, 55–57
Woodpecker, 44–46
Worden, Edward, 331–32
World War I. See First World War
World War II. See Second World War
Wright, Dick, 314
Wright, Elaine, 252–55

Yeo, Commodore, 37
York Regiment, 31, 52–53
Young, Lieutenant, 196
Young, Mark, 262
Ypres, 116–18, 119–22, 135, 164
Yster, 90
Yugoslavia (former), 435–42, 451
Yugoslavians, 377–78, 380–82, 447,
    448, 450

Zabotin, Nikolai, 315, 316, 318–21
Zeppelins, 144–45
Zonnebeck, 164–65